Children's
Literature
Review

Guide to Gale Literary Criticism Series

When you need to review criticism of literary works, these are the Gale series to use:

If the author's death date is: **You should turn to:**

After Dec. 31, 1959
(or author is still living)

CONTEMPORARY LITERARY CRITICISM

for example: Jorge Luis Borges, Anthony Burgess,
William Faulkner, Mary Gordon,
Ernest Hemingway, Iris Murdoch

1900 through 1959

TWENTIETH-CENTURY LITERARY CRITICISM

for example: Willa Cather, F. Scott Fitzgerald,
Henry James, Mark Twain, Virginia Woolf

1800 through 1899

NINETEENTH-CENTURY LITERATURE CRITICISM

for example: Fedor Dostoevski, Nathaniel Hawthorne,
George Sand, William Wordsworth

1400 through 1799

LITERATURE CRITICISM FROM 1400 TO 1800
(excluding Shakespeare)

for example: Anne Bradstreet, Daniel Defoe,
Alexander Pope, François Rabelais,
Jonathan Swift, Phillis Wheatley

SHAKESPEAREAN CRITICISM

Shakespeare's plays and poetry

Antiquity through 1399

CLASSICAL AND MEDIEVAL LITERATURE CRITICISM

for example: Dante, Homer, Plato, Sophocles, Vergil,
the Beowulf Poet

Gale also publishes related criticism series:

CHILDREN'S LITERATURE REVIEW

This ongoing series covers authors of all eras. Presents criticism on authors and author/illustrators who write for the preschool through high school audience.

SHORT STORY CRITICISM

This series covers the major short fiction writers of all nationalities and periods of literary history.

ISSN 0362-4145

volume 14

Children's Literature Review

Excerpts from Reviews,
Criticism, and Commentary
on Books for Children
and Young People

Guest Essay, "The Child's Monopoly
of Story," by Margery Fisher

Gerard J. Senick
Editor

Melissa Reiff Hug
Associate Editor

Gale Research Company
Book Tower
Detroit, Michigan 48226

STAFF

Gerard J. Senick, *Editor*

Melissa Reiff Hug, *Associate Editor*

Susan Miller Harig, *Senior Assistant Editor*

Motoko Fujishiro Huthwaite, *Assistant Editor*

Sharon R. Gunton, *Contributing Editor*

Jeanne A. Gough, *Permissions & Production Manager*

Lizbeth A. Purdy, *Production Supervisor*
Kathleen M. Cook, *Assistant Production Coordinator*
Suzanne Powers, Jani Prescott, Lee Ann Welsh, *Editorial Assistants*

Linda M. Pugliese, *Manuscript Coordinator*
Donna Craft, *Assistant Manuscript Coordinator*
Jennifer E. Gale, Maureen A. Puhl, Rosetta Irene Simms, *Manuscript Assistants*

Victoria B. Cariappa, *Research Supervisor*
Maureen R. Richards, *Research Coordinator*
Mary D. Wise, *Senior Research Assistant*
Joyce E. Doyle, Kent Graham, Eric Priehs, Filomena Sgambati, Laura B. Standley, *Research Assistants*

Janice M. Mach, *Text Permissions Supervisor*
Kathy Grell, *Text Permissions Coordinator*
Susan D. Battista, *Assistant Permissions Coordinator*
Mabel E. Gurney, Josephine Keene, *Senior Permissions Assistants*
H. Diane Cooper, Anita L. Ransom, *Permissions Assistants*
Eileen H. Baehr, Melissa Ann Kamuyu, Martha A. Mulder, Kimberly F. Smilay, Lisa M. Wimmer, *Permissions Clerks*

Patricia A. Seefelt, *Picture Permissions Supervisor*
Margaret A. Chamberlain, *Picture Permissions Coordinator*
Colleen M. Crane, *Permissions Assistant*
Pamela A. Hayes, Lillian Tyus, *Permissions Clerks*

Arthur Chartow, *Art Director*

Library of Congress Catalog Card Number 75-34953
ISBN 0-8103-0349-3
ISSN 0362-4145

Computerized photocomposition by
Typographics, Incorporated
Kansas City, Missouri

Printed in the United States

CONTENTS

PREFACE

As children's literature has evolved into both a respected branch of creative writing and a successful industry, literary criticism has documented and influenced each stage of its growth. Critics have recorded the literary development of individual authors as well as the trends and controversies that resulted from changes in values and attitudes, especially as they concerned children. While defining a philosophy of children's literature, critics developed a scholarship that balances an appreciation of children and an awareness of their needs with standards for literary quality much like those required by critics of adult literature. *Children's Literature Review (CLR)* is designed to provide a permanent, accessible record of this ongoing scholarship. Those responsible for bringing children and books together can now make informed choices when selecting reading materials for the young.

Scope of the Series

Each volume of *CLR* contains excerpts from published criticism on the works of authors, author/illustrators, and illustrators who create books for children from preschool through high school. The author list for each volume is international in scope and represents the variety of genres covered by children's literature—picture books, fiction, folklore, nonfiction, poetry, and drama. The works of approximately fifteen authors of all eras are represented in each volume. Although earlier volumes of *CLR* emphasized critical material published after 1960, successive volumes have expanded their coverage to encompass criticism written before 1960. Since many of the authors included in *CLR* are living and continue to write, it is necessary to update their entries periodically. Thus, future volumes will supplement the entries of selected authors covered in earlier volumes as well as include criticism on the works of authors new to the series.

Organization of the Book

An author section consists of the following elements: author heading, author portrait, author introduction, excerpts of criticism (each followed by a bibliographical citation), and illustrations, when available.

- The **author heading** consists of the author's full name followed by birth and death dates. The portion of the name outside the parentheses denotes the form under which the author is most frequently published. If the majority of the author's works for children were written under a pseudonym, the pseudonym will be listed in the author heading and the real name given on the first line of the author introduction. Also located at the beginning of the introduction are any other pseudonyms used by the author in writing for children and any name variations, including transliterated forms for authors whose languages use nonroman alphabets. Uncertainty as to a birth or death date is indicated by question marks.

- An **author portrait** is included when available.

- The **author introduction** contains information designed to introduce an author to *CLR* users by presenting an overview of the author's themes and styles, occasional biographical facts that relate to the author's literary career, a summary of critical response to the author's works, and information about major awards and prizes the author has received. Where applicable, introductions conclude with references to additional entries in biographical and critical reference series published by Gale Research Company. These sources include past volumes of *CLR* as well as *Contemporary Authors, Something about the Author, Something about the Author Autobiography Series, Yesterday's Authors of Books for Children, Contemporary Literary Criticism, Twentieth-Century Literary Criticism, Nineteenth-Century Literature Criticism, Dictionary of Literary Biography,* and *Authors in the News.*

- **Criticism** is located in three sections: **author's commentary** and **general commentary** (when available) and within individual **title entries,** which are preceded by **title entry headings.** Criticism is arranged chronologically within each section. Titles by authors being profiled are highlighted in boldface type within the text for easier access by readers.

The **author's commentary** presents background material written by the author or by an interviewer. This commentary may cover a specific work or several works. Author's commentary on more than one work appears after the author introduction, while commentary on an individual book follows the title entry heading.

The **general commentary** consists of critical excerpts that consider more than one work by the author being profiled. General commentary is preceded by the critic's name in boldface type or, in the case of unsigned criticism, by the title of the journal.

Title entry headings precede the criticism on a title and cite publication information on the work being reviewed. Title headings list the title of the work as it appeared in its country of origin; titles in languages using nonroman alphabets are transliterated. If the original title is in a language other than English, the title of the first English-language translation follows in brackets. The first publication date of each work is listed in parentheses following the title. Differing U.S. and British titles of works originally published in English follow the publication date within the parentheses.

Title entries consist of critical excerpts on the author's individual works, arranged chronologically by publication date. The entries generally contain two to six reviews per title, depending on the stature of the book and the amount of criticism it has generated. The editors select titles that reflect the entire scope of the author's literary contribution, covering each genre and subject. An effort is made to reprint criticism that represents the full range of each title's reception—from the year of its initial publication to current assessments. Thus, the reader is provided with a record of the author's critical history.

Entries on author/illustrators will occasionally feature commentary on selected works illustrated but not written by the author being profiled. These works are strongly associated with the illustrator and have received critical acclaim for their art. By including critical comment on works of this type, the editors wish to provide a more complete representation of the author/illustrator's total career. Criticism on these works has been chosen to stress artistic, rather than literary, contributions. Title entry headings for works illustrated by the author being profiled are arranged chronologically within the entry by date of publication and include notes identifying the author of the illustrated work. In order to provide easier access for users, all titles illustrated by the author/illustrator will be boldfaced.

Beginning with *CLR,* Volume 14, the series will feature entries on prominent illustrators who have contributed to the field of children's literature. These entries are designed to represent the development of the illustrator as an artist rather than as a literary stylist. The illustrator's section is organized like that of an author or author/illustrator, with two exceptions: the author introduction presents an overview of the illustrator's styles and techniques rather than outlining his or her literary background, and the commentary written by the illustrator on his or her works is called illustrator's commentary rather than author's commentary. Title entry headings are followed by explanatory notes identifying the author of the illustrated work. All titles of books containing illustrations by the artist being profiled as well as individual illustrations from these books are highlighted in boldface type.

- Selected excerpts are preceded by **explanatory notes,** which provide information on the critic or work of criticism to enhance the reader's understanding of the excerpt.

- A complete **bibliographical citation** designed to facilitate the location of the original book or article follows each piece of criticism.

- Numerous **illustrations** are featured in *CLR.* For entries on illustrators, an effort has been made to include illustrations that reflect the characteristics discussed in the criticism. Entries on major authors who do not illustrate their own works may also include photographs and other illustrative material pertinent to the authors' careers.

Other Features

- A list of **authors to appear in future volumes** follows the preface.

- A **guest essay** appears before the first author entry. These essays are written specifically for *CLR* by prominent critics on subjects of their choice. Past volumes have included essays by John Rowe Townsend, Zena Sutherland, Sheila A. Egoff, Rudine Sims, Marcus Crouch, Anne Pellowski, and Milton Meltzer. Volume 14 contains Margery Fisher's "The Child's Monopoly of Story." The editors are honored to feature Mrs. Fisher in this volume.

- An **appendix** lists the sources from which material has been reprinted in the volume. It does not, however, list every book or periodical consulted for the volume.

- *CLR* volumes contain **cumulative indexes** to authors, nationalities, and titles.

- The **cumulative index to authors** lists authors who have appeared in *CLR* and includes cross-references to *Contemporary Authors, Something about the Author, Something about the Author Autobiography Series, Yesterday's Authors of Books for Children, Contemporary Literary Criticism, Twentieth-Century Literary Criticism, Nineteenth-Century Literature Criticism, Dictionary of Literary Biography,* and *Authors in the News.*

- The **cumulative nationality index** lists authors alphabetically under their respective nationalities. Author names are followed by the volume number(s) in which they appear. Authors who have changed citizenship or whose current citizenship is not reflected in biographical sources appear under both their original nationality and that of their current residence.

- The **cumulative title index** lists titles covered in *CLR* followed by the volume and page number where criticism begins.

Acknowledgments

No work of this scope can be accomplished without the cooperation of many people. The editors especially wish to thank the copyright holders of the criticism included in this volume, the permissions managers of many book and magazine publishing companies for assisting us in securing reprint rights, and the staffs of the Kresge Library at Wayne State University, the University of Michigan Library, the Detroit Public Library, and the Wayne Oakland Library Federation (WOLF) for making their resources available to us. We are also grateful to Anthony J. Bogucki for his assistance with copyright research.

Suggestions Are Welcome

In response to various suggestions, several features have been added to *CLR* since the series began:

- Since Volume 3—**Author's commentary,** when available, which presents the viewpoint of the author being profiled.

  —An **appendix** listing the sources of criticism in each volume.

- Since Volume 4—**Author portraits** as well as **illustrations** from works by author/illustrators, when available.

  —**Title entries** arranged chronologically according to the work's first publication; previous volumes listed titles alphabetically.

- Since Volume 5—A **guest essay,** when available, written specifically for *CLR* by a prominent critic on a subject of his or her choice.

- Since Volume 6—**Explanatory notes** that provide information on the critic or work of criticism to enhance the usefulness of the excerpt.

  —A **cumulative nationality index** for easy access to authors by nationality.

- Since Volume 8—Author entries on retellers of traditional literature as well as those who have been the first to record oral tales and other folklore.

  —More extensive illustrative material, such as holographs of manuscript pages and photographs of people and places pertinent to the authors' careers.

- Since Volume 10—Occasional entries devoted to criticism on a single work by a major author.

- Since Volume 12—Entries on author/illustrators featuring commentary on selected works illustrated but not written by the author being profiled.

- Since Volume 14—Entries on prominent illustrators featuring commentary on their styles and techniques.

Readers are cordially invited to write the editor with comments and suggestions for further enhancing the usefulness of the *CLR* series.

AUTHORS TO APPEAR IN FUTURE VOLUMES

Aardema, Verna (Norberg) 1911-
Adams, Harriet S(tratemeyer)
    1893?-1982
Adams, Richard 1920-
Adler, Irving 1913-
Ahlberg, Janet 1944- and Allan 1938-
Anderson, C(larence) W(illiam)
    1891-1971
Arnosky, Jim 1946-
Arundel, Honor (Morfydd) 1919-1973
Asbjörnsen, Peter Christen 1812-1885
    and Jörgen Moe 1813?-1882
Asch, Frank 1946-
Avery, Gillian 1926-
Avi 1937-
Aymé, Marcel 1902-1967
Bailey, Carolyn Sherwin 1875-1961
Ballantyne, R(obert) M(ichael)
    1825-1894
Banner, Angela 1923-
Bannerman, Helen 1863-1946
Barrett, Judi(th) 1941-
Barrie, J(ames) M(atthew) 1860-1937
Baum, L(yman) Frank 1856-1919
Baumann, Hans 1914-1985
Beatty, Patricia Robbins 1922-
    and John 1922-1975
Behn, Harry 1898-1973
Belloc, Hilaire 1870-1953
Berenstain, Stan(ley) 1923- and
    Jan(ice) 1923-
Berger, Melvin H. 1927-
Berna, Paul 1910-
Beskow, Elsa 1874-1953
Bianco, Margery Williams 1881-1944
Bishop, Claire Huchet
Blades, Ann 1947-
Blake, Quentin 1932-
Blos, Joan W(insor) 1928-
Blumberg, Rhoda 1917-
Blyton, Enid 1897-1968
Bodecker, N(iels) M(ogens) 1922-
Bødker, Cecil 1927-
Bonham, Frank 1914-
Brancato, Robin F(idler) 1936-
Branscum, Robbie 1937-
Breinburg, Petronella 1927-
Bridgers, Sue Ellen 1942-
Bright, Robert 1902-
Brink, Carol Ryrie 1895-1981
Brinsmead, H(esba) F(ay) 1922-
Brooke, L(eonard) Leslie 1862-1940
Brown, Marc Tolon 1946-
Browne, Anthony (Edward Tudor)
    1946-
Bryan, Ashley F. 1923-
Buff, Mary 1890-1970 and Conrad
    1886-1975

Bulla, Clyde Robert 1914-
Burch, Robert (Joseph) 1925-
Burgess, Gelett 1866-1951
Burgess, Thornton W(aldo) 1874-1965
Burkert, Nancy Ekholm 1933-
Burnett, Frances Hodgson 1849-1924
Butterworth, Oliver 1915-
Caines, Jeannette (Franklin)
Carlson, Natalie Savage 1906-
Carrick, Carol 1935- and Donald 1929-
Chambers, Aidan 1934-
Chönz, Selina
Christopher, Matt(hew F.) 1917-
Ciardi, John (Anthony) 1916-1986
Clapp, Patricia 1912-
Clark, Ann Nolan 1896-
Clarke, Pauline 1921-
Cohen, Barbara 1932-
Colby, C(arroll) B(urleigh) 1904-1977
Colman, Hila
Colum Padraic 1881-1972
Cone, Molly 1918-
Coolidge, Olivia E(nsor) 1908-
Coolidge, Susan 1835-1905
Cooney, Barbara 1917-
Courlander, Harold 1908-
Cox, Palmer 1840-1924
Crane, Walter 1845-1915
Cresswell, Helen 1934-
Crompton, Richmal 1890-1969
Cunningham, Julia (Woolfolk) 1916-
Curry, Jane L(ouise) 1932-
Dalgliesh, Alice 1893-1979
Daly, Maureen 1921-
Danziger, Paula 1944-
Daugherty, James 1889-1974
D'Aulaire, Ingri 1904-1980 and Edgar
    Parin 1898-1986
De la Mare, Walter 1873-1956
Denslow, W(illiam) W(allace)
    1856-1915
De Regniers, Beatrice Schenk 1914-
Dickinson, Peter 1927-
Dillon, Eilís 1920-
Dillon, Leo 1933- and Diane 1933-
Dodge, Mary Mapes 1831-1905
Domanska, Janina
Drescher, Henrik
Duncan, Lois S(teinmetz) 1934-
Duvoisin, Roger 1904-1980
Eager, Edward 1911-1964
Edgeworth, Maria 1767-1849
Edmonds, Walter D(umaux) 1903-
Epstein, Sam(uel) 1909- and Beryl
    1910-
Ets, Marie Hall 1893-
Ewing, Juliana Horatia 1841-1885
Farber, Norma 1909-1984

Farjeon, Eleanor 1881-1965
Field, Eugene 1850-1895
Field, Rachel 1894-1942
Fisher, Dorothy Canfield 1879-1958
Fisher, Leonard Everett 1924-
Flack, Marjorie 1897-1958
Forbes, Esther 1891-1967
Forman, James D(ouglas) 1932-
Freeman, Don 1908-1978
Fujikawa, Gyo 1908-
Fyleman, Rose 1877-1957
Galdone, Paul 1914-1986
Gantos, Jack 1951-
Garfield, Leon 1921-
Garis, Howard R(oger) 1873-1962
Garner, Alan 1935-
Gates, Doris 1901-
Gerrard, Roy 1935-
Giblin, James Cross 1933-
Giff, Patricia Reilly 1935-
Ginsburg, Mirra 1919-
Goble, Paul 1933-
Godden, Rumer 1907-
Goodall, John S(trickland) 1908-
Goodrich, Samuel G(riswold)
    1793-1860
Gorey, Edward (St. John) 1925-
Gramatky, Hardie 1907-1979
Greene, Constance C(larke) 1924-
Grimm, Jacob 1785-1863 and Wilhelm
    1786-1859
Gruelle, Johnny 1880-1938
Guillot, René 1900-1969
Hader, Elmer 1889-1973 and Berta
    1891?-1976
Hague, Michael 1948-
Hale, Lucretia Peabody 1820-1900
Haley, Gail E(inhart) 1939-
Hall, Lynn 1937-
Harnett, Cynthia 1893-1981
Harris, Christie (Lucy Irwin) 1907-
Harris, Joel Chandler 1848-1908
Harris, Rosemary (Jeanne) 1923-
Haywood, Carolyn 1898-
Heide, Florence Parry 1919-
Heine, Helme
Heinlein, Robert A(nson) 1907-
Highwater, Jamake (Mamake) 1942-
Hoberman, Mary Ann 1930-
Hoff, Syd(ney) 1912-
Hoffman, Heinrich 1809-1894
Holland, Isabelle 1920-
Holling, Holling C(lancy) 1900-1973
Hughes, Langston 1902-1967
Hughes, Shirley 1929-
Hunter, Mollie 1922-
Hurd, Edith Thacher 1910-
    and Clement 1908-

Hyman, Trina Schart 1939-
Ipcar, Dahlov (Zorach) 1917-
Iwasaki, Chihiro 1918-1974
Jackson, Jesse 1908-1983
Janosch 1931-
Johnson, Crockett 1906-1975
Johnson, James Weldon 1871-1938
Jones, Diana Wynne 1934-
Judson, Clara Ingram 1879-1960
Juster, Norton 1929-
Kelly, Eric P(hilbrook) 1884-1960
Kennedy, (Jerome) Richard 1932-
Kent, Jack 1920-1985
Kerr, (Anne-)Judith 1923-
Kerr, M. E. 1927-
Kettelkamp, Larry (Dale) 1933-
King, (David) Clive 1924-
Kipling, Rudyard 1865-1936
Kjelgaard, Jim 1910-1959
Kraus, Robert 1925-
Krauss, Ruth (Ida) 1911-
Krumgold, Joseph 1908-1980
La Fontaine, Jean de 1621-1695
Lang, Andrew 1844-1912
Langton, Jane (Gillson) 1922-
Latham, Jean Lee 1902-
Lauber, Patricia (Grace) 1924-
Lavine, Sigmund A(rnold) 1908-
Leaf, Munro 1905-1976
Lenski, Lois 1893-1974
Levy, Elizabeth 1942-
Lightner, A(lice) M. 1904-
Lofting, Hugh (John) 1866-1947
Lunn, Janet 1928-
MacDonald, George 1824-1905
MacGregor, Ellen 1906-1954
Mann, Peggy
Marshall, James 1942-
Masefield, John 1878-1967
Mayer, Marianna 1945-
Mayne, William (James Carter) 1928-
Mazer, Harry 1925-
Mazer, Norma Fox 1931-
McCaffrey, Anne (Inez) 1926-
McGovern, Ann
McKee, David (John)
McKillip, Patricia A(nne) 1948-
McNeer, May 1902-
Meader, Stephen W(arren) 1892-1977
Means, Florence Crannell 1891-1980
Meigs, Cornelia 1884-1973
Merrill, Jean (Fairbanks) 1923-
Miles, Betty 1928-
Milne, Lorus 1912- and Margery 1915-

Minarik, Else Holmelund 1920-
Mizumura, Kazue
Mohr, Nicholasa 1935-
Molesworth, Mary Louisa 1842-1921
Moore, Lilian
Morey, Walt(er Nelson) 1907-
Mowat, Farley (McGill) 1921-
Naylor, Phyllis Reynolds 1933-
Neufeld, John (Arthur) 1938-
Neville, Emily Cheney 1919-
Nic Leodhas, Sorche 1898-1969
Nielsen, Kay 1886-1957
North, Sterling 1906-1974
Norton, Andre 1912-
Ofek, Uriel 1926-
Ormondroyd, Edward 1925-
Ottley, Reginald (Leslie) 1909-
Oxenbury, Helen 1938-
Parish, Peggy 1927-
Peck, Richard (Wayne) 1934-
Peck, Robert Newton 1928-
Perl, Lila
Perrault, Charles 1628-1703
Petersen, P(eter) J(ames) 1941-
Petersham, Maud 1890-1971 and
    Miska 1888-1960
Picard, Barbara Leonie 1917-
Platt, Kin 1911-
Politi, Leo 1908-
Price, Christine 1928-1980
Pyle, Howard 1853-1911
Rackham, Arthur 1867-1939
Rawls, Wilson 1919-
Reeves, James 1909-1978
Richards, Laura E(lizabeth) 1850-1943
Richler, Mordecai 1931-
Robertson, Keith (Carlton) 1914-
Rockwell, Anne 1934- and Harlow
Rodgers, Mary 1931-
Rollins, Charlemae Hill 1897-1979
Ross, Tony 1938-
Rounds, Glen H(arold) 1906-
Rylant, Cynthia 1954-
Sandburg, Carl 1878-1967
Sandoz, Mari 1896-1966
Sawyer, Ruth 1880-1970
Scarry, Huck 1953-
Scott, Jack Denton 1915-
Sebestyen, Ouida 1924-
Seton, Ernest Thompson 1860-1946
Sharmat, Marjorie Weinman 1928-
Sharp, Margery 1905-
Shepard, Ernest H(oward) 1879-1976

Shotwell, Louisa R(ossiter) 1902-
Sidney, Margaret 1844-1924
Silverstein, Alvin 1933- and Virginia
    B(arbara Opshelor) 1937-
Sinclair, Catherine 1800-1864
Skurzynski, Gloria (Joan) 1930-
Sleator, William (Warner) 1945-
Slobodkin, Louis 1903-1975
Smith, Doris Buchanan 1934-
Smith, Jessie Willcox 1863-1935
Snyder, Zilpha Keatley 1927-
Spence, Eleanor (Rachel) 1928-
Sperry, Armstrong W. 1897-1976
Spykman, E(lizabeth) C. 1896-1965
Steele, William O(wen) 1917-1979
Stevenson, James 1929-
Stolz, Mary (Slattery) 1920-
Stratemeyer, Edward L. 1862-1930
Streatfeild, (Mary) Noel 1897-1986
Taylor, Sydney 1904?-1978
Taylor, Theodore 1924-
Tenniel, Sir John 1820-1914
Ter Haar, Jaap 1922-
Thiele, Colin 1920-
Thompson, Julian F(rancis) 1927-
Titus, Eve 1922-
Tolkien, J(ohn) R(onald) R(euel)
    1892-1973
Trease, (Robert) Geoffrey 1909-
Tresselt, Alvin 1916-
Treviño, Elizabeth Borton de 1904-
Turkle, Brinton 1915-
Twain, Mark 1835-1910
Udry, Janice May 1928-
Unnerstad, Edith (Totterman) 1900-
Uttley, Alison 1884-1976
Ventura, Piero (Luigi) 1937-
Vining, Elizabeth Gray 1902-
Waber, Bernard 1924-
Wahl, Jan 1933-
Walter, Mildred Pitts
Ward, Lynd 1905-1985
Wells, Rosemary 1943-
White, T(erence) H(anbury) 1906-1964
Wiese, Kurt 1887-1974
Wilkinson, Brenda 1946-
Wyeth, N(ewell) C(onvers) 1882-1945
Yates, Elizabeth 1905-
Yonge, Charlotte M(ary) 1823-1901
Yorinks, Arthur 1953-
Zemach, Harve 1933-1974 and Margot
    1931-
Zion, Gene 1913-1975

Readers are cordially invited to suggest additional authors to the editors.

GUEST ESSAY

The Child's Monopoly of Story
by Margery Fisher

Which came first, the child or the story? Which is more important, the child or the book? That these questions should even be considered suggests that there is something amiss in the world of children's literature. For many decades the trend in the assessment of stories for children has been almost entirely child-oriented. With a nervous respect, librarians, teachers, and publishers hasten to consult children about their tastes, trying without much success to translate such comments as "very exciting" or "too long and boring" into a comprehensible brief for those persecuted individuals who actually produce the books.

Children's authors can be allocated to two camps. There are those who say firmly that they write for themselves—perhaps Beatrix Potter was the first to make this claim. This is hardly a statement to take too literally. It is obvious that regarding subject, syntax, length, and to some extent vocabulary, *The Tale of Peter Rabbit* (1902) was addressed to a child. What Beatrix Potter meant was that in devising a tale to help a sick child to recover, she was bound to satisfy herself that she had found the right style and approach for the occasion and that the story was as good a piece of literature *for its purpose* as she could make it. All the same, the impulse of creation remained exclusively personal.

In the second camp are those writers who for one reason or another start with the reader's hypothetical desires, as if there could ever be a standard unisex child to whom a story might be addressed. This is particularly the case with the domestic tale for the middle years (roughly, seven to eleven or so), the years when reading becomes either a lifelong habit or a chore. Thinking, then, of this hypothetical child, the author conscientiously runs through a list of possible subjects—a ghost or a treasure in the attic of an old house, a lost dog, sibling rivalry, a smuggler unmasked—and chooses potentially interesting plots not from personal inspiration but from a survey of the market, from a list of recent publications, or from the results of a survey of what the top class of a junior school has just enjoyed. This wretched author, pressured by public opinion and confused by the inconsistencies and prejudices of critics, draws up a list of priorities. Will her readers understand words of more than two syllables? Where can she inject the desirable humor? Where should she place the token ethnic character, and has she balanced the genders properly? Small wonder that when this writer puts pen to paper, inspiration has gone out of the door and the skeleton of the book collapses for want of flesh and muscle.

These are, of course, extremes. In the middle are authors who write because they want to, because they start with an idea, a setting, or a character and let it work inside them while, quite legitimately and sensibly, they assemble the practical facts of markets and comparable works and make the necessary technical decisions about length, prose style, direction of the plot, and so on. They have, these ideal writers, enough confidence in their own motives to let the future of carping critics and opinionated child-guardians look after itself. Yet, however sure they may be of their own intentions, however determined to set their own standard and keep to it, there remains one last, inescapable convention. A story for children is about children. It has a child at the center.

What does this mean? Something more than the mere fact that the narrative is mainly concerned with a child. Incidents will be chosen that are likely to interest a reader of around the same age and experience as the characters; events and characters will be conceived from the point of view of the child, within a child's wavelength. This *should not* mean that the child has total monopoly of the story, enclosed in a bubble of importance. When this happens the book will lack breadth and substance and will do nothing to help the young reader to grow mentally and emotionally, to reach out beyond himself. When adult characters draw aside and leave the young hero or heroine in isolation, the dialogue, incidental description, motive, and character development of the story are inevitably weakened.

The convention of the vanished parent is one of long standing. For decades, mothers have been whisked off to hospital for operations demanding long periods of convalescence; fathers have accepted assignments in distant countries and have taken their wives along; grannies, aunts, or old friends have sent requests for urgent help; and, of course, in every case the most careful arrangements for guardians have broken down after the parents have vanished over the horizon. The motto under which this device has dominated junior literature for so long is that famous telegram in Arthur Ransome's *Swallows and Amazons* (1930) sent by Captain Walker to his four children, their ages ranging from fifteen to nine, in answer to their demand for total independence in sailing their dinghy on the lake where they spend the holidays—"BETTER DROWNED THAN DUFFERS IF NOT DUFFERS WON'T DROWN." A useful device, certainly, and one which in the hands of sensible authors has produced some of the most lively domestic tales of our time, but one which, used unintelligently, has stultified and diminished this type of junior fiction to a disastrous extent by destroying its essential reality.

I can best define what I mean by essential reality by referring to Philippa Pearce's *A Dog So Small* (1962) as an example of a story where a child is placed right at the center but with the family all round him—father, mother, siblings, grandparents—offering their view of him just as he gives his view of them. The boy's search for a dog of his own is paramount, emotionally and in terms of the plot, but he acts within the constraints of his world and is aware of interests other than his own. From time to time the focus shifts from Ben—to his sister, who is preparing for her wedding, to his father's work on the London Underground, even to Tilly, his grandfather's old spaniel, preoccupied with a neighboring dog. None of these characters takes the center of the stage long enough to divert attention from the main line of the story. Simply, the world *outside* Ben is present, warmly and actually, widening the scope of the book for the alert reader.

Given the junior readership of seven to eleven or so which I have in mind and the approximate length of stories for this age range, the author has to keep a delicate balance in the treatment of young and adult characters. To suggest the point of view or the angle of vision of an adult is, to my mind, as essential as it is useful to the health of a book, but to go further, towards analysis or development of adult interests, is to shift the focus away from the child, who should be the center of the action. The quality of a writer may often be judged by the treatment of adult characters in a book designed for middle-year readers.

I offer as an example a book by Jenifer Wayne for readers from eight or so, *Sprout's Window-Cleaner* (1971). This is the second of a group of five short domestic narratives centering on a boy of five or six. This young hero is what critics are prone to call a "real person" by virtue of three simple details. First, his universally accepted nickname comes from the unruly tuft of hair by which he may be physically recognized; then, his abiding curiosity about life, matched with an abounding self-confidence, is expressed both in his eager, forthright mode of speech and in the way he initiates events; finally, he has one obsession, with elephants, which provides, as it were, a refrain running through all the books as well as many opportunities for amusing incidents. What happens in the books depends on Sprout and on the chosen details about him which are made clearly accessible to young readers. But—and this is important—Sprout acts within his environment and in relation to other people, including adults, who have their own constraints and preoccupations.

In *Sprout's Window-Cleaner* these adults are not all placed in the story in the same way. Their function differs, their positions are carefully balanced. Sprout's competent, unflappable mother, much occupied by the anarchic behavior of Sprout's infant sister Tilly, is nicely contrasted with the nervous, headache-ridden mother of Sprout's school friend Raymond. The window-cleaner, provided with routine Cockney idiom, is present in the story for the sake of the plot, to comment usefully on the burglary in the flat where Raymond lives—which brings a new experience to Sprout—and to offer the necessary adult aid to the small boy when he confronts the burglar.

One seemingly extraneous character, Miss Crabbe, has another function altogether. According to Raymond, who lives in the flat above her, she is an old lady who is always cross. Sprout thinks otherwise, after he has gone to investigate the "burglar's mess" which must, he supposes, be different from any other and which, therefore, he is bound to investigate. When the visiting police constable moves from the upstairs flat to question Miss Crabbe, as owner of the house, Sprout peers at her, this cross woman with "thousands of wrinkles," from under the man's arm:

> [He] could see Miss Crabbe's back as she led the way into her sitting-room. It was a very large grey back, with a sort of rounded stoop. Then she turned, and he saw her front. Raymond was right, there certainly were thousands of wrinkles; there was also a very long nose, and very small eyes, and when she spoke there were big teeth that stuck out at the sides almost like tusks.
>
> Sprout had never seen a person who looked more like an elephant. He liked her at once. . . .then the constable started to ask Miss Crabbe whether she had noticed anything

unusual that morning; whether she had been in all the time; whether anybody had called; whether she had ever seen any man or men lurking about in the road outside.

"I'm afraid I can't help you," said Miss Crabbe; her voice was very gentle and polite and surprisingly young. She might be quite a *girl* elephant, Sprout thought. "You see, I hardly ever go out, I have everything sent. I hardly *look* out, for that matter!" And she gave a smile which was all tusks and apologetic friendliness. "So I'm sorry to say I think you'll find me what I believe they call a dead loss."

By this time she had sunk her vast grey bulk into a vast green chair; the policeman moved, and Sprout was left out in the open by the door.

"Good gracious!" said Miss Crabbe, "a *very* young policeman!"[1]

An unpromising character for a book for children—unattractive, elderly, and with no obvious part in the story—Miss Crabbe moves forward and brings a new dimension into it. Jenifer Wayne made no mistakes in creating her. She did not distract the attention from Sprout; indeed, we see her through his eyes. Yet it is a double view. As she stands in the garden watching the policeman at work we see her as he does, "blinking her little eyes and watching them as a wise and friendly elephant would watch mice who were supposed to be trained."[2] But she is a person in her own right, a self-sufficient woman who, because she has no social graces, talks to the two small boys in a perfectly natural, equal tone. She reveals a robust sense of values. When Sprout breaks the lustre bowl she has lent him for a school competition, she says roundly, "Whatever does one old pot matter—why, it's not even alive!"[3] Besides, the tea she provides for them, to celebrate their success, is exactly right, including three shortbread elephants with currant eyes and split almond tusks. " 'One each,' smiled Miss Crabbe. 'My mother taught me to make them when I was a little girl. I still have her old tin elephant-cutter.' "[4] The small coincidence is one of many which hold the story together. Skillfully planned as it is, it is notable for the balance of characters and, above all, for the broadening of emotional scope in consequence of this plain, elderly spinster, a vindication of the way a story lives by the vitality of the people in it. The child in the center, without monopolizing the tale, is thrown into relief in an unexpected way as he responds to a woman who seems to him an extension of the elephants who fill his mind.

Children from the earliest years have to adapt to the irruption into their lives of unheralded adults; yet this obvious enlargement of their own restricted territory is represented exceptionally rather than normally in the books which supposedly reflect experiences similar to their own. In this regard it is worth noting that stories for the nurseries of English middle-class families in the nineteenth century more often than not contained a broader range of characters than those of our time, for a book might be read to the children in a family, various in age, and each would be expected to take as much from the book as he or she was capable of understanding. The range of characters and attitudes in stories like Mrs. Ewing's *Lob-Lie-by-the-Fire* (1872) or *A Flat Iron for a Farthing* (1874) is very striking; it has taken writers the best part of a century to work back to that breadth of reference. Mrs. Ewing, in the mid-Victorian period, was fortunate in her audience. Only one decade later, the books of Mrs. Molesworth were more deliberately addressed to a narrower age range, and the use of baby talk, the careful simplicity of vocabulary and syntax, the firm authorial direction and comment, show limitations not to be found in Mrs. Ewing's civilized, humane, and gloriously rich writing which held out possibilities of pleasure to children of all ages.

Mrs. Molesworth comes nearest to her predecessor, perhaps, in *Rosy* (1882), though the story is still consciously framed for really young listeners. One of her less well-known nursery tales, the narrative describes how the heroine, a pretty, spoilt eight-year-old, upsets her mother's plan to offer a happy home to Beata, daughter of family friends who have to spend a year or two in India. Jealous of Beata and determined to remain the center of attention, Rosy sulks and makes mischief, as frank about her unpleasant moods as she is about her genuine efforts to "be good." However, this is not a simple tale of a naughty child who learns to master her faults, for a great deal of her disagreeable behavior is due to a trait which is basically good, a hatred of hypocrisy. When people "pretend," as she puts it—when, for instance, her subservient governess fails to discipline her because she is afraid of losing her post—Rosy is insolent, unacceptably but understandably. Miss Pinkerton is, in fact, seen as an example of misguided adult behavior; the point is made firmly and in a way that extends the story beyond the simple exposition, in the dogmatic, moralistic tone of the time, of youthful misdemeanor and the road to virtue.

Even more striking in its implications is the role of Nelson, maid to Rosy's aunt, who has insinuated herself into that household by sycophantic service and who has been the chief agent in the indulgences which have made Rosy so vain and demanding. The intermittent appearance of this morose, jealous, intrusive woman brings a new dimension into the book. Her impudence, her malice towards the innocent Beata ("I don't like them secrety sort of children"[5]), her ostentatious "darlings" and sentimental attitude to Rosy make her a significant *adult* mirror for the child's misguided but more forgivable mischief. In fact, at certain moments Nelson dominates the story with something of the power of the bad fairy in a traditional tale. Her character, hinted at rather than deliberately analyzed for obvious reasons of balance, still stretches beyond the limits of a nursery chronicle. The same implications of adult emotions and behavior may be seen in the sad situation of the widower Mr. Craven and its effect on his delicate, cross-grained son Colin in Frances Hodgson Burnett's *The Secret Garden* (1911), a book which is read at many ages and many times and with each reading brings new insights.

It is this pattern of coexistence, this rich variety in the provision of characters, so clearly discernible in the work of Mrs. Ewing and visibly being altered and eroded in the family stories of E. Nesbit, which we must encourage in the present if children's fiction is not to be diluted and confined by over-anxious considerations of suitable subjects and styles for a narrow age range of readership. It is the death of a book to begin with the question "What does a child want to read?" There is a right time and place for technical considerations of length or vocabulary, of what has to be stated and what may be inferred or suggested. However, the genesis of a story must be natural and unconstrained. It may be a piece of reminiscence rising of itself from the writer's own childhood and finding its own tone from this.Whatever starts the train of thought and the process of creation, the idea will be investigated and hammered into shape by a writer whose childhood still exists within the adult personality. The continuity of emotional experience from childhood to maturity is at the root of any story for the young. It is this continuity, exemplified in individuals and in the successive generations of a family, that ensures the layered richness of four books by Alan Garner which in the ten years since their publication have been grouped under the title the "Stone Book Quartet": *The Stone Book* (1976), *Granny Reardun* (1977), *Tom Fobble's Day* (1977), and *The Aimer Gate* (1978).

These four books cover six generations of craftsmen working in stone, iron, or wood in a part of England, the Cheshire environs of Manchester, which Alan Garner has called North Mercia and from which he has drawn an idiom and a vocabulary—designedly Anglo-Saxon and unlatinate—as sturdy and as variable as the stone which dominates the landscape. The four stories are linked through sixty or seventy years by physical details—a clay pipe dropped in a potato clamp by Robert the stonemason is by chance dug up by his grandson Joseph, himself a grandfather, in the presence of *his* grandson William; the steeples of church and chapel, the weathercock on the one and the clock on the other, stand in one story after another as symbols of the long life of stone and iron and the family memory of the craftsmen who worked on the buildings and their furnishings.

The continuity which concerns me here is the more elusive one of character and heredity. In each book a child stands square in the center. In *The Stone Book,* Mary is made aware of the past when her stonemason father takes her deep into a mine and shows her the print of a prehistoric hand, and when he makes for her, just by the smoothing and strength of his hands, a simulation of a prayer book in a split stone within which is revealed the fretting of a fossil fern. In *Granny Reardun,* Mary's son Joseph, on his last day at school, faces the fact that he wants to work in iron rather than in the stone whose properties he has learned all through his childhood through watching his grandfather work. In *The Aimer Gate,* Joseph's son Robert perceives, so far as his youth allows, the effect of a World War on his father, who made horseshoes for the cavalry, and his uncle, on leave from the Front, who shoots the rabbits in the cornfield as alternative targets. Finally, in *Tom Fobble's Day,* Joseph, on the last day of his working life as a smith, makes a sledge for his grandson William, who triumphantly asserts *his* link with the land of his forebears as he flies down a steep hill under searchlights with the sound of Heinkels in his ears.

In each child lives the adult of the future: for each child an adult (most often a grandfather) provides, in reminiscence, in example, or just through an affectionate familiarity, a foretaste of the future and an impulse from the past, so that the child is seen as a member of a family, equal but not greater in importance. Instead of the artificial isolation in which the young central character so often stands and which so greatly impoverishes a story, the child in each of Alan Garner's books has a natural position in which he is at once an individual and a part of his inheritance. In the last book of the group (last, that is, according to the internal chronology, in fact the third in date of publication), William's grandfather, worker in iron, explains the significance of the two horseshoes which have their special place in the chimney of the old man's house:

> Your Grandma and me, we'd have let every stick of furniture go first, and the house, before we'd have parted from them. They're our wedding. They're your Father and your Uncles. They're you. Do you not see? They're us!

> Your friends and your neighbours give them to the wedding. No one says. It happens. And it happens as the smith's at his forge one night, and happens to find the money by the door. And he makes the shoes alone, swage block and anvil: and we put them in the

chimney piece. Mind you, I'd know Tommy Latham's work anywhere. But we don't let on. It's all a mystery.[6]

The mystery of identity and inheritance, one of several threads in these brilliant, close-honed stories of local and family continuity, is offered to young readers who will find what they are capable of finding at the first and, one hopes, at subsequent readings. There has been no thought of what a reader of this or that age could or could not "understand." It is in the quality of the writing and in the breadth of reference between the old and the young who move the stories along by their actions and reactions that the books make their mark as literature, as food for growing minds.

They make their mark in the breadth of social reference as well—for Alan Garner's four books reach beyond family to local history, to a close community owing its atmosphere and its continued existence to the raw materials and the social conditions of available work. There is a certain literary quality which Robert Bridges, writing of Shakespeare, called "populousness," the capacity to suggest areas of life and of character outside or on the fringes of a play or a novel. Relatively short books for the middle years of readership can, if the writer wishes, convey a sense of community, of a particular place where other people exist independently of the child at the center of the story, stirring us to imagine their doings beyond what we are told.

Leila Berg's *A Box for Benny* (1958) was far ahead of its time in surrounding a small boy with the exuberant, vigorous, varied life of a dominantly Jewish working-class quarter of Manchester. Nothing in the book could be called inaccessible to readers making a first venture into independent reading but, following as they will the efforts of small Benny to find a shoebox for a seasonal street game, they will glimpse a wide world of the city. The streets Benny visits in his search, the people he meets, are linked by the peripatetic figure of the ragman, whose advice inspires the quest. Disappointed at being given a balloon in exchange for tattered woollen garments, Benny complains, "I never get what I want" but he is told, "You keep on giving, love. And one day you'll get the thing you want."[7] For a long time the child is doubtful, for swapping gets him no nearer to the coveted shoebox. Sometimes he is cheated; ruthless Becky offers a dirty cigaret packet in exchange for a powder compact, insisting that it has a secret sign in it leading to treasure. Sometimes he gives cheerfully; blind Mrs. Taylor was supposed only to have a sniff at the scent bottle with its faint aroma of attar of roses, but her delight compels his generosity. Disappointment, hope, ultimate triumph—from stage to stage he moves through a world of other people's concerns, as he minds a neighbor's fractious baby, bargains for bagels with a street-merchant, visits his two grannies (Bobby-with-the-hens and Bobby-with-the-wine). A small world but a rich one, and one to extend the horizon of the child who reads. For as children extend their geographical range, moving outwards from home to more and more distant landmarks, so their experience is widened by meeting more and more people and identifying them by their place in the community.

A sense of place and a sense of people—these inseparable necessities in story are likely to be missing in books where a young character is too exclusively used to provide its motive power. In any list of writers whose books may be confidently given to readers under twelve, those who convey a sense of community, of populousness, will be preeminent—among them Betsy Byars, Eleanor Cameron, and Paula Fox in America, Ruth Park and Nan Chauncy in Australia, Jan Mark, Robert Leeson, and William Mayne in England. Mayne, in particular, has created a living world in each of his books. *A Parcel of Trees* (1963) moves from the author's central, congenial point of a girl looking for privacy in a small house to a picture of a West Country village, complete and authentic in weather, topography, and social structure and in the deployment of characters of all ages, from old Mr. Monsey through middle-aged Mr. Ferriman, a lawyer with a sly sense of humor, and henpecked gambler Tom Royal, down to the lads of the village and then to fourteen-year-old Susan and her intrusive small sister Rosemary, who seldom speaks but conveys meanings—usually hostile—by shrugs, gestures, and inimical glances. When the loft is ruled out as a possible refuge by Susan's father, the village baker, chance leads her to a small triangle of land cut off from the Brown's garden by the railway and its embankment that was once part of the baker's garden.

The railway's claim to this enclosure of nettles and apple trees proves shaky; if Susan can prove it has been in continuous use for twelve years he may, Mr. Ferriman advises, be able to make out a case for her. She identifies, and dates, the small graves with headstones recording pet dogs, the skeleton of a horse, the burnt shed, each relating to an incident in the past whose actors are still alive; as each point is made the panorama of the village and its interlocking inhabitants becomes clearer. William Mayne has taken a subject suitable for readers of a certain age and has treated it with the proper balance of setting and character, the gradual unfolding of a narrative pattern which we expect from a novel as a piece of literature.

In the years between seven and eleven (with the qualification that age groups are always provisional and liable to overlap at either end), children become readers. Whether or not they become, and remain, confirmed readers depends on the quality of the books they find, or are given, during these years. They need a variety of stories, some within their capacity and experience, others stimulating them to jump ahead of themselves, and in these stories, I believe, they need a breadth of reference far beyond the "child at the center." We do not expect a policy of artificial isolation in the novels we read as adults; old ladies do not wish to read exclusively of geriatrics or young men to concern themselves solely with the exploits of young men. Children need not be expected to have their attention confined to their peer groups in fiction. Indeed, if they are offered books of such restricted interest and purpose, books in which children stand centrally on the stage and adults are kept virtually passive in the wings, they are likely to lose interest in that most rewarding and life-enhancing branch of literature, the novel. Reading full, rich tales which have been written out of a fulness of interest rather than with any dominant prescription of age-interest, a child may go on to become a lover of literature as one of the major pleasures and essentials of a full life.

Notes

1. Jenifer Wayne, *Sprout's Window-Cleaner* (London: Heinemann, 1971), 23.
2. Ibid., 27.
3. Ibid., 93.
4. Ibid.
5. Mrs. Molesworth, *Rosy* (London: Macmillan, 1882), 45.
6. Alan Garner, *Tom Fobble's Day* (London: Collins, 1977), 52-4.
7. Leila Berg, *A Box for Benny* (Leicester, England: Brockhampton, 1958), 17.

Bibliography

Berg, Leila. *A Box for Benny.* Illustrated by Jillian Willet. Leicester, England: Brockhampton, 1958.

Burnett, Frances Hodgson. *The Secret Garden.* Illustrated by Charles Robinson. London: Heinemann, 1911.

Ewing, Mrs. *A Flat Iron for a Farthing; or, Some Passages in the Life of an Only Son.* London: Bell, 1874.

_____. *Lob Lie-by-the-Fire; or, The Luck of Lingborough and Other Tales.* Illustrated by George Cruikshank. London: Bell, 1872.

Garner, Alan. *The Aimer Gate.* Illustrated by Michael Foreman. London: Collins, 1978.

_____. *Granny Reardun.* Illustrated by Michael Foreman. London: Collins, 1977.

_____. *The Stone Book.* Illustrated by Michael Foreman. London: Collins, 1976.

_____. *Tom Fobble's Day.* Illustrated by Michael Foreman. London: Collins, 1977.

Mayne, William. *A Parcel of Trees.* Illustrated by Margery Gill. London: Penguin, 1963.

Molesworth, Mrs. *Rosy.* Illustrated by Walter Crane. London: Macmillan, 1882.

Pearce, Philippa. *A Dog So Small.* Illustrated by Antony Maitland. London: Constable, 1962.

Potter, Beatrix. *The Tale of Peter Rabbit.* London: Warne, 1902.

Ransome, Arthur. *Swallows and Amazons.* London: Cape, 1930.

Wayne, Jenifer. *Sprout's Window-Cleaner.* London: Heinemann, 1971.

Margery Fisher is an English author, critic, editor, and lecturer. Considered one of the most respected contributors to the field of children's literature criticism, she is well known as the author of *Intent upon Reading: A Critical Appraisal of Modern Fiction for Children* (1961; revised edition, 1964), a survey of children's books from approximately 1930 through 1960 which is recognized as a contemporary classic, and as the editor and publisher of *Growing Point,* a reviewing journal which has appeared regularly since 1962. Fisher has also written the critical sources *Matters of Fact: Aspects of Non-Fiction for Children* (1972), *Who's Who in Children's Books: A Treasury of the Familiar Characters of Childhood* (1975), and *The Bright Face of Danger* (1986), an analysis of the adventure story, as well as the biographies *Shackleton* (with James Fisher, 1957), *John Masefield* (1963), and *Henry Treece* (1969), and the novel *Field Day* (1951). She served as the editor of *A Scrapbook of Ashton* (1954), *A World of Animals* (1962), *Open the Door* (1965), and Richard H. Horne's *Memoirs of a London Doll* (1967). Formerly the children's books editor of the *Sunday Times,* London, Fisher has been contributing articles on children's literature to newspapers and magazines since the 1960s. In 1966, she received the first Eleanor Farjeon Award, which is presented to a children's literature professional of extraordinary achievement, and was chosen to deliver the first May Hill Arbuthnot Lecture in 1970. Fisher is a member of the International Board on Books for Young People (IBBY) as well as the International Research Society for Children's Literature. She has also served on juries for the Hans Christian Andersen Award and the Biennale of Illustrations Bratislava, and has organized courses in reading and writing for pleasure for the National Federation of Women's Institutes.

Children's
Literature
Review

Aesop

620? - 564? B.C.

Greek fabulist.

(Also transliterated as Aesopus and Esop) Aesop is credited with defining and popularizing the fable as a literary genre. Although fables predate Aesop and are generally regarded as the work of many cultures in different eras, western fables are usually associated with him. Aesop's fables are considered an important part of the popular culture of the English-speaking world; phrases such as "sour grapes," axioms like "familiarity breeds contempt," and allusions to characters in tales such as "The Hare and the Tortoise" have become part of our everyday language. As a literary form, fables are brief didactic stories characteristically featuring anthropomorphic animals whose simple actions lead directly to a pithy moral lesson appended at the end. Stressing self-preservation, common sense, moderation, and planning, fables often contain satirical or cynical observations on human nature. The severity of these reflections is balanced by the wisdom and humor of the tales, qualities abundant in the Aesop versions. These fables, noted for establishing the animal story as the genre's characteristic mode of expression, are distinguished by the gracefulness with which they allow readers to learn about the virtues of humanity while laughing at its foibles. Originally created to instruct and entertain adults, Aesop's fables now belong to children, who enjoy the stories for their cheerfulness and the antics of their animal characters.

Although he is considered immortal as a storyteller, the real Aesop may never have existed. Reputed to be a Phyrgian or African slave whose wit earned him his freedom as well as a violent death, Aesop is thought to be the first to use fables during times of political tyranny, when direct speech is risky. The fables of Aesop were probably first recorded about 300 B.C. by Demetrius Phalereus, founder of the Alexandria library. Since then, hundreds of international editions have appeared. Prominent early collections include a first-century Latin verse rendition by Phaedrus and a second-century Greek verse compilation by Babrius, whose work is the basis for many later versions. In England, Aesop has enjoyed much popularity. William Caxton, the first English printer, produced an edition in 1484, and numerous school versions were in use by the end of the sixteenth century. In 1692, Sir Roger L'Estrange, a Tory pamphleteer, compiled a comprehensive collection of Aesop's fables that is significant for being the first children's edition and for including political applications as well as morals for each fable. Reverend Samuel Croxall featured Whig political commentary in his 1722 edition, which was utilized or adapted throughout the eighteenth century by such personages as John Newbery, the first notable English publisher for children. Over the centuries, Aesop's fables have inspired many eminent writers including Geoffrey Chaucer, Jean de la Fontaine, Joel Chandler Harris, and Rudyard Kipling, as well as such illustrators as Thomas Bewick, Gustave Doré, Arthur Rackham, and Alexander Calder. Today, Aesop is called "the children's Homer," and is held in the same esteem as the Grimm brothers and Hans Christian Andersen.

Since antiquity, Aesop's fables have been regarded with critical as well as popular acclaim. Although reviewers and ed-

ucators have sometimes found the didacticism of the stories excessive and their cynicism harmful to children, they applaud the succinctness, simplicity, and wisdom of the fables, and consider the talking animals device an excellent teaching tool. There is every indication that Aesop will remain an enduring favorite with children, adaptors, storytellers, and illustrators.

JOHN LOCKE

[The following excerpt is from an essay originally published in 1693.]

[When by] gentle ways [the child] begins to be able to read, some easy, pleasant book, suited to his capacity, should be put into his hands, wherein the entertainment that he finds might draw him on, and reward his pains in reading; and yet not such as should fill his head with perfectly useless trumpery, or lay the principles of vice and folly. To this purpose I think *Æsop's Fables* the best, which being stories apt to delight and entertain a child, may yet afford useful reflections to a grown man; and if his memory retain them all his life after, he will not repent to find them there, amongst his manly thoughts and serious business. If his Æsop has pictures in it, it will entertain him much the better, and encourage him to read when it carries the increase of knowledge with it. . . . (pp. 119-20)

John Locke, "Some Thoughts Concerning Education," in his The Educational Writings of John Locke,
edited by John William Adamson, Edward Arnold,
1912, pp. 21-180.

SAMUEL RICHARDSON

When there are so many editions of *Æsop's fables,* it will be
expected, that some reasons should be given for the appearance
of a new one; and we shall be as brief on this head, as the
nature of the thing will admit. Of all the *English* editions, we
shall consider only two as worthy of notice; to wit, that of the
celebrated Sir *Roger L'Estrange,* and that which appears under
the name of *S. Croxal,* subscribed to the dedication. And when
we have given an account of what each says for his own performance, it will be our turn to offer some things to the reader
with regard to our present undertaking.

> When first I put pen to paper upon this design,
> says Sir *Roger,* I had in my eye only the com-
> mon school book, as it stands in the *Cambridge*
> and *Oxford* editions of it, under the title of
> **Æsopi Phrygis Fabulae; una cum nonnullis var-
> iorum auctorum fabulis adjectis:** propounding
> to myself, at that time, to follow the very course
> and series of that collection; and, in one word,
> to try what might be done by making the best
> of the whole, and adapting proper and useful
> doctrines to the several parts of it, toward the
> turning of an *excellent Latin manual* of morals
> and good counsels, into a *tolerable English one.*
> But, upon jumbling matters and thoughts to-
> gether, and laying one thing by another, the
> very state and condition of the case before me,
> together with the nature and the reason of the
> thing, gave me to understand, that this way of
> proceeding would never answer my end: in-
> somuch that, upon this consideration, I con-
> sulted other versions of the same fables, and
> made my best of the choice. Some that were
> *twice or thrice over,* and only the self-same
> thing in other words; these I struck out, and
> made one specimen serve for the rest. To say
> nothing of here and there a *trivial,* or a *loose
> conceit* in the medley, more than this; that such
> as they are, I was under some sort of obligation
> to take them in for company; and in short, *good,
> bad* and *indifferent,* one with another, to the
> number, in the total, of 383 fables. To these I
> have likewise subjoined a considerable addition
> of other select *Apologues,* out of the most cel-
> ebrated authors that are extant upon that sub-
> ject, towards the finishing of the work.

And a little farther,

> This *Rhapsody* of *Fables,* says he, is a book
> universally read, and taught in all our schools;
> but almost at such a rate as we teach *Pyes* and
> *Parrots,* that pronounce the words without so
> much as guessing at the meaning of them: or,
> to take it another way, the boys break their teeth
> upon the shells, without ever coming near the
> kernel. They learn fables by lessons, and the
> moral is the least part of our care in a child's
> institution: so that take both together, and the
> one is stark nonsense, without the application
> of the other; beside that, the doctrine itself, as

we have it, even at the best, falls infinitely short
of the vigour and spirit of the fable. To supply
this defect now, we have had several *English*
paraphrases and essays upon *Esop,* and divers
of the followers, both in prose and verse. The
latter have perchance ventured a little too far
from the precise scope of the author upon the
privilege of a poetical licence: and for the other
of antient date, the morals are so insipid and
flat, and the style and diction of the fables so
coarse and uncouth, that they are rather dangerous than profitable, as to the purpose they
were principally intended for; and likely to do
forty times more mischief by the one, than good
by the other. An emblem without a key to it,
is no more than a *Tale of a Tub;* and that tale
sillily told too, is but one folly grafted upon
another. Children are to be taught, in the first
place, what they ought to do: 2dly, the manner
of doing it: And, in the third place, they are to
be inured by the force of instruction and good
example, to the love and practice of doing their
duty; whereas, on the contrary, one step out of
the way in the institution, is enough to poison
the peace and the reputation of a whole life.
Whether I have in this attempt, adds Sir *Roger,*
contributed or not, to the improvement of these
fables, either in the wording, or the meaning
of them, the book must stand or fall to itself:
but this I shall adventure to pronounce upon
the whole matter, that the text is *English,* and
the morals, in some sort, accommodate to the
allegory; which could hardly be said of all the
translations or reflections before mentioned,
which have served, in truth, (or at least some
of them) rather to teach us what we should *not*
do, than what we *should.* So that, in the publishing of these papers, I have done my best to
obviate a common inconvenience, or, to speak
plainly, the mortal error of pretending to erect
a building upon a false foundation: leaving the
whole world to take the same freedom with me,
that I have done with others.

Thus far Sir *Roger L'Estrange.* Now we come to what the other
gentleman has to say *for himself,* or rather, as he has managed
the matter, what he has to say *against* Sir *Roger,* the depre-
ciating of whose work, seems to be the cornerstone of his own
building.

> Nothing of this nature, says he, has been done
> since *L'Estrange*'s time worth mentioning; and
> we had nothing before, but what . . . was so
> *insipid and flat in the moral, and so coarse and
> uncouth in the style and diction, that they were
> rather dangerous than profitable, as to the pur-
> pose for which they were principally intended;
> and likely to do forty times more harm than
> good.* I shall therefore only observe to my reader
> the insufficiency of *L'Estrange*'s own perfor-
> mance, as to the purpose for which he professes
> to have principally intended it; with some other
> circumstances, which will help to excuse, if
> not justify, what I have enterprized upon the
> same subject.

Now this purpose for which he principally intended his book, as in his preface he spends a great many words to inform us, was for the use and instruction of children; who being, as it were, a mere *rasa tabula*, or blank paper, *are ready indifferently for any opinions, good or bad, taking all upon credit; and that it is in the power of the first comer, to write saint or devil upon them, which he pleases.* This being truly and certainly the case, what devils, nay, what poor devils, would *L'Estrange* make of those children, who should be so unfortunate as to read his book, and imbibe his pernicious principles! Principles coined and suited to promote the growth, and serve the ends, of popery and arbitrary power. Though we had never been told he was a pensioner to a Popish prince, and that he himself professed the same unaccountable religion, yet his reflections upon *Aesop* would discover it to us: In every political touch, he shews himself to be the tool and hireling of the Popish faction: since even a slave, without some mercenary view, would not bring arguments to justify slavery, nor endeavour to establish arbitrary power upon the basis of right reason. What sort of children therefore are the *Blank Paper*, upon which such morality as this ought to be written? Not the children of *Britain*, I hope; for they are born with free blood in their veins, and suck in liberty with their very milk. This they should be taught to love and cherish above all things, and, upon occasion, to defend and vindicate it; as it is the glory of their country, the greatest blessing of their lives, and the peculiar happy privilege, in which they excel all the world besides. Let therefore *L'Estrange*, with his slavish doctrine, be banished to the barren deserts of *Arabia*, to the nurseries of *Turkey, Persia,* and *Morocco,* where all footsteps of liberty have long since been worn out, and the minds of the people, by a narrow way of thinking, contrasted and inured to fear poverty and miserable servitude. Let the children of *Italy, France, Spain,* and the rest of the Popish countries, *continue this tedious declaimer,* furnish him with blank paper for principles, of which free-born *Britons* are not capable. The earlier such notions are instilled into such minds as theirs indeed, the better it will be for them, as it will keep them from thinking of any other than the abject, servile condition to which they are born. But let the minds of our *British* youth be for ever educated and improved in that spirit of truth and liberty, for the support of which their ancestors have often bravely exhausted so much blood and treasure.

Thus we see the chief quarrel of the worthy gentleman is against the *Politicks* of Sir *Roger;* and we heartily join with him on this head. Sir *Roger* was certainly listed in a bad cause as to politicks, and his reflections have many of them a pernicious tendency. But the time in which he wrote, within view, in a manner, of the civil wars so lately concluded, and the anarchy introduced by them, to so great an extreme of one side, was so naturally productive of an extreme on the other, that many very great men of that time fell into the same error with Sir

Wood engraving by William Caxton, England's first printer, from the first English edition of Aesop's Fables *(1484). Caxton's translation was considered the standard version of the fables during the middle ages.*

Roger: and perhaps a charitable mind, duly reflecting upon this, and not intent upon *partial* or *selfish* views, would have found something to have said, if not in *excuse,* yet in *extenuation,* of the fault.

The Doctor, for such I am told the gentleman is, proceeds to strengthen his own cause, by further observing,

> That *L'Estrange* (as he every where calls the deceased knight) made not fair reflections upon the fables in political points: that *Æsop,* though a slave, was a lover of liberty, and gives not one hint to favour *L'Estrange's* insinuations: But that, on the contrary, he takes all occasions to recommend a love for liberty, and an abhorrence of tyranny, and all arbitrary proceedings: that *L'Estrange* (again!) notoriously perverts both the sense and meaning of several fables, particularly when any political instruction (*for this is still the burden of the Doctor's song*) is couched in the application;

and then gives an example in Sir *Roger's* fable of the **"Dog and the Wolf"**; and further objects against the Knight,

> that he has swelled his work, which was designed for the use of children, to a voluminous bulk; and by that means raised it to an exorbitant price, so as to make it unsuitable to the hand or pocket of the generality of children.

And here follows a very extraordinary conclusion of the Doctor, which we shall give *verbatim:*

> If I were, *says the good man,* to put constructions upon the ways of Providence, I should fancy this prolixity of his was ordered as a preservative against his noxious principles; for however his book may have been used by *Men,* I dare say, few *Children* have been conversant with it.

So that we see, at last, all the terrible apprehensions of the mischiefs of Sir *Roger's* book, are merely the effects of the good Doctor's imagination, which, it is generally said, has run away with his judgment in more instances than the present.

If this then be the case, we presume to hope, that, even in the good Doctor's opinion, there will not be any necessity to banish poor *L'Estrange* to the barren deserts of *Arabia*, to the nurseries of *Turkey, Persia*, and *Morocco;* nor that he should be confined to the children of *Italy, France, Spain*, and the rest of the Popish countries; but, for the sake of the excellent sense contained in his other reflections, where politicks are not concerned; for the sake of the benefit which the *English* tongue has received from his masterly hand; for the sake of that fine humour, apposite language, accurate and lively manner, which will always render Sir *Roger* delightful, and which this severe Critick has in some places so wretchedly endeavoured to imitate: for all these sakes, I say, let him remain among us still, since our author thinks he can do no harm to *Children*, and *Men* may be supposed guarded by years and experience; and the rather, if it be only to shew the difference between a fine original, and a bungling imitation; and that no prating *Jays* may strut about in the beautiful plumage of the *Peacock*.

The Doctor proceeds, and fixes a stigma on the second Volume of Sir *Roger*'s Fables, and, in the main, I join with him in it; for, as a Book of Fables, it is truly unworthy of that celebrated hand; and for that reason we have made very little use of it in our present edition; though we cannot but apprehend, that he was put upon it rather by the importunity of booksellers, encouraged by the success of the first volume, than by his own choice or judgment: and, after all, some allowance ought to be made for his circumstances, and his years, being, as he tells us, on the wrong side of fourscore when he wrote it.

It is but just to transcribe the concluding paragraph of the Doctor's preface.

> Whether, *says he,* I have mended the faults I find with him, in this, or any other respect, I, must leave to the judgment of the reader: professing (according to the principle on which the following applications are built) that I am a lover of liberty and truth; an enemy to tyranny, either in Church or State; and one who detests party-animosities, and factious divisions, as much as I wish the peace and prosperity of my country.

We greatly applaud this pompous declaration of the good Gentleman's principles: but though we might observe, that he has strained the natural import of some of the Fables, near as much one way, as Sir *Roger* has done the other, and may be censured for giving too frequently into political reflections, which had, on all occasions, if the book be meant for Children, better be avoided, where the moral will bear a more general and inoffensive turn; yet we shall only observe, that had this gentleman, who clothes himself in the skin of the departed knight, and, at first fight, makes so formidable an appearance in it, lived in the days of Sir *Roger*, and had Sir *Roger* lived in his, it is not impossible that the sentiments of both might have changed.

What I mean, is, the *Restoration* of Monarchy under King *Charles* II, made these now exploded doctrines as much the fashion then, as the glorious *Revolution* under King *William* III has made the Doctor's principles the fashion now. And for aught that appears from the *moderation* of the Doctor's principles, if we may judge of a Man's temper by his disposition, as shewn in several instances of his preface, had the Doctor lived when Sir *Roger* did, he might have been the *L'Estrange* of the *one Court;* as *L'Estrange*, had he been in the Doctor's place, might have taken orders, and become Chaplain in the

other. If the living Gentleman reflects, as he ought, upon the little mercy he has shewn to the dead, he will not think this too severe. And the comparison will appear the less invidious, to any one who considers, that Sir *Roger* suffered for his principles, bad as they were: and the Doctor, we hope, for the sake of the *publick*, as well as for his *own sake*, will never be called upon to such trials.

We have thus set the pretensions of the two gentlemen in a proper light: it remains for us, now to say something of our own undertaking.

The usefulness and benefit of such a work to children is allowed on all hands; and therefore we shall not insist upon a topick, which has been so much laboured by the gentlemen who have gone before us.

We have seen, that the only objections which a scrutinizing adversary, who had it in view to supplant the Knight, and thrust himself into his place, can find against him, are the *political* part, and the *bulk* and *price* of the performance: as to the rest, on comparing the works, we find a very great disparity between them: we therefore were assured, that we should do an acceptable service, if we could give the *exceptionable reflections* a more *general* and *useful* turn; and if we could reduce the work to such a size as should be fit for the *hands* and *pockets* for which it was principally designed; and at the same time preserve to Sir *Roger* the principal graces and beauties for which he is so justly admired: and this only, though we found afterwards, on a closer review, a necessity of going further, was our *first* intention.

We were the rather prevailed upon to take this liberty with Sir *Roger*, because he ingenuously declares, in what we have quoted from his preface, 'That he was under some sort of obligation to take into his medley, as he modestly calls it, here and there a trivial or a loose conceit, for company.' An obligation imposed upon him, we presume, by his unhappy circumstances (and which hardly those could excuse), in order to add to the bulk of his book, which he first published in folio.

This, with other proper alterations, &c. where the sense and poignance of the fable and reflections would best bear it, we thought would give us the opportunity of answering the objection about the *bulk* and *price*. And on looking closer into the subject, we found sufficient reason to justify our opinion.

Thus then, instead of banishing Sir *Roger* to the desarts of *Arabia*, we confess that it was our intention, every-where, except in his *political reflections*, to keep that celebrated writer close in our eye: And in some places we have accordingly contented ourselves with the inferior glory of having only abridged him, where we could not, with *equal* beauty and propriety, give words and sentences different from his own; rather choosing to acknowledge our obligations to so great a master, than to arrogate to ourselves the praises due to another.

We have not, however, spared any of those conceits, as Sir *Roger* calls them, which we imagined capable only of a trivial, or liable to a loose construction. We have also presumed to alter, and put a stronger point to several of the fables themselves, which we thought capable of more forcible morals. And instead of the political reflections, we have every where substituted such as we hope will be found more general and instructive. For we think it in no wise excusable to inflame children's minds with distinctions, which they will imbibe fast enough from the attachments of parents, &c. and the warmth of their own imaginations. But nevertheless, we must add, that wherever the fable *compelled,* as we may say, a political turn, we have, in our reflections upon it, always given that preference to the principles of LIBERTY, which we hope will for ever be the distinguishing characteristic of a *Briton.* (pp. i-xii)

If thus we have banished from Sir *Roger* all that his most partial enemy could except against him; and have preserved all that has gained him the approbation of the best judges: If we have avoided the faults of both gentlemen (and we think we could point out, if we were put upon it, where the one has been faulty as well as the other; and a thousand instances wherein he has infinitely fallen short of the author he aims to supplant): why should we not presume, that there may be room for this performance, which we now present to the publick? To whose judgment we therefore submit it; and are willing to stand or fall by its determination. (p. xiv)

. . . . .

We have had the history of Æsop so many times over and over, as Sir Roger L'Estrange observes, and dressed up so many several ways, that it would be but labour lost to multiply unprofitable conjectures upon a tradition of so great uncertainty. Writers are divided about him, almost to all manner of purposes; and particularly concerning the authority even of the greater part of those compositions that pass the world in his name: for the story is come down to us so dark and doubtful, that it is impossible to distinguish the original from the copy; and to say, which of the fables are Æsop's, and which are not; which are genuine, and which are spurious; beside, that there are divers inconsistencies upon the point of chronology, in the account of his life (as Maximus Planudes and others have delivered it), which can never be reconciled.

This is enough in all conscience to excuse any man, says Sir Roger, from laying over-much stress upon the historical credit of a relation that comes so blindly and so variously transmitted to us; over and above, that it is not one jot to our business (further than to gratify an idle curiosity) whether the fact be true or false; whether the man was strait or crooked; and his name Aesop, or (as some will have it) Lochman: in all which cases the reader is left at liberty to believe his pleasure. (p. xv)

> *Samuel Richardson, in a preface and "The Life of Aesop," in* Aesop's Fables *by Aesop, edited by Samuel Richardson, 1740. Reprint by Garland Publishing, Inc., 1975, pp. i-xiv, xv-xxxiv.*

OLIVER GOLDSMITH

[The following excerpt is taken from an essay originally published in 1784.]

[Æsop] was a person of a remarkable genius, and extraordinary character. . . . [He] had a great soul, and was endowed with extraordinary mental qualifications; his moral character approached to a degree of perfection to which very few have attained. He appears to have had a true sense of morality and a just discernment of right and wrong; his perceptions and feelings of truth were scrupulously nice, and the smallest deviation from rectitude impressed his mind with the greatest antipathy. No considerations of private interest could warp his inclinations so as to seduce him from the paths of virtue; his principles were stedfast and determined, and truly habitual. He never employed his great wisdom to serve the purposes of cunning; but, with an uncommon exactness, made his understanding a servant to truth. Historians have given many instances of his wit and shrewdness, which were always em-

ployed in the service of virtue, philanthropy, and benevolence. (pp. i-ii)

His Fables are allegorical stories, delivered with an air of fiction, under various personifications, to convey truth to the mind in an agreeable manner. By telling a story of a *Lion, Dog,* or a *Wolf,* the Fabulist describes the manners and characters of men, and communicates instruction without seeming to assume the authority of a master or a pedagogue. (p. iii)

The writer of [Æsop's] life prefixed to Dodsley's **Fables** compares him to Dean Swift, but with very little propriety; for he has a delicacy in all his wit which the Dean of St. Patrick's was a total stranger to; and, what is more strange, he had nearly as much Christianity.

It has been doubted if he was the inventor of Fables; but it is certain he was the first that brought that species of writing into reputation. Archilochus is said to have written Fables one hundred years before him; but it would appear that those stories were not written for posterity like those of Æsop. The Fables of Æsop were written in prose, though the images that are in them afford good scope for a poet, of which Phrædus has given an elegant specimen. Æsop writes with great simplicity, elegance, and neatness; the schemes of his Fables are natural, the sentiments just, and the conclusions moral. Quintilian recommends his Fables as a first book for children. . . . (p. viii)

The great excellency of Æsop's manner of writing is, that he blends the pleasing and the instructive so well as to instruct and please at once. . . .

[Æsop's] Fables have immortalised his memory, and will hand down his name to the latest posterity. (p. ix)

> *Oliver Goldsmith, "Life of Aesop," in* Bewick's Select Fables of Aesop, *by Aesop, 1784. Reprint by Cheshire House, 1932, pp. i-ix.*

THE PROSPECTIVE REVIEW

[Though] Aesop has been a good deal pressed upon the attention of "the youth of the British isles," we apprehend it has not been with much success: the pithy meaning in which the point of the story lies is lost upon him, and all that he cares for is any humour which may be embodied in the telling. . . . The tales gather an interest as elucidating the pictures; and that is all. Fables are not milk for babes by any means. (p. 55)

> *"Fictions for Children," in* The Prospective Review, *Vol. II, No. XLI, February, 1855, pp. 51-82.*

EDWARD SALMON

Aesop's fame in the nursery is so great as to appear almost as fabulous, at least in its historic aspects, as the themes of which he treats. It would be an interesting and far from uninstructive inquiry for some one, who could give the time to it, to attempt to determine the influence which Aesop, or rather the marvellous collection of fables associated with the name of Aesop, has had on the minds of men. Throughout the ages, in the midst of ignorance and superstition, in the homes of rich and poor alike, Aesop has secured a place. It would be an endless task to enumerate the editions through which he has passed or the various methods in which it has been sought to lay his teaching before the nymphs of the nursery. Even now only two others can claim to storm that particular section of the household with anything like equal success—Grimm and Andersen. . . . Aesop is distinguished first by brevity; second, by the manner in which his moral is generally hung in an epigrammatic

Uncredited German woodcut from Aesop's Life and Fables, *Ulm, about 1476-77. This was the most popular edition of the fifteenth century.*

and easily to be avoided form at the end of his narrative.
(pp. 564-65)

> *Edward Salmon, "Literature for the Little Ones," in* The Nineteenth Century, *Vol. XXII, No. CXXVIII, October, 1887, pp. 563-80.*

ANDREW LANG

"Esop."

He sat among the woods, he heard
    The sylvan merriment; he saw
The pranks of butterfly and bird,
    The humours of the ape, the daw.

And in the lion or the frog—
    In all the life of moor and fen,
In ass and peacock, stork and log,
    He read similitudes of men.

"Of these, from those," he cried, "we come,
    Our hearts, our brains descend from these."
And lo! the Beasts no more were dumb,
    But answered out of brakes and trees;

"Not ours," they cried; "Degenerate,
    If ours at all," they cried again,
"Ye fools, who war with God and Fate,
    Who strive and toil: strange race of men,

"For *we* are neither bond nor free,
    For *we* have neither slaves nor kings,
But near to Nature's heart are we,
    And conscious of her secret things.

"Content are we to fall asleep,
    And well content to wake no more,
We do not laugh, we do not weep,
    Nor look behind us and before;

"But were there cause for moan or mirth,
    'Tis *we*, not you, should sigh or scorn,
Oh, latest children of the Earth
    Most childish children Earth has borne."

     ·   ·   ·   ·   ·

They spoke, but that misshapen Slave
    Told never of the thing he heard,
And unto men their portraits gave,
    In likenesses of beast and bird!

(pp. 2-3)

> *Andrew Lang, " 'Esop'," in his* The Fables of Aesop *as first printed by William Caxton in 1484: History of the Aesopic Fable, Vol. I, edited by Joseph Jacobs, David Nutt, 1889, pp. 2-3.*

JOSEPH JACOBS

[*The following excerpt is taken from an essay originally published in 1894.*]

It is difficult to say what are and what are not the *Fables* of Aesop. Almost all the fables that have appeared in the Western world have been sheltered at one time or another under the shadow of that name. I could at any rate enumerate at least seven hundred which have appeared in English in various books entitled *Aesop's Fables*. L'Estrange's collection alone contains over five hundred. . . .

Aesop himself is so shadowy a figure that we might almost be forgiven if we held, with regard to him, the heresy of Mistress Elizabeth Prig. What we call his fables can in most cases be traced back to the fables of other people, notably of Phaedrus and Babrius. It is usual to regard the Greek Prose Collections, passing under the name of Aesop, as having greater claims to the eponymous title; but modern research has shown that these are but medieval prosings of Babrius's verse. (p. v)

     ·   ·   ·   ·   ·

Most nations develop the Beast-Tale as part of their folk-lore, some go further and apply it to satiric purposes, and a few nations afford isolated examples of the shaping of the Beast-Tale to teach some moral truth by means of the Fable properly so called. But only two peoples independently made this a general practice. Both in Greece and in India we find in the earliest literature such casual and frequent mention of Fables as seems to imply a body of Folk-Fables current among the people. And in both countries special circumstances raised the Fable from folklore into literature. In Greece, during the epoch of the Tyrants, when free speech was dangerous, the Fable was largely used for political purposes. The inventor of this application or the most prominent user of it was one Aesop, a slave at Samos whose name has ever since been connected with the Fable. All that we know about him is contained in a few lines of Herodotus: that he flourished 550 B.C.; was killed in accordance with a Delphian oracle; and that *wergild* was claimed for him by the grandson of his master Iadmon. When free speech was established in the Greek democracies, the custom of using Fables in harangues was continued and encouraged by the rhetoricians, while the mirth-producing qualities of the Fable caused it to be regarded as fit subject of after-dinner conversation along with other jests of a broader kind (''Milesian,'' ''Sybaritic''). This habit of regarding the Fable as a form of the Jest intensified the tendency to connect it with a well-known name. . . . About 300 B.C. Demetrius Phalereus, whilom tyrant of Athens and founder of the Alexandria Library, collected together all the Fables he could find under the title of *Assemblies of Aesopic Tales.* . . . This collection, running probably to some 200 Fables, after being interpolated and edited by the Alexandrine grammarians, was turned into neat Latin iambics by Phaedrus, a Greek freedman of Augustus in the early years of the Christian era. As the modern Aesop is mainly derived from Phaedrus, the answer to the question ''Who wrote Aesop?'' is simple: ''Demetrius of Phaleron.''

In India the great ethical reformer, Sakyamuni, the Buddha, initiated (or adopted from the Brahmins) the habit of using the Beast-Tale for moral purposes, or, in other words, transformed it into the Fable proper. A collection of these seems to have existed previously and independently, in which the Fables were associated with the name of a mythical sage, Kasyâpa. These were appropriated by the early Buddhists by the simple expedient of making Kasyâpa the immediately preceding incarnation of the Buddha. A number of his *itihâsas* or Tales were included in the sacred Buddhistic work containing the ''Jātakas'' or previous-births of the Buddha, in some of which the Bodisat (or future Buddha) appears as one of the Dramatis Personae of the Fables; the Crane, *e.g.,* in our **''Wolf and Crane''** being one of the incarnations of the Buddha. So, too, the Lamb of our **''Wolf and Lamb''** was once Buddha; it was therefore easy for him—so the Buddhists thought—to remember and tell these Fables as incidents of his former careers. It is obvious that the whole idea of a Fable as an anecdote about a man masquerading in the form of a beast could most easily arise and gain currency where the theory of transmigration was vividly credited.

The Fables of Kasyâpa, or rather the moral verses (*gathas*) which served as a *memoria technica* to them, were probably carried over to Ceylon in 241 B.C. along with the Jātakas. About 300 years later (say 50 A.D.) some 100 of these were brought by a Cingalese embassy to Alexandria, where they were translated under the title of ''Libyan Fables'' . . . , which has been earlier applied to similar stories that had percolated to Hellas from India; they were attributed to ''Kybises.'' This collection seems to have introduced the habit of summing up the teaching of a Fable in the Moral, corresponding to the *gatha* of the Jātakas. About the end of the first century A.D. the Libyan Fables of ''Kybises'' became known to the Rabbinic school at Jabne, founded by R. Jochanan ben Saccai, and a number of the Fables translated into Aramaic which are still extant in the Talmud and Midrash.

In the Roman world the two collections of Demetrius and ''Kybises'' were brought together by Nicostratus, a rhetor attached to the court of Marcus Aurelius. In the earlier part of the next century (c. 230 A.D.) this *corpus* of the ancient fable, Aesopic and Libyan, amounting in all to some 300 members, was done into Greek verse with Latin accentuation (choliam-

bics) by Valerius Babrius, tutor to the young son of Alexander Severus. Still later, towards the end of the fourth century, forty-two of these, mainly of the Libyan section, were translated into Latin verse by one Avian, with whom the ancient history of the Fable ends.

In the Middle Ages it was naturally the Latin Phaedrus that represented the Aesopic Fable to the learned world, but Phaedrus in a fuller form than has descended to us in verse. A selection of some eighty fables was turned into indifferent prose in the ninth century, probably at the Schools of Charles the Great. This was attributed to a fictitious Romulus. Another prose collection by Ademar of Chabannes was made before 1030, and still preserves some of the lines of the lost Fables of Phaedrus. The Fables became especially popular among the Normans. A number of them occur on the Bayeux Tapestry, and in the twelfth century England, the head of the Angevin empire, became the home of the Fable, all the important adaptations and versions of Aesop being made in this country. One of these done into Latin verse by Walter the Englishman became the standard Aesop of medieval Christendom. The same history applies in large measure to the Fables of Avian, which were done into prose, transferred back into Latin verse, and sent forth through Europe from England.

Meanwhile Babrius had been suffering the same fate as Phaedrus. His scazons were turned into poor Greek prose, and selections of them pass to this day as the original Fables of Aesop. Some fifty of these were selected and, with the addition of a dozen Oriental fables, were attributed to an imaginary Persian sage, Syntipas; this collection was translated into Syriac, and thence into Arabic, where they passed under the name of the legendary Lôqman (probably a doublet of Balaam). A still larger collection of the Greek prose versions got into Arabic, where it was enriched by some sixty fables from the Arabic Bidpai and other sources, but still passed under the name of Aesop. This collection, containing 164 fables, was brought to England after the Third Crusade of Richard I, and translated into Latin by an Englishman named Alfred, with the aid of an Oxford Jew named Berachyah ha-Nakdan (''Benedictus le Puncteur'' in the English Records), who, on his own account, translated a number of the fables into Hebrew rhymed prose, under the Talmudic title *Mishle Shu'alim (Fox Fables)*. Part of Alfred's Aesop was translated into English alliterative verse, and this again was translated about 1200 into French by Marie de France, who attributed the new fables to King Alfred. After her no important addition was made to the medieval Aesop.

With the invention of printing the European book of Aesop was compiled about 1480 by Heinrich Stainhöwel, who put together the Romulus with selections from Avian, some of the Greek prose versions of Babrius from Ranuzio's translation, and a few from Alfred's Aesop. To these he added the legendary life of Aesop and a selection of somewhat loose tales from Petrus Alphonsi and Poggio Bracciolini, corresponding to the Milesian and Sybaritic tales which were associated with the Fable in antiquity. Stainhöwel translated all this into German, and within twenty years his collection had been turned into French, English (by Caxton, in 1484), Italian, Dutch, and Spanish. Additions were made to it by Brandt and Waldis in Germany, by L'Estrange in England, and by La Fontaine in France; these were chiefly from the larger Greek collections published after Stainhöwel's day, and, in the case of La Fontaine, from Bidpai and other Oriental sources. But these additions have rarely taken hold, and the Aesop of modern Europe is in large measure Stainhöwel's, even to the present day. The first three-quarters of the present collection are Stainhöwel, mainly in Stainhöwel's order. Selections from it passed into spelling and reading books, and made the Fables part of modern European folk-lore.

We may conclude this history of Aesop with a similar account of the progress of Aesopic investigation. First came collection; the Greek Aesop was brought together by Neveletus in 1610, the Latin by Nilant in 1709. The main truth about the former was laid down by the master-hand of Bentley during a skirmish in the Battle of the Books; the equally great critic Lessing began to unravel the many knotty points connected with the medieval Latin Aesop. His investigations have been carried on and completed by three Frenchmen in the present century, Robert, Du Méril, and Hervieux; while three Germans, Crusius, Benfey, and Mall, have thrown much needed light on Babrius, on the Oriental Aesop, and on Marie de France. Lastly, I have myself brought together these various lines of inquiry, and by adding a few threads of my own, have been able to weave them all for the first time into a consistent pattern.

So much for the past of the Fable. Has it a future as a mode of literary expression? Scarcely; its method is at once too simple and too roundabout. Too roundabout; for the truths we have to tell we prefer to speak out directly and not by way of allegory. And the truths the Fable has to teach are too simple to correspond to the facts of our complex civilisation; its rude *graffiti* of human nature cannot reproduce the subtle gradations of modern life. But as we all pass through in our lives the various stages of ancestral culture, there comes a time when these rough sketches of life have their appeal to us as they had for our forefathers. The allegory gives us a pleasing and not too strenuous stimulation of the intellectual powers; the lesson is not too complicated for childlike minds. Indeed, in their grotesque grace, in their quaint humour, in their trust in the simpler virtues, in their insight into the cruder vices, in their innocence of the fact of sex, *Aesop's Fables* are as little children. They are as little children, and for that reason they will forever find a home in the heaven of little children's souls. (pp. 104-10)

> *Joseph Jacobs, in a preface and "A Short History of the Aesopic Fable," in* The Fables of Aesop *by Aesop, edited by Joseph Jacobs, 1894. Reprint by The Macmillan Company, 1964, pp. v-vi, 104-10.*

G. K. CHESTERTON

Æsop embodies an epigram not uncommon in human history; his fame is all the more deserved because he never deserved it. The firm foundations of common sense, the shrewd shots at uncommon sense, that characterise all the Fables, belong not to him but to humanity. In the earliest human history whatever is authentic is universal: and whatever is universal is anonymous. In such cases there is always some central man who had first the trouble of collecting them, and afterwards the fame of creating them. He had the fame; and, on the whole, he earned the fame. There must have been something great and human, something of the human future and the human past, in such a man: even if he only used it to rob the past or deceive the future. (p. v)

The historical Æsop, in so far as he was historical, would seem to have been a Phrygian slave, or at least one not to be specially and symbolically adorned with the Phrygian cap of liberty. He lived, if he did live, about the sixth century before Christ, in the time of that Crœsus whose story we love and suspect like

The Lion and the Mouse. Engraving by British artist Wenceslaus Hollar for John Ogilby's The Fables of Aesop *(1665), which is considered the first artistic translation of the tales for the young.*

everything else in Herodotus. There are also stories of deformity of feature and a ready ribaldry of tongue: stories which (as the celebrated Cardinal said) explain, though they do not excuse, his having been hurled over a high precipice at Delphi. It is for those who read the Fables to judge whether he was really thrown over the cliff for being ugly and offensive, or rather for being highly moral and correct. But there is no kind of doubt that the general legend of him may justly rank him with a race too easily forgotten in our modern comparisons: the race of the great philosophic slaves. Æsop may have been a fiction like Uncle Remus: he was also, like Uncle Remus, a fact. It is a fact that slaves in the old world could be worshipped like Æsop, or loved like Uncle Remus. It is odd to note that both the great slaves told their best stories about beasts and birds.

But whatever be fairly due to Æsop, the human tradition called Fables is not due to him. This had gone on long before any sarcastic freedman from Phrygia had or had not been flung off a precipice; this has remained long after. It is to our advantage, indeed, to realise the distinction; because it makes Æsop more obviously effective than any other fabulist. *Grimm's Tales,* glorious as they are, were collected by two German students. And if we find it hard to be certain of a German student, at least we know more about him than we know about a Phrygian slave. The truth is, of course, that *Æsop's Fables* are not Æsop's fables, any more than Grimm's Fairy Tales were ever Grimm's fairy tales. But the fable and the fairy tale are things utterly distinct. There are many elements of difference; but the plainest is plain enough. There can be no good fable with human beings in it. There can be no good fairy tale without them.

Æsop, or Babrius (or whatever his name was), understood that, for a fable, all the persons must be impersonal. They must be like abstractions in algebra, or like pieces in chess. The lion must always be stronger than the wolf, just as four is always double of two. The fox in a fable must move crooked, as the knight in chess must move crooked. The sheep in a fable must march on, as the pawn in chess must march on. The fable must not allow for the crooked captures of the pawn; it must not allow for what Balzac called "the revolt of a sheep." The fairy tale, on the other hand, absolutely revolves on the pivot of human personality. If no hero were there to fight the dragons, we should not even know that they were dragons. If no adventurer were cast on the undiscovered island—it would remain undiscovered. . . . Fables repose upon quite the opposite idea; that everything is itself, and will in any case speak for itself. The wolf will be always wolfish; the fox will be always foxy. Something of the same sort may have been meant by the animal worship, in which Egyptian and Indian and many other great peoples have combined. Men do not, I think, love beetles or cats or crocodiles with a wholly personal love; they salute them as expressions of that abstract and anonymous energy in nature which to any one is awful, and to an atheist must be frightful. So in all the fables that are or are not Æsop's all the animal forces drive like inanimate forces, like great rivers or growing trees. It is the limit and the loss of all such things that they cannot be anything but themselves: it is their tragedy that they could not lose their souls.

This is the immortal justification of the Fable: that we could not teach the plainest truths so simply without turning men into chessmen. We cannot talk of such simple things without using animals that do not talk at all. Suppose, for a moment, that you turn the wolf into a wolfish baron, or the fox into a foxy diplomatist. You will at once remember that even barons are human, you will be unable to forget that even diplomatists are men. You will always be looking for that accidental good-humour that should go with the brutality of any brutal man; for that allowance for all delicate things, including virtue, that should exist in any good diplomatist. Once put a thing on two legs instead of four and pluck it of feathers and you cannot help asking for a human being, either heroic, as in the fairy tales, or unheroic, as in the modern novels.

But by using animals in this austere and arbitrary style as they are used on the shields of heraldry or the hieroglyphics of the ancients, men have really succeeded in handing down those tremendous truths that are called truisms. If the chivalric lion be red and rampant, it is rigidly red and rampant; if the sacred ibis stands anywhere on one leg, it stands on one leg for ever. In this language, like a large animal alphabet, are written some of the first philosophic certainties of men. As the child learns A for Ass or B for Bull or C for Cow, so man has learnt here to connect the simpler and stronger creatures with the simpler and stronger truths. That a flowing stream cannot befoul its own fountain, and that any one who says it does is a tyrant and a liar; that a mouse is too weak to fight a lion, but too strong for the cords that can hold a lion; that a fox who gets most out of a flat dish may easily get least out of a deep dish; that the crow whom the gods forbid to sing, the gods nevertheless provide with cheese; that when the goat insults from a mountain-top it is not the goat that insults, but the mountain: all these are deep truths deeply graven on the rocks wherever men have passed. It matters nothing how old they are, or how

new; they are the alphabet of humanity, which like so many forms of primitive picture-writing employs any living symbol, in preference to man. These ancient and universal tales are all of animals; as the latest discoveries in the oldest prehistoric caverns are all of animals. Man, in his simpler states, always felt that he himself was something too mysterious to be drawn. But the legend he carved under these cruder symbols was everywhere the same; and whether fables began with Æsop or began with Adam, whether they were German and mediaeval as Reynard the Fox, or as French and Renaissance as La Fontaine, the upshot is everywhere essentially the same: that superiority is always insolent, because it is always accidental; that pride goes before a fall; and that there is such a thing as being too clever by half. You will not find any other legend but this written upon the rocks by any hand of man. There is every type and time of fable: but there is only one moral to the fable; because there is only one moral to everything. (pp. vi-xi)

> *G. K. Chesterton, in an introduction to* Aesop's Fables *by Aesop, translated by V. S. Vernon Jones, Doubleday Page & Co., 1912, pp. v-xi.*

WILLIS L. PARKER

Tradition has it of the Fables of Aesop that they are reading matter for little children. So they are, indeed; but not for little children solely. (p. v)

It is doubtful if Aesop ever wrote down a single one of his fables, or dictated them with any expectation that they would be collected. The first recorded compilation was made nearly three centuries after their narrator's death. Therefore Aesop as we have him has been stirred through a host of compilers and editors of great and little merit: Demetrius Phalereus, Babrius, Nicostratus, Martin Luther, Planudes, Erasmus, Ranuzio, Roger L'Estrange, Samuel Croxall, et cetera ad infinitum. Who among these were translators and who were counterfeiters and adulterators is largely guesswork. Nor were the fables surely original with Aesop. There were fabulists famous in Asia before him, and some of those stories which are in the Occident ascribed to the Greek are in the Orient credited to the Arabian Bidpai or Milpay.

The personality of Aesop was striking in the extreme; only to striking personalities does legend accrue in such measure. That he was a self-made man is a matter of record. Of his intellectual quality there is direct testimony in the account of his matching of wits at Croesus's court with Solon of Athens and Thales of Miletus. Of his humor there is evidence in a number of the fables whose authenticity is reasonably certain ("**The Lark and Her Young Ones**," "**The Town Mouse and the Country Mouse**," and others).

Like most self-made men, Aesop was conservative, and his conservatism reached to cynicism and indifference in the face of established abuses; "**The Fox and the Hedgehog**" was meant to caution the citizens of Samos against hastily unseating a grafting magistrate, lest his successor be worse. This deduction as to character is further supported by the similar intention of "**The Frogs Asking for a King**," designed to warn the Athenian citizenry that the tyranny of Pisistratus might be preferable to the tyranny of whomsoever a revolution could seat in his place.

That a man so tolerant, humorous, and vital should be remembered by such smug precepts as the morals to "**The Ant and the Grasshopper**" and "**The Hare and the Tortoise**" has annoyed many people. That Aesop was abandoned entirely to the domain of the mush-and-milk school of moralists aroused . . . [resentment]. (pp. vi-vii)

Aesop was such a strong personality that his contemporaries credited him with every fable ever before heard, and his successors with every fable ever told since. The contentious Martin Luther believed the fables to be the work of no one man but the sum of precepts from the greatest minds of history. Aesop is more than a man or a mind in history; Aesop is an enduring idea. . . . (p. viii)

Willis L. Parker, in an introduction to The Fables of Aesop *by Aesop, edited by Willis L. Parker, Illustrated Editions Company, 1931, pp. v-viii.*

J. H. DRIBERG

[There is a] debt which we owe to Aesop and which civilization owes to Africa. For many of the fables which the African slave wrote down for posterity in the country of his adoption are still current to-day in the country of his origin. Despite the transmutations they have suffered in their cultural migration their parenthood is still recognizable. They have acquired a new infection of morality: virtue is rewarded and wickedness punished: the evildoer does not "get away with it" as he so often does in Africa: the malicious joker falls into the snare which he sets for others, though we may perhaps see here the origin of the malice which was Aesop's own undoing. Certainly there is more than a trace of malice in many of his stories, and in African folk-tales the hare, the father of mischief-makers, is compact of malice, cunning, falsehood, trickery and all the dubious elements which go to the making of a shady company-promoter.

How nearly he kept to his originals may be seen in his fable of the Wulf and of the Dogge, the moral of which, as Caxton remarked, is that "lyberte or freedome is a moche swete thynge," or in the fable of the Two Rats, in which we learn that it "better worthe is to lyve in poverte surely than to lyve rychely beyng ever in daunger." What is this but the story of the Dog and the Jackal, current to-day in the folk-repertoire of so many tribes? The dog having visited the jackal repays his hospitality by inviting him to a meal at his kind master's village. "Truly," cries the jackal, after seeing the dog soundly thrashed, "truly I, even if I live in the bush, am better off than you."

The crane, who was appointed their lord and master and ate up all the frogs, finds his prototype in many creatures as destructive of their subjects' lives. The fable of the Good Man and of the Serpente is reflected in the habitual kindness shown to snakes by many tribes: for snakes are the repositories of the souls of ancestors and they are cherished therefore and invited to live in the houses of men by daily gifts of milk. When the good man "was angry ageynste the serpent and took a grete staf and smote at hym . . . and felle ageyne in to grete poverte" as a result, his fate was what a good animist might have predicted for him. Frogs are still as arrogant as they were 2,400 years ago, when their ancestor puffed itself up to bovine proportions and burst: they never learn, it seems, but go on bursting themselves in the old way, and all because . . . they bring in the rain—the proof of which lies in the fact that after a drought frogs croak with the first rains.

Less well known is the fable of the Foxe and of the Cocke. Caught by a trick—for the cunning fox had flattered the cock into singing—the cock in his turn tricked the fox into speaking, whereon "the cok scaped fro the foxe mouthe and flough upon a tree"—of which the moral is that "over moche talkyng letteth: and to moche crowynge smarteth: therfore, kepe thy self fro over many wordes." Is this not one with the guinea-fowl, which, caught in a hunter's snare, kept first his daughter, then

his son, then his wife and finally the hunter talking and arguing, and incidentally bragging, till with a sudden flutter of wings it flew out from the cooking pot, in which it had been placed alive, and (as the African tersely puts it) left the family and their friends to the joy of anticipation? "Words," it cried, as it flew away, "never cooked a guinea-fowl."

Then there is the Montayn whiche shoke, and all the people were "aferd and dredeful, and durst not wel come ne approche the hylle"—till they discovered that it was a mole which "caused this hylle shakynge," when "theyr doubte and drede were converted into Joye." There are hundreds of stories like this one in Africa, which tell of the fears and doubts of a people coming into a new country. The Lango, for example, coming to marshy lowlands from their old mountain homes were at first afraid to walk more than a cautious step at a time, lest the not too solid earth should engulf them, and their fears were only dissolved by the sight of an antelope running at full speed in front of them. But more often than not the modern fabulist reverses Aesop's order of things and tells how what is apparently harmless is found to be disconcerting or dangerous. In this class of stories is the enchanted stook of stubble, behind which two lovers lay in secluded contentment, till they were dragged back from their transports by the harsh voice of the stook—an uncompromising bachelor—telling them to be gone or he would turn them into slugs.

The Asse that frightened all the Beestes by his braying and would even have frightened the lions, if he had not been a party to the experiment, recalls the proverb which Aesop must have known that a roaring lion misses his prey. Even a cursory reading of his fables is enough to show how often Aesop embroidered this motif: for then, as now, the virtue of silence was well esteemed.

Assuredly, if Aesop was not an African, he ought to have been. For his fables, for all their gloss of an alien orthodoxy, have the fragrance of African forests, the malice of the hare that tricked the leopard to matricide, and the versatility of the chameleon who, sharing the cunning of the hare, possesses nevertheless an ambiguous morality which places it definitely on the side of the angels. (pp. 857-58)

J. H. Driberg, "Aesop," in The Spectator, *Vol. 148, No. 5425, June 18, 1932, pp. 857-58.*

F. J. HARVEY DARTON

[The following excerpt was originally published in 1932.]

Of all printed matter which could be adapted for the use of children when Newbery set up in business, 'Aesop' was the most obvious item. The fables had been in English print ever since Caxton finished his translation from the French on March 26, 1484. . . . He did not mean this text, any more than he meant *Reynard the Fox* (1481), for children. . . . He chose fables 'for to shewe al maner of folk what maner of thyng they ought to ensyewe and folowe. And also what maner of thyng they must and ought to leve and flee, for fable is as moche to seye in poeterye as wordes in theologye.' No one has ever achieved a straightforward purpose in better English. Caxton's *Aesop*, with infinitely little modernization, is the best text for children today. (p. 9)

There were two lines of descent for *Aesop* in England, until it became definitely a 'family' book and so a children's book. One was through the schools, the other through fashionable society. (pp. 9-10)

Aesop narrating his fables. Painting by Italian artist Roberto Fontana. The Granger Collection, New York.

English school versions began to grow numerous in the latter half of [the sixteenth century]. The compulsory use of our native tongue in the more numerous and no longer ecclesiastical schools had a rapid humanizing effect, and, though the fables were as a rule used only as a vehicle for teaching both Latin and English, they took on something of local colour and something of each translator's personality; one sees behind them, often, a man speaking to children, as well as a pedagogue teaching pupils. (p. 10)

[Before] George III's reign was half over, the Fable had passed, like an embryo, through the literary and social changes of its full growth. It had been something not far from folk-lore long before, had been regimented for schools and decked out for fashion. It had been Everyman's and now was Everychild's. (p. 23)

> *F. J. Harvey Darton, "The Legacy of the Middle Ages: (i) Fables," in his* Children's Books in England: Five Centuries of Social Life, *third edition, Cambridge University Press, 1982, pp. 9-31.*

W. G. WADDELL

Why should not Aesop's *Fables* be used for Greek reading in schools? The stories are interesting, many of them are beast-fables, and the vogue of *Uncle Remus* proves that that type of story has still a wide appeal. The moral tone of the *Fables* is high, yet not so impossibly high as to inspire rebellion or disgust; and wisdom is nicely blended with humor. . . .

Aesop is for children of all growths. . . . (p. 162)

[Aesop] resembles Socrates both in wisdom and in not committing his thoughts to writing; but perhaps the best analogy is conveyed by the well-deserved title, "the Children's Homer." (p. 163)

"Aesop, speaking timely words in his wise fables and inventions, and all the while playing in serious earnest, persuades men to be sensible." So says Agathias in his epigram on the statue of Aesop. The Aesopic fables teach, in especial, "the social virtues—fidelity in friendship, gratitude for kindnesses, love of work, acceptance of destiny, candor and truth, moderation in all things." (p. 164)

The fables often introduce the gods, sometimes giving us the entrée into Olympus. There is, for example, the fable which George Eliot enjoyed as a child and again later in life, "she laughed till the tears ran down her face in recalling her infantile enjoyment of the humor in the fable of Mercury and the Statue Seller." Hermes (or Mercury) in disguise once asked a sculptor the price of two statues, and was told that the statue of Zeus was to be one drachma, that of Hera, more than one drachma.

Seeing also an image of himself and expecting that as messenger and god of gain he would be highly esteemed, he asked the price; but the sculptor replied, "Why, if you buy the other two, I'll throw this one in for nothing." (p. 165)

There is much point in the fable which tells how War, being the last in the divine lottery for wives, found Hybris (Arrogance or Brutality) alone remaining; however, he fell violently in love with her and married her. That is why he accompanies her about wherever she goes.

Even those stories which are familiar to us from childhood's days often have in their Greek form some added detail which strikes the imagination. For instance, after Boreas had blown furiously upon the wayfarer only to make him don one garment the more, the Sun in his turn shone to such effect that finally the traveler "stripped and went off to bathe in a river that flowed near by." (p. 166)

The humor of the *Fables* is of several different types. There is the cynical humor of the gods who, when an impostor had failed to fulfil a vow, took revenge by bidding him go to the seashore where he would fetch . . . 1000 drachmae. Overjoyed, he hastened to the beach, fell in with pirates, was sold by them as a slave, and thus fetched 1000 drachmae.

Of a more pleasant type of humor are the stories of the dishonest or ignorant doctor. One rogue, who was attending an old woman for an eye ailment, would steal her furniture while her eyes were closed with unguents. When the cure and her furniture were both at an end, the doctor demanded the fee agreed upon, and as the woman refused to pay, he brought her before the magistrates. Her plea was that in point of fact the treatment had made her eyes worse, for previously she had seen all the furniture in the house, whereas now she could see not a single piece. (pp. 166-67)

In the beast-fables the lion naturally has chief place as the king of beasts. When a fox taunted a lioness with never bearing more than one cub at a time, "Yes, one cub," she retorted, "but a lion!"

Animals have reason to be critical of human beings. One day as he stood beside a cottage, a famished wolf overheard an old nurse scold a crying child with the words: "Stop crying, or else I'll throw you to the wolf this instant." Thinking she really meant what she said, the wolf waited long; but when evening had fallen he heard the woman this time soothing the child and saying: "If the wolf comes here, my child, we'll kill him." On hearing this, the wolf set off, saying: "This is a place where they say one thing and do another."

"The fable," says G. K. Chesterton, "must not allow for what Balzac called 'the revolt of a sheep' "; yet the sheep may of course upbraid the unskilful shearer: "If it is my wool you are after, don't clip so close; if it is my flesh you desire, slay me once and for all and rid me of this gradual torture."

Similarly the ass, usually portrayed as the type of stupidity, may at times outwit the wolf. Once, while pretending to have a thorn in his foot, the ass begged the wolf to pull it out with his teeth,—"lest," he added, "when you eat me, it should stick in your throat." But while the wolf was acting as doctor, the ass kicked him on the mouth, breaking his teeth; then he galloped off.

Aetiological tales are to be found among the Aesopic fables as well as in the other derived collections. The tortoise got her shell through the anger of Zeus because she alone had failed to attend his marriage feast. Next day, on being asked the reason, tortoise replied: "There's no place like home," or, more literally, "One's own home is ever best." Thereupon Zeus in his indignation condemned her from that time forth to carry her home upon her back wherever she went. (pp. 167-68)

[We] find an elaborate example [of an aetiological tale] in the **"Bat, the Bramble, and the Seagull."** To their trade partnership, the bat contributed borrowed money, the bramble cloth, the seagull a quantity of copper. After losing all in a storm, the seagull ever looks for copper to be cast up on the beach; the bat, in dread of her creditors, shuns the daylight; the bramble catches the clothes of passersby, seeking to recognize her lost materials. . . .

Almost all the fables treat of persons or animals; one exception is **"The Lamp."** Drunken with oil and gleaming brightly, a lamp boasted that it gave more light than the sun himself. Just then a breath of wind came whistling past and at once quenched the lamp. Relighting it, some one called: "Shine, lamp, and be silent; the light of the stars never fails." (p. 169)

Phaedrus used to be much read in English schools; and this gives us a final argument to support the introduction of the Greek Aesopic fables into the present curriculum.

If a publisher should be enterprising enough to bring out a book of *Aesopi Fabellae* or *Selections from Aesop* for school use, it would induce many to stray along this bypath of Greek literature. (pp. 169-70)

W. G. Waddell, "A Plea for Aesop in the Greek Classroom," in The Classical Journal, *Vol. XXXII, No 3, December, 1936, pp. 162-70.*

MARK VAN DOREN

If such a Greek as Aesop lived in the sixth century, B.C., he is now generally supposed to have recited rather than written his fables. There are legends concerning a man of that name who appeared at banquets and in the market place with stories of animals which carried a human meaning. But there is no record that he preserved them in anything better than his memory, and it is certain that the collection of tales now known as *Aesop's Fables* cannot be traced back nearer to his time than a thousand years. Far from decreasing the interest of the *Fables,* this adds to their importance; for it is clear that not one man, named Aesop or otherwise, and not even one generation of men invented them. They are the invention of the human race, and their origins are legion. At a particular place and time a particular man may have hit upon the device of the animal tale to render the expression of his ideas more piquant, or more safe; but it is likely that no such thing took place. Fables, like proverbs, cannot be traced to their source. They seem to have been current always and everywhere, just as they are immediately meaningful to any member of the race who hears them for the first time. The wisdom of mankind, and sometimes its cynicism, is imprisoned in these stories as sunlight was once assumed to sleep in gems. The fox and the grapes, the lion and the mouse, the fox and the raven, the town mouse and the country mouse, the ox and the frog—it is hard to imagine how we should get along without them if they were suddenly taken away. Or rather it is not hard. Equivalent stories would be concocted to fill their place. They are necessary to our thought and speech. (pp. 135-36)

Mark Van Doren, "Aesop and Jean de la Fontaine: Fables," in The New Invitation to Learning, *edited by Mark Van Doren, Random House, 1942, pp. 135-49.*

LIN YUTANG, JACQUES BARZUN AND MARK VAN DOREN

[*The following excerpt is taken from a discussion of the fables of Aesop and Jean de la Fontaine given as part of the radio series* Invitation to Learning.]

[*Mark Van Doren*]: One of the earliest books I can remember is the **Fables** of Aesop. As a matter of fact, they were read to me before I could read myself. Did you have an experience similar to this in China, Mr. Lin?

[*Lin Yutang*]: I read them as a child, too, and enjoyed them.

Van Doren: You mean these same stories?

Lin: Yes, Aesop's **Fables.** I read them in Chinese, though.

Van Doren: Later on, were you able to find them in English?

Lin: Oh, yes, but I never cared for them that way. I enjoyed them most in Chinese.

Van Doren: Did you have a similar experience, Mr. Barzun?

[*Jacques Barzun*]: Similar in general outline, yes. It is the *Fables* of La Fontaine, of course, that most French children are brought up on. (p. 138)

Van Doren: Is the value of fables, considered in their simplest form, for children or for adults? . . .

Lin: I think that the writer of these fables, whoever he was, really meant them for adults. It was a sly way of taking revenge on mankind by libeling the animals. I feel that all these fables are libels upon our fellow creatures; they are not so sly, so crooked, so hypocritical as man. The man who invented the fable really meant it for adults, I think.

Van Doren: That's interesting. You come to the defense of the animals.

Lin: Yes, definitely.

Van Doren: I think we might all agree there. The animals are being misused. Nevertheless you do say, I gather, that the morals or the points of the fables have an applicability to human life in its mature stages.

Lin: Exactly. That is why they are so universally appreciated, because they are really dissections of human nature, not of animal nature. Remember the story of the sour grapes? Why, it is only man who would do that. The animal just walks away; he doesn't moralize about it. It is we, the crooked men, who do that.

Barzun: I quite agree with you. You are attacking not only the writer of the fable as a libeler, but you are attacking the intelligence of man as a reflective being, aren't you, Mr. Lin?

Lin: Well, not exactly. We do reflect, and the writer of fables himself is reflecting; but he is performing a useful task when he satirizes us by means of animals. It is a good examination of man, I think.

Van Doren: Man is certainly acquainted with his weaknesses, with his vices. Yet he does not like to admit them; or rather, if he is willing to admit them, he is willing to admit them only in the roundabout way of attributing them to the animals—or else to the whole of the human race excluding himself.

Lin: And the readers who are human beings take it more kindly, because it's cloaked in that way, than if the writer of the fables were to say: Men are crooked; men are hypocritical. Human readers wouldn't like that.

Barzun: It is characteristic, it seems to me, of the fable that it flourishes particularly under tyranny or absolutism. Aesop is supposed to have written under the tyrants of Greece. (pp. 139-40)

Van Doren: I came across a note in the volume I was reading to the effect that the fables of Aesop were very much relished by certain officials of China in some past-century—I've forgotten which century. . . . Until these same dignitaries began to understand that the stories were against them, were to their disadvantage. Then they suppressed them. . . . Perhaps the people, however, kept on reading them.

Barzun: But what bothers me a little bit about the fable is perhaps symbolized in the fact that we call the conclusion of it a moral. Very frequently, don't you think, we ought to call it an *im*moral?

Van Doren: The word "moral" has never pleased me, unless it meant generalization. I should say that that is about all the word means. The text always ends up by saying: Well, what this really means in general is so and so.

Barzun: Still, the pedagogical intent of the fable is very clear, and if you followed in order all the fables of Aesop you would be the most contradictory being in the world; you'd be doing one thing at one time and another at another; you'd be cunning in order to overreach your enemies and your cunning would defeat you. What do you think of that?

Lin: I think Aesop never meant to be systematic. He was a Greek, I believe, and it is an obsession with modern Europeans that they must be systematic; they mustn't contradict themselves. An Oriental or Asiatic doesn't bother himself about it. He wants to observe human nature; he makes a comment here, he makes a comment there, and that is all. Whenever Aesop saw a point about humanity, he recorded it; he didn't work out a system.

Van Doren: Whenever men act this way, this is the way they act. The same objection, Mr. Barzun, could be made, and is often made, against proverbs. There is a proverb, isn't there, a folk-saying, which covers every conceivable circumstance?

Barzun: But at least the proverb is a simple saying; it doesn't pretend to be a literary form and to be useful. What strikes me

The Dog and the Shadow. Wood engraving by English artist Thomas Bewick from his Select Fables of Aesop *(1784). Bewick is recognized for raising the artistic level of the woodcut and for being the first major artist to illustrate books for children.*

as particularly unfortunate about the use of Aesop's fables is that for the most part they deal only with the surface aspect of the situation. Take for example the one of the traveler who was taken in by a satyr and who first blew on his hands to make them warm and then blew on his broth to make it cool. This enraged the satyr, who threw him out of his house. That is an absurd moral, isn't it? You should use your breath for exactly those two purposes.

Van Doren: That fable has never struck me as characteristic. The reason we remember it is the phrase "to blow hot and cold." When we now say "to blow hot and cold," we are talking about something that Aesop apparently did not consider. We are finding a moral Aesop did not find. On the other hand, there survive among us at least a half dozen fables which seem to me to have the greatest point—the fox and the grapes, the dog in the manger, the goose that laid the golden eggs, the boy who cried "wolf, wolf."

Barzun: There is a question in my mind, Mr. Van Doren, whether some of these aren't over-simplifications. For example, I should like to defend the fox who said "sour grapes." Isn't it a perfectly sound experience of every one of us that inability to do something makes us reflect on the entire situation and see features in it that we didn't see at first? And it's never been proved that the grapes weren't sour as well as unreachable.

Van Doren: I couldn't help thinking a minute ago—I'm not agreeing with you, by the way, Mr. Barzun; I think you're all wrong—when Mr. Lin remarked that the fox walked off without saying anything—I couldn't help wondering how Mr. Lin knew what the fox was saying or not saying. Possibly the animals have processes which would astonish us.

Lin: But the sophistication of calling it "sour grapes" is distinctly human.

Barzun: Whether animals think or not, they are at our mercy because we are the only ones that write fables.

Van Doren: Of course, the matter of simplification or over-simplification is a very interesting one. To me the whole point of the fables is that they are absolutely simple. No other kind of story can be as short as this and say so much.

Lin: I think so, too. But I should like us to consider whether they are still good today, or whether we should think they are antiquated because they are simple.

Barzun: I'd like to jump into the breach and say that as a strict genre in the form which Aesop bequeathed it to us, it is antiquated. Not in the sense that we can't go back to it and enjoy it as children, or even later, but that anyone who should attempt to add to the number of fables in that simple form would find his labor in vain.

Van Doren: Of course, one reason for that would be that a man making such an attempt would be making it, say, in the year 1942, while thousands of years have gone by during which these fables have grown. Aesop, so far as we can discover, is not the author of any fable that we know, although he may be the origin in some sense of them all. This whole body of literature is of the greatest and slowest growth, so that no one man operating at any time could be expected to add very much to it; just as no individual, even in a lifetime, could create a significant number of proverbs. They are all infinitely old. I quite agree with you that the authority of the fables comes perhaps from their age.

Barzun: Not only that, but granting that they have a real understanding of human nature embodied in them, still that is what you might call rudimentary understanding. It seems to me that the world today and for the past few centuries has needed a deeper understanding, more intelligence than is displayed here, and of a different kind.

Van Doren: Again I must say just the opposite of that. The trouble with the world today may be that it cannot see things as simply as Aesop saw them.

Lin: I agree wtih you. If we cannot any longer write simple things, the joke is on us. We have lost simplicity of mind; we are too sophisticated, and I think that is a distinct disadvantage rather than an advantage. (pp. 140-43)

Van Doren: [Many] things for me were illuminated by reading Aesop this time. He has four or five fables which apply directly and with a really terrible conclusiveness to the past ten years of relations between the United States and Japan. In each of them he represents an animal as having betrayed his future—destroyed himself in the end—by having given to an enemy something with which that enemy was to return and finish him. (p. 145)

Barzun: Aesop preaches cunning and roundabout means and a disregard of moral values on every other page, doesn't he?

Van Doren: [What] about the story of the tortoise and the hare? The moral of that seems to be, doesn't it, that the tortoise was right—the slow, regular, steady plodder won the race. Which animal in that case do you prefer?

Lin: I prefer the hare. My sympathy is all with the hare. The trick of these fables is that you can turn any of them around any way you like. I would never sympathize with a plodding student; I would sympathize with the man who looks upon learning as an exploration, as a joy, a pleasure, and if I were telling the story I would make the hare symbolize that.

Barzun: But are you willing to have a world in which there are both hares and tortoises, which is my desideratum?

Van Doren: Perhaps the trouble is with the way we are applying the story of the tortoise and the hare. Now, the analogy between a tortoise and a hare who are racing to reach a certain point at a certain time and two students—of whom one is a grind and the other is brilliant and unsteady and erratic—is not perfect, because there is no point at which a student is supposed to arrive. He is supposed to become something on the way.

Barzun: And certainly there are functions in life to be fulfilled by both types of mind. A statistician must be a tortoise, I think.

Lin: But the point about learning, specifically about learning, is that the man who arrives anywhere is the man who enjoys it, not the man who looks upon the process of learning as a torture.

Van Doren: I suppose that is true. One interesting question, it seems to me, has arisen here: Are the findings of Aesop about human nature on the whole unflattering to human nature? Does he seem to be most interested in weakness and vices? Would you call him cynical, Mr. Barzun?

Barzun: The charge is allowable. . . . (pp. 146-47)

Lin: I think Aesop is essentially cynical; he is a satirist. He wanted to satirize mankind, and any satirist, as you know, takes a rather cynical view of human nature.

Van Doren: I've never been sure that the word "cynical" was quite right. All such men are merely telling you that if you go out among men you will find them in general to be behaving in this way. This is what you can expect to find. But Aesop also understands that you may find something you don't expect, namely, virtue; but virtue is an unpredictable thing; indeed it is an ineffable thing, something about which we can say nothing, something which we have no right to count on.

Lin: He observes human nature very realistically, but we must also say this, that he has a kind of humor; he is able to laugh at human nature. That is the way we all should be. (pp. 147-48)

> *Lin Yutang, Jacques Barzun, and Mark Van Doren, "Aesop and Jean de la Fontaine: Fables," in* The New Invitation to Learning, *edited by Mark Van Doren, Random House, 1942, pp. 138-49.*

JAMES REEVES

Why have people delighted to hear and repeat [*Aesop's Fables*] for over two thousand years? In the first place, they are clear and simple and easy to remember. Secondly they are wise and sensible, and we see at once that they are true. True to what? They are true to humanity because, although they are mostly about animals, Aesop's animals represent different sides of human nature. The lion stands for kingliness, the ass for obstinate stupidity, the fox for cunning, the sheep for simplicity, the wolf for greed and savagery towards the defenceless. In this way, the various sides of our nature can be seen to be at war with one another; the weak and simple are the victims of the strong and cunning; pride goes before a fall; meddlers often come to harm; patience and skill triumph over life's difficulties. We read *Aesop's Fables,* not to discover these truths, nor just for the neatness and simplicity of the stories; we read them because, through our pleasure in the stories, we recognize the truths we have always known, but which we delight to meet again in novel form.

The virtues which Aesop praises are not the heroic ones—desperate courage, self-sacrifice, high endeavour; they are the peasant virtues of discretion, prudence, moderation and foresight. They bring hope and consolation to ordinary people, assuring them that the slow can sometimes win the race, that a proud creature may be indebted to a very humble one, that those who lay up store for the winter will be rewarded, and that even the strongest tyrant will fall. That is why Aesop, who—if there ever was such a person—had more than ordinary wisdom, has always had the affection and regard of ordinary people. (pp. v-vi)

> *James Reeves, in an introduction to* Fables from Aesop *by Aesop, adapted by James Reeves, Henry Z. Walck, Inc., 1962, pp. v-vi.*

CLIFTON FADIMAN

"He killed the goose that laid the golden eggs."

"Yes, but who'll bell the cat?"

"He's a wolf in sheep's clothing."

"Fine feathers don't make fine birds."

"Sour grapes!"

"Don't be a dog in the manger."

"Don't count your chickens before they're hatched."

You may have heard people use these sayings, or you may have read them somewhere, or you may have said them your-self. They're so familiar that they seem to be part of the language. (p. 111)

[People] have been enjoying these fables for thousands of years, partly because, though simple, they are quite wise and funny—and partly because they're about animals. I said they were simple. That's true, but some are cleverer than you might think at a first quick reading. Take, for example, **"The Lion and the Statue."** . . . That's pretty smart.

Some have a rather grim wisdom, like **"The Eagle and the Arrow."** . . . Others are just charming, like **"The Old Woman and the Wine Jar."** . . . (This is one of the few fables not about animals.)

It's interesting to compare fables with the fairy stories you've read. . . . Fairy tales make better reading, I think, but fables are shrewder, crammed with common sense. They make us feel that thousands of years ago human beings learned from daily living the same tough, practical lessons you and I have to learn today. *Familiarity breeds contempt* is just as true now as it was long ago when Aesop illustrated the statement through the actions of the Fox and the Lion. (pp. 112-13)

> *Clifton Fadiman, in an afterword to* The Fables of Aesop *by Aesop, edited by Joseph Jacobs, Macmillan Publishing Company, 1964, pp. 111-13.*

ROBERT B. DOWNS

Typically, the Aesopic fable is brief, simple, and direct; the language clear and unpretentious, apparently artless. It is dramatically effective, though, in bringing out a witty, emotional, or didactic point. To serve his practical purpose—the teaching of a moral lesson—the fabulist incorporates folklore, tradition, superstition, and sophistry. Frequently he does violence to the facts of natural history—quite aside from the literary device of dumb animals or inanimate cities, trees, mountains, rocks, and rivers talking to one another.

The moral significance gives the fable unity and makes of it a work of art. To insure against the point's being missed or lost, it is always spelled out, in a kind of Q.E.D. statement, as the fable's conclusion, often in the form of a proverb. Nevertheless, as the Aesop editor and translator Lloyd W. Daly observes, in his *Aesop Without Morals:* "Far from being highly moral stories, the fables are not always even conducive to moralizing . . . the vast majority of the tales . . . serve as examples, usually horrible, of human behavior." They embody both the wisdom and the cynicism of mankind, dissecting human rather than animal nature. Satire is therefore a common element in the fables. Cunning, trickery, and other devious methods are rewarded, while the honest and well-meaning, but stupid, individual may suffer disaster for his ineptness and lack of guile. Thus Aesop is essentially a satirist who inclines toward a cynical view of human character. It is ironical that, like Swift's *Gulliver's Travels,* while they were meant for adults, the fables are now read chiefly by children. Daly in his comprehensive, unexpurgated translation specifically states that this version "is not intended for the edification of the young."

It has been objected that Aesop took unfair advantage of the animals and unjustly libeled them in attributing human behavior to innocent beasts. At least three rationales have been suggested. First, from the standpoint of primeval man, with whom the fable originated, animals were almost brothers, and there seemed nothing incongruous in giving them human characteristics. Second, as civilization advanced, men would have resented and found unpalatable being depicted as hypocritical,

The Hare and the Tortoise. Wood engraving after the French artist J. J. Grandville from Fables de la
Fontaine *(1838). According to critic John J. McKendry, "no English writer ever equalled La Fontaine,
whose retelling gives the fables a position they have only in France, that of a major literary monument. . . ."*

weak, dishonest, and sly—all traits clearly implied in the Aesopic fables. Finally, and closely related to the second point,
the fable flourishes under tyranny and dictatorship; subtle satire
voiced by animals is tolerated by the despot who would ruth-
lessly suppress direct criticism.

The influence of Aesop's fables on popular thought and formal
literature has been far-reaching. Innumerable Aesopic expressions and moral teachings have become common currency.
Note, for example, "fishing in muddy waters," "out of the
frying pan into the fire," "the goose that laid the golden eggs,"
"the dog in the manger," "the boy who cried wolf," "the
hare and the tortoise," "the wolf in sheep's clothing," "the
fox and the sour grapes," "the ass in the lion's skin," "the
bundle of sticks."

Literary figures who have emulated, paraphrased, or been inspired by Aesop are numerous. The great beast-epic known as
the "History of Reynard the Fox," dating from about the tenth
century A.D., consists of independent episodes of a fabulous
nature woven together. Among other medieval specimens are
Geoffrey Chaucer's "The Nun's Priest's Tale" and John Lydgate's tale of "The Churl and the Bird." Of modern fabulists,
the most renowned is the seventeenth-century French author
Jean de La Fontaine. La Fontaine's first fables were based

mainly on Aesop as told by Phaedrus; later, he was considerably influenced by Persian and Indian examples. In England,
Sir Roger L'Estrange in the seventeenth century wrote satirical
bestiaries as vehicles for his political opinions, and the verse
fables, also often political satires, of John Gay were popular
in the eighteenth century. Subsequently, Gotthold Lessing in
Germany, Leo Tolstoy and Ivan Krylov in Russia, and Joel
Chandler Harris (Uncle Remus) in the United States were some
of the eminent writers who utilized fable motifs in short stories.
Twentieth-century English and American authors have also
followed the form effectively in such creations as Rudyard
Kipling's *Jungle Book,* George Orwell's *Animal Farm,* and
James Thurber's *Fables for Our Time.*

Aesopic fables and their predecessors represent the earliest
stage of literary art. Apparently they possess an irresistible
appeal for man at every cultural level from the savage to the
savant. The secret of their charm lies in their simplicity, directness, native shrewdness, and a curious combination of na-
iveté and sophistication. In a sense, the fables are the essence—
a kind of distillation—of the universal experience and age-old
wisdom of the race. (pp. 33-5)

Robert B. Downs, "Famed Fabulist," in his Famous
Books: Ancient and Medieval, *Barnes & Noble, Inc.,
1964, pp. 31-5.*

CORNELIA MEIGS

[The Aesop stories] went through many hands. . . . Even through all these changes of hands, they have not lost the touch of some original genius, their reflection of the instinctive friendship between man and the animal kingdom, their cheerful presentation of human weaknesses recognizable to anyone, even the very young reader. It is difficult to imagine what our English speech ever did without recourse to the early bird, to the fox and the sour grapes in whom the simplest person can see himself, to the tortoise who has brought encouragement to generations of plodders. (pp. 30-1)

> Cornelia Meigs, *"The Multiplying Leaves: The Printed Word—Caxton, Aesop, Malory,"* in A Critical History of Children's Literature *by Cornelia Meigs and others, edited by Cornelia Meigs, revised edition, Macmillan Publishing Company, 1969, pp. 22-31.*

ROBERT G. MINER, JR.

The basic English children's edition of *Aesop's Fables* is by Sir Roger L'Estrange and came out in two volumes, 1692 and 1699. After establishing in his introduction that his book is "for the Use and Edification of Children," L'Estrange goes on to insist that

> Nothing spoils Young People, like Ill Example; and that the very Sufferance of it, within the Reach of Their Ken, or Imitation, is but a more Artificial way of Teaching them to do Amiss . . . Now this Medly, (such as it is) of Salutary Hints, and Councels, being Dedicated to the Use, and Benefit of Children, the Innocence, of it must be preserved Sacred too, without the least Mixture of any Thing that's Prophane, Loose, or Scurrilous, or but so much as Bordering That way.

A normal enough sentiment, of course, but interesting in the light of some of the fables that follow it. . . . [For] example:

"Socrates and Calisto"

There happen'd a Dispute betwixt Socrates and Calisto; the One, a Famous Philosopher, and the Other, as Famous a Prostitute. The Question was only This; which of the Two professions had the greater Influence upon Mankind. Calisto appeals to Matter of Fact, and Experiment: for Socrates, says she, I have Proselyted Ten times as many of Your People, as ever you did of Mine. Right, says Socrates, for Your Proselytes, as you call them, follow their Inclinations, whereas Mine are forc'd to work against the Grain. Well well! says Lais (Another of the same Trade,) the Doctors may talk their Pleasure, of the force of Virtue and Wisdom, but I never found any Difference yet, in all my practice, betwixt the Flesh and Bloud of a Fornicator, and that of a Philosopher; and the One Knocks at my Door every jot as often as the Other.

No philosophers and fewer fornicators knock on children's doors these days. The difference in attitudes that this suggests may be significant.

The L'Estrange edition of *Aesop* set me thinking about other editions of *Aesop,* before and after 1699. Were there any? What were they like? Where did they come from? What or who was

Aesop, for that matter? And did all this bear looking into, anyway? Perhaps there was more to Aesop and his fables than that certain dusty ennui that I remembered from my childhood—after all, that courtesan had a point, didn't she? And if only I had heard of it when young, things might have turned out differently. As it was, I had had to wait for High School and Freud to discover what any well-bred eighteenth century tot would have known from his nursery days.

Even the briefest of histories of *Aesop's Fables* is complicated. It turns out that there were, for instance, several *hundred* editions and variations of *Aesop* before L'Estrange. Beginning, it seems, sometime in the sixth century, B.C. And in at least a score of basic languages. None of these editions were for children (children, of course, were not invented until the seventeenth century); but much of the content of these editions came to be considered particularly suitable for children (which is an interesting fact in itself: must certain kinds of great basic literature eventually end up the exclusive property of children—folk tales, ballads, fables, myth, the Bible?).

It seems likely that a man named Aesop did exist in Greece in the sixth century, B.C. He was a slave, seems to have lived in Samos, and most probably died a violent death at the hands of the Delphinians. Joseph Jacobs, the eminent Aesop scholar, argues that Aesop did not invent the "beast-tale with a moral" (as he calls it) but rather invented a new use for it [see excerpt dated 1894]. Before Aesop it was used to amuse children; Aesop used it to convince men, to make political points in the age of the tyrants when direct speech could be unhealthy. Even indirect, metaphorical stories seem to have been unhealthy for Aesop, however, and for one reason or another he was killed in 671 B.C. by outraged citizens of Delphi—perhaps for making a point too well.

After his death fables continued to be attributed to him and his influence can be traced through references in Plato, Aristotle, Xenophon, Herodotus, Aristophanes. Socrates is even said to have turned some *Aesop* into verse while awaiting death. After the founding of the democracies in Greece, fables became part of the rhetorical tradition and continued to grow as a form: they were considered the exclusive property of the well-educated and a sophisticated way to make a point. (pp. 9-10)

The history of English editions of *Aesop's Fables* begins with Marie of France's assertion about [King] Alfred's version. Whether or not he actually produced one is questionable (there is an *Aesop* by *an* Alfred in the 1170's—some years after King Alfred's death), but the story ought to be true. It would be appropriate that Alfred, attempting to revitalize his ravaged society, should have chosen to translate *Aesop* into the vernacular as a basic text for popular education. Nothing is really known about "King Alfred's" *Aesop,* but the idea of there having been one then, and for that reason, helps emphasize the very real connection between *Aesop* and education (and, therefore, children) that developed in England several centuries later.

England was the home of *Aesop* in the centuries following King Alfred, and the popularity of the fables with the Normans led to numerous French versions (done in England) and to the inclusion of several fables in the Bayeux Tapestry of the twelfth century. The fables then show up in the popular literature of anecdote—and in sermons—of the thirteenth and fourteenth centuries. Collections of fables appropriate for use in sermons (one wonders what *they* include) were made by Holkot, Bromyard and others. And of course Chaucer, Lydgate and Gower all used some fables in their works.

It was not until the fifteenth century that another complete English collection of *Aesop* appears. That was Caxton's edition of 1484 and one of the very first books printed in English. Interesting enough in itself, this fact takes on added significance when you realize that Caxton took the time to translate, as well as print, it: all this for *Aesop* while Caxton was engaged in his frenetic attempt to print everything of importance to his time. *Aesop,* then, was important (and popular: Caxton was sensitive to popular needs) in the fifteenth century. With Caxton's help it became more so. Because from his time onward a surprising number of important men begin to mention Aesop in their writing, usually with the same particular focus: learning and children.

In *The Book Named the Governor,* printed in 1531, Sir Thomas Elyot was quick to grasp the potential of *Aesop* for the education of children. Elyot develops a theme that is echoed again and again in the years leading up to L'Estrange's *Aesop* of 1692:

> After a fewe and quicke rules of grammer, immediately, or interlasyge it therwith, wolde he redde to the childe *Esopes fables* in greke: in which argument children moche do delite. And surely it is a moche pleasant lesson and also profitable, as well for that it is elegant and brefe, (and not withstanding it hath moche varietie in wordes, and ther wis moche helpeth to the understandinge of greke) as also in those fables is included moche morall and politike wysedome.

In Elyot's view, *Aesop* should be the very first book a child reads. His argument for *Aesop* is little changed by the time it is used by L'Estrange:

> For as the Foundations of a Virtuous and a Happy Life, are all laid in the very Arms of our Nurses, so 'tis but Natural, and Reasonable, that our Cares, and Applications toward the Forming, and Cultivating of our Manners, should Begin There too. And in Order to Those Ends, I thought I could not do better, than to Advance That Service under the Veyle of Emblem, and Figure, after the Practice, and the Methods of the Antients. . . . For Children must be Ply'd with Idle Tales, and Twittle-Twattles; and betwixt Jeast and Earnestness, Flatter'd, and Cajol'd, into a Sense, and Love of their Duty. A Childs lesson, must be fitted to a Childs Talent and Humour. . . .

Between Elyot and L'Estrange several prominent men talk about *Aesop,* among them Sir Philip Sidney, Francis Bacon, and John Locke. Before them, however, and just after Elyot, comes an illuminating event in the history of *Aesop* and its connection with learning. *Aesop* was such a popular and influential book, apparently, that William Bullockar used it as the best way to make his point. In 1585 he brought out his *Aesopz Fablez in tru Ortography,* spelled new, to convince his fellow countrymen of the excellence of his method of spelling.

Both Sidney and Bacon make essentially the same comment about *Aesop.* They are primarily interested in how *Aesop* works, both emphasize its power to instruct and delight at the same time: through indirection and entertainment the fables elevate

Painting of Aesop by Spanish artist Diego Rodriguez de Silva Velasquez. The Bettmann Archive, Inc.

the human mind. Locke's emphasis is different. He is interested in the proper reading for children and what influence it can have. He suggests that what is needed in England is an edition of the fables specifically for children. Which is where L'Estrange got the idea.

By the time L'Estrange's version begins to come out in 1692, *Aesop* is not only one of the basic books in Western (and an even more basic book in English) culture, but also a vitally important book for children (according to the adults, anyway). Children's books are beginning to exist in response to the discovery that children exist and what they first read could be a matter of first importance.

The eighteenth century experienced a great expansion of books for children under the energetic John Newbery and others of his business-like mien. Not unexpectedly, *Aesop* figured prominently in this development. It is not that there were so many different versions, but rather that unrecorded numbers of bits and pieces of Aesop appeared as chapbooks and pamphlets. These appeared continually—and promptly disappeared. From overwork (this, too, is in the proper Aesopic tradition: scholars note for example that only three copies of Caxton's *Aesop* survive today and only one of them in decent shape. The rest have been thumbed out of existence. How many other popular, much printed books can that be said for?). Two major new versions of *Aesop* did appear during the eighteenth century, one by the Reverend Samuel Croxall in 1722 and another by (of all people) Samuel Richardson. Croxall's *Aesop* was a translation, not merely a revision of L'Estrange or Caxton, and it is less extravagant—and less earthy—than L'Estrange's. At the same time it is livelier than Caxton's. Croxall, too, had children in mind when he did his edition. Each fable was supplied with a drawn conclusion, and the book ends:

> It is not expected that they who are versed and hackneyed in the paths of life should trouble themselves to pursue these little loose sketches of morality; such may do well enough without them. They are written for the benefit of the young and inexperienced; if they do but relish the contents of this book, so as to think it worth reading over two or three times, it will have attained its end; and should it meet with such a reception, the several authors originally concerned in these fables, and the present compiler of the whole, may be allowed not altogether to have misapplied their time, in preparing such a collation for their entertainment.

In his introduction to the 1889 edition of Caxton's *Aesop*, Joseph Jacobs has something to say about both L'Estrange and Croxall.

> He (L'Estrange) inflicted on *Aesop* the indignity of "applications" in addition to "morals"; these were intended to promote the Jacobite cause. . . . L'Estrange was succeeded on the Aesopic throne of England by the Rev. S. Croxall, whose reign lasted throughout the eighteenth century, and whose dynasty still flourishes among us in the *Chandos Classics*. It says much for the vitality of Aesop that he has survived so long under the ponderous morals and "applications"—Whig against L'Estrange's Jacobitism—with which the reverend gentleman loaded his author.

With characteristic earnestness, Richardson attempted to correct these "excesses" by neutralizing *Aesop*. His version is entitled *Aesop's Fables, With Instructive Morals and Reflections, Abstracted From All Party Considerations, Adapted to all Capacities*. It does not seem to have been popular and may serve as a lesson to those who try to purge literature for children of all living and breathing blemishes.

The point about these eighteenth century editions is that they reflect the attitudes and prejudices of their times towards children and literature for children. As did the L'Estrange edition for its time. Which brings us to a further point: Since *Aesop* is such a basic book in England through the ages, and since as a basic book it came naturally to be thought of as a basic book for children, then perhaps we could tell something about that intangible and elusive something in the air that characterizes different ages by looking carefully at what each did to its *Aesop*s. More specifically for our purposes, it would seem to me, at least, that Aesop might prove a quick and convenient indicator of the basic attitudes of an age toward its children and what they read. The idea deserves a thorough look. It also suggests related questions that may have some light shed on them in the process.

What, for example, gives Aesop its longevity? Its almost universal appeal (among the better known languages *Aesop* has

appeared in are the following: Chinese, Basque, Bengali, Breton, Catalan, Esperanto, Estonian, Gascon, Hindustani, Icelandic, Marathi, Hyanja, Pushto, Sanskrit, Serbo-croat, Swahili, Tonga, Turkish, Welsh)? Is it that animal stories appeal somehow to that ancient human wish to belong? Maybe to hear of animals making our mistakes, proving our points is somehow comforting in an anthropomorphically primitive way. Or maybe the necessary impersonality of an animal fable tickles the fancy: objective and simple that way, life seems subject to solid, comfortable, consistent laws. No ifs and buts about what an animal does.

Another question that arises is related to changes in moral values. Which of the fables is consistently repeated in every age? Which for children? Which not? And why? Is it still fashionable, for instance, to be happy with one's lot? or emulate the tortoise in a nuclear age? And how did the eighteenth century react to a fable chastising the monkey for wanting to cover and decorate his private parts?

And what of American *Aesops*? It would not be surprising to see them take on different shape from English ones—or would it? Is there anything of the pioneer in, say, the boy who cried wolf, or the wolf in sheep's clothing? the dog in the manger? Is Sour grapes a tale to suit post-colonial tastes?

Of course the psychological, scientific, and sociological claims on *Aesop* cannot be neglected. Anne Caldwell, author of *Origins of Psychopharmacology from CPZ to LSD*, has suggested that the connection between fables and hallucinogens needs exploring (any child prone to nightmares can verify that, I bet). And what about some sort of statistical-sociological study of the relationship between the number of editions of *Aesop* in any age and its intensity of feeling for its children? The possibilities, like the versions of *Aesop,* seem endless.

Perhaps after all this we shall discover that *Aesop* is one of those books that future millennia (if there are any) will say were vital to our civilization (look, after all, at the sheer numbers) but which we never noticed because it was so thoroughly basic. (pp. 11-14)

> *Robert G. Miner, Jr., "Aesop as Litmus: The Acid Test of Children's Literature,"* in Children's Literature: Annual of the Modern Language Association Seminar on Children's Literature and The Children's Literature Association, *Vol. I, 1972, pp. 9-15.*

MARY F. THWAITE

[Perhaps] the oldest book of all on the child's bookshelf today [is] *Aesop's Fables*. In every age this has had the distinction of being approved and adapted for youth. In style the Aesopian fable is akin to the folk-tale, but unlike most traditional lore, it had the good fortune in the ancient world to be moulded into an acceptable and enduring form. Often made into a schoolbook and burdened with additional moralities, it never lost those pristine characteristics which endeared it to young or unsophisticated minds. Brevity in telling, clarity of style, animal characters behaving like human beings, pithy lessons about conduct and shrewd dealing—these were features to give life to the fables in every generation since their invention. There is little of high ethical purpose in the episodes. They are more like a fascinating looking-glass reflecting the follies of mankind. The long familiarity of the people with these old fables can be gauged by the number of sayings from them which are now a part of our common speech, such as 'sour grapes', 'a dog in the manger', 'a wolf in sheep's clothing', to quote a few of the best-known examples. (p. 8)

The Fables of Aesop, versified, retold, adapted, moralised or modernised in various ways have been a perennial part of children's literature, and this was especially the case after printing brought them easily within the child's reach. They are to be found in all kinds of medleys and miscellanies for youth, as well as in numerous separate editions. When John Newbery brought out his first book for children in 1744, he included four of them with new style moralities in the form of little letters from 'Jack-the-Giant-killer'. The infinite ways Aesop has been adapted for the child are truly astonishing. (p. 9)

> *Mary F. Thwaite, "Sources: Printing—Its Heritage and Promise," in her* From Primer to Pleasure in Reading, *revised edition, The Horn Book, Inc., 1972, pp. 1-10.*

MARGARET BLOUNT

Aesop's Beast Fables, tongue-in-cheek human substitutions, have always been in favour. Perhaps from Caxton's time onwards, they have been regarded as the right books to give to children, recommended by educationists from Locke onwards. They are part of most people's early experience and are the very roots of that kind of humanisation which turns animals into facets of human character, and many writers have changed and revived them. Animals are here 'used' rather than presented and they point the way directly to those moral and satirical tales which were intended, from Swift to Orwell, to show the human race how it ought to behave. (p. 26)

Aesop, the oldest and most influential animal story teller of all, used the attractive power of animals and narrative to get at his audience in a peculiar way, and the method has been seized on, enlarged, used and copied until, in the last century, the animal moral tale becomes almost wearisome. The genius of Aesop was to use the animal as a fixative, in an unforgettable way.

Prudence pays better than greed; or, it is better to keep what one possesses than to lose it while trying to gain the unattainable. This is easy to say but horribly cumbersome to *imagine*. 'A man's reach should not be greater than his grasp' is easier. Easier still is 'a bird in hand is worth two in the bush', which brings with it a Bewick picture of a man with a gun and two dogs and a pheasant; most brains supply pictures which fix abstractions. What Aesop did was to reverse the process so that the image comes first, and so no one forgets the dog dropping the bone to try to grasp the one that is only a reflection. Aesop well knew the power of a story and the graphic, simplified short cut that animals made towards human attention; if the same story began with a man crossing a bridge with a piece of meat in his hand all sorts of other considerations would enter, the least of which being why the man should be silly enough to mistake his reflection for reality. (p. 34)

Aesop's fables have none of the humour of folklore, none of the warm satisfaction of fairy tale—the sudden turn of fortune before the happy ending. They have surface justice or an amused shrug. They have a resemblance to folk tale in their short, plain, factual lack of light and shade, but there the likeness ends. Aesop's animals, behaving not like animals at all but as propositions in Euclid, or, as G. K. Chesterton suggests, pieces in games of chess [see excerpt dated 1912], are interesting because they are the very beginning of that typecasting which animals have found so difficult to shake off since; but there is a flatness about the stories, a cynical assessment of human nature at its lowest, an acknowledgement that often the good and innocent are duped and that good works often pay, not

because they are good, but because nature is sometimes arranged that way.

The people in Aesop are non-figures, the farmer, a man, a boy, an old widow; their interaction with the animals does not seem to belong to any golden age when the animals could speak and people understand, and even Mr McGregor, shadowy as he is, has more character. The people, like the animals, have to be ciphers. If they had any real, complex human attributes, all kinds of chemical reactions might set in and spoil the experiment. The tendency, on reading Aesop, has been to applaud, to remember, and lastly to add one's own moral, to decide perhaps that the Fox that lost the grapes was the most sensible beast ever. 'Some men, when they are too weak to achieve their purpose, blame the times,' says the Greek; but the story also tells one not to bother about what one cannot have. Roger l'Estrange's *Aesop*, 1692, pictures the Fox 'turning off his disappointment with a jest', a kindly interpretation, equally valid, and Samuel Croxall in 1722 was uneasy about the grapes for a different reason—grapes did not grow wild in England and foxes did not like them anyway.

L'Estrange was doubtful about Aesop's moral values, and thought that they might be 'more dangerous than profitable'; but Locke, in his essay on education [see excerpt dated 1693], had no doubts at all. Aesop was the best book to offer to children to encourage them to read; because it 'may afford useful reflections to a grown man; and if his memory retain them all his life after, he will not repent to find them there, among his manly thoughts and serious business. If his Aesop has pictures in it, it will entertain him much the better.' (p. 36)

> *Margaret Blount, "Folklore and Fable," in her* Animal Land: The Creatures of Children's Fiction, *William Morrow & Company, Inc., 1975, pp. 23-41.*

P. GILA REINSTEIN

People often think of Aesop's fables and the folk tales of the brothers Grimm together, since both are collections of traditional folklore, classics of children's literature, and important sources of American popular culture. Both are retold in elementary school readers; both are regularly selected by artists for reinterpretation and reissue as picture books. Political cartoonists and advertising campaign designers take advantage of the public's familiarity with Aesop and Grimm for purposes of their own. Aesop and Grimm appear to have been adopted by and incorporated into our culture, to the degree that few children grow up today without somewhere along the way absorbing the plight of Cinderella and the fate of the tortoise and the hare. Sometimes these stories are first encountered in library books or school texts, but more often they are introduced through the popular culture, by way of animated cartoons, Sesame Street or Walt Disney adaptations, mass marketed books like those published by The Golden Press, and in the most traditional manner, by word of mouth. (p. 44)

[Aesop's] fables are not simplistic children's stories, but highly intellectual exercises which take abstract ideas and translate them into formalized dramatic encounters. Jakob and Wilhelm Grimm, in contrast, were nineteenth century philologists and students of German regional culture. They gathered the tales which bear their names from diverse sources, and their interest in the stories was not primarily child oriented; they were studying folklore and the history of words in the spoken German language. Over the years, both Aesop's fables and the Grimm's folk tales became the property of all the people, not only intellectual orators, not only scholars of language and folk lit-

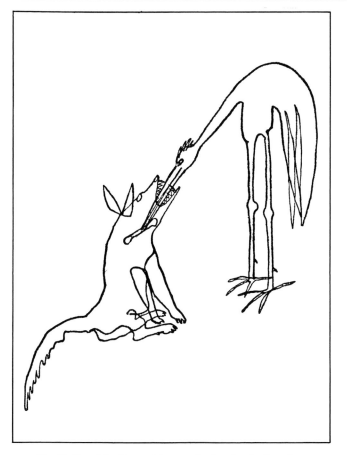

The Wolf and the Crane. Linecut of a drawing by American artist Alexander Calder from Fables of Aesop according to Sir Roger L'Estrange *(1931). The Metropolitan Museum of Art; Gift of Monroe Wheeler, 1949 (49.89).*

erature; and both have become the special property of children. (p. 45)

The fables and the fairy tales both convey values which our society respects. Each collection of Aesop's fables presents a fairly consistent world view, a philosophy, a prescription for right behavior. It is the same with the brothers Grimm. (p. 46)

Although there are some exceptions, taken all together, the fables teach pragmatic lessons: they recognize that the world is a dangerous place, full of exploiters, bullies, and false friends. Love counts for little; it exposes you and foolishly allows you to relax your defenses. The fables teach self-protection and the value of hard work. Goodness is rarely rewarded, but evil is often revenged. The fables recognize that in the real world, might does make its own right—unfair, perhaps, but true, nonetheless.

To put it mildly, Aesop's fables are not idealistic. They do not recognize miracles. The world is what it is: the enemies, the people in power, are tyrannical lions, tricky foxes, vindictive snakes; the victims, the little people, are vain crows, foolish donkeys, self-important rabbits, and ill-advised lambs. No one is perfect—neither oppressor nor oppressed—and no one can change who he is. The best you can do, according to the fables, is to stand up for yourself, selfishly, if need be, since you can expect no one else to stand up for you; trust only yourself; expect to be attacked and have the sense to lie low when

threatened; and, if you are lucky, take your revenge when you get the chance.

The world of the folk tales collected by the Grimms recognizes enemies and dangers, but unlike the world of the fables, it also allows for perfect goodness and the possibility of coming through a trial unscathed, and resting on that one victory happily ever after. Aesop's fables present no ideal characters, no heroes, no heroines. The fairy tales, in contrast, offer many models of perfection.... While Aesop's fables urge watchful cleverness, the fairy tales suggest trust and patience as the better way: after all, miracles can happen. Cinderella can go to the ball in a dress that rains down on her from a tree. Sleeping Beauty may have to wait for a century, but ultimately she awakens to love at first sight.... And most significantly, what is dead can be made alive again. (pp. 47-8)

The Aesopic fables suggest that evil is commonplace. The Germanic folk tales present evil in more terrible guises, but also show that the virtuous victims are ultimately better off for having tangled with the evil. (p. 49)

Aesop's and the Grimms' stories, although not native to America, have nonetheless been absorbed into the American folk and popular culture and can, therefore, be presumed to express ideas and values important to our culture. Because of the all-but-universal familiarity of American children with many of the fables and fairy tales, I have taught Aesop and Grimm to students in children's literature courses at two different colleges, to give them adult perspectives on material which they "have always known." The students in one group attended a four-year state college in New England; those in the other group were enrolled at a two-year community college, a branch of the City University of New York. Interesting as the differences between Aesop and Grimm are, almost as interesting are the different reactions of the students to the fables and the fairy tales.

Their response seems to vary with their own socioeconomic background. Students in children's literature classes at the New England college were predominantly young, single, white, and middle to lower-middle class. The students in comparable classes in New York City were predominantly older (30-60 years old), married and raising children, black or Hispanic, and working class or on welfare. The four-year college students were mostly straight out of high school, often idealistic, and relatively innocent of the ways of the world. The community college students, in contrast, had lived in the world—and a particularly rough, urban world.

Many of the state college students found Aesop's fables unpleasantly cynical and felt that they were inappropriate reading for small children, but made interesting intellectual exercises for children of 10 or older. These students believed that it was wrong to take from small children their sense of safety, their trust in loving adults who would shelter them from danger. On the other hand, these same students felt that the folk tales of Grimm fostered kindliness, loyalty, and love, qualities they highly prized. They felt that children should be exposed to the fairy tales early, starting as young as 3 or 4 years old, to encourage imaginative and moral development, and they felt that the exposure should continue lifelong.

The community college students did not share these views at all. The city-wise older students discovered in Aesop much of the wisdom they felt their children needed to help them cope with the life of the streets, and they agreed among themselves that Aesop was the very book to read to small children of about

4 or 5 years old, before sending them out of the house alone to play or walk to school. As for the fairy tales of the Grimms, the City University of New York students enjoyed studying them, but reacted with cynical laughter to some of the idealistic and, to them, totally unlikely behavior of the protagonists. These students felt that the Grimms' stories ignored reality and taught lessons appropriate for Sunday school but not for weekday use. Since most of them were churchgoers and believers, they felt uncomfortable about this inconsistency, but they couldn't avoid it: they did not want their children victimized. They could not afford to teach their children to be sweet, passive, and trusting when the world was so clearly Aesopic to them, so full of predatory lions, wolves, and foxes ready to swallow their children up, and once swallowed, chewed and digested, not magically restored to life unharmed. They saw themselves and their children as the lambs, the reeds, and the ants of Aesop's fables, the powerless creatures who must lie low, use their wits when threatened, and work hard the rest of the time. (pp. 50-1)

The fables and folk tales perform different functions. The former teach self-preservation, acknowledging the difficulties of life for ordinary people in the real world today—and, apparently, in every era of the past 25 centuries, if the continuous manuscript and publication history of Aesop's fables is any indication. Survival cannot be taken for granted; loved ones cannot always protect each other from harm. There are no apparent rewards for goodness, no assurances that justice will triumph. Fables are, and have always been, useful for the presentation of cautionary lessons to the underdogs in Western civilization. (p. 52)

P. Gila Reinstein, "Aesop and Grimm: Contrast in Ethical Codes and Contemporary Values," in Children's literature in education, *Vol. 14, No. 1, (Spring), 1983, pp. 44-53.*

AGNES PERKINS

We are so familiar with Aesop's stories that we seldom look closely at just what they are saying and how they are saying it; as Aesop himself would say, "Familiarity breeds contempt." We may dismiss them as we do much of the didactic literature of the past as too moralistic for modern taste. But a rereading of Aesop convinces me that the fables are not so much lessons advocating moral goodness as sharply ironic, and often humorous, pictures of human foibles. . . .

We know little about Aesop the man. . . . More important than speculation about Aesop as a person is that the Western body of fable from the oral and early written traditions has been assembled and known by his name. (p. 60)

What lessons . . . do Aesop's fables teach? A surprising number condemn, not evil intent, but foolishness. The frogs who want a king find themselves with a tyrant whose appetite they do not survive. The donkey who, seeking a lighter load, twice deliberately falls into the water so that the salt he is carrying will wash away, discovers how stupid his trick is when he is loaded with sponges. The frog who tries to blow himself up as big as the ox bursts in the attempt. The goat, seeing a fox in the well, jumps in without considering how he will get out, and the fox, having climbed out with the aid of the goat's back, laughs at him. Often foolishness is combined with vanity. Chaucer's Nun's Priest's tale of Chanticleer is based on an Aesop's fable. **"The Fox and the Crow"** is a similar tale, in

which the fox gets the crow's cheese by flattery. Others concern foolishness combined with greed. The man kills his goose which lays golden eggs in an attempt to achieve more wealth; the widow overfeeds her hen, hoping to get twice as many eggs, but instead makes the hen so fat that she stops laying entirely. The milkmaid, planning all the good things she will get when she sells the milk and raises chickens, stumbles and spills the milk and so has nothing. The boy, reaching into the jar and taking a fistful of nuts, finds he cannot get his hand out again because he has grabbed too many. Some teach that one should be content with his place in life. The donkey masquerading in the lion's skin is recognized and beaten for his pretentions; the ass who envies the war horse decides, on the day of the battle when the horse is killed, that its humble, hard-working life is better after all. A few of the fables promote cooperation. The old man teaches his sons that together they are strong, individually weak, when he shows them how easy it is to snap a single stick and how difficult to break a bundle. The great trees sacrifice their small neighbor, the ash, to the woodcutter who wants an axe handle, and soon find themselves victims of the axe.

This last is a good example of the negative presentation of the lesson, a method frequently found in Aesop: not "cooperate and you will save yourselves," but "fail to cooperate and you will be destroyed." In fact, the lesson itself is often not a moral in the sense of an exhortation to a virtuous act, but a cautionary anecdote followed by an application that would hardly be a desirable pattern to follow. When the fox invites the stork to dinner and serves its food on a flat plate and the stork returns the invitation with a dinner served in a narrow-necked jar, the "moral" that follows is, "One bad turn deserves another."

The lessons of Aesop's fables are less directions to righteousness or goodness than patterns of practical advantage; they are not about how to lead a good life but about how to get along in the world. They present practical "peasant wisdom" in a tone that is realistic, even callous. No sympathy is wasted on the boy who cries "Wolf!" and loses his sheep or, in some versions, his life. No tears are shed over the sick lion who is mistreated by his subjects or over the lion in love, who allows his claws to be trimmed and his teeth extracted until he becomes a laughing stock. No pity is extended to the man who lets his young wife pick out all his white hairs and his elder wife pluck out all the black ones, until he is bald. The characters' suffering is the way of the world and results from their own foolishness; it serves them right!

Most of us do not enjoy being preached at. Most moralistic literature is short-lived, and one might expect that, in the modern world at least, such tales would be relegated to those with a taste for the obscure or quaint. Instead, they are continually being revived in new collections or used as subjects for dramatizations and picture books. I suspect that their continued popularity is not because of any moral value they promote, in the sense of piety or virtue, but because they take a sharp, satiric view of the world and make us laugh ironically at the faults we recognize in our neighbors and, all too often, in ourselves. (pp. 61-2)

Agnes Perkins, "The Five Hundreth Anniversary of Aesop in English," in Children's Literature Association Quarterly, *Vol. 9, No. 2, Summer, 1984, pp. 60-2.*

Mitsumasa Anno

1926-

Japanese author/illustrator and illustrator of picture books.

Anno is recognized for extending the boundaries of the picture book genre and for being one of its most inventive producers. Japan's most internationally acclaimed contemporary illustrator, he is regarded as an artistic genius whose skillful draftsmanship and sense of design have prompted *Kirkus Reviews* to call him "the nursery Escher." Anno is well known for the variety of his texts and illustrations as well as for his ability to give pictorial expression to elusive impressions of time and space. He creates intriguing compositions that range from delicate paintings and trompe l'oeil to heavily detailed double-page spreads and incorporate tricks of perspective, optical illusions, anamorphosis, and visual jokes and puzzles. A former elementary school art teacher well-versed in how children learn, Anno combines the roles of artist, scholar, and educator in all of his works, and challenges his audience to see the world, both intellectually and imaginatively, from a different visual perspective. Many of Anno's works are concept books which present complex mathematical, scientific, and philosophical ideas through simple stories elucidated by either naive or sophisticated line drawings and watercolors; he has worked with several collaborators on these books, including his son Masaichiro. Based on Anno's visits to Europe, Great Britain, and the United States, his four wordless "journey" books—*Anno's Journey* (1977), *Anno's Italy* (1978), *Anno's Britain* (1981), and *Anno's U.S.A.* (1983)—follow a lone horseman on his travels and cleverly juxtapose historical periods with mind-stretching literary and cultural allusions. Anno has also written a folktale, *The King's Flower* (1976), and devised *All in a Day* (1986), a picture book in which he makes a plea for peace and joins nine international illustrators in depicting what children around the world are doing on January 1. Although many of his works introduce difficult abstractions and terminology, Anno characteristically adopts a playful, whimsical tone and often includes insightful forewords or afterwords.

Regarding him as one of the most innovative illustrators in children's literature, critics esteem Anno for the breadth of his intellectual and artistic vision, the diversity of his illustrative techniques, and the skill with which he translates abstract principles into visual entities. Despite occasional comments on the difficulty of some of his books for a young audience, reviewers judge Anno's works to be universally valuable and stimulating introductions to varied concepts.

Anno has received numerous adult- and child-selected awards both in Japan and internationally. *Topsy-Turvies* won a German Children's and Youth Book Award commendation in 1973. *Anno's Alphabet* earned a Kate Greenaway Medal commendation in 1974, the *Boston Globe-Horn Book* Award in 1975, the Christopher Award in 1976, and the Golden Apple Award from the Bratislava International Biennale in 1977. *Anno's Counting Book* was selected as a *Boston Globe-Horn Book* Honor Book in 1977, and *Anno's Journey* received the *Boston Globe-Horn Book* Award in 1978. *The Unique World of Mitsumasa Anno* won the Bologna Children's Book Fair First Prize for Graphic Excellence in Books for Youth in 1978, and *Nippon no uta (Anno's Song Book)* earned the same pres-

Courtesy of Mitsumasa Anno

tigious award in 1980 in the category of books for children. In 1984, Anno won the Hans Christian Andersen Illustrator Medal for his body of work.

(See also *CLR*, Vol. 2; *Something about the Author*, Vols. 5, 38; *Contemporary Authors New Revision Series*, Vol. 4; and *Contemporary Authors*, Vols. 49-52.)

AUTHOR'S COMMENTARY

[The following excerpt is from an interview by Hisako Aoki.]

[Hisako Aoki]: You were born and grew up in Tsuwano, which is in the western part of Japan. Please tell us something about it.

[Mitsumasa Anno]: Tsuwano is in a valley surrounded by mountains. As a child I always wondered what was on the other side of the mountains. . . .

On the other side of the mountains were villages with rice fields, and beyond these rice fields was the ocean, which seemed to be very, very far away. When I reached the ocean for the first time in my life, I tasted it to see if it was really salty.

Because my world was cut off from the outside world, first by the mountains and then by the ocean, the desire to go and see what lay on the other side grew stronger. (p. 137)

Aoki: You left Tsuwano after graduating from high school to study further, did you not?

Anno: Yes. But what I remember most vividly is the homecoming: how I got off the train at the station, feeling happy and proud and a bit shy at the same time, thinking how much I had matured being away from Tsuwano but that the town would accept me as I was. Hermann Hesse expresses this very feeling as "mein übermütiges Heimkehr-Gefühl" in his book *Schön ist die Jugend.* When I read how Hermann Hesse, as a student, went home to Calw, getting off the train at the end of the town, walking by the river, and crossing the bridge, my heart ached because everything was exactly the same with me. The only difference was the fact that there wasn't a storks' nest in Tsuwano. I could almost fit to his text my illustrations of the scenery of Tsuwano.

Because Hesse's words so perfectly matched my own homecoming as a student, I felt that I had to go to Calw to see if it really looked the same. And when I went, it was completely different. I took a few photographs and drew some sketches and came back. I showed them to someone, together with the sketches I had done of Tsuwano before, and said, "They are different, aren't they?" He answered, "No. They are surprisingly similar. They almost look alike."

Then it dawned on me that the sketches and photographs of Tsuwano and Calw represent the world as seen through my eyes, and they are my own compositions—which other people may see differently. I believe that this is one of the reasons for drawing, writing, photographing, or expressing oneself in any form. Through a creative work, people may experience something which they may not have experienced before.

Aoki: In other words, a work of art offers us an opportunity to see with the eyes and to sense with the heart of the creator. And we can widen our scope by appreciating such a work.

Anno: Yes, I think this is what teaching art is all about. Once I was an elementary school art teacher, and from my experience I must say that this process works reciprocally. As a teacher I tried to present material to pupils so that they could widen their scope of understanding and self-expression. At the same time I learned a lot from them.

Children's way of seeing is actually different from that of adults; teachers and parents should understand this and not base everything on adult standards. For example, children's sense of perspective is different from ours, partly because their faces are smaller and their eyes are closer together. In addition, their experience is more restricted, so they have less to base their judgment on. (pp. 138-39)

Aoki: Do you have anything to say regarding elementary school textbooks in Japan?

Anno: I feel that recently the importance of creating images while one reads has been overstressed. Once I was asked to do some illustrations for a Japanese language textbook in order to encourage children to form images while reading. I refused because I believe that the world created by words and the world created by images are different. One does not necessarily have to create definite images while reading. And being able to create images should not be regarded as the most important

criterion of effective writing. It goes wider and deeper than that.

Aoki: Now you sound more like a writer than an illustrator. But you are in fact the author of several books. What you have just said applies to picture books, doesn't it? If the text is written so that the readers may easily picture the situation, there is no need to illustrate it. The contrary can also be said.

Anno: Very often I hear that because some of my books do not have any text, they are difficult to understand. I really do not know how to respond to such a comment.

Aoki: A good example of such works is *Anno's Alphabet* . . . , which you made for an English-speaking international public as well as for Japanese people. What did you learn from that experience?

Anno: Well, it certainly taught me that each nation uses the book in keeping with its own cultural background, and each has different associations of ideas and images with certain letters and words. This meant I had to be very careful in collecting the most universal images. I could not have done it without help from a few English-speaking people.

For example, about my illustration of a devil an American said that it was not the kind of devil she knew. I had to laugh and ask if she had ever seen a devil. But seriously, I believe that a nation's culture is reflected in the way in which something invisible is given a certain form. And it is true that we Japanese tend to imagine devils and angels quite freely because in the past a wide variety of their images have come into Japan from different countries.

Anyway, with this topological book I want my readers to work to discover for themselves as many as possible of the points I have illustrated. And I hope that doing this gives them as much pleasure—and as many problems—as the book gave me in putting ideas together on the page.

Aoki: Later you worked on more books without words. How did the idea for your first "journey" book originate?

Anno: I went to Europe and visited Scandinavia mainly, and then I traveled to England and south through Germany. I was not aware of it when I was working on the book, but having my traveler begin his journey by landing in a boat may be a reflection of the Japanese way of thinking. A German artist possibly would not have started his journey that way. My purpose for traveling was not merely to see more of the world but to get lost in it. I did often get lost and faced many difficulties, but under such circumstances there were always unexpected discoveries and interesting experiences waiting for me.

My second journey book is *Anno's Italy*. . . . (pp. 139-41)

Aoki: Your third journey book took us to England. So where will your fourth journey book take us?

Anno: Well, I went to the United States last fall. So my fourth journey book will be about the U.S.A.

Aoki: Did you travel around by car?

Anno: Yes, most of the way by car. At first, from Boston to New York, Washington, D.C., Williamsburg, and Atlanta. It is almost impossible for the average Japanese to realize how big America is. Driving from Atlanta to New Orleans, for example, I saw cotton fields for miles and miles and then corn fields which seemed to go on endlessly. I was excited at first, but after a while I had the urge to escape from the same scenery.

Aoki: From New Orleans did you go to the West Coast?

Anno: It was my original plan to go to the West Coast and back to Japan. But when I got as far as Albuquerque, I felt I had to go to St. Louis.

Aoki: Why?

Anno: As a child I loved Tom Sawyer and Huckleberry Finn, and Mark Twain meant America to me. So I just had to meet them before going back to Japan. (pp. 142-43)

Aoki: I look forward very much to seeing your America in the next journey book. It seems to me that you are always working on something which interests you and fascinates you at the same time. Is that right?

Anno: Yes, in that fact I can say I'm lucky. Recently I have been captivated by mathematics and have worked on several books in that field for both children and adults.

Aoki: How do you actually set about producing something?

Anno: I try to work very thoroughly on whatever I have in hand. For example, I am constantly asked to create many different kinds of small pieces. Often these coincide with a major idea of mine, but as I'm always worried about getting things done by a deadline, these small works are inclined to get finished first. Then I feel free to concentrate on what I want to do myself.

My room is full of piles of unfinished work which is in fact already completed in my mind. What stimulates its completion is a phone call asking whether some work is ready or not. After giving an affirmative answer, I go back to the particular work and finish it off.

My atelier looks terribly crowded and messy, but I like it that way, for I can see everything to be done and also what's in progress, and I don't have to hunt for things. Everything is visible! In the same way I only wish that what is in my mind were visible to you. Then you would see what books are coming out of me in the future. (pp. 144-45)

> *Hisako Aoki, "A Conversation with Mitsumasa Anno,"*
> *in* The Horn Book Magazine, *Vol. LIX, No. 2, April,*
> *1983, pp. 137-45.*

GENERAL COMMENTARY

TEIJI SETA AND MOMOKO ISHII

The most internationally known Japanese illustrator of children's books today must be Mitsumasa Anno.... This ex-[elementary]-school-teacher attracted attention as soon as he brought out his first book, *Fushigi na E (Strange, Strange Pictures),* ... which was immediately introduced to Switzerland, Denmark, and America where it was published as *Topsy-Turvies: Pictures to Stretch the Imagination.* . . . The world he creates with his fine incisive lines is a strange one. His pictures range from unusual presentations of three dimensional shapes to finely delineated decorative backgrounds. He is a born artist with a special vision of his own, and it has been said that there has not been a day since his childhood when he has not drawn. (p. 56)

> *Teiji Seta and Momoko Ishii, "Where the Old Meets*
> *the New: The Japanese Picture Book," in* Illustrators
> of Children's Books: 1967-1976, *Lee Kingman, Grace*

Allen Hogarth, Harriet Quimby, eds., The Horn Book,
Inc., 1978, pp. 44-57.

GRACE ALLEN HOGARTH

[Anno was] fascinated during his childhood by mathematics for the perfection of "its perfect world without tricks." He found that mathematics helped him to see the physical world as it is and to discover its beauty. He worked for several years as a teacher in primary school and, during this time, he found it difficult to reconcile the perfect world and the real one. However, when he discovered Escher's art-work he learned the way to express these two opposites simultaneously.... [*Topsy-Turvies*] was inspired by Escher. Since then he has worked at the illustration of children's books until, finally, with *Anno's Alphabet* he has come to feel freer and has learned that the more elaborately and freely he works, the closer he comes to his childhood's dream of the beautiful world of mathematics.

> *Grace Allen Hogarth, "Biographies of Illustrators*
> *Active 1967-1976: Mitsumasa Anno," in* Illustrators
> of Children's Books: 1967-1976, *Lee Kingman, Grace*
> *Allen Hogarth, Harriet Quimby, eds,* The Horn Book,
> *Inc. 1978, p. 96.*

BRENDAN GILL

Prominent in any contemporary group of writer-artists is Mitsumasa Anno . . . whose increasing fame has caused his name to reduce itself among his devotees to a simple "Anno"—a sacred password, the very uttering of which is capable of turning total strangers into friends. At least half a dozen of Anno's works have been translated from Japanese into English over the past several years. The latest of them is *The Unique World of Mitsumasa Anno*—by bad luck, the least felicitous of his titles. (Surely publishers should know by now that "unique" is even more tiresome an adjective than "wonderful." It conveys nothing except an awareness of its own exhaustion.) Fortunately, the book is far superior to the title and serves as an admirable introduction to Anno's quirky and mischievous nature, which combines to an uncanny degree the analytical and the intuitive. He is an artist-writer at once playful and in dead earnest; his mind rejoices in pranks, and the pranks must be as logical as they are comic. If their outrageousness is not highly reasonable, he will find no use for them. "I am," he seems to say, "a teacher disguised as a clown. I have something hilarious and serious to tell you."

The dust jacket of *The Unique World* is itself a prank. At first glance it appears to be a package, wrapped in brown paper, stamped, addressed, and bound with heavy twine; one is tempted to look for a pair of scissors with which to cut the twine. The trompe l'oeil having been successfully seen through we discover that the contents of the book consist of more pranks—drawings of objects, many of them impossible to experience in the real world (the so-called Escher staircase is one of them). The drawings are based sometimes upon physics and sometimes upon folklore and are accompanied by texts drawn from an unexpectedly diverse mingling of sources. Freeman Dyson, Oscar Wilde, Friedrich Nietzsche, Ambrose Bierce, Yoshitoshi Sugiyama, and St. Matthew are surely surprising bedfellows, or bookfellows; what they have in common is the relish with which Anno uses quotations from their writings as captions for drawings of a striking (and cunningly calculated) inappositeness—an inappositeness raised to the level of genius.

An introduction to Anno as useful as *The Unique World* is *Anno's Medieval World,* in which he supplied both text, and drawings and in which his bent for teaching is fully exploited. We are charmed and amused and we are also instructed. In an afterword, Anno notes that the book could have possessed a longer title—"I might have called it, How People Living in the Era of the Ptolemaic Theory Saw Their World." That, he claims, is what the book is about, but we as readers will feel free to contradict him; the book is about the sunny interior of Anno's mind, which is not only Copernican, but Pickwickian.

If still another introduction to Anno's books were required to lure us into the Anno cult, then let me recommend with all my heart, especially for children, *Anno's Italy,* in which Anno the writer is entirely suppressed in favor of Anno the artist. Page after page of ravishing watercolors depict an Italy that none of us has ever encountered but that we recognize at once as the true Italy—the Italy of our hearts' desire, in which men, women, children, dogs, cats, horses, sheep, cows, and birds dwell in happy comity together. It is an Italy in which St. Francis of Assisi is likely to be come upon as we round the next corner, and we need show no surprise if he proves to be carrying a balloon in one hand and a lark in the other. Not a word of text is needed, even to point out certain pleasing secret references tucked away in treetops and green fields. Here is Anno's hand, lightly touching the page; we share with him as if from one moment of creation to the next the springtime freshness of the wonders that flow out of it. (p. 19)

> *Brendan Gill, "The Amazing Anno," in* Book World— The Washington Post, *November 9, 1980, pp. 11, 19.*

ELAINE MOSS

Being Japanese and overflowing with the desire directly to communicate truths about people, legends, religion, architecture, art, mathematics, science to the world, poses a problem: Japanese is not a universal language. But painting is. Mitsumasa Anno has used his pen and brush to delight adults and children everywhere with his challenges to their power of reasoning, his enlightened—and enlightening—view of European culture. His two alphabet books are included here as hors d'oeuvres, appetisers preparing the palate for the special flavour of his travels in place and time. (p. 38)

Why did Anno choose to paint a carved wooden interrogation mark for the jacket and the half-title page of his *Alphabet*? If you can answer this *question* correctly you will have gone some way towards discovering what the artist is asking of you. For his *Alphabet* is composed of paintings of carved letters, their joints and angles startling the reader into an appreciation of trompe l'oeil painting, since no craftsman could join or plane letters the way Anno has painted them. Look at the interrogation mark again—closely. How is the curved upper part of the sign joined to the dot below? Ah! Now you can answer *two* questions. Why did Anno use the question mark—and how many question marks are present in the picture of *the* question mark? (p. 39)

Believe it or not, a second Anno alphabet [*Anno's Magical ABC: An Anamorphic Alphabet*] which is a challenge to the eye—and, here, to the mathematical brain. For this is an alphabet—or rather two alphabets, the upper and lower case—drawn on the anamorphic projection, each letter illustrated with a full-colour *A*ngel, *B*alalaika, *C*assette on a similarly distorting projection. In order to read the letters, identify the painted objects, you use a reflecting cylinder—a circular tin stripped of its paper wrapping, or the piece of foil thoughtfully provided with the book by the publishers. And readers wishing to make

their own anamorphic projections are given full instructions in the centre of this 64-page full-colour picture book. Start at either end. . . . (pp. 39-40)

[In *Anno's Journey,* there] is no point in journeying with Anno (who represents himself in his paintings as a tiny figure on a horse) through Europe unless you are prepared to travel slowly with your eyes skinned. If you have patience, . . . you will be rewarded. For as Anno ambles through the green countryside, through villages, through towns, stories unfold—a romance, a race. And here and there a familiar piece of landscape (Van Gogh's Bridge at Arles), a group of people (Millet's Reapers), a folk tale in action ("The Great Big Enormous Turnip") or a musical phrase (the opening bars of Beethoven's Ninth Symphony on a shop sign) will stop you in your tracks. But Anno clip-clops on over the hill, away to fresh horizons, silent (for there is no text here), observant, and once again, as in the *Alphabet,* using trompe l'oeil for your entertainment: children throwing quoits—on to a steeple; a statue (Anno on his horse) being led *off* its pedestal! (p. 40)

There is a great deal of difference between knowing that the world is round and understanding the explosive impact of that knowledge on the people of the Middle Ages, who believed it to be flat. In this brilliant picture book [*Anno's Medieval World*] painted on a simulated parchment background, Anno traces the story of the world-in-the-universe from Ptolemaic Theory through Copernicus to Galileo. And meanwhile the flat earth, inhabited by people who believed in witchcraft and alchemy, becomes first curved, then semi-circular, global, floating in space as man discovers the microscope, the telescope, navigational instruments. Text (adapted by Ursula Synge) and pictures magically capture the beliefs of our pre-Renaissance ancestors— and help us to understand our own. (pp. 40-1)

> *Elaine Moss, "Mitsumasa Anno," in her* Picture Books for Young People, 9-13, *The Thimble Press, 1981, pp. 38-41.*

TADASHI MATSUI

With his highly original works, Mitsumasa Anno has carved out his own particular niche in the long annals of picture-book history. He has extended the range of expression of the picture-book genre and thereby created a special world of wonder and enjoyment. Moreover, his books have already played their part in bringing East and West closer together.

Although his picture books were born in Japan, they have travelled widely in Europe and the U.S.A. and are much appreciated everywhere they go. Therefore I think it is reasonable to say that Anno's books demonstrate how it is possible to transcend cultural and social differences and reveal the universality of human interest, sympathy and pleasure. A similar universality is found in the field of modern music.

Anno's first picture book was *Fushigi na e (Topsy-Turvies).* . . . As a result of that book he became known as "The Japanese Escher," but his many picture books published since then have been distinguished by a keen sense of originality. It is certainly true that *Fushigi na e* was influenced by the work of the Dutch artist Escher, but Anno has established a considerable scientific reputation in his own right. Indeed, this book gave birth to the expression "Anno's Steps" in the vocabulary of scientists.

One important feature of Anno's achievements in the world of picture books has been his ability to find pictorial expressions for difficult phase and space concepts. He has the unusual skill of digesting many topological themes and incorporating them

The King was just a little uneasy when he saw the huge pincers and again when the dentist tied him down in his chair. But everyone pushed or pulled and at last out came the tiny bad tooth and the King's enormous toothache was over.

From The King's Flower, *written and illustrated by Mitsumasa Anno. William Collins Publishers, Inc., 1979. Copyright 1976 by Kodansha, Tokyo. Reprinted by permission of Philomel Books.*

in his books: Penrose's Triangle, Necker's Cubic, Schröder's Steps, Moebius's Strip, Perpetual Motion, to name but a few. The result of this process is the creation of a unique kind of picture book art.

The fruit of his labours in this field was the publication of ***ABC no hon (Anno's Alphabet)*** . . . , in which many of his ideas were crystallized. I feel sure that the alphabet designs moulded by Anno will long play their part in the history of lettering. Anno has commented on his book:

> As a Japanese I have never felt very close to the alphabet, and it is therefore possible for me to regard the letters of the alphabet quite objectively as materials with which to design freely. I think that Europeans have a deep cultural relationship with the alphabet, and as a result find it difficult to achieve the sense of detachment from it that is so easy for me. The art of lettering carries on its shoulders the weight of a long and dense history of design, and that perhaps handicaps people's ideas in some way.

Another feature of Anno's ***ABC no hon*** is his use of arabesque frames for his pictures. These designs are distilled from the essence of traditional decorative arts: that essence has been absorbed, digested and reborn as Anno's Arabesque. I feel that Anno's excellent ideas, careful attention to detail and elaborate draughtsmanship raise the artistic value of the book's vision to a high level.

From the points I have made so far, it may seem as though Anno's talent is simply a combination of intellectual games and a fine 3-dimensional sense of design. But one is also struck by his sharp observation of nature and landscape and also his skilful and lyrical handling of stories. These characteristics are well exemplified in ***No no Hana to Kobito-Tachi*** (*Wild Flowers and Little People*, . . .) and, at a slightly more advanced level, in the three volumes of ***Tabi no Ehon*** (***Anno's Journey***, *Anno's Journey II* and *Anno's Journey III*, . . .). These are all extremely popular picture books.

Anno is a master at the use of the 'trompe-l'oeil.' A good example is his book ***Mori no Ehon*** (*Anno's Strange Woods*, . . .) and there are countless examples to be found in the ***Tabi no Ehon*** series together with many other tricks. Anno's readers seem to share his delight in visual tricks and are easily led into his ***Tabi no Ehon*** world by way of his vivid picture story. Perhaps the real hero of these books is the architecture; Anno places great emphasis on the architectural backgrounds to his illustrations. It is as though Anno has somehow grasped, and is able to express, the real essence of the picture book: not just something to look at, not just a visual delight, but a whole new world to enter into.

Anno picks his elements from many fields—sciences, literature, the visual arts—and arranges them in his characteristic way with intelligence, humour and a host of tricks. He organises his forms carefully and presents them to us in picture-book style. As a result he has developed an attractive new world and extended the range of possibilities for picture book creation.

Finally, I should add that Mitsumasa Anno is also a distinguished educator and a leading essayist in Japan. It is rare indeed to come across an artist with his combination of talents. (pp. 36-7)

Tadashi Matsui, "The Art of Mitsumasa Anno,"
translated by Michiko Takemura and Stuart Atkin,
in Bookbird, *Nos. 1 & 2, March 15 & June 15, 1982,*
pp. 36-7.

LEONARD S. MARCUS

Among the more adventurous picture books to appear in the United States in the last dozen years have been those of the Japanese illustrator, painter, and teacher Mitsumasa Anno. Few artists, past or contemporary, have presented so fully realized a vision of the picture book as a distinctive form, or approached their work with so spirited a taste for experiment as has Anno. His books are on themes as various, and one might at times have thought unlikely, as anamorphic illusion, the mathematical concept of factorials and the Ptolemaic world view, as well as on such more conventional picture book themes as the alphabet and first numbers. Perhaps the most characteristic quality of Anno's illustrations, whatever his subject happens to be, is the open-endedness of their imaginative forms; Anno's knack, that is, for making books that readers must complete with their own understandings, fantasies, words. All art of substance remains open-ended to some degree, subject to interpretation. But Anno's books engage different readers in distinctly different levels of mental activity; they arise out of a deep knowledge of the stages of children's mental development, and more generally, of the types and habits of human perception, from simple recognition and naming to the poetic ranges of metaphor-making. A child who returns to Anno's best books at intervals of a year or more is apt to find that they correspond to changes in his or her own interests and awareness.

Even the *Alphabet* and *Counting Book,* which have as their starting points basic grade school lessons, are not only concerned with sets of facts to be memorized once and for all, but with relationships between facts, with orders and classes of facts and experience. Thus from the latter book one not only learns to count in whole numbers, but realizes that counting, quantifying, and measuring are activities useful all one's life—for playing jumprope and for earning one's living. The *Counting Book*'s clever plan, according to which illustration details (trees, houses, fish in the stream) always occur in multiples equal to the number being presented transforms a rote lesson into a whimsical game of hunting for additional examples of the number within each picture. The *Counting Book* follows the pattern of a cumulative counting song like "The Twelve Days of Christmas." By this device, Anno indirectly introduces the concept of addition. He continues the book through the number twelve instead of the more usual counting book limit of ten; in addition, the double page illustrations turn out also to represent the months of the year, a calendar. Learning from such a densely constructed, suggestive book as this becomes a process of gradual recognition, of not-having-to-be-told.

To speak of "readers" of Anno's wordless picture books is appropriate because his pictures are of a kind that *tend toward language.* The *Alphabet* and *Counting Book,* among others, directly concern the basic signs of written language, but this is only their most obvious link to the language realm. Much

that at first glance seems merely decorative in the illustrations turns out to have a specific verbal reference or association. A reader of the *Alphabet,* for instance, mentally draws up a list of the plants and animals pictured in the ornamental border for the letter P and recites: "parrot, pea, pumpkin, poppy"—a tongue-twister stumbled upon, decoded. To discover the tongue-twisters, visual puns, and other plays-on-wordlessness half-hidden in the books, one must first have begun to think in terms of names and naming, as young children learning to talk do, pointing incessantly to nearby objects and announcing their names: "Moustache! Grandpa! Tree!" From a developmental standpoint, one of the earliest levels on which Anno's books involve readers is that of naming.

The child who proudly says: "Tree!" also means to say: "That tree is *not* me!" A sense of self emerges, in other words, with a growing sense of the familiarity of one's surroundings and world. A corresponding pattern may be observed in young children's art, in which each hilltop, cow, and car is typically rendered as a thing apart, a picture symbol that may be considered the visual equivalent of a name.

In some of his books more than others, in the *Counting Book,* for instance, more than in the *Journey,* Anno has worked in a naive style reminiscent of children's art. Stylistic affinities of this kind can easily become mere affectations, but in Anno's case the simplicity and clarity of the drawings, rendered in an agile line with often the suggestion of a humorous curl or twist to it, are encouragements to children to read details in terms of their names. Thus Anno's child-like manner results from his understanding of younger children. (pp. 34-5)

Puzzle interest is another level of understanding on which Anno engages readers in several books. Among them the first two of his to have been reprinted in the United States were *Topsy-Turvies* and *Upside-Downers.*

When first examined, *Upside-Downers* appears to be a wordless collection of gently amusing watercolor paintings. However, the pictures are looked at upside-down, different and equally convincing images take their place. When the page is returned to its original position, the first picture reappears, the second one having slipped from view. Illusions of this kind . . . call attention to the limits of our ability to see, to know by seeing. For no matter how often we turn the pictures one way or the other, long after we have become aware of their doubleness, we still register only one image at a time. It is as though we wear mental blinders that permit only a single, partial reading. We do. To see, then, such pictures show us, is largely a mental act, the mind sorting, selecting, interpreting all that the eye naively witnesses; *Upside-Downers* represents an enticing skewing of the rules of perception as worked out by artists and psychologists.

Another well-known example of visual subversion of this kind is the graphic art of M. C. Escher. In Escher's "impossible figures," as psychologists of perception call them, stairways, corridors, flat and curved surfaces swerve back from their vanishing points to join up in fantastic structures that defy definition within our familiar three-dimensional world. Space reels out from and back on itself. Up and down have no meaning. The familiar orienting cues of "solid" space dissolve.

Escher's wryly intellectualized riddle world draws inspiration from Alice's Wonderland dream and in turn has inspired the whimsically castled and pennanted fantasies of Anno's *Topsy-Turvies,* in which little people calmly climb Moebius-stairways that lead them up and down walls and across ceilings. The main departure Anno makes from Escher's vertiginous art appears in the former's festive tone, in the complete lack of menace in his delicate watercolor and line paintings. (pp. 36-7)

Thoughts about infinity may occur to children at a very early age. This is an insight Anno's works all implicitly acknowledge. Young children may lack the means to reason or to communicate abstractly about such matters, but as Bruno Bettelheim has observed, "the child's fantasies are his thoughts." From this standpoint, Anno's impossible figure paintings are a kind of mental gymnastic apparatus on which the young may exercise their first glimmerings of a world beyond measure.

Upside-Downers, the Escheresque *Topsy-Turvies,* and more recent books like *Anno's Animals,* the *Magical ABC,* and *Unique World,* are puzzle anthologies, clever inventions arranged in series like ducks in a row. But in other Anno books, the form of the book becomes enmeshed in its contents. In *Dr. Anno's Magical Midnight Circus,* an early instance of this, and in the *Alphabet, Counting Book,* and *Journey,* more recent examples, page and book assume metaphorical meanings, heightening readers' participation. This metaphoric binding of form and content creates a third level of understanding on which certain of Anno's books may be read. (pp. 37-8)

The metaphor of book-as-magic-performance is the premise of Anno's first exploration of the picture book as symbolic form. *Dr. Anno's Magical Midnight Circus* consists of *trompe l'oeil* pages within pages in which clowns become artists who paint lions that spring suddenly to life, threatening to devour the puffed-up ringmaster, slapstick authority figure. In among circus props—hoops, cages, and balancing balls—one sees artists' ink bottles, scissors, and paper, all larger than life—or have these tools and materials somehow arrived in a miniature Wonderland world of the artist's invention? As in surrealist works like René Magritte's painting "Personal Values," there is no way of gauging scale in Anno's illustrations, of grounding our perceptions in that usually relied-upon way. Through such "liberation from all obligations of dimensions," which [Gaston] Bachelard calls "characteristic" of the imagination's activities, Anno involves the plainest of everyday objects in a metaphoric realm.

Relying less on puzzle illusions than on poetic metaphor, *Anno's Alphabet* represents a deepening of the experiment of merging content and form. The *Alphabet's* title page is much delayed. Before one arrives at it, one first sees a painting of a blossoming tree; then, an image of the stump left after the tree has been chopped down. A branch of the tree, still attached to the stump, doubles as the axe handle—a suggestion that subject and object, ends and means have begun somehow to merge. One thinks of the tree from which the pages for the book in one's hand was made, then of the tree depicted on its pages, and realizes that by reading the book in one's hands one is continuing the process of making it right up to the present moment.

In succeeding pages (we still haven't gotten to the title page), there is an image of a block of wood in a carpenter's vise; then one of a solid wood "book" carved from the block. Finally, the title *Anno's Alphabet* appears, followed by pages of alphabet letters, also apparently carved from the block, as are many of the objects chosen to illustrate them—a wooden French horn for H, a wooden typewriter for T. Gradually a metaphor has taken form, pointing to similarities between one living thing, a blossoming tree, and a word, a book, language.

Anno's letters, skillfully and beautifully rendered as carvings in woods, are large and clear for young children just learning the alphabet. The illustrations accompanying each letter depict objects for early talkers to name. Most likely it is older readers who notice that the decorative line borders framing each double page are each different, each constructed of floral, animal, and other elements, the names of which begin with the letter presented on the same page; the alphabet letters when closely examined prove to be impossible figures: more naming, more puzzle interest. Readers must also eventually be drawn in to some extent by the visual splendor of the *Alphabet,* which is undoubtedly one of the most accomplished works of picture book art to be published in years.

Just as many-sided is *Anno's Journey,* a wordless book that is a mass of colorful detail, a picture narrative, and a poetic meditation in narrative form. Without a written text as guide, readers are left to invent stories of their own, which may or may not concern the little man whose journey by boat and on horseback forms the one narrative lifeline or thread running through the book from beginning to end. The artist's vantage point is a view from above, what Bachelard might have called a daydreamer's prospect, which permits us to see more of the passing scene than the little man does. We observe: a wedding, a funeral, children playing, and adults at work—a fully rounded pastoral world of boatmen and birds, fieldworkers and idlers, windmills and horse-drawn carts. As in the narrative picture scrolls of the eighth-century Japanese artist Kibi, activity is emphasized over personality, the characteristic over the individual. The reader remains free to ignore the little man and be diverted by seemingly endless other goings-on, to "stray from the path" as it were; though, far from implying a grave outcome for readers whose attention wanders, Anno's book is a heartfelt encouragement to daydream, question, reimagine the world.

Scattered among the *Journey's* scenes are details from European master paintings and storybook characters like Red Riding Hood and Goldilocks: allusions to be uncovered and recognized by some readers, as in a treasure hunt, and simply accepted by others as particulars of the *Journey's* thickly inhabited world. Unobtrusively, such references also imply that art and life are continuous with each other; that the imagination is not so much an escape from the real as it is its extension beyond workaday limits.

In sequels to the *Journey—Anno's Italy, Britain,* and *U.S.A.—* the hunt or puzzle element plays a larger and perhaps more intrusive role. Much of the mystery that makes the *Journey* such an evocative and involving fantasy arises from the fact that we recognize its setting only in a general way. Just as we do not know much about who the little man on horseback is, we don't know quite where he is, or when in time we have encountered him. An enticing state of not-knowing—the essence of the old storyteller's gambit "once upon a time"— propels us inward, leaving us to rely on our wits and on our powers of observation to find our way through the *Journey* which, in the process, becomes *our* journey, too.

But in the more recent travel books, the role that the artist casts the reader in has changed in emphasis and become more that of a sightseer than an adventurer finding his or her way through unfamiliar territory. In *Anno's U.S.A.,* for example, glimpses of Colonial Williamsburg, the great American desert, the Capitol, Independence Hall, midtown Manhattan, and dozens of other recognizable locales predominate. The invitation to the journey, in becoming more structured, more a matter, that is, of identifying known sights (and the characters, historical or imaginary, associated with them) has been reduced to something like a tourist's itinerary.

In *U.S.A.,* Anno seems to have experienced difficulties in organizing and selecting his material, problems that one finds few if any traces of in the earlier travel books. His technical mastery as a watercolorist and draftsman remains as sure-handed as ever. But certain transitions, particularly the one leading into a view of present-day Manhattan, are awkward, unprepared-for. Being essentially pastoral, that is, tied to the cyclical rhythms and continuities of village life and the changing seasons, Anno's vision is ill-suited to skyscrapers (which look stranded incongruously in the book's middle illustrations) and cars (represented only by a few quaint, antique specimens) among other symbols of industrial and postindustrial American life that harken back not to some timeless past but merely to the *historical* moment that gave rise to them. Reading the pastoral *Journey,* one has the sensation of having entered headlong into a mythic world—much as when one gazes at the array of stones set out in a Japanese meditation garden, or at a bonsai tree, or at one of the miniature sculptural ruins of the contemporary artist Charles Simonds. But *Anno's U.S.A.,* like a Disney theme park of methodically selected and scaled-down prairie plains and Pilgrim settlements, seems capable mainly of amusing and perhaps of informing.

The variety and ambitiousness of Anno's picture book experiments have, on the whole, been extraordinary. His *Medieval World,* chronicling the West's momentous discovery that the earth is a sphere that revolves around the sun, is a good example not only of clear and concrete narrative writing for children (really, for the lay person of any age), but of skill at lightening the solemn occasion of a history lesson by pictorial means. His *Mysterious Multiplying Jar,* a demonstration of the mathematical concept of factorials, does not quite reconcile its subject material to the picture book format, divided as it is into two unintegrated sections, a picture part and a follow-up explanation. But attempts at dispelling the dread that many children develop toward math are rare, and one respects and looks with expectation beyond this initial effort. Both books also point to a fuller understanding of Anno's esthetic, implying as they do that, contrary to accepted wisdom, an interest in science and mathematics is compatible with an interest in art; that art and science represent different approaches to the common end of exercising human perception beyond known limits.

In *The World of M. C. Escher,* C. H. A. Broos writes that

> no one knowing Escher's preference for Lewis Carroll will be surprised that he underlined the following passage by the mathematical physicist J. L. Synge: "In submitting to your consideration the idea that the human mind is at its best when playing, I am myself playing, and that makes me feel that what I am saying may have in it an element of truth."

The spirit of play that pervades Anno's work is its unifying principle, the bond that holds together its various levels of appreciation and meaning. Readers enter Anno's realm at their ease, without the apprehensiveness with which they might approach school or the adult world at large, and find their level, as we find ours, whether it be that of namer, puzzle-solver, daydreamer-storyteller-poet, or some other. Anno addresses every reader with an exclamation that is also a question, the Lion's question in *Through the Looking-Glass*—"What's this!''—to which one feels inclined to answer with another

question, the Unicorn's possibly: "Ah, what *is* it, now?" Thus, seeing and making, and learning and playing become forms of one another, looking-glass activities in the fluid imagination of Anno's knowing art. (pp. 40-4)

> *Leonard S. Marcus, "The Artist's Other Eye: The Picture Books of Mitsumasa Anno," in* The Lion and the Unicorn, *Vol. 7-8, 1983-84, pp. 34-46.*

PATRICIA CRAMPTON

[Mitsumasa Anno was] a clear winner [of the Hans Christian Andersen Award] both for his technical mastery and for his ability to involve the child in his work, as if every page were a new game for the mind and senses. (p. 5)

Mitsumasa Anno has published over 70 books which have increasingly played a part in bringing the art and understanding of East and West closer together. Long known and loved throughout Europe and the USA as well as in his native Japan, Anno has received [numerous international prizes] . . . and every possible Japanese picture book prize.

Anno's originality is by now legendary, yet he succeeds in exciting a universal response—almost as if the reader had been waiting for just such a book, but had never believed it could really happen. An intellectual artist of astonishing range, Anno has succeeded in conveying, in pictures of great beauty, extremely complex scientific concepts such as perpetual motion, Möbius Rings, etc. His concern has always been with topology and the beauty of the mathematical world, and this is evident in all his works.

The *ABC No Hon (Anno's Alphabet)* . . . is still one of his most impressive works, with its combination of clean, three-dimensional designs for the lettering, with exuberantly decorative frames illustrative of flora and fauna beginning with the letter in question—in other words, the reverse of the usual of the alphabet in picture books.

Sophisticated as they are, most of Anno's books can also be pure fun for children, something which can be studied only as they play with it, an object which demands, and receives, their total participation. *Sakasama (Upside-Downers), Tabi No Ehon (Anno's Journey), Tsubo No Naka (Anno's Mysterious Multiplying Jar), Kazoete Miyo (Anno's Counting Book)* are just a few of the works which have gained so much fame and given so much delight all round the world. (p. 8)

> *Patricia Crampton, "The Hans Christian Andersen Awards 1984," in* Bookbird, *No. 2, June 15, 1984, pp. 4-10.*

PATRICIA CRAMPTON

[*The following excerpt is taken from a speech given by Crampton, the 1984 Hans Christian Andersen Award jury president, at the presentation ceremony.*]

It has become almost a truism to say that Anno's work is uniquely successful in communicating to both east and west. . . . (p. 5)

Mitsumasa Anno was born in Tsuwano, in a valley surrounded by mountains, but in his lifetime, he told an *Observer* journalist, he has seen the beautiful countryside in which he grew up decimated into an urban wilderness. He laments the loss to the children of today, but he does not just sit crying in the wilderness. "In all his work he creates and celebrates an alternative world, transmitting to his less fortunate readers the

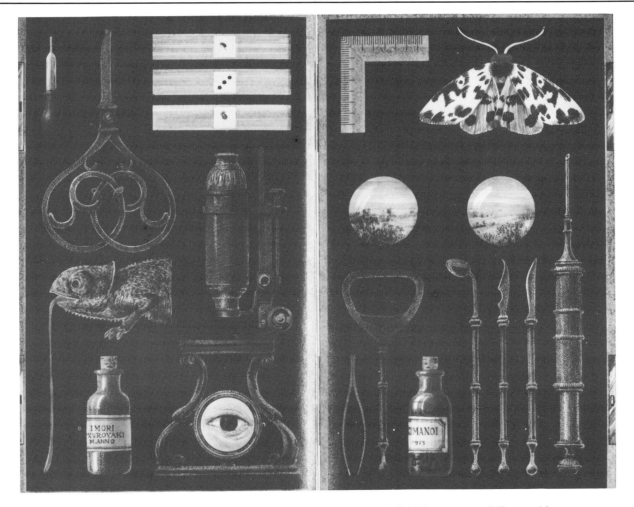

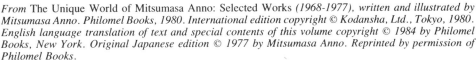

From The Unique World of Mitsumasa Anno: Selected Works *(1968-1977), written and illustrated by Mitsumasa Anno. Philomel Books, 1980. International edition copyright © Kodansha, Ltd., Tokyo, 1980. English language translation of text and special contents of this volume copyright © 1984 by Philomel Books, New York. Original Japanese edition © 1977 by Mitsumasa Anno. Reprinted by permission of Philomel Books.*

flowers, trees, ancient cities and historic places that they may never see.'' When you look at the finished book, he told the Sydney newspaper, *SCAN,* last year, ''you may feel that this entire book has a detailed plan, but when I first start to create a particular book I have mountains and rivers, or an ocean. . . . Then perhaps where there is a river *there is always a bridge*''. This is the nub: the river flows, the story moves on, but rivers flow only in one direction: then comes the bridge, Anno's bridge, and a bridge is the span between two banks, a bridge is essentially the bearer of two-way traffic. Thus it is that the man from the East is able to give back to us, in his journeys through the West, what the West has meant to him. Thus it is that he gives to children, in his books, a world of original invention, a mystery conveyed in the most apparently prosaic of our learning tools (think of the **ABC No Hon** . . . or **Anno's Mysterious Multiplying Jar**), and the children in turn are magnetized, magicked, into participation: he crosses the bridge to them and they return with him, are ''lost'' with him, in books which demand as much as they bestow. His originality is by now legendary, yet he succeeds in exciting a universal response—almost as if the reader had been waiting for just such a book, but had never believed it could really happen.

Of the books in which he conveys, in images of great beauty, such complex scientific concepts as perpetual motion or the Möbius Ring, he said: ''Actually I have 13 books which are related to mathematics. I am not necessarily a specialist, but I had a fascination about these types of ideas, although I did not think they were necessarily mathematical ideas. I did not intentionally create a marriage between mathematics and art, but I have that type of mind. Some people think that mathematics and art are very different, but I feel that they are actually the same from the viewpoint of creativity.'' I know of no other artist who has successfully built that particular bridge, with the possible exception of Escher, but his mathematical puzzles give me vertigo, whereas the ''marriage of mathematics and art'' in Anno gives me pure satisfaction.

It is not for me, a layperson, to attempt to analyse Anno's (as it seems to me) perfect use of the page, his endlessly inventive, delicate and humorous draughtsmanship, the subtlety and vivacity of his colours. We in IBBY are very far from the first, and I am sure we are also very far from the last, to honour him as an artist—for that must be the word, in Anno's case, rather than illustrator. We rejoice tonight in celebrating

Anno1984, and we look forward with relish to Anno 2000 and after. (pp. 5-6)

Patricia Crampton, "There Is Always a Bridge," in Bookbird, *No. 4, December 15, 1984, pp. 4-8.*

MARTIN GARDNER

If you and your children, or children you know, have not yet discovered Mitsumasa Anno you are in for fantastic treats. For two decades this Tokyo artist, with his delightful style, his puckish humor and his deep love of science and mathematics, has been creating absolutely marvelous books for children. I have been an admirer of his for a long time, indeed I wrote the introduction to a book of his five years ago [see excerpt dated 1980 for *The Unique World of Mitsumasa Anno*]. Mr. Anno is sometimes likened to Maurice Escher because of his fondness for geometrical structures and visual mind-benders. In the book that introduced him to American readers in the 1970's, *Anno's Alphabet,* each letter is drawn as an "impossible" object made of wood. Many of his other books swarm with optical tricks, upside-down pictures, hidden animals, mazes, mirror pictures and endless other jokes and surprises.

Anno's Journey was the first of his classic "journey books." These are picture books without words, but every picture so filled with wondrous details that both children and adults return to its pages, each time discovering amusing and beautiful things never before noticed. A child of any age can spend weeks studying the objects in *Anno's Flea Market*—his "love song to the past," as a reviewer described it last year on these pages [see excerpt dated August 26, 1984 for *Anno's Flea Market*]—without exhausting its subtle nuances.

Many of Mr. Anno's dozens of books are designed to teach mathematics to very young children. Most of them are available, alas, only in their original Japanese, but we are fortunate to have some in English. Is there any better way to introduce children to the first 12 numbers than by giving them *Anno's Counting Book*? Its exciting pages depict scenes from January through December, each landscape filled with sets of objects to be counted by the number of the month. There is even a church clock in each picture that shows the time from 1 to 12. Addition and subtraction? There is no more pleasant way for a child to learn the meaning of these operations than by turning the pages of *Anno's Counting House.* . . .

Anno's Mysterious Multiplying Jar is an incredible blue-and-white porcelain jar containing many things—islands and mountains and houses with cupboards that hold small jars exactly like the original. Not knowing they are being taught, child readers learn what few adults know—the meaning of "factorial." . . .

I know of no more painless way to introduce a bright child to the meaning of what logicians call the "binary connective" of "if . . . then" than to give the child *Anno's Hat Tricks.* You too will learn some elementary logic, including a way of diagramming deductive reasoning with a "binary tree," from the "Note to Parents and Other Older Readers" at the back of the book.

Martin Gardner, "The Fun of 'If . . . Then'," in The New York Times Book Review, *November 10, 1985, p. 52.*

ZENA SUTHERLAND AND MAY HILL ARBUTHNOT

An outstanding Japanese artist, Mitsumasa Anno has a sense of humor that pervades all of his distinctive books; his love of

mathematics is also obvious, especially in *Topsy-Turvies* . . ., an elegant compilation of mathematical impossibilities in space, with drawings that flout deliberately all known rules of perspective. His line and watercolor paintings are beautiful in detail, and his experience as a book designer has contributed to the handsomeness of the page layouts. Few of Anno's books have much text, but their language is universal. In *Anno's Alphabet* . . . the woodgrain letters are beautifully framed by decorative black and white borders; in *Anno's Journey* . . . the artist records European art and architecture quite seriously but cannot resist a visual joke here and there (a gatehouse is engraved with "Anno 1976"); and in *Anno's U.S.A.* . . . he does the same sort of mixture of places and cultural jokes delightfully. In *Anno's Animals* . . . his love of humor and trompe l'oeil produce a forest full of hidden animals. Anno's draftsmanship is impeccable, his use of color restrained and sophisticated.

Zena Sutherland and May Hill Arbuthnot, "Artists and Children's Books: Mitsumasa Anno," in their Children and Books, *seventh edition, Scott, Foresman and Company, 1986, p. 150.*

KAZOETE MIYŌ [ANNO'S COUNTING BOOK] (1975)

If Anno has previously functioned as the nursery Escher, he turns up here in the guise of a kindergartners' Grandma Moses. Still there is more ado in these charming primitivist landscapes than meets the careless eye. Numbered one through twelve in the right-hand margins, each double-page picture represents the same rural scene at a different hour of the day and month of the year, and in the left margin colored blocks stack up correspondingly (with a new column beginning at eleven). Within the picture a community grows—from one house, pine tree, leafy tree, child, adult, and animal to twelve of each; along the way more roads and bridges appear, activity steps up, groupings shift—and, best of all, Anno lets children discover it all for themselves, without a word of direction. However you add it up, it's a plus for your preschool collection.

A review of "Anno's Counting Book," in Kirkus Reviews, *Vol. XLV, No. 9, May 1, 1977, p. 483.*

The very best dish to set before the king's children is *Anno's Counting Book* . . ., one of the few truly intelligent counting books ever produced—and a work of art besides. . . . Anno's village is alive in his lovely watercolor paintings, and every child will be subtly, irresistibly pulled in, counting trees and trucks, flowers and fish, ducks and diapers. Ambrosia to be consumed by the child and enjoyed by the parent in the sharing.

George A. Woods, "Pleasures for the Eye," in The New York Times Book Review, *May 1, 1977, p. 28.*

Mitsumasa Anno is a Japanese illustrator who brings a new dimension to children's illustration. At first glance his counting book is deceptively simple but each double spread repays careful observation time and time again. . . . In its sense of scale and careful placing of groups and sets of figures as well as in the continuity of amusing detail from page to page this is an outstanding children's book—one to treasure from generation to generation.

A review of "Anno's Counting Book," in Books for Your Children, *Vol. 12, No. 4, Autumn, 1977, p. 7.*

The children's picture-book, as an art form, gets cleverer all the time, and not always for its own good. **Anno's Counting Book** is an exercise in observation. Starting with Zero and an almost blank page it progresses to 12, adding all the time to the same scene, the complexities increasing in strict arithmetical degree. It is all, in the literal and figurative sense, "calculated". Much as one admires the mind behind this experiment, it may be more difficult to love the book—although teachers may well disagree. (pp. 271-72)

> *M. Crouch, in a review of "Anno's Counting Book,"*
> *in* The Junior Bookshelf, *Vol. 41, No. 5, October,*
> *1977, pp. 271-72.*

ŌKINA MONO NO SUKINA ŌSAMA [THE KING'S FLOWER] (1976)

Children's book artists must hitch their pictures to a tale. You can lead a child to culture, but you can't make him think—without a story.

Proof positive can be found in Mitsumasa Anno's **The King's Flower**. . . . Here the prodigious draftsmanship of one of Japan's leading children's authors is totally in the service of a narrative imagination. An early Renaissance European king wants everything he has to be the biggest: Big is beautiful and best. Elaborate hoists and pulleys are needed to help him eat with his gigantic fork and knife; pincers the size of a meeting hall are needed to pull his tooth; when he fishes in the castle moat he must catch a whale, nothing less. He orders the biggest flowerpot ever made to grow the biggest tulip ever seen, but even he must wait until the flower grows. At last it appears: very small—one tulip in a very big pot—but very beautiful. The contrast between the king's small body and his gargantuan possessions is carefully worked out: The mechanical world of his will is humorously played off against the natural world of his body and of the tulip. The moral and political message is clear, but unobtrusive. The illustrations—both line and color—are sharp and clear and clever, with something of the earth tones of late Maurice Sendak in the palette. A first-rate picture book, one of the best of the season.

> *Nora Magid, "Concerning This and That," in* The
> New York Times Book Review, *April 29, 1979, p.*
> *46.*

Anno has used sizes and shapes wittily in earlier books; here he makes size the focus of a story about a foolish king. . . . There is food for thought here, although not all children will respond to the provocative hints. They will undoubtedly all enjoy the nonsense of Anno's concept, the humor of the pictures, and the exquisite details of the precisely drawn and handsomely composed pages.

> *Zena Sutherland, in a review of "The King's Flower,"*
> *in* Bulletin of the Center for Children's Books, *Vol.*
> *33, No. 1, September, 1979, p. 1.*

The series of amplifications provides the kind of humor readily appreciated by small children, while some details may only be perceived by those more sophisticated. . . . With clarity and a brilliant use of color Anno presents his story in a medieval setting. The originality of his graphics serves a tale for which an afterword underscores the message: "We must be content, and recognize that each flower, each worm, is something natural and indispensable." (pp. 522-23)

> *Virginia Haviland, in a review of "The King's*
> *Flower," in* The Horn Book Magazine, *Vol. LV, No.*
> *5, October, 1979, pp. 522-23.*

In **The King's Flower** the reader enjoys comical images based on incongruous size relationships. There is a gigantic bed for the perfectly average-sized king, a chocolate bar too large to haul through the gates of the city, and enormous pincers to pull out the king's bad tooth—a dental problem resulting from that indulgence in sweets.

But this farce becomes suddenly solemn as the author makes the tale explicitly moralistic. The king tries to grow a giant tulip and is disappointed by its normal dimensions. Yet he finds it very beautiful. This turn in the plot reveals a desirable reform in the king—a broadening sensibility. But it lessens the tale's consistency of tone when the author spells out the lesson: "Perhaps biggest is not best after all." An allegory is much more effective when its theme remains implicit.

As in other books by Mitsumasa Anno, the illustrations here are magnificent in both conception and execution. Colors are muted and offer contrasting shades in the objects placed against a stark white background. Textures are rich in their patterns, and line functions as both contour and embellishment. Freely curved shapes are placed against rigid verticals, and the background areas tend to be large, bold, and solid. The ridiculous little king appears in and out of various settings: His out-of-scale possessions are precisely drawn and very humorous because of the exaggerated size contrast.

The arrangement of all these elements is impressive. The little patterned trim around each page is a warm finishing touch—a nice balance to the small, heroic flower.

> *Donnarae MacCann and Olga Richard, in a review*
> *of "The King's Flower," in* Wilson Library Bulletin,
> *Vol. 54, No. 6, February, 1980, p. 391.*

TABI NO EHON [ANNO'S JOURNEY] (1977)

Anno's journey through some lovely northern European countryside and picturesque old towns is on one level an uneventful one: a man in gray rows to shore, buys a horse, and simply rides it through the changing scenes. But there is much to observe en route, and Anno makes of the venture an exercise in spotting the action—and the allusions. Most obvious, besides all sorts of shops and trade signs, are the busy people: performers, bathers, flower vendors, tourists, children everywhere at play, and men and women at their work in fields, streams, and streets. There is a footrace in progress, a duel and a wedding (parts of an ongoing sequence), a prisoner escaping, a street market, a fair, and a parade in which Sesame Street characters mingle with more traditional marchers. And there are countless other such sly injections from the Pied Piper, Red Riding Hood, and other nursery tale characters to figures and bits from paintings by Seurat, Millet, and others. Inspired in part by the traditional semi-narrative scroll paintings of Anno's native Japan, this works well in the picture-book format. But as there is no one story to follow through and no center of interest anywhere—and as the tiny, isolated and numberless details can become as much a strain as a challenge, its appeal at the picture-book level is questionable.

> *A review of "Anno's Journey," in* Kirkus Reviews,
> *Vol. XLVI, No. 7, April 1, 1978, p. 365.*

From Anno's Journey, *written and illustrated by Mitsumasa Anno. Collins-World, 1978. Copyright ©
1977 by Fukuinkan Shoten Publishers, Tokyo. All rights reserved. Reprinted by permission of Philomel
Books.*

The best book of the season—it will be a classic forever—is
a wordless book by a Japanese, ***Anno's Journey***. . . . The book
moves chronologically from the Age of the Horse to the Age
of Steam. Anno is playful: Look carefully and you'll find a
bust of Beethoven in a window, a Ping-Pong game in progress,
Don Quixote and windmill, and reproductions of the "Bridge
at Arles," "The Angelus," and other great works of art. I've
been through the book four times, and I'm sure I've still missed
a lot. A bargain, and a wonderful look at the way people live.
For children eight to eleven. And me. And you. . . .

> *William Cole, in a review of "Anno's Journey," in*
> Saturday Review, *Vol. 5, No. 17, May 27, 1978, p.
> 58.*

An artist's Europe, a scholar's Europe, is hidden cunningly in
linked scenes through which a tiny figure . . . rides on a hired
horse through vineyards and orchards, villages and towns, past
schools, cathedrals, markets, mills, railway stations, always
detached, always moving on, a solitary figure to be hunted for
in each crowded page. Flattering the pleasure for those who
find, more deeply hidden, echoes of Post-Impressionist pictures
or characters from fairy-tale: strong the pleasure, too, for those
who like pictures that are anecdotal, who can extend in imagination dramatic events glimpsed on the way through the book—
a race, carnival dancing and pipe-and-drum bands, a street-
corner orator collecting an audience, a flitting, an escaping
prisoner. . . . There is no end to the surprises in this book, a
desert-island standby if ever there was one. Endless ingenious
detail delineated in meticulous line and exquisitely related colours, with a witty mixture of periods and allusions—this is a
book for every age, now and for many years to come.

> *Margery Fisher, in a review of "Anno's Journey,"
> in* Growing Point, *Vol. 17, No. 2, July, 1978, p.
> 3368.*

Anno, a consummate craftsman, crowds his pictures with incredible amounts of activity, yet avoids any sense of clutter.
He is somehow able to suggest continuity in noncontinuous
situations or uniqueness in redundant ones. He is a master of
incongruity and unobstrusive humor. Never obvious, he does
not call attention to particular elements in his pictures, but
allows the reader to discover in initial and subsequent readings
previously overlooked visual jokes and allusions. Both the content and the mode of presentation are unique in picture books,
so children's traditional modes of response will be inadequate
to this work. (p. 85)

> *Barbara H. Baskin and Karen H. Harris, "A Se-
> lected Guide to Intellectually Demanding Books: 'An-
> no's Journey'," in their* Books for the Gifted Child,
> *R. R. Bowker Company, 1980, pp. 84-5.*

MORI NO EHON [ANNO'S ANIMALS] (1977)

Mitsumasa Anno, the brilliant writer and illustrator of ***The
King's Flower*** and other works (the most celebrated children's
book author of Japan) has given us 15 woodland scenes in ink
and watercolor, mostly green and brown and dull in effect.
Within these unexceptional and uninteresting sketches he has
concealed dozens of animals (or parts of animals) of different
sizes. Such hide-and-seek books can be great fun, but in this
case the bewildered parent and child can spend many, many
frustrating minutes searching for the bunny and the skunk.
Because the pictures themselves are dull, the search becomes
homework, and once the animals are found you can pitch the
book in the corner with the used-up puzzle and coloring books.
Growl. Mr. Anno is usually much, much better than this.

*Harold C. K. Rice, in a review of "Anno's Animals,"
in* The New York Times Book Review, *November
11, 1979, p. 66.*

Like all the Japanese author-illustrator's picture books, Anno's latest is a landmark and far different from whatever the versatile artist has created before. Double-page spreads—in shades of green, black and white—are wordless scenes of a magic woodland. It takes concentration and acute eyes to detect the teeming wildlife camouflaged by trees, bushes, the waters of a pond and other natural covers. Children and their parents will find it exhilarating to make a game out of spotting cheetah, gorilla, fox, llama, jackal, hornbill, a duck—a veritable zoo of cunningly placed creatures in astonishing, fool-the-eye paintings. Since fair is fair, clues to each scene appear on the last page. These, however, accompany a note pointing out that searchers will find even more elusive figures if they really try.

A review of "Anno's Animals," in Publishers Weekly,
Vol. 216, No. 22, November 26, 1979, p. 52.

Page after page (after page after page) of leafy green foliage which yields—if you look hard—hidden animal forms. . . . Were the animals actually hidden in the deep woods (camouflaged, that is, by the foliage), this might have some point; but it's simply artistic sleight-of-hand, the old hide-and-seek game in a naturalistic setting—and one that, limited almost entirely to trees and branches, quickly becomes monotonous. The final foolishness is the list of animals at the close—keyed, by number, to unnumbered pages. For the usually inventive Anno, a feeble performance altogether.

A review of "Anno's Animals," in Kirkus Reviews,
Vol. XLVIII, No. 4, February 15, 1980, p. 209.

ANNO MITSUMASA NO GASHŪ [THE UNIQUE WORLD OF MITSUMASA ANNO: SELECTED WORKS (1968-1977)] (1977)

AUTHOR'S COMMENTARY

Once someone said, upon seeing my pictures, "You amuse yourself by fooling people; you can't draw without a mischievous spirit."

I really wanted to counter by saying, "The spirit of noble humanity causes me to do so." If, however, I had to admit it, I should say that his words were correct. The more I think of playing tricks on my audience, the better I can concentrate power in my pictures.

My pictures are like maps, which perhaps only I can understand. Therefore, in following my maps there are some travellers who get lost. There are those who become angry when they discover they have been fooled; but there are also those who enter into the maze of my maps willingly, in an attempt to explore their accuracy for themselves.

Nakahara Yūsuke invented the phrase "representational truth" to express the logical appearance of the truth that is perceived by the eye, but which exists only in pictures and not in reality. In this case it is right to interpret the word "representational" as referring to an image, reflection, portrait, shadow, or vision.

Although in this world of "representational truth" the perspective method shows a two-dimensional picture of a three dimensional object or scene, this is not inconsistent. And if one looks at it "mathematically," it is quite perfect.

Centuries ago, the discovery of the perspective method brought about a great change in the history of painting; for a long time thereafter, this discovery dominated the general development of art; but the great artists of the modern age have tried to escape the restrictions of the perspective method and have succeeded in doing so. Escher, Dali, and Magritte, the elders of the Surrealist school, provided me with instructive examples and made it much easier for me to cast off those same bonds.

And as I freed myself of those bonds, I became aware of a new "representational truth," one which was subtly interwoven with futuristic ideas of topological geometry. Those who find it difficult to accept this concept might well consider the following example: "Because of the development of better transportation facilities, some parts of the United States and Europe have grown closer to Tokyo than remote parts of Japan." This example is no longer one of relative or even "representational" truth, but of reality itself.

If I were living in an earlier age my pictures would make people feel uncomfortable, and I might be condemned and severely penalized. Fortunately, today in what appears as an irrational and topsy-turvy world, my maps of what I perceive to be the universal realities do not seem to be so strange.

My kind of picture is difficult to explain verbally, and when one gives an explanation, the words seem to become trite. However, since there are those who may expect more from a book than a mere series of pictures, I decided instead of explanations, to quote relevant passages from the works of famous authors and to place the pictures with them.

There is an immeasurable distance between the pictures and the quotations but also a delicate relationship exists due to their juxtaposition. Through this delicate relationship I can express curious feelings which could not be expressed in words alone or pictures alone. (pp. 47-8)

As for the titles of the pictures, I was asked to include them by way of explanation. I deliberately wrote them, however, in enigmatic form to make them difficult to read. I hope thus to allow the reader to experience something similar to the puzzles that exist in my own thoughts, as they decipher the titles. (p. 48)

Mitsumasa Anno, in a postscript to The Unique World
of Mitsumasa Anno: Selected Works (1968-1977),
edited and translated by Samuel Crowell Morse, Philomel Books, 1980, pp. 47-8.

Japanese graphic artist, painter, and illustrator Anno creates impossible worlds much in the tradition of Escher, Magritte, and Dali. His distortion of perspective and his mathematical puzzles are reminiscent especially of Escher, but, unlike Escher, for Anno the pictorial is never secondary. It is Anno's colorful graphic style and sense of humor that redeem his visual games from the fact that they aren't always profound. **"The Outside of an Insideout Bottle Is a Sea of Wine"** shows Anno at his most clever, but others in this collection of 41 plates lack the surreal genius that could take them beyond the ordinary. There is little analysis of the illustrations; instead, the images are juxtaposed with quotations from literature, science, and philosophy.

*Daniel J. Lombardo, in a review of "The Unique
World of Mitsumasa Anno: Selected Works
(1968-1977)," in* Library Journal, *Vol. 105, No. 21,
December 1, 1980, p. 2492.*

In the Western world 1980 could be *Anno Anno,* the year of Anno, the year that Mitsumasa Anno, former art teacher and now one of Japan's leading artists as well as a top book illustrator, ceases to be known only to a small group of devoted admirers.

Some Anno addicts claim to have discovered him as early as 1970 when his *Topsy-Turvies,* a fantastic book of "impossible pictures," became available outside Japan. Others were introduced to him during the next few years by such equally mind- and eye-dazzling books as *Upside-Downers, Maze, First Books of Mathematics, The Theory of Set, Dr. Anno's Magical Midnight Circus,* and *The Stone Brain Computer.*

My own discovery of his work came in the mid-seventies with *Anno's Alphabet.* So startling was this volume in its departure from the usual *ABC* book (A is for Apple, B is for Bear . . .), so filled with optical tricks and visual jokes, that I knew at once that a remarkable new artist was at work in Japan and that it would only be a matter of time until the world heard about him. (p. 4)

[In] 1978 there was published *Anno's Journey,* to me the most entrancing picture book for children in half a century. The following year brought us *Anno's Animals,* with its ingeniously hidden pictures, and a translation of *The King's Flower,* a gentle fable reminding us that big is not always beautiful.

His publishers now have given us the first collection of Anno's individual works of graphic art: *The Unique World of Mitsumasa Anno.* The book contains only a fraction of the artist's work during a ten-year period, pictures executed mainly to amuse himself and his friends, then offered to anyone of any age who enjoys representational art that plays with mathematics, science and paradox.

Of special interest, both to mathematicians and psychologists who study optical illusions, are Anno's "impossible figures.". . . . Some of them are not perceived as impossible at first glance. You may have to study carefully the wooden crate on page 12, and what seems to be a familiar "Chinese puzzle" on page 13, to see why they are impossible. The same is true of the curiously truncated cube on page 35. If a cube is sliced as shown, the cross-section has to be a hexagon. There is no way it can have an elliptical border. The illustrations on pages 11 and 18 are variations on what is sometimes called the "Escher staircase" because M. C. Escher used it in several of his pictures. Actually this marvelous illusion was invented by two British scientists, the geneticist L. S. Penrose and his physicist son, Roger.

The picture on page 37 is an example of what is called "anamorphic art.". . . . The reflection of Anno's picture, in the cylinder's side, will astonish you!

Anno's work has been likened to that of Escher and René Magritte, and there is something to be said for both comparisons. Like Escher, Anno is fascinated by geometry and optical illusions. Unlike Escher he is not interested in unusual shapes that tesselate the plane, nor does he, like Escher, confine his work to black and white. He is more like Magritte in his use of color, his whimsical humor, his surrealistic juxtapositions of objects never seen together. He is, of course, no imitator of either artist. He is Anno, native of Japan, citizen of the world—a man at home with science and mathematics, knowledgeable about modern culture, seeing all things from his own subtle perspective.

Perhaps Anno's art is not for you. There are those who find Escher's pictures frigid and uninteresting. There are those to whom Magritte's paintings are no more than garish conundrums. (pp. 4-5)

As for me, I am unashamed to count myself a member of the rapidly growing Anno cult. I am among those who find the future richer in potential visual pleasure because we do not yet know what amazements the skillful fingers of this pictorial prestidigitator will show us next. (p. 5)

> *Martin Gardner, in a foreword to* The Unique World of Mitsumasa Anno: Selected Works (1968-1977), *edited and translated by Samuel Crowell Morse, Philomel Books, 1980, pp. 4-5.*

Drawn from the artist's individual works, the collection presents forty astonishing pictures to challenge and delight the imagination. . . . [Anno's] exercises in optical illusion and delusion are far more than brilliantly clever tricks; they are dazzling intellectual conceptions executed with almost impossible perfection. Knowledgeable about universal culture, Anno has linked each of the paintings and drawings with quotations from famous writings, . . . not as literal interpretations but to set up relationships and analogies that transcend the meanings of the pictures presented alone. Thus, teasing the intellect and revealing new possibilities in the graphic art are verbal samples representing worldwide figures—from St. Augustine and Chaucer to Alexander Dumas and Charles Darwin. . . . [This is] an elegant volume.

> *Ethel L. Heins, in a review of "The Unique World of Mitsumasa Anno: Selected Works (1968-1977),"* in The Horn Book Magazine, *Vol. LVII, No. 1, February, 1981, p. 71.*

The Japanese artist Mitsumasa Anno is best known here for his picture books for the young. They are exceptional works; some—like the splendid *Alphabet*—using brilliant devices of trompe l'oeil; some teaching numbers or tracking history through the movement of tiny people and animals in delightful double-spread landscapes. His last—*Anno's Mediaeval World,* about the shock of change from Ptolemaic belief to Copernican—follows this technique.

All these books are signposts to the arresting *Unique World of Mitsumasa Anno,* the first selection in book form to appear of his individual works of graphic art. It is not a child's book by intent, but (as Martin Gardner points out in his Foreword) it is for "anyone of any age who is intrigued by representational art that plays with mathematics, science and paradox" [see excerpt dated 1980]. Each of the 40 plates presents a visual thought of the teasing Anno kind. Under each is a passage from some Eastern or Western writer. . . . Here is **"The Cantankerous Coffee Cup,"** a superb cup on its matching saucer.

Actually, the handle is inside. The sugar cube changes its shape as you look. Brillat-Savarin provides the comment. Turn to the medieval **"Endless Staircase."** Does it work? Yet if not why not? Text is from Wilde *(De Profundis):* "Suffering is one very long moment. We cannot divide it by seasons. . .''. In **"A Very Involved Conversation"** two eighteenth century characters, facing each other, speak by telephone. The intertwining wires, miles of them, form an exquisite frame to the scene. Text is from Bierce's *Devil's Dictionary.* Here's Pisa's Leaning Tower, perfectly upright. But the neighbouring buildings lean. **"The Outside of an Insideout Bottle is a Sea of Wine"** is another theme. So is **"We can Weigh Ourselves with**

the Scales We Use to Weigh Others.'' Most striking of all, perhaps, is the last, **"Will the Sun Rise Again?"**, a ravishing ocean-piece in blue, in which is floating pensively a bright red circular sun.

Anno admits his debt to Escher, Magritte and Dali, especially in the areas of perspective. (He does not mention da Vinci; no doubt he feels no need). But his idiom, like his graphic skill, is his own. "My pictures are like maps, which perhaps only I can understand," he can say. Their very preciseness makes them a perfect medium for this witty and disturbing acrobat of ideas.

> *Naomi Lewis, "Up an Endless Staircase," in* The Times Educational Supplement, *No. 3373, February 13, 1981, p. 26.*

TABI NO EHON II [ANNO'S ITALY] (1978)

Country scenes, town scenes, city scenes (Rome, Florence, Venice), tiny locals laboring, tiny revelers performing, tiny tourists gawking; clusters of buildings with steep red tile roofs and striated stone walls . . . and in these assorted environs, a familiar image here and there: the Babe in the Manger, Pinocchio, the Last Supper, the Three Little Pigs, John the Baptist, Cinderella, the Crucifixion. This particular intermix of curiosa in an already foreign setting seems not only pointless but triflingly capricious—and an utter waste of a lot of talent.

> *A review of "Anno's Italy," in* Kirkus Reviews, *Vol. XLVIII, No. 6, March 15, 1980, p. 359.*

Pilgrims, pirates, and princes; shepherds, sages, and rogues.

These are just a few of the motley characters meandering across the delicately hued pages of Mitsumasa Anno's delightful pen and ink paean to European culture, legend, and religion.

Ostensibly a children's book, **Anno's Italy,** like Lewis Carroll's allegorical tales of enchantment, weaves a richly hued tapestry that can fascinate the very young with its magical simplicity and entice the older reader with its erudite symbolism and technically masterly illustrations. . . .

Anno's pen slips in and out of illusive time channels, so that one finds on the same page and in the same hamlet Pinocchio pursued by an irate Geppetto, a bicycling paperboy delivering morning papers, and a haughty Renaissance grande dame receiving admiring glances from men in modern garb.

There are all sorts of subtle and wry surprises for the discerning reader to discover in this evocative fantasy. There is no text, but the visual impact of the characters alone forms sentences, and their movements construct paragraphs. And as allegories should, **Anno's Italy** transcends illusive age barriers as well as time periods. (p. B12)

> *Kristina L. C. Lindborg, "Travelling in Pictures," in* The Christian Science Monitor, *May 12, 1980, pp. B12-13.*

The worlds of past and present—real and imaginative—merge. . . . The artist is equally adept at rendering tiny figures and the soaring architecture of Florence, Rome, and Venice. Each page—depicted from an aerial perspective—is as carefully composed and uncluttered as a Breughel painting, offering a myriad of treats to the eye and the imagination. (p. 284)

> *Kate M. Flanagan, in a review of "Anno's Italy," in* The Horn Book Magazine, *Vol. LVI, No. 3, June, 1980, pp. 283-84.*

Being all things to all men is no mean feat, as St. Paul long ago confided to the Corinthians. But the Japanese illustrator Mitsumasa Anno has surely mastered the art of engaging all eyes—and through the eyes, the minds and imaginations—of viewers of all ages. From his earliest wordless work, **Topsy-Turvies** . . . , this ever inventive picture-book artist has been steadily expanding his audience's sense of visual wonder.

In the present sequel to **Anno's Journey** . . .—the book is, in fact, called *My Journey II* in Japan—Anno's unflappable hero on horseback travels through an Italy verdantly rendered in 21 double-page panoramas. Voyaging through time as well as space, and hitting a surprising number of esthetic high points of Western civilization en route, Anno gives us, in a single picture: A charming Tuscan landscape, its verisimilitude unruffled by the presence of biblical shepherds; Adam and Eve being expelled from Eden (à la Michelangelo); the Virgin Mary being visited by the Angel of the Annunciation (as pictured by Fra Angelico); Tarzan swinging through the trees; a witch nonchalantly riding her broomstick; and a fairytale wolf on the prowl.

Depending upon the breadth of one's frame of reference, other Italianate vistas reveal such a mixed bag of literary treasures as Lewis Carroll's white rabbit consulting his watch, Aesop's tortoise outrunning the hare, Shylock about to exact his pound of flesh, and Rapunzel letting down her impressively plaited hair from atop a genuine campanile. All this plus the Ponte Vecchio, an awesome view of Brunellesco's cathedral cum Giotto's bell tower in Florence, and renaissance masterpieces including Leonardo's "Last Supper" and Botticelli's "Three Graces." Beyond this, there are visual jokes: e.g., a dachshund whose head appears at one side of a building viewed in the distance, his rear end with tail at the other.

A small child will be content simply to find Anno's hero in each busy scene; a curious older child can learn how barrels are made and iron bells cast; and a sophisticated adult could spend hours trying to uncover all of Anno's subtly secreted visual references. It is a remarkable graphic feast—too rich to be savored in any single viewing—or reviewing.

> *Selma G. Lanes, in a review of "Anno's Italy," in* The New York Times Book Review, *August 17, 1980, p. 18.*

TENDŌ SETSU NO HON [ANNO'S MEDIEVAL WORLD] (1979)

[Mitsumasa Anno's] illustrations here are vital and original, encouraging us to take a new look at some old concepts. Each double page has an illuminated border that frames a globe or segment of a globe dotted with figures, buildings, ships, fountains, machinery, animals. Action takes place in an ocherous glow that owes something, perhaps, to the gilded backgrounds of Byzantine and medieval religious painting, while Anno's skill with figures and landscapes may remind us of the prints of such Japanese masters as Hokusai and Hiroshige. (p. 60)

As concerns the text, however, some of Anno's gambles have not paid off so well. Evidently, his ambition was to give us a sort of condensed history of Western cosmology, from primitive animism through modern science, and if one were able to take the entire narrative as allegory or fable the author might have been successful. Unfortunately, by alluding to (though

From Anno's Flea Market, *written and illustrated by Mitsumasa Anno. Philomel Books, 1984. Text translation copyright © 1984 by Philomel Books. Original Japanese edition copyright © 1983 by Kuso-Kubo. All rights reserved. Reprinted by permission of Philomel Books.*

not actually naming except in an annotated chronology at the back of the book) such historical personages as Marco Polo, Copernicus, Giordano Bruno and Galileo, he has committed himself to a specific historical framework.

Perhaps the book's title is unintentionally accurate in that Anno's medieval world is not that of many modern historians. For example, the appearance of the plague in Europe was not attributed exclusively to the work of witches, and the notion that the earth is flat was not . . . widely accepted during the time of Columbus. On the contrary, it was known among the educated as a vulgar error, rather on a par with the current right-wing flirtation with creationism, as opposed to evolution. Of much greater impact on medieval (Ptolemaic) cosmology was the Copernican theory that the earth was not the divinely ordained center of the universe, and on the development of this concept, Anno's narrative is lucid and informative.

How much you care about these matters may depend on how much extra-textual explanation you are ready to give the children in your life. Certainly Anno's illustrations are beautiful and fascinating in themselves. Perhaps the best approach to them would be to supply your own palimpsest or interlinear gloss. (pp. 60, 62)

> Georgess McHargue, *"Early Explorers," in* The New York Times Book Review, *November 9, 1980, pp. 60, 62.*

The assorted concepts and terms are ipso facto confusing; the various beliefs are unrelated; and in the course of their pre-

sentation, the central problem—of a flat or a round earth, of a fixed or a rotating sphere—is lost sight of entirely. It's questionable, too, whether this historical scheme—ringing in "an astronomer from the north," "an astronomer from the south," and a "monk [who] was burned at the stake"—is a particularly appropriate way of putting these ideas across. What, after all, does a medieval world-view mean to young children? (The pictures, less crowded than usual, are as usual deft.)

> *A review of "Anno's Medieval World," in* Kirkus Reviews, *Vol. XLIX, No. 2, January 15, 1981, p. 71.*

No one could accuse this book of being unambitious. It attempts, through a sequence of elaborately-decorated pages by Mitsumasa Anno, and a text also his though adapted by Ursula Synge, to explain the values, both secular and religious, of the medieval world. Since this period is one of the most complex transitions in man's history the enterprise is a bold one and while applauding the venture I must admit to a serious discomfiture with the results. . . . The afterword is an exemplary text, spare and elegant, and is a personal exposition on the author's motives; but how many people—let alone children—need an afterword?

The text veers dangerously between intensely compacted propositions and vast over-simplifications—Galileo 'explained' in a sentence and a half. The pictures, too, in Anno's exquisite and delicate line and colour wash, compress a whole sequence of facts, reflecting the technique, one supposes, of the medieval miniaturists who crammed whole events into the space of an illuminated capital. What, one wonders, will a child make of one plate showing not only a group of European medieval peasants around a village well but in the background a Parthenon in perfect repair. The point of that juxtaposition requires knowledge outside the text provided.

If this sounds ungenerous, it is not so intended. One's sympathy is with Anno for this is clearly a project dear to his heart. He appears to have been trapped inside his 'children's author' reputation and his work has been presented as a picture-story book, which plainly it is not. (pp. 35-6)

> *Gabrielle Maunder, in a review of "Anno's Medieval World," in* The School Librarian, *Vol. 29, No. 1, March, 1981, pp. 35-6.*

Anno baffles me. Here is an artist equal in graphic ability and in intellect. He clearly knows just what he is doing. I wish I were equally sure. In **Anno's Medieval World** he encapsulates the history of the middle ages in a few pages of minutely detailed pictures and brief text and then, as if this were not enough, he shows the destruction of that world through the ideas of the Renaissance. The constant factor in all this is the world itself, a level horizon which grows gradually more globe-like until we see the world in space. The book is presented as if on parchment, cracked and stained by centuries of use, and this illusion is extended even to the laminated covers. Clever certainly, as is the scholarly Afterword, but I am not sure whether it really comes off. Too clever by half?

> *M. Crouch, in a review of "Anno's Medieval World," in* The Junior Bookshelf, *Vol. 45, No. 2, April, 1981, p. 60.*

MAHŌ TSUKAI NO ABC [ANNO'S MAGICAL ABC: AN ANAMORPHIC ALPHABET] (with Masaichiro Anno, 1980)

Anno's Magical ABC, by Mitsumasa Anno (with lettering by his son, Masaichiro) preserves Anno's reputation as one of the most visually inventive makers of picture books today. Here he revives an unusual optical technique found in both Western art and 17th-century Japanese art—anamorphosis—in which images are distorted, requiring the viewer to see them from a different perspective. In this "Anamorphic Alphabet," Anno's letters and their accompanying pictures do not become clear until one rolls the shiny, reflecting paper in the book's back pocket into a tube and places it in the center of the page.

Presto! The abstract pictures and letters take their proper shape—a zipper, a yacht, an elf, or a tricycle. There are, in fact, two alphabets in the book (one of objects and people, the other of animals), and the book can be read backwards or forwards. Anno's instructions for creating an anamorphic alphabet are tucked in the middle between the two ABC's.

Anno is clever, and his significance as a children's book maker is that he encourages children to perceive the world more imaginatively. However, his **Magical ABC** strikes me as being just too gimmicky, sacrificing the thoroughly refreshing character of his earlier books (**Anno's Alphabet** or **Anno's Journey**) for an optical illusion which, once its learned, is somewhat repetitive. Still, it is an eye-opening book..., and should intrigue a visually sophisticated youngster, one who has seen everything. (pp. 14, 19)

> *John Cech, "The Alphabet Angle," in* Book World— The Washington Post, *May 10, 1981, pp. 13-14, 19.*

Since the book requires a sheet of mirror paper (bent into a tubular column) to correct the proportions of the paintings and letters on the pages, it may be too frail for library collections—but what a nice gift item!... When the mirror page is placed over a central circle, the pictures, ink and watercolor, are seen in proper proportion. They are quite beautiful. This example of anamorphic art is intriguing, not the best way to learn the alphabet, perhaps—since the letter can't be seen at the same time as the picture when the paper tube is held at the center of the page—but a fine way to enjoy another example of the inventive whimsy of one of Japan's most distinguished illustrators.

> *Zena Sutherland, in a review of "Anno's Magical ABC: An Anamorphic Alphabet," in* Bulletin of the Center for Children's Books, *Vol. 35, No. 2, October, 1981, p. 21.*

Anno's Magical ABC is an unusual book of its genre in several ways. It is really two books in one. Holding the book one way, one reads upper-case letters and sees various objects corresponding to the letters. Held the opposite way, one reads lower-case letters and animals.... Clearly an ABC book for those beyond the beginning stage, Anno's selections stretch vocabulary as well as visual imagination. Objects range from cassette to faun to yak to ocarina. This anamorphic alphabet is a winner; inventive and captivating, it shows the very familiar as never seen before. It's the classiest game book around.

> *George Shannon, in a review of "Anno's Magical ABC: An Anamorphic Alphabet," in* School Library Journal, *Vol. 28, No. 4, December, 1981, p. 48.*

Anno is the least predictable of artists. Each of his books has introduced some unfamiliar idea or viewpoint, and here is another. At first sight the book, which is reversible like Rex Whistler's unforgettable *Oho,* seems to have gone mad. The alphabet and its accompanying drawings are distorted out of recognition. For the interpretation of this riddle the publisher provides a piece of mirror paper which, wrapped around a cylinder and placed in the centre of each page, reflects letters and pictures in all their elegance and humour. The device is undeniably clever and intriguing. Whether it is really worth the effort is perhaps open to doubt. However, the artist does not think so. He has been to great pains to get the book just so, and it is as fine a production as we have seen this year. I have clear evidence that it can stimulate the young reader to imitation, however difficult the technical processes—which Anno describes in detail—may be.

> *M. Crouch, in a review of "Anno's Magical ABC," in* The Junior Bookshelf, *Vol. 46, No. 1, February, 1982, p. 13.*

TABI NO EHON III [ANNO'S BRITAIN] (1981)

The four books reviewed [*Anno's Britain,* Margot Zemach's *Jake and Honeybunch Go to Heaven,* Arnold Lobel's *Ming Lo Moves the Mountain,* and Chris Van Allsburg's *Ben's Dream*], the cream of this year's early vernal crop, are by a few of our best contemporary illustrators. Among them these artists have accumulated three Caldecotts and four runner-up awards. Clearly, only a technicality (foreign citizenship and residency) has kept the fourth artist, Mitsumasa Anno, un-awarded.

With or without that circular silver seal, Anno is an original and talented man at the top of his field, in this case the tender green expanse winding through *Anno's Britain.* The book begins with the small blue-clad pilgrim who was rowing out of view at the end of *Anno's Italy.* Still at the oars, he is now approaching the white cliffs of Dover. We follow him over the roads and fields of ''this other Eden,'' through pretty towns and villages, and literary and historical pantomimes take place wherever he goes.

This book is wordless because it needs no words; the journey is sufficient narrative. Each double page, a tapestry of tiny, easy brush strokes, is alive with surprises: Tom Tom the Piper's son careers by on his stolen pig, Stonehenge looms in the distance. Alice, Peter Pan and Tink, Bottom the Weaver and the Queen herself are only a few of the illustrious extras who walk in and out of these scenes. A skilled draughtsman with a faultless sense of scale and design, Anno also has a splendid gift, mostly unused here, for illustrative legerdemain. This extremely attractive British Baedeker is the third in his travel series. *Anno's Alphabet,* an earlier book, in which the artist reveals himself as a magician, remains one of a kind. (pp. 31, 46)

> *Karla Kuskin, ''The Complete Illustrator,'' in* The New York Times Book Review, *April 25, 1982, pp. 31, 46.*

Children owning this book will cherish it for years as they learn about the culture and countryside of England, Scotland and Wales, relishing anew what they've learned elsewhere about Britain's art and folklore.... The artist paints broad, detailed scenes depicting characteristic terrain and structures: Stonehenge, Canterbury, the Tower of London, etc. The pictures show plain folk going about their business but a careful scrutiny reveals more: past and present heroes of British history like Robin Hood, Isaac Newton, Queen Elizabeth II and more. Previous Anno books have been described as ''classic'' and ''remarkable.'' The new title deserves no less.

> *A review of ''Anno's Britain,'' in* Publishers Weekly, *Vol. 221, No. 20, May 14, 1982, p. 215.*

[This] is a pastiche, an intermixing of people and things from a millenium of history in totally cohesive scenes tied together only by the wanderer on his horse. The point of view is always the same, as if we were atop a 200-foot flagpole. Thus we can see over walls and down roads; but we can also see full figures rather than tops of heads. And such figures: stonemasons building a castle; Mother Goose characters; the Beatles.... Anno, like [Piero] Ventura and [Peter] Spier and [M.] Sasek, can miniaturize humanity and create wonderfully informative and entertaining scenes that invite us to join them again and again in journeying into their perceptions of our world.

> *Kenneth Marantz, in a review of ''Anno's Britain,'' in* School Library Journal, *Vol. 29, No. 1, September, 1982, p. 102.*

The third of Anno's journeys brings him to Britain, and a Britain which must seem curious to the natives. True, there are familiar things depicted in the artist's characteristic, exact drawings: London, Canterbury and Windsor, Willy Lott's cottage and King Alfred in Winchester, Stonehenge and the Royal Observatory. But is Britain quite so quaint and olde-worlde? Surely the rider who appears in every picture is wearing blinkers as is his horse. But perhaps I am being too serious about a book which is also good fun, with a host of details awaiting the reader's discovery.

> *M. Crouch, in a review of ''Anno's Britain,'' in* The Junior Bookshelf, *Vol. 46, No. 5, October, 1982, p. 178.*

10-NIN NO YUKAI NA HIKKOSHI [*ANNO'S COUNTING HOUSE*] (1981)

Once more, Anno has used his unique gifts as an artist and teacher to create a triumph of invention and splendor. A note preceding the wordless pages explains how children can play games with numbers. An afterword offers suggestions to grownups on helping little ones ''experience the immense beauty and intellectual pleasure'' in the world of numbers. Pictures of two nobly constructed houses appear with windows cut out. Through the windows, boys and girls get glimpses of the occupants and count as they move, one by one, out of one house and into the other. There are several intricate steps in the game, illustrated in radiant watercolors and fine ink drawings. The fun begins all over again at the end, where kids can track the moves in reverse order. *Anno's Counting House* will endure, in the company of all of his previous books, treasured by all ages.

> *A review of ''Anno's Counting House,'' in* Publishers Weekly, *Vol. 222, No. 20, November 12, 1982, p. 66.*

With the conviction that children learn best if they are intrigued and amused and also that the concepts of numeracy can and should be absorbed as numbers are manipulated, the artist has devised an ingenious but lucid sequence of pictures in which ten children move one by one from a house on the left hand side of each opening to one on the right, each time taking various objects with which the empty house is gradually furnished. He suggests many games to be played with the pages, involving matching, comparing, sorting and so on; his deft deploying of the cheerful characters, the artful humour and charm with which he presents them, attests both to his uniquely delicate and exciting art and his shrewd, pleasing methods as an educator.

> *Margery Fisher, in a review of ''Anno's Counting House,'' in* Growing Point, *Vol. 21, No. 5, January, 1983, p. 4018.*

This counting book is, perhaps, the most didactic of all Anno's inventive works.... In ''A Note to Parents and Other Adults,'' some of the theory of learning which guided Anno is explained, and some activities are suggested that go beyond the mathematical self-learning by fixating on the children's costumes or the furnishings of the houses. The ''story line'' is ultra-simple so such extensions are useful ways of seeking complexity in the visual design components.... Anno retains his meticulous eye and sly sense of humor. There is no way to keep from becoming involved, if not in the basic addition and subtraction needed to account for the movement of children, then even more surely in the curious reorganization of all kinds of objects. Some carping adults may object to five trousered boys and five skirted girls; but the clothes are European as are the houses. And such houses—each roof shingle is articulated, each brick has a character all its own. The contrast of black-and-white interiors with the full-color children helps us attend to the latter's number and actions. This is a book that can naturally draw curious adults and youngsters together. It is one of Anno's best as far as I'm concerned: practical, amusing and engaging.

Kenneth Marantz, in a review of "Anno's Counting House," in School Library Journal, *Vol. 29, No. 7, March, 1983, p. 155.*

'We have ways of making you enjoy numbers' is the aim; neither [*Anno's counting house* nor *The first book of numbers* by Angela Wilkes and Claudia Zeff] is likely to achieve it without huge input from adults. Both are picture books, with text essential to their use, but their reading level is out of step with their numeracy level. Anno's book is impenetrable without reading the foreword; even then, serious difficulty is encountered. The visual detail is complex and tedious. Ten children move from one house to another, gradually, but there is little to interest the reader, except cut-out windows, which suggest numerical conclusions at variance with the desired learning. . . .

[Don't] buy either book as a teaching resource unless you have plenty of time to make work cards to accompany it.

Terry Downie, in a review of "Anno's Counting House," in The School Librarian, *Vol. 31, No. 2, June, 1983, p. 127.*

TSUBO NO NAKA [ANNO'S MYSTERIOUS MULTIPLYING JAR] (with Masaichiro Anno, 1982)

Masaichiro Anno collaborated with his famous artist father, Mitsumasa, in creating **Anno's Counting House,** and has teamed up with him again to produce this fascinating companion book. Beautiful paintings illustrate the pages inducing children to imagine a blue jar full of water, the water becoming an ocean, with a ship sailing on it to an island with two countries, each with villages containing a number of houses. Superbly demonstrating the conception of factorials in mathematics, the text and pictures combine to present a lesson in a palatable form as well as the pleasure of looking at pictures that only Mitsumasa Anno could invent. Although the book is for children, it will be snapped up by the artist's adult fans also.

A review of "Anno's Mysterious Multiplying Jar," in Publishers Weekly, *Vol. 223, No. 18, May 6, 1983, p. 99.*

The mathematically naive may not grasp the power of numbers to build to enormous sums. Here Anno uses his graphic skills to help readers visualize the concept of *factorials*. He uses 10 x 9 x 8 x 7 x 6 x 5 x 4 x 3 x 2 x 1 to provide a visual sense of the result: 3,628,800. Beginning with one island with two countries, each of which has three mountains, etc., the pages disclose Anno's typically detailed ink and watercolor drawings of the objects. After the entertaining pictures (we only get the 3 mountains, not 3 x 2 mountains) he becomes the teacher and uses tiny red dots as counter. But after 8! (8 factorial) with its 40,320 dots covering 2 pages, he gives up the visuals and relies on words to take us the rest of the way. Then he mentions other ways we can use the concept in our daily life. But the pictorial section somehow doesn't tie in enough with the more didactic stuff. Yet, if you want a book that does a good selling job on the factorial concept, this one works. (pp. 114-15)

Kenneth Marantz, in a review of "Anno's Mysterious Multiplying Jar," in School Library Journal, *Vol. 30, No. 1, September, 1983, pp. 114-15.*

A carefully delineated blue-and-white porcelain jar becomes the magic object which transports readers from the realm of fantasy to the fascinating world of mathematics. A brief, rhythmic text coupled with precise drawings begins ostensibly as a sim-

ple counting book describing the contents of the jar. . . . By repeating the sentences in the first part of the text in conjunction with mathematical sentences and red dots representing the quantities involved, the book moves logically and elegantly from the concrete to the abstract in a manner readily understood by anyone with a rudimentary knowledge of multiplication. The afterword extends the concept by indicating when an understanding of factorials would be useful. Once made clear, the concept is unforgettable, but the book entices the reader to return for further appreciation of the artistry with which it was designed. (pp. 588-89)

Mary M. Burns, in a review of "Anno's Mysterious Multiplying Jar," in The Horn Book Magazine, *Vol. LIX, No. 5, October, 1983, pp. 588-89.*

The Anno books are now widely known and dearly loved by many children. Perhaps the favourite is **Anno's Britain** with the perfection of drawing and painting of which the Japanese are so distinguished and is a delight not only to children but to adults as well. **Anno's Counting Book** and other of the more educational titles are understandable, clear and also very beautiful. To this reviewer the key word for this latest Anno book is "*mysterious*". I can follow the delightful pictures and the simple arithmetic until I find myself again back to one jar and move forward into numerical patterns that leave me panting far behind. However, a twelve-year-old, whom I consulted, thinks the book "*wonderful*" and a perfect way to teach maths, so I can recommend it without hesitation.

A review of "Anno's Mysterious Multiplying Jar," in Books for Your Children, *Vol. 18, No. 3, Autumn-Winter, 1983, p. 18.*

TABI NO EHON IV [ANNO'S U.S.A.] (1983)

Like other books of Anno's in which he has a traveler who journeys through a country, this begins with rural scenes, takes a traveller into more heavily populated areas, and ends with an embarkation. Anno deliberately mixes costumes, vehicles, and other representations of various periods in the handsome double-page spreads that are beautifully composed; his use of color and perspective are admirable; his command of architectural drawing is impressive. What may appeal most to readers, however, are the small visual jokes that enliven the pages: the lions of the New York Public Library on a parade float, the policeman and ducks from *Make Way for Ducklings,* Tom Sawyer painting the fence. Delicious.

Zena Sutherland, in a review of "Anno's USA," in Bulletin of the Center for Children's Books, *Vol. 37, No. 4, December, 1983, p. 61.*

Of course there are no rules here, neither of history proper nor proportion nor juxtaposition of real and fictional characters. Anno is a visual trickster who liberally lards each double-page scene with humorous surprises. Children will have to be sharp to pick out Laurel and Hardy moving a piano down a colonial Boston street, Tom Sawyer painting the fence or Ben Franklin flying his kite. That's the game to play in every square centimeter of each page. Anno's fine scratchy line creates animated sets which children will view from a bird's eye vantage point. His color is applied transparently to suggest rather than to dominate. Even in the Thanksgiving parade scene the hues are subtly used, orchestrated to blend with myriad details in the cityscape. Hours of good looking here for children with some

From Anno's U.S.A., *written and illustrated by Mitsumasa Anno. Philomel Books, 1983. Copyright ©*
1983 by Kuso-kobo. All rights reserved. Reprinted by permission of Philomel Books.

knowledge of American art and literature as well as history. (p. 70)

Kenneth Marantz, in a review of ''Anno's U.S.A.,''
in School Library Journal, *Vol. 30, No. 5, January,*
1984, pp. 69-70.

As usual, the pages are wordless and there is no key to their contents, so a child unfamiliar with Philadelphia's Independence Hall would be at a loss to recognize it here without adult assistance. Anno's emphasis is on rural, pre-industrial age America, and his mention in an afterword of the ''forest wilderness'' of Kansas will raise eyebrows in the Sunflower State. The 21 spreads are drawn on a scale so miniature that considerable detail has been omitted, although the artwork is painstaking and carefully composed. Due to its American orientation, even libraries that have passed up other Anno picture essays will want to consider this.

Karen Stang Hanley, in a review of ''Anno's U.S.A.,''
in Booklist, *Vol. 80, No. 11, February 1, 1984, p.*
811.

I recently made a very interesting trip across America. It took about an hour—longer, if you count the time spent revisiting several places. I ''journeyed'' through *Anno's U.S.A.* . . . by Mitsumasa Anno, a Japanese illustrator of exceptional talent and whimsical bent.

Working in watercolor and ink, Anno creates exquisitely detailed landscapes, imaginatively and very actively inhabited by people and animals, as well as by characters from literature, music, and art.

As in all his journey books, Anno's ''lone traveler,'' in garb reminiscent of Robin Hood's, rides horseback through farm and village, town and countryside. Apparently oblivious to the hustle and bustle around him, he calmly appears somewhere in each scene. (Finding him may require great patience and a persistent eye.)

The fun, of course, lies in one's own journey—in this case, through the United States, moving west to east, and back and forth in time. When the lone traveler finally departs from the East Coast, for instance, he encounters Columbus's crew arriving on the Santa Maria.

During my trip, I recognize Washington, D.C., by the Capitol in the foreground. People in horse-drawn buggies lag behind others in early Ford cars. A politician delivers a long-winded speech from a podium. In this deceptively simple scene, a keen-eyed observer notices pleasant anomalies: Little Orphan Annie with Daddy Warbucks and her dog, Sandy; Charlie Chaplin on roller skates, and, near the politician, Dorothy holding forth with the Tin Man, the Cowardly Lion, and the Scarecrow.

It took several ''visits'' to Boston before I noticed Hester Prynne, scarlet letter delicately painted on the bodice of her dress, standing among folks on the village green. In the distance, a man on horseback gallops, arm upraised, toward an inn: Paul Revere in the middle of his historic ride.

Elsewhere in Boston, mothers push baby carriages, children stroll the streets, vendors hawk their wares, and two men struggle to move a piano. Suddenly, I realize the two men are Laurel and Hardy.

Equally delightful surprises appear in other areas of the country; Whistler's Mother on her rocking chair in a cottonfield; the Wright Brothers and their plane somewhere in Arizona; characters from Sesame Street in the Deep South.

Anno obviously has a sharp eye. Through illustrations alone, he depicts the vastness, history, and culture of America. And he allows us to make our own journeys: to make our own discoveries as we will, and to see different things each time we travel through the book. He wisely shows us that his ''lone traveler'' is really each one of us.

> Carole Brissie, "American Odyssey," in The Christian Science Monitor, July 6, 1984, p. B2.

NOMI NO ICHI [ANNO'S FLEA MARKET] (1983)

Mitsumasa Anno's silence is his great achievement as an author. His books are unique, not because they are wordless (or almost so) but because they so completely enlist the intellect and the imagination of the reader, solely through visual means. His wonderfully airy drawings and his storytelling combination of panoramas and details imply a narrative but never tell a conventional tale. He is a visual poet as much as a storyteller— the meaning of his work is never crisp and clear (although the drawings themselves are), and the books unfold more like a scroll than a sequence of pages, in beautiful, slow, nuanced stages.

His narratives take on form by accumulation—the layering of visual clues through angles, white spaces, architectural details and small incidents that take place in country landscapes or in cities. (Mr. Anno understands the delicate balance and fine distinctions between rural and urban space, and he makes the reader appreciate their interdependence.)

In Anno's Flea Market, he has given us another demanding and supremely rewarding promenade through time. This market is an essay on our past, using the language of objects. It is also an enormous personal museum, with the galleries organized according to the artist's quixotic and droll sensibility. Unexpected and improbable human action swirls around the tables and racks of old objects. So a monocled man wearing a top hat presides over a table full of old eyeglasses and optical devices (binoculars, lorgnettes, pince-nez, magnifying glass). Just to the right of the table is Charlie McCarthy, seated on the knee of Edgar Bergen. But the fellow presiding over the eyepieces is also Charlie McCarthy. Above them is a display of dolls and puppets in great variety and number, including such celebrities as Pinocchio, Pulcinella and a version of Gumby. And included among the children surrounding Edgar Bergen and Charlie McCarthy, making a guest appearance, is Kermit the Frog.

The pages are packed with vintage clothes—dresses, suits, underwear, shoes, boots, hats, furs and more. Above the displays on one page is a stage where a fashion show of antique dresses is being paraded before an audience in the dress of the same vaguely 19th-century period. Next to a table of shoes and boots, a group of women is waiting to try on a single slipper. They are all dressed in a more or less contemporary fashion, but the man trying each foot to fit the slipper is dressed, oddly, in the costume of an indeterminate past, while his attendants are all of the Renaissance, a period in which the Prince's search for Cinderella might take place.

These are just two examples of the book's sly and playful surprises. The objects themselves are a delight; it is as if one were wandering through a two-dimensional museum of utilitarian arts, a printed Shelburne Museum. The sheer breadth of objects in Mr. Anno's collection—and his ability and ambition to draw each one so that it is readily identifiable—is an ex-

traordinary achievement. As in any true-to-life flea market, there are unfamiliar objects that once had a function but are now baffling. Since Mr. Anno has organized the book by genres of things, there are clues to be followed in the adventure of identifying these mystery objects.

Anno's Flea Market is, finally, a love song to the past, to the integrity of beautiful handmade things and the history each one contains. And while the drawings are unaccompanied by words, in a short prologue Mr. Anno writes, "Each of these old things has a tale to tell us if we will stop to listen. Each has been used in the past by someone's grandmother or great grandfather or mother." In an equally short epilogue, Mr. Anno tells of an old and beautiful wooden bowl that caught his own eye in a flea market: "My beloved wooden bowl evokes in me thoughts of its first owner and user and of the craftsperson who carved its satisfying proportions."

> Edward Koren, in a review of "Anno's Flea Market," in The New York Times Book Review, August 26, 1984, p. 23.

I opened Anno's latest book with high hopes, and found myself unaccountably disappointed. I say 'unaccountably', as this book is very much in his familiar style. Heavily detailed and itemised drawings fill the pages, and the colours are his usual mix of delicate and sophisticated tones of sepia and grey—all of which works so delightfully in the Medieval world and The king's flower. So what is wrong with this one?

Firstly, I think, it's very hard to 'read'. There's no narrative thread to the pictures, and no text to help. Not only are historical periods jumbled together, with past and present cohabiting, but there is no scale: large objects like steam engines are drawn the same size as pewter jugs. To begin with, I thought Anno was going to provide readers with a key in the shape of a peasant family bringing their goods to the market-place on a hand-cart. There they were on the first spread, and on the second; but try as I might I failed to find them thereafter until they reappeared on the concluding page. It would have helped if they'd been there all the way through, and given a centre to these busy pages.

What, I wonder, was Anno's purpose in portraying all the historical periods together? Was it to demonstrate continuity in the life of markets? 'Every single object in the market has a story behind it', says the preface. But how many children read prefaces? And isn't it the obligation of the artist to make his intention plain through his art? The suggestion is that we should search through the pictures and find as many disparate objects as we can; but reading pictures should build a 'map' in your head. My mind remained stubbornly confused.

Perhaps I'm being unfair, and rewriting Anno's book for him; but I was doing what all readers do—trying to make a pattern— and failing.

> Gabrielle Maunder, in a review of "Anno's Flea Market," in The School Librarian, Vol. 32, No. 3, September, 1984, p. 223.

Gradually the spaces on the page—and inside a good part of the town—fill with an apparently limitless array of objects, from grand pianos to toothbrushes. On several pages a theme may be discerned: the neatly-displayed items belong to a class (clothing, household or farm implements, toys, musical instruments, weapons or food); but many fascinating entrants are a challenge to identify. There is an undeniable appeal to this book, and its usefulness as a stimulus to social and cultural history is obvious; Anno clearly hopes to inspire children to be conservators and collectors as well as mathematicians. Yet, with its glut of minutiae, it never achieves the enthralling sense of unfolding adventure to be discovered on *Anno's Journey* . . . , or in *Anno's Britain*. . . .

> *Patricia Dooley, in a review of "Anno's Flea Market," in* School Library Journal, *Vol. 31, No. 1, September, 1984, p. 98.*

I really don't know what to make of Anno. His new book represents an enormous expenditure of physical and imaginative energy. It is drawn with exquisite care. Is it worth while? I don't know.

His flea market, where you can 'buy anything from an elephant to a flea', takes place in a medieval walled town, and the fine drawings of walls and towers, colonnades and fountains provide the common feature that helps to stabilize the pages and connect the incredibly detailed drawings of market stalls crammed with miscellaneous treasure and rubbish. You can literally buy anything in the flea market, and there is an equally varied assembly of customers. Some of these are ordinary peasant types, others less predictable. In a corner Cinderella tries on her shoe. In the green market Popeye and Olive Oil debate the relative merits of tinned and fresh spinach. Among a litter of nautical items a mermaid confronts a prospective buyer. An itinerant painter provides his sitter with the fine bust that nature has denied her. It is all good fun. It is also very exhausting, so much happening that the effect becomes diffused. Compare, say, a picture-book by Raymond Briggs, and see how a book gains by a concentration of disciplined effects. One must respect and admire Anno for the wealth of his imagination and the skill with which he meets the technical demands of his invention, and yet fail to feel for his vision and his humour the warm glow that comes from personal involvement. (pp. 200-01)

> *M. Crouch, in a review of "Anno's Flea Market," in* The Junior Bookshelf, *Vol. 48, No. 5, October, 1984, pp. 200-01.*

AKAI BŌSHI [ANNO'S HAT TRICKS] (1984)

[*Anno's Hat Tricks was written by Akihiro Nozaki.*]

Anno's thirst for knowledge to share with the world's children is the impetus to his creation of books singular in style and substance. With Nozaki, a mathematician, the renowned author-artist has [created] this problem-solving primer, stunningly illustrated. A sporty fellow asks the reader to be Shadowchild, the amorphous figure in gray in the colorful paintings of little Tom, Hannah and the puzzle presenter. The readers must use rudimentary binary logic to tell whether the interlocutor sets a white or red hat on Tom and Hannah and Shadowchild in texts progressing from cinchy to tough as there are more . . . two red and one white and . . . Hmmmm. The examples may drive grownups wild with frustration but, for boys and girls born into the computer age, figuring out even the hard ones may be duck soup.

> *A review of "Anno's Hat Tricks," in* Publishers Weekly, *Vol. 227, No. 21, May 24, 1985, p. 70.*

Anno, a celebrated illustrator with many picture books to his credit, has here teamed up with a teacher of mathematics and computer science. The result is an unusual book with great

charm and a gentle manner of exposition calculated to disarm children who might otherwise be put off by repeated appeals to their powers of abstract reasoning. The illustrations are a delight—the figures of Tom and Hannah being varied, sometimes very subtly, from page to page with a marvellous economy of line.

> *Michael Lockwood, "Getting into Gear," in* The Times Literary Supplement, *No. 4286, May 24, 1985, p. 589.*

Anno is among the cleverest of today's picture-book makers, which is, no doubt, why the point of his books sometimes escapes me. . . . The problems [in *Anno's Hat Tricks*], which make adults think a bit, will probably present little difficulty to children experienced in computer studies. In fact I rather suspect that they will dismiss the book as kid's stuff. . . . Anno himself squeezes every bit of interest he can out of his drawings, but they remain basically pictures of two children and a shadow. Clever, certainly, but potentially boring too. . . .

> *M. Crouch, in a review of "Anno's Hat Tricks," in* The Junior Bookshelf, *Vol. 49, No. 4, August, 1985, p. 176.*

SOCRATES AND THE THREE LITTLE PIGS (1985; British edition as Anno's Three Little Pigs)

[*Socrates and the Three Little Pigs was written by Tuyosi Mori.*]

The wolf, Socrates, is a philosopher. His friend is Pythagoras the frog. To keep his cross wife quiet, wolf ought to catch a pig. But which? Now starts a complex mathematical game. It defeats me but I recommend this book none the less. Apart from the jolly pictures, it's the only version I know to give the wolf fair treatment.

> *Naomi Lewis, "Unreluctant Feet," in* The Observer, *April 20, 1986, p. 25.*

In this version of the well-known nursery tale, the wolf is Socrates no less, with Xanthippe his wife ravenously in attendance. Prior to eating the three little pigs, Socrates tries to work out their current deployment between five cottages. Thereby he raises them to the power of digits in a full scale exercise in combinational analysis, mathematical permutations and combinations. These are laid out in page after exquisitely designed page. I don't doubt for a second that Anno and Tuyosi Mori, his collaborator, have got their logic right. Nor am I surprised that Socrates and Xanthippe lose their appetite for bacon in the end. This is the perfect book for a toddler with advanced computer skills or a systems-analyst of whimsical disposition. When I next come across either I shall recommend it heartily.

> *Chris Powling, in a review of "Anno's Three Little Pigs," in* Books for Keeps, *No. 38, May, 1986, p. 30.*

Anno's Three Little Pigs is a picture book, but for juniors and above. It explains, through a whimsical variation on a fairytale, with most charming little illustrations, mathematical permutations and combinations, with combinatorial analysis. . . . Given Tuyosi Mori's skill and clarity in explanation and Anno's glorious humour and delightful colour, this book is a real breakthrough in mathematical teaching.

M. Hobbs, in a review of "Anno's Three Little Pigs," in The Junior Bookshelf, *Vol. 50, No. 3, June, 1986, p. 106.*

ALL IN A DAY (1986)

Mitsumasa Anno has a wish for the world's children, and he's making it just in time for Bologna. There you'll find, on display, Anno's *All in a Day,* a children's book on which he collaborated with nine other artists, in his hope for children that "by the time you grow up and learn about such things, this earth will have become a better place for you to live on, a place where everyone is always happy and friendly." . . .

Anno's books have found a wide audience among both children and adults. His enthusiasm for detail draws readers to his pictures as they look for the visual jokes that fill each page. And his concept books—*Anno's Counting House, Anno's Mysterious Multiplying Jar, Anno's Magical ABC,* and the just-published *Socrates and the Three Little Pigs*—combine sophisticated scientific, philosophical and mathematical ideas with simple stories.

All in a Day, which was first published in Japan, was conceived as a contribution to the cause of peace and understanding among the children of the world. Artists from around the globe—Raymond Briggs, Ronald Brooks, Gianvittore Calvi, Eric Carle, Zhu Chengliang, Leo and Diane Dillon, Akiko Hayashi and Nicolai Y. Popov—have lent their talents to one frame of each spread. The book begins on January 1 in households all over the globe. Each artist follows one child through a day, through the heat of an Australian summer, the firecrackers of a Chinese New Year, the bustle of an open air market in Kenya, portraying a moment in time with a universal perspective.

Kim Fakih, "World Artists Contribute to New Anno Book," in Publishers Weekly, *Vol. 229, No. 12, March 21, 1986, p. 47.*

Here's a book to reckon with. What a brilliant idea to take one day all round the world and show what is happening in Moscow, Tokyo, Australia—all round the world at the same time. . . . [There's] superb quality all round too. This is a book to generate lots of discussion including questions like, "What time is it now?" Life will never be simple again! It is a pleasure to welcome such an original treatment of a fascinating idea which will literally widen horizons and lay foundations in its own way for better international understanding.

Anne Wood, in a review of "All in a Day," in Books for Your Children, *Vol. 21, No. 3, Autumn-Winter, 1986, p. 7.*

Anno has set out to accomplish much with this volume, and too much information is carried by the graphic content. The variety of illustrative styles and interpretations by the artists will require many examinations before children will be able to integrate them. Complex in concept, minimal in plot, *All in a Day* is nonetheless a great success at conveying the warmth, richness, and variety of people. It will be welcomed by thoughtful browsers and for use with groups in order to stimulate discussion about the brotherhood of man. (pp. 139-40)

Carolyn Noah, in a review of "All in a Day," in School Library Journal, *Vol. 33, No. 7, March, 1987, pp. 139-40.*

Randolph Caldecott

1846-1886

English illustrator of picture books, fiction, and fables.

Caldecott holds an enduring place in children's book illustration as the creator of works that herald the modern picture book. Acknowledged for introducing the technique of animation into picture book art, Caldecott is also highly regarded for his pioneering work in extending textual meaning with humorous, mildly satiric illustrations. A member with Kate Greenaway and Walter Crane of the triumvirate known as "Academicians of the Nursery," Caldecott is considered the greatest of the three artists. His reputation rests on sixteen picture books—occasionally called toy books—that mainly feature traditional nursery rhymes and songs. Published in pairs, these works include *The House that Jack Built* and *The Diverting History of John Gilpin*, written by William Cowper (1878); *Elegy on the Death of a Mad Dog*, written by Oliver Goldsmith, and *The Babes in the Wood* (1879); *Sing a Song for Sixpence* and *The Three Jovial Huntsmen* (1880); *The Farmer's Boy* and *The Queen of Hearts* (1881); *The Milkmaid* and *Hey Diddle Diddle* with *Baby Bunting* (1882); *A Frog He Would A-Wooing Go* and *The Fox Jumps over the Parson's Gate* (1883); *Come Lasses and Lads* and *Ride a Cock Horse to Banbury Cross* with *A Farmer Went Trotting upon His Grey Mare* (1884); and *An Elegy on the Glory of Her Sex, Mrs. Mary Blaize*, written by Oliver Goldsmith, and *The Great Panjandrum Himself*, written by Samuel Foote (1885). The books have been reissued in a variety of formats since their initial publication: in a single volume, in two collections of eight titles each, in four collections of four titles each, and in miniature editions of each title. Employing deceptively simple but sweeping line drawings and subtle pastels, Caldecott expressed his love of life, animals, and late 18th-century English countryside locales in these works with spontaneity, gaiety, and charm, while depicting an honest vision of life that incorporates both joy and tragedy.

Already recognized for the variety and excellence of his adult art, Caldecott began illustrating for children in 1878 at the invitation of Edmund Evans, a noted wood engraver and printer who had also worked with Crane and Greenaway. Evans proposed that Caldecott choose and illustrate two picture books per year, which Evans would then produce. This combination of talents led to a financially successful partnership that continued for eight years until Caldecott's death. Characteristically drawing in sepia applied with a brush rather than a pen, he composed an average of three uncolored, less detailed pictures for every colored, formal one. Given free artistic rein by Evans, Caldecott studied what he called the "art of leaving out," whereby he utilized the fewest possible lines to convey expression and action. His pictures are not mere visual renditions of the text; a major aspect of Caldecott's genius lies in the invention of scenes and characters that complement the words and add a logical, realistic, and sometimes poignant subplot to the story.

Admired by such artists as Vincent Van Gogh, Paul Gauguin, Beatrix Potter, L. Leslie Brooke, and Maurice Sendak, Caldecott created a fluid style in which there is a sense of continuous movement from page to page. Action may flow from the top of one drawing to the bottom of the next or from a close-

The Bettmann Archive, Inc.

up to a more distant scene. People and animals dance, gallop, and participate in the action, causing Sendak to assert that "Caldecott breathed life into the picture book." Exhibiting a similar range of emotion and ability to capture the essence of a subject, Caldecott's other illustrated works for children include the fables of Aesop and La Fontaine in addition to three works by the popular Victorian children's writer, Juliana Horatia Ewing—*Jackanapes* (1883), *Daddy Darwin's Dovecot: A Country Tale* (1884), and *Lob Lie-by-the-Fire; or, the Luck of Lingborough* (1885). Influential since their publication, Caldecott's illustrations have waned in popularity to some degree in recent years. However, they are still esteemed by most scholars and respected as the inspiration for the Caldecott Medal, given annually since 1938 to the artist of the most distinguished American picture book published within each year.

Nearly unanimous in their admiration for Caldecott, critics have praised him particularly for his originality, as seen in his ingenious visual adaptations of texts, precedent-setting use of movement between pictures, and ability to illustrate a story thoroughly in only a few lines. They also laud his insight into human nature, instinctive grasp of what appeals to children, and accurate depictions of people, animals, and topography. Over the last century, most reviewers have agreed with F. J. Harvey Darton's assessment that "no other artist quite united so easily as he for children the qualities of humour, draughts-manship and intuitive interpretation."

(See also *Something about the Author*, Vol. 17.)

ILLUSTRATOR'S COMMENTARY

[The following excerpt is from a letter written by Caldecott to Horatia Gatty, editor of Aunt Judy's Magazine *and sister of Juliana Horatia Ewing for whom Caldecott illustrated several books.]*

[As] I believe very much in realistic work—not in opposition to—but as equally worthy with—ideal work—when the object is to teach, enlighten, or—(same thing)—innocently interest and amuse—I wish it to be fairly judged as to its *reality*. Its reality is its strongest or *only* reason for existing. I admit that some of the subjects which I choose fail and are unnecessary when they are not as realistic as I can exhibit them. And I am content to consider that they—my attempts at realistic draw-ings—are *all* unnecessary if people say they are not "like". I do not think that I often fully succeed—I rarely do anything like what I want—but I believe that the exact representation of ordinary people and life is not a bad thing to shew to the people who live that life, and as I see in the works of others so very, very little exact and true representation of it, why I—with great self-denial, for I yearn for pure forms, graceful lines and noble subjects—rush in—pencil in hand—and let drive at the people. Some say I hit them—anyway they pay well for it—which last fact brings out my self-denial in startling relief! (p. 140)

> *Randolph Caldecott, in a letter to Miss Gatty on August 25, 1879, in* Yours Pictorially: Illustrated Letters of Randolph Caldecott, *edited by Michael Hutchins, Frederick Warne, 1976, pp. 139-41.*

GENERAL COMMENTARY

MRS. EWING

[Ewing was a popular English children's writer for whom Caldecott illustrated three books. The following excerpt is from a letter she wrote to her husband in early 1879.]

Do you remember those books that came out this Christmas. . . . *John Gilpin* and *The House that Jack Built* illustrated by a man called Caldecott? I was *daft* about them—the draughtmanship so nervous and fine—the whole artistic satisfactoriness so completely free of *trick* and so thoroughly the outcome of labour. The other day I wrote some doggerel in the Hood irregular metre [later published as *A Soldier's Children*] . . . and was seized with a longing that Caldecott should illustrate it. I boldly sent it to Routledge [her publisher]—and offered to waive remuneration for myself if he would bring it out with Caldecott. He wrote very civilly and said at least Caldecott should see the lines of which he spoke very sugardly. But I have ever since been regretting I couldn't get at Caldecott himself. . . . I asked [Miss Mundella, a friend,] if she knew Caldecott. She does! She thinks what a combination if *he* illustrated *me*—and in that spirit she is going to try and combine us at luncheon! Alas! alas! he is dying of heart disease.

> *Mrs. Ewing, in a letter to her husband in 1879, in* Mrs. Gatty and Mrs. Ewing *by Christabel Maxwell, Constable Publishers, 1949, p. 208.*

PERCY FITZGERALD

Mr. Caldecott has attracted the attention of all true connoisseurs from the sort of unique and special flavour attached to his works. Delicacy, originality, variety, and a graceful humour, are his characteristics. A singular life and motion is imparted to his figures, and above all there is dramatic force, showing that he had thoroughly possessed himself of the spirit of his authors. He has been a very diligent workman, and the public which has made special favourites of certain of his works would be astonished to see what abundant claims he could put forward to their favour. As an illustrator he is among the first. Any one of taste will find it easy to estimate him by recalling the effect of his pictures the first time he was fortunate enough to see them. (p. 630)

In a feeling for landscape—conveyed by a few broken lines, and stretching away so as to open up a far stretch of country—our artist is wonderful. There is a tenderness and significance amazing, considering the means employed. (p. 631)

Some of [the] more ambitious scenes are given with an extraordinary breadth, and really reflect not only the animation of the situation, but have the additional merit of actually transcribing the landscape. The scene of Gilpin's flight along the high-road affects one like a farce. We almost hear the galloping of the horses, the flapping and screaming of the ducks. But any one that has been at Edmonton will recognise the fidelity of the picture—the faint red of houses by the roadside overlaid with dust, the old-fashioned faded tone of the whole, the bare high-road, the curious tone of sleepiness. Here, again, is feeling. This and some others, if effectively framed, would adorn the walls of a room.

In the ***Mad Dog*** . . . there is one of these charming views—a bit of landscape, a sort of fringing to a common, a row of old redbrick houses, half hidden by trees, delicately tinted, as it were, and which opens up in a very suggestive way all the associations which such scenes furnish, and which are so difficult also to describe. The "lie" of the ground is wonderfully given, and offers the rich sinuosities of such places. So, too, in the ***Babes*** . . . , the little church in the distance and the scrap of village. (pp. 631-32)

One of [Caldecott's] happiest expressions is that of motion—swift breezy motion; a fluttering dress, something blown away, a horse galloping, birds flying—this is conveyed with startling effect. I defy the most rigid anchoritish muscles not to relax after gazing for a few moments at the large picture in ***John Gilpin***, where the geese are fluttering and flapping in the air under the horse's feet in their strange composite motion, half flying, half running, with idiotic plunges. We almost seem to hear their agonising cackling. So, too, with the rout of mounted people in pursuit of Gilpin, the different modes of eager riding, the head bent down, &c., the amused faces, the graceful women rushing to the gates, the natural air of surprise and enjoyment, the general tone of bustle and excitement—all is wonderfully dramatic.

His girls' faces have a singular charm. Many of the most interesting are not pretty in form or outline, but have the strongest force of expression. (p. 632)

He excels in [the] dramatic power of devising varieties of faces. Here is where the average illustrating artist is deficient, all faces being more or less of a conventional kind. But Caldecott abounds in varieties of most expressive faces. He seems to dip into his mind for curious forms of expression, and has a surprising faculty of furnishing faces that will satisfy our ideal of something where a great deal of finesse is in question. It is easy to express farce or tragedy, but there are innumerable intermediate emotions of a character more difficult to define. . . . Oddity is really conveyed by an expression of the eye or a curious smile on the lips. But Caldecott has the art of conveying this mental expression without twisting the features. (p. 633)

It is when comparing him with another artist, Mr. [George] Du Maurier, whose girls' faces have a charm of their own, that we see Caldecott's special gift. Du Maurier does not aim at the intellectual or mental; his characters have all the features of a type of the soft English composure and placidity—a fine contour and brilliant eyes. Caldecott's, however, pique from their originality and distinctness, and the lurking expression within.

Dramatic instinct is difficult to discriminate, and still harder to describe. But it can be indicated by an example. Mr. Caldecott was giving an illustration of the Yule Log burning and crackling on the hearth, with its glowing ashes, smoke, &c. Now, the effect of this—the associations of the genial warmth—it would seem to many, could be best conveyed by a vivid picture of the log and blaze itself. But this is not the effective way. Our artist introduces two dogs, seated in front, and with their backs to us, gazing intently on the blaze, and enjoying the warmth in that curiously reflective fashion which can be noted in dogs. Now, this at once imparts a vital interest to what before had been but a mere mechanical effect: we can supply the lazy relish of the creatures—their luxurious delight. This spirit of dramatic conception is carried out in the most abundantly fruitful way. Yet one is puzzled to discover the secret. The result certainly is that the dogs have a curious fascination as of companionship, and we find ourselves looking at them again, as at something living.

Besides the true interpretation of the author's meaning, there is the art, the dramatic one, of seizing on merely what is *essential;* rejecting all that, however pretty, would not express the incident. Let the reader test most of his pictures by this. Not only is there dramatic treatment in the materials of a scene done to his hand, but our artist can devise, and legitimately, out of a hint, a whole dramatic scene. In the *Mad Dog,* for instance, the simple line, ''The dog it was that died,'' becomes a really vivid event—the dog discovered dead on a common, the genial red houses fringing it, and the man in his walk coming on it, and calling to a labourer in the distance. Indeed, the whole, by the surroundings and background, becomes a local village story. And ''I vow and declare,'' as Lady Blarney would say, it will be impossible to think of Goldsmith's lines for the future without calling up this mortuary scene. (pp. 633-34)

Mr. Caldecott, like other artists, can use the modelling tool with skill. I fancy, on the whole, that, with his power and colour, atmospheric effect, and movement, his true domain would be the more enduring one of oils and canvas. Our artist has moreover great strength as a draughtsman. He is fearless and secure in his knowledge, so that his hand obeys his inspiration; nor is he disturbed by any fear that the result may be incorrect. Note particularly the drawing of legs in different positions, when that position is conveyed by the outline—courageous as a skater's curve on the ice—and independent of all aids from shading, which covers up so much bad drawing. Witness those of the godly man and others in the *Mad Dog.* I fancy the little outlines, alternated with the vivid coloured sketches, suffer from the contrast, and appear poor. They might

be bolder, and with a little shading; the companionship of colour and outline is wrong artistically. Mr. Caldecott's quality is delicacy and colour. However this may be, the public may be as much congratulated on the possession of such an entertainer as on its own good taste and sagacity, which from the first recognised and heartily appreciated so good an artist. (p. 635)

Percy Fitzgerald, ''Randolph Caldecott,'' in The Gentleman's Magazine, *Vol. CCXLVI, January-June, 1880, pp. 629-35.*

W. E. HENLEY

In his way [Mr. Caldecott] is the most graceful and charming of modern illustrators—a Nursery [William] Small, so to speak; and, moreover, in his way he is the most popular also. Three or four years ago he was, comparatively speaking, unknown. He had produced a good many excellent designs, but he had not succeeded in fixing the public eye nor in touching the public heart. Then, in 1878, he brought out the first of his incomparable picture-books, and became famous at once. They made more noise and gave more pleasure than all the pictures of the year, and between old folks and young there was a contest of admiration over them. They were better than popular, they were fashionable; and under their shadow a crop of imitations and adaptations sprang up like mushrooms. Old England entered into a kind of pictorial apotheosis; and Young England suddenly awakened to the exquisite quaintness of mobs and short waists, and the daintiness and charm of spencers and sandal-shoes and narrow skirts. The times became teacup times once more; and within the Victorian age . . . there grew up a tiny artificial Age of Anne. . . . And Mr. Randolph Caldecott—the grace of Dolly Varden, and the beauty of Beatrix Esmond, and the tenderness and charm of Mr. Austin Dobson's old-world Muse to the contrary—would have seemed the great first cause of it all. (pp. 208-09)

[Mr. Caldecott] made a complete conquest of the general public by producing his famous versions of *John Gilpin* and *The House that Jack Built.* To my mind they are a great advance upon [his works for adults]. The drawing is better, both as drawing and as expression; the gesture is larger and more assured; the fun is richer and more spontaneous; the invention is more facile and abundant; there is more of creation and less of research; the charm, the fancy, the gaiety, have grown stronger, and less deliberate, and more personal; and there is proof in twenty places of a true and delicate sense of simple colour, and of an uncommon ability in its arrangement. Never before had Mr. Caldecott drawn such fresh and winsome girls as the Maiden All Forlorn and John Gilpin's customers and servant-maid, and certain among the spectators of the ride. Never had he produced figures so true in gesture and so full of spirit as the Man All Tattered and Torn and the Calender, and the bruised and broken Gilpin, and the wondering Waiter, and the horsemen in the hue and cry. Never before had he contrived to make his animals so comic and personal and so true. The Rat that ate the Malt is a kind of creation; so is the Cat that ate the Rat, so is the humorsome, ill-favoured, sulky, cynical ruffian—a Quilp among curs!—that worried the cat. The vein thus opened was wrought yet deeper next year in *The Babes in the Wood* and *The Mad Dog.* They are hardly so successful as their two predecessors, and they deal with subjects that are far from being agreeable and acceptable; but they contain some excellent work for all that. The Wicked Uncle and the Ruffians of the first are not at all good; but the Babes themselves are very pretty and innocent and touching, and the friends they make in the woods are friends worth knowing. *The Mad Dog* is altogether superior. The Man is a veritable creation; and the Dog—whether philandering with the Man, or listening to the promptings of the fiend Jealousy; or going off his wits, with infinite determination and a humour of frenzy in every hair on his coat; or fading away, as one who has seen a Boojum, into the quiet sunset—is even better than the Man. Our last year's Christmas Box was more acceptable by far; for it consisted of *The Song for Sixpence*—with its wonderful noise of Blackbirds, its delightful King and Queen, its charming Washer-Maiden, and its heaps of comic Courtiers: to say nothing of its value as exegesis, and its freshness and novelty as a commentary on an ancient and most mysterious legend—and of *The Three Jovial Huntsmen,* with its Gothamitish heroes, its exquisite glimpses of landscape, its fine differentiation of character, and its varied spirit of adventure. What Mr. Caldecott has in store for us next Christmas is yet to be seen. . . . Meanwhile, whatever it is, it can hardly be other than charming; and it will certainly receive a warm and earnest welcome.

Whatever it is, too, we may be sure that it will have something to do with that pleasant Eighteenth Century which, from Anne to George, Mr. Caldecott has conquered to himself in Art, even as Mr. Austin Dobson has done with it in verse; so that now none dare to attempt it with his pencil under pain of killing comparison with the author of *John Gilpin* and the *Song for Sixpence,* just as none dare to write about it, in dread of the poet of Rosine and Madame Placid. . . . They are absolute over "the times of Paint and Patch," are these two artists. They reign in them like two æsthetic Kings of Brentford, *arcades ambo, et cantare pares*—though I suppose the poet is the better workman as well as the soldier spirit; and of their rule there is not a circumstance but is wholesome and kindly and beautiful. . . . [Mr. Caldecott] is a kind of Good Genius of the Nursery, and—in the way of pictures—the most beneficent and delightful it ever had. It is as if he had lived and worked under the special protection of an æsthetic Fairy Godmother, who made an artist of him wholly and solely that millions of children might be made glad. He has fulfilled his destiny quite royally. He is a Prince of Picture Books. Under his sway Art for the nursery has become Art indeed. Between the toy-books of thirty and twenty years ago and the toy-books of present years the difference is that between a post-chaise and the Flying Scotsman. Such works as Mr. Crane's *Baby's Bouquet* and *Baby's Opera,* and Miss Greenaway's pleasant *Birthday Book,* and Messrs. Sowerby and Emmerson's *Afternoon Tea,* would once have been considered luxuries only fit for dukelets and princelings. Now they are within every one's reach; and for a shilling apiece you can purchase the picture-books of Mr. Caldecott, which are better and bonnier than them all. The printer, the publisher, the engraver, and the paper-maker have gone ahead surprisingly, and the artist has gone with them. The Art of the nursery was primitive and abominable. . . . It was difficult to fall in love with any Cinderella, any Twoshoes, any Goldenlocks but one's own. Now Mr. Caldecott has come, and it seems impossible to be enamoured of any but the artist's. His work, with its freshness and its charm, its vivacity and spontaneity, its admirable gaiety and kindliness, is one of the prettiest facts in child-life. He has given to infancy a new pleasure, and to its governors a new influence for good. His books are not only delightful to have as books; you have but to take them to pieces, and group and mount the pictures under glass, to have one of the most charming decorations imaginable. In this form his work may become an important factor in the process of unconscious education to which all children are subjected. To be constantly familiar with what is cheerful in spirit and pretty and pleasant in fact, is to take something of these qualities into one's life and one's self. I can conceive

it possible and likely that there are many boys and girls alive just now who, wittingly or unwittingly, when they are grown men and women, will owe much to Mr. Caldecott, and be all the better for the place he had in their infancy. (pp. 211-12)

> *W. E. Henley, "Randolph Caldecott," in* The Art Journal, *1881, pp. 208-12.*

JULIANA HORATIA EWING

[*The following excerpt is taken from a letter written by Ewing to Caldecott.*]

I think you stand alone!—For an 'all-roundness' of genius in "illustrating" humanity, and human surroundings, with a delicate dexterity that is delicious to anyone who has *any* knowledge of *your* art, and with an absence of tricks and mannerism which seems to me only to be found in the highest order of any art whatever!

And this is not because I fail to appreciate that we are very rich just now in character sketchers of very high order. . . .

And yet—I think you have no peer! . . . I believe your work will be gathered up again and treasured by those who *know* and *love* their fellow creatures—the world around them—and the gifts of hand and eye—when Mr Crane and Miss Greenaway are out of fashion for the mass and fatiguing to the elect!!!!!!

> *Juliana Horatia Ewing, in a letter to Randolph Caldecott on December 9, 1882, in* Yours Pictorially: Illustrated Letters of Randolph Caldecott, *edited by Michael Hutchins, Frederick Warne, 1976, p. 89.*

PUNCH

[*Caldecott contributed many pen-and-ink drawings to* Punch *from 1872-83. The following excerpt is a poem paying tribute to Caldecott upon his death.*]

Too early stilled that happy hand
　　That limned old English life, love, leisure,
That waked glad laughter through the land,
　　And sent our playrooms wild with pleasure.
Too early stilled! Dumb Fate hath willed
　　One of its cruellest of crosses;
For, faith, our hearts are often thrilled
　　With lesser griefs at larger losses.

We loved the limner whose gay fun
　　Was ever loyal to the Graces;
Who mixed the mirth of *Gilpin's* run
　　With willowy forms and winsome faces:
Who made old nursery lyrics live
　　With frolic force rejuvenated,
And yet the sweetest girls could give
　　That ever pencil-point created.

From "Bracebridge Hall" to "Banbury Cross"
　　His fancy flew with fine facility.
Orchards all apple-bloom and moss,
　　Child sport, bucolical senility,
The field full cry, snug fireside ease,
　　Horse-fun, dog-joke his pencil covers,
With Aldermen and hawthorn-trees,
　　Parsons and squires, and rustic lovers.

Sure never pencil steeped in mirth
　　So closely kept to grace and beauty.
The honest charms of mother Earth,
　　Of manly love, and simple duty,

Blend in his work with boyish health,
   With amorous maiden's meek cajolery,
Child-witchery, and a wondrous wealth
   Of dainty whim and daring drollery.

And all that flow of fun, and all
   That fount of charm found in his fancy,
Are stopped! Yet will he hold us thrall
   By his fine Art's sweet necromancy,
Children and Seniors, many a year,
   For long 'twill be ere a new-comer
Fireside or nursery holdeth dear
   As him whose life ceased in its Summer.

"Randolph Caldecott: In Memoriam," in Punch, *Vol. XC, No. 2329, February 27, 1886, p. 106.*

HENRY BLACKBURN

[*Blackburn was an author, journalist, and editor who encouraged Caldecott to pursue a career as an artist. Caldecott produced several illustrations for* London Society, *a magazine which Blackburn edited, and illustrated two of his books,* The Harz Mountains *(1872) and* Breton Folk *(1880). In the following excerpt from his personal memoir of Caldecott, Blackburn praises his friend's work.*]

About [July, 1874] it was suggested to Caldecott to make studies of animals and birds, with a view to an illustrated edition of *Æsop's Fables*, a work for which his talents seemed eminently fitted. The idea was put aside from press of work, and when finally brought out in 1883 was not the success that had been anticipated. This was principally owing to the plan of the book.

As Caldecott's *Æsop* was often talked over with the writer in early days, a few words may be appropriate here. Caldecott yielded to a suggestion of Mr. J. D. Cooper, the engraver, to attach to each fable what were to be styled "Modern Instances," consisting of scenes, social or political, as an "application." Humorous as these were, in the artist's best vein of satire, the combination was felt to be an artistic mistake. That Caldecott was aware of this, almost from the first, is evident from a few words in a letter to an intimate friend where he says:—

Do not expect much from this book. When I see proofs of it I wonder and regret that I did not approach the subject more seriously.

Circumstances of health also in later years interfered with the completion of what might have been his *chef d'œuvre*. (pp. 94-6)

As this memoir has to do with Caldecott's earlier career, and particularly with his work in black and white, the artistic value of his illustrations in colour, especially in his **Picture Books,** can only be hinted at here.

Caldecott's Picture Books are known all over the world; they have been widely discussed and criticised, and they form undoubtedly the best monument to his memory. (pp. 204-05)

Caldecott, of all contemporary artists, owed his wide popularity to the wood engraver, to the maker of colour blocks, and to the printing press. No artist before him had such chances of dispersing facsimiles of daintily coloured illustrations over the world. All this must be considered when his place in the century of artists is written. (p. 206)

About the year 1879 Caldecott became acquainted with Mrs. Ewing, which led to his making many illustrations for her,

such as the design for the cover of *Aunt Judy's Magazine,* and notably the illustrations to that "book of books" for boys, **Jackanapes,** and to **Daddy Darwin's Dovecot,** and others. (pp. 208-09)

Looking back, but a few months only, at the passing away of two such lives—the author of **Jackanapes** and the illustrator of the **Picture Books . . .**—the loss seems incalculable.

In the history of the century, the best and purest books and the brightest pages ever placed before children will be recorded between 1878 and 1885; and no words would seem more in touch with the lives and aims of these lamented artists than a concluding sentence in **Jackanapes,** that—their works are "a heritage of heroic example and noble obligation."

The grace and beauty, and wealth of imagination in Caldecott's work,—conspicuous to the end,—form a monument which few men in the history of illustrative art have raised for themselves. (pp. 209-10)

Henry Blackburn, in his Randolph Caldecott: A Personal Memoir of His Early Art Career, *1886. Reprint by Singing Tree Press, 1969, 216 p.*

FREDERICK LOCKER-LAMPSON

It seems to me that Caldecott's art was of a quality that appears about once in a century. It had delightful characteristics most happily blended. He had a delicate fancy, and his humour was as racy as it was refined. He had a keen sense of beauty, and, to sum up all, he had *charm*. His old-world youths and maidens are perfect. The men are so simple and so manly, the maidens are so modest and so trustful. . . .

Frederick Locker-Lampson, in an extract from Randolph Caldecott: A Personal Memoir of His Early Art Career *by Henry Blackburn, 1886. Reprint by Singing Tree Press, 1969, p. 207.*

GEORGE Du MAURIER

[Randolph Caldecott was] a true illustrator, if ever there was one. That is, an enhancer of the charm and humour of his text, whose art seems of the slightest—a very few strokes were enough for him to work wonders with. It is magic! Grace, charm, beauty, humour, character, pathos—all were his; and he was as skilled in landscape and animals as in the human figure, and "good alike at grave or gay." There is also his immortal series of picture-books, equally beloved by old and young and middle-aged, by babies even—a gallery that never palls. (p. 352)

George Du Maurier, "The Illustrating of Books from the Serious Artist's Point of View—I," in The Magazine of Art, *Vol. 13, November, 1890, pp. 349-53.*

EDMUND EVANS

[*Evans was the most respected English wood engraver and color printer of Victorian children's books. He commissioned Walter Crane, Kate Greenaway, and Caldecott to contribute to a series of colored picture books which helped establish the trio as the most eminent illustrators of their time. Since the actual date of the following excerpt is unknown, it is here dated 1905, the year of Evans's death.*]

I was much impressed by [Randolph Caldecott's] early work known in London: **Old Christmas** and **Bracebridge Hall** by Washington Irving; there were many illustrations to each, drawn

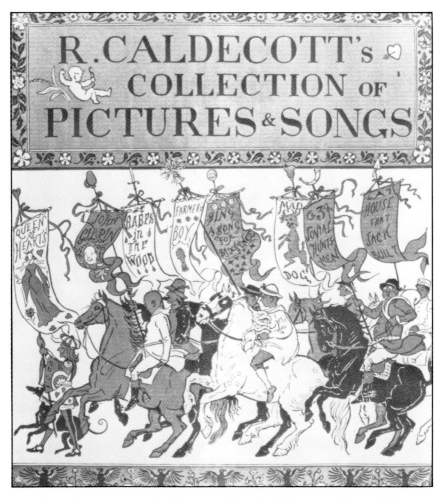

Cover illustration from R. Caldecott's Collection of Pictures and Songs *(1883).*

on wood and engraved by James Cooper. . . . I believe they sold very largely: anyway they should have done for they were most fascinating books, very well printed and got up generally. I thought Randolph Caldecott would be just the man to do some shilling toy books which I was anxious to do, so I appointed a meeting with him at his lodgings in Great Russell Street, Bloomsbury. He liked the idea of doing them as I proposed, and fell in with me very pleasantly, but he would not agree to doing them for any fixed sum: feeling sure of his own powers in doing them, he wished to share in the speculation—said he would make the drawings—if they sold and paid, he would be paid, but was content to bear the loss if they did not sell, and not be paid: so I agreed to run all the risk of engraving the key blocks which he drew on wood: after he had coloured a proof I would furnish him, on drawing paper, I would engrave the blocks to be printed in as few colours as necessary. This was settled, the key block in *dark brown*, then a *flesh tint* for the faces, hands, and wherever it would bring the other colours as nearly as possible to his painted copy, a *red*, a *blue*, a *yellow*, and a *grey*. (I was to supply paper, and print 10,000 copies, which George Routledge & Sons have published for me.) I asked him to come and see me at my house at Witley, which he did, and we talked over the subjects of the two first books. We agreed to publish together, in the Autumn of 1878, *The House that Jack Built* and *John Gilpin*. Shilling Toy Books, at that time, generally had blank pages at the back of the

pictures: I proposed to have no blanks at all in these books: these slight illustrations were little more than outlines, but they were so racy and spontaneous. R. C. generally drew them from his friend where a man was wanted: his cats, dogs, cows, showed how thoroughly he understood the anatomy of them. If the sketches came all right, he let them pass—if he was not satisfied with the result, he generally tore them up and burned them. They were made in pen and ink on smooth-faced writing paper, post 8vo size, photographed on wood, and carefully engraved in 'facsimile'—Process work was not sufficiently perfected at this time to reproduce the drawings by this method. I shewed him some drawings by Kate Greenaway which I had photographed on wood and engraved in the usual way, also some similar drawings which I had reproduced by this process, but R. C., Kate Greenaway and myself liked the engraved ones best. The subjects were used in the edition of Mavor's *Spelling-Book* illustrated without coloured illustrations by Kate Greenaway, only—I particularly wanted R. Caldecott to join with Kate Greenaway in illustrating this book, but K. G. was dead against it, so, as usual in such cases, I had to give way: K. G. got her way! I still feel sure R. C. would have been of immense value and the Public would have taken cheerfully to the book, which, I am sorry to say, they did not. . . . These two Caldecott books took immediate possession, or rather, the Public were very anxious to get possession of them. The 10,000 copies sold before I could get another edition printed. We produced two new Toy Books each year. . . . (pp. 55-8)

I always regret I did not ask R. C. where he got *The Three Jovial Huntsmen* from: I know he wrote the verse, The City Alderman.

The sale of the Toy Books increased so that I printed 100,000 first edition: they were bound in volumes, 4 books or 8 in each volume with paper covers, cloth up the back. R. C. made a special drawing for these volume covers. After the sixteen books were completed, I printed 1,000 copies in larger-sized paper, each copy numbered and signed by the publisher and printer. This 'Edition de Luxe' sold immediately they were printed: I wished I had printed three or four thousand instead of one thousand. Kate Greenaway often stayed with us at Witley during the time these drawings were being made; it was refreshing to see her keen enjoyment of these spontaneous drawings when I brought them down for her to see. The R. C. *Sketch Book* was not a success; why, I never could understand. Later on, R. C. illustrated a shilling edition of Mrs Ewing's delightful little stories, *Jackanapes, Daddy Darwin, Lob Lie-by-the-Fire*. . . . Caldecott was a good man of business—he made good terms with Mrs Ewing to be paid one penny a copy—if they sold badly or well, this arrangement was quite satisfactory to Mrs Ewing, for she got these clever drawings without the responsibility of paying a round sum down. (pp. 58-9)

> Edmund Evans, "The Reminiscences: Randolph Caldecott, Kate Greenaway and George Eliot," in his The Reminiscences of Edmund Evans, *edited by Ruari McLean, Oxford at the Clarendon Press, 1967, pp. 55-76.*

MARTIN HARDIE

It is [Edmund Evans] that we have to thank for the delightful coloured plates by Caldecott, Greenaway, and Crane, that during the last thirty years have won the affection of old and young. Most of all, perhaps, are those of us indebted, who are young enough to remember the joys of our childish days, when *Under the Window*, **The Three Jovial Huntsmen**, and *The Great Panjandrum Himself,* delightful beyond all books that we had ever seen or imagined, were gift-books new and fresh. Where are they now, all those dear companions of our nursery days? Perhaps they were too dear, too well-thumbed to live. One looks back across the years, and thinks of them with sorrow and regret, as of friends departed. Did they survive, they should hold a place of honour in the bookcase that we cherish most. (p. 266)

[Walter Crane, Randolph Caldecott, and Kate Greenaway] have been grouped under the title of 'Academicians of the Nursery,' and their names have long been household words. As contemporary illustrators of children's books they must always be linked together, though all have gifts peculiarly their own, with a style as distinct and individual as possible. (p. 270)

Kate Greenaway and Randolph Caldecott both died at a comparatively young age; Mr. Walter Crane is the only one of the trio now alive. For the sake of convenience, however, one must use the present tense throughout in speaking of these three artists and their work together. All three of them, distinct though their styles are, work to a large extent on common ground. They grasp the fact that the child's book need neither be childish nor priggishly instructive; that the child mind is essentially receptive, and that designs inherently beautiful will find ready appreciation from young as well as old. In consequence, they have made the ideal books for children; not books ostensibly intended for the young, while coquetting with grown-ups under their false disguise; but books full of real fascination

for the child mind, and at the same time instinct with charm for the 'Olympian,' who still is fortunate enough to retain something of childhood's happy spirit. The child, it must be remembered, 'moves about in worlds not realised'; he still has eyes for wonderment, a mind receptive and impressionable, overflowing with fancy and imagination, with a literal preference in his play for symbolism rather than reality: make-believe is the essence of his being. The child, too, is serious in his fun, and all three artists have adopted just that right attitude of playful gravity which is the key to childhood's heart.

The work of these three artists, morever, owes much of its success to an air of convincing sincerity. They work as if they could not help it, for the sheer joy of working; and they laugh, and make others laugh, with a humour that is irrepressible. Every picture shows that the painter's heart and soul was in it, and reveals the fact that it was made for his own satisfaction no less than for the delight of youthful spectators. In technique also there is this point of similarity, that all of them take into consideration the method by which their drawings are to be reproduced, and study its obvious advantages as well as its obvious deficiencies. The result is that in their individual way all display consummate skill in working with pure colours and flat tones, with a simple and direct treatment that adapts itself to the scope of the wood-engraver and the colour-printer from wood-blocks. (pp. 270-72)

[Caldecott] studied the 'art of leaving out as a science,' believing, to use his own words, that 'the fewer the lines, the less error committed.' Phil May has been credited with the invention of drawing in terse, dramatic outline that is never strictly outline at all, and it has been stated that his style was caused by the exigencies of the cheap Australian printing presses. There is, in my opinion, little in his actual technique that you do not find already fully developed by Caldecott. In both cases the economy of means and apparent simplicity suggested by the final drawing were only achieved by endless studies. Nobody knows the true inwardness of Phil May's work till he has seen his carefully finished pencil studies. The same statement is equally true of Caldecott; and, to give a single instance, among the original drawings by him at [The South Kensington Museum] are no less than nine careful studies for the small and insignificant fox that adorns the Aesop fable of the Fox and the Stork. Another striking example of apparent simplicity is the famous sketch of the mad dog dancing. At first sight it is in outline, broken perhaps, but outline for all that—a rapid and effective sketch. Now analyse it, and you will find that it is composed of over two hundred and fifty separate strokes of the pen, not one of which is meaningless or unnecessary. (pp. 279-80)

[Caldecott's] world lies in the past, among the old manners and customs of eighteenth-century England, not the eighteenth century of Pope and Sheridan, amid the elegant and dissipated beau-monde of the town; but rather that of Oliver Goldsmith, amid simple country life with its 'homely joys and destiny obscure.' He excelled in expressing fresh and breezy scenes of the English squirearchy in manor-house and hunting-field. His work is full of eloquent design, an abundance of kindly humour, an inexhaustible store of fancy—all expressed in attractive colour. (p. 280)

Ostensibly picture-books for children, [Caldecott's picture-books] were in reality works of art full of subtle charm and rare originality. Every variety of talent the artist possessed finds its full display in his ingenious adaptation of nursery rhymes, old ballads, and the comic poems of the eighteenth century. In his colouring he employed flat tints of great variety, sometimes making finished water-colour drawings, but more often making a pen-drawing first, and then colouring a proof of the wood-engraving sent by the printer. (p. 281)

With *The House that Jack Built* and *John Gilpin* Caldecott set himself a very high standard, which he nevertheless managed to sustain with only an occasional falling off, due partly to want of complete sympathy with his subject, partly to failing health. *John Gilpin* seemed inimitable, yet it was followed in 1879 by the fascinating *Elegy on the Death of a Mad Dog,* and by *The Babes in the Wood.* The complete list continues as follows:—*Three Jovial Huntsmen* and *Sing a Song for Sixpence* (1880); *The Queen of Hearts* and *The Farmer's Boy* (1881); *The Milkmaid, Hey-diddle-diddle, the Cat and the Fiddle,* and *Baby Bunting* (the last two in one volume, 1882); *The Fox jumps over the Parson's Gate,* and *A Frog he would a-wooing go* (1883); *Come Lasses and Lads, Ride a Cock Horse to Banbury Cross,* and *A Farmer went trotting upon his Grey Mare* (the last two in one volume, 1884); *Mrs. Mary Blaize* and *The Great Panjandrum Himself* (1885). (pp. 281-82)

The work of these 'academicians of the nursery' is well worth treasuring, and the number of volumes that have passed unscathed through years of nursery life must be comparatively small. Yet even Kate Greenaway's books, which are the rarest of all, can now be purchased for a 'mere song.' Before many years have passed they should be worth their weight in gold. (p. 282)

> *Martin Hardie, "Edmund Evans, Crane, Greenaway, and Caldecott," in his* English Coloured Books, *1906. Reprint by Rowman and Littlefield, 1973, pp. 266-82.*

WALTER CRANE

It was some time in 1877, I think, that our friend Mr. Thomas Armstrong brought Randolph Caldecott to our house. He never looked strong, and his quiet manner, low voice, and gentle but rather serious and earnest way of speaking did not suggest the extraordinary vivacity and humour of his drawings, though an occasional humorous remark may have betrayed a glimpse of such qualities. He consulted me as to his plans and dealings with publishers in regard to the picture-books he was then preparing (Edmund Evans again being the printer), the series which afterwards became so popular, and I think he may have benefited a little by my experience in the same sort of work— I mean as regards publishing arrangements—as his books were brought out at a shilling, and he was able to secure a royalty on them, which I could never get on my sixpenny toy-books.

His first was *The House that Jack Built,* which appeared in 1878, so that Caldecott's work and Miss Greenaway's books for children became known to the public about the same time. . . . His picture-books became immensely successful, and I think perhaps he caught the more popular English taste to some extent by his introduction of the sporting element. His *Three Jovial Huntsmen* will not easily be forgotten. (pp. 183-84)

> *Walter Crane, "Life in the 'Bush,' 1873-79," in his* An Artist's Reminiscences, *1907. Reprint by Singing Tree Press, 1968, pp. 154-208.*

JOSEPH PENNELL

There is a side to Caldecott's drawing which, though it has been almost altogether ignored, is really the only side to be considered by the student. This is his power of showing expression and action by a few lines, often by a single line of his brush used as a pen. There is no one in England who has ever equalled him in this, and I very much doubt if any one anywhere ever surpassed him. I do not see how it would be possible to give with fewer lines the intense expression of the cat stealthily approaching the mouse. But curiously enough, although there are several other cats in *The House that Jack Built,* there is not one which comes near it, unless, perhaps, I except the cat worried by the dog in which, however, the dog is characterless, while the intense expression which characterizes the cat I give is wanting in all the others.

Again, has anybody ever given such a delightful absurdity as this of the dog [in *Elegy on the Death of a Mad Dog*], who to gain some private ends, went mad and bit the man? It is the concentration of action and expression. Could anything be finer than the two dots for eyes which glitter with madness, or the aimless expression of the fore paws and the undecided pose of the whole body? You have not an idea in which direction the dog will spring, but you are very sure you ought to get out of the way. The big dog, too, sitting among broken pots and plates, is fine, but Caldecott simply could not work out a foreground. When a man draws plants and flowers and grass, I at once compare him with Alfred Parsons; if he cannot give them so well as Parsons, it is useless for the student to turn to his work. Parsons worked from nature; Caldecott out of his head.

Caldecott's drawings were done with a brush used as a pen, in sepia or some other liquid color. But unless the printing is in brown, as in the Picture Books and *Æsop's Fables,* it is impossible to give any idea of his work. It cannot be reproduced in its proper value, and absolutely the only object in using this brown ink is to make work for engravers and color-printers. (p. 231)

It would be almost impossible to give a better idea of bounding free motion than in [the] stag from the *Æsop,* with the whole of Scotland stretching away behind him, though probably the lines in the shadow were better in the original drawing. Then look at the happy fox after he has fooled the stork, and the innocent young lamb, probably just before he entered on his discussion with the wolf. Take this lamb technically, I cannot conceive of anything more innocent and childlike; it would be simply absurd to attempt to copy such a drawing and yet everything you want is in it. It shows Caldecott's marvellous power in expressing a whole story in a few lines, technically worthless for any one else; in his hands perfect. But the minute he went beyond this expression in pure outline, only to be surpassed by the cleverness of handling of Caran D'Ache and the Japanese, he began to fall off. Caldecott was not able to express with many lines what he could indicate with one. If a man can express so much in one line as he did, he is really great; no one can follow him. If you have the same ability, you can do the same thing in your way; if you have not, your imitation of his way is sure to be artless and valueless. I know it will be said that there are cases in which Caldecott drew figures and elaborated landscape well; perhaps there are, but they are very rare exceptions, and even in these exceptions his work cannot be compared with Charles Keene. What I want to show is every man's best work, and what I have shown is, I think, Caldecott's. (pp. 231-32)

> *Joseph Pennell, "Of Pen Drawing in England," in his* Pen Drawing and Pen Draughtsmen: Their Work and Their Methods, *The Macmillan Company, 1920, pp. 183-270.*

JACQUELINE OVERTON

There is a sense of freedom in all [Caldecott's] drawing—never was an artist who could tell so much with so few lines—he knew his power in that direction and delighted in it. But Caldecott's sketches were not dashed off as quickly as one might imagine. (p. 116)

[It was] about 1877 or 78 that he began the work that will probably be longest remembered—his picture books, and again Edmund Evans is to be thanked for urging him to do them. Walter Crane's toy books had established a high standard, and before beginning his own work in that field Caldecott went to call on Crane to ask his advice about contracts with publishers, etc. A most congenial friendship resulted and Walter Crane was always generous in his praise of Caldecott's work.

Leslie Brooke, an artist of today, who "upholds the fine tradition of English picture-book making established by Walter Crane and Randolph Caldecott," says that "Caldecott is an extreme instance of instinctive drawing," and never is that more truly shown than in his picture books. One feels he let himself go for the children, and all his natural sweetness and gayety of spirit, all his love of life out-of-doors and particularly the English out-of-doors are reflected from the pages of the old nursery jingles, full of children and old folks, huntsmen and country characters. Animals abound in them, horses and dogs and birds—the pages are full of action. Was ever so hurly-burly a chase imagined as that instituted by those "headlong, horn-blowing, cheek-bursting and hopelessly futile Three Jovial Huntsmen?"

A Farmer Went Trotting Upon His Grey Mare, John Gilpin's Ride and *The Fox Jumped Over the Parson's Gate* were subjects after his own heart, while England in the spring comes out of every page of *The House that Jack Built, The Farmer's Boy* and the old May Day ballad, *Come Lasses and Lads.*

The Queen of Hearts, A Frog He Would a-Wooing Go, Hey Diddle Diddle and *Sing a Song for Sixpence* are all treated in a cozy, homey manner with enough tarts, blackbird pies, pots of honey and frosted cakes about to make one's mouth water.

Austin Dobson says that in his picture books Caldecott's pencil "played the most engaging variations. Who, for example, ever before conceived of Madam Blaize as a pawnbroker, because—

> She freely gave to all the poor,
> Who left a pledge behind?

And where else had the world been shown the authentic, academic presence, the very 'form and pressure' of the 'Great Panjandrum Himself,' with the little round button on top?"

Those who were familiar with the country around Whitchurch were always discovering familiar bits in Caldecott's picture books. He must have loved Malpas Church tower for it appears in no less than three books: *Baby Bunting, The Fox Jumps Over the Parson's Gate* and the *Babes in the Woods,* while you can walk down the main street of Whitchurch just by opening *The Great Panjandrum.* . . . (pp. 117-18)

There never have been any picture books quite like these of Caldecott's, before nor since. The spirit of them is so fine and gentle, the fun in them so real that they make a never-ending appeal to children and grown people alike, who have a love of beauty and action. Originally they were published singly in paper cover for a shilling. Later, an edition was published of several bound together in three books: *Picture Book No. 1, Picture Book No. 2* and *The Panjandrum Picture Book.* Still later the toy books were all bound together in a large edition entitled *The Complete Collection of Pictures and Songs.* . . . (p. 118)

In the summer of 1878 he and Mr. Blackburn made a trip into Brittany that delighted Caldecott's sense of the picturesque. (p. 119)

Mr. Blackburn writes: "Apart from the artistic material so abundant everywhere, Caldecott's love of animals and knowledge of them, his interest in everything connected with farming, markets, country life and surroundings, roused him to exertions at Carhaix which none but the most hardy 'special artist' would have attempted. . . . He made some extraordinary rapid sketches in colour with the brush direct, without a touch of the pencil or anything to guide him. Few sketches of this kind exist, excepting rough notes in books not intended for the public. In the evening the figures in the streets and at the inns had to be noted down."

Caldecott and Mrs. Ewing met in London in 1879, when "*Jackanapes* was simmering in her brain." She had greatly admired his work and wanted him to illustrate for her, and he was the ideal person to do it, for they had many tastes and interests in common. He made the pictures for *Jackanapes,* that splendid story of a gallant boy and a gallant horse, also for *Daddy Darwin's Dovecot,* in which he drew birds to his heart's content, and for *Lob Lie-By-The-Fire,* and they might have done many more things together had their lives been spared.

In speaking of Caldecott's love of birds one must not forget a charming little vellum-bound book called *The Owls of Olynn Belfry.* The author bears the initials A.Y.D., the book bears no date at all, so that it is difficult to know when the drawings were made. It is seldom we find him picturing a fairy, but there is a delightful Fairy Queen in this book, dancing the minuet with a portly old owl. (pp. 119-20)

> *Jacqueline Overton, "'Tuppence Colored': Walter Crane, Randolph Caldecott and Kate Greenaway," in Contemporary Illustrators of Children's Books, edited by Bertha E. Mahony and Elinor Whitney, 1930. Reprint by Gale Research Company, 1978, pp. 110-25.*

F. J. HARVEY DARTON

[*The following excerpt was originally published in 1932.*]

[Three artists of the 1860s], in spite of other work, have come to be regarded in a special degree as benefactors of the young—Randolph Caldecott, Walter Crane and Kate Greenaway. They made the modern 'picture-book'.

Of the three, Caldecott had the most robust and, so to speak, humane personality. The other two seem like artists first and ordinary people afterwards. You always feel that Caldecott is not thinking of a picture, but of folk and lovable dogs and horses and flesh-and-blood hybrids like his fellow-Englishmen. When he illustrated the *Elegy on the Death of a Mad Dog* . . . , he saw with Goldsmith's own humorous eyes:

> The dog and man at first were friends;
>   But when a pique began,
> The dog, to gain some private ends,
>   Went mad, and bit the man.

It is quite clear, from the pictures, that that is what did happen; from the persons drawn, it is inevitable. Those *must* have been the adventures of even so excellent a man, and of a capering dog to whose burial marched six black Cocker spaniels with

Illustration from Hey Diddle Diddle *(1882).*

long silky ears. You understand the man and the dog, and their feelings, and Goldsmith's feelings. Caldecott understood men and dogs too, and that was the secret: he *liked* them, as Goldsmith did.

His early death . . . was a great loss, and though to some extent (chiefly for 'grown-up' books) his place was filled by the no less lovable Hugh Thomson, no other artist quite united so easily as he for children the qualities of humour, draughtsmanship and intuitive interpretation. He did not become part of his authors to the same extent as, say, Tenniel in *Alice* or Hughes in *Sing-Song.* But he could identify himself as fully with new work—in the illustrations to Mrs Ewing's tales, for example—as with the old which he lifted out of the costume-piece atmosphere into reality. Pictures were like speech or writing to him: his natural talk. (pp. 277-78)

> *F. J. Harvey Darton, "The Sixties: 'Alice' and After,"*
> *in his* Children's Books in England: Five Centuries
> of Social Life, *third edition, Cambridge University*
> *Press, 1982, pp. 252-92.*

BERTHA MAHONY MILLER

Walter Crane, Randolph Caldecott, Kate Greenaway are three great names in the history of picture books and books for children. (p. 674)

Randolph Caldecott's Picture Books are all in print and they have a simplicity, and economy and verve of line that are distinctly modern, or rather, ageless. Caldecott's drawings picture an English countryside and leisurely way of life of a passed time but they picture it with humor, gaiety and merry kindness. And while the times in which Caldecott lived were more leisurely than ours, there's a lot of speed in his Picture Books. *The Three Jovial Huntsmen,*—stronger as riders than as philosophers—ride up hill and down dale and stop to look and comment upon this and that. . . . A colored full-page picture records their stopping places, but the fast black and white drawings show them at canter or gallop. . . . And surely no one has run faster through the pages of a book (unless it is William Nicholson's "Clever Bill") than Caldecott's *John Gilpin.* His *Fox Jumps over the Parson's Gate,* and the Hounds after him go, *The Farmer goes Trotting upon his Grey Mare,*

a little boy and his sister *Ride a Cock-Horse to Banbury Cross, Hey Diddle, Diddle,* The Cat and the Fiddle, The Cow jumps over the Moon, and the villagers run wildly from *The Mad Dog* but the dog dies at the end from the man-bite and not the other way around. *The Queen of Hearts, Sing-a-Song for Six-pence, The Milkmaid, Come Lasses and Lads, A Frog He Would a-wooing Go, The Great Panjandrum Himself*—there's life and fun and nonsense in all of them—in all except *Babes in the Wood;* that is too sad for most little children. Whether it was an old nursery song like *The Farmer's Boy,* or a folkish tale like *Mrs. Mary Blaize,* Caldecott put into his books the folk he saw in his part of England and the funny way he saw them.

We tend in these times of ours to be too serious, too earnest. There is too little gaiety. Too little nonsense. Some families, ours included, treasure the books of Randolph Caldecott . . . for the gaiety and the nonsense that is in them. Ever since our grand-daughter was two years old, whenever she has come to visit us, we have placed the *Caldecott Picture Books* on a table beside her bed for early morning perusal. Now she is six and still enjoying them. One summer recently a little Finnish girl was a member of our household. She was four years old, had been living with her father and mother on a remote farm and spoke only Finnish. When she appeared in my study at inopportune times, as she often did, the *Caldecott Picture Books* could be depended upon for nearly an hour's quiet, absorbing interest, the black and white drawings giving just as much pleasure as the colored ones. At the end of the summer Thelma could "read" *The House That Jack Built.*

It is one of the wonderful, magic things of our world that the work of a happy-hearted young man born almost a hundred years ago should be delighting young and old today. (pp. 674-76)

[Caldecott] is described by more than one friend as being "the very embodiment of sweetness, simple-mindedness, generosity and honour." All these qualities are in his Picture Books . . . and in all his work. But there is also that gay and vigorous humor, sometimes nonsensical, which has gone flowing through the years, brightening days for those who have had the good fortune to meet it and putting its impress upon later artists, Hugh Thomson and L. Leslie Brooke, among others. (p. 677)

> *Bertha Mahony Miller, "Caldecott's Picture Books,"*
> *in* Publishers Weekly, *Vol. 132, No. 9, August 28,*
> *1937, pp. 674-77.*

ANNE THAXTER EATON

The Randolph Caldecott picture books . . . should be on a child's bookshelves along with Mother Goose. The poems and verses which he illustrates have the swing and rhythm a child enjoys, and his drawings provide a whole gallery of vigorous figures in lively humorous situations. *The Farmer's Boy* with its animals is a fine first picture book for the baby, to be followed as he grows older by all the rest of the delightful Caldecott volumes. . . . (p. 52)

Caldecott's pictures have the action which so delights the youngest children: away go the Three Jovial Huntsmen, horns blowing, red coats flashing; out into the village street run the wondering neighbors in *An Elegy on the Death of a Mad Dog;* John Gilpin, visibly breathless, is whisked along wigless; and in *Come, Lasses and Lads* the boys and girls seem literally to "jig it, jig it, jig it" from page to page. This great draftsman has, however, given us more than motion and typical English landscapes, for he presents us with whole communities of real individuals. Examine attentively the faces in *The Diverting History of John Gilpin,* in *Mrs. Blaize,* and in *A Farmer Went*

Trotting; notice the expression on the faces in *Come, Lasses and Lads,* from the young folk who dance around the Maypole to the stern parent awaiting the belated return of her daughters, and we realize why it is that Caldecott can never be outgrown and why those interested in fine draftsmanship and in humorous observation of human nature turn back to him all their lives to find refreshment. (pp. 283-84)

Anne Thaxter Eaton, "Through Magic Doorways," and "Artists at Work for Children," in her Reading with Children, The Viking Press, 1940, pp. 41-64, 281-309.

BEATRIX POTTER

[*The following excerpt is from a letter to the American librarian Jacqueline Overton.*]

I never met Caldecott. My father bought some of his work, through a dealer, and he could easily have made Caldecott's acquaintance; but he did not do so.

We bought his picture books eagerly, as they came out. I have the greatest admiration for his work—a jealous appreciation; for I think that others, whose names are commonly bracketted with his, are not on the same plane at all as artist-illustrators. For instance, Kate Greenaway's pictures are very charming, but compared with Caldecott—she could not draw. Others who have followed him were careful, correct draughtsmen, but lifeless and wooden. Besides; Walter Crane and Caldecott were the pioneers; their successors were imitators only. (pp. 180-81)

No doubt Caldecott's health affected his work—he was consumptive. How sorry we were to hear of his breakdowns. . . . We were all interested when he achieved success, because he had been a clerk in a Manchester bank. He must certainly have had some art training, for instance in perspective, but I gathered that he was an original genius. . . . What one remembers is the tragedy of his lungs. But he had reached the summit. He would never have done finer work than *John Gilpin.* The later picture books declined a little; though there is one of my first favourites in the last—the *Great Panjandrum*—the maid and the cabbage leaf. I *know*—because *I* tried to draw cabbages when I drew *Peter Rabbit.* (p. 181)

He was one of the greatest illustrators of all. (p. 183)

Beatrix Potter, in a letter to Jacqueline Overton on April 7, 1942, in her Beatrix Potter's Americans: Selected Letters, edited by Jane Crowell Morse, The Horn Book, Inc., 1982, pp. 180-83.

ALICE M. JORDAN

All across America, from Maine to California, in the children's rooms of the public libraries, March will have special significance this year of the centenary of Kate Greenaway and Randolph Caldecott. For it is, happily, through the libraries that their picture books are kept in perpetual remembrance. . . .

And in many a story hour for little children the pictures of these two artists will be shown, lest they be missed in the abundance of more recent books. However, the librarians guard against that, as no picture book lists are considered complete without the names of Randolph Caldecott and Kate Greenaway. (p. 9)

While we think of Kate Greenaway as capturing the sweetness of childhood in her books for children, we do not expect from her the sheer rollicking fun that we find in Randolph Caldecott. His incomparable *Picture Books* are among the "musts" for every young child. Discerning elder relatives in the United States are wont to choose *The Farmer's Boy* . . . as a first book for a new grandchild. Where else will you find all the farm animals so expressively portrayed? (pp. 11-12)

First of the sixteen picture books, *The Diverting History of John Gilpin,* was published in 1878, and I know of one family in which the third generation is now enjoying that precious early edition . . . in all its fresh colour and clarity of line. Maybe the paper covers are worn by much handling, but the original gaiety and grace are there for the children to see. . . . (p. 12)

And how spontaneous is the fun, how free and untrammelled the fancy, how lively the action, how rich the details on every page! Apart from Caldecott's sure feeling for colour, which brightens some of the scenes, his work in black and white invites repeated study. Note the faces of the three purposeful customers, whose entrance to the linen draper's shop delays John Gilpin while the chaise, bearing six precious souls, rattles down Cheapside, tagged by a fringe of reckless urchins. What variety of expression lightens the faces of the bystanders and participants, as the famous ride follows its destined course, and the pursuit ends ineptly, even as Gilpin reaches home.

Besides *The Diverting History of John Gilpin,* two other long poems are included in the picture book group, inspired by the eminent engraver and printer, Edmund Evans, whose ability and discerning taste meant so much to both Caldecott and Kate Greenaway. These are the *Elegy on a Mad Dog* and *Mrs. Mary Blaize;* all the others are chosen from nursery rhymes and tales.

In these humorous poems there is full play for the wit and vivacity so thoroughly enjoyed by adults, who can see the comic side of human nature, and appreciate the hand of caricature, in the *Punch* tradition.

Anyone examining Caldecott's illustrations for these memorable *Picture Books* cannot fail to be captivated by his masterly treatment of animals. With dogs of all sorts he must have had a secret understanding, for every breed comes alive from tip of ear to end of tail, at his touch. Few of these nursery books lack pictures of them. There is the expressive circle surrounding the mad dog at his death, there are the panting escorts of Gilpin's wild flight, the pack of hounds in *The Three Jovial Huntsmen,* the mischievous puppy who worries the cat, the dogs who accompany the young squire, as he sets forth to seek his fortune, in *The Milkmaid* (but here, we believe, the cows are more important).

Caldecott liked horses, too, both for drawing and riding. His choice of subjects gives play to his keen studies of the workhorse, the hunter, and the family horse. All the inhabitants of the barnyard, from horses to ducks, have a place in *The Farmer's Boy,* for that young lad must needs care for them all. Here the lambs playing round him, as he pipes to them, are very engaging, and here the pigs take on individuality.

In no less fascinating manner Caldecott presents the humblest types in the animal world, the red fox who jumps over the parson's gate, and the troublesome raven; he enlarges upon the inimitable graces of Miss Mousey, as she coyly accepts the wooing of Mr. Frog, and introduces a host of birds and domestic fowls. Only one who really knew rural life could ever have drawn the splendid cock greeting the morn, the noisy blackbirds who came out of the pie, the lily white duck, the flock of geese.

Children, everywhere, who are fortunate enough to possess the matchless *Picture Books,* thus have a source of unfailing pleasure all through their nursery years, and beyond.

But Randolph Caldecott has given American children more than laughter, priceless though it be. By his skilful artistry he introduces them to English landscape, with its rivers and trees, the hunting field, the farm with its cows and milkmaids, villages at festival time, with a merry Maypole dance, towns and their rows of neat, red brick houses with casement windows. These all broaden the horizon in a mechanized age.

Out of the Caldecott books we draw a sense of companionship with the man himself. He seems to share with us his quick warm sympathies, his kindly understanding of animal and human foibles, his wholesome mirth. His personality must have been rare and lovable; it is no wonder that children hovered over him as he sketched. (pp. 12-14)

> *Alice M. Jordan, "Kate Greenaway and Randolph Caldecott: An American Tribute," in* The Junior Bookshelf, *Vol. 10, No. 1, March, 1946, pp. 9-14.*

ELEANOR GRAHAM

We remember Randolph Caldecott chiefly for his Picture Books, which contain the very essence of the English country life. . . . (p. 21)

[During] 1878 he was studying the question of "the art of leaving out." . . . [His] strength of line is well shown in nearly all his Picture Book work. (p. 25)

Walter Crane sounds wistful in reported comments on the great success of Caldecott's Picture Books, and Kate Greenaway seems to have felt him as something of a rival of her own, even while she appreciated the greater strength of his work. Crane has, I suppose, suffered most in the passage of time, Caldecott least. Human nature changes little, and his observation was deep and shrewd. He used more reality than imagination and tempered everything he did with a robust wit, never smirched by archness. (pp. 26-7)

> *Eleanor Graham, "Randolph Caldecott," in* The Junior Bookshelf, *Vol. 10, No. 1, March, 1946, pp. 21-7.*

HILDA VAN STOCKUM

Few artists have achieved so much in so short a time as Randolph Caldecott. Perhaps he felt that he would not live long, for his work matured surprisingly fast. When he illustrated Washington Irving's *Old Christmas* and *Bracebridge Hall,* he was still influenced by the style of the period with its intricate shading. We have to know him well to recognize his hand in those pictures. His early drawings for *The Graphic* are also less original and vigorous than the later ones, but he soon gets into his stride and his illustrations for *Æsop's Fables* and Mrs. Ewing's books—*Jackanapes, Daddy Darwin's Dovecot, Lob Lie-by-the-Fire*—are masterful.

It is, however, to Caldecott's Picture Books that I am confining this paper—those books which I knew and loved as a child—as this gives me the advantage of two points of view, one of the past, the other of the present. Thinking of those early years, made bright by Walter Crane, Kate Greenaway, Tenniel, Leslie Brooke, Beatrix Potter, Elsa Beskow, Willebeek Le Mair and, of course, Caldecott, I notice a peculiar thing. Whereas the other artists have all left me a legacy of definite, stationary pictures which I can pull out of the cupboard of my mind and examine at leisure—the goose that WAS a goose, Peter Rabbit

entangled in a net, Alice swimming in her tears—I don't remember any particular picture of Caldecott. But at the sound of his name, as to the tune of a Pied Piper, a procession of little figures comes dancing past—horses with red-coated riders, shaggy dogs, loving couples, children, kings, queens, dishes, and a cow jumping over a moon. So I have come to the conclusion that Caldecott provided me with my first movies.

When leafing through his Picture Books it is this ebb and flow of perpetual motion which strikes one first. Other artists like to dwell on the scenes they are creating, either from contemplative joy in their beauty or from a psychological joy in their social values. Not so Caldecott. He is always aiming at the next picture; his very figures seem to be pointing to it; one cannot wait to turn the page and see what happens next. I even have an odd feeling that if one kept one's hand still the pages would turn over by themselves!

As an artist, I am interested to see how Caldecott achieves this effect of continuous movement. I think he does it through a lavish use of horizons; his people are either coming at you, large as life, or vanishing over a hill. You can never be sure of them; now they're here, now they're gone. There lies the great contrast with Leslie Brooke, who belongs to the "Come-gather-round-and-I'll-tell-you-a story" kind of drawing. One has a sense of living in Johnny Crow's Garden; but if one day John Gilpin should fail to slow down and leaped headlong from the white cliffs of Dover, no one would feel surprised.

It is this vigorous action which endears Caldecott to children, who don't look at pictures to admire, but to participate. As a daughter of mine put it, they want to be "in the book."

The next characteristic of Caldecott's work seems to me to be its joyousness. When I had grown up, and hadn't looked at my old Picture Books for a long time, I happened to pick up one day *The Three Jovial Huntsmen.* Wave upon wave of scarce remembered happiness came sweeping over me, tumbling me back into the wonderland of childhood. Of course, to me, *Three Jovial Huntsmen* is the most typically Caldecott of all his books. It is the one that comes first to mind. And it is also the most English of his books, with its Pickwickian characters. It starts off with that lovely house—doesn't it speak of early morning tea, roaring fires, plum pudding and punch? The joviality of the huntsmen is apparent right away, when the middle one salutes the sparrows. It is obvious he has nothing on his mind, has a good digestion, and is prepared to find anything on God's earth entertaining. They are kind huntsmen, too; they pity the poor scarecrow, cheering him up, for he strains after them rapturously as they career away again over several more pages. They are like small boys, detached and happy, examining everything they meet. Next, it is a stupid old grindlestone who becomes so enamored of them that it pursues them to the indignation of the farmer and his wife and their scandalized house.

No wonder the huntsmen are exhausted after all that. The reader can rest for a moment as they mop their brows and allow their horses to drink. But soon they are off again, greeting a calf who responds to their merry mood as do the children, who wouldn't be children if they didn't. The pig, however, in the nakedness of his complacency, scares the huntsmen back into the open where one of them promptly comes to grief, showing the proper use of his horn. Meanwhile Mr. Caldecott shows us the proper use of the pen, drawing with a few strokes a drama in the distance: the other huntsmen discover their loss and, veering round, lead back the riderless steed.

Finally they come to the climax of their trip and frighten a loving couple out of their wits like the bad boys they are. Then back again to their comfortable house as the sun goes down. One senses the healthy glow of the hunters in the still evening light, and their complete love for one another. Here is all the exuberance and consolation of childhood. And one feels one has made the trip oneself and leans back to rest a while.

Let us take two versions of *John Gilpin*—the one illustrated by Caldecott, the other done a little later by Charles E. Brock. It is obvious that Mr. Brock has seen Caldecott's work and admired it. His characters have a strong resemblance to Caldecott's, even to the details of clothing. Otherwise the style is quite different. Mr. Brock makes precious, shaded pictures, very beautiful in themselves but not suited to the spirit of the poem. There is such a shining finish of detail that the story limps with it, whereas one races through Caldecott's with a flicker of pages. Also, Caldecott gives his scenery a generous share in the action, while Mr. Brock's backgrounds could be moved from one picture to another without affecting the story at all.

This participation of nature in Caldecott's pictures is seen, for instance, in the colored picture where John Gilpin tries to turn his horse around. Here the swallows dance madly about in the air, the donkey brays dismally, and the distant houses prick up their chimneys. Even when Mr. Caldecott's houses are indifferent they are purposely so: they seem to be saying, "I'm only a house, I'm not in on this; you can't expect it of me." Whereas Mr. Brock's houses aren't saying anything, but seem to have strayed out of a book on "how to draw houses in correct light and shade." This is not to run down Mr. Brock, who draws charmingly, but to use him as a yardstick by which to measure Mr. Caldecott's excellence.

Every artist knows how easy it is to be led away from the main theme through interest in some detail; to enjoy drawing a tree, a horse, a gown, and forget the action. But Caldecott always sacrifices the lesser for the greater. If one line can do it, no two lines are used. Nor is he in love with line itself. . . . With Caldecott, the story is supreme. Even the grass on the ground adds to the general effect—either waving wildly or twinkling with merry little dots or regarding itself peacefully in a pond. When the "man all tattered and torn" in *The House that Jack Built* leads away "the maiden all forlorn" the daisies bow respectfully before the Power of Love.

One of my favorite books as a child was *The Queen of Hearts*. I always loved the King, he seemed so kind; and the Queen was so pretty, and their baby so adorable. Incidentally, only a democratic nation could produce pictures making such good-humored fun of royalty. The picture in which the royal family of Hearts saunter in the garden, and the King picks a blushing little flower for the Queen, is a masterpiece of irony. Mr. Caldecott doesn't believe a word of all this sweetness and light, but he is too polite to say so.

The knave is truly a knave, only one instantly guesses that he lacks the spirit to keep it up, while the cat knows it all. Can't you see her tail waving, "I told you so"? And doesn't she enjoy playing the informer, like a garrulous neighbor in a murder mystery? And oh, how his sin preys on the miserable knave who flees all glances while the clocktower points to eternal values. He gets away with his booty to the disgust of the town but now he thinks every moment that he has been discovered, especially when the Queen happens to use him as a target for her arrows. And when dinnertime comes, and four cherubs clamor in vain for the tarts, the major-domo is summoned. The cat is in the limelight again and explains it all, whereupon righteous anger descends upon the King—his very mustache cries to heaven. The knave gets a more passionate beating than ever was given with so few strokes, while the sobbing infants try to hold back the King and lose their crowns in the process.

Meanwhile a flirtatious King of Clubs has taken advantage of the situation and is dancing with the Queen.

The cat's sense of justice is satisfied and she purrs as she watches the knave chased forth by the jeers of his colleagues. But the end is not yet. Sniffling, the knave returns the tarts to the enthusiastic infants and then breaks down utterly, unable even to hold up his halberd, after which he makes virtue out of necessity and it all ends with a great moral display upon which the skeptical Mr. Caldecott declines to comment further.

One could go on like this endlessly, enjoying story after story with all its silent byplay: Mr. Panjandrum actually explained; nursery rhymes receiving proper endings in the pictures, if not in the words; minor characters getting tacitly their due. Everywhere the same candid simplicity; no display of artistic fireworks, no pomposity, no evasion. Like a child, Mr. Caldecott goes to each work he illustrates, taking in all the meaning and all the ramifications of meaning and unstintingly bringing out each point. He is like his own jovial huntsmen—no creature is too mean for his attention, his affection, and his humor. And always, everywhere, this tremendous vitality and love of life in all its forms. How meager would be our knowledge of England, how many pictures poorer, without this great draughtsman who makes his country live for us—the ditches, the fields, the thin snow, the cottages, the towns and the wonderful ladies! Where else but in England can one find ladies and gentlemen at the drop of a hat?

So let us take off our hats to that deftest of all gentlemen, that humorist, that artist, that friend—RANDOLPH CALDECOTT. (pp. 119-25)

Hilda Van Stockum, "Caldecott's Pictures in Motion," in The Horn Book Magazine, *Vol. XXII, No. 2, March-April, 1946, pp. 119-25.*

MARIA CIMINO

It is good to be celebrating . . . the 100th anniversary of Kate Greenaway and Randolph Caldecott who were born within five days of each other. . . . Their names are well known and their books are beloved by the children who have been looking at their pictures all these years, unconsciously absorbing their first and for some perhaps their only, glimpse into English life and history. . . . [Who] can look at the robust and rollicking life in every line of Randolph Caldecott without feeling the very origins of the nursery rhymes and their commentary on English life, character and humor? (p. 652)

[Unlike Kate Greenaway,] Randolph Caldecott is not concerned with recapturing moods but rather with recreating situations, for there is nothing contemplative about a drawing by Randolph Caldecott. Instead, there is the situation, seen so keenly that one is convinced that it could not have been otherwise. One feels the activity of his imagination and how he is constantly thinking of every nuance and possibility that might contribute to the humor of a situation. His drawings move on the page with speed and vitality. His smallest stroke, in his most reposed drawing, is vibrant with the idea he is expressing. Nor are his pages crowded. The great wonder of it all is how much drama, sense of space and distance, period and personality he is able to convey with just a few lines.

All this is packed into the leisurely pages of his nursery rhymes. Here are the animals and people of England giving to small children their first glimpse into English folklore. Those remarkable **Three Jovial Huntsmen** who tell better than any serious book about England's great sport, hunting, how the countryside looks and how English country folk are. Boys twelve years old will read the rhyme aloud carried away by the rhythm and gusto of Caldecott's drawings, *"Look Ye There!"* A small girl, not yet two, turns again and again to **Hey Diddle Diddle** demanding the rhyme with long pauses at the page where the cow jumps over the moon. Then there is **The Queen of Hearts,** my own favorite. No valentine could be better than the wonderful picture sequence of humor for this rhyme. **The Farmer's Boy** grows better with each reading, there are so many new things to discover in the drawings. As for **John Gilpin,** never was such a profusion of animals and people so remarkably catapulted into John Gilpin's dilemma. The pages in full color tell much. Children linger over them, but they like even better the line drawings in Caldecott's picture books, for breathing space, where one may speculate upon the drama that went before and what is to follow. (pp. 652-53)

Maria Cimino, "K. G.—R. C.: 1846-1946," in Library Journal, Vol. 71, No. 9, May 1, 1946, pp. 652-53.

MARY GOULD DAVIS

When the children look at Randolph Caldecott's picture books they turn the pages very slowly. Each page tells a story, first in the action, then in the characters and, finally, in the little details that children love to linger over. Their eyes turn occasionally to the words on the opposite page, but only for a moment. Then they go back to the pictures. Often the poem or the nursery rhyme that is illustrated is known to them; but Randolph Caldecott's interpretation of that rhyme is a new and delightful adventure. Their eyes follow John Gilpin in his mad gallop over the countryside and through the narrow streets of an English village; they scan the wintry fields for the tiny distant figures of the Three Jovial Huntsmen; they linger soberly on the bedroom scene, in **The Babes in the Wood,** where the old Nurse brings the Babes to say good-bye to their dying parents. Little boys sometimes look slightly sheepish as they follow the romantic history of **A Frog He Would A-Wooing Go,** but little girls smile and glance at one another with that look that is purely feminine—and as old as Eve.

Caldecott's creative imagination is never more in evidence than in the story of the lovelorn frog. He is so gallant, so appealing in his green coat and pale blue waistcoat, with his hat under his arm and a bouquet of flowers for his ladylove in one hand. He is carrying a cane, too, and the people who are fishing in the river stare at him in admiration as he goes by. When he meets Mr. Rat and they start off together they are tiny figures in the background while, in the foreground, a mother and her two little girls sit under a tree and watch them.

It is when they come to Miss Mousie's house that the excitement really begins. How charming and demure she is in her white muslin dress with a wide ruffle around her neck and a pink sash tied around her slender waist! She serves them beer in tall glasses from a flagon that might be a family heirloom. Mr. Frog drinks freely, but his wooing is always uppermost is his mind. Little girls linger for a long time over the drawing where he is kissing Miss Mousie's tail, while Mr. Rat sits in

a chair against the wall with his legs crossed and the glass of beer in his hand. Mr. Rat does not look jealous; he looks bold and comfortable and perhaps a bit sleepy. . . . The drawing of "a cat and her kittens came tumbling in" is an original interpretation. It is good to hear the children chuckle over it. Here is Miss Mousie's cottage surrounded by trees, in green leaf, and a garden. A father, a mother and two children are standing in the path watching with interest while Mrs. Pussy, dressed in flowered muslin, creeps cautiously up the steps, followed by three kittens, also dressed in flowered muslin, their full skirts draped neatly over their tails. They look very respectable! Nevertheless, they get Mr. Rat and Miss Mousie, while Mr. Frog jumps out of the window—only to meet his tragic end when "a lily-white duck comes and gobbles him up."

It pleases the children that Caldecott made the King and Queen so youthful in **Sing a Song for Sixpence.** The interior of the counting house where the boy King is counting out his money repays long study. On the outside a footman has his ear pressed against the door while two agitated gentlemen, a Grenadier Guard, and another footman watch him anxiously. Inside, in the pleasant room, there is a clock, a calendar and a statue of St. George and the Dragon on the mantlepiece; and on the wall hang two very interesting paintings: one of Jack defying a truly terrible giant, and one of Robinson Crusoe and his man Friday. The crown is laid carefully on a velvet cushion on the table within reach of the King's hand. The Queen's parlor is even more repaying. The paintings on the wall there are of Red Riding Hood, The Babes in the Woods, and Bo-Peep. There is a very regal-looking doll sitting on a chair beside the Queen; and in a cupboard near by is a group of puppets—Italian, by the look of them. You may be very sure that the children miss none of this! How tempting the honey looks with the loaf of crusty bread beside it. And how good the jars of jam look in **The Queen of Hearts.** The children count them over: apricot,

Illustration from Sing a Song for Sixpence *(1880).*

black currant, peach, strawberry, raspberry, green gage, and three more jars that one cannot quite make out. (pp. 7-10)

Younger boys and girls have a great affection for Baby Bunting. That little round face beneath the famous "rabbit skin" when the baby stands on a chair, with the rabbit ears sticking up cockily and the "rear" of the skin dragging behind him, is irresistible. A nice touch is the drawing of the family dog, a spaniel, ears and tail up, following the baby's father when he starts off to shoot the rabbit. All that can be seen of father is the back of one foot disappearing around a corner of the wall; but you know exactly how the dog will feel if he is left behind.

Although one feels that Caldecott cared more for dogs than for cats, he has drawn some very effective members of the cat family. There is the family in *A Frog He Would A-Wooing Go*, there is the angry cat in *The House that Jack Built* and, best of all, there is the cat in *Hey Diddle Diddle* who played the fiddle so well. We see him first with the fiddle in his hands bowing graciously to four adorable children who are evidently lost in admiration of his powers. In another scene—the one when everyone begins to dance—the cow and the two pigs with rows of buttons up and down their fronts are just "stepping out" while the cat, dressed in a bright red coat, sits on a brick wall and fiddles vigorously. Even the two roosters are dancing, but "the little dog" sits quietly beside the wall and smiles. It is only later that he "laughs to see the sport." Over the two "dish ran away with the spoon" drawings the children spend a long time. How demure the Spoon looks as she sits on the bench with the Dish beside her. The cat is sitting on the dresser, still fiddling, and even the plates on the shelf above him have developed legs and are just about to jump down and join in the dance. . . . It is often the little boys who discover in *The Milkmaid* that the snobbish-looking grayhound who comes with the "Sir" is approaching the farm collie with the same question that his master is asking "the pretty maid." Obviously, he gets very much the same answer. In the last drawing the collie is chasing the grayhound out of the field as enthusiastically as the milkmaids are chasing the fine gentleman.

As one grows older the picture books that linger longest in memory are perhaps *The Three Jovial Huntsmen* and *The Fox Jumped Over the Parson's Gate*. Here is the very heart of England; the roads, the wintry fields, the graceful bared branches of the trees. As we follow the huntsmen the melody of

Do ye ken John Peel?

keeps time to their galloping feet. Is it the Parson's mother who sits flat on the ground with a horrified expression while the hounds stream through the garden? Although the hounds will stop for nothing, we must pause a moment to study the gravestones in the churchyard. Says one: "Underneath lie the remains of Peter Piper who Picked a Peck . . ." The next one is "erected to the memory of Timothy Blowhorn." You cannot quite read the inscription on the others in the drawing where Nancy is coming out of the church on the arm of her soldier, but how lovely Nancy is in her poke bonnet wreathed with daisies and her white dress and yellow sash. (pp. 10-13)

Perhaps Caldecott's most original interpretation is of Mrs. Mary Blaize in Dr. Goldsmith's poem. This picture book does not mean so much to the little children as it does to the older boys and girls who are able to appreciate its gentle satire. In "she freely lent to all the poor who left a pledge behind," Caldecott makes Mrs. Blaize a pawnbroker. She stands behind the counter in a very interesting shop holding a young gallant's watch, while with the other hand she pushes two coins toward him.

In the next drawing a less attractive gentleman is leaving his waistcoat on the counter while he hastily buttons his coat over the place left vacant. How cold, how hard her face is as she turns away from the man who is trying to get even a small sum for his golden heart. In this drawing the little "R.C." that appears on every one is traced on the tablet hanging from the counter. Doubtless, Mrs. Blaize kept it there to record her dubious transactions. We feel not too much regret as we come to the final picture of Mrs. Blaize being carried into the churchyard in her coffin.

Why did Caldecott make the Great Panjandrum Himself a college professor in cap and gown with a Latin Grammar under one arm and a very realistic bundle of switches in his hand? He completely loses his dignity—to the joy of the children—in the game of catch-as-catch-can, and after it is over he looks so utterly exhausted that we can only feel sorry for him. The Great She-bear in this book is an unfailing favorite. She walks sedately along the village street with its lovely vistas, her dress of muslin dotted with red roses, with her neat red shoes and a red sash. She is carrying a basket for her marketing and an umbrella. The people who turn to look at her are amused and interested—and not at all frightened.

The children's faces are very sober as they turn the pages of *The Babes in the Wood*. Three generations have grieved over their sad fate. How many grandfathers and grandmothers there must be today who remember vividly those two adorable children and the wicked uncle with his pointed red beard and his black velvet doublet and hose.

After Caldecott's death in 1886, Frederick Warne issued a facsimile of the original sketches in ink for *The House that Jack Built*. And in the Parker Collection is the notebook, of the same size as the picture books, in which he made, in pencil, the first sketches for *The Babes in the Wood*. Most of his notebooks are the "pocket" kind, long and narrow, bound in black cloth. There are twelve of them in the Parker Collection, and one can spend hours, even days, going over them. It is fascinating to trace the evolution of the scenes and the characters in the picture books. Here are the five mournful hounds who grieve over the death of the Mad Dog. It is a source of great satisfaction to the children that, in the finished design, Caldecott added the impressive black-edged card inscribed "In Memory of Toby." In the notebooks, too, are the hens and roosters that appear in *The Farmer's Boy*, and the swans. There are also many studies of pigs.

Pages are filled with the details of pigs: snouts, little eyes, tails, backs, legs. It is interesting to note the difference between Caldecott's pigs and the pigs of Leslie Brooke, who so worthily upheld the Caldecott tradition in English picture books. Leslie Brooke drew many of his pigs as reputable citizens of an orderly world, living in neat well-furnished cottages with portraits of their porcine ancestors hanging on the walls. Caldecott's pigs are more realistic. See them at the trough, waiting to be fed, in *The Farmer's Boy*. See the one wallowing happily in the mud in *The House that Jack Built*. True, the pigs who are dancing in *Hey Diddle Diddle* have rows of elegant buttons up and down their fronts. And, in *The Farmer's Boy*, there is an elderly pig in spectacles who is laboriously spelling out the word "Mary" with blocks. In *The Three Jovial Huntsmen* the pig is fat and jolly. . . . Perhaps the most convincing pig of all is indicated in an early notebook and found in its final form in Hallam Tennyson's rhymed version of *Jack and the Beanstalk*, published by Macmillan in the year of Caldecott's death.

The studies of birds in the notebooks are especially interesting. Every possible detail is drawn, with marginal notes indicating corrections to be made for the final drawings. The notebooks are not always dated, so one does not know how many of these penciled sketches formed the basis for the hens and roosters, the ducks and swans in the picture books. Some were probably used for the illustrations in Mrs. Frederick Locker's *What the Blackbird Said*. Possibly Caldecott used them in his oil paintings of storks and pelicans for decorative screens. (pp. 10-17)

The Caroline Miller Parker Collection at The Houghton Memorial Library at Harvard has many of the original drawings for the picture books, as well as the pocket notebooks, many first editions and a collection of personal letters. In The New York Public Library is one page of the original drawings for *John Gilpin*. In their publication, year after year, the picture books have had unbroken continuity. . . . Today, after two world wars and the bombing of London, all four of the volumes bound in boards and fourteen out of the sixteen single volumes are available. The enchanting little "miniature" edition is out of print. The Parker Collection has the full set in single volumes and one copy of the four bound in boards. (pp. 20-1)

[Children] have learned to think of England as Caldecott drew it—the England that can never die. Not the thing that man's hands have fashioned and that can be destroyed, but the very land itself: the fields that are green again with every spring, the little hills of Shropshire softly rounded against the sky, the walled gardens and quiet churchyards. Even the most exacting expert can find no fault with Caldecott's drawing of the domestic animals, while his humor, his tolerance, his integrity as an artist bring his people to life on every page—all sorts and kinds of people from the members of Parliament to the kindly, weather-beaten old farmers at the cattle fairs.

That contemporary artists appreciated Caldecott's work is shown by the tributes paid him at the memorial exhibition of his pictures in Manchester in 1888. It was held at the Brasenose Club; and the official catalogue in the Parker Collection quotes the speeches from famous people of the day. Vincent van Gogh valued his sketches highly. In a letter to Anton Ridder van Rappard in 1883 he speaks of collecting the sketches published in English magazines: "Caldecott does such splendid work," he says. There is a nice tribute to him from a contemporary (now known only as A.T-B), in the preface to the facsimile edition of the first sketches for *John Gilpin*. "For Randolph Caldecott was a creator," he says, "a maker of types, and we have waited for him long. Once and for all he has shown us John Gilpin, once and for all the Man that the Mad Dog Bit and the Mad Dog itself, and the Three Jolly Huntsmen and many an old friend more." (pp. 21-2)

As long as books exist and there are children to enjoy them, boys and girls—and their elders—will turn the pages of the Caldecott picture books. They will follow John Gilpin's wild ride through pages that glow with vitality and color. They will feel the cold of the wintry English fields with the Three Jovial Huntsmen. They will grieve with the robins who covered the tiny bodies of the Babes in the Woods with autumn leaves, and laugh with the pigs who danced to the cat's fiddle. They will sit with the little Queen in her parlor "eating bread and honey" and walk with the lady-bear along the streets of an English village. New artists, new trends, new techniques will come and be welcomed. But Randolph Caldecott and his engraver, Edmund Evans, will remain unchallenged in their field. (p. 22)

[The "modern instances" in *Some of Aesop's Fables with Modern Instances*] have little appeal to children and they are definitely dated. Otherwise, boys and girls would like the drawings for the *Fables*. Among them are some of Caldecott's most expressive dogs. (p. 30)

Caldecott's feeling for birds must have made his drawings for *Daddy Darwin's Dovecot* a labor of love. His pocket notebooks are filled with the details of birds, some of them with penciled notes beside them indicating changes that he would make in the finished drawing—little directions like "longer beak" or "front hock like this" or "inside hock." . . . In 1881 George Routledge published Mrs. Frederick Locker's little book *What the Blackbird Said*. It was illustrated by Caldecott with four drawings in black and white, showing three birds, a robin, a blackbird and a rook—or crow.

Another proof of his skill in making birds express all sorts of emotions is in the illustrations for a book called *The Owls of Olynn Belfry*. We do not know just who the author, A. Y. D., is but we feel fairly certain that she was a lady. . . . Caldecott's characterization of the owls is individual and amusing and some of the other drawings are lovely in design. There is one of the homesick governess, Mlle. Marie, sitting under a tree pining for her native France. In the setting of an English garden she looks very French—and very attractive. There is a scene showing a churchyard with figures of the village people in the foreground and the church and belfry in the background. Best of all is a drawing, that would delight the children, of the old owl solemnly leading a tiny and exquisite fairy queen in a quadrille. The old gentleman is in formal evening clothes and is a bit conscious of his feet. He is pointing them neatly, but they are an owl's claws just as his head is an owl's head, with its wise eyes and rather prissy mouth.

We do not know just when Caldecott made the drawings for Hallam Tennyson's rhymed version of *Jack and the Beanstalk*. It was published by Macmillan in the year of his death—1886. Some of the drawings are in pencil, unfinished, but so well engraved that they are as clear as crystal. His treatment of the contrast in size between Jack and the giant and his wife is fascinating. The giant's house, his possessions and his wife are all in scale. Jack is always a tiny, defiant figure in the foreground. There is mischief and courage in every line of him. How children today would love these drawings! The giant is huge and clumsy and rather stupid, but his wife is a jolly, roly-poly person. The only thing about her that is frightening is that she is unusually *large*. The castle, as Jack sees it from the top of the beanstalk, is a thing of dreams—piled towers and turrets against the sky. The quality of humor in this book reminds us a little of Frank R. Stockton and his illustrator—E. B. Bensell. While Jack stands at the door of the giant's kitchen, watching the giant's wife and unseen by her, she is carefully basting a young elephant which she is evidently preparing for her husband's dinner. Neatly trussed and stuffed it lies in the huge pan on its side, looking very brown and tempting. In the drawing where Jack has the hen under his arm and is rushing for the beanstalk, he is running so fast that you can feel the push of the wind against him. This tale has been a favorite with the children for centuries. It would be very exciting if the children of today could have Caldecott's interpretation of it.

While he was making these illustrations and working away at his painting and modeling, the picture books were parading gaily in to and out of the presses. Boys and girls were claiming them, and they were winning praise from even the most carping critics of art and literature. . . . How many members of an older generation in America today think of the English countryside in terms of Caldecott's fields and farmyards and village streets? When we see England for the first time it is familiar to many of us because we knew as children the Caldecott picture books. (pp. 37-40)

It is tragic that he could not have lived to picture the American scene. His tolerance and gaiety, his genius for background and characterization might have made a record of great and lasting value. (p. 40)

Beside his published drawings Caldecott made drawings for two alphabets. They are both in color, four and three-quarter inches by four and five-eighths. The "sporting" alphabet is in rich browns and greens and yellows, illustrating scenes of hunting, fishing, rowing, swimming, etc. The other one is very much like the picture books. In it his humor and his imagination are given full play. In the drawing that represents the letter U a man is walking along a village street in the rain carrying a very impressive umbrella. At his feet stands a tiny green frog who is apparently just getting ready to walk along beside him. He carries a large green lily pad! Both these alphabets are now in the Parker Collection. (p. 42)

It is easy to see in both his letters and his sketches that *people* fascinated Caldecott—all sorts and kinds of people. If he saw them as slightly ridiculous, pompous, conceited or self-conscious he drew them that way. But there is no malice in his interpretation. They were figures in a scene that told a story—funny, sad, romantic, commonplace. Not even the smallest detail is left out of the story. It is all there for us to read.

His art stands, too, for the unchanging things—for the precious possessions that are common to all men; for the fields and hills and streams, for the flight of birds and the companionship of friendly animals, for the beauty of bare trees in winter and the delicate color and outline of their branches in spring. There was no fixed idea in his mind, apparently, of making an "arrangement" of his background and his models. There is always design, but it is Nature's design rather than his own. He saw things as they are. Even when he gives Miss Mousie a white muslin dress she remains a mouse; just as Mr. Frog in his green coat and flowered waistcoat remains unmistakably a frog. And through it all runs his humor, the gaiety that is to the children his most endearing quality. The laughter that is their tribute to him is quiet laughter; not loud guffaws, but a smile, that dawns in their eyes and touches their lips, or a low chuckle. He never puzzles them with broad caricature. To them he is always reasonable. Through his fertile imagination and his artist's skill they find the story—and are content. (pp. 42-4)

A fellow artist who knew [Caldecott] well said, after his death, that his name would "remain till the end of our art and literature a household word." He was speaking, probably, only of England. For his birthday party in 1946 we might blow out the hundred candles with one long, steady breath and wish that his name might be "a household word" to all the children of all the world. (p. 44)

> *Mary Gould Davis, in her* Randolph Caldecott, 1846-1886: An Appreciation, *J. B. Lippincott Company, 1946, 47 p.*

MARCIA BROWN

Some books for children can be returned to again and again, not only because the child enjoys repetition, but because he will always find in them the reward of enjoyment.

Such books are those of the artist whose name is given to the greatest honor we confer on an illustrator of children's books, Randolph Caldecott. From the insipid, oversweet atmosphere of many of our picture books today, it is like stepping out of doors into a fresh wind to enter his picture books. Here are vitality in every line, sweep, humor without acerbity that never had to worry about age-levels or suitability for children because it was born of rich observation of and enthusiasm for life itself. Here is such a thorough familiarity with the English countryside and its people that these scenes and characters could have sprung from no other soil. And all that is essential is clear to the youngest mind and yet stimulating to the adult who returns to it again and again. Much has happened in illustration and bookmaking since Caldecott's time, but the positive quality of his spirit remains in our best picture books. (p. 388)

> *Marcia Brown, "Distinction in Picture Books," in* The Horn Book Magazine, *Vol. XXV, No. 5, September-October, 1949, pp. 383-95.*

ANNE EATON

Never perhaps was there a maker of pictures for children who felt so instinctively what children want. Caldecott's animals come to life on the page, one feels the rush of wind that removed Gilpin's hat and wig as he galloped through Islington, one enters the cosy room with the Frog Who Would-A-Wooing Go, watches him gallantly kiss Miss Mouses's tail, while his friend, Mr. Rat, serenely sits in a chair against the wall and drinks a glass of beer. *The Farmer's Boy, The Three Jovial Huntsmen, The Fox Jumped Over the Parson's Gate* bring the English countryside before the reader's eyes. There are sly touches of character, the severe face glimpsed at the window tells us that the pretty maid late in returning from the Maypole dance in *Come Lasses and Lads,* will receive a grim welcome. To look at Caldecott's pictures is excellent training for children, never was so much told with such an economy of line. The fun in them is so genuine, the spirit so gay and at the same time so gentle that they are fine examples of true humour.

Caldecott illustrated three of Mrs. Ewing's books. They worked together happily, for they had much in common; each admired the other's work and when Mrs. Ewing was planning her famous *Jackanapes,* she asked Caldecott to make her a picture to "write to," saying that she knew he had profound sympathy with horses and he "must not be afraid to trust her with the ghost of a Posting House, horses, highwaymen and an old Postillion," though "if a coloured sketch would be easily concocted out of a laddie with an aureole of yellow hair on a red-haired pony full tilt among the geese over a village green," he was to give her "the decayed Postillion in pen-and-ink" [see excerpt dated August 4, 1879 for *Jackanapes* (1883)]. The frontispiece which Caldecott made to this specification is one of the best known and best loved of Caldecott's drawings. (pp. 252-53)

> *Anne Eaton, "Widening Horizons, 1840-1890: Illustrators Who Were More Than Illustrators," in* A Critical History of Children's Literature *by Cornelia Meigs and others, edited by Cornelia Meigs, Macmillan Publishing Company, 1953, pp. 244-58.*

ELIZABETH NESBITT

In the creation of picture books, Randolph Caldecott, Walter Crane and Kate Greenaway . . . established all-time precedents. Caldecott in particular set high standards of technical excellence, of imaginative insight, storytelling detail, humor and gayety, beauty of color and line and background. (p. 399)

> *Elizabeth Nesbitt, "A Rightful Heritage, 1890-1920: The March of Picture Books," in* A Critical History of Children's Literature *by Cornelia Meigs and others, edited by Cornelia Meigs, Macmillan Publishing Company, 1953, pp. 399-406.*

LILLIAN H. SMITH

To look at Randolph Caldecott's picture books is to find oneself in gay and lively company. His unfailing humor, his affectionate, observant interest in animals and his robust lighthearted enjoyment of the out-of-doors are found in all of his sixteen picture books for children. (p. 120)

A few words will supply Caldecott with ideas for many pictures. His pictured comments are not only on the bare text. His imagination seizes on all the successive steps, both before and after any situation, and on the byplay of minor as well as major characters who may or may not be mentioned in the text. It is as if he is saying to the children, "Look, this is how it all happened."

Caldecott's strength, which is the weakness of both Walter Crane and Kate Greenaway, is his power to give personality to both human and animal characters. His pen and ink sketches, often overlaid with bright but not gaudy color, are a study in expression with a minimum of line. Whether it is amusement, dejection, deference, disapproval, expansiveness or recoil, his drawing makes every emotion unmistakable and graphic. His nursery-rhyme picture books are full of action, humor and fancy and show to a high degree that essential quality of storytelling. (pp. 120-21)

> *Lillian H. Smith, "Picture Books," in her* The Unreluctant Years: A Critical Approach to Children's Literature, *American Library Association, 1953, pp. 114-29.*

FREDERICK LAWS

> This is the sort of book we like
> (For you and I are very small)
> With pictures stuck in anyhow
> And hardly any words at all.
>
> You will not understand a word
> Of all the words, including mine;
> Never you trouble; you can see
> And all directness is divine.
>
> Stand up and keep your childishness:
> Read all the pedants' screeds and strictures;
> But don't believe in anything
> That can't be told in coloured pictures.

G. K. Chesterton wrote these lines in a child's copy of one of Caldecott's picture books. It is high praise but well deserved. Randolph Caldecott's reputation is safe in the nursery. Babies today take as keen a delight in his picture books as their grandparents did, and prove themselves consistent art critics. This may explain why his work is neglected by adults and why he has been given no place in the hierarchy of English artists. He has, it is true, no claim to rank with those major artists whose work is as absolute as mathematics or philosophy. He lived within the limitations of his talent and had no ambition to be other than a good craftsman and a man of his time. But his talent was genuine and he used it well; some of the things he did were perfect in their kind. In a short life he proved himself

one of the great English illustrators. Caldecott was a good Victorian, and his marginal commentary on the way of living of his contemporaries lacks the preservative anger of the satirist who sees his contemporaries with the eyes of the future. But for all that his recording pencil was neither dishonest nor superficial. Caldecott was no political reformer like his rival Walter Crane, nor did he use his pencil to express a righteous indignation about the condition of England or the nature of man. There is good reason to suppose that he disliked the times he lived in, but it has to be deduced from what he left out of his pictures rather than from what he put in. (pp. 61-2)

In the Puritan cant of modern aesthetics he may be said to have 'escaped' from the ugly reality of his times to the country and the past. But his country was no fantasy world of a weekending Georgian. He knew country life from the small farmer's point of view and drew it without sentimentality. He sees the countryside not as landscape but as farming land or hunting country, and the people on it are not the nymphs and swains of pastoral convention. His shepherds shear their sheep and his milkmaids know how to milk. He had a remarkable visual memory and used his Whitchurch experience many years after he had left the place. Malpas Church can be recognized in three of the picture books, Whitchurch High Street in *The Great Panjandrum*, and a local inn line for line in *Old Christmas*.

It was at Whitchurch, too, that Caldecott's enthusiasm for hunting first developed. Following hounds was his favourite amusement. . . . Rather jealously Walter Crane wrote: 'I think perhaps he caught the more popular English taste to some extent by his introduction of the Sporting element. His *Three Jovial Huntsmen* will not easily be forgotten.' . . . His early work shows a great admiration for John Leech, though he lacked Leech's passion for accuracy of hunting detail. (pp. 63-4)

The poems which Caldecott raised almost to the true fame of anonymity included two by Oliver Goldsmith—the *Elegy on the Death of a Mad Dog* from *The Vicar of Wakefield* and his *Elegy On The Glory of Her Sex Mrs. Mary Blaize*. . . . Neither of these poems were meant for children though Goldsmith, through his friendship with [John] Newbery, wrote more for children than for adults. They are nonsense in a way, but the verbal nonsense of paradox and anti-climax, rather than the image-nonsense of dream poetry. Caldecott made them live by ignoring their critical wit and exploiting every 'sympathetic' touch for all it was worth. The Mad Dog himself is a famous charmer:

> The dog and man at first were friends
> But when a pique began,
> The dog, to gain some private ends,
> Went mad, and bit the man.

In three drawings Caldecott makes it clear that the friendship was based on the gift of bones, that the pique was a matter of jealousy of a cat and that the madness was an unfortunate private matter which 'the wondering neighbours' were impertinent to discuss.

Caldecott's choice of Robert Bloomfield's *Farmer's Boy* needs no explaining. It illustrates itself with a new animal on every page which those young persons who have learnt few words can nevertheless greet with appropriate noises. *John Gilpin* by William Cowper is more an older child's book. The riding and the misfortunes make active pictures, but babies may agree with Miss Greenaway that the accidents and sufferings of a nice old man are more distressing than funny.

Samuel Foote's **Great Panjandrum** is queerest of all. Foote wrote it to annoy the actor Macklin, famous for his Shylock. Macklin retired from the stage to keep a coffee-house and hoped to attract custom to it by giving lectures. Foote knew that sooner or later he would boast of his actor's skill in memorizing anything at a single hearing, and attended his lecture armed with **The Great Panjandrum**. This was a piece of nonsense from which each vestige of consecutive thought, every memory aid of association and all sane meaning had been carefully excluded. Where Caldecott found it I cannot imagine. . . . But he *did* find it, and in no time dons and clergymen were sending translations of it into the Greek or Hebrew to *Notes and Queries,* and the young had adopted it as an excellent difficult thing to learn by heart.

His illustrations for this Dadaist masterpiece are an extreme example of his method of work and the peculiar fitness of his sort of imagination for the entertainment of small boys and girls. It is clear that he did his first drawings while telling a story to a child on his knee. The book of *Lightning Sketches For The House That Jack Built* proves that. (pp. 79-80)

Caldecott had kept the severely literal visual imagination which I believe to be characteristic of young children. The thing imagined for them is not of another order of reality from the thing seen. After all, you can see it in your head. They are willing to accept flexible conventions in imagining, will grant for the sake of fun that a cloud is very like a camel or Father like a bear. Yet their fancy has hard edges and is not at home off the solid earth. Until corrupted by whimsical elders, they prefer what they know or can see to fanciful inventions.

In picturing the Panjandrum, Caldecott leaves no point unsharpened and no bridgeable gap unbridged.

> So she went into the garden to cut a cabbage-leaf to make an apple-pie; and at the same time a great she-bear, coming down the street, pops

Sketching under difficulties. From Breton Folk: An Artistic Tour in Brittany *(1880), written by Henry Blackburn.*

its head into the shop. What! no soap? So he died, and she very imprudently married the Barber; and there were present the Picninnies, and the Joblillies, and the Garyulies, and the great Panjandrum himself, with the little round button at top; and they all fell to playing the game of catch-as-catch-can, till the gunpowder ran out at the heels of their boots.

The She-Bear goes down a real street—in Whitchurch. The regrettable shortage of soap directly causes death. The round button at top of the Panjandrum proves him a schoolmaster, and the gunpowder which ran out at the heels of the boots of the dancers, though unexplained, is clearly drawn in.

He brought the same thoroughgoing habits of realistic visualization and explanation to nursery rhymes, and the purist may object to such hard-and-fast interpretation. His most elaborate piece of exposition comes in *Sing a Song of Sixpence* which he changed to a Song *for* Sixpence without authority. The lines:

> Sing a song for sixpence
> A pocketful of rye
> Four-and-Twenty blackbirds
> Baked in a pie.

are given eight pictures. An old lady gives a little girl sixpence, presumably for having sung. The girl gives it to a man chopping wood. The man buys or acquires a poacher's pocketful of rye which he takes home. His children set a blackbird trap in the snow, and evidently catch twenty-four birds which their mother bakes in a pie. This *looks* a likely story, but it is more probable that the first two lines of the song mean nothing at all. However, parents with children who ask Why? are fully covered. And the birdtrap picture is a very charming colour design. Humanitarians may disapprove of the whole blackbird incident. I can only report that at the age of three a kindly daughter of mine found the picture with the birds beginning to sing a sad one, on the grounds that the little girl with the spoon might get no dinner.

Another piece of rationalizing one might regret is the lowness of the moon jumped over by the cow. But no parent will regret the introduction of pigs to explain what fun the little dog laughed at. An insufficiency of pigs is one of the great faults of modern children's books.

The most famous of all Caldecott's drawings came in his first picture book—**The House That Jack Built**. The Dog that Worried the Cat sits there exhausted by his effort but happy in the consciousness that that effort has been virtuous, while behind him threatens the unsuspected, inevitable cow. Tragic irony and the madness of pride could not be more precisely expressed.

Story and picture have merged so closely in these books that to pick out a single page as a specimen of drawing is like removing a line from a sonnet. Each sketch depends on what went before and what comes after. The girls opening the gate here have been eavesdropping on the proposal scene just ended and will join the indignant heroine in chasing the kind gentleman. The dog slinking off on the right has been making up to the milkmaid's dog before and will be driven away by it afterwards. His set pieces in colour sometimes achieve dignity—the fine lady on a white horse is unquestionably handsome—and they have vigour and gaiety always. But his great achievement is the creation of a fluid style of pictorial storytelling which is as natural and as pleasant as friendly conversation. (pp. 80-3)

Frederick Laws, "Randolph Caldecott," in The Saturday Book, *Vol. 16, 1956, pp. 61-83.*

IRENE SMITH

The love and knowledge of country life, and his innate gaiety, never deserted Randolph Caldecott. His accurate memories, based upon a rural boyhood, and the drawings and models which were his earliest pastime bore their fruit in such universal favorites as *The Farmer's Boy, A Farmer Went Trotting upon His Grey Mare,* and *Three Jovial Huntsmen.* When you turn the pages of a Caldecott picture book you are in England. It is England on a sunny day with a wind blowing off the heath. The village streets, houses, and old stone walls stand deep-planted in their native earth. In fields and towns, people and animals trip, parade, chase, and run. Everything and everybody in the picture participate in it and add something to its liveliness. (pp. 27-8)

Irene Smith, "Three Bookmen True," in her A History of the Newbery and Caldecott Medals, *The Viking Press, 1957, pp. 11-28.*

MAURICE SENDAK

[*Sendak received the 1964 Caldecott Medal for* Where the Wild Things Are. *The following excerpt is taken from his acceptance speech of June 30, 1964.*]

[I am going to] turn to the work of Randolph Caldecott and define the single element that, in my opinion, most accounts for his greatness. . . . [He is] one of my favorite teachers.

I can't think of Caldecott without thinking of music and dance. *The Three Jovial Huntsmen* beautifully demonstrates his affinity for musical language. It is a songbook animated by a natural, easy contrapuntal play between words and pictures. The action is paced to the beat of a perky march, a comic fugue, and an English country dance—I can hear the music as I turn the pages.

I am infatuated with the musical accompaniment Caldecott provides in his books, for I have reached for that very quality in my own. (p. 345)

No one in a Caldecott book ever stands still. If the characters are not dancing, they are itching to dance. They never walk; they skip. Almost the first we see of The Great Panjandrum Himself is his foot, and its attitude makes us suspect that the rest of his hidden self is dancing a jig. . . . [Caldecott] was endowed with a fabulous sense of lively animation. . . . Characters who dance and leap across the page, loudly proclaiming their personal independence of the paper—this is perhaps the most charming feature of a Caldecott picture book. Think of his three clowning huntsmen, red in the face, tripping, sagging, blowing frantically on their horns, receding hilariously into the distance and then galloping full-blast back at you. It has the vivacity of a silent movie, and the huntsmen are three perfect Charlie Chaplins.

One can forever delight in the liveliness and physical ease of Caldecott's picture books, in his ingenious and playful elaborations on a given text. But so far as I am concerned, these enviable qualities only begin to explain Caldecott's supremacy. For me, his greatness lies in the truthfulness of his personal vision of life. There is no emasculation of truth in his world. It is a green, vigorous world rendered faithfully and honestly in shades of dark and light, a world where the tragic and the joyful coexist, the one coloring the other. It encompasses three slaphappy huntsmen, as well as the ironic death of a mad, misunderstood dog; it allows for country lads and lasses flirting

and dancing round the Maypole, as well as Baby Bunting's startled realization that her rabbit skin came from a creature that was once alive.

My favorite example of Caldecott's fearless honesty is the final page of *Hey Diddle Diddle.* After we read "And the dish ran away with the spoon," accompanied by a drawing of the happy couple, there is the shock of turning the page and finding a picture of the dish broken into ten pieces—obviously dead—and the spoon being hustled away by her angry parents, a fork and a knife. There are no words that suggest such an end to the adventure; it is a purely Caldecottian invention. Apparently he could not resist enlarging the dimensions of this simple nursery rhyme by adding a last sorrowful touch.

Caldecott never tells half-truths about life, and his honest vision, expressed with such conviction, is one that children recognize as true to their own lives. (pp. 346-47)

Maurice Sendak, "Caldecott Award Acceptance," in The Horn Book Magazine, *Vol. XL, No. 4, August, 1964, pp. 345-51.*

MAURICE SENDAK

Along about 1877 Randolph Caldecott began his illustrations for some of the [Mother Goose] nursery rhymes, and no artist since has matched his accomplishments. Caldecott breathed life into the picture book. The design of his books, so deceptively simple, allowed him the greatest possible freedom in interpreting the verses. . . . As in a song, where every shade and nuance of the poem is illumined and given greater meaning by the music, so Caldecott's pictures illuminate the rhymes. This is the *real* Mother Goose—marvelously imagined improvisations that playfully and rhythmically bounce off and around the verses without ever incongruously straying. If any name deserves to be permanently joined with that of Mother Goose, it is Randolph Caldecott. His picture books . . . should be among the first volumes given to every child. (p. 38)

Maurice Sendak, "Mother Goose's Garnishings," in Book Week—The Sunday Herald Tribune, *October 31, 1965, pp. 5, 38.*

MARGARET C. GILLESPIE

The Caldecott Award which presently is conferred annually to the illustrator of the most distinguished children's book of the year, is well-named, indeed. Caldecott's own delightful picture books represent the innovation of an important trend in children's books. Here, for the first time, we have a tremendous creative talent in craftsmanship being expended in the making of lovely picture-reading for young children. The sensitive charm and unfailing good humor of this remarkable artist shine through his drawings and speak out from them today as they did when he created them. (pp. 112-13)

Margaret C. Gillespie, "Landmarks in Literature for Children: Memorable Moments in Illustrating," in her History and Trends, *Wm. C. Brown Company Publishers, 1970, pp. 107-14.*

BARBARA BADER

[Randolph Caldecott] is the English illustrator who animated children's picture books, winging the eye from page to page and running away with the story line. . . .

[Spontaneity] and vivacity and identification with the text . . . constitute his enduring qualities. . . .

Caldecott and his contemporaries Walter Crane and Kate Greenaway used traditional material perforce; but while they pictured a scene in a nursery rhyme, he set the rhyme to pictures and extended it. There is implicit comment, even counterpoint in his vignettes: Baby Bunting wrapped in a rabbit skin attracts a gallery of curious, quizzical rabbits—are they brothers under the skin? Without changing or adding a word, Caldecott has created something both richer and more intimate.

He doesn't embellish the rhymes, he inflects them, taking children into his confidence as it were; and in fact one reads his pictures.

Barbara Bader, "Has Caldecott's Name Been Taken in Vain?" in The New York Times Book Review, *March 21, 1971, p. 34.*

PERCY MUIR

[Despite] some splendid animals in **The House that Jack Built**, this is greatly surpassed by **John Gilpin** if only for the two superb double-spreads of colour, one showing Gilpin careering through a toll-gate to the consternation of a flock of geese and the wonder of the onlookers, the other of the six mounted gentlemen raising the hue and cry. But in these, as in all the series, the gaiety and freshness of the colour does not detract one whit from the admirable consistency of the line drawings.... [The] economy with which he secures his effects is astonishing, more especially for its novelty.... Caldecott leaves out every inessential feature and thus, almost for the first time, shows a grasp of the proper use of the wood-engraver's craft. Not quite for the first time, for Crane had seen it almost as clearly in, for example, *Mrs Mundi*, but allowed himself to be seduced into less effective trickiness and mannerism. Crane, moreover, in even his simple drawings, was essentially a decorator, whereas Caldecott is a true illustrator. (p. 167)

Caldecott had a strong sense of humour, and an even stronger sense of good humour. Thus, although the drawings are not primarily funny, they are extremely good fun. Consider how elegantly he emphasises Goldsmith's gentle humour in **Mrs Blaize** by causing the reader to turn the page before the point is made. Quite early in the series, ... Caldecott had chosen another of Goldsmith's parodies of funereal poetry taken from *The Vicar of Wakefield*—**An Elegy on the Death of a Mad Dog**. This is one of the most brilliant of the series. The drawing of the dog posed against wooden palings on waste land is one of the best things he ever did in colour. Facing it is a page of snippets of text illustrated with dogs of many kinds that no other artist of his day could have done.

John Gilpin has already been mentioned. The excellence of the monochrome drawings should be especially remarked. The three customers placidly arriving at the Cheapside draper's shop, with boys in the background cutting capers on hitching posts while others exhort the coachman to 'whip behind' at the two youngsters hanging on the back axle, the leg and tail denoting the scampering horse with the mud-spattered pedestrians, are all full of life and movement, every one a triumph.

It would be tedious to continue a catalogue of choice pieces with which the reader is already familiar or can readily become so. Caldecott's invention never flagged. For the second series he changed to an oblong format and varied his style accordingly. The last of them, **The Great Panjandrum**, ... is as lively and inventive as any of them; and if any one doubts it let him try improving on the scenes where 'gunpowder ran out of the heels of their boots'.

Caldecott died in 1886; but he had already decided to do no more of the Toy-Books. Outside of them there is comparatively little of great consequence.... (pp. 168-69)

He illustrated three books by Mrs Ewing, ... all containing some capital things. (p. 169)

He was incomparably the most rewarding artist that [Edmund] Evans ever worked with. (p. 170)

Percy Muir, "The Advent of Colour," in his Victorian Illustrated Books, *B. T. Batsford Ltd., London, 1971, pp. 149-78.*

MARY F. THWAITE

[Randolph Caldecott is] perhaps the greatest artist of the three picture-book makers who worked with Edmund Evans.... [His series of picture-books] brought a new quality into such publications for young children, for the artist was not merely illustrator, but a storyteller with a pencil like quicksilver. He had a great power of line, a keen sense of humour, and a love of dogs, horses and the countryside, especially evident in that racy and vigorous work, **The Three Jovial Huntsmen**.... [Caldecott's] lively, clever picture-books have lost little of their savour with the years and are regularly reprinted. (pp. 197-98)

Mary F. Thwaite, "Flood Tide—The Victorian Age and Edwardian Aftermath: Picture-Books and Books for Young Children," in her From Primer to Pleasure in Reading, *revised edition, The Horn Book, Inc., 1972, pp. 188-200.*

JOHN ROWE TOWNSEND

[Randolph Caldecott] offers a strong contrast to Crane; his style is spare and wiry, and he is first-class in scenes of action. His **John Gilpin** ... is still the best of the many illustrated versions of Cowper's poem. Nobody else has matched Caldecott's picture of Gilpin in mid-ride, clinging desperately to the horse's mane as geese fly, almost audibly squawking, from under its hooves, dogs chase after it, and passers-by stare in bewilderment from the roadside. And Caldecott's rustic dancers in **Come Lasses and Lads** ... look ready to dance right out of the page. (pp. 150-51)

John Rowe Townsend, "Pictures That Tell a Story," in his Written for Children: An Outline of English-Language Children's Literature, *revised edition, 1974. Reprint by J. B. Lippincott, 1975, pp. 142-62.*

MICHAEL HUTCHINS

[In 1875, Caldecott] illustrated Louisa Morgan's **Baron Bruno**. It was the first children's book he attempted, and the stories and his illustrations are quite unlike what was to become his normal work for children. The stories resemble some of Grimm's tales, and the drawings are heavily detailed and over-finished, like the early drawings for **Old Christmas**. (p. 3)

By 1877 Edmund Evans needed a new illustrator if he was to continue with one particularly successful part of his engraving and printing business. For twelve years or so he had produced children's books which Walter Crane had illustrated, but now Crane did not want to produce any more sixpenny titles. Evans was the most skilled engraver and printer of coloured illustrations in England and Caldecott a relative newcomer, but Evans made only one stipulation when he asked the young man to illustrate two picture books: they were to cost a shilling.

The stories, and how they were to be treated, were entirely Caldecott's choice. He made a blank dummy book and rapidly drew 'a number of sketches in the rough, page for page as they will appear'.

The dummy for *The House that Jack Built* shows how close the printed book was to these first sketches. Detailed descriptions can be as easily written from the few lines on every page of the dummy as from the printed book itself.

Before publication day [in 1878 for *The Diverting History of John Gilpin* and *The House that Jack Built*] Caldecott sailed for France, and when the books were reviewed he was staying at Cannes, where:

> 2 or 3 notices have been read by the visitors to this hotel and I am asked if I am any relation to the gifted artist. 30,000 of each book, *Gilpin* and *House,* delivered to Xmas—50,000 of each expected to sell straight away. Hope so. I get a small royalty—a small, small royalty.

Without exception the reviews were full of praise. The enthusiasm of *The Times* reviewer [see excerpt dated December 24, 1878 for *The Diverting History of John Gilpin; The House That Jack Built* (1878)] was carried along for three hundred words and it was natural that he should end with a comparison with Evans's former protégé:

> In a few strokes, dashed off apparently at random, he can portray a scene or an incident to the full as correctly and completely, and far more lucidly, than does Mr Crane in his later and more elaborate style.

Caldecott—as an illustrator of picture books for children—had begun spectacularly.

So confident was Evans that the plans for the next pair were already advanced. Caldecott wrote:

> Some of those designs [for *The Babes in the Wood* and *The Mad Dog*] were made when I was very very stomachily seedy at Florence and most were arranged and planned there. I scribbled out the plan of 1 book in the train between Florence and Bologna.

Until the end of his life Caldecott was now committed during the spring and early summer of each year to selecting the titles, planning and producing the original drawings for a pair of picture books. (pp. 4-5)

Any of the sixteen picture books, which are most people's introduction to Caldecott, tells something of the man. The prodigality with which he drew shows at once how fast he worked and that even the shortest text gave him a long sequence of ideas.

His great rivals, who also had the benefit of Edmund Evans's skills, were Kate Greenaway and Walter Crane. All three illustrated *Sing a Song of Sixpence.* Kate Greenaway, in *April Baby's Book of Tunes* has just one illustration; Crane in *Baby's Opera,* puts the verses and four small illustrations on a single page; Caldecott made eight coloured and twenty-two black-and-white illustrations.

The difference between the three books is far more than just this. By changing a word in the title—his book is *Sing a Song for Sixpence*—Caldecott adds a dimension to the original rhyme which is completely lacking in Crane's and Miss Greenaway's pages. He tells a story which is far more complex and involved than appears at first reading.

Here, and in every picture book, is certain evidence of the clever amateur—the clever man who, in the older sense of the word, loves to draw. They show just how accomplished an illustrator he was, for at no point does he merely put the words of a text into visual form. With each illustration Caldecott adds something quite unique to the story.

Why was the maiden forlorn in *The House that Jack Built?* Because, says Caldecott, she had seen the dog tossed, killed and buried. Why, in *The Frog who Would A-wooing Go,* did the frog ask the rat to go with him to Miss Mouse's house? Because he was too shy to go wooing alone.

Caldecott has his chosen text as initial inspiration, but his skill as a storyteller takes over. It is this, the ability to weave one story around another, coupled with the mastery which produces pictures not fixed in time, that makes his picture books as enjoyable today as when they were first published. (p. 6)

> *Michael Hutchins, in an introduction to* Yours Pictorially: Illustrated Letters of Randolph Caldecott, *edited by Michael Hutchins, Frederick Warne, 1976, pp. 1-12.*

WILLIAM FEAVER

[Randolph Caldecott] left behind him in picture books and pictorial journalism a vision of a nut-brown, pale pea-green, hunting-pink Old England. [Thomas] Rowlandson's England, tidied, mellowed, with smiles instead of leers.

Compared with Caldecott, Walter Crane . . . was heavy-handed and altogether too set on opulent effects. Miss Greenaway, his main rival, was limited to a few winning poses. Like [Aubrey] Beardsley, Caldecott thrived on restrictions. His style was shorthand. The characters only rarely stepped out of period dress into Du Maurier urban-contemporary. The Caldecott country, developed over fifteen years, was a blend of Shropshire and Kent, a land recently enclosed, where every copse teemed with wildlife, where archetypal Arts and Crafts villages housed jolly, gaitered farmers, demure milkmaids, mad dogs and Parson Woodfords. A brilliant combination of free drawing (as though straight off the thumbnail) and tonal restraint (line and colours to suit the engraver or blockmaker) gave his work a spontaneous yet age-old character. He was Beatrix Potter's greatest inspiration. . . .

The biggest batch of letters [in *Yours Pictorially: Illustrated Letters of Randolph Caldecott*] is Caldecott's correspondence with Mrs Ewing between 1879 and her death, in mid-collaboration, in 1885. He illustrated *Jackanapes, Daddy Darwin's Dovecot* and *Lob Lie-by-the-Fire* for her and the relationship flourished. This exchange of progress reports, fee negotiations and queries as to plot development and precise details of dress and manner, is revealing not only for the light thrown on Caldecott's business and drawing methods but for its demonstration of the relationship that had to develop between an author and illustrator if there were to be any illuminating result. Not that Caldecott's *Jackanapes* illustrations were anything like his best work: he was always at his best enlarging on nursery rhymes. Mrs Ewing went into ecstasies as the roughs appeared ("Your embryo hero on his pony is so delicious") but the flattery was a means of coaxing faithful renderings out of him. Her intentions, his interpretation, her thanks. . . .

Working with Mrs Ewing he was the supplier of aerating touches, of cover appeal and frontispiece attraction. In *Jackanapes,* as in *Hey Diddle Diddle, Sing a Song for Sixpence* and in his letters, he sought to please, to entertain, worried less about his status than his royalties.

William Feaver, "In Caldecott Country," in The Times Literary Supplement, *No. 3906, January 21, 1977, p. 64.*

AIDAN WARLOW

Of all the great Victorian children's illustrators, one likes to see Randolph Caldecott's work remembered. His edition of John Gilpin was admired not only by Maurice Sendak but by Van Gogh and Gauguin. He illustrated his stories with a wit and deftness of line that E. H. Shepard imitated but never rivalled, always managing to supplement the narrative with delightful subplots which precisely complement the text.

Aidan Warlow, in a review of "John Gilpin and Other Stories," in The School Librarian, *Vol. 26, No. 1, March, 1978, p. 83.*

DAVID PREISS

Second to no illustrator of any age, Caldecott is inevitably linked to his enduring imagery of Aesop's fables, Mother Goose, jovial huntsmen, John Gilpin, colorful country genre scenes similar in style but superlative in execution to those of his contemporary Kate Greenaway, and, of course, *Old Christmas.* There is little wonder that, despite Caldecott's everlasting Englishness, each year The Caldecott Medal is awarded to the illustrator of America's most distinguished picture book for children.

David Preiss, in a review of "The Randolph Caldecott Treasury," in American Artist, *Vol. 42, No. 436, November, 1978, p. 24.*

MAURICE SENDAK

To me, [Randolph Caldecott's] work heralds the beginning of the modern picture book. There is in Caldecott a juxtaposition of picture and word, a counterpoint that never happened before. Words are left out—but the picture says it. Pictures are left out—but the word says it. It is like a bouncing ball; it goes back and forth. In short, it is the invention of the picture book. (p. 11)

The word *quicken,* I think, best suggests the genuine spirit of Caldecott's animation, the breathing of life, the surging swing into action that I consider an essential quality in pictures for children's books. Sequential scenes that tell a story in pictures, as in the comic strip, are an example of one approach to animation. In terms of technique, it is no difficult matter for an artist merely to simulate action, but it is something else to *quicken,* to create an inner life that draws breath from the artist's deepest perception.

Happily, Caldecott was endowed with a fabulous sense of lively animation. Characters who leap across the page, loudly proclaiming their personal independence of the paper—this is perhaps the most charming feature of a Caldecott picture book. His illustrations for *The Queen of Hearts* are an instance of his extraordinary development of this new form. He takes off sedately enough by picturing his theme ("The Queen of Hearts, she made some tarts") simply and straightforwardly. Then begin the purely Caldecottian inventions, the variations that enrich and build the nursery rhyme into an uproar of elaborate and comical complications. He accomplishes this not with flowing drawings in sequence across each page, but with tremendously animated scenes that rush from page to page. The delightful crescendo reached at the line "And beat the Knave

full sore" is worth describing: in the background Caldecott pictures the Knave being soundly trounced by the King to the rhythm of a minuet danced gracefully in the foreground by a lady and gentleman of the court.

The word *quicken* has another, more subjective association for me. It suggests something musical, something rhythmic and impulsive. It suggests a beat—a heartbeat, a musical beat, the beginning of a dance. To conceive musically for me means to quicken the life of the illustrated book. I've long felt that children respond most spontaneously to illustrations that have a sense of music and dance and are not something just glued onto the page. And since music is the impulse that most stimulates my own work, it is the quality I eagerly look for in the work of the picture-book artists I admire.

It is, of course, impossible to know whether Randolph Caldecott related his own work to music, but it is also impossible to imagine his not being conscious, at least to some extent, of his musical sympathies. His pictures abound in musical imagery; his characters are forever dancing and singing and playing instruments. More to the point is his refinement of a graphic counterpart to the musical form of theme and variations, his delightful compounding of a simple visual theme into a fantastically various interplay of images, his clever weaving in of black-and-white sequences of drawings that both amplify and enrich the color pictures. (pp. 11-12)

[*The Three Jovial Huntsmen*] is a veritable song-and-dance fest with its syncopated back-and-forthing between words and pictures. It has a galloping, rhythmic beat that suggests a full musical score. . . . (p. 12)

His *Hey Diddle Diddle* and *Baby Bunting,* too, exemplify the rhythmic syncopation between words and images—a syncopation that is both delightful and highly musical. In most versions of *Hey Diddle Diddle,* the cow literally jumps over the moon. But here, the cow is merely jumping: the moon is on the horizon in the background and, from this perspective, only gives the *appearance* of being under the cow. In this way, Caldecott is being exceedingly logical, since he obviously knows the cow can't jump over the moon. But within his logic he shows you, on the color page, two pigs dancing, the moon smiling, the hen and the rooster carrying on—all of it perfectly acceptable to him and to us. Yet Caldecott won't go beyond a certain "logical" point: the cow *seems* to be jumping over the moon, but in fact it's just leaping on the ground—and, still, this is bizarre enough to make the milkmaid drop her pail of milk.

Now there's a reason for her dumping over the milk, for when you turn the page to read "The Little Dog laughed to see such fun," you might well have taken this line as a reference to the cow's having jumped over the moon. It refers, however, to the spilt milk—or whatever was in that pail—now being gobbled up by the two pigs, while the cow stares from the corner watching it all happen, and the maid looks down, perplexed, perhaps annoyed. So Caldecott has interjected a whole new story element solely by means of the illustrations, adding and ramifying, like a theme and variations, on top of the line, image upon image.

And from this absurdity and silliness, you turn the page to find one of his greatest and most beautiful pictures—"And the Dish ran away with the Spoon," accompanied by a drawing of the happy couple, obviously in love. Then there is the shock of turning the page and finding a final picture of the dish broken into ten pieces—obviously dead—and the spoon being hustled

Illustration from Baby Bunting *(1882).*

away by her angry parents, a fork and a knife. . . . So it all ends tragically. The pounding, musical quality of the book culminates in this strange final note. And that's Caldecott: words taking on unobvious meanings, colors, and dramatic qualities. He *reads* into things, and this, of course, is what the illustrator's job is really about—to interpret the text much as a musical conductor interprets a score.

The situation in **Baby Bunting** is a bit more conventional: the baby's getting dressed, Father's going a-hunting, looking a little ridiculous as he disappears behind a wall, followed by that wonderful dog trotting after him. But Father's frantic hunting is ineffectual, and all comes to naught. So they rush off to town to buy a rabbit skin. And this, of course, is pure Caldecott: the father dressed in hunting regalia with his dog, unable to kill a rabbit, finally winding up in town to *buy* the skin.

Father brings the rabbit skin home to wrap the Baby Bunting in, and what follows is a scene of jollity: the baby dressed in that silly garment, everyone rushing around, pictures on the walls from other Caldecott picture books. Then there is the lovely illustration of Mama and Baby.

And now again, Caldecott does the unexpected. The rhyme ends (''To wrap the Baby Bunting in''), but as you turn the page you see Baby and Mother strolling—Baby dressed in that idiotic costume with the ears poking out of his head—and up on the little hillside a group of about nine rabbits playing. And the baby—I'd give anything to have the original drawing of that baby!—Baby is staring with the most perplexed look at those rabbits, as though with the dawning of knowledge that the lovely, cuddly, warm costume he's wrapped up in has *come* from those creatures. It's all in that baby's eye—just two lines, two mere dashes of the pen, but it's done so expertly that they absolutely express . . . well, anything you want to read into them. I read: astonishment, dismay at life—is this where rabbit skins come from? Does something have to die to dress me?

After the comedy of what has preceded, the last scene again strikes that poignant note. Caldecott is too careful and too elegant an artist to become melodramatic; he never forces an

issue, he just touches it lightly. And you can't really say it's a tragedy, but something hurts. Like a shadow passing over quickly. It is this which gives a Caldecott book—however frothy its rhythms, verse, and pictures—an unexpected depth at any given point within the work, and its special value.

When I came to picture books, it was Randolph Caldecott who really put me where I wanted to be. Caldecott is an illustrator, he is a songwriter, he is a choreographer, he is a stage manager, he is a decorator, he is a theater person; he's superb, simply. He can take four lines of verse that have very little meaning in themselves and stretch them into a book that has tremendous meaning—not overloaded, no sentimentality in it. Everybody meets with a bad ending in **A Frog he would a-wooing go.** Frog gets eaten by a duck, which is very sad, and the story usually closes on that note. But in Caldecott's version, he introduces, oddly enough, a human family. They observe the tragedy much as a Greek chorus might—one can almost hear their comments.

In the last picture, we see only Frog's hat on a rock at the stream's edge, all that remains of him. And standing on the bank are a mother, father, and two children. It's startling for a moment, until you realize what Caldecott has done. It is as though the children have been watching a theatrical performance; they're very upset, obviously. There are no words— I'm just inventing what I think it all means: Frog is dead, it alarms them, and, for support, they are clinging to their parents. The older child, a girl, clutches her father's arm; the younger holds fast to his coat. The mother has a very quiet, resigned expression on her face. Very gently, she points with her parasol toward the stream and the hat. The father looks very sad. They're both conveying to the children, ''Yes, it is sad, but such things do happen—that is the way the story ended, it can't be helped. But you have us. Hold on, everything is all right.'' And this is impressive in a simple rhyming book for children; it's extremely beautiful. It's full of fun, it's full of beautiful drawings, and it's full of truth. And, frankly, Caldecott did it best, much better than anyone else who ever lived. (pp. 12-14)

Maurice Sendak, ''Randolph Caldecott: An Appreciation,'' in The Randolph Caldecott Treasury, *edited by Elizabeth T. Billington, Frederick Warne, 1978, pp. 11-14.*

BENNY GREEN

There are a few creative artists who penetrate the cerebral defences before any awareness is upon us that such creatures as creative artists exist at all. Dickens is certainly one of them, Carroll another, Hans Andersen probably a third. That for English-speaking readers Randolph Caldecott is part of this select company there can be no question. Even if we do not always know him by name, we recognise instantly the contours of the country he created. One glance and immediately we are at ease within its boundaries, know its every crook and nanny, gaze on the colourations and configurations of its landscape with the mingled sadness and affection of a traveller coming home. During the last hundred years there can hardly have been a British child who has not been confronted by a Caldecott illustration, and being confronted, has accepted the delightful challenge of exploring it from margin to margin. Caldecott's **Hey Diddle Diddle,** his **House That Jack Built,** his **John Gilpin** have become an intrinsic part of our awareness of the world, and of ourselves. . . .

[Where] Caldecott's power to evoke resides [is] in the fact that even if we happen not to find his illustrations attractive, they have become so deeply embedded in our consciousness that we cannot help responding to them. They are the very stuff of childhood, and are not to be sloughed off on some hypercritical intellectual level.

Benny Green, "Bitter-Sweet," in The Spectator, Vol. 242, No. 7857, February 10, 1979, p. 22.

SELMA K. RICHARDSON

Caldecott captured much in a few strokes of his pen and in his shilling books has given us superb examples of economy of line in animated scenes. Largely self-taught he assiduously developed his techniques and skill. That he could transfer to paper with great speed what he saw and envisioned is convincingly shown in his "lightning sketches" for *The House that Jack Built* and the illustrations that decorate so much of his correspondence. Without the familiar advice of a mentor, Caldecott seemed to know to seek his subjects in his surroundings, although for the picture books and the Washington Irving, a Georgian flavor was given to customs and garb. His picture books were unlike any seen before. In his depiction of people and animals in perpetual motion and his leading of the reader from front cover to ending, he surpassed his notable contemporaries, Crane and Greenaway. (p. 33)

In over a hundred years the analytical studies of Caldecott are limited to the 1946 commemoratives: Hilda van Stockum, *Horn Book,* [see excerpt dated March-April, 1946]; and Mary Gould Davis's "appreciation" [see excerpt dated 1946]. . . . Might our colleagues in art history and criticism be urged to bring to bear on picture books their special knowledge of the craft and skill of artists, the requirements of creating and reproducing in various media, and the climate of art periods?

Henley in an issue of *The Art Journal* of 1881 [see excerpt above] before all sixteen books had appeared, opined that Caldecott "has fulfilled his destiny quite royally. He is a Prince of Picture Books. Under his sway Art for the nursery has become Art indeed" [see excerpt dated 1881]. Would not the approaching centenary of Caldecott's death be an auspicious time to "crown" him with the publication of superb facsimiles of the sixteen lively picture books in colorful, stiff-card covers and to commission a critical study that deals with the milieu in which Caldecott lived and worked, discusses his illustrations for authors of children's books, and culminates in an analysis of the picture books? Then, the reason this British illustrator is a worthy choice for the name of a prestigious American award might be crystal-clear. (pp. 36-7)

Selma K. Richardson, "Randolph Caldecott," in Children's Literature Association Quarterly, Vol. 6, No. 4, Winter, 1981-82, pp. 32-7.

JON C. STOTT

Although Caldecott has been praised for the variety and range of his artistic talents, his reputation rests on his sixteen picture books for children. At their best, for example in *Hey Diddle-Diddle. . . , John Gilpin's Ride,* and *A Frog He Would a-Wooing Go. . . ,* they represent a perfect blend of text, art, and engraving. In choosing texts, Caldecott seems to have selected those which best complemented his style and gently satiric bent. The rhythmic quality of the language was important, as it could be harmonized with the rhythmic, flowing quality of the art. Each of the works contained a great deal of action and, with the exception of *The Babes in the Wood. . . ,* all were capable of humorous interpretation. The focal point in many of the narratives is some kind of ridiculous disaster: John Gilpin is carried off on a runaway horse; a courting frog is devoured

by a duck; a dog bites a man and dies. Much of the action takes place on horseback and in the country, allowing Caldecott to indulge his love of drawing horses and rural scenes. Seldom are the actions of the main characters performed in solitude; generally there are crowds and thus the artist has opportunities to include many satiric sketches.

Caldecott's art work has made the picture books the classics they are. The simplicity of line, the accurate depiction of topography, animals, and people, the subtle use of color, and the fluidity and rhythm of the pictures are all qualities of his work that critics have constantly praised. Caldecott's pictures are far more than illustrations: they are interpretations and extensions of the actions. His sense of narrative development seems to have been a major principle in his illustrations. This can be seen in *Bye Baby Bunting. . . ,* where the pictures expand the meaning of the simple four line lyric into a story of a father's long, frustrating, and unsuccessful hunting trip.

This interpretation and extension of meaning is achieved by Caldecott's inclusion of details not found in the words. In *An Elegy on the Death of a Mad Dog. . . ,* the reasons for the dog's turning on his master are made clear in the illustration: the man is paying attention to a kitten while the dog sulks in the corner. In *A Frog He Would a-Wooing Go,* the suitor's actions are watched by a human family which is at first amazed, but which becomes more and more concerned as the drama progresses to its disastrous conclusion. This use of detail is best seen in the three pictures which accompany the single line "And the dish ran away with the spoon" in *Hey Diddle-Diddle.* The first shows the elegantly dressed dish running from a party with a dainty spoon, much to the amazement of the onlookers: a wine decanter, a pitcher, and several plates. The second shows the two lovers sitting quietly, shyly, and lovingly together on a bench, while the third reveals the outcome of their precipitous actions. Father knife and mother fork sternly lead their daughter home, while the dish, surrounded by four mourning plates, lies in pieces on the floor, the victim of either his own rash acts or the father's anger.

With the exception of *The Babes in the Wood,* so untypical of Caldecott's work in many ways, and apparently a concession to Victorian pathos, the general tone of the picture books is humorous and gently satiric. Caldecott once wrote to a friend, "Please say that my line is to make to smile the lunatic who has shown no sign of mirth for many months." Although human foolishness, vanity, and hypocrisy are portrayed in the pictures, the tone is not caustic. The foolish suitor who rejects a milk maid who has no dowry is shown being unceremoniously lifted onto the back of a bucking cow; John Gilpin, so dignified as he starts on his ill-fated ride to Edmonton, clings to the horse's mane as his wig and hat fly off behind; the three jovial huntsmen stare stupidly at a pig which they mistake for a "Lunnon alderman." (pp. 70-1)

Jon C. Stott, "Randolph Caldecott," in his Children's Literature from A to Z: A Guide for Parents and Teachers, McGraw-Hill Book Company, 1984, pp. 69-71.

SONIA LANDES

[A] study of picture books should begin with Randolph Caldecott, the illustrator for whom the medal was wisely named. Aside from his robust style and freedom of line, Caldecott's greatest contribution to illustration lay in his ability to enlarge the dimensions of the text and enhance its meaning. He did this in two ways: one, by inventing characters; two, by additions to the plot.

Let us take the well-known nonsense rhyme, *Hey Diddle Diddle.* The words are a sequence of *non sequiturs.* They tell us about a cat and a fiddle, about a cow jumping over the moon, about a dog that laughs, and a dish running off with a spoon. Caldecott manages to extract meaning from these words by joining the *non sequiturs* together. Giving the fiddle to the cat starts a merry round of strange happenings, the last and most interesting of which is a love story. Caldecott first hints at the romance by having the dish and the spoon sit out a dance; then they elope. "The dish ran away with the spoon" may be the last words of the song, but not of the story. An additional page, with no words at all, shows the irate parents, the knife and fork, dragging their errant daughter, the spoon, away from her love, who lies shattered upon the floor.

"Sing a Song of Sixpence" is a mix of nonsense and plot, in spots almost unintelligible. Once again Caldecott invents meaning. He changes the "of" of the title to "for," making *Sing a Song for Sixpence,* and begins to put the puzzle pieces together. A little rich girl, ever so kindly, gives a poor man sixpence for his song. He runs to buy a pocket full of rye, which he scatters around a trap to catch the blackbirds to bake in a pie. As the ragged family, sitting eagerly around the table, cuts open the pie, the birds begin to sing. (As early as 1549, an Italian cookbook speaks of a pie of live birds. The birds are placed in a ten-inch-high, very thick pastry, which is then covered with a lattice crust so the birds can breathe. The pie is then rushed to the table.) "Wasn't that a dainty dish to set before the king." Dainty meaning delicious? Dainty meaning worthy? Matter for etymologists.

And who are the king and queen? They are the children Caldecott wrote for. He fills their world with their fairy tale characters. The proper decor for this queen's parlor is Little Red Riding Hood, Hansel and Gretel, and Little Bo-Peep. In the king's room are heroes for boys: Jack, the Giant Killer (the Victorian two-headed variety of giant) and Robinson Crusoe. There is something for the grown-ups, too. The maid has a handsome and affectionate soldier ready to console her—after the loss and return of her nose.

Other additions to the rhymes: A cat in *The Queen of Hearts* tattles on the knave of hearts who stole those tarts. What's more, this all-knowing cat points, with a paw, in the direction of the thief. The daddy "gone a hunting," has a bad day and *buys* the rabbit skin at a store. Later, a bunch of rabbits stare in utter amazement at the little girl, wrapped in kin skins.

That was a hundred years ago. Today's illustrators are still following in Caldecott's footsteps, inventing characters and stories, while substantially increasing the art and devices of the picture book. (p. 51)

> *Sonia Landes, "Picture Books as Literature," in* Children's Literature Association Quarterly, *Vol. 10, No. 2, Summer, 1985, pp. 51-4.*

ANITA SILVEY

We do not laud and praise the father of the picture book for his technique, his facility, his art—but rather for his sense of liveliness, exuberance, movement, and economy. His works are not to be framed and enjoyed in museums; they are an integral part of a book and work in close conjunction with the text. Caldecott did not illustrate material merely to display his artistic ability; he illustrated material because it would make a lively text for a book—most important, for a picture book.

For almost fifty years now, the American Library Association has honored Caldecott with an award that bears his name. Some of the choices—*Where the Wild Things Are . . . , Make Way for Ducklings . . . , Sylvester and the Magic Pebble . . . ,* and *The Little House . . .*—without a doubt mirror Caldecott's vision of picture books and illustration. But I cannot help feeling that lately the award has gone, as Barbara Bader states, to those books which stress a completely different conception of a picture book. High art, high gloss, decoration, emotionless embellishment seem to be the most recent standards for what we are calling distinguished. If the award were called the Madison Avenue Medal, the trend would not be so painful. Possibly we need to rename it. Possibly we need to rethink the criteria—because I do not honestly believe that in 1986 Randolph Caldecott could win the award named after him.

> *Anita Silvey, "Could Randolph Caldecott Win the Caldecott Medal?" in* The Horn Book Magazine, *Vol. LXII, No. 4, July-August, 1986, p. 405.*

KATE FLINT

Caldecott's reputation rests on a group of sixteen books. Neither attempting original subjects, like Kate Greenaway, nor tackling a varied range of texts, like Walter Crane, he largely employed texts from traditional rhymes and songs, to which he added Cowper's "John Gilpin", Foote's "Panjandrum", two poems by Goldsmith and Edwin Waugh's "Three Jovial Huntsmen". The toy books repeatedly glance back with nostalgia to a pastoral image of the eighteenth century: a world of quiet fields, hunting horns and boots, men in wigs and simpering girls in flounced dresses. Hints of modernity occur only in his disdain for the bounding margin, and in the Japanese delicacy of the blossomed apple bough on which the blackbirds perch in *Sing a Song for Sixpence.* At his most sentimental, he is embarrassing, as in the plate which shows a chubby Baby Bunting listening to a large-eyed, Louis Wain-style cat playing the fiddle. Happily, these are not the aspects of Caldecott's work which have proved a lasting influence on the many subsequent illustrators who have acknowledged his importance to their work. Beatrix Potter claimed to have a "jealous appreciation" of him [see excerpt dated April 7, 1942; Edward] Ardizzone spoke of his "robust splendours" alongside Rowlandson, [George] Cruikshank and [John] Leech; Maurice Sendak commended the "rhythmic progression through the pages, a sense of music and dance". All learnt from the freshness with which he tackled each particular combination of word and text, from the energy and economy of his draughtsmanship. . . .

> *Kate Flint, "The Urge to Illustrate," in* The Times Literary Supplement, *No. 4368, December 19, 1986, p. 1426.*

BRIAN ALDERSON

[Caldecott's] small collection of sixteen books represents both a culmination in the Victorian craft of picture-book making and a model for the blending of words and pictures in books for young children. The praise of contemporary lay-critics was echoed by Caldecott's fellow-professionals (not always a natural reaction among artistic brethren) and more recent practitioners of the art of the picture book, from Beatrix Potter and Leslie Brooke to Edward Ardizzone, have acknowledged his pre-eminence. In the United States the major annual award for picture books is named after him—the American Library Association Caldecott Medal; his three jovial huntsmen were in

1924 neatly adopted as an emblem for the leading review journal of children's books, the *Horn Book Magazine;* and there has been no better assessment of the qualities of his books than that given in a series of critical parerga by the American illustrator Maurice Sendak [see excerpts dated 1964, 1965, and 1978]. . . .

[Caldecott] figures as *primus inter pares* in an essentially English style in the creation of children's picture books. Chauvinistically or not, one can argue that this 'English' style is a touchstone for the judging of all picture-book art, embodying as it does a flexible and richly responsive interplay between text and illustration with an emphasis throughout on the quality of line rather than on less essential features of *chiaroscouro* and colouring. (p. 8)

. . . . .

[When Kate Greenaway saw Randolph Caldecott's] new drawings for **Hey Diddle Diddle,** she wrote to Frederick Locker: 'They are so uncommonly clever . . . I wish I had such a mind' [see excerpt for this title dated 1882.]

The winning candour of this praise is the more attractive for coming from an illustrator whose name was so closely linked with Caldecott's (some people even thought they were married). For while her *Under the Window*—scheduled for publication in 1878—was delayed for a year, the first of the Caldecott Toy Books were one of the successes of that autumn; and, while, in critical terms, her books were to win a constant admiration from an audience that believes that children's books are the province of thin fancy, she (like Mrs Ewing) recognised that, with **The House that Jack Built** and **The Diverting History of John Gilpin** he was reuniting a rich inventiveness with rock-solid technique. Children's picture books which for so long had been visited only fitfully by those within the great tradition were now all-too-briefly to benefit from the hand of the master.

It could be objected that, by comparison with other picture-book artists of his time, Caldecott chose an easy route for himself. Unlike Kate Greenaway he did not attempt original subjects; unlike Walter Crane he did not tackle a varied range of texts. . . . His reputation rests centrally on a group of sixteen books, all made to a similar pattern, and mostly employing texts from traditional rhymes and songs. Cowper's *John Gilpin,* two poems by Goldsmith, Foote's *Panjandrum* and *The Three Jovial Huntsmen* by Edwin Waugh are near enough to 'traditional' not to seem out of place.

What is of consequence here though is not the limited range of material and the recurrent eighteenth-century background but the varied interpretive and graphic skills which Caldecott brings to bear on them. Every theme is recognised as having a character of its own which is explored with great consistency and without reference to any previously established practice. Thus, for instance, **John Gilpin** is treated with a kind of scrubbed realism and the **Huntsmen** with deeply affectionate satire; **Sing a Song for Sixpence, A Frog he would A-wooing Go,** and **Come Lasses and Lads** exhibit in varied ways Caldecott's famous device of introducing a pictorial sub-text to the main narrative; **The Great Panjandrum Himself** welds intentionally disparate nonsense into comic unity, and—perhaps greatest of all—the **Elegy on the Death of a Mad Dog** is indeed that. Where readers may find only comedy in the poem, Caldecott—dog-man to the bottom of his hunting boots—turns the irony on its head. Yes—the dog it was that died.

Every narrative within the Toy Books is a coherent and individual interpretation. At the same time, the parts that go to make up that interpretation are almost always executed with the utmost skill and intelligence. It is drawing that lies at the root of this—not just its exactness, but its economy too. . . . In working on such drawing he was certainly in the temper of his times. When he first came to London he had—literally—sat at the feet of Du Maurier, whom he then called 'the greatest master of drawing in line that we have', and in his work for the magazines he shows a flair for composition and a fastidious wit that link him to that peerless *Punch* man John Leech. With his ready embracing of past times though, in the Washington Irving illustrations and throughout the Toy Books, he turns himself into a benign disciple of Rowlandson, whose bag-wigged merchants, flouncing girls, busy children and eager dogs find an idealised milieu amid the pastures and wainscotting of Caldecott's trim world.

Nor should one detract from Caldecott's use of colour. He and Evans between them achieved some marvellous atmospheric domestic and landscape scenes—the high-point always being the light and airiness of the English countryside in winter. But in both the colour-plates and the sequences of sepia drawings that make a unity of the books it is Caldecott's pen that does the work. Whether he is describing or fantasising, animating real or imagined creatures or household objects he shows complete command of the drawn-line.

It is said that Caldecott's widow was unhappy about the publication in 1899 of his **Lightning Sketches for 'The House that Jack Built'** and there were doubts about the wisdom of issuing his preliminary drafts for the edition of **Jack and the Bean-stalk** that he was working on when he died. Nevertheless, evidence of this kind gave a wider proof than was hidden away in sketch-books and illustrated letters of the work that went into the creation of such apparently spontaneous entertainments. **Jack and the Bean-stalk** was to be the first step in a new direction for illustrating children's books. . . . [One] can feel nothing but deep regret that the pioneer would not be the one to follow the road. (pp. 79-83)

> *Brian Alderson, in a preface and ''Randolph Caldecott,'' in his* Sing a Song for Sixpence: The English Picture-Book Tradition and Randolph Caldecott, *Cambridge University Press, 1986, pp. 7-10, 79-83.*

BARON BRUNO; OR, THE UNBELIEVING PHILOSOPHER AND OTHER FAIRY STORIES (1875)

[Baron Bruno *was written by Louisa Morgan.*]

[**Baron Bruno**] was one of Caldecott's first books for children. . . .

It is of interest because the illustrations disclose Caldecott's lack of freedom as an illustrator. The drawings are detailed to the point of being overfinished, as was the custom of the time. Only in the illustration of Fidunia feeding the geese does one capture a feeling of motion and excitement in the hungry goslings.

Certainly the illustrations do not hint at the joy and movement which would burst forth when Caldecott illustrated old rhymes more familiar to him.

> *Elizabeth T. Billington, ''Selections from the Work of Randolph Caldecott: 'Baron Bruno','' in* The Randolph Caldecott Treasury, *edited by Elizabeth T. Billington, Frederick Warne, 1978, p. 105.*

THE HOUSE THAT JACK BUILT; THE DIVERTING HISTORY OF JOHN GILPIN (1878)

[The Diverting History of John Gilpin *was written by William Cowper.*]

In his new versions of *John Gilpin* and the *House that Jack Built* . . . Mr. Caldecott has approved himself the possessor of qualities so precious and so rare as to put a writer at fault for adequate terms of approbation. He is a humourist of genius, and a draughtsman of genius also; and the feeling for colour displayed in his larger drawings is simply delightful.

As a humouristic inventor, his gift is remarkable. Not only does he create his type so masterfully as to give it an appearance of finality, he can also vary it infinitely, and maintain its original features under the action of a score of emotions. His John Gilpin is the most smug and jovial cit ever drawn; and, what is of still greater importance, he is himself and none other through all the fortunes of that wild ride of his; one has as good and complete an idea of him from the last drawing as from the first. Again, the Dog of the *House that Jack Built*— the Dog that worried the Cat and got tossed by the Cow with the Crumpled Horn—is as strong and sure an example of creative art as *John Gilpin;* while of the Man all Tattered and Torn one might use still higher terms if one could only find them. I do not know of anything so comic in art, indeed, as Mr. Caldecott's Dog. To see this great creature looking round a corner at the Cat is to understand La Fontaine, and to know that here at last is a man to illustrate him. But this is, after all, the Dog's least notable moment. He appears in the next picture; and what an appearance it is! Such a glum, brutal, misanthropical specimen of doghood as he is were capable of anything. One knows at once that he only rejoices in doing evil, and one is almost prepared for the wonderful smile of ill-humoured repletion that appears upon him when he has worried

the cat—for the extraordinary look of surprise and terror that he wears in air high over the crumpled horn. On the other hand, the happy tatterdemalion, as he climbs the style, and tiptoes over the field to where the Maiden all Forlorn is sitting lonely, is fairly bursting with joviality and delightfulness; they peer out at his holes and glorify his patches: it makes one good-tempered to look at him.

These and their fellows are admirably drawn. Mr. Caldecott is of the rare artists who never waste a stroke, who give you in a dozen scratches the effect that some men fail to produce by an elaborate system of composition and design. A fine suggestiveness is his, and with a rarity and assurance of touch almost unequalled he maps out a wide and living champaign in a few masterful lines. It is not possible, I think, to praise too highly the wonderful little bits of background he has achieved in these two books. A gate, a fence, a tree, a cottage, a blade or two of grass, grow real under his hand, and would be, but for the spirit and truth of the figures they assist, too good and striking for accessories merely. So right and so apt are they, indeed, that one gets to look on them almost as natural objects, kept in their normal place and having their normal value determined by the frank and fanciful life they environ.

A word as to Mr. Caldecott's sentiment. It is full of fancy, but it has its roots in a just and kindly sympathy with real, objective nature. Whether he is comic, or passionate, or fantastic, his line is instinct with force and aptitude, his effect is perfectly produced. His picture of the waiter wondering, watch in hand, why John Gilpin does not appear is a piece of pure comedy in black and white; the figure of the forlorn maiden wending homeward on the arm of her ragamuffin is so full of quiet happiness as to be one of the loveliest and most effective things in art; his wonderful view of morning, as reflected in the rosy, crinkled face of the Priest all Shaven and Shorn, is perhaps the best and highest of all. (pp. 481-82)

Illustration from The Diverting History of John Gilpin *(1878), written by William Cowper.*

W. E. Henley, "Mr. Caldecott's Picture-Books," in
The Academy, n.s. Vol. XIV, No. 341, November
16, 1878, pp. 481-82.

Dear old *John Gilpin's Ride* was never better illustrated than
it is this year by Mr. R. Caldecott, who has also furnished *The
House that Jack Built* with a new series of pictures. The last
is, of this set, *the* book for children. It is full of fun; and that
picture where the sly Dog, after successfully worrying the
unfortunate Cat, is seated, smiling to himself in a self-satisfied
manner, in happy ignorance of the proximity of a terrible Nem-
esis in the shape of the Cow with the Crumpled Horn, is
inimitable.

*A review of "John Gilpin's Ride" and "The House
that Jack Built," in* Punch, *Vol. LXXV, December
14, 1878, p. 276.*

Mr. R. Caldecott's latest caricatures should not be overlooked
by purveyors for the nursery. His *John Gilpin* and *House that
Jack Built* . . . are *sui generis*, and irresistibly funny as well
as clever. One hardly knows which to admire most—the full-
page color prints, or the outline sketches in the brown ink of
the text. Happy the generation that is brought up on such
masters as Mr. Caldecott and Walter Crane!

"Mention of . . . ," in The Nation, *New York, Vol.
XXVII, No. 703, December 19, 1878, p. 389.*

The child who receives as a Christmas present either the *Diverting History of John Gilpin* or the *House that Jack Built* . . . ,
as illustrated by R. Caldecott—or both, if so much happiness
be permitted to childhood—will be an uncommonly fortunate
child. Admirable as the illustrations to children's books have
now become, this latest work of Mr. Caldecott's overtops them
all. Where both are so good, it seems almost invidious to
assume that one is less good than another; but we feel inclined
to give the preference to the *House that Jack Built,* if only for
the sake of that inimitable dog chuckling over his late successful
passage of arms with the cat, unconscious of the near approach
of the avenging cow whose crumpled horn he is soon so painfully to feel. The expression of satisfaction on that dog's face
no words can adequately portray; Landseer himself never in-
fused more soul into an animal's features. An admirable figure,
too, is that of the "Man all tattered and torn" (an Irishman,
obviously, in Mr. Caldecott's idea) stealing up to kiss the
"Maiden all forlorn," but looking, however, remarkably nice
to kiss. But, indeed, all the pictures in this exquisite little
gallery are so good that it is difficult to say which is best. In
the other book we like most, perhaps, the last of the large
coloured pictures, when the hue and cry after Gilpin is at its
height, as he rattles along on his homeward, though involun-
tary, journey. In this the idea of hurry and tumult is very well
depicted, and some of the faces are excellent, notably that of
the old man at the finger post; but, indeed, were it not for the
House that Jack Built, the *Diverting History of John Gilpin*
would itself be supreme. Mr. Caldecott has the admirable faculty of informing his pictures with plenty of life and variety,
and yet never confusing or overloading them. The untutored
eye of a child can catch at a glance the true meaning of all he
has drawn as easily as it can take in the distinct utterances of
its big alphabet. In a few strokes, dashed off apparently at
random, he can portray a scene or an incident to the full as
correctly and completely, and far more lucidly, than does Mr.
Crane in his later and more elaborate style. This we hold to
be the very essence of all illustration for children's books.

*A review of "Diverting History of John Gilpin" and
"House that Jack Built," in* The Times, *London,
December 24, 1878, p. 9.*

Great as the [1860s] undoubtedly were in the annals of book
illustration they did not give us any notable "Gilpins." (p. 99)

[It] is a genuine pleasure to come to the name of Randolph
Caldecott, who stands—without fear of competition—as the
greatest illustrator of Cowper's poem. With its companion,
The House that Jack Built, John Gilpin formed the first pair
of the famous "Picture Books" that so entertained both children and grown-ups of last century. . . . [The] success of the
book was (to quote Blackburn) "beyond expectation": nor was
ever success more deserved. Caldecott's method—that of strong
outline supported by flat colour—was not new; . . . but its effect
was charming. Moreover it contained no artistic subtleties to
puzzle the non-technical.

Caldecott makes John a pleasant figure, likeable and homely.
The contented Gilpin, smoking his church-warden (with wifely
arm on his shoulder) in the first picture, is recaptured in the
final illustration, which shows John embracing his loving
spouse—whilst over her shoulder he contrives a most prodigious wink to us—his beholders. Nor are the intervening pictures less good. Betty, as she assists the bold linendraper into
his "long red cloak," looks undeniably attractive, and sympathy is felt for the dainty lady whose dress—when John "threw
the wash about"—is so bespattered with dirt, but the *tour de
force* is undoubtedly the double-page illustration in the middle
of the book. This shows John, mounted on a powerful bay, as
having just passed through the turnpike gate and settling down,
very grimly, to his uncomfortable journey. Hat and wig have
gone, stirrups have been lost, but the precious stone bottles
(with their "curling ears") are as yet intact. Geese fly cackling
before the onslaught, and a tribe of barking dogs follow after.
People—alarmed at the noise—run to window, door and garden
gate, whilst a small child tumbles face-downwards in its hurry
to escape the mad rush. A picture few can pass without chuckling audibly!

It is interesting to study the original sketch for this illustration,
and as this was secured by the Victoria and Albert Museum at
a sale of Caldecott relics, we can fortunately reproduce it.
Although the main features of the later picture can be clearly
seen, it will be noticed that the background differs materially;
also that the ranks of the canine followers have been augmented
in the later production. . . . [The] cover of the "John Gilpin"
book should be mentioned, as its embellishment is clever. John
is seen early in his mad career with his fine cloak still unloosed.
A signpost (behind which a damsel shelters) bears the indication that the book is "One of Randolph Caldecott's Picture
Books," whilst a small dog, tearing along to enjoy the fun,
bears the letters "R. C." on its collar. (pp. 199-200)

*H. T. Kirby, "John Gilpin in Picture: Some Illus-
trators of Cowper's Famous Poem," in* The Book-
man, *London, Vol. LXXXI, No. 483, December, 1931,
pp. 198-201.*

**ELEGY ON THE DEATH OF A MAD DOG; THE BABES IN THE
WOOD** (1879)

[Elegy on the Death of a Mad Dog *was written by Oliver Goldsmith.*]

Mr. R. Caldecott's 'Picture-Book' is increased by the addition
to *The House that Jack Built* and *John Gilpin* of *The Babes in*

the Wood and Goldsmith's *Elegy on the Death of a Mad Dog.* . . . The Gilpin will probably remain the favorite, and the artist has shown a grievous want of taste in treating humorously the tragedy of the Babes; but the Mad Dog is mirth-provoking enough.

"Mention of . . . ," in The Nation, *New York, Vol. XXIX, No. 755, December 18, 1879, p. 428.*

SING A SONG FOR SIXPENCE; THE THREE JOVIAL HUNTSMEN (1880)

ILLUSTRATOR'S COMMENTARY

[*The following excerpt is taken from Caldecott's letter to the editor of the* Manchester Guardian.]

Your notice of my work—as is shown in my picture books and elsewhere—has hitherto given me unalloyed pleasure and gratification, and in your journal of the 20th inst. you continue to give me praise by saying some very encouraging and flattering things about the quality of the designs in **The Three Jovial Huntsmen,** just published; but you add thereto some comments which may cause my friends who are amongst your constant readers to shake their heads over my seeming falling off in virtue and generosity.

You use these words: "The text is, we believe, though no acknowledgement of the fact is made, the production of Mr Edwin Waugh." Now, my friend, Mr Waugh, has written, by the help of his fertile imagination, a version of this not at all unknown ballad upon the lines handed down by tradition, and it is printed in his cheerful little book called *Old Cronies.* In a letter to me he said, "With respect to the song, 'The Three Jovial Hunters', I have written two or three additional verses, and altered some of the others a little. Of course, you are quite at liberty to use it in any way you like." I have, therefore, taken out six of his verses, disrespectfully changing a word here and there; also mark the difference of title; and have added two brand new verses of my own. Your readers can judge from this statement of what my text truly is—whether I could have explained it in a suitably brief preface to my simple picture book, or whether I was called upon to explain it at all. I may here remark that I supposed all Lancashire people knew *Old Cronies* by heart.

And towards the close of your observations is the passage: "Mr Caldecott has been greatly helped by the excellence of the engraving, which is, we believe, the work of a well-known Manchester artist (whose name might, perhaps, have been given). Mr Caldecott can afford to be generous to his *collaborateurs.*" Mr Edmund Evans, the engraver and printer of the book, who sends me the piece of your journal in which the notice appeared, is glad to have your opinion of the engraving, because it is his work, with the exception of three of the small uncoloured designs, . . . which were engraved by the artist to whom you give credit for the reproduction of the whole. The said artist is a clever engraver, and I persuaded Mr Evans to take advantage of his proffered help.

When I say that the profits of the other people connected with these books are larger than mine, I hope that those who still think I want all the glory will be comforted by knowing that I do not get all the money. (pp. 252-53)

Randolph Caldecott, in a letter to the editor of the Manchester Guardian on November 24, 1880, in Yours Pictorially: Illustrated Letters of Randolph Caldecott,

edited by Michael Hutchins, Frederick Warne, 1976, pp. 252-53.

[*The following excerpt is taken from a letter written by Juliana Horatia Ewing to Caldecott.*]

How can I bless you enough for [**The Three Jovial Huntsmen**] . . .? [My sister and I] have already sent the Jovial 3 in all directions—not only across country as is proper at this season but across the sea! The Pig is of course a universal favourite—and he is delightfully comic—and very naked—but I think my favourites of all are pages 19, 20 and 21. The boy and *the bird* at page 20 are so living a picture of "bursting with happiness" in the sweet seasons of youth (and hunting) and all outdoor and country joys that it makes one feel young again and strong again to look at them! (p. 80)

I am *charmed* with my huntsmen. I must also say how very much I admire [**Sing a Song for Sixpence**]. When you showed us the sketches I remember being so greatly struck with the happy thought of genius by which you had put the arras with the hunting scenes behind the young king and queen. The effect is grander and more royal than any vista of vast rooms could have been. But as I have once or twice been "cheeky" enough to express my grudge of your pencil being used to immortalise sea-side trippers or other ungraceful episodes—I must say how intensely I am charmed by the peculiar *grace* of the song. The king in his counting house is exquisite, his pictures and knick-knacks are admirable but the teachings of tradition, the dignifying effects of state—and the general pressure of *noblesse oblige* in that most royal and most fascinating little couple and their surroundings are most refined and most perfect. Not perhaps the least in one sense, though the tiniest, is the deliciously dignified little pair and their page issuing from the distant yew hedge archway. (pp. 80-1)

And after all this—I believe you won't believe it anything but the military element which makes me so delighted with [**Sing a Song for Sixpence**]! And I'm free to confess that it adds its usual sparkle to the scenes of everyday life!

And oh, *how* well you'll do soldiers some day when you're too big a swell to do anything for me!! Pages 24 and 25 are *too* good! The girl is a model of pose and grace, but dear old sentry-go is delightful, though I trace a tendency to treat with some levity the Defenders of our Hearths and Homes (!) especially about the legs. But the "portrait of an officer" in the frontispiece is all that could be wished and I think you must allow that he adds much to the picture. Page 30 is perfect. The distant group—the *rage* of the blackbird (I *do* congratulate you on having expressed by almost identical strokes fury there, and rapture in the bird . . . [in **The Three Jovial Huntsmen**])—the beauty of the maid and the *prompt support of the military* are truly excellent. Finally it may seem an impertinence to congratulate you on the virtues of honesty and thoroughness—but it is very pleasant to see you surpass yourself where your success is already sure and you might *scamp.*

Shall you ever be able to do **Jackanapes** for me? But I fear my work doesn't "fetch" your sympathies as yours does mine! I quite agree with you that you could not do it otherwise than with the care you give to these. But I think we could afford you your just terms; and I should like them in this style rather than more highly finished (as in **Bracebridge Hall**) to go with the coloured frontispiece. I hate to bother you—but I know that when I hold my peace other people snatch you, and you know I have a charming letter of yours signed "your future illustrator". How wrong it is to break faith with a lady. I know I need not impress on your chivalrous mind! Large be your royalties on these nice books!! (p. 81)

Juliana Horatia Ewing, in a letter to Randolph Caldecott on November 17, 1880, in Yours Pictorially: Illustrated Letters of Randolph Caldecott, *edited by Michael Hutchins, Frederick Warne, 1976, pp. 80-2.*

Both the black-and-white drawings and color reproductions [in *Sing a Song for Sixpence*] show why the artist has been singled out for setting such high standards of picture book illustration. Of more than historical interest, the action, precision, and individuality of his work will please youngest nursery rhyme fanciers of today as much as those of a century ago.

Betsy Hearne, in a review of "Sing a Song of Sixpence," in Booklist, *Vol. 74, No. 8, December 15, 1977, p. 686.*

Of the sixteen picture books that Randolph Caldecott created between 1878 and 1885, *The Three Jovial Huntsmen* . . . is one of the better remembered. Active, spirited, friendly, humorous, and oh-so-very-English, the book in many respects epitomizes Caldecott's style and subject matter. With this and the others of his very successful toy books (each of which sold in the tens of thousands in their paperback format—the "yellow backs" that Edmund Evans printed in three colors and sold at railroad stations), Caldecott effectively established the dynamic new form of the modern picture book: a vital means for both verbal and visual storytelling.

Caldecott's three droll equestrians have become virtual symbols for excellence in the art of the picture book, occurring as they do in the relief that is emblazoned on the Caldecott Medal and in the logo of the *Horn Book Magazine.* Yet today, for the most part, Caldecott's contributions to children's literature are taken for granted, without much discussion or study. Or, perhaps worse, there is a begrudging acceptance of the inviolate status that is often conferred upon Caldecott in the standard surveys of children's literature. "He's something like Shakespeare," a local children's librarian once told me. "You've got to have him on your shelves because you've heard for so long how good he is. But tastes have changed and his books are dust-catchers. Nobody looks at him anymore, except in library school."

Caldecott's "problem" is one shared by many other "classic" writers or author/illustrators: their works simply are not read today, let alone analyzed and pondered, debated and reevaluated. This neglect is especially true for artists working in the mixed media of the picture book form. With the exception of a few major figures, the hierarchy of subjects in children's literature criticism deemed acceptable for serious scrutiny has tended, until rather recently, to leave out picture books in favor of what are thought to be more verbally complex and sophisticated forms. And when the critic's attention has turned to the picture book, it is usually not to the work of nineteenth-century author/illustrators like Caldecott, but rather to contemporary figures who are making use of the most modern printing and reproduction techniques and speaking directly to current tastes. As one of my students once quipped, Caldecott might very well not win the award that was named after him.

Yet criticism is an act of remembering, of recollection and sometimes of retrieval. My purpose here is to remember one of Caldecott's better known books. In a number of respects.

The Three Jovial Huntsmen is quintessential Caldecott, with its iconography of the hunter, coursing the English countryside, merrily blowing his horn, but there is more—much more—to Caldecott and his work than this now stereotyped image suggests. *The Three Jovial Huntsmen* offers a sweeping sense of Caldecott's special qualities as an illustrator and creator of picture books. Remembering this one chapter of Caldecott's sixteen-book corpus of works for younger children will help, hopefully, to recall the whole.

From the opening pages of *The Three Jovial Huntsmen,* the reader is immediately surprised by one thing: Caldecott's utter simplicity of style. His lines and pages are open, unclogged by embellishment, free to move. The modern eye has come to expect (most likely because it is spoiled, visually saturated) something bold and unusual, both in color and form, to get and hold its attention. It is sure to be taken aback by Caldecott's earth tones and the relatively few colored plates that do appear in the text (there are three uncolored line drawings for every colored picture). Yet even in the colored engravings that accompany Caldecott's text, one is drawn to the characters themselves rather than to detail or color. The colors are flat, even in well-preserved first editions, and this allows Caldecott to carry the reader along on this wild ride over the countryside by virtue of his line. The Caldecott line is swift, sure, and nimble because it is unencumbered by fussiness over detail or modeling, and it is not reduced to background by chromatic textures.

Caldecott had been influenced significantly, as anyone who drew in pen and ink in nineteenth-century England had to be, by the tradition of popular line drawing and illustration established by such masters as Cruikshank, Phiz, Rowlandson, Leech, and Tenniel. Caldecott's own earliest training as a professional artist had been as a "special reporter" for the illustrated British newspapers and magazines (like the *Graphic* and *Punch*) when line drawings were still the accepted and, for all practical purposes, the only cheap means of visually recording news events. As Caldecott developed as an artist, he recognized that his talent lay with this "line," as he punned, and not in the more prestigious media of water colors or oils. In fact, in his later years, he refused commissions in these media, preferring what he felt to be the more expressive, spontaneous vehicle of the pen and ink drawing.

The breakthrough that he made in children's illustration was that he applied this sense of line to picture books in a way that was uniquely different from the works of his two chief contemporary competitors, Kate Greenaway and Walter Crane. Greenaway and Crane also published their works with Caldecott's publisher, Edmund Evans, and in spite of the fact that they cherished Caldecott's friendship, they were also somewhat jealous of Caldecott's talents and tremendous popular success with the picture books. While Crane usually relied on sumptuous colors, forms, and ornamental elements (or highly stylized outlines when he turned to black and white), and Greenaway allowed detail to dominate her almost invariably static drawings, Caldecott brought a freedom of movement to his illustrations. . . . Among more recent commentators on Caldecott's work, Maurice Sendak identified Caldecott's musical line and its "quickening" power as the key to understanding Caldecott's work in the Picture Books [see excerpt dated 1978].

Throughout his career, Caldecott worked at distilling this technique, using the fewest possible lines to tell his stories: "the fewer the lines, the less error committed," he wrote to Henry Blackburn, his biographer, friend, and the publisher of some of his early drawings and travel sketches. His sketchbooks and finished drawings for his picture books bear out this principle: everywhere they are daubed with white ink to remove detail and, in essence, to release the energy of the work. The effect is to involve readers imaginatively in the material. We must, in a sense, "fill in the blanks" by actively participating in the book, adding the floor boards in the dining room where we meet the huntsmen eating, finishing the bricks in the wall that provides border to explode the huntsmen into the reader's world, making up the stubble in the spring field that they course over, inventing the expressions on the faces of the farmers or maidens who watch the huntsmen from a distance.

Another aspect of the active interplay between Caldecott and his audience is the artist's cheerful anticipation of readers' questions, his way of making our need for qualifying detail a part of his own imaginative process. Thus, he has the huntsmen burst onto the scene, in full red-coated, puffy-cheeked splendor on the opening page of the book; but he realizes that before they can reasonably be expected to do this, he must back up on the next page and give them their breakfast. After all, who can be expected to ride all day without a breakfast? He solves this problem through one of those "lightning sketches" in the brown ink he favored (and recommended to Kate Greenaway) which shows the huntsmen, in all their gawky imperfection, quaffing mugs of ale and awaiting another brace of roast capon or grouse from the innkeeper to get them going. All the while, a demure maiden waits, at the end of the table near the door, with the hunting cap and a belt belonging to one of the group, until the chaps are finished and on their way. One might ask, why are they "jovial huntsmen"? Well, it is nearly eight o'clock, and the men seem to be in no hurry to take to the field; a late start won't matter to them, for they are having a splendid time already. We first come to know them as older men—one stout and bald, the middle one lean, tall, and angular, and the third, small and energetic. After this introduction we will see them become more and more youthful as they ride along, caught up in the spirit of the chase—a chase, not to corner some poor fox, but rather to explore and, as three boys might, to turn the facts of the world around them fantastically upside down, to play with its contingencies and to celebrate their profound enjoyment of one another's company.

In *The Three Jovial Huntsmen* and in each of the other picture books, we see Caldecott building a similar kind of logic into his recreations of things that is as surrealistically undemanding of probability as nursery or nonsense rhymes. A child could conceivably ask, "How *does* a cat play a fiddle?" Caldecott respects the question and teases out an answer: he ties the cat's wrist to the fiddle bow with a ribbon. There is nothing unnatural or condescendingly easy about the imaginative bridges Caldecott constructs in the picture books. Children must work for the answers to those literal questions, and they must be willing to suspend their disbelief and bend their emerging rationality to get the jokes that provide the stopping points in *Hey Diddle Diddle* or the huntsmen's journey across the countryside.

Each time the huntsmen come across a new quarry—a scarecrow, a millstone, a bull-cow, a group of children, a pig, or a pair of lovers—the verbal and visual lines of the poem intersect and the improbable can happen. Sendak has described the huntsmen as "three perfect Charlie Chaplins" [see excerpt dated August, 1964]; and, indeed, they are clowns who are compelled to fool around with the world as they find it. They are what the Dakota Sioux call "the contraries," those whose license it is to reverse conventional expectations, doing the

opposite of what any "sane" person or, in this case, determined hunter would do under similar circumstances. In the Lancashire folksong that Caldecott draws on for his text, the first hunter always gives a literal explanation for whatever they have stopped to investigate. He is the straight man, the norm, whose opinion every reader is sure to take initially. And he is quickly overruled by a "contrary" vision. We don't know which of the other huntsmen objects to his interpretation of what he has seen, it could be the second or the third. In any case, he is outvoted, thus allowing reason to be turned inside out; a far-fetched alternative is always the other two huntsmen's preferred opinion. So a "boggart" in a field becomes, satirically, "just a ge'man farmer, that has gone an' lost his way" and a "gruntin', grindin' griddlestone" turns into "nought but an' owd fossil cheese, that somebody's roll't away." The jokes build, incrementally, until the huntsmen's "insane" humor becomes, transparently, a game, both among themselves and for their audience. They are not such "fools" as they may at first have appeared to be. We see through their mask when they kindly insist that the group of school children they meet are "no but little angels, so we'll leave 'em to their play." Finally, the cat is out of the bag when they observe that the "two young lovers in a lane" are just "two poor wanderin' lunatics—come, let us go away." We know that the inverted vision of the huntsmen has found the truth that once more reverses perception, this time letting the huntsmen land on their feet, solidly in reality: lovers *are* often like "lunatics," so *who* is really crazy?

Attempts to define the nature of genius often single out its ability to see new possibilities or relationships between old or common things. Certainly this is true of comic genius. In studying the verbal experimentation of younger children, Kornei Chukovsky came to the conclusion that, between the ages of two and five, children traverse a period in their development when they have gained a mastery of their language and suddenly begin to take sophisticated liberties with it. They become, in short, "linguistic geniuses." Caldecott's visual and verbal games speak directly to this time in children of expansive verbal fantasy. Personally, he remained sensitive throughout his life to this highly charged, creative phase of associative thinking and brought its qualities into the picture books, using visual jokes to corroborate the verbal fantasy. In *The Three Jovial Huntsmen*, for instance, inanimate objects, like scarecrows or millstones, do come alive, in response to the huntsmen's imaginative ability to transform them. The more one looks at the pig, the more he does resemble a well-fed London politician; and the lovers—especially the overprotected gentleman—are surely behaving erratically, given the harmless, good-natured spirit of the huntsmen we have become familiar with by this late point in the book.

In children's humor, there is an additional element that is located in the sympathetic identification most children make between themselves and whoever is the object of a joke. The child and the fool are therefore especially close and share a common ground. In their own way, each is innocently unself-conscious and susceptible to the pitfalls that line the path of any experience. Both are prone to falling down a lot and in a variety of ways (which, in fact, one of the huntsmen does in the book, finally having to climb a tree and blow his horn to get the attention of his friends). As a result of these accidents, the child fears appearing ridiculous to less charitable, older eyes. Caldecott had taken his own tumbles; and, because he could play and laugh about them afterwards, he could exorcise their effects, which might otherwise be devastating. He frequently took occasion to joke in letters to friends about the poor health from which he suffered throughout his relatively short life. (pp. 110-16)

Less dramatically, but apropos of *The Three Jovial Huntsmen,* Caldecott found room to jest about the spills he took while riding. . . . (p. 116)

Caldecott acknowledges and, in doing so, embraces these moments of vulnerability in himself and in others, usually through humor. This willingness to realize the comic and thus to transform these painful accidents establishes a bond of sympathy with his audience—particularly with children. Caldecott's material may not work with sober adults or older, more serious-minded children, though one would like to think his books show both groups how to transcend defeats and laugh at themselves and the spills they take. . . . As though to underscore this difference between adults' and children's responses to life's pratfalls, Caldecott has his jovial huntsmen sent off with expressions of alarm or irritation by all the adults they encounter in the book. But the children understand the huntsmen's game and wish them well, waving them on to further adventures.

In the end, we are always brought back to that sense of movement that permeates Caldecott's picture books. Sendak described this element as "a spontaneous, rushing quality" in his "Appreciation" of Caldecott [see excerpt dated 1978]. He went on:

> The word *quicken,* I think, best suggests the genuine spirit of Caldecott's animation, the breathing of life, the surging swing into action that I consider to be an essential quality in pictures for children's books. Sequential scenes that tell a story in pictures, as in the comic strip, are an example of one approach to animation. In terms of technique, it is no difficult matter for an artist merely to simulate action,

Illustration from The Three Jovial Huntsmen *(1880).*

but it is something else to *quicken,* to create an inner life that draws breath from the artist's deepest perception.

One obvious way that Caldecott achieves this "quickening" in the structure of *The Three Jovial Huntsmen* is through the alternation of colored engravings with line drawings. The latter serve to sweep the reader along, moving him back and forth across the pages. We pause with the huntsmen at the fully worked, colored pages, as they contemplate their "catches" and deliver a verse of the poem. But, true to his subject, as soon as the verse has been read and the joke has just barely had its absurdity digested, the huntsmen race on to another encounter.

Generally, it is assumed that a picture book will "read" visually as well as verbally, from left to right. However, Caldecott breaks this "rule," doing what comes most naturally for the organic whole of the book. The pictures, the visual action of the book, are multidirectional like a hunt. The chase doubles back on itself, seeming to force the reader's eye back on the left margin where he has begun to "read." Then it gallops over a hill, taking the eye to the top of the page; and, once again, it pauses for a rest and another verse. No words are necessary to explain what the huntsmen are doing between verses. In fact, Caldecott constructs the book so that his text and illustrations do not merely repeat one another. Instead, they are truly complementary, one beginning where the other ends, one providing a visual or verbal harmony or counterpoint to the melody line of the other. This duet between illustrations and words has led admirers like Sendak to acknowledge Caldecott's achievement as, in essence, "the invention of the picture book."

Perhaps more than any of his other picture books, *The Three Jovial Huntsmen* was Caldecott's celebration of movement and humor, of the countryside and its characters, of language and line. In terms of his personal experience, the book was also his exultant expression of his own participation in life. Like the huntsmen, who return to an inn, empty-handed but full-hearted, at the end of their outing, so Caldecott also came home many times (and here, brings the reader there) tired, happy, and satisfied. The ride, the game itself, was more important than any tangible goal. In fact, a fox doesn't even make an appearance in the book, as he frequently doesn't in the chase of life. When the creature finally does take the stage in *The Fox Jumped Over the Parson's Gate,* he outsmarts all his pursuers. Caldecott puts him in the saddle on a horse's back, to chase the last of the hunters out of the book.

Caldecott might not win his own award today, but this dismissal would occur only because modern (or, rather, postmodern) readers have forgotten how to look—carefully, slowly, deeply into the clear, flowing pages of a Caldecott Picture Book. To return to Caldecott is not a regression but, as I suggested at the outset, an act of remembering. And Memory, we know, is the mother of the Muses—and maybe of criticism as well. (pp. 116-19)

> *John Cech, "Remembering Caldecott: 'The Three Jovial Huntsmen' and the Art of the Picture Book," in* The Lion and the Unicorn, *Vols. 7-8, 1983-84, pp. 110-19.*

THE MILKMAID; HEY DIDDLE DIDDLE AND BABY BUNTING (1882)

[The following excerpt is taken from a letter written by Kate Greenaway to Frederick Locker.]

I've been to call on the Caldecotts to-day with Mrs Evans. My brother showed me some of his (Mr. Caldecott's) new drawings yesterday at Racquet Court. They are so uncommonly clever. The Dish running away with the Spoon—you can't think how much he has made of it. I wish I had such a mind.

Kate Greenaway, in a letter to Frederick Locker on May 24, 1882, in Kate Greenaway *by M. H. Spielmann and G. S. Layard, G. P. Putnam's Sons, 1905. p. 89.*

JACKANAPES (1883)

[Jackanapes *was written by Juliana Horatia Ewing. The following letters present Ewing's correspondence with Caldecott regarding his illustrations for the book.*]

4 August 1879

My sister [Horatia Gatty] is writing to say how good it will be for [*Aunt Judy's Magazine*] if you *are* able to let me have a coloured sketch to write to before very long—but I am sure we neither of us want to feel the least "hustled", so don't get (metaphorically speaking!) out of breath.

But I am now becoming so nervous under the honour of interpreting you! that I want to give you a hint of my weakest points—than which nothing is stronger—and one is that I am an absolute, hopeless, unredeemable stick at *mere* middle class modern life. A rising young family in sandboots and frilled trousers with an overfed mercantile mamma will simply congeal my few brains. I only say this because I fear that you may try to *draw down to me* and give me a subject ready-made for a writer of nice little stories!

It must inevitably seem to you that the more obvious and everyday the situation the more help you have given me, but the truth is, nothing is *so* hard as to extract the pathos that lies beneath "Philistinism". Forgive my saying that though my art may do it, I doubt if yours can! You only with your "fateful lines" burn in upon one's brain for perpetual contemplation what it takes such large efforts of human and super-human sympathy to forget!!!

Tell me if you would prefer me to give you the least suggestion.

What I should like best of all would be if you would do a rough coloured sketch of anything that pleases you, and if you would pack it up with one or two pen and ink scratches of *any* quaint groups or figures that float before your mental retina!

Putting them together will be *my* game! and I hope you may think it worth the candle. But trust my imagination please, and if you will send me several *scraps* I shall be very grateful. (pp. 75-6)

P.S. and N.B.! Don't give me a fat baby with a coral—though all England would rise up and call you blessed if you did— and put in dogs or ravens or cockatoos or any such babies at your will.

Lady's postscript: It has this moment struck me that you have profound sympathy with horses, and with the haunting memories round old houses. Don't be afraid of trusting me with the ghost of a posting house, horses, highwaymen, and an old postillion.

But N.B. if you do let your genius run along an old coach road give me one sketch of an almost baby lad learning to ride "like

a jackanapes never off" on a donkey (but not, oh *not*!!! at the seaside).

Take it any way you like. If the coloured sketch would be easily concocted out of a laddie with an aureole of warm yellow hair on a red-haired pony, full tilt among the geese over a village green (the geese to include pretty frightened members of my sex!), give me the decayed post house and postillion in pen and ink. (p. 76)

. . . . .

21 August 1879

If I tell you that your letter pleased me almost more than the sketch I fear your modesty may lead you to underestimate my entire delight and satisfaction with the latter—so I won't say so!

I will only say how very pleasant it is to find that you have not taken very justifiable "huff" at suggestions which might have seemed presumptuous, and how very grateful I am to you, 1st for doing it at all (the full favour of which I assure you I don't underestimate!), and secondly for trying to do it to please me! It is very pretty of you to leave me so many graceful openings for refusing to be inspired by your drawings but I cling to it as tightly as 'our' hero to his red pony, and my head *will* be stupid if I can't hammer something out of it to illustrate you!! (pp. 76-7)

[If] by any amount of brain-thrashing I can fit the design with words the least worthy of it—and please you one half as you have pleased me, I shall be very proud. . . . (p. 77)

. . . . .

[*On December 5, 1882 Caldecott wrote Ewing that "I know I shall not come up to your expectations about* Jackanapes.*" The following excerpt is from her response to this assertion.*]

9 December 1882

One thing I *won't* let you say—that there is the remotest fear of your not being able to "satisfy me".

It's a moral, mathematical and mechanical impossibility that you could fail to do so.

I am too "far-gone" a lover of your pencil; and if the designs proved entirely different from my expectations, I should only see deeper designs in your work, and expound you as Ruskin does Turner!!!!

I doubt if you know, and it seems almost impertinent in me to express, the charm your work has for me. (p. 89)

Juliana Horatia Ewing, in three letters to Randolph Caldecott on August 4 and August 21, 1879 and December 9, 1882 in Yours Pictorially: Illustrated Letters of Randolph Caldecott, *edited by Michael Hutchins, Frederick Warne, 1976, pp. 75-6, 77, 89.*

SOME OF AESOP'S FABLES, WITH MODERN INSTANCES (1883; also published as *The Caldecott Aesop*)

ILLUSTRATOR'S COMMENTARY

[Some of Aesop's Fables, with Modern Instances *was adapted by Alfred Caldecott. The following excerpt is from a letter Caldecott wrote to Frederick Locker-Lampson, a poet and friend for whom Caldecott illustrated* London Lyrics *(1881).*]

As to the Title-Page of my selection of *Fables*—they are not treated very seriously—so that it is not necessary to have a severe title.

I fear that "select Fables" would suggest a very respectable gathering of highly instructive Fables with morals elegantly and wisely pointed—in which, for instance, "the man and his 2 wives" could not come—harmless though it be. And I do not want people to be deceived into the notion that they are going to buy all the Fables of Aesop. So I think we shall have to say *Some of Aesop's Fables with modern Instances* &c, &c.

This is more in the spirit of my designs, sketches and scribblings—and yet is not too irreverent—I admit its tendency towards flippancy.

"Twenty Fables" &c would be too auction-like and cause irritable folk to ask "Why twenty?" "What twenty?" and to fancy that they are the 20 I like best.

Keeping out the words "1st Selection" is judicious: because, if these don't take, of course I will not trouble the world with others.

> *Randolph Caldecott, in a letter to Frederick Locker-Lampson on February 18, 1883, in* Yours Pictorially: Illustrated Letters of Randolph Caldecott, *edited by Michael Hutchins, Frederick Warne, 1976, p. 239.*

It was in [the] grand traditions of British sporting and satiric illustration that Randolph Caldecott produced his unique embellishment of the ancient fables.

Few texts would have been more suited to Caldecott's special talents than Aesop's fables. (p. 4)

It was while working on [Washington Irving's *Old Christmas* and *Bracebridge Hall*] that Caldecott first considered an edition of Aesop.... [Engraver James David] Cooper suggested as a novelty that a "modern instance," or an example from contemporary life (either political or social), might be attached to each fable as an "application" of the moral. This conception amused the artist, and so his proposed edition embraced both his great affection for the English countryside and his pointed observation of Victorian life.

For its text the artist employed his brother, Alfred Caldecott, a fellow of St. John's College, Cambridge, where he taught English literature, took prizes for political economy, and was noted for his musical compositions. The scholar was obviously not in full sympathy with his brother's handling of the classic material. As indicated by the preparatory note, Alfred hoped to make an authentic translation from the Greek, Roman, and French originals, but Randolph's finished sketches were taken from traditional English retellings which differed in places from the old renderings. As the drawings had been executed some time before the translation, and Randolph was reluctant to submit revisions, the professor succumbed and felt obligated to explain in the preface the discrepancies between the archaic and his new versions.

Due to the artist's poor health, the original scheme for the collection was abandoned in favor of a modified selection of the popular fables. Several drawings dropped from the book were published in *The English Illustrated Magazine,* and eleven unpublished designs were exhibited at the annual show of the students of the Chester School of Art. (p. 6)

Characteristically Caldecott was disappointed with his efforts. "Do not expect much from this book," he warned a friend. "When I see proofs of it I wonder and regret that I did not approach the subject more seriously." Not everyone agreed with his harsh appraisal of the book. Joseph Pennell, the American etcher and critic, found in the Caldecott *Aesop* the finest examples of the illustrator's "marvellous power in expressing a whole story in a few lines." "It would be impossible," Pennell wrote in *Pen Drawing and Pen Draughtsmen,* . . . "to give a better idea of bounding free motion than in this stag from the *Aesop,* with the whole of Scotland stretching away behind him" [see excerpt in General Commentary dated 1920]. The American also admired the laughing fox that fooled the stork, and the lamb before he met the wolf: "technically I cannot conceive of anything more innocent and childlike; it would be simply absurd to attempt to copy such a drawing, and yet everything you want is in it." One may easily conclude with Paul Gauguin, when he spoke of Caldecott's animal sketches, "That was the true spirit of drawing."

Surely the *Aesop* is a perfect example of what Caldecott called "the art of leaving out as a science." He argued that "the fewer the lines, the less error committed." This theory should not suggest any carelessness in the planning or execution of the book. Despite his great facility with pen and brush, Caldecott made numerous preliminary sketches for each design in the completed volume. A large collection of these abandoned drawings, mostly for the spot decorations, still survive in the Victoria and Albert Museum. None, however, appears overworked; each is as fresh and spontaneous as a quick thumbnail sketch or a study by a Chinese master. As a comparison between the printed engravings and the original drawings (now in The Houghton Library, Harvard University) proves, J. D. Cooper masterfully preserved in wood the integrity of Caldecott's sketches in brown ink. (pp. 7-8)

> *Michael Patrick Hearn, in an introduction to* The Caldecott Aesop *by Alfred Caldecott, Doubleday & Company, Inc., 1978, pp. 3-8.*

Although the adaptations by Alfred Caldecott are simply written and the illustrations of Randolph Caldecott can be savored by children, the political and social overtones of the pictures and the scholarly quality of the lengthy introduction make the book most appropriate for an older audience, particularly those interested in literary or book art history. The Caldecott brothers present amusing instances of contemporary (Victorian) life in their interpretation; two pages are devoted to each fable, with a literal picture. For **"The Wolf and the Lamb,"** for example, on the left a wolf drooling at a lamb, and a Victorian scene on the right (one man points out a "no fishing" sign to another, then contentedly sits down on the same spot as soon as his victim is out of sight, and begins to fish).... [The] pictures are as deft and witty and vigorous as only Caldecott can make them—but most of them have a latent content that requires a sophistication few children have.

> *Zena Sutherland, in a review of "The Caldecott Aesop," in* Bulletin of the Center for Children's Books, *Vol. 32, No. 6, February, 1979, p. 93.*

This is lesser Caldecott, as he himself recognized, and in no respect a book for children. To the 20 fables are appended "modern instances," meaning that **"The Fox Without a Tail"**—who denigrates all tails—is followed by a drawing of a Vic-

THE DOG AND THE WOLF

A Wolf, seeing a large Dog with a collar on, asked him: "Who put that collar round your neck, and fed you to be so sleek?" "My master," answered the Dog. "Then," said the Wolf, "may no friend of mine be treated like this; a collar is as grievous as starvation."

The Dog and the Wolf. Illustration from Some of Aesop's Fables, with Modern Instances *(1883), adapted by Alfred Caldecott.*

torian spinster-type similarly telling three comelier ladies, "Nonsense, my dears! Husbands are ridiculous things and are quite unnecessary!" The illustrations for the fables proper are far more literal and finicky than is usual with this audacious artist—an effect heightened by their being hand-colored (with watercolors) in the volume from which this reproduction was made. This is not, altogether, Caldecott's animal drawing— *or* social comment—at its spontaneous, vivacious best, which would seem to limit the book to comprehensive historical collections where Michael Hearn's Introduction [see excerpt dated 1978] . . . will be properly appreciated.

A review of "The Caldecott Aesop," in Kirkus Reviews, Vol. XLVII, No. 4, February 15, 1979, p. 201.

[*The Caldecott Aesop*] will be of more historic interest than it will be a first-choice Aesop for children. . . . After each tale and its illustration there is a small commentary-sketch that pictures a contemporary example of each, and displays Caldecott's gift for satiric cartooning on political or social themes. While this does date the treatment, and many references will be lost to children, there are so few examples to hand of this aspect of Caldecott's art that this Aesop is especially welcome for the profuse instances of his skill and imagination as well as of the wit and bite of his pen.

Ruth M. McConnell, in a review of "The Caldecott Aesop," in School Library Journal, Vol. 25, No. 9, May, 1979, p. 58.

A FROG HE WOULD A-WOOING GO; THE FOX JUMPS OVER THE PARSON'S GATE   (1883)

Altogether we may say that [in her designs for *Little Ann and Other Poems* and *Almanack for 1884* Kate Greenaway] shows no falling off in her work.

Not so Mr. R. Caldecott. His two picture-books—***The Fox Jumps over the Parson's Gate,*** and ***A Frog he would a-Wooing Go*** . . .—are unworthy of the series which they continue. The colored drawings particularly are so poor and so little characteristic as to make the familiar initials seem counterfeit. In the outline sketches there is here and there a trace of Mr. Caldecott's genius, but they are mostly below his average. (p. 494)

"Children's Books," in The Nation, New York, Vol. XXXVII, No. 963, December 13, 1883, pp. 493-95.

[The illustrations from *A Frog he would a-wooing go*] represent a new departure by Caldecott in illustrating for children. . . .

A study of the drawings discloses the influence they bore on the work of Beatrix Potter, L. Leslie Brooke, and later illustrators.

At the time of their publication the reviewer for *The Nation* [see excerpt above] . . . wrote that the colored drawings in Caldecott's newest work were "below his average" and "unworthy of the series." Today they are considered some of Caldecott's finest work.

Elizabeth T. Billington, "The Picture Books: Miscellaneous Selections from the Picture Books," in The Randolph Caldecott Treasury, edited by Elizabeth T. Billington, Frederick Warne, 1978, p. 279.

DADDY DARWIN'S DOVECOT: A COUNTRY TALE (1884)

ILLUSTRATOR'S COMMENTARY

[*Daddy Darwin's Dovecot was written by Juliana Horatia Ewing. The following excerpts are from letters Caldecott wrote to Ewing in response to her comments about his pictures for the book.*]

22 January 1884

D. D.'s Dovecot would, of course, make a nice illustrated book; and, if you would entrust it to me, I think I could make the drawings in April—not before. I would make as many drawings as you can afford to reproduce. If you think of having it fully illustrated and by yours obediently, could you be so good as to lend me any little sketches of the villages, farmhouses, churches, &c, &c of the locality in which the scene of the story is laid—or of any details of local costume. (pp. 107-08)

. . . . .

6 July 1884

Here are 2 drawings corrected. I have taken out and put in again the face of young lady and boys and have added terrier. I have also taken out and re-put in chin and mouth and eye of young lady in garden. (I have also made the chin lighter in Phoebe Shaw returning from church: but I do not return it for inspection.) And *all* this in warm weather and with hay still about. Better if you had had the drawings in the month of April! You are not even decided yet—process or engraving? I wished to know which before making the drawings—I should not have used white for process. (Remarks about process further on.)

Your letter is interesting because of the remark about my heroines having passed their first youth and I feel quite pleased that you have made it. Mrs R. C. is—and has been—of this opinion—and so am I to a great extent (explanation further on). But the instance which you give—p. 17, *Milkmaid*—I do not feel to be applicable. I have smoked a cigarette over it and I consider the girl to be only about 20—and the mother in the frontispiece to be old enough to have a son of 17.

And I cannot allow that the parson's daughter was not—before alteration in face and figure—quite correct for 19. I am not saying that she was nice; but, according to my experience, possible and even common. The healthy country people that I have known—milkmaids and parson's daughters—have been quite women at 19. And I maintain that altho' I seldom represent, or try to represent, girls of 15 and 16, yet my young women are seldom more than 25—generally about 20—and at 20 the first bloom of youth is certainly over. You will smile at my assured way of putting it. I find that many artists—illustrators—fight shy of representing the age of 15 or 16. It is, however, a difficult thing to draw small faces in ink so that

all observers shall agree as to the age represented. And 'figures' vary so much that one cannot lay down laws about them.

I may remark here that milkmaids in the dairy districts that I know do not marry as early as those in your experience.

What you say of chins is true—I make a note of it—but the suggestion to 'give a touch more size to the eyes' makes one think that one must be careful in accepting—or rather in acting upon—criticisms of this kind. Mr Blackburn used to say that I was the only man who would alter—I like to do so when I am sure it would be better, although the certainty may be forced upon me by a critic who regards things with different eyes from mine. I have altered the eye of the lady in question: but I have made it rather smaller. It was monstrously large before and not in its right place. It is a very cheap way of making a pretty face to draw large eyes, and then the effect is not intellectual, unless the brow is massive—which will tend to give an imp-like look to the head. Of imps there are 2 kinds—small-brained and large-brained.

I have always been struck by the truthful value given to faces by artists who know how to keep down the eyes. Du Maurier is good in this way—Leech was not so in female faces—in *woodcuts*—and they often looked rather silly.

If I had enlarged the eye in question the distance from eyebrow to underlid would have been greater than distance from underlid to bottom of nostril.

Pardon me for going into these details: as you are a good and valued critic I can pardon myself. (pp. 112-13)

Do not think I have been doing your work hurriedly or carelessly. The drawing of *D.D. and P. daughter* is one of 5 made, and I was obliged to let one go at last.

My ***Picture Books*** are not yet completed, and other matters press upon me: but I do no work hastily. (p. 114)

Randolph Caldecott, in two letters to Juliana Horatia Ewing on January 22 and July 6, 1884 in Yours Pictorially: Illustrated Letters of Randolph Caldecott, edited by Michael Hutchins, Frederick Warne, 1976, pp. 107-08, 112-14.

[I want] to pour out my delight and gratitude for the Gaffers [a picture later used as the frontispiece for ***Daddy Darwin's Dovecot***]!

It is hardly possible fitly to tell you how I appreciate the sympathy you have shown and the trouble you have taken in depicting the scene and all its local colour.

In the latter you have been quite marvellously successful. (p. 83)

You have given the spirit of the men and the spirit of the country, and I know what that means as to careful reading of my M.S. and kindly sympathy with the home life thereof! Many, many thanks! . . .

I hope you gain some comfort from knowing that "whatsoever things are pure and whatsoever things are lovely" in home scenes of landscape and of humanity—always tempt one to say "How like Caldecott". (p. 84)

Juliana Horatia Ewing, in a letter to Randolph Caldecott on November 23, 1881, in Yours Pictorially: Illustrated Letters on Randolph Caldecott, edited by Michael Hutchins, Frederick Warne, 1976, pp. 83-4.

LOB LIE-BY-THE-FIRE; OR, THE LUCK OF LINGBOROUGH (1885)

ILLUSTRATOR'S COMMENTARY

[Lob Lie-by-the-Fire *was written by Juliana Horatia Ewing. The following excerpts are from letters Caldecott wrote to Horatia Gatty, Ewing's sister, who worked with him on the production of the book during Ewing's final illness and after her death on May 13, 1885.*]

27 April 1885

(I send to E. Evans to-day the 7 drawings which are approved for him to go on with.)

I should like to have a little further criticism of the 4 drawings kept apart from the 7, so that, if possible, I could modify or alter them.

The drawing-room scene is a little "tight" and not simple enough in treatment—this I can perhaps do over again. N.B. The rather fat lady on left was not intended for one of the little old ladies.

In scene with lawyer and 2 ladies—are ladies not satisfactory, or lawyer—or all? He is dressed as country lawyers were wont to be attired at that time.

In baby-finding scene—I do not think the hand of lady is wrong. It has a mitten on it, and I thought I was happy in shewing the shape of the wrist. It looks just a little funny—I could bring the arm and elbow *out* a little more. You do not praise the babe's leg. It is copied from the leg of one of Luca della Robbia's most beautiful Infant Saviours—and he is very great at infants—the best of all the Italians—I think.

If the sailor is not considered a pleasing subject to depict—I'll leave him out. I could make my drawing of him more winning as to expression of face—and I think the figure would give variety to the book and please some people. I think a little of the rugged gives force and contrast and counteracts the namby-pamby. (pp. 153-54)

I made a new drawing of tea-party and sent it to Evans. I did not put more sentiment into it, so I thought it would not interest you—I felt sure that it was a better drawing than the 1st attempt, and had something in it I wanted to shew. (p. 154)

. . . . .

11 June 1885

Here are 9 drawings to *Lob*—1 of them is, however, but a second version of another, and you will please to mark that which you like the better.

The child and wreath I suggest as a finial to the book, and it can be reduced a little in size.

I fear that Mr Evans will feel somewhat "done" when he sees all the drawings (he has had the others in his hands for some time) because he has promised to engrave them on wood, and they are more important and have more work in them than former books. I do not propose to do any more—except perhaps a cover-design.

I have put a little more work into these than I intended because I have felt that I was working towards helping to keep Mrs Ewing's memory green—although many more important things will tend to do that. (p. 154)

. . . . .

13 June 1885

I again send you the 'Highlander and boy' which I have altered according to your suggestion. I do not think *I* can make it better than it now is. The costume is from a Waterloo picture. I at first made the kilt rather short because I have often observed that soldiers of unusual height wear usual-sized garments. I have added considerably to the weight of the body, and I have altered the nose. Is not this a Lowland nose now?—the old nose I have seen in Highlanders, who are akin to the Welsh, I believe.

I read in the story of an officer with a sword "clattering after him" and from the description of his dress I suppose him not to be a field-officer. If not, would he not wear a claymore. Perhaps I am quite in a muddle over this. Very likely.

As to more military scenes, I do not think I mentioned any number, because I had not then considered that part of the book and the cockatoo portion. Now I am of opinion that to put more than the 2 I have made (the boy running in snow and this enclosed) would unduly illustrate that part of the book and not fairly distribute the cuts over the whole. Then that part is but short and the most dramatic scenes—the outpost duty on cold night scenes—are almost undrawable. The chief figures in this military portion are Mac. and John, and it seems to me unnecessary to repeat them—more especially as they are often drinking. The death-bed scene I consider to be too well told by the author to be trifled with by the illustrator—apart from the seriousness of the subject.

The title and cover design (which will be one) will have the Highlander somewhereabout: but I think he should not be prominent, for I hear opinions that his is not the most interesting part of the book. (p. 155)

Randolph Caldecott, in three letters to Miss Gatty on April 27, June 11, and June 13, 1885, in Yours Pictorially: Illustrated Letters of Randolph Caldecott, *edited by Michael Hutchins, Frederick Warne, 1976, pp. 153-56.*

───────────

THE RANDOLPH CALDECOTT PICTURE BOOK   (1976)

Randolph Caldecott is a perennial favourite if only because he arouses such nostalgia in the older generation; and in *The Randolph Caldecott Picture Book* are reproduced four of his classics: *The Diverting History of John Gilpin, The House that Jack Built, The Queen of Hearts* and *The Farmer's Boy*. This new edition is as authentic as it could be, with the line-drawings and original typeface in sepia. Modern children are likely to confuse *The Farmer's Boy* with Old Macdonald who had a farm, and those in London may find it hard, if salutary, to reconcile John Gilpin's almost rural ride through "Edmonton so gay" with the horrors of the North Circular Road. The full-page colour illustrations stand the test of time remarkably well; the "Priest all shaven and shorn"—from *The House that Jack Built*—opening his casement window at dawn to see the "Cock that crowed in the morn" is particularly happy, and in *The Queen of Hearts* nothing could be slyer than the Knave, depicted slipping the tarts into his medieval sleeve, watched by the kitchen cat.

Felix Pickering, "Gilpin Rides Again," in The Times Literary Supplement, *No. 3900, December 10, 1976, p. 1546.*

The humour, verve and gaiety of Caldecott's work in colour or black and white are evident, as is his ability to relate illustration to text.

His use of the black and white double page spread without words does not interrupt the action but rather skilfully leads the reader on to the next stage of the story. Time has not lessened the appeal of his illustrated nursery rhymes and they compare favourably with many modern versions. . . . Both [*The Randolph Caldecott Picture Book* and *The Kate Greenaway Book*] merit a place in any collection devoted to the study of children's literature, but it would be sad to think that we did not also ensure that the picture books of these two artists find their way into the hands of children for whom they were created.

> *Enid M. Osborne, in a review of "The Randolph Caldecott Picture Book," in* Library Review, *Glasgow, Vol. 25, No. 8, Winter, 1976-77, p. 332.*

The resurgence of the graphic arts between 1860 and 1880 . . . included the work of some highly original children's book illustrators such as Walter Crane, Kate Greenaway and Randolph Caldecott. In fact, it's no exaggeration to say that these are seminal figures in the field. . . . Kate Greenaway's world is one of delicately-poised, sweetly pretty children, in an arcadian countryside, while Randolph Caldecott's much tougher, more masculine, approach offers us a robust hunting England full of vividly characterised individuals, with a rollicking humour that goes back to Rowlandson. This can be well seen in *The Diverting History of John Gilpin,* the first of four of his classic books which make up *The Randolph Caldecott Picture Book.* It shows him as a master of line drawing, full of vigour and verve, which marvellously brings John Gilpin's famous ride to life as he scatters geese, dogs and children before him on his wild gallop. . . . Caldecott produced books in which each picture is an integral part of the design of the whole book.

Perhaps part of Caldecott's success as an artist derives from the fact that he came late to book illustration, after an early career as a Shropshire bank clerk where he was deeply involved in country life, living in an old farmhouse, going fishing, shooting and hunting, and attending the local cattle markets and fairs. This intimate knowledge of country life went into his drawings, even though his inspiration was not drawn from his own contemporary world but looked back to the late eighteenth and early nineteenth century. Only rarely do his characters step out of period dress, for the Caldecott country is a sort of pre-industrial Shropshire, with villages full of jolly, gaitered farmers and demure milkmaids. And yet his art is also centred on closely observed incidents from the real world, which he recreated with a few fluid lines, like the breezy drawing of the fashionable lady being splashed by mud from the flying hoofs of John Gilpin's horse, or the snorting animal seen from the rear as it gallops down the road. Marvellously dynamic pictures like the three which show the cow with the crumpled horn tossing the dog, that worried the cat, that killed the rat, that ate the malt, that lay in the house that Jack built, make most of today's nursery rhyme picture books seem stiff and unresponsive. In fact the four Caldecott toy books reproduced here more than hold their own among all the modern products of sophisticated technology, where lavish colour printing often has to make up for the poverty of imagination and artistry.

> *Lavinia Learmont, "Classical Picture Books," in* Books and Bookmen, *Vol. 22, No. 9, June, 1977, p. 62.*

RANDOLPH CALDECOTT'S JOHN GILPIN AND OTHER STORIES (1977)

Impossible to overlook among the new publications is this collection of lyrics and illustrations, imbued with the spirit of a recognized genius. Caldecott added his personal touches to Cowper's verses about *John Gilpin* as well as to the other gems here: *The House that Jack Built, A Frog He Would A-Wooing Go* and *The Milkmaid.* The paintings and drawings are full of life, whether they show raucous geese scrambling in fright from Gilpin's bounding runaway horse, delicate figures in a pastorale dance, or any goings-on. The book hasn't lost a bit of freshness since it appeared first, back in 1878. The new edition will undoubtedly be snapped up by collectors, by everyone who values art.

> *A review of "Randolph Caldecott's John Gilpin: And Other Stories, in* Publishers Weekly, *Vol. 213, No. 9, February 27, 1978, p. 157.*

Four of Caldecott's works collected here offer exemplary samples of the robust action, economy of line, and attention to detail that the nineteenth-century artist brought to his work. Alternating brown line sketches with rich, full-color illustrations, Caldecott's representative art infuses nuances of humor that add extra dimensions to John Gilpin's ruinous ride, Jack's burgeoning house, the frog's disastrous courting session, and the milkmaid's timely revenge. Authentic backgrounds accurately portray the surroundings of the artist's own world, while his sly wit and innate ability to entertain reach easily across the span of time.

> *Barbara Elleman, in a review of "Randolph Caldecott's John Gilpin and Other Stories," in* Booklist, *Vol. 74, No. 17, May 1, 1978, p. 1428.*

Here is a useful reminder, if one is needed, of the first undoubted genius of the children's picture-book, a masterly technique and a roving imagination at work in an England which is no less attractive for being a never-never land. Superb draughtsmanship is wedded to wit and to a sure and affectionate observation. No wonder young Edwin Lutyens, conditioned to these books in childhood, grew up to design houses as lovely and as improbable as those which flowered from Caldecott's imagination.

> *M. Crouch, in a review of "John Gilpin and Other Stories," in* The Junior Bookshelf, *Vol. 42, No. 3, June, 1978, p. 134.*

Modern day youngsters and their teachers can get the same sense of fun as earlier generations. The large-sized book with full-colored Victorian illustrations exhibits a large-sized talent that has been a long-lasting favorite. Caldecott . . . gets more action, expression, and humor into a few strokes than more belabored works of art. The drawings enhance less-than-extraordinary works of poetry. Good to compare with the Greenaway collection.

> *Ruth M. Stein, in a review of "Randolph Caldecott's John Gilpin and Other Stories," in* Language Arts, *Vol. 56, No. 6, September, 1979, p. 688.*

Alice Childress

1920-

Black American author of fiction, dramatist, and scriptwriter.

Although she has published only four works for children, Childress is recognized as an outstanding creator of realistic young adult novels and well-crafted plays. She is best known for her first book, *A Hero Ain't Nothin' but a Sandwich* (1973), a revealing picture of a thirteen-year-old heroin addict. Childress is also the author of *Rainbow Jordan* (1981), a sensitive examination of maternal neglect and the healing bonds between generations. Portraying lifelike characters and complex situations with power and realism, Childress describes black adolescents faced with finding love and security in urban environments. Both of her novels contain such themes as the effects of racism and poverty, accepting love from a parental figure, adjusting to loss and loneliness, the importance of family, and learning to believe in oneself. Well-respected as an adult playwright, Childress structures her chapters as new acts or scenes and employs dramatic techniques such as the monologue to provide narration and build characterization. The novels are also distinguished by natural black dialect, inclusion of positive adult role models, and use of unresolved endings; although her stories do not conclude happily or neatly, Childress leaves them open to believable, hopeful conclusions. Considered a writer of awareness, sensitivity, eloquence, and directness, Childress provides young readers with books which are regarded as encouraging and uplifting despite the harshness of their subjects.

Childress gained immediate rapport with the teenage audience after the publication of *A Hero Ain't Nothin' but a Sandwich*. Set in Harlem, the book is told in the first person by protagonist Benjie Johnson as well as by several different characters with varying interests in him: his stepfather Butler Craig, his close friend, his teachers, and even his pusher. In addition to its popularity, *Hero* became immediately controversial. Banned from several school libraries, it was one of nine works which reached the Supreme Court in a book banning case. Childress adapted *Hero* into a film in 1977. Her other works include *When the Rattlesnake Sounds* (1975), a one-act play for young adults which looks at three days in the life of black abolitionist Harriet Tubman, and *"Let's Hear It for the Queen"* (1976), a humorous play for elementary school readers which is based on "The Queen of Hearts" nursery rhyme. Both plays are considered expertly written, enjoyable to read and produce, and easy to stage.

While noting her storytelling ability and the success of her narrative style, critics especially applaud Childress's objective, in-depth characterizations. Several observers commend the exceptional skill with which she delineates Butler Craig and Rainbow Jordan; she is also saluted for portraying Benjie Johnson with sympathy and understanding without condoning his behavior. Reviewers praise Childress as a writer of books which offer an insightful look at the toll of poverty and bigotry through their inclusion of universal themes, nondidactic presentations, and appealing child and adult characters who support each other and discover their own inner strength.

A Hero Ain't Nothin' but a Sandwich was chosen as a National Book Award finalist and won a Jane Addams Honor Award

© Jerry Bauer

in 1974; it was also selected for the Lewis Carroll Shelf Award in 1975. For her screenplay, Childress received the first Paul Robeson Award for Outstanding Contributions to Performing Arts from the Black Filmmaker's Hall of Fame in 1977. *Rainbow Jordan* received a Coretta Scott King Award honorable mention in 1982.

(See also *Contemporary Literary Criticism*, Vols. 12, 15; *Something about the Author*, Vols. 7, 48; *Contemporary Authors New Revision Series*, Vol. 3; *Contemporary Authors*, Vols. 45-48; *Dictionary of Literary Biography*, Vol. 7: *Twentieth-Century American Dramatists*; and *Dictionary of Literary Biography*, Vol. 38: *Afro-American Writers after 1955: Dramatists and Prose Writers*.)

AUTHOR'S COMMENTARY

Events from the distant past, things which took place before I was born, have influence over the content, form, and commitment of my work. I am a descendant of a particular American slave, my great grandmother, Annie. Lincoln's proclamation of emancipation did not automatically release all held in bondage. Many "owners" held back the news of "freedom" and continued to exact unpaid labor. Public pressure finally brought about a legal deadline for the release of those held in bondage. Draped in rags, my great grandmother was taken to the center of the city of Charleston, South Carolina, and there she was abandoned at the age of thirteen. A white woman, Anna Campbell, found her crying and after hearing her story offered to share her home. ''I have a five-room house and very little money. You are welcome to stay with me and we can try to be of some comfort to each other.'' Annie's relatives had been sold away to other places and were unknown to her. She took the last name of her benefactor—Campbell.

Mrs. Campbell's son was a seaman. He visited his mother whenever his ship docked in Charleston harbor. He sailed away, never to return, when Annie became pregnant with his child. Mrs. Campbell assured my great grandmother that she knew the child was her son's. The baby was a girl. They named her Eliza, after a character in Harriet Beecher Stowe's *Uncle Tom's Cabin,* the young mother who took flight to freedom across an icy river, while pursued by the hounds of slaveholders. When Anna Campbell died she left a letter stating that Annie and Eliza Campbell were to become the owners of her small house and all furnishings. At that time laws forbade Negroes inheriting property rights over any white, related claimant. Out-of-town cousins came to town and claimed the Campbell place. Annie was illiterate but kept Eliza in school through the fifth grade and made it possible for her to read and write. The child was very intelligent and continued to read and so to educate herself in current events, history, poetry, and art. She married a mill-hand slave descendant and they raised seven children in abject poverty. They sent their children out to become apprentices and learn trades—tailoring, dressmaking etc. Some managed to stay in school through grade eight, none went higher.

Eliza, my grandmother, raised me. I had to wring such stories out of her. She was not fond of remembering her mother's account of slavery and the mockery of so-called freedom. Her own life was very hard, Annie's was bleak. I never planned to become a writer, I never finished high school. My daughter was the first college graduate on my mother's side of the family. Time, events, and Grandmother Eliza's brilliance taught me to rearrange circumstances into plays, stories, novels, and scenarios and teleplays. I recall teachers urging me to write composition papers about Blacks who were ''accomplishers''—those who win prizes and honors by overcoming cruel odds; the victory might be won over racial, physical, economic, or other handicaps but the end result had to inspire the reader/audience to become ''winners.'' This trend continues in a flood of how-to and inspirational books which give counsel on how to beat out competition, how to become the lone winner in a field of five hundred . . . or millions. I turned against the tide and to this day I continue to write about those who come in second, or not at all—the four hundred and ninety-nine and the intricate and magnificent patterns of a loser's life. No matter how many celebrities we may accrue, they cannot substitute for the masses of human beings. My writing attempts to interpret the ''ordinary'' because they are not ordinary. Each human is uniquely different. Like snowflakes, the human pattern is never cast twice. We are uncommonly and marvelously intricate in thought and action, our problems are most complex and, too often, silently borne.

I concentrate on portraying have-nots in a *have* society, those seldom singled out by mass media, except as source material for derogatory humor and/or condescending clinical, social analysis. Politically I see my Black experience, my characters, and myself in very special circumstances. Participation in po-

litical parties has not given us power and authority over our lives. We remain in the position of petitioners, or at best pressure groups trying to plead and press one faction against another. Over the years, our Black leaders have been forced to act as intermediaries between Blacks and the President of the United States. I wonder why no President considers himself our leader. Somehow he manages to convince himself that certain citizens are outside of his sphere. The presidential contribution is to give some minimal hearing and consideration to our ''representatives''—who fill him in on the problems of those who are not white. Our leaders, in exchange for minimal progress, are sent home, where they must urge us to vote for ''the lesser of two evils.'' Either/or is too confining a pattern to solve the complexity of racism. Too often we Black writers are image-building for others to measure our capability, acceptability, or human worth. The Klan instinct attacks the mind and persecutes thought even when not organized into Klaverns.

The Black writer explains pain to those who inflict it. Those who repress and exclude us also claim the right to instruct us on how best to react to repression. All too often we follow their advice. Many of us say we are not ''Black'' writers, but only writers. The long fight for social justice bends our creative effort in many either/or directions. Few white writers are bound by so many limitations. They are not faced with racial persecution transcending class, sex, economics, or religion. The marketplace is white and there we are daily reminded that our writing is not considered universal. We are told that ''the best'' is that subject matter applicable to the whites of the world; to the same extent it may acceptably touch upon the Black experience. That measure of ''universality'' and ''common experience'' places shackles on a writer's pen. The Black writer needs no such mental measuring to enjoy the works of Peretz, Sholom Aleichem, Sean O'Casey, Guy de Maupassant, Shakespeare, and a host of ''others'' whose lives have been spent outside of our boundaries.

We are the only racial group within the United States ever forbidden by law to read and write. The law also forbade any white to teach us to read. After generations of such laws, while slave labor made profits and founded fortunes for others, we are besieged with accusations of ''inferiority'' in learning skills. We and the Native Americans were the only citizens or aliens legally forbidden to enter libraries, concert halls, theaters, and public schools. In order to change such laws we spent many lives and much money and time. Any who allied themselves with us had to pay similar penalties.

The political atmosphere of a country shapes the intellect of the majority of its citizens—toward conformity. Even when a writer seeks to evade and omit all that is political, because it is politic to do so, that then becomes political. In the U.S.A. we profess and proclaim freedom of thought and expression; certain thoughts are seldom presented via mass media or financially rewarded to the same extent as the ''popular'' view. The constant presentation of murder as a form of casual amusement and the blatant sexual exploitation of children are presented as art forms and enjoy a more lucrative market than works which confront social and political issues in depth. Such works are frequently derided and labeled controversial.

Artists are economically tempted away from serious topics. The Black artist finds most opportunity and reward in the field of ludicrous comedy, refuge in laughter. That labeled ''serious and controversial'' is silently considered dangerous ground. We usually wait for whites to interpret global affairs and form government policy toward foreign countries. That ''minority'' leadership which shows independence of thought and action is often silenced, imprisoned, or mysteriously murdered. No, one cannot kill an idea but it may be delayed for a long while. We read storm warnings and keep our small craft near shore. Writers are encouraged to "keep 'em laughing" and complain "with good humor" in order to "win" allies. The joke is always on ourselves. The only white face in a minstrel show is Mr. Interlocutor, the questioner. He asks the blackface comedian, "Who was that lady I saw with you last night?" He answers, "Dat was no lady, dat was my wife!" The reliable joke brings a reliable laugh. The humor would fall flat on the ears of some revelers if it turned, ever so slightly: "Dat was no lady, dat was *your* wife!"

As long as we are subliminally trained to recognize other racial feelings above our own, our ideas are in danger of being altered even before they are written. It becomes almost second nature to be on guard against the creative pattern of our own thought. Shall I ease in this bit of truth or that? Perhaps I can make a small point in the midst of a piece of nonsense. We often make a great noise in the other direction and try to "mouth whitey to death"; blowing off steam can be a grand but harmless substitute for even small action. Self-censorship also knows how to disguise itself in long, strong, pointless diatribes against ourselves. "We don't vote! We don't know how to take a joke! We don't need to speak Black English!" And on and on: "Black women sleep with their fists balled up!" Consider *Black English* and the furor it causes. "Zis and zat" when uttered by the French is considered charming, but "dis and dat" as an Africanism is ridiculed as gross and ugly. The echo of European accents and linguistic spillovers into American "English" fall easily upon our ear. Africanisms cause a shudder. Many Blacks now say hail and farewell with the Italian *ciao*. So what? Maybe I shoulda stood in bed and not sperl ya day awready. Okay? Like enough with the jabber and the bla, bla, bla. Got it? See what I mean?

I try to bend my writing form to most truthfully express content; to move beyond the either/or of "artistic" and politically imposed limitations. I never planned to become a writer. Early writing was done almost against my will. Grandmother Eliza gently urged, "Why not write that thought down on a piece of paper? It's worth keeping." Writing was jotting things down. The bits and pieces became stories. Writing was a way of reminding myself to go on with thoughts, to take the next step. Jottings became forms after I discovered the public library and attempted to read two books a day. Reading and evaluating form, I taught myself to know the difference of structure in plays, books, short stories, teleplays, motion picture scenarios, and so forth. Knowledge of such form and much content taught me to break rules and follow my own thought and structure patterns with failure and success. I acquired a measure of self-discipline, to make myself write against my will in the face of a limited market.

Because I wrote, people began to think of me as a writer, they *asked* to perform and publish what I had written. I had started a "career" as an actress with the American Negro Theatre, went to Broadway with *Anna Lucasta,* was nominated for a Tony award. Radio and television work followed, but racism, a double blacklisting system, and a feeling of being somewhat alone in my ideas caused me to know I could more freely express myself as a writer . . . and yet. My stories and plays were usually labeled controversial and some were banned from a few school libraries and by several local television outlets when shown on national network. I do not consider my work controversial, as it is not at all contrary to humanism.

My books tend to read somewhat like plays because theater heavily influenced my writing. I think mainly in terms of visual, staged scenes and live actors in performance—even in a novel. The novel and film allow for more wandering and changing of "setting." The stage play, confined to one area, taxes the imagination more than other forms. It is the greatest challenge because it also depends heavily on the cooperation of many other individuals with several approaches to creative expression—the director, the producer, set, scene and lighting people, costumer etc.

The new surge toward cable and cassette may prove to be a most hopeful area for Black and other "minority" writers. Cassettes, sold over the counter like tapes and records, will give theater a broader audience freed from the unspoken but imposed restrictions of stage, screen, television, and film. Without an imposed measure of "universality" our audience will be found in homes and on the college circuit, by selection. Being a woman adds difficulty to self expression, but being Black is the larger factor of struggle against odds. Black men and women have particular problems above and beyond the average, in any field of endeavor. Again, I remind you, I've heard some of us say, "I am not a *Black* writer, I'm a *person,* an *artist.*" I've never heard any whites decry being *white* for fear that being *white* and a *person* might cancel one or the other. Being white comes in handy in most parts of the world . . . even in a few Black countries. In South Africa and the United States it is a definite plus in the matter of progress. A Black writer *is a person* and there should be no room for contradiction. The twisted circumstances under which we live is grist for the writing mill, the loving, hating and discovering, finding new handles for old pitchers, and realizing there is no such thing as *the* Black experience; the pain and pleasure is many-faceted and the honest writer can only reveal absolute belief—be it right or wrong according to the belief of others. Time and events allow for change on both sides. Of course, the greatest challenge is trying to write well. With all of its trials, for me there is no creative process more fulfilling than that of writing.

In *A Short Walk* [a novel for adults], *A Hero Ain't Nothin' But a Sandwich,* and *Rainbow Jordan* I used a monologue style and first- and second-person storytelling and placed past, present, and future in and out of the usual sequence—while progressing story line. A central narrative is told by several characters even though one is the lead. Story differs and point of view changes as plot progresses. The Japanese film classic *Rashomon* unfolds a story of rape. Told by several characters, each gives a different account of the same event, but only one is telling the truth. In my stories the characters all have different points of view, but all are telling the truth. (pp. 111-16)

While one is creating a character there are glad moments of divorce from one's own conscious theories and beliefs. We can be taken over by a character. I was tempted to remove "The Pusher" from *A Hero Ain't Nothin' But a Sandwich:* the villain was too persuasive, too good at self-defense, too winning in his sinning; however, he is the toughest form of street temptation, so I let him live. The book was banned from the Island Trees School Library, case still pending along with several others after going through two courts. It was also the first book banned from a Savannah, Georgia, school library since *Catcher in the Rye* was banned during the fifties. Writing is indeed exciting and the joy of creation, though tedious at times, is the highest form of compensation. Well, I can't find a thought to better this old one. . . . (p. 116)

Alice Childress, "A Candle in a Gale Wind," in
Black Women Writers (1950-1980): A Critical Evaluation, *edited by Mari Evans, Anchor Books, 1984,*
pp. 111-16.

GENERAL COMMENTARY

ALLEEN PACE NILSEN AND KENNETH L. DONELSON

Two of Alice Childress' novels are studies in loneliness and
quiet heroism. *A Hero Ain't Nothin' But a Sandwich* could
have easily been a sociological treatise about a young drug
user, but Benjie is no sociological specimen. Neither is his
would-be stepfather, Butler Craig, one of the noblest creations
of modern young adult fiction. Butler saves Benjie's life, and
later, when Benjie admits his mistakes and apologizes, Butler
makes clear what the quiet hero is, though Butler would never
have admitted he was in any way heroic. . . . (p. 221)

In *Rainbow Jordan,* Rainbow is a fourteen-year-old girl who
lives some of the time with her immature mother, Kathie, and
when her mother leaves for places unknown, Rainbow lives
with Miss Josie who runs a temporary way-station for children
with problems. Although the adults should serve as hero-models
for Rainbow, in a reversal of normal roles, Rainbow emerges
as the strongest of the three, the most admirable, the most
deserving of emulation by readers. (pp. 221-22)

> *Alleen Pace Nilsen and Kenneth L. Donelson, "Life*
> *Models: Of Heroes and Hopes," in their* Literature
> for Today's Young Adults, *second edition, Scott,*
> *Foresman and Company, 1985, pp. 208-57.*

A HERO AIN'T NOTHIN' BUT A SANDWICH (1973)

AUTHOR'S COMMENTARY

I put aside any fear of writing on themes which seriously affect
our lives. *A Hero Ain't Nothin' But a Sandwich* has created a
fiery dialogue, pro and con, between librarians, teachers, parents and students, on the subject of drug abuse and the written
word. The book is startling because I wanted the attention of
the reader, without glossing over the subject matter to make
it other than it has proven to be . . . a tragic destruction, particularly of the young, by adults who profiteer from misery.
The art of living cannot be taught or learned by rote, so I
believe we should encourage our children to make inquiry and
seek answers, directly, with honesty, through reading and open
discussion in the home as well as at school. Young People
send me admirable letters which show they have no difficulty
in deciding *against* participation in the drug scene, expressing
deep concern and regret for those who ruin their lives by using
false bravado as a form of rebellion. Their letters let me know
that "cinema verite," in writing, exposes the land mines and
booby traps to be found on the contemporary scene. Now, and
in the future, I hope we continue to enjoy great classics and
the beautiful fairy tales of Grimm and Andersen, but with the
full understanding that "Sleeping Beauty" no longer sleeps . . .
and times grow "curiouser and curiouser."

> *Alice Childress "The People behind the Books: 'A*
> *Hero Ain't Nothin' but a Sandwich'," in* Literature
> for Today's Young Adults *by Kenneth L. Donelson*
> *and Alleen Pace Nilsen, Scott, Foresman and Com-*
> *pany, 1980, p. 427.*

There are too few books that convince us that reading is one
of the supreme gifts of being human. Alice Childress, in her
short, brilliant study of a 13-year-old black heroin user, *A Hero
Ain't Nothin' But a Sandwich,* achieves this feat in a masterly
way by telling a real story of the victims of today's worst urban
plague, heroin addiction, and it reaffirms the belief that excellent writing is alive and thriving in some black corners of
America.

Benjie Johnson is a hero and a victim in this story, though he
would be the last to see himself as either. In Benjie's ghetto
world there are few recognizable heroes; everyone there is a
victim of the life that numerous black people experience daily;
even childhood is almost nonexistent for him. (pp. 36, 38)

Though Benjie is vulnerable, he is not innocent, and the story
tells of those who are affected by his near addiction to "skag"—
most severely, his mother and his stepfather, Butler, who is a
hero in his own right. . . .

This is a family whose members suffer in turn, for dope has
changed Benjie into its enemy in their midst. The other characters of the book encounter the family in its sorrow and near
dissolution and are more or less concerned by the tragedy and
speak of it. . . .

Even the stone-hearted pusher, Walter, is allowed his say. . . .
(p. 38)

Walter is cold and tough, like the streets he stalks each day.
Benjie knows the hardness of the pavement and people, knows
that it grinds away the tenderness of youth and innocence. Yes,
in Benjie's Harlem a hero ain't nothin but a sandwich. . . .
[The] analogy is national in scope and extremely apt. An identity crisis stalks the children of the black community to their
very graves!

This surprisingly exciting, entertaining book demystifies the
pusher and the problem he sells by centering on the unwitting
victim, Benjie, and the disintegration of a black family. With
their own voices the people in this story tell the truths of their
lives. The writer uses her considerable dramatic talents to ex-
pose a segment of society seldom spoken of above a whisper;
she exposes the urban disease that hides behind the headlines
of drug abuse, the child junkies, drug rehabilitation programs
and the problem of sheer survival in the black urban community.

There is a suggestion of hope in this book, but there is also
the unconcealed truth. This truth is well-known but up to now
has been a well-kept secret. You don't even have to be heroic
to discover it. Just read. (pp. 38, 40)

> *Ed Bullins, in a review of "A Hero Ain't Nothin' but*
> *a Sandwich," in* The New York Times Book Review,
> *November 4, 1973, pp. 36, 38,40.*

[*A Hero Ain't Nothin But a Sandwich*] tackles the grim topic
of teenage addiction head on and contrives no happy ending,
but her strong novel is so charged with vitality, personality
and tension that it is anything but defeatist. . . . [It is written
in] a tough, trenchant Harlem idiom and through the viewpoints
of a number of brilliantly delineated people around Benjie. . . .
Despite the cynical title . . . and the total absence of message,
the implicit theme of individual responsibility will do for an
affirming flame; at the end it's still not clear whether alibiing
Benjie will face up to his responsibility, but we know that
Butler, who has accented his with exhilarating—and realistic—
resolution, will be hanging in there whatever comes. (p. 7C)

Sada Fretz, "A Long Sad Tale," in Book World— The Washington Post, *November 11, 1973, pp. 6C-7C.*

[Playwright Alice Childress] has initiated a writing style untried in black children's books, thus far.... The trueness of the book holds even to the end, with the suggestion that Benjie might have shaken his habit left hanging. It's a very powerful story....

[*Hero*] indicates the limitless possibilities which we can expect in black children's books from now on.

Judy Richardson, in a review of "A Hero Ain't Nothin' but a Sandwich," in The Journal of Negro Education, *Vol. XLIII, No. 3, Summer, 1974, p. 398.*

Alice Childress' experience as playwright and actress is revealed in the brilliant characterization and dialogue in *Hero*.... It is told honestly in the vital, but strong, street idiom of Harlem.... While each monologue is part of the story, it also presents a different point of view and helps to develop a gallery of memorable characters. (p. 54)

Hero is not just a family of blacks and their problems: it deals with themes and experiences that are universal, such as rejection, love, the importance of family ties, poverty, and the problems of growing old. It also depicts the frustration and despair of lives warped by discrimination and want; at the same time showing that people must believe in themselves. Lastly, it is a horrifying picture of the effects of dope that make a fine boy become an enemy in his own home. (pp. 56-7)

John T. Gillespie, "Understanding Social Problems," in his More Juniorplots: A Guide for Teachers and Librarians, *R. R. Bowker Company, 1977, pp. 51-74.*

The three novels herein discussed [*A Hero Ain't Nothin But a Sandwich*, *Daddy Was a Number Runner* by Louis Meriwether, and *Nilda* by Nicholasa Mohr] deal with young people growing up in poverty. Poverty is not a subject to be taken lightly, so when an author decides to tackle it, he or she assumes an added responsibility. Writing about poverty commits the writer to a serious treatment; it is not merely enough that the book be entertaining. I am tempted to say that such a book must shed some light on the social and political forces that create poverty, but many great books have been written which avoid all references to politics, though the characters are poor people. Why then apply this criterion to the books at hand? The ready answer is that they owe it to the spirit of the time. These books would not have been published, would not have been written, were it not that the political unrest of the past decade made it popular for publishers to seek out these kinds of books. They, in fact, exploit the currency of a political and social problem, and in so doing, they incur the responsibility of dealing with it with some degree of critical insight. *A Hero Ain't Nothin But a Sandwich* . . . is the only one of the three books which is totally acceptable from both an aesthetic and a political point of view. (p. 6)

A Hero Ain't Nothin But a Sandwich succeeds where both of the other books fail. The circumstances from which the story is wrought are similar to those found in the other two books, but the treatment is quite different. (p. 12)

A Hero abandons the one-point-of-view structure. Each chapter is essentially a monologue delivered by each of the different participants in the story. This allows for utmost flexibility in portraying the conflicting interest of the several characters. It is difficult, though not impossible, to show a situation in all its complexity and yet convince a reader that it is a child's perception. Alice Childress avoids this predicament with a most felicitous result. No doubt the fact that she is a playwright has a great deal to do with her ability to let each character speak for him or herself.

The monologue technique not only has the advantage of describing the action from several vantage points, but it also enables the author to clearly show the discrepancy between what one character thinks he or she is doing and what is perceived by the others, without violating the integrity of any of them. This discrepancy between intention and result is most obvious in the case of Nigeria Greene, a black teacher in Benjie's school. He is, to hear him speak, a gung-ho black nationalist. He tries instilling in his pupils a sense of black pride. That, he feels, comes first, over and above any academic skill he might be able to impart to them. His room is decorated with portraits of Marcus Garvey, W. E. B. Du Bois, and Malcolm X. He constantly runs at the mouth about those blacks who cow-tow to whitey's ways. But he is unable to escape the fact that being a teacher puts him in an economic bracket that pulls him toward the style of life more consistent with the white middle class than with most of his fellow blacks in Harlem. Nigeria Greene seems confused by this phenomenon, and the only thing he can do to protect himself from this inner conflict is to spout more rhetoric.

The portrait of whites is more realistic in this book, more compassionate, and at the same time, because it is believable, more scathing. Bernard Cohen, Benjie's other teacher, is the typical middle class liberal. He wants to do a good job, but he is confused as to what that means. He doesn't want to rock the boat. When he notices Benjie's nodding off, he assumes the boy stays up late watching television. He doesn't want to have to deal with turning a kid in. He only takes action after Nigeria forces the issue. Bernard Cohen is no less confused than Nigeria. Cohen fears that blacks will drive him out of his job, and that keeps a muffled racism alive in him. The principal, the only other white in the book, is counting the days to his retirement.... He is not a stupid man, nor an evil one. He is only an ordinary man trying to do a job too big for him.

The book conveys very strongly the message that we are all human, even when we are acting in ways that we are somewhat ashamed of. The structure of the book grows out of the personalities of the characters, and the author makes us aware of how much the economic and social circumstances dictate a character's actions. We see how people are forced to deviate from their moral standards by the exigencies of their economic self-interest. This is achieved without neglecting to observe the psychological complexity of each human being. Every character is presented as unique. There are no evil characters in the book, though there are evil consequences: a perfect example of hating the sin, but not the sinner.

A Hero has a strong but simple dramatic structure. The story builds to a climax which is resolved in an optimistic denouement. Benjie, as a potential junkie, is the ultimate repository of all the evil that racism and capitalism can inflict upon human beings. The main drama is played out between him and his step-father, Butler Craig. Butler is the strongest person in the book, the only one who is able to come to a clear resolution of his inner conflict, and the only one who is able to reach Benjie. It is interesting to note that Butler is a working class black, in contrast with Nigeria Greene, who despite his rhetoric is unable to see and accept Butler for what he is. Butler, on the other hand, has Nigeria pegged from the beginning: Butler says: "... seems like I'm knowing him, but he can't know me; however I don't hold that against him.... The cat is strainin' so hard to get to me, till I just have to encourage him." Butler comes across as a heroic character, worthy of admiration (something missing from both *Daddy* and *Nilda*), yet the reader is able to identify with his struggle in trying to deal with Benjie. Benjie too is sensitively drawn. The author, without condoning or relieving him of the responsibility which is rightfully his, shows him becoming a junkie, but does not lose sight of the fact that he is a child who is hurting, in trouble, and worthy of our sympathy.

A Hero Ain't Nothin But a Sandwich works, both on an aesthetic and political level, because it is true to its characters. As always, the ultimate criterion for judging a novel must be honesty. Other qualities may be lacking but if the treatment is inherently truthful, the effect will be powerful enough.... In the final analysis, the political content, also, can only be judged on how honestly the characters have been portrayed. What is politics after all? The backbone of radical politics is a humanistic ethic. It seems from the tenet that human needs come first, that every human being is equal, and that an equitable method of distributing the available goods is possible and desirable. None of the books here discussed deal directly with these issues. There is no reason why they must, if only they supply honest characterization, and give the reader some insight into human behavior. Alice Childress, in successfully portraying the complexity of character, has been able to show the effect of economic class and historical antecedent on the people she writes about. (pp. 13-15)

> *Miguel A. Ortiz, "The Politics of Poverty in Young Adult Literature," in* The Lion and the Unicorn, *Vol. 2, No. 2, Fall, 1978, pp. 6-15.*

The important differences between novels and films become particularly apparent when the same author treats a story in both media, as Alice Childress did when she wrote the screenplay for *A Hero Ain't Nothin' But a Sandwich* (1978), based on a novel she had published five years earlier.

Like other novels directed at an adolescent audience, the story has an adolescent, Benjie Johnson, as its central character. (p. 236)

The mood of the novel is stark, and the reader shares Benjie's hopelessness. He does not know where his real father is and agonizes over this fact. Because his mother is busy with her job and her new love, he feels excluded from her life. Butler makes efforts to be a father to him, but Benjie is unable to relate to him and feels that he has stolen Rose's love from him.

In school, Benjie encounters such diverse role models as Nigeria Greene, a fiery black nationalist who makes racial pride the main study in his classes; Bernard Cohen, a Jewish teacher who worries about the decline of traditional learning in general and about the influence of Greene's teaching methods in particular; and the principal, who is just trying to hold on until his retirement three years hence.

Besides narratives by these characters, we also find various other points of view represented. Benjie's grandmother believes that her particular brand of religion-superstition is the answer to his problem; a neighbor woman has designs on Butler and thinks Rose is foolish to let Benjie or anyone else come between her and such a fine man; a pusher, Walter, denies that he is doing anything particularly bad and maintains that if he

didn't supply his customers someone else would. Several boys Benjie's age are portrayed in the book, including his only real friend, Jimmy-Lee, who has broken the dope habit, and with whom Benjie must then break if he is to rationalize his own heroin dependence. There are also some "dope friends," Carwell and Kenny, and another pusher, Tiger.

The first-person narration form is particularly effective in bringing out the uncertainty and ambiguity the various characters feel about their own identities; their stories provide an effective parallel to Benjie's own confusion and uncertainty.

The book is extremely powerful, and Benjie is a character we care about. Though he indulges in considerable adolescent self-pity, he is not without saving graces. (pp. 236-37)

We also care about Rose, who longs to express her love for her son but finds herself only able to criticize, and about Butler, who sincerely loves Rose and is fond of Benjie but who though he works hard to support both them and Benjie's grandmother is keenly aware that he has no official status in their lives.

The novel's ending offers no easy solutions to Benjie's problems, but it leaves us hopeful.... We do not know for sure that Benjie will actually come, but the understanding that he and Butler have begun to achieve suggests that he has at last begun to have a hero in his life, and it strongly implies that if he does not come that day he will come soon.

Both the problem portrayed and the characters are clearly realistic, and what might easily have been a preachy or sentimental book becomes in Childress's hands a sensitive, honest view of life, the way things are today. Because of her skillful use of first-person narrations, the characters—and not just the problem (drugs)—are important. This is not always true of "problem novels" for young readers. (pp. 237-38)

The first change one notices [in the film] is that the setting has been changed from Harlem to Los Angeles, presumably because it was cheaper to film location shots near the Hollywood studio. Obviously, a drug problem such as Benjie's might as easily be found in Los Angeles as in Harlem since no locale or level of affluence is immune from drugs today, but, the effect of moving Benjie from what is clearly an ugly, threatening environment, as portrayed in the novel, to the movie's world of beautifully landscaped parks, palm trees, and beachfront, is to mute the dreariness that characterizes Benjie's environment in the book. (p. 238)

Even more significant than the shift in setting, however, is the change from the multiple first-person narration form of the book to the dramatic objective viewpoint of the camera eye. The power of the novel in illuminating the characters' inner frustrations and confusions is largely lost through this change. Nowhere is this more evident than in the characters of Nigeria and Cohen, who seem much weaker in the film than in the novel. The very sharp, deep conflict between them and their values—as well as the genuine concern for their students that forms a mutual bond between them—is reduced in the film to a superficial playground confrontation.... In the case of Benjie and Butler, however, the characters are both so well developed that we do not miss having their first-person narrations.

The roles of some characters are given either greater or lesser emphasis in the film than in the novel. Rose seems more of a real person in the film than in the novel, where she was a rather shadowy figure. The principal does not appear in the film, and we do not particularly miss him. The grandmother and her religion are given somewhat less prominence in the movie, the neighbor woman is completely eliminated; both changes work well in the film. The four characters of Benjie's dope world acquaintance are effectively combined into two in the movie, each being given enough of a role to make him seem real. Butler's role is significantly increased in the film—so much so that he seems almost equal in importance to Benjie. This may give the movie a real problem with respect to its intended audience. The book is clearly aimed at young adolescents. . . . The movie, with its "PG" rating, is apparently trying to appeal to the whole family, thus the greater emphasis on Butler and Rose and their problems. However, a young adolescent would likely not be able to relate to Butler's problem of establishing his role as the father, for instance. The movie is almost *too* much Butler's story, and there is a mild schizophrenia in point of view. The book, in spite of the multiple first-person narration form, is very clearly Benjie's story. (pp. 238-39)

In fact, from the very beginning of the film Butler seems so clearly concerned about Benjie that it is difficult for the viewer to understand why the boy holds him at arm's length for so long. In the book, this side of Butler is far less apparent until late in the story.

The plot of the novel moves more or less straight forward in normal chronology, though there are some overlaps in time because of the changes in narrators, who frequently comment on the events already mentioned and commented on. In the book, this effectively brings out the various viewpoints and is not really distracting or confusing to the reader. Nevertheless, the movie's straightforward presentation may be somewhat easier for young people to follow.

There are several changes in the sequence of events from novel to film. For instance, the encounter between Benjie and Jimmy-Lee in which the latter declares that he is not going to use dope any more because "I got somethin' better for a dollar to do," takes place early in the book. This is a signal to the reader that despite his protestations to the contrary Benjie is becoming so addicted to heroin that he prefers to break off this important relationship, since Jimmy will no longer join him in his habit. In the movie, this scene appears almost at the very end and therefore only indicates that Benjie is continuing in what we already know is a serious drug habit. Its usefulness in helping us follow Benjie's descent into drugs is lost in the movie.

In fact, the movie never makes it sufficiently clear how or why Benjie becomes addicted to drugs. To show that Benjie is becoming hooked, the filmmaker resorts to the device of repetitive scenes showing him using the drugs and earning money for this habit by delivering drugs. In the movie, the whole time lapse from Benjie's first use of marijuana to when we know that he is, in fact, unable to quit heroin, seems altogether too brief and unrealistically sudden. And the question of *why* Benjie takes drugs remains quite puzzling. Though bothered by the fact that he does not know where his real father is, he appears to have no other problem. Because of the shift in setting and some other changes as well, Benjie's environment seems neither hostile nor threatening. At home, he is surrounded by people who care about him, even though they have their own needs and preoccupations too. And in school he even seems to be something of a star. There is a scene in Nigeria's class in which Benjie is able to amaze the whole class, teacher included, with his knowledge about a particular black leader. And in Bernard Cohen's class, he is asked to read aloud a composition for which he is publicly praised and given an "A".

The scene is apparently used to show two things: first, assigned to write about a member of his family, Benjie has selected his mother, thus revealing her importance to him as his only remaining parent. Second, when as part of his praise Cohen says, "Keep this up and some day you'll be somebody," Benjie replies, "I'm somebody now." We are confronted with a common adolescent problem: the feeling that adults don't give them credit for being someone *now,* and focus too much on what they *may* grow up to be. The scene thus fulfills some valid functions in the movie, but combined with the scene in Nigeria's class it also suggests that Benjie's school provides a generally supportive atmosphere. In the book, the praise Benjie receives for the paper about his mother is said to be something that happened years before the time of the book, and it is not typical of his school career. There is no equivalent in the book of the scene in Nigeria's class.

In addition, the Benjie of the novel tells us several times that one of his problems is that he feels betrayed by Nigeria Greene, who, along with Cohen, has turned him in for drug use. Though the movie does show the two teachers taking him out of class when he is obviously stoned, it does not emphasize for us the importance that this betrayal has for Benjie because it has not made sufficiently clear how he has idolized Nigeria.

A time shift that is even more troublesome than the one involving Benjie's encounter with Jimmy-Lee concerns the change in the relationship between Benjie and Butler. In the book, after Butler has saved his life, Benjie writes "Butler is my father" one hundred times. This indicates that Benjie finally realizes that Butler does indeed care for him, and suggests to the reader that the boy is accepting Butler's role in his life. Also, because Benjie slips this paper into Butler's coat pocket, where Butler is sure to find and read it, Butler is given more justification for taking off work to meet Benjie at the Drug Rehab Center. In the movie, Benjie writes "Butler is my father" much earlier, *before* Butler has saved his life—and so far as we know Butler never sees the piece of writing. Thus, the movie Benjie's motivation for trying to get off drugs—like his motivation for getting on them—is not fully clear, and the movie Butler does not have the same motivation to wait for Benjie at the Rehab Center.

Several scenes and elements in the movie do not appear in the book, and some of these are extremely effective. Although the encounter group scene in the hospital, in which other patients bombard Benjie with their views about drugs, seems to add little, Nigeria's oration at Carwell's funeral is touching and effective. The still photographs of Benjie as he goes through the various stages of withdrawal in the hospital are a brilliant directorial choice and heighten our horror at Benjie's predicament.

Moving pictures, however, are clearly better at vividly portraying some scenes than are either stills or word pictures. For instance, the rooftop scene in which Benjie's life is in danger gets our adrenalin flowing far better in the visual medium than in Childress's novel. Along with Benjie, we hang precariously by one hand as Butler strains to pull us up.

The ending of the movie is revealing of the overall differences between the two forms. In the movie, when Butler waits for Benjie at the Rehab Center, the boy actually appears; in the book Butler only waits and hopes. The movie ending is weaker in consequence, but the change is necessitated by the differences in chronology and motivation mentioned earlier. The reader was led to believe that Benjie will appear, because this would be the logical result of his realization of Butler's love for him and of his acceptance of the older man as his hero.

But since moviegoers have not had this clear motivation for Benjie to change, they need to be shown that the boy does indeed intend to change.

The experience of viewing a movie based on a book need not—cannot—be the same as that of reading the book. Whereas the book is more subtle in its portrayal of people and uncompromising in its presentation of the environment in which they live, the movie sharpens the individual portraits but softens the environment. However, we care deeply about the people in both book and movie, and that is one of the important tests of any story presentation, whether verbal or visual. (pp. 240-43)

> *Elbert R. Hill, "A Hero for the Movies," in Children's Novels and the Movies, edited by Douglas Street, Frederick Ungar Publishing Co., 1983, pp. 236-43.*

WHEN THE RATTLESNAKE SOUNDS: A PLAY (1975)

A short, strong, one-act play, set in a Cape May, New Jersey, summer hotel where Harriet Tubman and two younger women work as laundresses to get money for Harriet's Underground Railroad work. There's friction between Lennie, righteous and dedicated, and Celia, a minister's daughter who has joined Harriet impulsively and now finds the work and the danger more than she bargained for. But with Harriet's encouragement and her sympathetic reminder of what their commitment means, Celia takes heart and the three women end up singing a hymn together as they scrub. Harriet's reminiscences evoking the atmosphere of other places and occasions make an effective and very simple way of "changing" scenes without changing sets; the play is easy to stage and its theme is easy to apply to any number of situations; thus it's an obvious choice for junior high production.

> *A review of "When the Rattlesnake Sounds," in Kirkus Reviews, Vol. XLIII, No. 23, December 1, 1975, p. 1340.*

Childress presents a tightly crafted one-act play that comments on fear and commitment to activist work. . . . From a practical standpoint the play is easy to produce, and the general dearth of high-quality dramatic material makes this small gem most welcome.

> *Denise M. Wilms, in a review of "When the Rattlesnake Sounds: A Play," in The Booklist, Vol. 72, No. 11, February 1, 1976, p. 765.*

[This short one-act play] conveys none of the promised insight into [Harriet Tubman's] "unwavering belief in God," or "her guiding strength". These concepts are merely mouthed by Harriet who is not as convincing nor as interesting as her two female recruits. Ms. Childress's inspired play is dull and flawed by too much rhetoric. Not shedding any new light on what is common historical knowledge, it fails to be compelling.

> *Patricia A. Spence, in a review of "When the Rattlesnake Sounds," in Children's Book Review Service, Vol. 4, No. 8, March, 1976, p. 70.*

There is little movement in this one-act drama, but a wealth of poignant dialogue. . . . Despite the lack of action, the play is moving because of its subject and impressive because of the deftness with which Childress develops characters and background in so brief and static a setting.

> *Zena Sutherland, in a review of "When the Rattlesnake Sounds," in Bulletin of the Center for Children's Books, Vol. 29, No. 9, May, 1976, p. 140.*

Generally, plays written especially for young people are reviewed as useful rather than as literary works. The new play, however, is a poignant celebration of courage, a beautifully crafted work drawn from the life of Harriet Tubman. Rather than attempting the usual chronological panoramic pageant, replete with trite dialogue and a cast of thousands, the author has wisely chosen to confine her drama to one act. . . . Skillful use of introductory notes, stage directions, and the scene-within-a-scene device gives insight not only into the life of the heroine who led hundreds of her people to freedom but also into the universality of human emotions. . . . [The] book offers the young reader a rare opportunity for an aesthetic experience while becoming aware of the techniques used by the dramatist to develop situation and characters.

> *Mary M. Burns, in a review of "When the Rattlesnake Sounds," in The Horn Book Magazine, Vol. LII, No. 3, June, 1976, p. 301.*

"LET'S HEAR IT FOR THE QUEEN": A PLAY (1976)

From the nursery rhyme about the queen of hearts who made some tarts, Childress has put together a very simple play for children to perform. The seasoning she adds includes some grade-school-Pirandello banter about this taking place "in the mind's eye" (essentially, the children play themselves playing the king, queen, knave, etc.) and a dash of contemporary language ("It bugs me just to look at you") and allusion ("Once I killed a dragon . . . right in front of the 24-hour-supermarket"). There's also a spot for a rock group to do a song of their choice, a most un-rocklike happy song for the king to perform, a quote from Shakespeare (". . . the slings and arrows of outrageous fortune. . .") for the knave, and an egalitarian happy ending with the much-abused knave ("They called me 'Your Lowness'") tried and forgiven—"a clear case of provoking." It's light as her majesty's pastry and not all that flaky—certainly not what you'd expect from Childress—but handy, at its level.

> *A review of "'Let's Hear It for the Queen'," in Kirkus Reviews, Vol. 44, No. 23, December 1, 1976, p. 1265.*

Despite the title, it is the Knave of the familiar rhyme . . . who is the central figure in a play that is easy to stage, block, and costume; hand props are minimal. . . . This hasn't the craftsmanship of the author's **When the Rattlesnake Sounds**, but it has brisk movement, humor, and a good role combination for children's play: a small cast but opportunity in some scenes for many bit players.

> *Zena Sutherland, in a review of "'Let's Hear It for the Queen'," in Bulletin of the Center for Children's Books, Vol. 30, No. 8, April, 1977, p. 120.*

Let's Hear It for . . . Childress who has written a witty script for young thespians based on the age-old lines, "The queen of hearts, she made some tarts all on a summer's day . . .". In this version, which uses the play-within-a-play technique . . . , the knave is punished by the king for questioning the government. The king decrees that he may not have any tarts which is why he steals them. The judge decides that the knave was "provoked" into thievery, thus the king and the knave are both deemed guilty of wrongdoing. All is forgiven; the queen agrees to make tarts daily; and the play ends in a song. The dialogue is realistic and appealing; the action is easy to stage; and this is a fine production as long as there's no objection to the situation ethics of the ending.

> *Susan P. Massie, in a review of "'Let's Hear It for the Queen': A Play," in* School Library Journal, *Vol. 23, No. 8, April, 1977, p. 53.*

RAINBOW JORDAN (1981)

As in *A Hero Ain't Nothin but a Sandwich* . . . , playwright Childress' main characters tell a story in alternating first-person chapters. It centers on 14-year-old Rainbow, whose 29-year-old mother Kathie has once again abandoned her in their New York City apartment, this time ostensibly in search of out-of-town work as a go-go dancer. Rainbow finds Kathie's irresponsibility increasingly difficult to excuse—to herself, to teachers, to her social worker and especially to her "interim guardian" Josephine, a 57-year-old dressmaker who sets high standards for herself and takes Rainbow in—even though she is barely coping with the blow of her husband's desertion. Rainbow also gives up on her much-loved boyfriend Eljay, who pressures her to have sex or lose him, and her shoplifting, sexually active best friend Beryl. Left in pain, alone, but true to herself, Rainbow comes to accept Josephine's support and guidance and even to comfort the older woman as she determines her *own*—not Kathie's, Beryl's, or Josephine's—way to live. Each word tells in this powerful, eloquent, revealing novel; the language is so polished that in doubt Rainbow speaks differently from when she is sure of herself. The memory of this exceptional heroine is likely to linger a long time.

> *Sally Holmes Holtze, in a review of "Rainbow Jordan," in* School Library Journal, *Vol. 27, No. 8, April, 1981, p. 137.*

Rainbow Jordan's mother is a free-spirited, 29-year-old black go-go dancer who tends to skip town with any passing boyfriend. At 14, Rainbow often seems the older of the two. Tough, proud, close-mouthed, she invents a whole stream of excuses for her mother every time she finds herself shunted off, once again, to the "interim home" run by Miss Josie.

Miss Josie, who has humiliations of her own to hide, treats Rainbow with tact and grace. Gradually, she and Rainbow come to care for each other—not in any instantaneous Hollywood style but with exactly the mixture of caution, hope and suspicion that you would expect from two such battle-weary people.

Rainbow is so appealing that she could carry this book on her own, but she doesn't have to. There's Miss Josie, who gives us her clearer view to balance what Rainbow tells us. (Rainbow says her mother looks like a model and has lovely long hair; Miss Josie says she looks like "'the lost girl' out of a TV show about crime and prostitution. A yard of wig hangs down her back to her hip. Her mouth forever shining with lipstick looking like a hemorrhage.")

And there's the mother herself—short-tempered, inconsistent, sometimes physically abusive, not much of a mother at all, really. Seen through Rainbow's adoring eyes, she's at least someone we can understand. ("Life is complicated," Rainbow says. "I love her even now while I'm putting her down.") In

fact, Rainbow's story moves us not because of the random beatings or financial hardships, but because Rainbow needs her mother so desperately that she will endlessly rationalize, condone, overlook, forgive. She is a heartbreakingly sturdy character, and *Rainbow Jordan* is a beautiful book. (pp. 52-3)

> *Anne Tyler, "Looking for Mom," in* The New York Times Book Review, *April 26, 1981, pp. 52-3, 69.*

Each of the three women speaks in turn, so that the intricate meshing of motivation, action, and reaction becomes a vivid pattern. Unlike *A Hero Ain't Nothin But a Sandwich*, in which the several narrators were used to intensify the picture of the protagonist, this shows both the pattern of the generations and the individuality of each speaker. . . . Three distinct voices, like spotlights, move and cross; crossing, they illuminate. (p. 189)

> *Zena Sutherland, in a review of "Rainbow Jordan," in* Bulletin of the Center for Children's Books, *Vol. 34, No. 10, June, 1981, pp. 188-89.*

Not all Black women write about Black women, and if they do, it's not always in quite the same consistent fashion as Childress. She grapples with, holds up to the light, peels away like onion layers the important subtleties, nuances, feelings and thoughts of our women. With an unusual combination of love, understanding, honesty, life experiences and wisdom, she shows us accurate, yet positive, images of our range and variety. Reading Childress, we are not unnecessarily arrogant about our revealed strengths, nor diminished or made dysfunctional when confronted by our weakness.

In *Rainbow Jordan,* Childress examines the relationships among three women. . . .

The book is well-constructed, unfolding from the point-of-view of each of the three women whom we come to know through their internal monologues, the ways in which they share their perceptions of each other and their conversations with each other. This is a tale with three storytellers. We see the poignancy of a middle-aged single woman who provides care for foster children and faces up to what she feels is ultimate loneliness without the man she loves. . . . (p. 24)

The idea of portraying three women, across three generations, using foster care and what is probably parental neglect as themes, is an ambitious project. The themes are painful, but Childress handles them well, resolving the difficult conflicts in realistic, sensitive, direct fashion and in ways that seem consistent with the characters.

Using the African-based language forms characteristic of the Black community, Childress energizes her characters; the language has intensity, pith, rhythm, volume, stillness. In places it sparkles. The author is adept at conveying warmth and other emotions, and she makes it possible for us to see African American language as a *literary* language. Each woman speaks in her form of language—with rhythmic pathos, humor, wryness, in rhyme, proverb, image and metaphor—about just how *she* sees and feels about the events that make up the story line of the book, and about her loss. For the book is most certainly about loss and alternatives for coping with it.

Comments not to be missed are those on Cinderella and Sleeping Beauty, sex education classes and Rainbow and her 3,000-year-old Egyptian sister. Feelings to be experienced—sorrow, suspense, fun, joy, resignation, understanding.

Bravo, too, to Childress for having Rainbow consider a number of well-thought-out and responsible birth-control alternatives, including abstinence as an important choice. But why does Rainbow ultimately decide to handle her boyfriend Eljay's consistent pressure to "give it up" in the way that she does? Rainbow's motives are not clear, and her apparent failure to make any decision about birth-control—even though she does not sleep with Eljay—might confuse readers, particularly those who need a positive model in weak moments.

The rainbow has had a particular cultural meaning to Black folks. Having nothing to do with the pot of gold, it has meant hope, faith, a better day. There is a sho-nuff *rainbow round Alice Childress' shoulder*. She has crafted a touching, powerful book. (pp. 24-5)

> *Geraldine L. Wilson, in a review of "Rainbow Jordan," in* Interracial Books for Children Bulletin, *Vol. 12, Nos. 7 & 8, 1981, pp. 24-5.*

Childress has an ear for dialect, idiom, and folk wisdom. She is an excellent author for children because her work is designed to uplift and encourage those who are hurt or confused. . . .

The tragic story of Rainbow, who was neglected by her mother but counselled by another woman, is treated by the author with sensitivity and humor. The book will not only stir up a young person's interest in reading, it will show young and old alike how adults are valuable role models. Childress' value to parents is that she understands the best of rural and urban experiences pertaining to the care of black children. Her message is clear. Any concerned, loving adult may "mother" someone else's child.

Young readers have a treat in store as they witness Rainbow grow up.

> *Carole E. Gregory, in a review of "Rainbow Jordan," in* Black Enterprise, *Vol. 12, No. 5, December, 1981, p. 22.*

Michael Ende

1929-

German author and author/illustrator of fiction.

Ende is internationally recognized for creating original, multi-level fantasies that extol the power of imagination. Best known for *Die unendliche Geschichte* (1979; *The Neverending Story*), he won global attention for writing this book, which is structured as a tale within a tale. Centering on the adventures of a lonely boy who reads about a beleaguered magic land which he later enters to become its hero, *The Neverending Story* stresses the need for belief in dreams in order to prevent annihilation, and has been adopted by antinuclear activists in West Germany. Printed in red and green type to distinguish between the story Bastian reads and the story in which he appears, the novel has been published in over twenty-five languages and has been filmed. Following the enthusiastic reception of *The Neverending Story*, the earlier *Momo* (1973; *The Grey Gentlemen*) gained worldwide acclaim as a contemporary allegory that condemns the dehumanization of modern existence. The book features Momo, a poor but wise girl whose talent for listening to people's secret dreams helps save them from time-thieves determined to rid the world of leisure and reflection. Illustrated by the author in black-and-white line drawings, the story can be read as both a tale for children and a social satire disparaging technological progress. Claiming that he does not write for children but for "the child within each of us," Ende published two additional juvenile books in England. *Jim Knopf und Lukas der Lokomotivführer* (1961; *Jim Button and Luke the Engine-Driver*) is the first of a two-volume work recounting the adventures of a little black orphan, Jim Button, and his engineer friend, while the picture book *Das Traumfresserchen* (1978; *The Dream-Eater*) is a fairy tale about a princess who has trouble sleeping.

Critics praise Ende for his inventive, entertaining, and universally relevant fantasies. While a few reviewers complain of some tedium, contrivance, and overstatement due possibly to stilted translations, most commentators agree that Ende's antiestablishment themes, unusual characterizations, and poetic whimsy have made him one of Germany's most popular authors.

Ende has won numerous European awards including the Deutscher Jugendliteraturpreis for *Jim Button and Luke the Engine-Driver* in 1961 and *Momo* in 1974. *The Neverending Story* won the Premio Europeo "Provincia di Trento" award in 1980 and the International Janusz Korczak Prize in 1981.

(See also *Contemporary Literary Criticism*, Vol. 31; *Something about the Author*, Vol. 42; and *Contemporary Authors*, Vol. 118.)

© *Jerry Bauer*

AUTHOR'S COMMENTARY

The child that I used to be is still alive in me today, and there is no abyss of adulthood separating me from him. Basically, I feel that I am the same person now that I was then, . . . a child who never loses its ability to wonder, to question, to feel excitement, who is vulnerable and exposed, who suffers, seeks comfort, senses hope . . . and who embodies our future until our dying day. (p. 9)

Essentially, I do not write for children at all. By this I mean that I never think of children while I am working, never consider how I should formulate my thoughts so that children will understand me, never choose or reject my subject matter as being suitable or unsuitable for children. At the very most I could say of myself that I write books which I myself would have enjoyed reading as a child. To write a fantasy is to embark on a journey to an unknown destination. It is just like starting 'the never-ending story'. It is a game . . . and it is at root amoral. (p. 10)

It is for this child in me, and in all of us, that I tell my stories. . . . I am not guided by pedagogical or didactic principles while I work. In every person there is a child who wants to play . . . beauty can exist only in free play . . . the wondrous is always beautiful; only the wondrous is beautiful . . . and for literature for children, or for the child in each of us, I add that children are susceptible to nothing so much as genuine humor. . . . (p. 11)

> *Michael Ende, in an extract from "20th IBBY Congress in Toyko," in* Bookbird, *Nos. 3 & 4, September 15-October 15, 1986, pp. 3-15.*

GENERAL COMMENTARY

ULRIKE MEIER

"Erzähl' mir keine Märchen!'' (''Don't tell me fairy tales'') is a modern German saying that writes off the fairy tale subject matter as belonging to the world of lies. . . .

Michael Ende, contemporary German ''storyteller,'' as he calls himself modestly, is one of the few writers who persevered in the idea that fairy tales do neither belong to the past nor a world of sheer fiction.

''Märchen are inner images. They are not, as many people believe, the description of an outer process, but rather the manifestation of an inner development in metaphorical form,'' he said. . . .

Ende's works, including ***Momo*** (1973) and ***Die unendliche Geschichte*** (*The Neverending Story*) (1979) have become cult classics around the world. So far his major writings have been translated into more than 30 languages.

> I seek the fairy tale form of writing for the simple reason that I believe that the basis of every culture needs a myth or a story rich in images. . . . This opposes the now predominant conceptual thinking, which is rigid and unequivocal. My little myths can and should be interpreted in many ways and yet they are unmistakable.

Hence, the reader actively participates in the evolution of the book. It is as much of an adventure to him as it is to Ende writing it down—or the hero living it. The author deliberately avoids any kind of explanation and lets the metaphors speak.

> Postwar literature has described man as a being fully determined by his outer world. It has played the game of questioning man's existence up to the point of no return. But it never tried to transcend this and give a *new meaning* to man.

> One of the reasons why my works enjoy such a wide readership may be, that I am talking about meanings, and not only about facts. . . .

Die unendliche Geschichte, which has reached sales of more than 3 million, tells the story of little Bastian who withdraws to the loft of his school, where he starts devouring a book called *Die unendliche Geschichte*. The world he is reading about soon becomes his as he cannot resist the call for help from the Childlike Princess of Fantastica. The book's lettering changes from green, the color for reality, to red, the fantasy world color.

All of Ende's literary work rests upon this combination of fantastic imagination and outer reality.

Born in 1929 in the south of Germany, Michael Ende grew up in an artistic surrounding, his father being a surrealistic painter. His wish was to write for the theater and only for this reason did he go to a drama school in Munich. Meeting by chance an old schoolmate, Ende was asked to illustrate some drawings for a children's book.

''I wrote the first sentence without knowing what was going to happen next. This turned out to be ***Jim Knopf und Lukas der Lokomotivführer*** (*Jim Button and Lukas the Engine-Driver*), the breakthrough for me at the age of 30.''

In 1962 a second volume entitled ***Jim Knopf und die Wilde 13*** (*Jim Button and the Wild 13*) followed. The adventure-fantasy, set in a ''country, which is not allowed to be'' over the seas, continents and poles, contains a number of elements based on myth-like fairy tale notions: Jim is the last descendant of Caspar, the Biblical king of the Moors, and a fictitious giant, a nymph, a Chinese princess as well as a number of physical and technological simplifications give the tale a universal and naive touch.

Ende claims he neither thinks of a specific readership when he writes nor does he lay down a plot before starting. He waits for the story to impose itself on him.

He also pretends not to have any specific message or pedagogical intention with his books—a fact which might come as a shock to the young Europeans who leave their hometowns in order to make the pilgrimage to Ende, in whom they see a guru if not a messiah.

In 1970, Ende left Germany . . . because he got fed up with having to justify his writing all the time.

''At the end of the '60s the famous 'escapism debate' started. All literature that was not realistic, politically engaged, socially critical or emancipatory was considered as 'flight' literature. I was called to account wherever I went . . . ,'' explains Ende.

Until . . . 1985, he lived in a little town on the outskirts of Rome, an area whose ambience seems to have had a considerable influence on the setting of ***Momo.***

Momo is the story of a little waif-like girl living in a deserted amphitheater whose main ability is to heal people by simply listening to them. Momo sets out to search for time, a value stolen by the gray people, characters who Japanese literary critics ironically interpret as the Japanese salaryman. . . .

Ende's works are considered to be ''positive utopia,'' and he states as one possible explanation for this label his faith in a

> world in which the conflicts belonging to a past and not being ours any more will finally be overcome.

> We have to overcome the materialistic positivism which still haunts our conscience more than we admit . . . And, under this aspect, fantasy is not a flight from reality. It is the capacity of forming new meanings, and bringing the old meanings in a new context. You may not realize it, but you live with a completely unmediated sense of reality.

> Giving a meaning to things, implies imagination and inner values. It is the task of literature and poetry to define these inner values and I hope to contribute as much as I can to make the culture of the 21st century worth living for,

says the author who refuses to be called a philosopher.

Ende is popularly associated with the Rudolf Steiner anthroposophical school of thought. Steiner, best known as the promoter of the Waldorf School movement in the 1920s, regarded man as having originally participated in the spiritual process of the world through a dream-like consciousness.

''I am not a product of a Waldorf School,'' says Ende, ''but I have been reading Steiner's works throughout my life. I have to admit that some of my main starting points in life have followed the confrontation with Steiner."

Ende attended the 20th Congress of the International Board on Books for Young People in Tokyo. Touching upon why he is writing for children, he states clearly that it is "for any child between 80 and 8 years" he puts words to paper.

> I believe, that there is a child in everyone of us. This child is capable of development, it has a future, needs hopes, is vulnerable and wants to be comforted. But, above all, it wants to play. This is the best part of us, the 'eternal juvenile' for which it is worth creating.
>
> Nowadays the child is homogenized from his schooldays on. The fact that we kill those children by killing their creativity is fateful. I believe that especially Japan will pay a high price for this one day.

Critics, who now speak about the "Ende phenomenon," some 10 years ago did not know how to treat his work, which does not fit into any of the traditional literary patterns. To declare the child-like consciousness in every being as the most important trait of man, and to further consider this consciousness as a global reality, did take quite a lot of courage, as Ende admits himself.

The fact that creating takes a lot more courage than destroying is no excuse to persevere in the present ignorance, Ende explains.

He concludes: "I believe that in order to tackle the present problem we need Märchen like mine. By descending into the inner world of images, man may be able to realize the original values of life."

> *Ulrike Meier, "Every Culture Needs a Myth: Ende," in* The Japan Times, *August 26, 1986, p. 10.*

JIM KNOPF UND LUKAS DER LOKOMOTIVFÜHRER [JIM BUTTON AND LUKE THE ENGINE-DRIVER] (1961)

[In 1961], a young German author was completing a two-volume work about Jim Knopf. This was Michael Ende, who neither had nor has the intention of becoming a professional writer for children, and *Jim Knopf* is the story of a little black foundling and his friend Lukas, the engine-driver, and of the engine as well, a mechanical marvel in its own right.

Now comic books about engines are strewn around almost as thickly as sand on the shore, for engines possess a symbolic value all their own within the world of technology. But with Michael Ende the value does not lie in this universal theme . . . but in the nature of the text. This is a most remarkable mixture of adventure and true poetry, fabulous and real worlds, witty dialogue and gay characterization. Although this is a first book, the imaginative content is handled with a confident mastery. The hackneyed themes of 'engines' and 'poor Negro children' and 'engine-drivers' are transformed in so fresh and original a manner and the story takes us into regions which, geographically, are so remote and, humanly, so many-sided, that it serves once again to prove that children's literature depends primarily not upon the subject matter but upon the way it is handled. The success of this book is also evidence that it is unwise to underrate the modern child's capability of accepting things which have to do with the imagination and the understanding. (p. 86)

Bettina Hürlimann, "Fantasy and Reality," in her Three Centuries of Children's Books in Europe, *edited and translated by Brian W. Alderson, Oxford University Press, London, 1967, pp. 76-92.*

MOMO: ODER, DIE SELTSAME GESCHICHTE VON D. ZEITDIEBEN U. VON D. KIND, DAS D. MENSCHEN D. GESTOHLENE ZEIT ZURÜCKBRACHTE; EIN MÄRCHENROMAN [THE GREY GENTLEMEN] (1973; U. S. edition as Momo)

The little girl Momo has the gift of true friendship. People love to spend time with her. But the Grey Gentlemen want everyone to save time—work faster, plan ahead, eat Snappy Snacks. In the end, beaten by Momo and Master Secundus Minutius Hora, the grey gentlemen destroy themselves.

This is one of the most original fantasies I have come across. It is firmly set in real city life, but the fantasy is all-pervading. Michael Ende accounts for each mode of existence to be found in the story, working everything out with delightfully inventive detail. The book builds up slowly, as befits its theme—use of time. The writing is a bit ponderous and prolix, betraying its German origin too clearly. Nusquam and Nunquam should have been translated. Misprints mar the excellent presentation; the author's illustrations are particularly pleasing. Despite the blemishes, a book not to be missed: the phrase "Save time" takes on a new dimension.

> *M. H. Miller, in a review of "The Grey Gentlemen," in* The Junior Bookshelf, *Vol. 39, No. 3, June, 1975, p. 197.*

Michael Ende, in *The Grey Gentlemen,* builds up with intricate and almost poetic detail a fantastic country in which it is easy enough to recognise the world we live and work in. There is a sociological message in this story of the sinister beings who appear in a certain town as the adversaries of Master Hora and delude the inhabitants into selling their spare hours and minutes for the sake of illusory material benefits. The takeover of Time would have been achieved if it had not been for the small girl Momo, a strange little being who lives in a deserted amphitheatre outside the town and who so far preserves her childhood values that she is a suitable ally for Master Hora in his stand against the invaders. The story is long, elaborately told in a dignified style shot with freakish humour that is not entirely funny (for example, the prophetic tortoise Cassiopeia has two sides to her nature). Michael Ende brings his story to an orthodox conclusion. In a scene of scintillating colour and strong drama Time and generous values prevail over the Gentlemen, who disappear like the mist and ash that they are. Love, leisure, common humanity are left to face the next challenge—and here is the ambiguity of the ending. As the author writes in a Postscript, "I have told you all this as if it had already happened. I might equally well have told it to you as if it had still to happen. As far as I am concerned, there is no great difference."

> *Margery Fisher, in a review of "The Grey Gentlemen," in* Growing Point, *Vol. 14, No. 2, July, 1975, p. 2657.*

The life-in-the-raw school likes to claim that fantasy and science fiction are pure escapism, but readers of the best examples of both genres know that there is often *more* freedom to examine issues of real importance when verisimilitude is not the main objective. There has, however, been an alarming trend in contemporary fantasy to fasten on fashionable subjects such as ecology, pollution, or sex-roles where worthiness is allowed to come before story-telling. *The Grey Gentlemen* confronts the vast and modish problem of the pace of life, but let those who dread the earnest allegory be reassured, for here is a story so ingenious in conception, so powerful in production that its message can safely slip unnoticed into the mind to linger after the splendid images begin to fade....

It's sad that so careful and inventive a plot should have such a slow and muddled opening....

> *Sarah Hayes, "Allegorical Action," in* The Times Literary Supplement, *No. 3826, July 11, 1975, p. 767.*

This is a modern parable for the young. As the world becomes more and more automated we must educate for leisure; we must show the next generation that there is more to life than material things. This is what Michael Ende is saying, and saying, I feel sure, in his own language very beautifully, but here I have two grumbles (and this was why I was rather put off at the beginning): he is badly served by both editor and translator, and the opening chapters are very clumsy. The brown print grew on me as did the book, which will, I am sure, grow on thoughtful readers over eleven for it can be read at many levels. (p. 339)

> *Joan Murphy, in a review of "The Grey Gentlemen," in* The School Librarian, *Vol. 23, No. 4, December, 1975, pp. 338-39.*

From Momo, *written and illustrated by Michael Ende. K. Thienemanns Verlag, 1973. © 1973 by K. Thienemanns Verlag in Stuttgart. Reprinted by permission of the publisher.*

Michael Ende's *Momo* has all the ingredients of the classic fairy tale: an idyllic world destroyed by forces of evil and reconstituted, a young innocent who is a central figure in the struggle and a colorful cast of supporting characters. Like Mr. Ende's ... *The Neverending Story, Momo* has been a best-seller in his native Germany. But it is a sophisticated fairy tale whose nuances of meaning are likely to appeal to adults more than children....

From the start Momo clearly represents the value of the past in a society dehumanized by progress. A psychoanalyst by nature, she enables those she knows to resolve their conflicts by talking about their histories....

Both Momo's calling and the novel's symbolic setting quickly establish it as an allegory about the fate of modern man. But Mr. Ende's tone is fanciful from the start. Rather than espousing or attacking an ideology, he goes after an impulse— the desire constantly to achieve, to produce, to "save time." Mr. Ende ingeniously personifies this force of evil in an army of "timesavers," "men in gray"....

The author has embellished his book with humorous drawings—in one, the directors of the Timesaving Bank are represented only by the identical derbies they wear—and there is a visual quality to the prose that J. Michael Brownjohn's translation effectively captures....

However, it is the author's absurd logic that really brings *Momo* to life. In another sequence, Mr. Ende parodies the aphorism "time is money" by literally treating hours, minutes and seconds as if they were capital. An individual has only to save and compound his time to increase his life span. The way Mr. Ende carries a concept like this to its preposterous conclusion lies at the heart of his artful brand of surreal satire.

Like all fairy tales, *Momo* has a happy ending. Momo discovers that the timesavers are really "time-thieves" and that time can't be saved because "time is life." Professor Hora engineers a "timequake" in which all the clocks stop so there is nothing left for the time-thieves to steal. Yet there is a haunting quality to Mr. Ende's tale: though camouflaged by all the whimsy, the society the timesavers create, with its fast-food restaurants and identical housing developments, turns from fantasy to starkly identifiable reality. While the author makes it obvious such banalities will perish from the world of his novel, he is also letting us know that as far as the real world is concerned, the nightmare is here to stay.

> *Francis Levy, "Punctuality Is the Thief of Time," in* The New York Times Book Review, *February 17, 1985, p. 34.*

German literature has long been strong on the semi-allegorical children's book that is surreptitiously (or not so surreptitiously) a statement of values for adults. I can think of Kaestner's *Emil and the Detectives*, Fallada's *Sparrow Farm*, Salten's *The Hound of Florence*, to say nothing of E. T. A. Hoffmann's "Nutcracker and the Mouse-King."...

[*Momo*] belongs in this category....

The idea is excellent and the imaginative detail is delightful. But somewhere in the middle Momo's gift is lost to sight, and the story turns into a world-saving cliff-hanger with a contrived ending. The strong point of the book turns out to be the characterizations, which are very fine, especially Cassiopeia, a tortoise who can see half an hour into the future and produce neon lettering on her shell....

Overall: well worth reading, but not as good as *The Neverending Story.*

E. F. Bleiler, "Semi-Allegory Delights in Spite of Flaws," in Fantasy Review, Vol. 8, No. 4, April, 1985, p. 19.

DAS TRAUMFRESSERCHEN [THE DREAM-EATER] (1978)

A delightful and unmistakably German contribution to the international picture book scene, Michael Ende's story . . . follows the basic fairytale pattern. The Princess of Drowsyland (oh catastrophe!) is unable to sleep for bad dreams. In a land where kindness and intelligence are gauged by ability to sleep, this is a disgrace. In a modern setting, the Queen irons the King's travel clothes before he sets out to discover the cure by questioning, among others, taximen and factory workers. At last he meets the eccentric Dream-eater in the frozen wastes, starving for bad dreams as a hedgehog needs snakes and snails. He gives the King a calling spell for the Princess (and all children who suffer such dreams). Annegert Fuchshuber's illustrations are as inventive as the plot.

M. Hobbs, in a review of "The Dream-Eater," in The Junior Bookshelf, Vol. 43, No. 2, April, 1979, p. 94.

DIE UNENDLICHE GESCHICHTE [THE NEVERENDING STORY] (1979)

[**The Neverending Story**] is a fantasy epic with all the requisite elements of the genre: chimerical creatures, exotic forests and mountains, unpronounceable proper names, a picaresque plot predicated on a Great Quest, magical swords and amulets, chivalric protocol, high melodrama, a virtuous empress, a heroic little fat boy and a moral vision of Manichaean simplicity. The novel is splashed generously with literary color but, as though that weren't enough, it is also printed in alternate sections of red and green type. Over all, the effect is lighthearted and festive. This rather large book is full of small charms and seems admirably suited for reading aloud, in installments, at the bedside of a 7-year-old child.

But a curious thing about **The Neverending Story** is that certain adults are evidently inclined to take it quite seriously. According to its American publisher, the book was first published in Germany "rather quietly, as a children's book. It began to touch a wider and wider circle of readers, and was adopted as a symbol by the peace marchers." Now rights have been sold in 27 countries, and the German director Wolfgang Peterson is at work on a film version. All this over an ingenuous book, inventive in its frills, conventional in its pieties, that combines some of the better features of Tolkien, *Peter Pan, Puff, the Magic Dragon* and *The Little Engine That Could.* But the fault is not Mr. Ende's. **The Neverending Story,** to its credit, does not seem to take *itself* very seriously.

Bastian Balthazar Bux is the fat and lonely little boy who steals a book, an alluring volume bound in copper-colored silk, printed in red and green type, and itself titled *The Neverending Story.* Having played hooky to read, through its miraculous pages Bastian enters a fabulous world where he performs great deeds of courage and evil.

Throughout the first half of Mr. Ende's novel, Bastian remains placed in the outer narrative frame, as the Reader; over his shoulder we watch while another young boy, Atreyu, pursues

From Momo, *written and illustrated by Michael Ende. K. Thienemanns Verlag, 1973. © 1973 by K. Thienemanns Verlag in Stuttgart. Reprinted by permission of the publisher.*

a Great Quest to save the life of the Childlike Empress. (The mythic resonance of Atreyu's name, in case you wondered, leads nowhere.) At the climax of that quest it becomes necessary for Bastian, the despised bookworm, to speak up himself and, in a moment of empathic transport, step across into the storybook world—Pirandello as played by the Muppets. The novel's second half follows Bastian through a course of challenges every bit as bizarre as those he had envied Atreyu, and eventually toward a lesson of growth and fulfillment he carries back into his mundane existence. It is all broad, innocent fun; nothing less, nothing more. (pp. 39-40)

David Quammen, "Fantasy, Epic and Farce," in The New York Times Book Review, November 6, 1983, pp. 14, 39-41.

This book is a cult object in Europe, a Book-of-the-Month Club Alternate in the United States, and is about to burst on our astonished gaze as an "epic film." Its publishers are taking huge ads to make sure we know all this.

Alas, it takes more than ballyhoo to make a book worthwhile. Just to open this one is to suffer disappointment and be vividly reminded that it began its life in Germany as a child's book, for how can anyone take seriously a book published in colored ink? Worse, the first letter of every chapter is muddily illuminated—on a full page, no less—and separated so far from the rest of the word that the puzzled reader is faced with cryptic words like "ladness."

The contents match the packaging. . . .

There are moments when Michael Ende's imagination takes wing, and he tells us of the terrifying "nothingness" that devours the landscape, and the huge luckdragons, "as light as a summer cloud," which "swim in the air of heaven as fish swim in water." But that hardly atones for the author's expectation that we'll take seriously a creature called "cheesiewheezie."

The Neverending Story has been praised for the lessons it teaches, and certainly it lays down some praiseworthy morals. The transformation of this hero is designed to teach the importance of loving, and no one could quarrel with that, but it is hardly a startling revelation. More interesting are Ende's convictions that fantasy plays a vitally important role in the world and needs to be protected, lest it turn into propaganda, and that to recognize what one is wishing for is as difficult as it is important.

But morals, if they are to do their job properly, must be whipped up vigorously into the plot and not allowed to just lie there in undigested lumps.

> *Pamela Marsh, "Praiseworthy Morals, Unwieldy Fantasy," in* The Christian Science Monitor, *November 9, 1983, p. 26.*

This book is about passion. So is every book that is worth reading—about the passion which makes more of life than is apparent at first glance. Early in the novel, . . . the author says: "Human passions have mysterious ways, in children as well as grown-ups". The mysterious way followed in those pages is the way of imaginative invention.

In *The Neverending Story* we read about a boy who is reading a book called *The Neverending Story.* He has escaped from regulated life to hide in a dusty attic above his school. . . . His attic has a strong symbolic connection with the dark rooms under the roof in Musil's novel *Törless* where the young rebels retire to hatch their plots. The quest is the same. They are searching for a world where human imagination can advance into impossible distance.

Michael Ende takes the step outside reality which remains only a suggestion in Musil's book. He creates an imagined world as fact. This world is Fantastica, an empire without known boundaries. Djinns and three-headed trolls flash across the page; there are giants who chew rocks and ride stone bicycles; dragons of course, and marvellous transformations like the desert where every night each grain of dry sand becomes a sprouting seed. In this land of unity beyond reason opposites always support each other in creative play. The beast, as everyone knows, is inevitably a beauty under the skin.

Fantastica is the land of stories, a world of fantasy which depends for every detail on the power of human invention. Even the geography is determined by wishes and is therefore without fixed outline. Michael Ende produces an amazingly complex and variable surface of figures and events to correspond to the spasmodic flexibility of human ideas when freed from the restraints of habit. But Fantastica is decaying, its Empress is sick. This means that humans are neglecting their power of imagination, because only humans can give the names which make and preserve Fantastica. The decline of Fantastica implies that the human world is sick too. Without fantasy the human world is impoverished. The two realms are interdependent. The apparent opposites of fairy-tale and reality support each other.

Ende is optimistic. To believe that Fantastica is a neverending story must mean he has faith in the healthy survival of the human imagination. It certainly survives in this book. There are some places where explanatory arguments bring philosophical implications close to the surface, but these are few and not too distracting. There's symbolic significance on every page, but the book can be read simply as a tale of magical adventure, pursuit and delay, danger, suspense, triumph. And always, throughout the book, there is the delight of this author's tremendous invention of strange figures which explode like Brueghel in print. The print, incidentally, is in red and green, a fairy-tale in itself.

> *Idris Parry, "A Land of Wishes," in* The Times Literary Supplement, *No. 4208, November 25, 1983, p. 1317.*

I wonder how much of the flavour of this epic fantasy has been lost in translation. It seems in style and in its pictorial elements to lack atmosphere of the kind carried on a tide of verbal exhilaration in the similar works of Tolkien and Ursula Le Guin. The power of naming and the image of the Water of Life, the inhabitants of the land of Fantastica, are drawn from sources that cross frontiers: we can all translate dragons and goblins into our own language. Yet none of the monsters and guardians of this world seem to rise inevitably out of their natural surroundings, as such basically primitive beings must do if we are to be stirred by their presence. The quest story is sustained with consistent inventiveness and its core, the initiation of a fat, diffident, unloved schoolboy of ten, is worked out logically and with emotional truth, with an unusual twist in the fact that Bastian enters his adventure by reading a book and slowly moving into it. Whether read as a fantasy–adventure or as an allegory of man's need for love and imagination, the book has a serious and relevant theme (sometimes, I feel, too heavily stated). With all its virtues of image, colour and argument, I found a certain detachment, a self-conscious effort in the book which stood between me and the emotional excitement which a narrative of this stature should be able to rouse in its readers.

> *Margery Fisher, in a review of "The Never Ending Story," in* Growing Point, *Vol. 22, No. 5, January, 1984, p. 4193.*

As 10 year-old Bastian Balthazar Bux settles down to read about the rock-chewer Pyornkrachzark from the Cheesiewheezie Mountains, murmuring to himself, "I must carefully apportion in my provisions", anyone who cares for linguistic vitality or imaginative integrity may be forgiven a quiet shudder. *The Neverending Story* is banal, pretentious, derivative, mind-numbing. It takes the reader on a daydream trip with Bastian to "Fantastica", a land where, as the old German fairytale puts it, "wishing still helped". Bastian enters Fantastica, gains miraculous powers, saves it from the "Nothing" which is eroding it, and in some unspecified way also heals our own world. The characters are simply names, the style is tired and lacklustre, the plot just an unstructured succession of easily surmounted obstacles placed between Bastian's depression on page 1 and his elation on page 396. Yet the book is an international best-seller. Why?

The key, I would guess, lies in the author's disparagement of "dull every-day reality", mirrored in Bastian's rejection of "books in which dull, cranky writers describe humdrum events in the very humdrum lives of humdrum people". The impulse behind *The Neverending Story*'s anodyne escapism is the same as that behind the concentration on the perverse and macabre in currently fashionable English literature: by presenting the extraordinary, which we all understand perfectly, to evade the ordinary, which we don't understand at all. The best fantasies force us to confront the ordinary, by showing the variousness, the complexity, the miraculousness of the simple fact of existence. The worst, like *The Neverending Story,* simplify, homogenize and defuse that various, complex, dangerous miracle. Wouldn't it be nice, such stories suggest, to live in that time when ''wishing still helped''; but the storytelling tramps of Victorian London recognized—who better?—that that ''was neither in my time, nor in your time, nor in anyone else's time''. *The Neverending Story* is a text without a context. One longs, to counteract its cloying denial of all the trivial detail which defines our humanity, for Gissing's character Biffen's resolutely humdrum novel of ''the ignobly decent'', *Mr. Bailey, Grocer.*

> *Neil Philip, in a review of "The Neverending Story,"* in The Times Educational Supplement, *No. 3523, January 6, 1984, p. 21.*

There is nothing new in publishers trying to hype fantasy novels into the same kind of mysterious fashionability that has fallen at various times upon *The Lord of the Rings* and *Watership Down,* but it seems to me that this time they have at last found a worthy cause. *The Neverending Story* is no mere copy of anything that has gone before; it is a story with a heart and soul of its own, and it has something important to say to us that we should attend to, whether or not we accept it.

Although *The Neverending Story* is an original work, it is closely related to several other recent books. The time has come, it appears, for paying serious attention to a particular question, and serious attention is being paid in the form of a number of novels which are truly outstanding. The question is the relationship between readers and fictions—especially fantastic fictions. *The Neverending Story* is about a boy, distressed by the circumstances of his own life, who takes refuge in a very special

book, which ultimately absorbs him into its fantastic substance. He becomes the creator of the fantasy, but a creator with crucially limited powers and with an urgent need not to be trapped within his own imaginary world. By this direct means the story explores, with allegory and direct commentary, the question of how the use of the imagination—and particularly the literary stimulation of the imagination—can enrich and transform the real business of living. It is a naive work in the best sense—which is to say that it is unashamedly bold in its inventions, giving the impression that the author is being uncommonly honest in opening up a route of access to something which is usually private and veiled. The adventures which Bastian Balthazar Bux reads—and later lives—in his neverending story are manifest stereotypes, echoing hundreds of recent heroic fantasies, but here we have the feeling of getting behind and inside the stereotypes, so that their very stereotype becomes a point of consideration; we are always being asked to think about their meaning and significance even while we can enjoy the ritual of their performance. (p. 29)

Critics of *The Neverending Story* will probably complain that it is over-sentimental, and that Bastian's eventual reconciliation with his ''real'' circumstances is a tawdry *deus ex machina.* Do not listen to such complaints. There are much more important things at stake here. *The Neverending Story* is not as brilliant as [Jeremy Leven's] *Creator,* nor is it as beautiful as [John Crowley's] *Little, Big,* but it is a brilliant and beautiful book nevertheless. The gimmick of printing the book in red and green (the two colors representing the ''real'' and ''imaginary'' worlds within the book) works well, and I hope that paperback publishers will not yield to the temptation of cutting costs by reverting to solid black. If they do, get the hardcover edition; this is a book that must be read as it is intended to be read, and in whose adventures the reader must be prepared to take a proper part. (p. 30)

> *Brian Stableford, ''Brilliant Invention, or Endless Tedium?'' in* Fantasy Review, *Vol. 7, No. 4, May, 1984, pp. 29-30.*

Jean (Guttery) Fritz

1915-

China-born American author of nonfiction, fiction, and picture books.

Fritz is one of the most popular contemporary writers of American biographies for children. Noted for her lively, conversational style, humor, and meticulous research, she selects amusing anecdotes as well as unusual facts and incidents to humanize textbook heroes and enliven dry accounts of the past. By writing works which are free of adulation, fabrication, and prejudice, Fritz provides children from preschool to junior high with a vivid sense of history and a better understanding of notable personalities. Her earliest publications include both fictional and nonfictional picture books that frequently feature animals. Beginning with *The Cabin Faced West* (1958), based on the family legend of her great-great-grandmother's dinner with George Washington, Fritz established a reputation for perceptive historical fiction. She continued to explore her American heritage with the well-known biographical picture book series about the founding fathers, each work entitled with a question, such as *Will You Sign Here, John Hancock?* (1976). Presented with an informal approach that belies the substantial scholarship behind it, the memorable cameos relate the subject's virtues and idiosyncracies with the touch of dramatic comedy that captures the primary grader. Fritz's deeper character studies for more mature students, concerning such complex personalities as the eccentric Stonewall Jackson and the traitor Benedict Arnold, examine motives in addition to deeds and stimulate reflective thought. Fritz's two autobiographical books—*Homesick: My Own Story* (1982), a kaleidoscope of her childhood memories of China until her arrival in America at the age of twelve, and *China Homecoming* (1985), an account of her visit to China fifty-six years later—are characteristically informative, entertaining, and revealing of period and place. A versatile and imaginative writer, Fritz has also ventured into fantasy and retold North American and Irish traditional tales.

Critics admire Fritz's literary craftsmanship, fully developed characterizations, whimsical style, and attention to authenticity. Well respected as a bicultural historian, biographer, and autobiographer, Fritz has enriched children's literature with her talent to delight as well as educate.

Fritz has received numerous awards both for individual books and her works as a whole. *And Then What Happened, Paul Revere?*, *Will You Sign Here, John Hancock?*, and *Stonewall* were designated *Boston Globe-Horn Book* Honor Books in 1974, 1976, and 1980, respectively. Fritz won the 1979 *Washington Post*/Children's Book Guild Nonfiction Award for her "total body of creative writing." *Where Do You Think You're Going, Christopher Columbus?* and *Traitor: The Case of Benedict Arnold* were American Book Award finalists in 1981 and 1982, respectively. In 1983, *Homesick* won the American Book Award as well as the Christopher Award and was also selected as a *Boston Globe-Horn Book* Honor Book and a Newbery Honor Book. *The Double Life of Pocahontas* was named a *Boston Globe-Horn Book* Award winner in 1984. Fritz received the 1985 Regina Medal, and in 1986 she was awarded the Laura

Courtesy of Jean Fritz

Ingalls Wilder Medal and was nominated for the Hans Christian Andersen Medal.

(See also *CLR*, Vol. 2; *Something about the Author Autobiography Series*, Vol. 2; *Something about the Author*, Vols. 1, 29; *Contemporary Authors New Revision Series*, Vols. 5, 16; *Contemporary Authors*, Vols. 1-4, rev. ed.; and *Dictionary of Literary Biography*, Vol. 52: *American Writers for Children since 1960: Fiction.*)

AUTHOR'S COMMENTARY

[The following excerpt is from Fritz's Regina Medal acceptance speech given on April 9, 1985.]

[I have begun to] overcome some of the awe I first experienced when I learned that I had received an award for the *body* of my work. Although I have written a good many books, I had never thought of my work as having a *body*. I found the idea a bit intimidating. Here, without even having set out to do it, I had apparently produced something substantial enough to have acquired a body. Well, you know how time is; it seems only yesterday when my editor was encouraging me to write a "long" book. My first book, *Fish Head*, was a picture book and I assumed that this was a format I would stick to. I couldn't conceive of being able to sustain a story through chapter after chapter and eventually turn out something fat enough to be considered, in layman's terms, a *real* book. (p. 21)

Taking the body apart and inquiring into the motive behind each book, I have to admit that what I find first and foremost is simple curiosity. How would a boy growing up in Salem, Massachusetts before the Revolutionary War decide which side he was on, especially if his father was a Tory? If I had lived then, how would I have decided? Would I have automatically taken the same stance as my family did? Or would events themselves have had sufficient impact to make me decide for myself? Again. How did such an oddball as Stonewall Jackson end up as such a hero? Here was a teacher who with all his eccentricities was the laughing stock of the student body but who as a general became not only the idol of the army but of civilians too, lady civilians especially who were just as aggressive in their devotion as Beatle fans have been in ours. And then there was Benedict Arnold. How could such a patriotic man who had again and again proved himself to be the "bravest of the brave"—how *could* he, I asked myself, sell out to the enemy?

As you can see, invariably the curiosity has been about human behaviour. I have always been a people watcher. Perhaps the most fortunate thing that ever happened to me was that I was brought up in an international community among such a range of lifestyles, such a variety of people that I started early wondering about them, noticing how different life was from the way grown-ups present it to children, looking for clues, eavesdropping, trying to figure everyone out, to find their stories. And of course I've been at it ever since. The past, it seems to me, offers the best possibilities for eavesdropping.

"Don't you ever write about people who are alive?" children often ask me.

I tell them, No. I prefer dead people. Their whole lives are there to be examined. And not just any dead people either. There are certain criteria that have to be met.

One. They have to be people children will ordinarily meet in school. Textbooks are so often both inaccurate and dull, a place where dead people just stay dead. I think of my job as bringing these people to life. I want to help change the traditional approach to history and convince children that the past is made of the same stuff that their own lives are made of. I want them to see not only the relevance of the past but the inescapability of it. How can we understand ourselves if we don't appreciate the part the past still plays in our lives?

My second criteria. The characters I write about have to be people whose lives lend themselves to story form, with sufficient drama, ups and downs, humor to hold a reader's interest. I have been asked many times why I don't write about Abigail Adams. Certainly I am fond of her; certainly she was admirable but I just cannot feel the story possibilities in her life. And as much as I like Jefferson, he was basically an intellectual and what makes him interesting to me is not what would make him interesting to children.

Third. I must find someone whom I have to figure out for myself on the basis of the evidence available. My favorite person in the Eighteenth Century is John Adams, yet in his own voluminous diaries and letters, he has explained himself so well that there is no challenge. On the other hand, I hesitated about Benjamin Franklin, for no one will ever know his secrets or secret thoughts. Witty, lovable, he was also a cagey man, always aware of exactly what image he wanted to present and

careful to reveal no more than that. But there were so many wonderful stories about him, I couldn't resist. Textbooks tell you about Franklin's kite experiments and his discovery of electricity but in order to appreciate his fascination with electricity, I think you have to know about his electrical picnic. If you have read my book, you know how he planned to kill a turkey by electric shock, roast it in a container connected to electric circuits on a fire lit by an electric bottle. And you know that he was so carried away with his performance that he became careless and was knocked out. But perhaps even now you can't really appreciate his courage unless you also know about the general timidity at the time about anything electric. Over a century later in 1891 when electric lights were first installed in the White House, neither President nor Mrs. Harrison had the nerve to turn on the switch. If anyone was going to get a shock, they said, let it be the servants.

Finally, my curiosity has to be sufficiently aroused so I know I can live with that person for a long time without getting bored. Sometimes I'm not even sure why a certain person speaks to me. I found Columbus, for instance, a difficult man to live with, but when my aunt, my father's sister, finished reading my book, she looked up at me in surprise. "You know," she said, "Columbus was just like your father." And he was.

As for Pocahontas, I identified with her quickly for in a way I, too, had led a double life. I, too, had seen the arrogance of white people trying to convert others to western ways. I do not think that when a writer brings his or her experience to bear on a subject, it influences the objectivity; at least it shouldn't but it does play a part in a writer's attraction to the subject matter. (pp. 21-2)

Often, however, the very people who make a fetish of praising the past turn out to be those who understand it the least. Our job, it seems to me, is to learn from the past, to see what we should discard as well as what we should hang on to. It isn't easy. In connection with my research into a new book on Sam Houston [*Make Way for Sam Houston*], I recently visited the Alamo, one of the most moving historical sites in our country. How can you not weep for that handful of valiant men who chose certain death to surrender? You may remember that at the end of the siege, according to the popular account, William Travis, the commander, drew a line on the ground with his sword and invited all who would stay with him to cross over. All did cross over, including James Bowie, sick with typhoid-pneumonia, who according to legend asked to have his cot carried over the line. But you don't always hear about the fifty-year-old volunteer who chose not to cross the line. He wasn't ready to give up life, he said, and he walked out of the Alamo, free, without impunity, to take up living presumably where he'd left off. Well, I admit, heartbreaking as are the heroes who died, I have a great deal of sympathy with that fifty-year-old man. I'm glad he walked away. History offers no easy answers but it does raise questions that cannot help but be a challenge to children if we let them be. How healthy is it, for instance, to be so entranced with the storybook ideal of a hero as these men clearly were? "God and Texas. Victory or Death." This was Travis' message to the outside world, yet in defending the Alamo he had deliberately disobeyed orders. Told to blow up the Alamo and fight the Mexicans on more auspicious ground, Travis and the defenders went their own way, confident of their heroics. History has not condemned them. How could it? Such brave men, so proud of their death—how can you not love them? Besides, you have to ask: had they not died at the Alamo, would Texas have been sufficiently aroused to win its independence? These are unanswerable questions, but when we tell the story, let's at least talk about alternatives, about heroes, and about that volunteer who walked away. It seems to me that history is the one place in the curriculum where we can discuss human nature, where children can bring out personal emotions, where they have a chance to extend their own short experience into a longer time span and to invigorate it with the experience of others.

So if curiosity has been my motive, I also see a subconscious sense of mission behind my work. I hear a lot from teachers and librarians today about the importance of providing children with role models. I understand the concern, yet making role models is not really the niche where I think I belong. I'm afraid if I set myself the task to create a role model, I might blunt my curiosity; I might be tempted to tamper with the truth; I might limit my cast of characters. "Role model" is a modern word and does not condone distortion, yet certainly it was a role model that Parson Weems was trying to create when he invented the story of George Washington, and the cherry tree. Of course, Washington, of all people, needed no inventions and I'm not suggesting that there *is* invention in modern so-called "role model" books, but I find something self-conscious, unappealing in the term itself. I have never looked for a role model, have never liked any real life role models that have been held up to me, and in general I'm afraid I'm perverse about the idea of trying to manipulate character by example. Not that people are not significantly influenced by other people (role models, if you insist), but as a writer I am uncomfortable with the limitations inherent in this way of teaching. Instead I hope children who read my books will be provoked to sympathy, to understand, to admiration sometimes, to disappointment at other times, to laughter, to tears. In the study of the past I want children to be introduced to the broad spectrum of human behaviour, to appreciate how people get to be what they are, and most of all to feel the full thrust of life, its ongoingness, the neverending bitter-sweet surprise of it all.

I had a letter from a boy who read my book on Benedict Arnold. He disagreed with my assessment of Benedict but I never received a letter that pleased me more. "Dear Mrs. Fritz," he wrote, "I have read your book on Benedict Arnold and enjoyed it too. But I just wanted you to know that in the aftermath of Saratoga I would have done just what he did. In this growing nation of ours, there is still one person who weeps for Benedict Arnold and that person is me." I couldn't answer his letter because he didn't sign his name and I was sorry. I would have liked him to know I weep too. The important thing about this boy's reaction was that he *cared*.

But if I can begin to recognize what lies behind my work, I must also ask if my work has in any way changed me. By exploring other people, I have inevitably been exploring myself too. Would I, I ask myself, write *The Cabin Faced West* now in the same way that I wrote it thirty years ago? In a roundabout way I was in a sense telling my own story, although I didn't realize it at the time. The heroine was ostensibly Ann Hamilton, my grandmother's grandmother, but in reality of course I was living through the isolation and loneliness of a childhood in China through the imagined loneliness of pioneer Ann. I told the same story in a direct way and in first person in *Homesick* but if you compare the two I think you will feel the double edge of homesickness in my own direct account that you don't get in the earlier fictional version. And if I had let Ann go back to Gettysburg, I wonder if I would have had the sense or

the courage thirty years ago to keep Gettysburg from being a perfect place. As it was, I had to send her cousin Margaret to her at the end of the book to compensate for the fact that the ending, from her point of view, was not a completely happy one. But I was a young mother when I wrote that book, more protective of children than I needed to be. With my own children I often tried to compensate when life went wrong; now I know you really can't. For myself, I was too much of a realist even as a child to expect anything to be 100 percent, but I did not expect my love for China to tear at me as it has throughout my adult life. Yet I think I have suggested in *Homesick* that might be the case.

Over the years I have become more secure, perhaps in part due to my books. I am less in need of a definite place to call home and I am definitely more eager for adventure. Indeed, I think that was what appealed to me when I wrote the book about St. Brendan. Here was a seventy-year-old man setting out across the open sea in search of Paradise and finding, at least according to every true-hearted Irish, the continent of North America. How could I not be drawn to this man, grouchy though he was? Actually, that was part of his attraction. It was a relief to find that not even a saint is perfect.

Much of my joy in producing this body of work has been that so many of the books have led to small adventures of my own. If I had not been writing about John Hancock, for instance, I would not have found myself in the Massachusetts Statehouse, walking across a plank where workers below me were digging in the ground, reinforcing the foundation. I stopped at the end of the plank and spoke to the curator who was with me.

"That's where I'd like to be," I said, pointing to the workers. I knew that the Statehouse was on property that John Hancock had once owned. "Have they found anything in their digging?" I asked.

Yes, as a matter of fact, they had. Just a few days before they had come across a large pile of bricks. "We've had them analyzed," the curator said. "They are the kind John Hancock used in his house and they are the right date."

I tried not to seem too eager. "What are you going to do with those bricks." I asked. The curator shrugged. They hadn't decided.

I got up the courage. "Just one brick," I said. "Do you think you could part with one brick?"

When I went back on the plane to New York that day, I had a brick wrapped up in a piece of newspaper. The brick sits in front of my fireplace now, a very proud souvenir of my small Eighteenth Century adventure—nothing compared to St. Brendan's, to be sure, but nevertheless a real touchstone to the past that I treasure.

There have been adventures in Virginia in search of Patrick Henry, in Ireland in search of St. Brendan, in London in search of King George, and most recently in Texas where in addition to tracking down Sam Houston's houses and battlegrounds, I found the out-of-the-way creek where he was baptized at the age of sixty. And I found a little-publicized letter by a young man baptised at the same time. Mrs. Houston, he said, stood on the banks of the creek, so happy that she shouted like a Methodist. Sam's mother-in-law was so happy that she donated a huge bell to the village of Independence where they lived. It is still there on display although it has neither hung nor rung since 1936 when its tower was knocked down by a hurricane. Perhaps finding a secluded Texas creek doesn't sound like much of an adventure but for a researcher whose time is largely spent in libraries, it rates high.

My biggest adventure, of course, was my trip back to China which I have written about in my new book *China Homecoming*. The Chinese told me that I had come at just the right time. If I'd come much sooner, I would not have been allowed the freedom or given the welcome I received. It was the right time for me too. Earlier I might not have been ready to bring the past and present together. They came together most dramatically one day when I asked our interpreter what had happened to the International Cemetery. Over the years I had been haunted by the fact that I had a sister buried in Communist China—so far away, so unreachable. Although I knew the cemetery would no longer be there, I needed to see where it had been.

The cemetery is now a children's playground, the interpreter said, and he took us to it. It was quite an elaborate playground with a gazebo in the center for musicians, swings, see-saws, jungle gyms, sand boxes, and many stone benches for grandmothers to sit on. As I watched the children playing, I thought this was certainly the best thing that could have happened to the cemetery.

But that night at the hotel I began to wonder if the cemetery was really in the right location. Perhaps this was what interpreters had been told to tell ex-China residents. So later in the week during an unscheduled afternoon, my husband and I walked back to the playground to look around, although I had no idea what I hoped to find.

Nevertheless, I walked around the edges of the playground, peering into unused corners, looking at the ground for some hint of the past. I kept telling myself what a hopeless search this was, but then leaning against a far wall was a broken stone lying on its side. There were letters printed on it. English letters. They said, *Sears*. There had been a date but it was no longer legible. Obviously it was part of an old gravestone.

Then looking at the playground, I noticed that the benches were similar granite stones placed on top of two cement supports. I went over to one and ran my hand along the underside. Yes, I could feel writing.

By this time the Chinese in the area were curious. What was this foreign woman up to, rubbing the underside of their benches? Near me there was a young woman with a small baby and I explained to her that this used to be a cemetery and I had a little sister buried here. These benches, I thought, had once been gravestones. She understood immediately and without any suggestion from me called several young men over to lift the stones from their stands. One by one, they placed them on the ground and turned them over.

Each was, as I had suspected, a gravestone. As they were turned over, I told the Chinese whose this had been. One a Norwegian died in 1896; this a Russian died in 1910; a young German girl, an American from Braintree, Massachusetts. My sister's stone was not there but it didn't matter any longer. I had uncovered a bit of lost history, a history that the Chinese would prefer to forget but history all the same. And it was the history to which I was tied to China.

I hadn't expected to feel this particular kind of tie but to me it was important. If felt it again one afternoon when we were visiting a museum that displayed relics from the beginnings of the Communist party. One room was devoted to the siege of Wuchang (a city across the river from us) which took place in

1926. Of course I remembered it well. The young guide pointed out a small cannon that had been used in the siege.

"It was placed on the hill above Wuchang, wasn't it?" I asked.

She looked at me in surprise. "Yes," she said. "How did you know?"

"I was here." I put my hand on the cannon. "I heard it."

Then I realized what I hadn't known before. China was not just part of me; I was part of China. Whether they had wanted me or not, I was part of its long unwritten history. I had been born here, lived here, and like the Chinese themselves, I had watched the river rise and fall, seen the moon come and go. I had waited out war. This sudden, intense sense of belonging to history only comes, I suspect, as a direct first-hand experience. On the other hand, I might not have had that experience had I not been prepared for it by books. It was books that had given me my hold on history in the first place. They go together—reading and writing, vicarious experience and real experience. Vicarious experience lights up one's personal life and in turn life itself makes vicarious experience more solid.

So it's not only thirty years of writing but thirty years of reading that have made me feel so much at home in various pockets of the world in various times. Of course you change. But if sometimes I feel my energy flagging, up to this point my curiosity shows no sign of becoming dull. I find life increasingly full of surprise. (pp. 23-5)

> *Jean Fritz, "Acceptance Speech: Regina Medal Recipient," in* Catholic Library World, *Vol. 57, No. 1, July-August, 1985, pp. 21-5.*

GENERAL COMMENTARY

CHARLOTTE S. HUCK

Jean Fritz has presented Paul Revere as a busy and sometimes forgetful human being in her humorous yet authentic picture-book biography *And Then What Happened, Paul Revere?*. She tells about the time Revere built a barn and put part of it on a neighbor's property, which really happened. He didn't always meet his deadlines either, producing a hymn book some eighteen months after he had promised it! A dreamer, he even left one page in his "Day Book" simply for doodling. The author does not debunk her character; she simply makes him come alive by admitting his foibles, as well as describing his accomplishments. Likewise in *Can't You Make Them Behave, King George?*, Fritz helps readers to think of the often-hated English monarch in a new way and to chuckle at his understandably human feelings. (p. 554)

> *Charlotte S. Huck, "Informational Books and Biography: Biography," in her* Children's Literature in the Elementary School, *third edition, Holt, Rinehart and Winston, 1976, pp. 550-82.*

BERNICE E. CULLINAN WITH MARY K. KARRER AND ARLENE M. PILLAR

Biographies about the people involved in the American Revolution give a serious view of their beliefs, sometimes a humorous glimpse of their foibles, and, ideally, a feeling that they were real people with blood in their veins. Jean Fritz decries the way we turn people from our past into stone statues to revere. She prefers to enter their world, match their words to their actions, follow the criss-cross of their public and private lives, and accept them finally as friends. Jean Fritz feels that a picture that shows a believable human being is preferable to one that idealizes the subject as a saint. . . .

Jean Fritz contends that humor is one of the most effective keys to appreciating the past and to seeing historical figures as fully human. Instead of stale facts about leaders of the American Revolution, she presents affectionate and well-informed biographical narratives. Each of her titles is a question: *Why Don't You Get a Horse, Sam Adams?, What's the Big Idea, Ben Franklin?, And Then What Happened, Paul Revere?, Where Was Patrick Henry on the 29th of May?, Will You Sign Here, John Hancock?,* and *Can't You Make Them Behave, King George?*. . . . Their brevity, humanizing personal insights, and humorous illustrations make these biographical narratives favorites. . . . (p. 347)

Jean Fritz's deep love for and pride in America enrich yesterday's history. . . . (p. 350)

> Bernice E. Cullinan with Mary K. Karrer and Arlene M. Pillar, "Historical Fiction and Biography," in their *Literature and the Child,* Harcourt Brace Jovanovich, 1981, pp. 329-82.

RICHARD AMMON

Perhaps you have seen them at national conventions—buttons inviting you to "Win Jean Fritz." Who is this prize? What can you expect if you are the lucky teacher who gets to have this author spend a whole week in your school?

As a frequent visitor to schools and libraries, Jean often finds herself surrounded by a semi-circle of children, each wiggling to get a little closer. The twinkle in her eyes seems to say that she has a special secret to share with only them. And of course she has. Jean loves telling tales about her Colonial American friends.

Sensing that she is a grown-up to be trusted, the youngsters bombard her with questions which she patiently answers. Perhaps it is her own sense of childhood that not only allows her to relate warmly to children but also enables her to reveal our forefathers as fresh, genuine characters.

Her recently published book, *Homesick* . . . , provides a delightfully honest glimpse of her childhood in China when her father was director of the YMCA in Hankow. In this personal account, readers can detect in Jean a free-spirited resolve. Warning her grandmother in America not to be disappointed, Jean wrote a letter to her saying, "I'm not always good. Sometimes I don't even try." And at the British school she attended, Jean steadfastly sang the words to *America* while the other childen sang *God Save the King,* even though that act of defiance got her into trouble with her classmates as well as with her "pinch-faced and bossy" teacher. (p. 365)

In *Homesick* we also learn that Jean always wanted to be a writer. Her first efforts, however, were marked not with reviews but with rejection slips. In fact, she hadn't even thought about writing for children until she took her son and daughter to the local library and discovered that there was no children's section. . . .

Although she has written numerous fiction and nonfiction books for children, Jean Fritz is perhaps best recognized for the . . . accurately crafted biographies of our founding fathers. She believes that children need to realize that these early leaders were not stale textbook characters but were real people, filled with the same foibles as people of today. Consequently, in each biography, Jean includes anecdotes, some quite humorous, that point up the humanness of each person.

For example, *Can't You Make Them Behave, King George?* . . . , is a portrait of someone who wanted to be a good king. Never intending to cause so much trouble, he simply wanted to punish the colonies. After all, he reasoned, if they broke away, what would happen to the rest of the empire?

Most amusing is Jean's description of King George's coronation, a ceremony of pomp and circumstance that turned into a fiasco. First, the guest were showered with sparks from 2,000 candles. Then it was discovered that there were no chairs for the King and Queen, no table for the Lord Mayor of London, and not enough food.

But the funniest episode occurred when

> Lord Talbot thought how clever it would be if his horse, instead of turning around, would back away from the king and queen. For days he trained his horse to walk backwards, and at the banquet that was just what it did. But instead of walking forward to the king and queen and *then* backing away, the horse backed its rear end right up to the king and queen.

In *Why Don't You Get a Horse, Sam Adams?* . . . , illustrator Trina Schart Hyman pictures Sam dressed shabbily because he was so passionate about the Revolutionary cause that he paid attention to little else. He even refused to ride because he couldn't gossip about the British from high atop a horse.

In *And Then What Happened, Paul Revere?* . . . , Jean shows that the most famous ride in American history did not come off without some hitches. Paul left in such a hurry that he forgot his spurs and left the door open, allowing his dog to escape. Luckily for Paul, the well trained canine saved the day (or rather, the night) by fetching Paul's spurs.

In *Will You Sign Here, John Hancock?* . . . , Jean characterizes the first signer of the Declaration of Independence as a friendly, handsome, generous man who wanted to be well liked. Consequently, it is no surprise to learn that Hancock's victories came not on the battlefield but at the dinner table where once he entertained 120 French officers for several days while they waited for their ships to be repaired.

Youngsters often ask Jean, "How do you find out about these people?"

"I like being a detective, a treasure hunter, an eavesdropper," she tells them. Jean insists upon doing her own research, her own discovering. First, she reads everything she can about that person. Then she seeks out primary sources—letters, newspapers, and other documents.

And when possible, she likes to travel to the site where the person lived. "While writing *Where Was Patrick Henry on the 29th of May?* . . . , I wanted to know what Virginia was like in late spring. What flowers were blooming? What fish were in the streams? And what trees grew on his thousands of acres of woodland?" (pp. 367-68)

When talking with children, Jean likes to present a slide show of illustrations from these biographies to demonstrate the interrelatedness of these American heroes. "I think it's important for children to understand that even though these people are represented in separate books, they worked together and in some cases, knew each other very well."

Jean believes that children need to have a realistic picture of the past in order to live honestly and intelligently. "They need to start early to think about the vicissitudes of human nature—what makes people behave as they do, how a person's strength may also be his greatest weakness, and how easy it is for people to fool themselves about their motives."

This interest in understanding character development explains why she wrote *Traitor: The Case of Benedict Arnold* . . . , a biography for intermediate grade and junior high school readers. "Here was a man who was so obsessed with being a hero that he went too far. He was, and still is a controversial figure whom I wanted to understand but couldn't defend."

Her opinion about history books was formed early. In *Homesick* . . . , she describes being in school back in America for the first time and opening the text to the chapter, "From Forest to Farmland." After skimming the pages she noticed that there wasn't any mention of people at all.

> There was talk about dates and square miles and cultivation and population growth and immigration and the Western movement, but it was as if the forests had lain down and given away to farmland without anyone being brave or scared or tired or sad, without babies being born, without people dying. . . .

"The problem with school texts and even some biographical series," Jean says forthrightly, "is that they are written without any style. Apparently, facts are inserted at appropriate places. Such books divest life of all emotion. Children need to become involved emotionally to know how people behaved, to know what they were really like. In schools, history is too often treated like a closed subject when it is in reality an open, lively one. Or, as Faulkner said, 'The past is never dead; it is not even past.'"

"Life is often paradoxical," she continued. "But by possessing a sense of continuity with the past, we can be free to change. If we are at home with history, we cannot deny the complexities of life." (pp. 368-69)

Jean writes slowly. "I use the stop-and-stall technique," she says. "I'm very word conscious and I'm sensitive to how a sentence will sound when read aloud. Consequently, I do a lot of re-writing and at day's end I'm lucky to have two typewritten pages. Children cannot believe me when I tell them that it takes me at least six months to write one book. To them, a half year seems like a long time to write one story."

That care in writing and commitment to research has paid off. . . . When she receives comments such as, "Your biographies aren't boring; they're like reading stories," her eyes radiate satisfaction. (p. 369)

Richard Ammon, "Profile: Jean Fritz," in Language Arts, *Vol. 60, No. 3, March, 1983, pp. 365-69.*

DONNA E. NORTON

Some very exciting biographies for young children are Jean Fritz's stories about Revolutionary War heroes. Patrick Henry, Samuel Adams, John Hancock, Benjamin Franklin, and Sam Houston seem to come alive through Fritz's inclusion of little-known information that makes these famous personages real and down-to-earth in children's eyes. Through these books children discover that heroes, like themselves, have fears, display good and bad characteristics, and may be liked by some and disliked by others. For example, Fritz adds humor to *Where*

Fritz as a young girl. Courtesy of Jean Fritz.

Was Patrick Henry on the 29th of May? by developing the theory that unusual things always seemed to happen to Henry on the date of his birth. She characterizes Henry not only as a great patriot, but also as a practical joker and a person filled with "passion for fiddling, dancing, and pleasantry." Similar insights enliven Fritz's biographies of other beloved figures from the revolutionary period. Fritz doesn't only write about supporters of American independence from Great Britain, however. In *Traitor: The Case of Benedict Arnold* Fritz develops a well-rounded characterization of a man who wanted to be a success and a hero, but who, in the eyes of most American colonists, was a dastardly betrayer of the cause. Fritz attracts the reader's interest in Arnold and prepares the reader for the apparently dramatic changes in a man who chose to support the British: "Benedict Arnold succeeded beyond anyone's wildest expectations—'the bravest of the brave,' George Washington called him in 1777. Yet three years later he was described as 'the veriest villain of centuries past,' and no one would have argued with that." . . . The incidents Fritz chooses to include develop many sides of Arnold's character and encourage readers to understand why he chose to join forces against his country. (pp. 572-73)

Donna E. Norton, "Nonfiction, Biographies and Informational Books: Biographical Subjects," in her Through the Eyes of a Child: An Introduction to

Children's Literature, *second edition, Merrill Publishing Company, 1987, pp. 569-77.*

VERNA BARGSLEY, NITA BECKMAN, JOAN DILGER, IRENE PEDERSEN AND OTHERS

Jean Fritz admits to one, maybe two, factual errors in all of her 30 books. As she tells her fans in grades four through eight, had she discovered earlier that Paul Revere's horse was named Brown Beauty, she never would have let the artist color the horse gray for the book jacket of *And Then What Happened, Paul Revere?*

Before she ever starts writing, Jean Fritz does extensive historical research, uncovering details that historians before her rarely reported. For *What's the Big Idea, Ben Franklin?* she found out not only that Ben did swimming tricks as a boy but which ones he did. He tried swimming with both legs tied together, and, perhaps as a prelude to his electricity experiment, learned to float on his back while flying a kite!

Fritz's respect for the facts extends to revealing even unflattering details about those who made history. In *Where Do You Think You're Going, Christopher Columbus?* she writes that a sailor named Rodrigo, not Columbus, was the first to sight land, but that Columbus took the credit and the prize for himself. In *Why Can't You Make Them Behave, King George?* she discloses that as a boy George wrote on one of his school assignments, "Mr. Caesar, I wish you may go to the devil." As an adult he once declared, "I wish nothing but good; therefore everyone who does not agree with me is a traitor or scoundrel."

Knowing the facts is important to children, says Jean, who advises that teachers approach social studies "with a little less reverence for the past." It's better that historical people are seen as people, not simplistic figureheads, she says, "Textbooks often expurgate facts or even falsify them. They'll say Patrick Henry's wife was sick but won't say she went insane. . . . A teacher might want to skirt some issues but we shouldn't dress up the facts. It's important to see that people can do great deeds even though they are imperfect. And knowing the details helps children understand the emotional effect on the characters."

As many teachers know, Jean Fritz's historical biographies for children lend themselves well to social studies and language arts classes. They can be used as supplements to texts, as a motivational way of involving children in the subject matter, and to help introduce the concept of doing library research. Plus, the award-winning books are wonderful stories in themselves. One of the many honors Jean has received was the *New York Times'* designation as outstanding children's biographer. (pp. 40-1)

> *Verna Bargsley, Nita Beckman, Joan Dilger, Irene Pedersen and others, "Is That a Fact, Jean Fritz?" in Instructor, Vol. 94, No. 1, August, 1984, pp. 40-4.*

SISTER M. SARAH SMEDMAN, O.S.B.

Several of Jean Fritz's big ideas are responsible for her becoming the originator and sole practitioner of a sub-genre of children's literature: carefully researched historical biographies of America's founding fathers and other fascinating figures, focused on a particular aspect of their personalities or lives, often articulated in a curious question which titles a story told with precision, vivacity, and wit. These stories illuminate our heroes as practical people with idiosyncracies and weaknesses

not unlike our own: people with whom we would feel at home in our living rooms or theirs, whom yet we admire exceedingly.

In her 1976 May Hill Arbuthnot Lecture, **"The Education of an American,"** Jean Fritz voiced several of the ideas which underlie the genre today synonymous with her name: that it is important that history be made to live for children, not as events and dates but as real people, individually and in communities; that, like all of us, childen must know where we have been in order that they may know where they are going; that children's imaginations must be educated to enable them to grow up able to adapt to the challenges of the future; and, finally, her commitment as a writer "to the proposition that to the best of [her] ability [her] words correspond to her experience."

Having been born in China of missionary parents and lived her first thirteen years there, Jean spent much of her childhood trying "to wrap [her] mind around" an issue most of us take for granted: what it means to be an American. Her biographies which demythologize American heroes formulate partial answers, but her historical novels about very real book children, like Brady and Ann Hamilton, and her own story, *Homesick,* come closest to capturing that essence. (p. 20)

No one who has read *Homesick,* child or adult, is likely to forget the robust patriotism of the young American, who upon first seeing her country, proclaimed from the ship's deck: "Breathes there the man with soul so dead / Who never to himself has said, / This is my own, my native land!" . . .

Nor can the reader fail to laugh and cry over the poignant idealism of the little girl at that moment as well as over the humor and pathos of so many moments when she worried about fitting in. . . .

[Those] concerned with excellence in children's literature . . . are grateful that our talented, fun-loving countrywoman with the good, strong Scottish name has written so many books worthy of it—short, to the point, which don't fool around. Spunky. Grateful that she imbided from her great-uncle Henry not only that "the simple life, homely virtues, and a full stomach are the backbone of America" but also the "tongue-in-cheek gusto" with which she has passed that message on.

Because Jean Fritz has recognized and used the power and the beauty of words not merely to mirror for children the mundane reality of today's world, as so many problem novels do, but to create what she has called the "secondary underground life that runs through childhood, paralleling the visible life, compensating for it and fortifying it;" because she has nourished young people's imaginations that they may learn to live with ambiguity with some degree of equanimity; because she makes children, and the child in each of us, aware of both the idealism and reality of ourselves as Americans, we . . . are privileged and proud to add to Jean Fritz's numerous other awards the 1985 Regina Medal for continued contribution to the excellence of children's literature. . . . (p. 21)

> *Sister M. Sarah Smedman, O.S.B., in an introduction to "Regina Medal Recipient—Jean Fritz," in Catholic Library World, Vol. 57, No. 1, July-August, 1985, pp. 20-1.*

ETHEL L. HEINS

[Jean Fritz], in the lineage of Laura Ingalls Wilder, . . . speaks unpatronizingly to young people, with directness, integrity, and a fine flair for enlivening the past.

Jean Fritz has been writing books for children since 1954, and her creative energy seems boundless. She began to publish historical fiction almost thirty years ago with *The Cabin Faced West* . . .—still in print!—a spontaneous, childlike pioneer story about her grandmother's grandmother in eighteenth-century Pennsylvania. There followed three more historical novels, each one centered on an adolescent boy responding to an era of chaos and crisis while, at the same time, coming to terms with his own inner conflicts: *Brady; I, Adam;* and *Early Thunder* . . . , a dramatic story set in Salem, Massachusetts, just before the official opening of the American Revolution.

In the Bicentennial decade Jean Fritz, proving that historical accuracy need not be solemn, gave us eight brief biographies of figures from American history—narratives brimming with vitality and candor and seasoned with a proper sense of the ludicrous, for she is convinced that "humor is one of the most effective keys for opening the past to children." And I have been fascinated that the titles of the books are all questions: *And Then What Happened, Paul Revere?, Why Don't You Get a Horse, Sam Adams?, Will You Sign Here, John Hancock?, Can't You Make Them Behave, King George?*. . . . For in dealing with historical leaders, Jean Fritz mistrusts reverence; these books emphasize the humanity as well as the heroism of our Founding Fathers. And in *Stonewall,* in *Traitor: The Case of Benedict Arnold,* and in *The Double Life of Pocahontas* . . . , she brings order to a mass of vivid detail and balances it with emotional truth to illuminate three complex personalities.

But the time finally came for Jean Fritz to plunge deep into memory and evoke her expatriate childhood in far-distant China. In reading *Homesick: My Own Story* . . . , I was struck by the power of her precise recall, which well matches that of Laura Ingalls Wilder; with a wry and often irreverent humor she summons the fierce ambivalence of an ebullient child loving her native city while passionately anticipating her new life as a real American. "My long exile was over," she once said. "I was ready to live happily ever after." And about the patient historical research that has been her preoccupation, she wrote, "No one is more patriotic than the one separated from his country; no one is as eager to find roots as the person who has been uprooted."

Jean Fritz's books share a quiet consistency: they have garnered awards, prizes, honors and, again and again, appear on all the best lists of all the best books. (pp. 430-31)

> Ethel L. Heins, *"Presentation of the Laura Ingalls Wilder Medal,"* in The Horn Book Magazine, *Vol. LXII, No. 4, July-August, 1986, pp. 430-31.*

ZENA SUTHERLAND AND MAY HILL ARBUTHNOT

[In *The Cabin Faced West*] there isn't much to console Ann. She misses her cousin in Gettysburg and there isn't another child in the pioneer country of Western Pennsylvania for her to play with until she finds a boy her own age. The high point of the story is a surprise visit from George Washington, an episode based on historical fact, but the most engaging incident is the one in which Ann's mother stops her work to play tea party with the lonely child.

Brady . . . is a more mature story, set in the years just before the Civil War. Living in an area where people's feelings are divided, Brady is embarrassed by his father's strong antislavery feelings until events move him to take a position of responsibility. Both books are smoothly written and are convincing in their setting and in period details, but *Brady* also has a depth

that stems from strong characterization and a vivid portrayal of the moral issues involved in the Abolitionist position.

Fritz's later novels, *Early Thunder,* set in 1775 Salem, and *I, Adam,* set in nineteenth-century New England, also have strong characters and serious discussions. We appreciate the problems of the characters, but we don't feel close to them. On the other hand, the humor of which Jean Fritz is capable shines forth abundantly in her *Who's That Stepping on Plymouth Rock?* . . . , *Can't You Make Them Behave, King George?* . . . , and *Where Do You Think You're Going, Christopher Columbus?*. . . . These are representative of the brief, factual tales for younger readers that are no less accurate than her more substantial stories. (pp. 409-10)

> Zena Sutherland and May Hill Arbuthnot, *"Historical Fiction: Jean Fritz,"* in their Children and Books, *seventh edition, Scott, Foresman and Company, 1986, pp. 409-10.*

SUSAN STAN

[Jean Fritz] has the great pleasure of hearing from hundreds of children that her work has made a difference in their lives. One letter from a young boy tells of his experience with *Homesick: My Own Story*: "For the first time I thought about what it would feel like to be a foreigner. I never thought about that before."

Homesick: My Own Story tells of Jean's feelings growing up in China as the only child of missionary parents. "I'd been trying to write that book for years and years and I couldn't find the right voice." When the right voice finally did emerge, it was as part of an image, that of her father's study. She begins the book, "In my father's study there was a globe with all the countries of the world running around it. I could put my finger on the exact spot where I was and had been ever since I'd been born. And I was on the wrong side of the globe."

When China was reopened to Westerners, Jean and her husband, Michael Fritz, quickly put in their names to visit. But when the time came to go, Jean was sick with an illness that required surgery. Looking back, she wonders if her sickness was not also a way of forestalling that trip. She was not ready to see China again: "I was scared I would lose the childhood I had been hanging on to."

Only after her father died, and with him the last connection to her childhood, was she able to write her story. "Then I could go to China," she explains. "My childhood was safe. It was down in black and white." She has been to China twice since then. *China Homecoming* tells of her first journey back; on the second trip, she conducted interviews and did research for a book about China's Long March of 1934-35. . . .

In reading *Homesick,* we meet a young Jean, intensely, single-mindedly filled with patriotism for an America she knows only second-hand. And in *China Homecoming,* we find an adult who recognizes that spending her childhood in China has created roots for her there that stand alongside her American ones. Fritz herself offers the suggestion that her overriding interest in American history—"trying to come to terms with what it has meant historically to be an American"—is a part of the process of finding her roots.

Each of Jean Fritz's books requires as much time to research as it does to write. She words her conjectures carefully: he *must have* felt, she *would have* thought. When she includes a character's words in quotes, it is because she has a source for that statement. If she finds a piece of information somewhere, she cross-checks it elsewhere to be sure it's accurate, a process that can lead her on a chase to libraries and museums throughout the country.

Because she spent over five years researching a book for adults about the American Revolution [*Cast for a Revolution: Some American Friends and Enemies, 1728-1814*], Jean Fritz feels particularly at home in that time period. Her well-known biographies for young people . . . are set in that era, as is her newest title, *Shh! We're Writing the Constitution.* Although she had no intention of writing this book, she says, she knew the people (she's speaking of George Washington, James Madison, and their contemporaries) very well. It was in early 1986 when, sick at home with the flu, she began receiving curriculum material on how to teach the Constitution. Her distaste for that material forced her hand, and she decided she had to write a book on the Constitution.

For Jean Fritz, history is full of idiosyncratic people every bit as interesting as people today. Yet children are not introduced to these people or to history in an enthusiastic and entertaining context. Instead, history is still being taught from the same kinds of stale textbooks that have failed to inspire generations of children.

Fritz would rather surprise children into learning. She avoids writing about obscure figures in favor of subjects that will fit into the classroom curriculum and provide a supplement—or an alternative—to the textbook. She recently shared her aim with a roomful of listeners. . . . In a comforting blend of forthrightness and graciousness that marks her character, she stated: "I would like to get rid of the history textbook."

Susan Stan, "Conversations: Jean Fritz," in The Five Owls, *Vol. 1, No. 5, May-June, 1987, p. 75.*

---

121 PUDDING STREET (1955)

This light comedy.has little more to it than a gratifying triumph over the whims of a fussy old lady but there are concurrent doings that trip the fantastic in a pleasurable sort of way. Mary, Ann, Christopher, Timothy and all the other children of Pudding Street dislike Miss Pursey who shuts her house and lot. Then Ann, the youngest, discovers Miss Pursey is a button collector and a consequent bribe opens the lot periodically to the kids. Then, for buttons, Miss Pursey decides to go off to Zanzibar, and in her absence Captain Happy buys 121 and lets the children run freely. Small plots and counterplots foil Miss Pursey's attempt to buy it back again when she returns from Zanzibar.

A review of "121 Pudding Street," in Virginia Kirkus' Service, *Vol. XXIII, No. 18, September 15, 1955, p. 703.*

This book has just the right balance between the natural and the highly improbable but utterly desirable. The figures move in a children's democracy, and parents are conspicuous by their absence from the scene. The only grownups allowed to assert themselves in the book are those who are wise enough to behave like children.

Readers who remember the author's previous book *Fish Head* will want to read her second offering and will not be disappointed.

Silence Buck Bellows, in a review of "121 Pudding Street," in The Christian Science Monitor, *January 12, 1956, p. 11.*

[Jean Fritz] has written another original story—a blithe one that hovers between extravaganza and realism. Things never work out like this in life but children often wish they would.

Ellen Lewis Buell, "A Summer's Tale," in The New York Times Book Review, *February 26, 1956, p. 30.*

THE LATE SPRING (1957)

A robin's flight North provides a focal point for Spring and makes a rather quiet book from Jean Fritz whose *Fish Head* and *121 Pudding Street* were more boisterous and witty. Down South, Robin R. takes his time making up his mind until the right combination of feelings and events sends him finally on his way.

A review of "The Late Spring," in Virginia Kirkus' Service, *Vol. XXV, No. 4, February 15, 1957, p. 137.*

It is a slight story, but it has charm and freshness and the kind of humor that makes the reader feel he is sharing a special joke with the storyteller. Like the text, Erik Blegvad's black-and-white pictures evoke the cold stillness of the days just before spring. . . .

Ellen Lewis Buell, "Tardy Robin," in The New York Times Book Review, *April 7, 1957, p. 28.*

THE CABIN FACED WEST (1958)

AUTHOR'S COMMENTARY

My first excursion into historical fiction was with the story of the dinner that my grandmother's grandmother, Ann Hamilton, had with George Washington. Her family had just moved over the Allegheny Mountains from Gettysburg to the western part of the state, now Washington County. One day as Ann was picking blackberries, a stranger on a white horse rode up. "Little girl," he said, "can you tell me what your mother is having for dinner tonight?" "Peas and potatoes," she answered. "And blackberry pie." The stranger smiled. "Would you tell her that General Washington would like to take dinner with her?"

The story has been handed down in our family, and Washington's diary records the fact that he "bated" one night at the Hamiltons. I started doing research on the period and place, almost blindly at first, picking up pieces as I went along, finding characters and threads for my plot as I became immersed in the period. County histories were one of the best sources for the book, and as I went over the records, I discovered not only that the families had lived far apart but that among those families there had been, as far as I could determine, no girls Ann Hamilton's age. Boys and babies there were, girls older and younger, but no one for Ann; and I, who had grown up lonely, far from what I considered home, knew how lonely Ann must have been, how rebellious she must have felt. As an adult, I also knew that at the time I had not appreciated the unique opportunities of my own childhood situation, and so I set about trying, as a writer for children does, not only to re-create the temper of childhood but to bring to it some of the wisdom that comes with maturity. I was both Ann Hamilton and someone trying to show Ann Hamilton the challenge of her own times. (p. 567)

Sometimes the joys of historical writing come even after the book is done. I shall always remember the day a year after *The Cabin Faced West . . .* was published when I first visited the hill where Ann Hamilton had lived. I had had no specific description to go by when I wrote the book, only a general description of that part of the country in the late 1780's which referred to the abundance of wild grapes. So, as I described Ann's home, I wrote about the grapes and as I pictured the scene, I always imagined a tangle of wild grapevines on both sides of the road. It is still farm country around Hamilton Hill, but this is, after all, the twentieth century and the book was largely imaginative. I could hardly expect the reality of today to resemble the landscape of two centuries ago, a landscape I had only dreamed up. Yet it was just as I had described it. The road, a dirt road, twisted and turned as I climbed the hill. Both sides of it were lined with wild grapes. I had the feeling that if I looked carefully I might still find the hoofprints of George Washington's horse.

But then, as I told myself later, even had the road been paved, even had the hill been built up, even had there been no wild grapes at all, I should have been looking for those hoofprints. A historical writer is always looking for old hoofprints, old footprints. They are still there, under the dust, under the pavement. And I am still looking for them. (p. 570)

> *Jean Fritz, "On Writing Historical Fiction," in* The Horn Book Magazine, *Vol. XLIII, No. 5, October, 1967, pp. 565-70.*

This is a brief, cozy little period piece, demonstrating Jean Fritz's versatility. Ann Hamilton was lonely for the chum she had left behind when her family moved to the early wilderness of western Pennsylvania. There were only the boys of the McPhale family, who seemed to be a shiftless group, unwilling to face the hardships of farming as pioneers. But Ann was caught up soon in helping roughneck Andy McPhale to learn to read, and ultimately in influencing his family to stick it out on the frontier. When George Washington comes to visit Hamilton Hill Ann finds the tedium of adjustment was all worth while. An easy reading chapter indicating the hardships which were part of the national heritage. . . .

> *A review of "The Cabin Faced West," in* Virginia Kirkus' Service, *Vol. XXVI, No. 2, January 15, 1958, p. 33.*

A well-written, interesting story of Ann Hamilton. . . . Based on the childhood of the author's great-great-grandmother, this is an appealing story with good characterizations. (pp. 1284-85)

> *Laura E. Cathon, in a review of "The Cabin Faced West," in* Library Journal, *Vol. 83, No. 8, April 15, 1958, pp. 1284-85.*

[*The Cabin Faced West*] is written with sympathy and sincerity. Family relationships are well portrayed, especially in a charming scene in which Ann's mother, although tired and busy, finds her daughter having a lonely tea party, and promptly joins her in imaginative play.

> *Zena Sutherland, in a review of "The Cabin Faced West," in* Bulletin of the Children's Book Center, *Vol. XI, No. 10, June, 1958, p. 109.*

A warm and childlike spirit pervades this simply told story. . . . The family picture, with Ann's teasing big brothers and the

Fritz, with her grandparents and her mother, after returning to the United States from China. Courtesy of Jean Fritz.

little baby she fondly called "Johnny-cake," will please children while it gives some understanding of what was demanded of wilderness settlers.

> *Virginia Haviland, in a review of "The Cabin Faced West," in* The Horn Book Magazine, *Vol. XXXIV, No. 3, June, 1958, p. 198.*

CHAMPION DOG, PRINCE TOM (with Tom Clute; 1958)

This true story of Prince Tom, a blonde cocker spaniel, will delight all dog lovers. Tom Clute and friendly young Nathan help Prince Tom become a trick dog and an obedience-trial champion and win the title "National Field Trial Champion" for his hunting ability. Prince Tom's main difficulty is in convincing humans of his many talents. Fast-reading, with helpful suggestions for dog training. . . . Good adult-children relationships. Recommended for all libraries patronized by grades 4-6.

> *Olive Mumford, in a review of "Champion Dog Prince Tom," in* Junior Libraries, *Vol. 5, No. 2, October, 1958, p. 155.*

The lovable dog's progress from trick dog and TV performer to obedience trials champion and finally to National Field Trial Champion of 1956 is affectionately told in a lively, appealing narrative.

> *Helen E. Kinsey, in a review of "Champion Dog, Prince Tom," in* The Booklist and Subscription Books Bulletin, *Vol. 55, No. 5, November 1, 1958, p. 136.*

THE ANIMALS OF DOCTOR SCHWEITZER (1958)

It was indeed a happy inspiration that led Jean Fritz to make this book, for what better introduction could children have to Dr. Schweitzer than an account of the pets he has had at his hospital "on the left-hand side of Africa" in the Ogowe wilderness. There is Monsieur le Pelican who appointed himself night-watchman for the doctor, Leonie and Theodore, the antelopes, and Thekla, the Red River hog so mischievous that he had to be sent to a zoo in London. There is Fifi, the chimpanzee, and many monkeys, Fritzi, Upsi, Romeo and Juliet, and Josephine, the wild boar, determined to go to church every

Sunday and to sleep under mosquito nettings even if she had to share the netting with a human being.

Children from eight up will enjoy these charmingly told anecdotes.... Through this book they will become aware of the Doctor's reverence for life, his great love of everything that lives, whether large or small.

> *"True Stories of Children in Other Lands," in* New York Herald Tribune Book Review, *November 2, 1958, p. 22.*

Jean Fritz has produced a warm, well-researched book on one phase of the great humanitarian's activities. With sensitivity and gentle humor, Mrs. Fritz tells the stories of the creatures who were given names and friendship by the doctor....

This is not a nature study, but an inspiring glimpse of one man's profound concern for all living things. Douglas Howland's realistic drawings and Mrs. Fritz's mastery of phrases make a book that should keep a child company for many years.

> *Ann McGovern, "'Patch of Gentleness'," in* The New York Times Book Review, *November 2, 1958, p. 44.*

The many children who are interested in animals, especially in tamed wild animals, will thoroughly enjoy these anecdotes of some ten of Dr. Schweitzer's special animal friends.... The author tells their stories with warmth and sympathetic amusement. As she does so, she etches in telling details of the Great Doctor's deep humanity and of the life in his Ogowe River village.... Many children have heard of Dr. Schweitzer or seen the film about him. These little stories will supplement their knowledge in a meaningful way.

> *Elizabeth Doak, in a review of "The Animals of Doctor Schweitzer," in* The Horn Book Magazine, *Vol. XXXV, No. 2, April, 1959, p. 145.*

HOW TO READ A RABBIT (1959)

There were all kinds of animals in the lending library: a mouse named Mickey, a snake named Sleuth, an owl named Goggles, even a skunk named Magnolia. This was a very special library, where children borrowed animals instead of books! Six-year-old Stephen fell in love with the little brown rabbit and yearned to take her home, but alas, he had to be 7 to borrow. Stephen suffered through animal after animal that his big brother brought home from the library, praying for the day the little brown rabbit would come for a visit. At last, one day she did, but under the most surprising circumstances; and because of the brown rabbit Stephen got a very special birthday present, 176 days ahead of time. The idea of an animal lending library is very clever, and, according to the author, such institutions really do exist. Many young readers will probably agitate for one in their own community. A pleasant story, which children will enjoy reading once over lightly.

> *Olga Hoyt, "Animals to Lend," in* The New York Times Book Review, *October 11, 1959, p. 36.*

Younger children will be as delighted with the very idea of an animal lending library as with the warm and amusing story in which Stephen's dream of a rabbit comes true in a most satisfying way.

> *A review of "How to Read a Rabbit," in* The Booklist and Subscription Books Bulletin, *Vol. 56, No. 12, February 15, 1960, p. 358.*

MAGIC TO BURN (1964)

A long and deftly-sustained fanciful story, written in a style that has vitality and smoothness; the story line is tight and well-paced, and the protagonist, a tiny creature named Blaze, is delightful. Blaze is a boggart, met by moonlight when Ann and Stephen were in England with their parents; they find him in their cabin aboard the homebound ship. Blaze does not take kindly to the United States—Blaze is anything but kindly by nature—and he is spoiled, querulous, and vain. When Stephen finds, among Blaze's effects, a valuable old manuscript, it enables him to get the homesick boggart back to his native soil, since the whole family flies back to England to verify the document. Nicely conceived and charmingly executed.

> *Zena Sutherland, in a review of "Magic to Burn," in* Bulletin of the Center for Children's Books, *Vol. XVIII, No. 5, January, 1965, p. 74.*

Jean Fritz has created a lively little character in her delightful fantasy, **Magic to Burn**. His name is Blaze.... Jean Fritz always writes a good story, but this, her first venture into fantasy, seems particularly fine. (pp. 354-55)

> *Charlotte S. Huck and Doris Young Kuhn, "Modern Fantasy and Humor: Lilliputian Worlds" in their* Children's Literature in the Elementary School, *second edition, Holt, Rinehart and Winston, Inc., 1968, pp. 353-55.*

WILL YOU SIGN HERE, JOHN HANCOCK? (1976)

The pantheon of the Founding Fathers is a daunting place. Crowded with idealized statuary, swept by the drafts of legend and infested with humbugs, it challenges honesty at every turn. Refreshing, then, to come upon this nicely executed mini-portrait of John Hancock, whose chief claim to our Bicentennial attention is the size of his signature on the Declaration of Independence....

Hancock had a keen sense of history, if not much stomach for its sometimes painful demands. Rich, pleasure-loving, vain, he passed through the Revolution in comfort, complaining occasionally of having to "ruff it"—which for him meant a temporary descent from silver to pewter utensils. King Hancock, some called him. But that was his style. He was also kind, generous and brave enough to have been one of the first to put personal safety and fortune into the battle against the Crown. So here is Hancock's story, warts and all, well told by Jean Fritz....

> *Robert Berkvist, in a review of "Will You Sign Here, John Hancock?" in* The New York Times Book Review, *May 2, 1976, p. 27.*

Jean Fritz goes rolling along, and we merrily after, through yet another fizzy tribute to our Founding Fathers. Unlike Ben Franklin ... who can't be pigeonholed, John Hancock is a pushover for the Fritz method. The most vulnerable, and humanizing, aspect of Hancock was clearly his overweening vanity, and Fritz plays the characteristic from every angle—an inventory of Hancock's nine fancy carriages; comparison of his increasingly grandiose signatures; even Hancock's own description of having to "Ruff it" during the war by doing without a candle snuffer and dining on tough turkey. . . . Trina Schart Hyman applies her confectioner's touch to the dandified goings on, and her caricatures of Hancock—looking appropriately pompous, outraged, or chagrined—catch the mood of affectionate iconoclasm. (pp. 636-37)

> *A review of "Will You Sign Here, John Hancock?"* in Kirkus Reviews, *Vol. XLIV, No. 11, June 1, 1976, pp. 636-37.*

It seems that the author couldn't stop, once she had got started on creating her witty and highly personalized portrayals of our Founding Fathers. Good. Thanks to her . . . , John Hancock is now among the historic *people* of our past, rather than figures in dry texts. (pp. 98-9)

> *A review of "Will You Sign Here, John Hancock?"* in Publishers Weekly, *Vol. 209, No. 26, June 28, 1976, pp. 98-9.*

As always, Jean Fritz writes with a light touch that belies the serious scholarship of her research and makes the conceited but good-hearted Hancock a truly believable man. The sly humor of Hyman's illustrations effectively underlies the tone of teasing affection. . . . (pp. 56-7)

> *Zena Sutherland, in a review of "Will You Sign Here, John Hancock?"* in Bulletin of the Center for Children's Books, *Vol. 30, No. 4, December, 1976, pp. 56-7.*

WHAT'S THE BIG IDEA, BEN FRANKLIN? (1976)

What we have here in this book about Benjamin Franklin is a clear triumph for the simple declarative sentence, something not very easily come by. **What's the Big Idea, Ben Franklin?** is neither cute nor is it simpering. Neither does it condescend nor shirk facts, nor does it romanticize nor pull out all the stops. It does not display any of the useless pedantry that may satisfy adults but only serves to confuse, bore or antagonize children.

Example: "Yet no matter how busy he was, Benjamin found time to try out new ideas. Sometimes he had ideas on why things happen the way they do. He wrote about comets. He formed a theory about hurricanes; they moved, he said, from the southwest to the northwest, contrary to the way winds usually move."

I could adduce similar examples anywhere in the book, because it is full of such tiny excellences. And, for a book so brief, it is remarkably inclusive—so inclusive, in fact, that it includes footnotes at the back. The reader—I hope there will be many readers—will learn a good deal about Franklin, the son of the Boston candlemaker, from his birth in Boston to his death in Philadelphia at the age of 84—Franklin, the printer and publisher, almanac maker, inventor, traveler, politician, sophisticate and citizen-patriot.

Congratulations to Mrs. Fritz. . . .

> *Gilbert Millstein, in a review of "What's the Big Idea, Ben Franklin?"* in The New York Times Book Review, *July 4, 1976, p. 16.*

The usual breezy, entertaining Fritz style masks the usual meticulous Fritz research in a brisk biography that is informal and informative. . . . Enough background information about colo-

nial affairs is given to enable readers to understand the importance of Franklin's contributions to the public good but not so much that it obtrudes on his life story.

> *Zena Sutherland, in a review of "What's the Big Idea, Ben Franklin?"* in Bulletin of the Center for Children's Books, *Vol. 30, No. 1, September, 1976, p. 10.*

Another light and lively biography of a Founding Father by the author of **Why Don't You Get a Horse, Sam Adams?** . . . , **Will You Sign Here, John Hancock?** . . . , and other question mark titles. Though few new facts are presented, this biography is distinguished from several others for this age level by its humanizing detail, amusing tone, and the perfect marriage of the cheery text with [Margot Tomes's] slyly humorous but accurate illustrations. Rollicking Bicentennial fare for all libraries.

> *Ellen T. Pugh, in a review of "What's the Big Idea, Ben Franklin?"* in School Library Journal, *Vol. 23, No. 1, September, 1976, p. 99.*

The details of Franklin's career . . . are presented for younger readers in a well-researched and documented narrative which reflects the humor, virtues, flaws, and zest for living characteristic of the subject. As in her earlier studies of Paul Revere and Sam Adams, the author successfully emphasizes and enlarges upon a particular trait—in this instance, the zeal for translating ideas into action—not to the point of caricature but rather as a child might instinctively distill the essence of a fascinating adult from close observation. . . . A balanced and vigorous biographical portrait. (pp. 507-08)

> *Mary M. Burns, in a review of "What's the Big Idea, Ben Franklin?"* in The Horn Book Magazine, *Vol. LII, No. 5, October, 1976, pp. 507-08.*

CAN'T YOU MAKE THEM BEHAVE, KING GEORGE? (1977)

Why can't you make this one funny, Jean Fritz? Perhaps the fact that we Americans demythologized King George some time back makes the details of his domestic life seem merely trivial and the many *faux pas* committed by his chief steward at the coronation less than refreshingly shocking. (The horse Lord Talbot had trained to back away from the King and Queen will very likely get a laugh when he backs *in* to them instead—but Fritz might have mentioned that the backing out was a polite custom observed by humans as well.) Another handicap no doubt is the absence of that shared affection which so clearly underlay the jokes on Paul Revere deprived of his horse or Sam Adams learning to ride one—and which generally made our patriots' foibles engaging. (Though King George might well have felt like "a father with a family of very, very disobedient children" when America started "acting up," it's hard to muster any filial indulgence.) Or maybe the problem lies in lackluster George himself; in any case, Fritz fails to project a personality that can make up for the shortage of history.

> *A review of "Can't You Make Them Behave, King George?"* in Kirkus Reviews, *Vol. XLV, No. 16, August 15, 1977, p. 854.*

There's a move toward equal time for the opposition in this typically cheeky Fritz sketch. . . . The only weakness is a conclusion that seems abrupt; in fact, it is an appended author's note that explains about George's later years. . . . (pp. 288-89)

> *Denise M. Wilms, in a review of "Can't You Make Them Behave, King George?" in* Booklist, *Vol. 74, No. 3, October 1, 1977, pp. 288-89.*

With her fine eye for detail, Fritz tells readers that the King made buttons, loved sauerkraut and fruit, and had his queen's hairdresser serve meals to cut down on the number of servants. She also adds a note about the King's affliction with porphyria, a disease now believed to be the cause of his bizarre behavior in later life. . . . Great fun and fascinating history.

> *Susan H. Lister, in a review of "Can't You Make Them Behave, King George?" in* School Library Journal, *Vol. 24, No. 3, November, 1977, p. 56.*

Another of Jean Fritz's witty, warts-and-all portraits of Revolutionary War leaders. What made her previous biographies so memorable was her ability to debunk almost-mythic heroes like Paul Revere with affection and good humor. This time, however, Fritz uses reverse strategy showing that George III, although obstinate and short-sighted, really wasn't such a bad fellow. As usual there are many humanizing tidbits (a reluctant Latin scholar, young George wrote, "Mr. Caesar. I wish you would go to the devil!"). (p. 22)

> *Jane O'Connor, in a review of "Can't You Make Them Behave, King George?" in* The New York Times Book Review, *November 6, 1977, pp. 22, 24.*

BRENDAN THE NAVIGATOR: A HISTORY MYSTERY ABOUT THE DISCOVERY OF AMERICA (1979)

While Fritz's jesting albeit affectionate approach may irk the devoutly religious (especially those with roots in the Emerald Isle), she has created a lively, provocative "history mystery," delivered in her familiar stylish prose. The question she explores is: Did St. Brendan sail from his native Ireland with a crew in a leather boat, across the Atlantic Ocean during the sixth century and discover America long before other claimants? Most of the accounts retold here come from the epic "Navagatio Brendani," author unknown, which has been a part of the classic literature of many languages since the 11th century, approximately.

> *A review of "Brendan the Navigator," in* Publishers Weekly, *Vol. 215, No. 26, June 25, 1979, p. 123.*

Fritz incorporates legend, speculation, and likely fact into her story of St. Brendan. . . . Her jaunty tone is a shade forced at first when she is treating Ireland's love for stories and enthusiasm for the new religion of Christianity, but Brendan's story itself, with all its fabrications and uncertainties, is a natural for her characteristic informal approach, which hinges on not taking her material too seriously.

> *A review of "Brendan the Navigator: A History Mystery about the Discovery of America," in* Kirkus Reviews, *Vol. XLVII, No. 13, July 1, 1979, p. 743.*

Fritz describes the life of St. Brendan, referring to miracles as though they were facts ("Then he commanded the ground to open. And it did.") and ending with a voyage across the seas to "paradise" that ended when an angel delivered a message that "God had other plans for the place" and therefore Brendan and his friends should go back to Ireland. While the postscript, entitled "Some New Clues," makes it clear that there is no corroboration for the fact that Brendan discovered America ("Ask any schoolchild in Ireland . . . and you'll hear . . . 'St.

Brendan discovered America.' ") only that a trip made in 1976-77 in a leather boat indicated that such a voyage would have been possible, the text may give readers the impression that the voyage was actually made in the sixth century. Fritz is, as always, in command of pace and style, but she's hampered by her subject, which doesn't often happen.

> *Zena Sutherland, in a review of "Brendan the Navigator: A History Mystery about the Discovery of America," in* Bulletin of the Center for Children's Books, *Vol. 33, No. 3, November, 1979, p. 47.*

STONEWALL (1979)

Fritz's trenchant, compassionate life of General Thomas Jonathan Jackson grips the reader and makes one understand why Stonewall is an honored legend in American history. . . . Most of his life Jackson endured as a loser, like [General] Grant, at almost everything he tried. Seeing him in that light, the reader is impressed by the man's determination to hone skills that made him a military genius, loved by his troops. The tragic irony of his death at age 39 is movingly described. It's really too bad that a slip here diminishes Fritz's sensitive writing and one of literature's most poetic and memorable utterances: "Let us cross over he [sic] river and rest under the shade of the trees."

> *A review of "Stonewall," in* Publishers Weekly, *Vol. 216, No. 9, August 27, 1979, p. 385.*

There is no adulatory writing, no overdramatization in this biography of the rigid, zealous, in some instances fanatical Jackson; Jean Fritz focuses on Jackson's prowess as a military leader, and most of the book is concerned with the years of the Civil War, but the early portion of the text so skillfully establishes Jackson's probity, eccentricity, and toughness that the later portion serves to amplify the personal portrait as well as to give a vivid picture of the war years. An extensive bibliography corroborates the evidence of careful research that permeates a well-written and carefully structured text.

> *Zena Sutherland, in a review of "Stonewall," in* Bulletin of the Center for Children's Books, *Vol. 33, No. 2, October, 1979, p. 27.*

Fritz skillfully uses the unpromising story of Jackson's early years before the Civil War to show how his obsessions were ultimately the stuff of heroism. . . . Fritz departs in this book from the light-hearted and witty approach used in her biographies for younger readers, e.g., **And Then What Happened, Paul Revere?** . . . and **Brendan the Navigator** . . . . **Stonewall** follows a more traditional route and, as such, is a superior example of biographical writing. Facts, remarks, and incidents are woven together into a picture of a complex and contradictory man. . . .

> *Shirley Wilton, in a review of "Stonewall," in* School Library Journal, *Vol. 26, No. 3, November, 1979, p. 76.*

Lives of Jackson are plentiful, for his mystique had begun before his death, but none, for all its brevity, surpasses Jean Fritz's. Writing for young people, she has managed to make Jackson's complexity clear without compromising either her information or her language; and she places him firmly within the context of an extraordinarily knotted period of American history. "Stonewall" Jackson was one of the strangest figures

America has ever chosen to regard as great. *Stonewall* gives us both the strangeness and the greatness. (p. 67)

> *Paxton Davis, "A Dark Destroyer," in* The New York Times Book Review, *November 11, 1979, pp. 57, 67.*

WHERE DO YOU THINK YOU'RE GOING, CHRISTOPHER COLUMBUS? (1980)

Jean Fritz has what amounts to perfect pitch when writing history or biography for young people. Naturally, reducing a life as well-documented as Columbus's to 80 pages must result in some simplifications of fact or context, but in this case they are not readily apparent. Mrs. Fritz's breezy narrative gives us a highly individual Columbus—vain, naïve, optimistic, inclined to self-pity, a master seaman but a poor administrator, a man who saw divine providence in the shape of an island, the flight of a bird. . . . [The] work of both author and [Margot Tomes the] illustrator is so consistently fine that they run the risk of being taken for granted. (p. 60)

> *Georgess McHargue, "Early Explorers," in* The New York Times Book Review, *November 9, 1980, pp. 60-1.*

The conversational narrative style of this biography, which is about 30 pages longer than her previous ones, is invitingly easy to read without any talking down. The excitement of landings, the eagerness and cruelties of European adventurers and the politics of exploration are vividly related. A large amount of information is smoothly conveyed. Her emphasis on Columbus' mystic fervor and obstinacy makes an interesting comparison with other accounts of Columbus available for this grade range. The author's usual supplementary notes are included, and an index has been added; a list of major sources would also have been welcomed.

> *Anna Biagioni Hart, in a review of "Where Do You Think You're Going, Christopher Columbus?" in* School Library Journal, *Vol. 27, No. 4, December, 1980, p. 58.*

This sprightly retelling of the familiar story of Columbus's life compares favorably with others by [Ingri and Edgar P.] d'Aulaire, [Alice] Dalgliesh, and [James T.] DeKay. Short and concise, the account of the major events in the life of the famous explorer is sprinkled with unusual humorous details. . . . Lacking the cadence and descriptive passages of d'Aulaire . . . , this is nevertheless more useful because of its index and notes, which supply details important to the story. A useful and very readable biography for those looking for slim books.

> *Janice P. Patterson, in a review of "Where Do You Think You're Going, Christopher Columbus?" in* Children's Book Review Service, *Vol. 9, No. 5, January, 1981, p. 34.*

The art of writing biography for younger children is a difficult one; the chief problem is to make complicated lives of the past with far-reaching consequences for the world accessible to readers whose understanding of history is limited. The author is a master of this precarious craft. In a simple, short biography of Columbus she has been extraordinarily successful in extracting the essence of the man—vain, stubborn, full of faith in his own destiny, deeply religious, and optimistic—and setting him in the context of his own time. . . . The horrors of the Spanish treatment of the natives of the West Indies are not ignored,

but humor is found in the small, revealing details of Columbus's dealings with the Indians as well as with his own people. The colloquial expressions add liveliness. . . .

> *Ann A. Flowers, in a review of "Where Do You Think You're Going, Christopher Columbus?" in* The Horn Book Magazine, *Vol. LVII, No. 1, February, 1981, p. 67.*

THE MAN WHO LOVED BOOKS (1981)

As expected, Fritz weaves folklore, fact and wit into another of her outstanding biographies. [Trina Schart] Hyman's drawings . . . are stylized, ornamental but slyly comic too, reflecting every nuance in the story of Ireland's St. Columba. Columba was a monk who loved his country and the books which were extremely rare in his time, the early sixth century. He would spend hours copying books by hand and caused a terrible war by copying one without permission. Remorse over the soldiers' deaths compelled the monk to do penance. Vowing never to set eyes on his homeland again, he sailed with a few followers to Iona where he served as a missionary. A crisis brought Columba back to Ireland temporarily but he kept his vow, as bemused readers will discover in this charming tale about the patron saint of book lovers.

> *A review of "The Man Who Loved Books," in* Publishers Weekly, *Vol. 219, No. 2, January 9, 1981, p. 76.*

Like **Brendan the Navigator** . . . , this sprightly bit of biography is "drawn from an old legend, much of which is certainly true." . . . This is told with the Fritz ease and some color, but St. Columba's story doesn't yield up the tales that Brendan's did. An agreeable extra.

> *A review of "The Man Who Loved Books," in* Kirkus Reviews, *Vol. 49, No. 5, March 1, 1981, p. 286.*

Using the light, anecdotal approach of her series on Revolutionary figures, Fritz writes about the Irish saint Columba. In a short text, which manages to capture an Irish tone, Fritz tells about Columba's love for books and his determination and efforts to copy as many books as possible, even if it required underhanded methods. Choosing to emphasize this part of his life, she only touches on his important role in spreading Christianity throughout Britain. The text incorporates stories such as his being fed an alphabet cake, and while most accounts attribute his self-imposed exile from Ireland to a battle fought over a kinsman, Fritz attributes the battle to anger over the High King's judgment against Columba about a book he copied without permission. There are touches of humor. . . . Pictures and text work beautifully together, making this picture-book biography of a little-known person a pleasant excursion into another time and place. (pp. 111-12)

> *Jane E. Gardner, in a review of "The Man Who Loved Books," in* School Library Journal, *Vol. 27, No. 8, April, 1981, pp. 111-12.*

Basing her narrative on legendary material, the author has told the story of the sixth-century Irish saint Columba. . . . The telling is direct and spirited, lilting and sensitively balanced, encompassing the bardic and the royal traditions of ancient Ireland as well as the joyful zeal of the saint.

Paul Heins, in a review of "The Man Who Loved Books," in The Horn Book Magazine, *Vol. LVII, No. 3, June, 1981, p. 317.*

TRAITOR: THE CASE OF BENEDICT ARNOLD (1981)

Fritz's gift for recreating the American past has won her awards and her biography of Benedict Arnold is bound to be universally acclaimed. It is a gripping story, related in the author's swift, eloquent style and perceptively recording examples of Arnold's twisted character, from his birth in 1741 through his betrayal of the Revolutionary forces and the aftermath of his treason. Fritz's descriptions of people involved in and/or affected by the trusted general's sellout to the British widen one's understanding. She is particularly moving in telling the story of Arnold's chief victim, Major John André. It's easy to see why the personable, brave spy incited compassion in American patriots as well as in the British when he was doomed to death by hanging. As compelling as a thriller, the book also shines as history, written the way it should be but seldom is.

A review of "Traitor: The Case of Benedict Arnold," in Publishers Weekly, *Vol. 220, No. 1, July 3, 1981, p. 147.*

Although Benedict Arnold is remembered as a traitor, Fritz' biography is a well-documented, nonjudgmental treatment of a man who followed through on his decisions. Arnold is portrayed as an ambitious, money-loving adventurer and decorated

Fritz visiting a school in Wuchan, China. Photograph by Michael Fritz. Courtesy of Jean Fritz.

hero who switched to the British cause because he believed this would help bring peace to the colonies and cash to his pocket. Fritz gives excellent coverage of the confusion and individualism of the American colonies and the Revolutionary War effort. The well-written and readable book provides a fresh analysis of Arnold's personality, his circumstances and his motives for action. This book could engender an understanding of the colonial period and, as shown by Arnold's life, the many considerations that affect adult decision-making.

Laura Mason, in a review of "Traitor: The Case of Benedict Arnold," in School Library Journal, *Vol. 28, No. 1, September, 1981, p. 136.*

How appropriate is an anti-hero in a book which proposes to do little else than tell a straight-forward tale of a traitor and which is intended for young people? Anti-heroes have been all the rage from time to time among adults. But their place in young people's literature prompts the use of a different set of criteria and thus, perhaps, a different evaluation. . . .

Have no doubt Benedict Arnold was an unlovable man: vain, overbearing, jealous and greedy, but author Fritz never urges her readers to hate him. Her approach to Arnold and his deed, the betrayal of West Point, is patient and understanding rather than condemnatory or scornful. In the end, of course, there is the moral lesson that such a base deed must be deplored. But the book allows history to deplore Arnold and what he did. This technique is likely to be more effective than an open statement.

If the wages of sin are death, the wages of Arnold's treason were rejection by the very society he sought to serve by his betrayal. Therein lies the core of this well paced biography and its appropriateness for young readers. Arnold had not acted out of principle, such as loyalty to the king or to the cause of Empire. He was not a true Tory and the Tories who had fled the colonies in rebellion did not accept him. He had acted out of self-pity and in the wake of his dereliction he went unpitied. That is as it should be and is a valuable lesson for one and all, of whatever age.

David H. Burton, in a review of "Traitor: The Case of Benedict Arnold," in Best Sellers, *Vol. 41, No. 10, January, 1982, p. 402.*

Fritz's biography equals her ***Stonewall.*** Both books exemplify criteria for good biographies—accuracy, interest, relevance to our times, and insight into the person, the period, and contemporaries. Footnotes are lacking, but bibliography, notes, and index document the sources. However cozy the style and informal the writing, the scholarship is solid, yet unobtrusive. Primary and secondary material are woven so neatly into the narrative, you scarcely notice the internal documentation. Fritz avoids the pitfall of Freudian psychoanalysis. She manages to clarify her protagonist and the positions he took, even though she cannot be accused of remaining unbiased. Arnold's "Case" appeals more than Stonewall's, partly due to the man's more flamboyant nature, and partly due to the tenor of the times. Arnold emerges as a man of little maturity, one who placed himself first, and who believed what was convenient. ***Traitor*** should have placed on the Newbery Honors list, at least.

Ruth M. Stein, in a review of "Traitor: The Case of Benedict Arnold," in Language Arts, *Vol. 59, No. 6, September, 1982, p. 605.*

THE GOOD GIANTS AND THE BAD PUKWUDGIES (1982)

Unified and enlivened by a wonderful oral cadence, this episodic recombining of several Wampanoag Indian legends tells of a giant, Maushop, who deserts his tart-tongued wife, Quant, for the charms of a green-haired sea maiden, Squant. Eventually, his failure to protect the local folk against the tiny devils known as pukwudgies results in the death of his five sons. Set in the Narrow Land (Cape Cod), the text is adjective-rich ("Maushop heard the singer's voice, liquid and larky, right beside him"), action-filled ("Roaring and wailing, the two stamped furiously all over the grassy place, crushing pukwudgies beneath their feet, catching them in their hands, and squeezing them until their eyes popped out") and playful ("They'd giggle their mean giggles and make nasty, slurpy, glug-glug noises like a swamp swallowing"). The union of format and content, however, is an uneasy one. Revolving around seduction and death, and centering on adult characters, the lengthy story is relatively complex in its language and its concerns, all of which denotes other than a picture-book audience.... This is a story that should be *told*, and to an older audience....

> *Kristi L. Thomas, in a review of "The Good Giants and the Bad Pukwudgies," in* School Library Journal, *Vol. 28, No. 9, May, 1982, p. 52.*

[A legend of the Wampanoag Indians] is told with flair and humor.... There's some crowding of plot, but it's compensated for by the style and the humor (especially in the terse New England speech pattern in dialogues between Maushop and his wife).... (pp. 187-88)

> *Zena Sutherland, in a review of "The Good Giants and the Bad Pukwudgies," in* Bulletin of the Center for Children's Books, *Vol. 35, No. 10, June, 1982, pp. 187-88.*

This is a conglomeration of several similar myths of the Wampanoag Indians of Cape Cod. Poorly turned into one myth, the story has no climax or moral. It deals with a family of good giants and some evil imps called Pukwudgies. The actions of both groups seem generally pointless. A poor representation of Indian mythology.

> *James F. Hamburg, in a review of "The Good Giants and the Bad Pukwudgies," in* Children's Book Review Service, *Vol. 10, No. 11, June, 1982, p. 103.*

Whether she deals with history or with legend, the author always sounds a clear note of authenticity. In a departure from her usual work she tells a tale about the Wampanoag Indians.... Characteristically, the author adds a final note explaining the source and her adaptation of the legends as well as the excellent reason for her laconic storytelling style. And she has provided fresh, unhackneyed material for [illustrator Tomie de Paola's] skill.

> *Ethel L. Heins, in a review of "The Good Giants and the Bad Pukwudgies," in* The Horn Book Magazine, *Vol. LVIII, No. 4, August, 1982, p. 391.*

HOMESICK: MY OWN STORY (1982)

AUTHOR'S COMMENTARY

When I started to write about my childhood in China, I found that my memory came out in lumps. Although I could for the most part arrange them in the proper sequence, I discovered that my preoccupation with time and literal accuracy was squeezing the life out of what I had to say. So I decided to forget about sequence and just get on with it.

Since my childhood feels like a story, I decided to tell it that way, letting the events fall as they would into the shape of a story, lacing them together with fictional bits, adding a piece here and there when memory didn't give me all I needed. I would use conversation freely, for I cannot think of my childhood without hearing voices. So although this book takes place within two years—from October 1925 to September 1927—the events are drawn from the entire period of my childhood, but they are all, except in minor details, basically true. The people are real people; the places are dear to me. But most important, the form I have used has given me the freedom to recreate the emotions that I remember so vividly. Strictly speaking, I have to call this book *fiction*, but it does not feel like fiction to me. It is my story, told as truly as I can tell it.

> *Jean Fritz, in a foreword to her* Homesick: My Own Story, *G. P. Putnam's Sons, 1982, p. 7.*

Jean Fritz describes, in a partial autobiography, the end of her childhood in China, when the turbulence of political transition made it imperative that the "white devils" leave. The book covers a two-year span and concludes with a happy child getting to know the grandparents and the family farm she had so longed to see; the author explains, in her preface, that she has compressed time and included some of her memories of earlier years [see Author's Commentary for this title]. No seams are visible; the story flows smoothly, richly, intimately. The descriptions of places and the times are vivid in a book that brings to the reader, with sharp clarity and candor, the yearnings and fears and ambivalent loyalties of a young girl.

> *Zena Sutherland, in a review of "Homesick: My Own Story," in* Bulletin of the Center for Children's Books, *Vol. 35, No. 11, July-August, 1982, p. 206.*

Fritz's telling never rises above the pedestrian; she does less justice to her own story than to those of the American history figures she has made real and human for children. Nevertheless the combination of author interest and unusual background should assure an interested readership.

> *A review of "Homesick: My Own Story," in* Kirkus Reviews, *Vol. 50, No. 17, September 1, 1982, p. 1002.*

Every now and then a book comes along that makes me want to send a valentine to its author. **Homesick** is such a book. I suppose all of us BICs (born in China) with literary ambitions have been urged at some time or another to record our childhood experiences. Now we don't have to. Jean Fritz has done it, putting her life and ours into a story as pungent and delicious as those meat dumplings we used to buy off the peddler's cart.

Fritz, who has made her place in children's and young adult literature telling other people's stories, from Paul Revere's to Stonewall Jackson's, now turns her eye for the revealing detail and her warm humor upon herself. With an historian's devotion to accuracy, Fritz has chosen to call the account fiction, recognizing the impossibility of recalling one's past perfectly. It is a wise decision, allowing the writer to reconstruct or create (who cares?) childhood scenes complete with dialogue.... (p. 13)

Fritz has gotten the voice of the book exactly right. It is the voice of a bright, imaginative, funny child, straining both towards growing up and towards that rainbow country where there are no beggars nor wars nor Communist mobs—the place where she will no longer be an exile.

This is Jean's story, and while Fritz never wavers from the myopic view of a child in telling it, she is still able to deliver the important people in Jean's life fully rounded. . . .

It is important to note that **Homesick,** while it contains many vivid observations, is not a book about China. It is the personal story of an expatriate child living through a very troubled time. (p. 14)

> *Katherine Paterson, ''An American Childhood in China,'' in* Book World—The Washington Post, *November 7, 1982, pp. 13-14.*

Seven well-constructed true episodes are so deftly written that they seem like carefully composed chapters of a novel, with young Jean as the central character and narrator. . . . (p. 41)

Mrs. Fritz is a practiced hand at narrative, and the reader of these seven stories is sometimes startled at the high professional polish she gives them and at the way the better tales, especially the first and third, round off in the tradition of fine storytelling. ''Am I dealing here with autobiography or skilled fiction?'' the alert reader asks, and Mrs. Fritz, anticipating that the question must arise, answers it forthrightly in her one-page foreword [see Author's Commentary for this title]. . . .

But how good are the stories as stories? They certainly show young Jean growing up, acquiring new understandings, reacting both to China and to the United States. They offer us an excellent portrait of the *amah* or governess, Lin Nai-Nai, and as much of her tragic story as a young girl would be able to appreciate. In the later episodes Andrea is a very real person and the divorce of her parents a wrenching affair. Two boys . . . are presented only briefly but with about the degree of attention a young girl in 1925 would accord them.

What impressed me was the felicitous way in which Mrs. Fritz uses children's language and conveys the attitudes of a faraway land and period. . . .

This book is worth reading. The young readers for whom it is intended will catch from it a sense of China and a feeling of how an American girl grew up in a strange land. Their parents who pick it up casually will, I feel sure, read it to the end, for it conveys a great sense of reality, and [the] compelling photographs—family snapshots not posed to perfection—prove that it all happened. (p. 57)

> *James A. Michener, ''China Childhood,'' in* The New York Times Book Review, *November 14, 1982, pp. 41, 57.*

In writing a memoir of her childhood in China, the author wisely decided, for the sake of storytelling, to take liberties with both time sequence and literal accuracy. . . . Told with an abundance of humor—sometimes wry, sometimes mischievous and irreverent—the story is vibrant with atmosphere, personalities, and a palpable sense of place.

> *Ethel L. Heins, in a review of ''Homesick: My Own Story,'' in* The Horn Book Magazine, *Vol. LVIII, No. 6, December, 1982, p. 649.*

As autobiography, the book measures up to Fritz's many award-winning works of fiction and nonfiction, in that the writing is rich in the telling observations of sights, sounds and people. The story describes gradual changes wrought by the unrest that grew into the revolution in China. But we are absorbed, for the most part, in the autobiographer's feelings, conveyed in humorous and moving anecdotes. . . . Readers will hope these chapters are a prologue to a second volume, with more rich entertainment and information about the life of a ''real American'' and a singularly gifted author. (pp. 59-60)

> *A review of ''Homesick: My Own Story,'' in* Publishers Weekly, *Vol. 222, No. 23, December 3, 1982, pp. 59-60.*

THE DOUBLE LIFE OF POCAHONTAS (1983)

AUTHOR'S COMMENTARY

[The following excerpt is taken from Fritz's Boston Globe-Horn Book *Award acceptance speech given on October 1, 1984.]*

The most difficult job I have had . . . of penetrating another culture came while I was working on *The Double Life of Pocahontas* . . . , and it is for this reason that [the *Boston Globe-Horn Book*] award today means so much to me. I didn't know if I should even try to write the book. I asked Jamake Highwater what he thought, and he encouraged me to go ahead. He was not one, he said, who thought a culture was closed to everyone outside that culture. We would indeed be lost if that were so. So I began—reading everything I could find written about Native American culture and finally books and records specifically about the Jamestown settlement. But there is so much hard evidence lacking. I was unhappy that I had sometimes to resort to words like *must, perhaps, might have;* yet there was no alternative.

There were many kinds of obstacles in my path. So many gaps in the record—and conflicting evidence. I read a recently published book by a prominent historian who suggested that Powhatan's brother Opechancanough had really been the Indian captured by the Spaniards in 1561. He had been given the name Don Luis in Spain, and he was returned to his homeland nine years later, in order to convert his tribe to Christianity. Instead, he murdered the Jesuits who had brought him and took a new name, Opechancanough, which the author maintained meant in Algonkian, ''He whose soul is white.''

If I accepted this version, it would certainly change my whole story, but I found it difficult to accept. The Jamestown settlers came to know Opechancanough well; would they not have detected his familiarity with Western ways? The settlers certainly made friends with many Indians who had no reason to keep such a secret and probably would not have. Yet in no account by the settlers is any such possibility mentioned. Moreover, when the settlers built Opechancanough an English house, they tell of his delight in the front door key which was such a wonder to him. He would go in and out of his house continually just for the pleasure of turning that key. Would a man who had lived a sophisticated court life in Spain be so entranced with an ordinary house key? It did not make sense to me.

So I went to the research library on Indian affairs in Chicago and talked to people there who seemed as dubious as I was. They gave me the name of a man in Virginia who was a specialist on the history of Jamestown. When I called him on the phone, he laughed and dismissed the idea. He knew about the publication I spoke of and was familiar with the theory, but sometimes, he said, a historian simply needs a new idea. This historian wanted so much to believe that Opechancanough was Don Luis that he persuaded himself that it might be so. Wishful thinking again.

As one final check I contacted the man at the Smithsonian Museum who is the expert on Indian languages. "Indians have no word for *soul*," he told me. "Moreover, the language spoken then has been lost to us, but I see no way that Opechancanough could be translated 'He whose soul is white.'"

I went on with my work, but the deeper I went into the subject, the more convinced I became that what happened in Jamestown to Indians is not so much different than what has been happening to them ever since. If Pocahontas was troubled by her two lives, that trouble continues. Expressing the painful split among Indians today, one Native American is quoted as saying: "Some days I am Indian, some days not." In the end when I finished the book, I sent it to Jamake Highwater for correction. He felt that I had caught the right spirit and had only one suggestion to make. When I use the word *sun*, he said, I should capitalize it. Of course. It seems to me I should have known that, and I am grateful that he pointed it out.

Like it or not, all of us are somewhat prisoners as well as recipients of our culture, but ever since writing this book, I find myself, like Pocahontas, thinking of trees as my sisters. I don't mention this to my friends, yet it has invigorated my perspective. (pp. 32-4)

Jean Fritz, "Turning History Inside Out," in The Horn Book Magazine, *Vol. LXI, No. 1, January-February, 1985, pp. 29-34.*

Pocahontas is remembered in school texts of a generation or more ago as a heroine, the Indian princess who saved the life of Capt. John Smith. Of course, the Indian point of view on Pocahontas is quite different. To them, she is the archetypal turncoat. After intervening to rescue Captain Smith (a gesture that may, after all, have been prearranged by her father, Chief Powhatan), Pocahontas watched relations between her people and the English go from bad to worse.

Married to an Indian at the age of 14, she was kidnapped by the Williamsburg settlers when she was 17; when her father failed to pay the ransom demanded for her return, she converted to Christianity and took an English husband, John Rolfe. Rolfe took his wife to England, where she became an object of curiosity, was snubbed by Captain Smith and died at 21 from the effects of the unfamiliar climate and white man's diseases.

Jean Fritz uses [Pocahontas's] poignant story to illustrate the clash between two cultures. Mrs. Fritz's plain-spoken style and ready wit bring this remote period of our history into lively focus for young readers. Equally important, she shows considerable sensitivity in imagining what Pocahontas must have thought of the strange newcomers who settled within her father's domain. This is especially commendable since it would have been all too easy to idealize Powhatan and his people and caricature the Williamsburg settlers, by all accounts as grubby and unenterprising as any lot of pioneers who ever sailed for the New World.

If there is a shortcoming to **The Double Life of Pocahontas**, it is a limitation imposed on Mrs. Fritz by the material itself. There are large gaps in the historical record, and at times

Pocahontas becomes a shadowy figure, retreating into the background of her own story. . . . (p. 53)

Joyce Milton, "Heroic Lives," in The New York Times Book Review, *November 13, 1983, pp. 41, 53.*

Jean Fritz has again brought to life a character in American history. Not a great deal is known about this Indian heroine but the author neither fictionalizes nor creates dialogue; instead, she often speculates, informing readers as to which statements are based on fact and which are expostulation. The notes at the end give further information and are followed by an extensive and impressive bibliography. It is this respect for fact in juvenile biographies that makes . . . *Pocahontas* outstanding in this genre. . . . While this book closely parallels Olga Hall-Quist's *Jamestown Adventure* . . . , it is told from the viewpoint of Pocahontas and quite clearly describes her "double life." . . . While this biography does not have the details of *Stonewall* . . . , or *Traitor* . . . , due to the lack of information available on the subject, it does portray a fresh viewpoint regarding Pocahontas' life and feelings.

Margaret C. Howell, in a review of "The Double Life of Pocahontas," in School Library Journal, *Vol. 30, No. 4, December, 1983, p. 66.*

Jean Fritz explores splendidly the impact of individual people, and one Indian girl in particular, on the course of history. Pocahontas: the princess, the friend, the captive, and the wife. It is her role as a cultural go-between that is questioned, investigated, and documented.

The author's technique of repeatedly posing questions within the narrative of the text initiates a similar response in readers to question and consider the given evidence. This is significant for she has, in essence, written a concise historical interpretation, based on extensive research and her own subsequent, articulate speculations. (p. 293)

Mrs. Fritz gives a rare and sensitive glimpse into the early annals of American history. Students should be alerted to the extensive detail and research in the writing. This should give them an appreciation for such historical endeavors and might encourage them to engage in their own historical speculation. (pp. 293-94)

Ronald A. Jobe, in a review of "The Double Life of Pocahontas," in Language Arts, *Vol. 61, No. 3, March, 1984, pp. 293-94.*

Although most historians now acknowledge that John Smith lied when he told of having been saved by Pocahontas, the popular conception remains unaffected. Jean Fritz's new "biography" will do nothing to change this. She reproduces the standard version, intact, with enough chunks of history of the Jamestown colony thrown in to make it book-length. There is plenty of speculative padding: "She would have" and "She must have" are common phrases. John Smith is portrayed as a hero, and there is more about him in this book than there is about Pocahontas. . . .

The reviews of this book have been uniformly positive. Kirkus called the book "buoyant and affecting." *Horn Book* found it to be "carefully researched," commended Fritz's "Forthright . . . disapproval of the exploitation of the native population" (it's hard to say where they found that), and spoke of the "transformation of an Indian princess into an English-woman." In fact, there is considerable emphasis on the trickery, savagery and childish naivete of the Native people: "Yet other Indians were not one bit friendly. Once they killed an English boy and shot an arrow right through President Wingfield's beard. Often they lay in the tall grass . . . waiting for someone to come through the gate. . . . Not even a dog could run out safely. Once one did and had forty arrows shot into his body."

And here's another quote: "Perhaps the strangers would leave soon, Powhatan thought. . . . In the meantime, he might get guns from the strangers. How he marveled at the power of guns!" The suggestion here is of a simple-minded person naively awed by the "power of guns" rather than of someone encountering a new technological achievement. And this is the same man who led a confederacy of 30 tribes, comprised of more than 9,000 people, in 200 villages. . . .

And surely it should not *still* be necessary to point out that there has never been such a thing as an Indian king, queen or princess?

It would serve no useful purpose to go through this book page by page, separating fact from fantasy. Suffice it to say that Fritz has added nothing to the little already "known" about Pocahontas, and that this little is treated with neither sensitivity nor insight.

> *Doris Seale, in a review of "The Double Life of Pocahontas," in* Interracial Books for Children, *Vol. 15, No. 5, 1984, p. 16.*

[Pocahontas] is recorded in school history books as the Indian who saved the life of Captain John Smith, married John Rolfe, and went to England. Jean Fritz's account of the girl's short life gives a clearer picture of the history surrounding her. In this carefully researched telling there is an honest look at both the unruly behavior of the colonists and the devious plotting of the Indians. The story of the life of the main character, Pocahontas, is extremely thought provoking. She is clearly the pawn of history and is trapped in the terrible dilemma of living between two cultures.

> *Stephanie Loer, in a review of "The Double Life of Pocahontas," in* The Horn Book Magazine, *Vol. LXI, No. 1, January-February, 1985, p. 29.*

CHINA HOMECOMING (1985)

As she relates in her fictionalized childhood memoir, **Homesick,** Fritz grew up in China yearning for the America she had never seen; here, 55 years after her departure at age 13, she returns—and finds, in a Hankou transformed, a few shards of her past: "China was not only part of me . . . *I was part of China.*" . . . Fritz has a lively historical imagination, as anyone familiar with her American-history re-creations for children well knows; she has the quality of remaining forever a child that she prizes (making telephone-contact with China-chum Andrea after publication of **Homesick,** she's disconcerted by this "new voice," relieved to hear "her old voice" at age 69); and she's engagingly unaffected—telling how she learned Chinese jokes in preparation for her trip, then how the jokes went off. Swatches of ancient and modern Chinese history are stitched into the narrative; and along with proclaiming both children and the elderly "the happiest people in China," Fritz makes some discreet observations about the constraints on those in between. The likeliest audience, though, consists of youngsters or adults taken with **Homesick**—who will share Fritz's satisfaction in her warm welcome, in no longer feeling the "outsider" and being able to call Hankou her hometown. (Below the relatively bland anecdotal/informational surface are some subtle sociocultural dynamics.)

> *A review of "China Homecoming," in* Kirkus Reviews, *Juvenile Issue, Vol. 53, Nos. 1-5, March 1, 1985, p. J-21.*

Books about contemporary China all too often have the same flaw: the events their authors chronicle were experienced through the distorting medium of official Chinese guides and interpreters. One feels the blunting presence of official China in the guise of those assigned to shepherd the foreign guests through their China experience. Such books are filled with paragraphs and sentences that begin "Then, we were told that . . ." or "When we were taken to . . .".

But Jean Fritz is a curious hybrid of China experiences. Because she lived in the city of Hankow (now Hankou) as a child until she was 13 . . . , she has experienced China directly. . . .

Her first book [**Homesick**] was filled with memories and sensations of her childhood; [this] sequel, although interesting and informative, lacks the same emotional power. When she finally gets her visa and arrives with her husband in Hankou, . . . to search for her old house, school and church after a 55-year absence, one expects to be drawn into her quest. Instead, the reader feels trapped on a rather prosaic tour hemmed in by guides, hotels and arranged trips to communes.

There are, however, several nice passages that suggest Mrs. Fritz's earlier book. When she describes her feelings as she once again looks up the stairs in her old house and remembers running up and down them so often as a young girl, her story comes alive. Ironically, what stands out about this book is not the drama of her homecoming, but the way in which she has woven discussions of China's past and present into her narrative. Here she is not striving to be dramatically captivating but to present information and explanation about China, and she does it very well. . . .

While **China Homecoming** may not notably succeed in its quest for "roots," it does go a long way in filling the void of thoughtful children's books on contemporary China. Using her own return to Hankou as a kind of trellis on which to hang a number of other historical and current observations about China, Jean Fritz gives us a very informative and clearly written view of that country, well within the reach of children and teen-agers. If I were taking my own son to China for the first time, as I hope soon to do, **China Homecoming** is a book I would want to have along.

> *Orville Schell, in a review of "China Homecoming," in* The New York Times Book Review, *June 23, 1985, p. 27.*

[This is] a record of a very personal search for roots and memories. It is also a rarely candid and objective picture of contemporary China. As both kinds of story it is wonderfully vivid, often touching, and it is written with a practiced grace and narrative flow.

> *Zena Sutherland, in a review of "China Homecoming," in* Bulletin of the Center for Children's Books, *Vol. 38, No. 11, July-August, 1985, p. 205.*

[Fritz's] account is clear and informal, though imbued with the excitement of an adult returning after fifty-five years. She observes such aspects of contemporary China as its communal

Fritz, rediscovering her childhood home in China. Photograph by Michael Fritz. Courtesy of Jean Fritz.

agriculture; its standard of living for young and old; its education, art, and recreation; its food and festivals; and of course its children. At the same time she points out, ''I am convinced that time doesn't really march neatly in a line from the past through the present to the future''; so she deftly intersperses the text with fascinating glimpses into China's four-thousand-year history and makes comprehensible its ordeals and upheavals of the past seven decades. One notes a personal intensity in her reporting. . . . With clarifying notes, an outline of Chinese history, and a bibliography. (p. 580)

> *Ethel L. Heins, in a review of ''China Homecoming,'' in* The Horn Book Magazine, *Vol. LXI, No. 5, September-October, 1985, pp. 579-80.*

MAKE WAY FOR SAM HOUSTON (1986)

[Fritz] has a genius for selection of details which illuminate her subject, neatly fit her careful design, and entertain the reader. Her new biography of Sam Houston is a fine addition to her impressive list of achievements.

Houston ''liked to do things in a big way or not at all.'' He also preferred to do them his own way. As a boy he was too busy reading to bother with school or conventional employment. By the time he was 21, he'd spent three years living with the Cherokees and fought heroically in the War of 1812 under General Andrew Jackson, his lifelong mentor. Taking up the law, his size, manner and charm got him elected to one office after another, including US congressman and governor

of Tennessee. Flamboyant, he sported a different costume for each role, not as turncoat but as man of many talents. But when his wife left him, he left the governorship and went back to the Indians, before going on to Texas, where he became first president of the Republic.

With her forthright, compact sytle, Fritz breezes through this welter of events and keeps them relevant and interesting. . . . Notes, bibliography, index.

> *A review of ''Make Way for Sam Houston,'' in* Kirkus Reviews, *Vol. 54, No. 5, March 1, 1986, p. 393.*

Sam Houston was the kind of larger-than-life hero about whom legends of Texan proportion have been woven. . . . In the hands of the fine biographer Jean Fritz, Houston's life retains its drama and vigor. . . .

Mrs. Fritz portrays his strengths—energy, vision, ambition and patriotism—without whitewashing his weaknesses—a hot temper, drunkenness and arrogance. The combination makes Houston a very human hero, no less admirable and much more compelling. . . .

Mrs. Fritz presents Houston in heroic terms to capture the imagination and admiration of a new generation hungry for heroes. The author proves that biographers writing for children can delineate whole eras through an individual life. In more than a dozen distinguished and engaging books, including *Can't You Make Them Behave, King George?* and *What's the Big Idea, Ben Franklin?* . . . , Mrs. Fritz has surveyed Revolutionary era America through the lives of several great men and one woman, Pocahontas. One hopes her further ventures into the 19th century will yield more heroines. The 1986 winner of the prestigious Laura Ingalls Wilder award and numerous other honors, she deserves every tribute.

At her best in this book, she is a skillful biographer and a graceful, entertaining writer. Mrs. Fritz engages her audience immediately by making Houston "ten or twelve" when she opens her story. Nor does she patronize by making up scenes or dialogue. She uses only direct quotations and provides end notes as well as a bibliography. Young readers will find the book fast paced and fact packed. But parents might volunteer to read *Make Way for Sam Houston* aloud because of its humor and vitality. Mrs. Fritz has told the story of a Huck Finn grown up.

> *Elisabeth Griffith, in a review of ''Make Way for Sam Houston,'' in* The New York Times Book Review, *March 16, 1986, p. 30.*

A canny politician, a successful military leader, an articulate and loquacious extrovert, Sam Houston was devoted, in his public life, to fair treatment for Indians, to the founding and preservation of Texas, and to preventing civil war in the United States. Fritz never fails to give him credit for achievements that contributed to improving any of those causes, but she never makes him a likable man, perhaps intentionally. Her research is always dependable, and is evidenced here by the notes and list of sources that precede the index. There are infrequent lapses in style (''At the time Americans argued if there should even be a war . . .'') but on the whole the writing is expectably competent if a bit heavy, and the pace and structure of the biography are good.

> *A review of ''Make Way for Sam Houston,'' in* Bulletin of the Center for Children's Books, *Vol. 39, No. 9, May, 1986, p. 165.*

Jean Fritz has done it again. In her tightly woven, well-researched biography of the Texas hero, she has demystified Sam Houston by presenting the facts of his life and providing interpretations. Her writing turns this larger-than-life character into a very real person.

Other biographers of Houston have joined the ranks of o.p., but even collections that still have them should make room on their shelves for this splendid biography. (pp. 90-1)

> *Therese Bigelow, in a review of ''Make Way for Sam Houston,'' in* School Library Journal, *Vol. 32, No. 9, May, 1986, pp. 90-1.*

SHH! WE'RE WRITING THE CONSTITUTION (1987)

No one writes history for children better than the latest Wilder Award winner; funny, pungent and impeccably accurate, her contribution to the plethora of books written for the Constitution's bicentennial should be at the top of everyone's purchase list.

Assembling attention-grabbing tidbits that illuminate personalities (Franklin observed that if the President's term wasn't limited there'd be no way to get rid of him short of shooting him), re-create conditions in the 18th century (delegates sweltered as windows were kept shut during a heat wave to keep out noise and flies), and give an excellent feel for the kind of

horse-trading that was required before an acceptable document was produced (it took 60 ballots just to settle on the Electoral College), Fritz surveys the background that made some kind of unity necessary (during the Revolution, when Washington asked some New Jersey soldiers to swear allegiance to the US, they turned him down flat), as well as events from the gathering of delegates (they trickled in from May to August) to the adoption of the Constitution by the states. She summarizes important features of the Constitution, especially the checks and balances it embodies, and the argumentative response that delayed ratification. A few amplifying notes and the text of the Constitution (as sent to Congress on September 18, 1787) are appended.

Lively and fascinating, this will be a delightful surprise to any child who stumbles on it as part of an assignment; it is sure to open minds to the interest and relevance of history.

> *A review of ''Shh! We're Writing the Constitution,'' in* Kirkus Reviews, *Vol. LV, No. 8, April 15, 1987, p. 637.*

[*Shh! We're Writing the Constitution*] is written in punchy prose. . . . But it opens with the striking statement that "after the Revolutionary War most people in America . . . were not ready to call themselves Americans. The last thing they wanted was to become a nation." But if opposition to an American nation was so widespread, why was the Constitution written, and how could it have been ratified?

Children, who are among the world's most rigorous logicians, will surely notice that the story does not hold together—which they often announce by saying the subject is "too hard" or they "don't understand." Allegiance to the American nation founded in 1776 was in fact far greater than Mrs. Fritz suggests. Instead, as other books note correctly, Americans' sense of common identity increased during the war with Britain—above all among the soldiers of the Continental Army. . . . (p. 42)

> *Pauline Maier, ''The Challenge of Children's History: Making It Vivid, Getting It Right,'' in* The New York Times Book Review, *May 17, 1987, pp. 42-3.*

Readers who know the historical work by Jean Fritz will look forward to reading her story of the Constitution in this bicentennial year. Those readers will not be disappointed. Without sacrificing historical accuracy, Fritz has used storytelling style to reconstruct the events of two hundred years ago. (p. 71)

Humor is evident in the episodes when various characters are shown to be ordinary human beings. During a short break, George Washington goes fishing for perch; Madison takes notes of all proceedings except the speeches by one delegate who talks too long and says nothing; Franklin sleeps through boring speeches; George Washington has a headache and upset stomach on his way to the convention. The research for this kind of detail is the reason for the strength of the story. (pp. 71-2)

The text of the book is relatively short because the author has avoided digressions to explain related events of the time. There is an extensive listing of notes following the story with references to specific pages. There is also a copy of the Constitution as it was written. This additional material is probably best left for a second or third reading so it does not interrupt a first reading. This is simply a good story that will last far beyond bicentennial time. (p. 72)

Norine Odland, in a review of "Shh! We're Writing the Constitution," in The Five Owls, *Vol. 1, No. 5, May-June, 1987, pp. 71-2.*

Fritz' account of the writing of the U.S. Constitution makes clear that the job was by no means an easy task. . . . As usual, Fritz' account is spiced with bits of detail that make the report come alive. . . .

The informed reporting that goes on here will give readers a new perspective on our government's beginnings, and perhaps the Constitution's stability is less likely to be taken for granted. An energetic, good-humored history lesson. . . . (pp. 1521-22)

Denise M. Wilms, in a review of "Shh! We're Writing the Constitution," in Booklist, *Vol. 83, No. 19, June 1, 1987, pp. 1521-22.*

Janni Howker

1957-

English author of fiction and short stories.

Howker is recognized as one of the most talented new creators of books for young people. Noted for writing powerful realistic fiction in a vigorous and well-crafted prose style, she is considered an incisive, passionate author who provides perceptive readers with rich, thought-provoking stories. Set in and near her home in Lancaster, England, Howker's three books convey the struggles of the working class and are written in colloquial Lancashire dialect. She explores adolescent frustration and growth through the characterizations of her young protagonists, who find individual strength and the illumination of experience through the choices they make and their relationships with older adults; she also addresses such topics as broken homes and family stress, death and loss, social injustice and prejudice, and mass unemployment and the resultant bonding within communities. Howker gained immediate acclaim with her first published work, *Badger on the Barge and Other Stories* (1984), a collection of five short stories. Underscored by a unique appreciation for senior citizens, each story highlights the healing capacity of a developing friendship between a lonely teenager and an independent elder. Her first novel, *The Nature of the Beast* (1985), is a mystery which parallels the devastation of a northern town when its most vital economic source—a mill—is closed with a series of attacks on the town by an unidentified animal, which the protagonist later discovers is an escaped circus panther. Howker presents this story through the first-person narration of a teenage boy whose anger at the tremendous hardships endured by his family and other mill workers turns into an obsession to destroy the beast. Centering on the deteriorating relationship between a father and son, she uses a turn-of-the-century Lancaster setting as the background for *Isaac Campion* (1986). In this book, ninety-six-year-old Isaac reflects back to age twelve and the effect on his life after the accidental death of a favored older brother and the ruin of the family business. In all of her works, Howker treats her subjects and themes unsentimentally; charged with emotion, her books are balanced by the warmth and humor with which she invests her writing.

Critics commend Howker as an author of unconventional, evocative works which feature vivid characterizations, well-delineated backgrounds, accurate dialogue, and colorful imagery. She is especially praised for skillfully and sensitively capturing the feelings of both adolescents and adults. While reviewers sometimes state that her use of symbolism, stock characters, and first person narration are intrusive, most applaud her energetic prose and predict that Howker will become a lasting favorite in children's literature.

Badger on the Barge was highly commended by the Carnegie Medal committee in 1984 and won the International Reading Association's Children's Book Award in 1985. *The Nature of the Beast* was selected as the Whitbread Book of the Year, children's novel section, in 1985, when it also received the Young Observer Teenage Fiction Award. *Isaac Campion* was highly commended by the Carnegie Medal committee in 1986.

(See also *Something about the Author*, Vol. 46.)

Reprinted by permission of Greenwillow Books

GENERAL COMMENTARY

STEVE LEWIS

Check your bookshelves. Have you got a copy of the very first *Brazen Voices*? You know, the magazine that came out each month as a record of the famous Lancaster readabouts. Why? Well these days being a local writer in Lancaster is like being a local writer in Bloomsbury between the wars. The place fairly bulges with playwrights, novelists, poets and the like and much of their work, fortunately for future generations of academics, has been documented in *Brazen Voices*. That first issue, published in January 1983, has turned out to be particularly historic though none of us knew it then; it marked the prose debuts of Frances Molloy and Janni Howker. . . .

While it is not possible to detect any impact 10 years spent in Lancaster has had on Frances' writing its effect on Janni Howker's work is far more evident. If you know the town at all you'll have no trouble recognising Freeman's Wood, The Canal, The Quay, even Levens Hall in the stories in *Badger on the Barge*. The same marked affection for the town and its environs runs through *The Nature of the Beast* too. The hero lives with his father and grandfather in a place that might almost be the Marsh and stalks the beast, or vice-versa, up in what could be the Lonsdale Fells.

Mind you, *The Nature of the Beast* is not the first novel she's written. That was *Fourth Wind,* written when she was 20 as an antidote to the claustrophobic emotions of the poetry she'd been producing through her adolescence. *Fourth Wind* dealt with the Mongol invasion of Russia in 150 colourful pages and was consigned to a shoe-box on completion, probably wisely. Two more novels followed as she worked her unsung apprenticeship, again neither sent out to publishers. "They were about me but disguised three millionfold," she says of them now, "I showed them to very few people."

Meanwhile her parents wanted to know when they were going to see some of what she was writing. So, at the end of 1982 Janni resolved to write a story for each of them and her two sisters. Determining to cast off the vestiges of former pretentions she set herself the task of writing a straightforwardly un-Borgesian narrative as clearly as she could. She was so taken by the results she decided to send out the first one she finished. As the directness and simplicity she'd aimed for had been achieved at least partly by using a child's perspective it seemed right to send it to Julia MacRae, whose list of children's and young adult's fiction she already admired. Like Frances her talent was recognised immediately.

That very unnuclear family at the heart of *The Nature of the Beast* is an interesting mark of Janni's ambivalence over feminism. Whilst she certainly agrees with many of the aims of the movement it would be hard to say that it significantly informs her work. "I couldn't have written the same story with a mother, daughter and grandmother," she says. Nearly all of her leading characters are male, even in those early novels. Two of the four stories in *Badger on the Barge* do feature young girls: "**The Topiary Garden**" in particular, in which Liz meets and is enlightened by Sally Beck, a woman who spent her girlhood disguised as a boy, but Janni readily admits that this has more to do with her own tomboyish adolescence than any overt political philosophy.

Virginia Woolves they may not be but Janni and Frances are certainly helping to mould Lancaster's status as the Bloomsbury of the eighties.

> Steve Lewis, *"Celebration of Women's Writing: Two Brazen Voices from Lancaster,"* in The Artful Reporter, *June, 1985, p. 13.*

JACI STEPHEN

At the age of 27, Janni Howker's writing career is already a remarkable success story. When we met in May, she was just preparing for a trip to New Orleans where her collection of stories, *Badger on the Barge,* was to receive the International Reading Association's first award for children's fiction. . . .

The feeling that she has at last "come home" is significant in Howker's development as a writer. Following a childhood spent on the move with her nomadic family, her return to [Lancaster] brought into focus an "extraordinary" world—"a world that everyone else took for granted". It provided the impetus for her to start writing as she, in the words of James Berry, "became aware of being full of feelings and points of view that could not be mentioned to anyone ordinarily".

The Lancashire setting of both Howker's books is a clear indication of the extent to which she has been influenced by her northern environment; likewise, her favoured use of northern dialect in them. The influence of Tony Harrison and Ted Hughes made her aware that she could use her own language and she describes the experience as being a "liberating" one: "It gave

me enormous wicked pleasure to be able to write colloquially at last, to taste the juice of my own language without having a teacher put a red pen through it. When I started to write, I had to forget most of the rules I'd learnt in English lessons."

Unemployment, "the harrowing of the north" as Howker calls it, has played a major part in her personal life and, as a result, is often reflected in her writing. *The Nature of the Beast,* set in a Lancashire village, deals specifically with its hardships and effects. This particular "local" problem and setting (in that the north is affected badly by unemployment), along with the use of dialect in both books, has not curtailed their appeal. Howker confesses to being "flabbergasted" at the response and, for the most part, feels that she has been "lucky" with reviews: "I'm always interested to see the type of reviews the book gets. *The Nature of the Beast* is about not just unemployment, but anger and pain. It's always pleasing when a reviewer picks up on the ambiguities". A recent review of the book in *The TES* "saddened" her, however [see excerpt dated April 26, 1985]: "It picked up on one incident. Mick's father is suffering from undiagnosed diabetes and the reviewer said that this was implausible—in fact, that it couldn't happen. It was actually based on a real case. Of course, you inevitably make yourself vulnerable when you write, but that sort of thing is still frustrating". . . .

Howker insists that she does not set out to write children's books. "Backhanded compliments infuriate me—'It's so good, it doesn't seem like a children's book'. My intention is to write good books . . . the best I can".

Howker's writing is indeed successful in blurring the distinction between writing for adults and children. The five stories in *Badger on the Barge,* each concerned with the relationship between a young and a much older person, are remarkable for their ability to bring two seemingly disparate worlds together. What unites them comes across as a sense of loneliness—in oneself, and therefore an intuitive recognition of it in another person. Howker sees loneliness as being common to every child, despite his/her background and levels of "happiness." It is to do with "the feelings of fear, confusion and puzzlement a child experiences—being 'by yourself' inside and lacking the facility to recognize that you're not alone in your feelings. It's a loneliness that is peculiar to childhood, rooted in a child's lack of experience."

> Jaci Stephen, *"Northern Lights,"* in The Times Educational Supplement, *No. 3597, June 7, 1985, p. 51.*

HEATHER NEILL

[Awards] and nominations have been sticking to this young writer like burrs for the past year or so. . . .

At twenty-eight she has become, on the strength of two books, a hot property in the publishing world—a slick commercial term she would probably hate. She lives in Lancaster, having returned to family roots from which she had been separated as a child by her father's career in the RAF. She married at nineteen (a relationship now over) and did a degree in Independent Studies at Lancaster University while helping her husband run a business which involved 'getting up at five to make breakfast for lorry drivers'. Her chosen subject, the Northern hero, led her to studies in archaeology, Icelandic and medieval myth and legend and to the production of dissertations, essays and a novel. More recently she did a year's creative writing course, mainly because the grant was more than the dole, but also to give herself 'official' time for writing—though she has published nothing from that period.

Nowadays Janni works part-time in a residential hostel for the mentally ill between writing and visiting schools to talk about her work. . . .

Janni Howker is notable for her honesty. She says, in so many words, that she hates cant and hypocrisy, especially the middle-class, liberal variety. It is a quality she shares with children whom she describes as 'shrewd little characters. A child will quickly suss out whether an adult is genuine or not.' This directness, coupled with an unsentimental warmth in describing relationships between young and old, marks her out as a distinctive new voice in writing for children and young adults. Not that she much likes categorization, having made no distinction herself between children's books and adult ones when she was growing up as long as they were exciting enough. She loathed the purpose-written American teenage novel which, she felt, patronizingly laid claim to entering the adolescent world and exploring its hang-ups.

The stories in *Badger on the Barge* were written as much for her family as for young readers and she has received favourable responses to them from groups widely varied in age and class. (p. 2)

She began with the story called **'Jakey'** written when she was twenty-five for her father. It was the first thing she had thought good enough to send to a publisher. . . . Julia MacRae asked for more and **'Badger on the Barge', 'Reicker', 'The Egg-Man'** and **'The Topiary Garden'** were added and published as a collection in 1984, each story dealing with the relationship between a child and a much older person. But before this apparently instant success Janni had written a full-length novel which she had no intention of trying to publish. ('It was me as Lawrence Durrell'). She was serving an apprenticeship: 'A carpenter doesn't put the first table he makes in the showroom. He expects to dismantle it and use the wood again.' Writing is a craft, but she adds later that if she didn't consider her work serious art she wouldn't do it. Analysing the process makes her uneasy, though, and she doesn't intend 'art' to mean that which is beyond most people's reach. It was her aim, she says, to make *The Nature of the Beast* readable by the real-life equivalent of its hero, Bill Coward, his redundant millworker dad and his old grandfather. . . . [The book] 'represents the very careful use of a limited vocabulary.' This about a book that has been greeted as 'poetic' by some reviewers and that contains a range of colourful and evocative images. 'It's closer to the oral rather than the literary tradition. But the images are all there in the spoken language, the lively images of working-class speech.'

'Image' is an apt word. Janni Howker would love to make a film, 'to be the director and the cameraman, too' and she 'sees' clearly the incidents as she writes them down. (She might have added smells and tastes, too: her work is full of images of the senses.)

How does she begin—with a character, plot or location? She grins: 'A bottle of cider.' She is too nice to want to be evasive but the jokey reply indicates her reluctance to talk about her work, especially to a stranger. She is anxious not to make too many general statements 'as if there were this great *oeuvre*. It's a great temptation to become an authority on my own work—after only two books.'

She admits that interviews are 'nerve-racking'. Writing, she says, 'comes from the most precious, most private part of me'. She'd much rather do it than talk about it, but she does answer the awkward question seriously. 'It begins when a character takes life on the page. I made several beginnings for *The Nature of the Beast* using the third person. They were dead, lifeless. Then I tried the first person. Bill Coward came alive and all I had to do was write it down. Every day for a month I'd work from nine until after midnight, waiting—with anguish sometimes—to see what would happen.' That was the first draft. The second took longer, but intensity is the keynote still. Janni Howker writes about people at points in their lives when they undergo an experience so intense that it alters their feelings and perceptions. And her method of working reflects that: there are bursts of concentrated activity for a month or two, then long periods when she is not writing.

The plot of *The Nature of the Beast* could have made a cosy, old-fashioned children's book: town and countryside are terrorized by a mysterious beast, which, boy-hero bravely discovers, is an escaped circus panther. But the novel is not like that at all. Bill Coward's thoughts, feelings—anger especially—and his relationship with his father and grandfather leap off the page. (Bill's mother is absent and Janni admits that so far she has found mature, younger women most difficult to write about. She explains this partially with a reminder about her own youth: 'When I wrote *Badger* I had spent more of my life being a child than an adult. . . . I'm very grown up now!') The plot line is not so very important—though it is subtly done—except as a means of understanding Bill and his background: a Lancashire town suffering under the scourge of unemployment. When Bill Coward found his voice and the writing took off, Janni Howker says that she found a weight of suppressed anger was released, anger at the effect of redundancy on her own family: 'Unemployment has dogged my life.'

This is not a pessimistic novel because there is warmth, humour and a will to survive in the main characters, but, for herself, Janni Howker finds it hard to be optimistic, 'The biggest difference between my childhood and the kids in this street is that we knew if you worked hard you'd do all right. At twelve they've given up hope. It breaks your heart. There's a difference too in that most teenagers think there's going to be a nuclear war in their lifetime. They have no belief in posterity and—it's an odd thing to say for a writer—but I don't think I have either. I try to be optimistic, but it's a matter of fiddling while Rome burns. Then the question is, what issues do you go on addressing?'

The concerns she has so far addressed have been to do with individual strength and community despair. Her old people in *Badger*—Jakey on his boat in the freezing weather, Miss Brady who will not bow to institutionalized authority, the Egg-man who lives in a perpetual dream idealizing the long-departed wife who had in fact made his life a misery, and all the rest—reflect Janni's feeling that 'it is an enormous shame that old people are so often presented as nuisances, sad or pathetic'. She has had friends among the old since childhood.

All the stories in *Badger* are set in 'an imaginary Lancaster, my Lancaster', while *The Nature of the Beast* is set further out where there are mill towns on the edge of the Pennines. Despite (or possibly partly because of) their very exact location, Janni Howker's books have sold remarkably well abroad. . . .

Nearer home success has brought her quite a following already in schools, especially local ones. She prefers to speak to children who have not been primed and who ask original questions. . . . 'Like "How old's your mother?" or "What's your favourite kind of balloon?" They really want to know.'

Has early success been a burden? 'So much has happened in the last year, my life has changed so much. I'm very glad of the attention, but the awareness and expectations are a bit frightening.' She indicates the mantelpiece with its cargo of recognition—a medal, a decanter and invitations—'I keep the awards downstairs, not in the study where I work.'

Janni Howker does not believe in cushioning children against strong emotion. 'Whenever you write about real people—and if you don't there's no point—you are bound to deal with touchy subjects. In what I'm doing at the moment there's quite a bit about death.' But she is not keen to discuss the work-in-progress in any detail since at the moment 'it's just a manuscript', not yet accepted for publication—though Julia MacRae is waiting eagerly to read the result of her labours. And if things go according to pattern plenty of other people, adults as well as children, soon will be too. (pp. 2-3)

> *Heather Neill, "The Nature of Janni Howker," in* British Book News Children's Books, *December, 1985, pp. 2-3.*

AMY SPAULDING

Outstanding books for older chilren from England [published in 1985] include . . . two books from an excellent new writer, Janni Howker. One book, *The Nature of the Beast,* is a brooding novel set in a town disrupted by a shutdown factory, while the other, *The Badger on the Barge and Other Stories,* is a collection of stories dealing with relationships between children and other adults. The books' styles and tones are very different, but in each, the reader gets to know real people. (p. 244)

> *Amy Spaulding, "A Potpourri of Bibliographies: Notable Children's Books, 1985," in* Top of the News, *Vol. 42, No. 3, Spring, 1986, pp. 243-47.*

TIM DOOLEY

Janni Howker's first books have brought her rapid and deserved success. Her vital, dramatic style has created in Bill Coward, narrator of *The Nature of the Beast,* an authentic voice of outrage against the moral and physical devastation of the industrial North, while the crisp, sympathetic stories of *Badger on the Barge* bring together young and elderly characters as fellow conspirators against blandness and conformity. (p. 6)

> *Tim Dooley, "All Sorts of Stuff: Fiction for Teenagers," in* British Book News Children's Books, *September, 1986, pp. 6-8.*

BADGER ON THE BARGE AND OTHER STORIES   (1984)

Janni Howker's noteworthy new talent has been deservedly acclaimed already. Doubtless, when the critics have finished with it, *Badger on the Barge* will be bought by every library in the land, and by teachers anxiously reserving chunks of capitation for their personal discovery. This set of five stories, each concerned with a relationship between young and old, is quality stuff: rich in metaphor and dense with "points for discussion".

The accomplishment in such a debut commands so much respect that it seems mean to express any reservations. But, if the immediate reaction was that they're heading for the classroom, the next churlish quibble is that this is where they've

come from. The writer's notebook looms large, and it's ominous news that Ms Howker is now studying for an MA in "creative writing". There is already enough of the exercise and formula here: the consummate architectonics poke through; the unity clamours faintly for attention; the occasional simile could have come from a junior school lesson. One longs for the passion, momentum and different kind of imperfection that a schooling in life, not in creative writing, would bestow.

Nevertheless, the tenderness found in **"The Egg Man"**—a brave venture into a minefield, if ever there was one—and the breathtaking suspense of **"Reicker"**—"And the night tightened one more turn . . . "—and the memorable atmosphere of **"Jakey",** and the fun and freaky-feminism of **"The Topiary Garden"** are not to be missed. As sound as a bell and as nice as they come. Tiny disappointments throughout, but my perception of these is commensurate with high and enthusiastic expectations of Janni Howker.

> *Ruth Kennedy, in a review of "Badger on the Barge & Other Stories," in* The Times Educational Supplement, *No. 3551, July 20, 1984, p. 21.*

The basic theme uniting the five substantial stories in this talented collection is the relationship between youth and age. In each tale a youngster is involved with a much older person: the action unfolds through the voice of adult experience as it fashions new attitudes and understanding in boy or girl.

Each pivot situation or character is unusual or exciting enough to seize the attention of young readers: eccentric Miss Brady cherishes a badger on board her barge; an ex-prisoner of war helps to catch a murderer who is holding a three-year-old child as hostage; lonely Isaiah Black is unable to accept the death of his beloved wife; ninety-one-year-old Sally Beck relives the years she masqueraded as a boy. Challenges and sharpened awareness help to transform brash misunderstandings, unkind taunts or jealousy into sympathetic and discriminating maturity.

Janni Howker's prose is lively and buoyant, carrying her story along with sprightly dialogue and vigorous narrative. For a first book, *Badger on the Barge* is an impressive achievement.

> *G. Bott, in a review of "Badger on the Barge," in* The Junior Bookshelf, *Vol. 48, No. 5, October, 1984, p. 216.*

Five stories built around the relationship between a child and an old person might seem too much of a prevalent motif. The old persons are all odd ducks, too—loners, social deviants of some sort, persons who confide in children, and need and trust them. Though one story could perhaps have been omitted without loss, each of Howker's five children grows in a different way: *how* is central, not the relationship per se. From any point of view, the title (and lead-off) story is the standout. Helen Fisher, delivering baskets from the school harvest festival to local pensioners, gets a grudging welcome from old Miss Brady, barge-dweller and—to Helen's horror and fascination—friend-in-need of a smelly, cranky old badger, Bad Bill. Helen's older, grammar-school brother Peter has been killed in a motorcycle accident, and Dad is inconsolable at the loss of his hope and pride. From the rapt scene in which Helen takes her parents to watch Bad Bill play on the barge, breaking the silence in the house, to her wheel-chair kidnapping of Miss Brady from the hospital, Dad comes out of "hibernation"—allowing himself to cry at fresh sight of Peter's pictures (Helen's temerity), and then to laugh aloud at that "old Badger," Miss Brady's, brazenness. In **"Reicker,"** a darker tale, two bored country-boys—each story has a different, distinct English setting—callously taunt an elderly, ex-German POW by calling him "Nazi"; one of the boys then saves the man from being mistakenly shot (in a murder-incident, a bit of pathetic local excitement), and apologizes for the Nazi-taunt. "When I was your age," old Reicker shrugs, "I was." **"The Egg-Man"** is a delicate parallelism, where any misstep would have been fatal: Jane's father is devotedly fashioning a feather-portrait of her mother as a birthday present, and to get him some brown feathers Jane invades the henyard of the crazy old egg-man—who takes her for his dead wife, and seeks to embrace her. **"Jakey"**—involving an emotionally-needy boy and a failing recluse-fisherman (who casts off to die)—is the most conventional, genre-wise; but it too has an insinuating twist in the boy's jealousy of fisherman Jakey's dependence on an older, hardier youth. **"The Topiary Garden"** again takes a girl out of the shadow of father and brother—through hearing how topiary-gardener Sally Beck, now 91, once had to don her brother's clothes to win her freedom. This is textured and layered work, from an auspicious newcomer, that succeeds as story and rewards close, reflective reading.

A review of "Badger on the Barge and Other Stories," in Kirkus Reviews, Juvenile Issue, *Vol. LIII, Nos. 1-5, March 1, 1985, p. J12.*

In each of these five stories a child begins to know what he or she can't know yet but will soon need to understand. After each illumination they are drawn back into childhood because it isn't time for them to meet this knowledge, though it is time for them to know it is there. Jakey's death follows his boat, 'grey and huge in the dark waters of the bay like a shark', the topiary garden turns 'what is natural into what's unnatural, like putting a tree in corsets'—the images are presented like little jewels to be understood when the time comes. There is a skilful use of children's rhymes, which are about the things children don't think adults will want to know they know. The backgrounds are precise and particular. These are good stories on any level, observant, written with a tender concern for language; but they are better than that. They are stories to learn from in the only way such things can be learnt.

Dorothy Nimmo, in a review of "Badger on the Barge and Other Stories," in The School Librarian, *Vol. 33, No. 2, June, 1985, p. 159.*

"October smelled of bonfires, even in Alfred Street. Down by the canal the yellow leaves of the big conker trees flickered and rustled like burning newspapers. In the still canal water black leaves floated on Helen's reflection." These evocative words begin Janni Howker's first book, a collection of five stories, set in England, each one a memorable encounter between a young person and an old one.

With the prose style and skillful dialogue of a far more experienced writer, the writer gently reminds the reader that, in an era when the young reign supreme, the old, who are often lonely, sometimes forgotten, sometimes misunderstood, have plenty to offer. . . .

Miss Howker's uncanny ability to reach into her past to recall childlike impressions and experiences, to project herself into the minds and bodies of the elderly, and to capture detail and dialogue, give the stories a life and liveliness not often found in children's literature today. The feelings evoked by the stories are at the same time rich, sparse and sharply uncompromising. . . .

The stories are not simply told and they are not easy reading. American children may stumble over some of the British colloquialisms, and in several passages British terms are not readily understandable from context. But the thoughtful reader (young or old) will find five gems—polished, smooth and sparkling—to treasure.

Ann M. Martin, in a review of "Badger on the Barge and Other Stories," in The New York Times Book Review, *October 6, 1985, p. 41.*

This is Janni Howker's first book, and the best collection for young people I have read in recent years. . . . In the title story a girl (whose family is in a state of grieving paralysis after the death of a son) meets an eccentric old woman who is caring for a badger. There is no sentimentality in the treatment of the woman, or the animal, or the family's grief. The contemporary adult world of these convincing, unpretentious stories is a troubled one—there is violence, victimization, sexual fear, illness, dying—but there is no heavy-handedness or despair, largely because the author is equally convincing about the funny, gritty world of sensitive and thoughtful youngsters. The women and girls have quiet, intelligent understandings with one another, especially in **'The Topiary Garden'**, a tactful yet firm account of a motherless girl whose life is determined by the expectations of her father and brother. These are stylish stories, written with a good sense of pace, a dramatic intensity of description, and a simple, direct form of narrative symbolism.

Victor Watson, "Fiction: 'Badger on the Barge and Other Stories'," in The Signal Selection of Children's Books 1984, *The Thimble Press, 1985, p. 23.*

THE NATURE OF THE BEAST (1985)

This first novel from a writer whose short stories for young people have met with critical acclaim has an immediate topicality with its treatment of the impact on a working-class community of the closure of its economic heart, the local mill. Billy's father and grandfather are among the men laid off. Their subsequent campaign against the closure is to come to nothing.

Howker's evocation of the despair, stress and hardship suffered at every level in this small Yorkshire town is well and angrily told, and in the first part of the book, told with a symbolic resonance that suggests a wider comment on the course of Thatcher's Britain. For, as the spectre of long term unemployment haunts the streets of Haverston, on the moors behind the town lurks the beast (hens and sheep have been found mauled), the embodiment of horror and destruction.

Howker's title suggests that she conceived "the nature of the beast" to be this wider threat, but her narrative does not sustain this interesting theme. In the second part of the book, the beast becomes flesh and blood (an escaped showground panther) and the story a routine, if excitingly told, adventure yarn as attention focuses on Billy's resolve to photograph and then kill the beast.

This uneven quality is also reflected in the unresolved and stereotypical references to Travellers (Billy has "a streak of gypsy blood" and therefore a fiery temper). Some of the minor characters are from rural soap opera casting—a crusty but kindly lord of the manor ("'. . . he doesn't suffer fools lightly'") and a motherly publican's wife ("'You've got nothing I haven't seen before, love,' says Ms Garnett, laughing. 'I've got two lads of my own, you know'"). A more recent stock character, the Insensitive-Social-Worker, makes an appearance on the last pages.

But my wish to believe Ms Howker's story was most severely tested when I reached her ludicrously inaccurate description of an undiagnosed diabetic suffering from a hyperglycaemic attack (the union organizer who fails to save the mill). We are told that the luckless Mr Dalton is taken to a hospital for "nervous breakdowns" and some weeks later (when he would have long since lapsed into a coma and died) that he is "probably a diabetic". Probably? The National Health Service may be seriously underfunded but this unlikely account of the inability of its doctors to diagnose a common medical condition is a foolish flaw in what is otherwise an unusual novel for teenagers with a strongly told and original first section.

Rosemary Stones, in a review of "The Nature of the Beast," in The Times Educational Supplement, *No. 3591, April 26, 1985, p. 26.*

The rare appearance of a truly individual talent is something to celebrate. Janni Howker writes with a dash and energy that make one feel she is newly minting a language of her own. The volume of stories, **Badger on the Barge,** with which she made a striking début last year, is now followed by **The Nature of the Beast,** a tale . . . told by a boy in the 'teens whose rapid, seemingly casual tones are as rough and rocky as the stony hillside over which he tracks an unseen beast. Does it really exist—perhaps an escape from a small over-wintering circus—or is it simply a symbol of the pressures and doubts that affect Billy, living at close quarters with a father morose with the threat of unemployment when the local mill is closed and a grandfather aggressively fighting off old age and dependence? Whatever the truth about the black creature which slaughters Chunder's fowls and leaves sheep torn and dying on the local farms, Billy is determined to track it down and destroy it, even if his friend Mick is less useful than he would wish as an ally. As for the reader, I defy anyone not to share Billy's belief. The boy's jagged moods of anger and resolve come across powerfully as he tells the story; his feelings can be surmised as he talks to friends, neighbours, grandfather, and the pictures he has of 'the nature of the beast' is as powerful. . . . A triumph of technique and of the bold deployment of feeling, this is a book to show the way towards strong, unmelodramatic, honest writing for the intelligent young. Billy, as a survivor of social disadvantage and personal inexperience, is a most memorable character.

Margery Fisher, in a review of "The Nature of the Beast," in Growing Point, *Vol. 24, No. 1, May, 1985, p. 4436.*

Janni Howker's gripping first full-length novel brings to life for the more fortunate the effect of the closures and mass unemployment of our times on so many communities, particularly in the North, through her narrator Billy, who brings vividly before us real people, real squalor and real language (not for the squeamish!). Billy, with gypsy blood in his veins, deserted by his mother at birth and brought up by his father and grandfather, is an extreme case, and extreme though credible in his awareness of what is going on in his Lancashire village when the mill closes, his understanding of people and his keen eye for nature and its detail on the moors above Haverston. . . . [The story of the beast loose on the moors] runs parallel to that of unions in conflict with unfair management which wins by trickery, and Billy's inner conflicts. Local farmers decide the beast is a dog, but when Grandfather's

breeding hen is destroyed, a tuft of black hair, a chance overheard remark about circus 'big cats', and the experience of Billy and his mate trying to photograph the beast send him searching in books: he finds a panther. By now, his life is in an inextricable mess, he has had pneumonia, his father has left him for work in Scotland, he is wanted by the law. With nothing to live for, he sets out to kill the panther armed only with an airgun. Fate momentarily favours him: the panther dies in a bog and Billy escapes. But his *Kes*-like, Catch 22 situation worsens. No-one believes him: a shot dog is credited with the killings. We are left with a strange, sinister open end: Billy, overhearing he is to be taken into care, sets out for the moors and the self-sufficient life he once dreamed about, vowing vengeance on the community which has destroyed him by greater damage than that of the Beast: both powerful and moving. (pp. 141-42)

M. Hobbs, in a review of "The Nature of the Beast," in The Junior Bookshelf, *Vol. 49, No. 3, June, 1985, pp. 141-42.*

Apart from the two contrapuntal plot elements—the economic disaster in the community and the mystery of the Beast—the story also makes incisive statements about social injustice and about the frustration of the young, adrift in an uncaring, hypocritical adult world. Neither grandiloquent nor sensational, the energetic writing is riveting in its powerful descriptive realism and its emotional wisdom and honesty. And although the background is bleak, the story essentially is not, for it ends not with despair but with defiance. (pp. 62-3)

Ethel L. Heins, in a review of "The Nature of the Beast," in The Horn Book Magazine, *Vol. LXII, No. 1, January-February, 1986, pp. 62-3.*

"Here's me, Bill Coward, Ned Coward's son and Chunder's grandson—nobody. Nowt."

These are the near-opening sentences of Janni Howker's novel. Caught in the sweep of the story it's easy to forget the anger of the words and their presage of tragedy.

Bill, Ned and Chunder—these three are the pivots of the story that Bill tells. . . .

The three circle round each other in a trio of discomfort and comfort, neglect and care: bacon sandwiches that drip butter down the fingers, the smell of chips from Danny's shop on cold nights: fry ups and shared beds and the commitment to each other that is more enduring than love. Stoical, observant, and judging, Bill chronicles it all.

The atmosphere is Dickensian, that of a northern town dominated by the moors and the chimney of the mill that has given the town its life—until the shadow of unemployment falls over the streets. Suspicion and anxiety cloud relationships: pride and resilience crumble. The threat of unemployment corrupts and corrodes.

And another Beast is on the loose—something . . . spreading destruction before it returns to the moors. . . .

The Beast becomes more than a symbol when Bill realises it must be a panther escaped from the circus. In epic fashion he sets out to slay the beast and claim the reward—the Beast is killed but he is humoured, cared for—and disbelieved.

Until in the final startling pages Bill is also threatened with the loss of freedom. Only then do we remember the anger of those opening sentences. He has killed the Beast but only to be confronted by a greater challenge. . . .

Remember the soldier of fortune who once tilted at windmills? *The Nature of the Beast* is not about unemployment or slaying a panther; it is about survival.

Janni Howker has written a deceptively discursive story beneath which lies a taut small masterpiece of anger and love.

> *Margaret Carter, in a review of "The Nature of the Beast," in* Books for Your Children, *Vol. 21, No. 1, Spring, 1986, p. 25.*

[In *The Nature of the Beast*] we're presented with a leap of imagination so bold we'd be left stranded were it not for the precise delineation of a place. Haverston is a community doubly devastated: by the closure of the local mill and by a marauding beast on the moors surrounding the town. The fusing of the two into the same predatory image could easily have seemed far-fetched but for the gorse-and-concrete, flesh-and-blood reality of the writing. This brings the action seeringly close to home. The progress of Billy Coward from victim to vigilante is like a prolonged scream of agony. . . . It's hard to envisage a more eloquent protest on behalf of the Billy Cowards of our society. Or a more gripping narrative for them (and the rest of us) to read.

> *Chris Powling, "Meet the Winners," in* Books for Keeps, *No. 39, July, 1986, p. 9.*

ISAAC CAMPION (1986)

The soft-focus world of the Hovis advertisements is never more than a twist of a phrase away in Janni Howker's compact new novella. It is deliberately evoked, and just as deliberately challenged and undercut. Isaac Campion, narrating the crucial events of his turn-of-the-century childhood, assumes an audience that thinks cobbles romantic, regional accents quaint; an audience that believes in the "good old days." The cosy glow of nostalgia is doused to the chill of a cold dawn, a scraped breakfast, a day's work ahead.

The deliberate harshness of perspective makes this book in many ways an urban counterpart of Rachel Anderson's brilliant *The Poacher's Son.* . . . There is behind both books a weight of feeling which makes them at once works of fiction and acts of witness to truths which other fictions have disguised. In this second sense, *Isaac Campion* is a triumph. Its feel for period is utterly convincing: in the pattern of relationships in a family and a community, as much as in the small telling details which Janni Howker observes so sharply.

As a story, however, *Isaac Campion* never quite makes full use of this cunningly evoked atmosphere. The decision to tell the story as first-person reminiscence limits both what the narrative can imply and what it can show. There is strain when Howker needs to make explicit for her readership matters which her narrator would surely pass without comment. Isaac the narrator is partly old man making urgent sense of his early memories, partly ruminative schoolteacher. One minute he is using "right broad speech", the next he is telling us, "This is the only way we have, you see, to go back into the past. This business of remembering. But it is false."

The limitation to one man's speech patterns, and the sense of violation when they are disrupted, is matched by the limitation to one point of view, which denies us, for instance, much sense of what is happening on the other side of Isaac's family's feud with the rival horse copers, the Laceys. We are left with Isaac as an old man observing himself as a boy observing fragments of one half of a story: excellent as far as it goes, but too narrow to chart fully the knot of tensions it describes.

The result of all this is to confine the book to over-familiar ground: the sensitive lad learning to pity as well as fear his savage-tempered, domineering father; the timid, uncomplaining mother with instincts of refinement; the silent, knowing uncles and the comically voluble one. They are truly and shrewdly depicted, but they are drawn from stock, none the less.

Janni Howker is a writer of considerable power: she knows how to sting and how to suggest. She is also a writer of real passion, and one can see her in this book staking out a parallel ground to that of Alan Garner's *Stone Book Quartet.* She too is not content that the lives of the labouring classes should be described in the words and the rhythms of the governing and recording classes. This book has neither the resonance nor the assured economy of the *Stone Book Quartet:* but in the cadences and cross-cutting of its dialogue, and in its sense of the emotions behind words, it provokes the comparison.

> *Neil Philip, "This Business of Remembering," in* The Times Literary Supplement, *No. 4363, November 14, 1986, p. 1291.*

[Howker] has written another glowing novel. . . .

Only the most sophisticated of readers will appreciate Howker's tale. The pace is leisurely, and Isaac narrates in the British dialect of his region and day, making the story tough going for the average American reader. But those who are up to it will find writing that is remarkably descriptive and compelling: the sounds of a quiet stable—"shod hoofs scraping on the flagstones. Soft spluddery thumps of dung. Deep-chested gentlemanly snorts." Isaac Campion, the character, is memorable; the novel is unforgettable.

> *A review of "Isaac Campion," in* Kirkus Reviews, *Vol. LV, No. 8, April 15, 1987, p. 639.*

For a reader of about eleven, girl or boy, to read this short, remarkable book is to be involved in several unforgettable rites of passage from childhood to adolescence, in understanding, reflection and, most significantly, reading.

First, the story . . . is passionate and painful. . . . Next, the author makes demands on the reader: to understand the voice of the narrator, including the dialectal forms that come from speech, and to see the movement of time in discourse—present events related to memory, past events retold as history, family history. This is possible because the writer helps the reader along, by direct address, lending eye and tongue to tune the dialogue and setting the events in the pattern of daily social habit. The whole text is a masterpiece of economy and directness. Only a full study of the verb tenses can make plain all the writer's skill.

The intense localness of the action, the skilful balance of violence and pity (the horses are both characters and symbols), the change in the characters, the feeling that the time has come to end the feudal exploitation of skill, the prevalence of old superstition, all these are subtly woven together. Within the course of the narrative we find harshness, of weather and social life, the abuse of children, the facts of sex and death, alongside a poetic recreation of wooden spoons stirring in pots and barrels rolling into a cellar. 'They used to make a lovely soft thuddery sound, those wooden casks, when they were rolled across cobbles.'

There are only eighty-four pages of short, highly particularised paragraphs, with never a word wasted, nor a sequence of dialogue out of place. This is the dramatic presentation of the modern novel for the young, fronting the scene as part of the action, fast-moving as TV makes inevitable, yet with the depth of understanding and feeling that only reading makes possible. It is another triumph for Janni Howker, and a chance for readers to get to grips with this as a reading experience before the visuals in the text, created in the inner eye of imagination, give way to the pictorial immediacy of the screen.

Margaret Meek, in a review of "Isaac Campion," in The School Librarian, *Vol. 35, No. 2, May, 1987, p. 153.*

Although *Isaac Campion* is categorized by the publisher as a novel for the over-10's, there is no impediment to this harsh little tale catching the eye of the over-20's. But this is always the hallmark of the best juvenile fiction. In the novella sandwiched between two letters to the author from an old man coming to the end of his days in an infirmary, there is the hint of a suggestion that this story is an imaginative realization of one of those taped social-history interviews. As the narrative begins to grip, and Janni Howker's now-celebrated gifts . . . begin to show themselves, whether her book grew out of somebody's talk, or out of her own head, becomes irrelevant.

Isaac Campion is a hard-hitting account of the time when, as the old man says in his epilogue, a child was just a "nuisance and a mouth to feed until you could do a day's work." The setting is urban Lancashire at the turn of the century, rough and pragmatic. Two families grind fatally against each other like the Montagues and Capulets. The narrator's family is in the horse trade, while its implacable rivals, the Laceys, are horse dealers beginning to push forward into the new automotive transport, electric trams and the like. But the rage between them has little to do with business rivalry, and everything to do with a kind of life-feeding hate.

What follows is the aftermath of a hideous accident when the 16-year-old Dan Campion fails to clear the spiked-rail fence the Lacey boy has challenged him to jump. . . .

There are two sensational occurrences in the book, the accident and the mating of the heavy horses by the stallioner, and Janni Howker proves what an exceptional writer she is by the economy of her descriptions of them. The effect is rather like glimpsing what one is not supposed to see, and then never being able to forget it. Quite an art to get this type of shock on the page. And then there is a sensation, this one offstage, so to speak, when a cargo of horses is lost in the wild Irish Sea, spelling financial disaster to Isaac's father and emotional havoc for himself.

Again, it is briefly told and barely dwelt on. . . . He thinks of them eventually washing to and fro in the shallows with their beautiful manes and tails floating like seaweed, and, of course, they are an image of his own overworked existence and his ending up in the geriatric ward. "I hope I come back as a bird next time, a swift or a swallow. . . . They have a damn good time. . . ." These are the hard-drinking Liverpool-Irish on the edge of migrating to America, people fighting for a footing in the world. If there is a lesson, it is that the old family ethos that is now looked back on with such approval and wistfulness contained a lot of now forgotten darkness and violence.

Ronald Blythe, "'A Mouth to Feed'," in The New York Times Book Review, *May 17, 1987, p. 45.*

Howker's ability to introduce the very taste and smell of a place as well as to write superlative dialogue and to show sensitivity to the needs and secret longings of old and young alike make her one of the most exciting young writers working today. In *Isaac Campion,* she offers the voice of a 95-year-old man, sharp-witted and somehow not quite bitter, and brings the tragedy and simple fortitude of his life into focus. Unlike her earlier two books, however, . . . this is such a mature, reflective story that it gives little natural entrance for young readers. Too good for those who read these reviews to miss and too mature for most of the children we serve, it probably belongs in the adult market but mustn't be lost for the sheer delight and perfection of the writing.

Sara Miller, in a review of "Isaac Campion," in School Library Journal, *Vol. 33, No. 10, June-July, 1987, p. 107.*

Taut, sharply honed, this forthright, brief novel carves an ineradicable niche in the reader's memory. Already acclaimed for her first two books, Janni Howker has, in this exploration of family relationships, surpassed her earlier achievements. . . . The structural device [a first-person narrative set between two letters to the author] is skillful for conveying a sense of immediacy in evoking the quality of life in the days before concern for child labor and compulsory education prolonged adolescence—before childhood, as we know it, was possible in a working-class family. . . . Perhaps in no other book for children have the reality of poverty and its effects on family relationships been so movingly portrayed, but the book is not a diatribe pro or con economic theories. Rather, it is a gut-wrenching view of a particular time, uncompromising yet not without humor. All this is accomplished in eighty-six pages—as simple and enduring as the inscription with which it ends—"ISAAC CAMPION 1888-1984." (pp. 469-70)

Mary M. Burns, in a review of "Isaac Campion," in The Horn Book Magazine, *Vol. LXIII, No. 4, July-August, 1987, pp. 469-70.*

Madeleine L'Engle (Camp Franklin)

1918-

American author of fiction and nonfiction, playwright, poet, and reteller.

L'Engle is considered one of the foremost American creators of juvenile fantasy and science fiction as well as a perceptive author of realistic family stories. Noted as an especially original writer for children and young adults, she weaves significant thematic concerns into her tales of home life, international intrigue, and imaginary journeys through time and space. Her intellectually and morally challenging books feature intricately structured plots as well as characters who grow in self-awareness and compassion through their experiences. Underlying her lively narratives are themes which reflect L'Engle's pervasive Christian faith and emphasize the force of a united, caring family. Best known for *A Wrinkle in Time* (1962), a fantasy hailed as the first work of science fiction for children to be regarded as genuine literature, and for a series of naturalistic, autobiographical stories about the Austin family, L'Engle has won a devoted following among thoughtful young readers.

A Wrinkle in Time combines such technical concepts as the tesseract, Einstein's theory of relativity, and Planck's quantum theory with philosophy, religious thought, literary quotations, and satire as L'Engle describes the Murry children's intergalactic rescue of their father. Recognized as one of the first science fiction novels to spotlight a female protagonist, it is also credited with introducing metaphysics to children's literature. The sequels that follow—*A Wind in the Door* (1973), in which teenager Meg saves younger brother Charles Wallace from life-threatening mitochondria, and *A Swiftly Tilting Planet* (1978), in which the deeds of Meg and time-traveler Charles Wallace keep the world from nuclear destruction—further reveal the physical and emotional development of the main characters while exploring cellular biology and astrophysics. In *A Wrinkle in Time*, L'Engle writes of the ultimate power of selfless love over evil; the other novels in the trilogy illustrate variations on this theme.

Meet the Austins (1960), which describes how twelve-year-old Vicky and her loving, close-knit household transform a spoiled orphan, is acknowledged as a milestone in children's literature for being one of the first family books to deal with death. Subsequent Austin novels—*The Moon by Night* (1963), *The Young Unicorns* (1968), and *A Ring of Endless Light* (1980)—and such cosmopolitan adventures as *Dragons in the Water* (1976) and *A House like a Lotus* (1984) continue to mix compelling storylines with value-clarifying issues like the nature of faith, the complexities of human relationships, and death as an affirmation of life. In addition to her novels, which reflect a variety of time periods and geographical settings and are filled with references to science, history, literature, art, and music, L'Engle has written poetry, drama, allegory, a collection of prayers, and retellings of Scripture. All of her books are written in L'Engle's spellbinding style, which is distinguished by its elegance and control.

Critics praise L'Engle as a spirited storyteller whose works reveal her skillful craftsmanship and personal integrity. Al-

© Jerry Bauer

though some reviewers note instances of overwriting, idealized characterizations, and overly complicated structure, the majority agree that L'Engle's absorbing stories and provocative themes have great appeal to young readers and stimulate them to confront life with courage and hope.

L'Engle has won numerous awards for both individual books and her works as a whole. *A Wrinkle in Time* won the Newbery Medal in 1963, the Lewis Carroll Shelf Award in 1965, and was a runner-up for the Hans Christian Andersen Award in 1964. *A Swiftly Tilting Planet* won the American Book Award in 1980; *A Ring of Endless Light* was designated a Newbery Honor Book in 1981. L'Engle received the University of Southern Mississippi Medallion in 1978 and the Regina Medal in 1984.

(See also *CLR*, Vol. 1; *Contemporary Literary Criticism*, Vol. 12; *Something about the Author*, Vols. 1, 27; *Contemporary Authors New Revision Series*, Vol. 3; *Contemporary Authors*, Vols. 1-4, rev. ed.; *Dictionary of Literary Biography*, Vol. 52: *American Writers for Children since 1960: Fiction;* and *Authors in the News*, Vol. 2.)

AUTHOR'S COMMENTARY

Long ago when I was just learning to read, and the world was (as usual) tottering on the brink of war, I discovered that if I wanted to look for the truth of what was happening around me, and if I wanted to know what made the people tick who made the events I couldn't control, the place to look for that truth was in story. Facts simply told me what things were. Story told me what they were about, and sometimes even what they meant. It never occurred to me then, when I was little, nor does it now, that story is more appropriate for children than for adults. It is still, for me, the vehicle of truth.

As for writing stories for children, whether it's fantasy or "slice-of-life" stories, most people are adults by the time they get published. And most of us adults who are professional writers are writing for ourselves, out of our own needs, our own search for truth. If we aren't, we're writing down to children, and that is serving neither children, nor truth.

I'm sometimes asked, by both children and their elders, why I've written approximately half of my books for children, and I reply honestly that I've never written a book for children in my life, nor would I ever insult a child by doing so. The world is even more confused now than it was when I first discovered story as medium for meaning, and story is still, for me, the best way to make sense out of what is happening, to see "cosmos in chaos" (as Leonard Bernstein said). It is still the best way to keep hope alive, rather than giving in to suicidal pessimism.

Books of fantasy and science fiction, in particular, are books in which the writer can express a vision, in most cases a vision of hope. A writer of fantasy usually looks at the seeming meaninglessness in what is happening on this planet, and says, "No, I won't accept that. There has got to be some meaning, some shape and pattern in all of this," and then looks to story for the discovery of that shape and pattern.

In my own fantasies I am very excited by some of the new sciences; in a *A Wrinkle in Time* it is Einstein's theories of relativity, and Planck's Quantum theory; tesseract is a real word, and the theory of tessering is not as far fetched as at first it might seem. If anyone had asked my grandfather if we'd ever break the sound barrier, he'd have said, "Of course not." People are now saying "Of course not" about the light barrier, but, just as we've broken the sound barrier, so, one day, we'll break the light barrier, and then we'll be freed from the restrictions of time. We will be able to tesser.

In *A Wind in the Door,* I turn from the macrocosm to the microcosm, the world of the cellular biologist, Yes, indeed, there are mitochondria, and they live within us; they have their own DNA, and we are their host planet. And they are as much smaller than we are as galaxies are larger than we are. How can we—child or adult—understand this except in story?

Concepts which are too difficult for adults are open to children, who are not yet afraid of new ideas, who don't mind having the boat rocked, or new doors opened, or mixing metaphors! That is one very solid reason my science fiction/fantasy books are marketed for children; only children are open enough to understand them. Let's never underestimate the capacity of the child for a wide and glorious imagination, an ability to accept what is going on in our troubled world, and the courage to endure it with courage, and respond to it with a realistic hope. (pp. 294-95)

> *Madeleine L'Engle, "Through the Eyes of An Author: The Search for Truth,"* in Through the Eyes of a Child: An Introduction to Children's Literature *by Donna E. Norton, second edition, Merrill Publishing Company, 1987, pp. 294-95.*

GENERAL COMMENTARY

MAY HILL ARBUTHNOT

Mrs. L'Engle's first notable book, **Meet the Austins,** is a fine realistic family story. The opening of *A Wrinkle in Time* suggests that it will be a similar kind of story. A storm is raging outside, but within the cozy kitchen Meg Murry and her brother, precocious five-year-old Charles Wallace Murry, are having hot cocoa with their mother. Into this family group comes a strange old woman, Mrs. Whatsit. She explains that she was "caught in a down draft and blown off course." But having finished her cocoa, she departs with one final word to the mother, ". . . there *is* such a thing as a tesseract." That is what the children's scientist father had been working on for the government when he disappeared. The next day, Meg, Charles Wallace, and Calvin O'Keefe, a friend, meet Mrs. Whatsit and two other strange old women, who warn the children that their father is in grave danger and that only they can save him and only if they are willing to tesseract. This involves the "fact" that the shortest distance between two points is not a straight line, but a fold or wrinkle. The children agree to try it. It proves to be a solitary, painful experience of blackness and terrifying force. . . . There follows in the complex course of the rest of the book a battle between good and evil, love and hate, that in spite of being complicated with science, philosophy, religion, satire, and allegory, carries the story on at a horrifying pace. (pp. 346-47)

This space allegory is neither as clear nor as beautiful as the Narnia series, but it is written in terms of the modern world in which children know about brainwashing and the insidious, creeping corruption of evil. The last third of the book is confused, but the fact that children and young people read it avidly suggests that they get more of its underlying significance than might be expected. It is a tribute to their growing maturity and to Madeleine L'Engle's writing, which is spellbinding. (p. 347)

[Isn't **Meet the Austins**] the first book in children's literature since *Little Women* in which the death of a loved one is handled so well?

The story begins in a modern kitchen where mother is preparing a gala dinner for a visiting relative. The small children are underfoot with dog and toys, the twelve-year-old daughter is doing her homework, and the record player is midway through Brahms' Second Piano Concerto when the telephone rings. It announces the death in an airplane crash of a beloved uncle, a distinguished test pilot, and his copilot. The scene that follows is handled with graphic details. The next night, realizing that the two oldest children are not sleeping, the mother gets them up and dressed and they drive up the mountain to talk. The children demand bitterly why God had to take a good man like Uncle Hal, and the mother replies, "Sometimes it's very hard to see the hand of God instead of the blind finger of Chance. That's why I wanted to come out where we could see the stars." They talk it out quietly in between long healing silences, and then they go home. Life goes on, but changed, with the spoiled orphaned child of the copilot in their home. The children's ups and downs, a serious brother-sister conflict, some funny and some grave situations—all develop against a background of family love. This is a fine family story, as unusual and provocative throughout as is its first chapter. (p. 445)

> *May Hill Arbuthnot, "New Magic" and "Here and Now,"* in her Children and Books, *third edition, Scott, Foresman and Company, 1964, pp. 326-75, 426-75.*

RUTH HILL VIGUERS

[*A Wrinkle in Time* is a] book that combines devices of fairy tales, overtones of fantasy, the philosophy of great lives, the visions of science, and the warmth of a good family story.... It is an exuberant book, original, vital, exciting. Funny ideas, fearful images, amazing characters, and beautiful concepts sweep through it. And it is full of truth. (p. 481)

[*The Arm of the Starfish*] is a story of spies and international intrigue, of family devotion, and the development of a boy's sense of values. Woven through it is the fascinating thread of prophetic advances in the biological sciences. Each of Madeleine L'Engle's books has been a testimony to her originality, breadth of knowledge, and her great resources of imagination and spirit. (p. 492)

In telling the story of a family's adjustment to a spoiled young orphan cousin who has come to live with them—and hers to the family—Madeleine L'Engle in *Meet the Austins* ... showed even deeper knowledge of young people than she did in *And Both Were Young*, one of the most perceptive books of its period. The Austin family is normal in its noise and minor quarrels, small disasters and confusion, but far from ordinary in its enjoyment of books and music, and its emphasis on fundamental values. Full of warmth and love and idealism, the book is also completely real. *The Moon by Night* ... in which the Austins take a camping trip from New England to the Southwest, North, and back across Canada is thought-provoking and exciting. The book is contemporary in feeling, incident, and characterizations, and the journey full of convincing adventures and unusually interesting encounters with people. (pp. 593-94)

> Ruth Hill Viguers, "Golden Years and Time of Tumult, 1920-1967: Worlds without Boundaries and Experiences to Share, in A Critical History of Children's Literature by Cornelia Meigs and others, edited by Cornelia Meigs, revised edition, Macmillan Publishing Company, 1969, pp. 446-83, 567-600.

JOHN ROWE TOWNSEND

Miss L'Engle's main themes are the clash of good and evil, the difficulty and necessity of deciding which is which and of committing oneself, the search for fulfilment and self-knowledge. These themes are determined by what the author *is;* and she is a practising and active Christian. Many writers' religious beliefs appear immaterial to their work; Miss L'Engle's are crucial. She is a thoughtful, highly intelligent, questioning Christian, and this means that, to her, the Christian faith is no simple affair but a mystery beyond human understanding. She well knows that she does not have, any more than Milton or any orthodox Christian writer ever since, the answers to the great and perennial problems. If God is good and all-powerful, why does evil exist? If God has foreknowledge, how can man have free will? Why does God not manifest himself? Where 'is' he, where 'are' heaven and hell? Miss L'Engle, I believe, sees clearly enough that the only possible answer to all these questions is, 'We do not know; we are not equipped to know.' As Uncle Douglas tells Vicky Austin in *The Moon By Night:*

> If there is a God, he's infinite and we're finite, and therefore we can't ever understand him. The minute anybody starts telling you what God thinks, or exactly why he does such and such, beware ... When I wasn't much older than you I decided that God, a kind and loving God, could never be proved. In fact there are, as

you've been seeing lately, a lot of arguments against him. But there isn't any point to life without him. Without him we're just a skin disease on the face of the earth, and I feel too strongly about the human spirit to be able to settle for that. So what I did for a long time was to live life *as though* I believed in God. And eventually I found that *as though* had turned into reality.

But Miss L'Engle has her certainties. The chief one, and clearly to her the chief commandment, is that we are to love one another. And a key centre of goodness on earth is, or is symbolized in, the life of a loving family.

> I think the closest we ever come in this naughty world to realizing unity in diversity is round a family table. I felt it at their (the Austins') table, the wholeness of the family unit, freely able to expand to include friends ... and yet each person in that unit complete, individual, unique, valued.

That is Canon Tallis in *The Young Unicorns*. Clearly both he and Uncle Douglas are expressing views with which the author is sympathetic.

So the Austin family, who are leading participants in three novels and have spiritual cousins in two more (the Murrys in *A Wrinkle in Time* and the O'Keefes in *The Arm of the Starfish*), are not merely characters; they are representatives of the kind of good to which in this imperfect world we can aspire. And perhaps they are a little too good to be true.

Two books, *Meet the Austins* ... and *The Moon By Night* ... are about the family life of the Austins, and are told in the first person by daughter Vicky, a young teenager. *Meet the Austins* is episodic, has no single story-line, and shows more than anything else the family reactions to a series of situations. *The Moon By Night* is the story of a coast-to-coast camping trip which is also a voyage of self-discovery for Vicky. The family is solid, warm and loving. Dr. Austin—it is significant, I am sure, that he is a healer—is an almost Godlike figure: kind but sometimes stern, authoritative, always knowing what needs to be done and able to do it. Mother is talented yet willing to give all to the family; and is as nearly perfect a mother as Dr. Austin is a father. John is the ideal elder brother: handsome, protective, resourceful, and improbably patient and understanding with the younger ones. Rob, the smallest, is bright and sweet and well-behaved; it is interesting that he is again and again referred to as a little boy and is always seen from a higher eye-level than his own. The girls are more human: Vicky has stirrings of adolescent restlessness, and younger sister Suzy even has plain ordinary faults. But then there are Uncle Douglas, and Aunt Elena, and Grandfather, who is a retired minister; and all three again seem to me to be a little too good. Not only that; I sense a certain smugness in the Austins. They *know* how nice and how cultured they are, and they appreciate themselves.... Artistic talent is present or latent in several members of the family, and the Austins attract talented friends. Singing is traditional with them, and when, in *The Young Unicorns,* Canon Tallis comes to dinner, they sing the Tallis canon in his honour, as a round, for grace. Why not? It would be a natural and charming gesture in such a family: and yet I must confess to a slight acidity in my reaction: Yes, they *would.*

Life in the Austin family is not entirely relaxed. Vicky, in both *Meet the Austins* and *The Moon By Night* seems to suffer undue guilt for very minor failings. Dr. Austin sometimes lectures her without apology:

> 'Vicky, I can just see you thinking, ''Mother and Daddy are sermonising again.'' Well, we're going to go on preaching, and,' Daddy's voice grew more serious, 'I expect you to listen.'

And both Dr. Austin and squarish elder brother John are distinctly stuffy when advances are made to Vicky by a cynical—but really quite harmless—boy called Zachary in *The Moon By Night.* Maybe it is just the result of a sense of inferiority in one who perceives himself to be neither as nice nor as cultured as the Austins, but I am afraid I cannot like them as much as the author does.

Madeleine L'Engle's novels do not confine themselves to family life, however. Her other aspect, as a writer for children and young people, is a remarkably different one. She is the author of—so far—three rapid-action adventure stories: *A Wrinkle in Time* . . . , *The Arm of the Starfish* . . . , and *The Young Unicorns*. . . . All three are to some extent science-based, and, indeed, *A Wrinkle in Time* is usually described as science-fiction. Miss L'Engle will clearly have no truck with any notion that science is either unfeminine or inimical to religion. In *A Wrinkle in Time,* the heroine's father is a scientist who has been experimenting with a means of short-circuiting time (necessary if vast distances in space are to be covered). In *The Arm of the Starfish,* experiments of a marine biologist which could have profound implications for people are the mainspring of the plot, while a means of control for the laser-beam plays an important part in *The Young Unicorns.*

The contrast between the family stories and the others is by no means complete, however. In the three action-novels, the L'Engle of the Austin books is still there. In fact, in *The Young Unicorns,* the Austins themselves are there, having moved from their quiet New England town to New York City. In these three books family relationships are found as a core of warmth and reassurance in baffling and dangerous situations. And the preoccupation with good and evil runs strongly through them all.

In *A Wrinkle in Time,* the clash of good and evil is at cosmic level. Much of the action is concerned with the rescue by the heroine Meg and her friend Calvin O'Keefe of Meg's father and brother, prisoners of a great brain called IT which controls the lives of a zombie population on a planet called Camazotz. Here evil is obviously the reduction of people to a mindless mass, while good is individuality, art and love. It is the sheer power of love which enables Meg to triumph over IT, for love is the force that she has and that IT has not. In *The Arm of the Starfish*—a swift, cloak-and-dagger, jet-age novel with an atmosphere somewhat reminiscent of Graham Greene's *The Third Man*—the hero's problem is to tell good and evil apart. Evil can have an attractive face; can cast doubt on good. The hero, Adam, is dazzled by sophisticated and 'spectacularly beautiful' Carolyn Cutter, who turns out to be on the wrong side; and he is warned by her against Canon Tallis, who in fact is good. Here it seems that the bad side aims to make corrupt use of scientific discovery, and the real triumph of good is not so much the defeat of villainy as the decision of the scientist Dr. O'Keefe to use the results of his research to benefit bad girl Carolyn. For, as Adam says, 'if you're going

to care about the fall of the sparrow you can't pick and choose who's going to be the sparrow'.

In *The Young Unicorns,* Miss L'Engle's Upper West Side story, the author seems to me to extend still farther her sense of evil as a positive thing and, perhaps, in some ways the mirror-image of good. Here much of the action takes place in a great cathedral and it turns out that the apparent Bishop—whose name, significantly, is Fall—had become a figure of evil, in league with delinquent gangs and with a villainous scientist prepared to misuse the laser device. Victory goes to the innocent: to the Austins and their friends, especially a young girl blinded in a sinister accident with the laser. The innocent, it seems, are protected by their innocence; the blind girl's blindness enables her, at the climax of the story, to save herself and others by finding a way through a warren of underground passages.

Miss L'Engle, it will be seen, has the nerve to present moral issues in black and white rather than in a steady, understanding grey. Audacity is something she never lacks. In *A Wrinkle in Time* she does not hesitate to enlist the greatest names on 'our' side in the battle against the powers of darkness:

> 'Who have our fighters been?' Calvin asked . . .
>
> 'Jesus!' Charles Wallace said. 'Why, of course, Jesus!'
>
> 'Of course!' Mrs. Whatsit said. 'Go on, Charles, love. There were others. All your great artists. They've been lights for us to see by.'
>
> 'Leonardo da Vinci?' Calvin suggested tentatively. 'And Michelangelo?'
>
> 'And Shakespeare,' Charles Wallace called out, 'and Bach! And Pasteur and Madame Curie and Einstein!'
>
> Now Calvin's voice rang with confidence. 'And Schweitzer and Gandhi and Buddha and Beethoven and Rembrandt and St. Francis!'

Most writers would, I think, be embarrassed by the thought of calling so magnificent a roll of honour in their pages, but Miss L'Engle has the wholehearted conviction that enables her to do this and get away with it. There is daring of another kind in the splendid yet shocking scene in *The Young Unicorns* when the robed Bishop is seen, resplendent on his throne and surrounded by young hoodlums, holding court in an abandoned underground railway station.

These three novels have their faults. In all of them the action is at times confusing. In *A Wrinkle in Time,* one sometimes has a sense of the derivative or second-rate, as for instance in the descriptions of the zombie planet. The outsize brain, pulsing away on a dais and controlling everything, could provoke a giggle rather than a shudder. In *The Arm of the Starfish,* the scenes between the hero and the siren Carolyn are quite unconvincing; surely no American student could be so mawkish. In *The Young Unicorns,* the sweetness of the relationships among the Austins and their friends gives a feeling that somewhere inside an apparently tough book is a soft centre. On the other hand, Miss L'Engle knows how to tell a story and can keep the reader turning the pages. She may confuse or embarrass or irritate him, but she is unlikely to bore him. (pp. 120-25)

John Rowe Townsend, ''Madeleine L'Engle,'' in his
A Sense of Story: Essays on Contemporary Writers

for Children, *J. B. Lippincott Company, 1971, pp. 120-29.*

SAM LEATON SEBESTA AND WILLIAM J. IVERSON

[With *A Wrinkle in Time*], science fiction for children attained a new seriousness. The book is one long crescendo. It begins realistically with the Murry family—Mrs. Murry, daughter Meg, younger son Charles Wallace, and the twins—comforting each other during an especially bad storm. A tramp arrives—or, rather, a creature from outer space—named Mrs. Whatsit. There is such a thing as a tesseract, she tells them. And soon Meg, Charles Wallace, and their friend Calvin have tesseracted and are sweeping away to other planets without any passage of time. Their immediate problem is how to rescue Mr. Murry, but even more is at stake: a gigantic evil force, named simply IT, must be overcome before it conquers the universe. This is great drama so long as the settings are clear, especially in the terrifying scenes of forced conformity. Eventually, however, abstractions supplant the action. The evil force can be defeated only by strongly willed love. Some of the dramatic force is lost, although many readers will testify that the sometimes confusing events in the latter chapters of the book are exactly right. L'Engle revisited the Murry family in *A Wind in the Door,* a story with an even more mystical conclusion.

L'Engle's *The Arm of the Starfish* tells of a marine biology student's involvement with the secrets of the regenerative process by which starfish grow new arms, a process which might be adapted to man. Someone is bent upon stealing the secret for evil purposes—but who? Is it Carolyn Cutter, who appears to be the heroine? Is it Canon Tallis, who appears to be the spiritual anchor for the story? The choice is more than an adventure story guessing game. It has to do with the theme: that good and evil aren't always easy to distinguish. The gang called the Alphabets in *The Young Unicorns* is recognizably evil. Their headquarters is under Columbia University and their activities include the use of a laser beam to dispose of their enemies. In both of these stories L'Engle has woven her theme into the fabric of plot and character; no departure from the action is needed in order to explain the significance. (p. 234)

Sam Leaton Sebesta and William J. Iverson, "Fanciful Fiction: Color Portfolio of Picture Books, Folk Literature, and Fanciful Fiction," in their Literature for Thursday's Child, *Science Research Associates, Inc., 1975, pp. 215-42.*

BARBARA PERRY

Are children's authors real people? Books by Madeleine L'Engle let the reader know that at least one is. Her books share her experiences and her philosophy of life.

Madeleine L'Engle in her autobiography, *A Circle of Quiet* . . . , tells us she grew up in New York and in Europe. Her father was a playwright and critic, and her mother was a musician. From them she received a desire and love for sharing the joys of music and writing.

L'Engle began writing while still in elementary school. It was her special talent and comfort while in European boarding schools. (p. 812)

The main characters in *And Both Were Young* . . . and *Prelude* . . . are gangling, awkward adolescents in boarding schools. They both love art, music, writing, and being alone like L'Engle. They even have a limp as she does. Meg, in *A Wrinkle in Time* . . . and *A Wind in the Door* . . . is a young Madeleine;

both have settings at Crosswicks [L'Engle's summer home in Goshen, Connecticut].

The Young Unicorns . . . is set in New York at the cathedral where the author works parttime. Canon Tallis in her stories is real. *The Twenty-four Days before Christmas* . . . is true in the special events which happen before Christmas. *The Other Side of the Sun* . . . , an adult novel, is set in Charleston, South Carolina, the birthplace of her mother. The list of likenesses is almost endless!

By looking at the list of her books, the author's wide interests are evident. She has written for every age, including fiction and non-fiction. (p. 813)

Certain themes do appear in L'Engle's work, whether it is poetry, science fiction, fantasy, or an autobiography.

One important theme found in all of her books, especially in *The Arm of the Starfish* . . . and *The Young Unicorns* . . . , is summarized in the following quote from an article by L'Engle, "The One-winged Chinese Bird":

> We are all part of humankind, and we can do nothing, absolutely nothing, in isolation. This theme is implicit in children's books . . .

Both of these books are science fiction and are very similar in plot structure. Both have surprise endings and plenty of action.

The Arm of the Starfish . . . is set on an island off Portugal. The science idea on which it is based deals with the regeneration properties of the starfish and the application of these properties to humans. There are two groups in conflict. The O'Keefes want to use their findings for legitimate scientific purposes; the other side wants to use the research for power and to make money. The password in this novel is a quote from Robert Frost which emphasizes our human responsibilities—"Only where love and need are one / is the deed ever really done / for Heaven and the future's sakes."

Likewise, *The Young Unicorns* . . . deals with a scientific conflict; here the laser is involved. The setting is in Manhattan, but it involves many of the same characters. Dave, a young reformed gang leader, is reminded of his role in humanity by the Rabbi.

> If no demand is put on you, then you are in a sense excluded.
>
> From what?
>
> Life itself. To be demanded of gives us dignity. . . .

L'Engle's two other similar, so-called science fiction works deal with this same theme but explore the more dominant idea of a "rampant evil threatening our universe." In her Newbery acceptance speech . . . she says, "Something in the universe is trying to make muffins of us" [see Author's Commentary for *A Wrinkle in Time*]. She is saying that Evil tries to make us alike. In *A Wrinkle in Time* . . . and in *A Wind in the Door* . . . Evil is pictured as a Dark Thing, the Shadow, the It, un-Naming.

The Evil is conquered for a time in both books, once in outerspace or macrocosm and once in inner space or microcosm. In both books Love is the conquering force. This idea is clearly stated. In *A Wrinkle in Time* Meg says

> Love!

That was what she had that It did not have.

How could she use It? What was she meant to do?

If she could give love to it perhaps it would shrivel up and die. . . .

A whirl of darkness. An icy cold blast. An angry resentful howl that seemed to tear through her . . .

Proginoskes, the cherubim in *A Wind in the Door,* tells Meg

Love. That's what makes persons know who they are. . . . I have to give myself away. . . . Love isn't how you feel. It's what you do. . . .

By comparing just these two short passages, the reader can recognize which of these two books, written eleven years apart, is better. *A Wrinkle in Time* is more coherent. The theme is more implicit; it teaches, not preaches. The action is more believable and dynamic. *A Wind in the Door* as an almost sequel fails to capture the reader the way *A Wrinkle in Time* does.

L'Engle considers both books to be fantasy. (pp. 813, 815)

Another idea found in most of Madeleine L'Engle's books deals with the metaphysical or ontological, as she calls it in her autobiography. This is the struggle between belief and disbelief in God. This theme goes beyond the conflict of good versus evil. L'Engle's personal soul searching is discussed in *A Circle of Quiet*. . . . It is also seen in the writing in her novels. It is Biblically stated in her Newbery winner

We look not at the things which are what you call seen, but at the things which are not seen. For the things which are seen are temporal. But the things which are not seen are eternal.

In her preface to *Lines Scribbled on an Envelope* . . . L'Engle admits she is Christian. Her poems are deeply personal; many speak of her faith.

Dance in the Desert . . . also has a religious theme and setting. It is the story of a young child and the crossing of the desert to Egypt by his family. Animals come and dance with the young child as they camp at night. The story builds to a climax; there is a two-page spread with the animals dancing around the child. The animals "swoop," "thud," and "the snake moves around the child's leg in sinuous swirls of affection, its undulating movements shimmering along the delicate length of its body." The imagery of this book is powerfully moving. Illustrated by Symeon Shimin, this is L'Engle's most aesthetically pleasing book. (p. 815)

In all of her writing the author uses quotes from famous literary sources. . . . Foreign phrases and unusual vocabulary add to the feeling of her writings. . . . By being selective, the language in her writing comes to life. It figuratively sets the tone for her story. This is especially true for her first pages which she says are the hardest to write. Since most of her books are not illustrated, her ability to set the tone using descriptive language is even more important. This ability can be seen in the following opening lines from *The Young Unicorns:*

Winter came early to the city that year. Josiah Davidson, emerging from the subway, his arms loaded with school books, shivered against the dank November rain which blew icily against his face and sent a tickle down the back of his

neck. He did not see three boys in black jackets who moved out of a sheltering doorway and stalked him. . . .

The titles of her books are also significant. "A Circle of Quiet" is a creek with a natural bridge at Crosswicks where the author goes to read and be alone. "The Other Side of the Sun" symbolizes death. "Prelude" fits Katherine, the main character, who is a pianist. (pp. 815-16)

[L'Engle's] ideas come from her experiences, her reading, and other people.

Knowing the background of this author, her intelligence, beliefs, and warmth, makes her books take on new meaning. L'Engle comes through as a real person! (p. 816)

> *Barbara Perry, "Madeleine L'Engle: A Real Person," in* Language Arts, *Vol. 54, No. 7, October, 1977, pp. 812-16.*

BOB DIXON

[The effect of Ursula K. LeGuin's *A Wizard of Earthsea, The Tombs of Atuan,* and *The Farthest Shore* is] to keep the social order as it is or even to go backwards.

Similarly, in L'Engle's *A Wrinkle in Time,* on one side there's a 'dark Thing' and on the other an elite, not wizards this time but certainly very special people, the Murry parents, who are presented as high-flying scientific intellectuals and their son Charles Wallace, a five-year-old with incredible mental powers, some of them mystic. There's no doubt as to which side God is on. Mr Murry says, 'we know that all things work together for good to them that love God, to them who are the called according to his purpose.' L'Engle has said that the book is 'against forced conformity of any kind' and also that she wrote it (while being a practising Christian) 'as a violent rebellion against Christian piety'. However, she admits to 'a feeling of religious spirit' in the book. Some of the best fighters in the cosmic struggle against the powers of darkness have come from earth, we read. Jesus heads the list and then come 'great artists' who have been, 'lights for us to see by'. On the 'light' side, of course, are the Murrys and the United States (Mr Murry is based at Cape Canaveral). Camazotz is one of the 'dark planets' and as it has, not surprisingly, been taken by many readers to represent a communist state, it's easy to see how religion is now being drawn into the world-wide political struggle.

A Wind in the Door is about the same family, the Murrys. Towards the beginning, in a rather odd reflection of Le Guin's main concern, we read that 'matter' is getting 'unbalanced'. In fact, Meg Murry, the young girl, says that things are 'falling apart'. Cosmic good and evil are curiously linked with conditions in the United States, in a way we're familiar with . . . from the comics. Mrs Murry says, incredibly, 'Here we are, at the height of civilisation in a well-run state in a great democracy.' She couples this, rather oddly, with 'And four ten-year-olds were picked up last week for pushing hard drugs in the school where our six-year-old is regularly given black eyes and a bloody nose.' It really does seem that they want to blame the dark, evil forces of the universe, here called the Echthroi. There doesn't seem to be much wrong at home as Mrs Murry keeps pointing out: 'In L.A. at last we have a president who is trying as honourably as a president can try in a world which has become so blunted by dishonour and violence that people casually take it for granted.' The Cherubim, a singular creature with a plural name, says to Meg, 'I have heard that your host planet is shadowed, that it is troubled' and says also that the Echthroi, which he describes as 'fallen angels', start all war. Then, we learn that they threaten 'the balance of the entire universe' and later that 'Charles Wallace is the point of equilibrium'. (I did say he was a special kind of child.) The note of bewilderment in Mrs Murry's comments isn't surprising. Nobody who looks at the world like that can hope to understand it. (pp. 151-52)

> *Bob Dixon, "The Supernatural: Religion, Magic and Mystification," in his* Catching Them Young 2: Political Ideas in Children's Fiction, *Pluto Press, 1977, pp. 120-64.*

CHARLOTTE S. HUCK

If there is a classic that emerges in the field of science fiction for children it may be Madeleine L'Engle's *A Wrinkle in Time*. . . . This story has many layers of meaning. It may be read for its exciting science-fiction plot alone, or it may be read for its themes of love conquering evil and the need to respect individual differences. It is a strange and wonderful combination of science fiction, modern fantasy, and religious symbolism. (pp. 292-93)

The theme of [*A Wind in the Door*] emphasizes the importance of every miniscule part of the universe in carrying out its purpose in living, to be all that it was meant to be. For the universe to thrive, the balance of life must be maintained. *A Wind in the Door* is a deeper, more complex book than *A Wrinkle in Time.* But L'Engle is capable of "kything" her message to perceptive children of 10 and up to whatever the reader's own age is . . .

The cast of characters [in *A Swiftly Tilting Planet*] is familiar yet grown older; faithful readers will be delighted to find Meg married to Calvin and expecting a baby. Once again L'Engle has given children a story that has action and suspense at the same time that it stretches their minds and spirit. (p. 293)

> *Charlotte S. Huck, "Modern Fantasy," in her* Children's Literature in the Elementary School, *third edition, Holt, Rinehart and Winston, 1976, pp. 246-303.*

SHEILA A. EGOFF

[Anne McCaffrey and Laurence Yep] are prototypical examples of the best science-fiction fantasy, combining, with reasonable success, qualities of both genres. Madeleine L'Engle's *A Wrinkle in Time* . . . is less definable, which is not in itself a fault. In this instance the confusion arises from writing that is eclectic rather than selective, innovative rather than original, and ultimately muddy in purpose and style. Although beginning with an Earth family environment, the action quickly moves into space, not by means of scientific technology but by "tesseracting" (kitty-cornering through space). Hailed as science fiction, it is similar in many ways to modern world-swapping fantasies based in Christian theology, such as C. S. Lewis's *Narnia Chronicles* or Ruth Nichols's *A Walk Out of the World*. L'Engle, too, attempts the conflict of good versus evil inherent in most major contemporary fantasies, but her pseudometaphysics and doctrinaire messages have neither the urgency of sociological science fiction nor the grandeur of the best fantasy. Without its space-opera costume, *A Wrinkle in Time* would simply be uninspired fantasy.

Both the plot and the characters of *A Wrinkle in Time* are strained. Meg and her five-year-old brother Charles Wallace can communicate mentally with one another and in a vague location in space they battle for the survival of civilization itself, fighting for genius, individualism, and human excellence in the face of an antihuman brain, which unfortunately rings too many bells with Dorothy's confrontation with the bogus great brain in *The Wizard of Oz*.

This kind of American pop history continues in the latent imperialism of L'Engle's subsequent book, *A Swiftly Tilting Planet*. . . . In this sequel to *A Wrinkle in Time,* Charles Wallace, now fifteen years old, travels, in his mind, on a unicorn through time and space, entering other people's minds and bodies in an effort to alter human destiny and free human will in a noncredible attempt to save world peace. Crammed with characters from different periods, the narrative is difficult to follow. One can only hold on to the thread that the president of a small South American state may or may not loose an atomic bomb upon the world because of the color of his eyes. They have to be blue!

Tampering with free will and history have been generally considered antithetical to the tradition of dramatic conflict. Unfortunately L'Engle ignores this canon. The ill effects thereof may be seen in a comparison with Alison Uttley's historical fantasy, *A Traveler in Time*. . . . In Uttley's book, Penelope Taberner goes back in time to the period of Mary, Queen of Scots, and finds herself caught up in the Babington plot to rescue the Queen. Penelope knows the end result and realizes the inevitability of historic destiny. The plot thus gains an extra dimension of tragedy as well as a greater understanding of the human condition. Both these elements are notably absent in L'Engle's works. Her constant vision of shortcuts through space seems to head her into a similar kind of casual disregard of the complexities of human life.

L'Engle also illustrates the propensity for overwriting so prevalent in much of science-fiction fantasy. Presumably in the attempt to create the imagery of first-rate fantasy, the writer's style often becomes overladen to the point of muddiness. Thus, in *A Wrinkle in Time* there are three good, witchlike characters reminiscent of Charles Kingsley's Mrs. Doasyouwouldbedoneby in *The Water Babies*. However, her writing makes these characters seem like parodies of Kingsley's clear-cut approach:

> "We cannot come to you now," Mrs. Who's voice blew to them like the wind. "*Allwissend bin ich nicht; doch viel ist mir bewisst.* [sic] Goethe. *I do not know everything; still many things I understand.* That is for you, Charles. Remember that you do not know everything." . . .
>
> "Tto alll tthreee off yyou I ggive mmy ccommandd," Mrs. Which said. "Ggo ddownn inntto tthee ttownn. Ggo ttogetherr."

L'Engle's strained writing and imagination falters even more when she moves outside of the domestic lives of her scientist family, as, for instance, when she has the mother making a meal on her Bunsen burner. In these deficiencies she is akin to that ubiquitous writer of science-fiction fantasy Andre Norton who, in such books as *Forerunner Foray* . . . and *No Night without Stars* . . . presents only vaguely described other planets. Both have either forgotten or are unfamiliar with Tolkien's dictum that:

> Anyone inheriting the fantastic device of human language can say *the green sun.* Many can then imagine or picture it. But that is not enough. . . . To make a Secondary World inside

which the green sun will be credible, commanding Secondary Belief, will probably require labour and thought, and will certainly demand a special skill.

Neither L'Engle nor Norton possess this "special skill."

L'Engle and Norton also are alike in their constant reliance on parapsychological ploys. The claims and counterclaims for the validity of extrasensory perception (ESP) are only of concern here as affecting literary skill in the commanding of belief. The two authors seek to convince by mere force of repetition, rather than by bolstering this imaginative concept with a base in reality. The works of both swarm with ill-defined characters and events. (pp. 147-49)

> *Sheila A. Egoff, "Science Fiction," in her* Thursday's Child: Trends and Patterns in Contemporary Children's Literature, *American Library Association, 1981, pp. 130-58.*

NANCY-LOU PATTERSON

Each of Madeleine L'Engle's three fantasies [*A Wrinkle in Time, A Wind in the Door,* and *A Swiftly Tilting Planet*] begins with the irruption into the ordinary world of a supernatural being. Meg and Charles Wallace Murry may not be ordinary children, but their world includes rain boots and hot cocoa, the paraphernalia of life as understood by many North American readers. In each fantasy the visitor has come to escort the children into an otherworld of conflict, where they achieve victory over evil. A being "who leads the way to the other world" is a psychopomp, a role generally played by an angel in Christian thought. Works like L'Engle's are part of what has been called "ethical fantasy," characterized by a battle between good and evil: "the Psychomachia, the *bellum intestinum,* the Holy War." Their major action occurs in a place beneath the level of consciousness, to which the ego must travel with the aid of a spiritual guide.

In *A Wrinkle in Time,* this escort is feminine and takes a triple form, "Mrs. Whatsit and her two friends".... (p. 195)

Besides these three weird sisters, there are two other feminine beings in *A Wrinkle in Time:* the unhappily named Happy Medium and the winsome Aunt Beast. The first enables Meg to see from afar what she needs to know, and the second heals her, body, mind, and spirit, after she rescues her father from the power of IT on the evil planet Camazotz. The children try to explain "our ladies" to Aunt Beast; the speaker is Meg's boyfriend:

> "Angels!" Calvin shouted suddenly from across the table, "Guardian angels!"...

At this, the ladies reappear and Meg faces her final challenge, to return to Camazotz and rescue Charles Wallace by the power of love.

Although the three sisters in this novel are finally identified as angels, the role of psychopomp is played in mythology by other entities which are also invoked. The centaur form of Mrs. Whatsit incorporates both the horse, the beast ridden to fetch the souls of the dead by the Valkyries, and the male human in his role as wise "master and teacher"—centaurs were the teachers of sacred wisdom in Greek myth. Further, the wind which brings the ladies is associated with the "generating pneuma, the breath of Life." This novel, and thus the whole trilogy, begins with the stereotyped storyteller's phrase, "It was a dark and stormy night." Mrs. Whatsit in her female form declares "Wild nights are my glory," in words which echo Emily Dickinson's poem:

> Wild nights! Wild nights!
> Were I with thee,
> Wild nights should be
> Our luxury!

The suggestion of sexuality in this phrase accords with the spiritually fecundating role of the wind, and the threefold female figures are derived from the triple goddesses who abound in mythology, whether as the three Fates, the three-faced Hecate, the triple fertility goddesses of the ancient Near East, the trifold Morrigan, or in a late incarnation as the three witches in *Macbeth.* The three ladies recently appear in Lloyd Alexander's *The Black Cauldron* ... as godmothers to the young hero Taran.

These figures are not goddesses for L'Engle, however, but angels, beings who come as messengers and supernatural aids, and their gender is thus appropriately fluid. Indeed, they are androgynous, even beyond gender, a conception even more daring, perhaps, than that of the masculine Oyarsa of MarsMalacandra and the feminine Oyarsa of VenusPerelandra in C. S. Lewis's space trilogy.

In L'Engle's second novel, the wind motif becomes explicit in the title, *A Wind in the Door* ... which refers to the visit of "a singular Cherubim".... (pp. 196-98)

[The Cherubim] is called by a plural title but is "a single creature," with a multitude of "merry eyes, wise eyes, ferocious eyes, kitten eyes, dragon eyes" ... and wings of ten-foot span, "covering and uncovering the eyes," surrounded by "spurts of flame." This apparition, exhibiting what has been called "the motif of polyophthalmia," appropriately takes the mandalic form in repose of "a misty, feathery sphere," and communicates directly with the minds of the children. At the novel's moment of ultimate crisis, a contest between the Echthroi or powers of negation, and Meg, the cherubim Proginoskes gives forth "a great cry" and flings himself as a sacrifice into the void.... All that remains is a single white feather: by his own choice he has given up his life to save his human charges.

The cherubim of Semitic myth are guardian figures. In *Genesis* they guard the gates of the Garden of Eden with a flaming sword, and in *I Kings 8:6-7,* they "opened out their wings over the place of the ark." But in *A Wind in the Door* the specific description used as a source for Proginoskes is *Revelation 4:8,* with its four living creatures, "each of them with six wings," and "full of eyes all round and within." The special trait of the cherubim is knowledge: the eyes, which are all-seeing because multiple, express their Assyrian origin as alert guardians of the throne, temple, or palace, but the One God who sees and knows all gives a sense of divine presence to this image. The name Proginoskes is from the Greek *Progignoskein,* to know. The novel turns upon the effort of Meg to save the life of Charles Wallace, afflicted by an illness in the microscopic portions of his body, and the same Greek word is the basis of "prognosis," the prediction of the course a disease will take. The feathers and scales of Proginoskes make him an animal rather than a human figure. He imparts the "enabling knowledge" of the future and of the course of an illness, which is given by an animal spirit to the Amerindian seeker on a vision quest.

In the third novel, *A Swiftly Tilting Planet,* a period of time has passed. Meg is married (to Calvin) and pregnant, and Charles Wallace is 15 years old, but they can still kythe: communicate without words. As always, it is Charles Wallace who first experiences the presence of the intermediary. He focuses upon a star, and sees a descending beam of light:

> Slowly the radiance took on form, until it had enfleshed itself into the body of a great white beast with flowing mane and tail. From its forehead sprang a silver horn which contained the residue of the light. . . .
>
> (pp. 198-99)

This being, obviously a unicorn, possesses wings, though they are not mentioned until fourteen pages later, where we read that "slowly great wings lifted and moved with the wind". . . . The unicorn gives his name: "You may call me Gaudior . . . that's Latin for *more joyful*". . . . (p. 199)

Gaudior too sacrifices himself, pouring light from the "blazing tip of his horn" . . . into the mind of a brain-damaged youth to ease his pain and fear; but later, brought out of the youth's mind again by the wind . . . , he rejoins Charles Wallace. (p. 200)

The story line of this many-layered novel is too complex to summarize, but the figure of the unicorn binds it together. Meg follows Charles Wallace's travels through the intricacies of the plot by kything, and there is a sense in which the unicorn is an image of their relationship. A unicorn, like an angel or a centaur, is a metamorph, a boundary-crosser. There are many examples of winged boundary-crossers in world mysticism: Garuda, the vulture god, is the mount of Vishnu; an ascetic in the *Rig Veda* cries that he has "mounted upon the wind." Mohammed rode upon the angelic mount, Buraq, a mule with wings and a woman's face, who represents "the contemplative mind."

The unicorn entered the Bible as a translation for *re'em,* a creature whose origins are variously derived from actual animals. The Near Eastern unicorn possessed wings. In Christianity this figure achieved what has been described as its "diverse, protean, symbolic, and mystic meaning." C. G. Jung devoted a major subchapter of his study of alchemy to "The Paradigm of the Unicorn." Because of its great variations of meaning, he found it to represent the union of opposites which was the alchemical goal. It combines "the theme of the single horn" in its meaning of "wild, rampant, masculine, penetrating force," with the image of its associated virgin as the "passive, feminine aspect," into a symbol of the *spiritus mercurius,* who is Christ. Again, the hollow horn of the unicorn as a cup represents the feminine aspect, while the piercing point represents the masculine. Something of this imagery appears when the newborn unicorn's horn pierces his encompassing eggshell in *A Swiftly Tilting Planet.* This androgynous quality is echoed in the concept of the Chinese unicorn, the *ch'i-lin,* of which the male is called *ch'i* and the female *lin.*

On the other hand, in specifically Christian thought, the Early Fathers of the Church saw the single horn as a symbol of the uniqueness of Christ, whose two natures, human and divine, existed in a manner which surpassed union and could only be expressed by undivided oneness. The unicorn Gaudior, then, is not only a psychopomp—as Hermes was called, the Shepherd of Souls—but the very image of Christ Himself, the Good Shepherd who can suffer, weaken, bleed, die, and be resurrected in His salvational relationship with humankind.

In the unicorn image, Love is presented not only as the intervention of a positive spiritual force, but as the action of a person. Each child goes to face the Adversary armoured and girded with the Love which is his or hers as a gift, freely given as Grace, and freely accepted by the action of his or her own will. The central theme of these books is that the battle of good and evil is won through love. The battlefield is the soul, the actual word used by Jung interchangeably with psyche. Passage to this place of inner conflict often appears in fantasy or myth as a portal, a threshold to be passed. But equally often, the passage takes place through the agency of an escort. In L'Engle's trilogy, these escorts, drawn from the deep sources of Western and Eastern mythology, are invested with rich and vivid life through her depictions of them. The epiphanies of these beings in her fantasies create a luminous delight: it is for these encounters that one rereads her works, watching their wonder unfold like rainbow wings.

In keeping with Christian thought, these figures of spiritual guidance are fully manifested and even multimorphic, while the evil spirits are insubstantial and empty—mere airs and noises—howls, smokes, chills, stinks, and shadows of negation. Because the spirit escorts are such intensely compelling realizations, endlessly delightful and unexpected, the evil beings sometimes approach monotony and predictability. One reads through their affairs with impatience to return to the presence of the good.

To put the matter fairly: does this presentation of the good characters as "altogether lovely" (*The Song of Solomon,* 5:16), and the evil characters as inevitably overcome by Love, make for an imbalance in the narrative structure? Does it weaken the suspense and hence the narrative thrust? Perhaps L'Engle's plots are so complexly constructed just in order to counter this possibility: victory is not in doubt, but the manner of its achievement may be. This is not to say that there is no narrative tension in her works. Far from it. Indeed, the outcome of the eucatastrophic structure (to use J. R. R. Tolkien's coinage) is not more inevitable than that of its tragic counterpart. And there *is* an implicit imbalance in the Christian world view: a moral universe with perfect balance would be a dualist universe, and its equal antagonists would render it static.

In L'Engle's works, as in the works of other Christian fantasists, the narrative gains its dynamism from the creative and attractive powers of the good characters. There is a dialectic in Christian literature in which the meeting of good and evil results in more and better good. The plot is always precisely this, that the corruption of the good created world by the forces of antibeing proves to be a *felix culpa,* a happy fault, whereby the action of God brings a new good, a new creation, even out of evil. In the central eucatastrophe, Christ does and is resurrected; death and evil do their worst and are bested. Dorothy L. Sayers once wrote that if this plot were boring, she did not know what could be interesting.

The central title suggests that this set of works could be called "The Wind Trilogy." Throughout the series, the symbol of wind appears as the operative spirit image, and the association of wind with each of the psychopomp figures makes clear that they are all images of spirit; indeed, the three novels may be read as meditations upon the Spirit, the divine wind or breath of the Holy Spirit in action in the world, expressed as trifold feminine wisdom, as masculine power, as angelic knowledge, and as the unifying unicorn. With guides like these, Madeleine L'Engle's child characters win their wars within. (pp. 200-02)

Nancy-Lou Patterson, "Angel and Psychopomp in Madeleine L'Engle's 'Wind' Trilogy," in Children's literature in education, *Vol. 14, No. 4 (Winter), 1983, pp. 195-203.*

KATHLEEN M. SUCHY

[The following excerpt is taken from Suchy's introduction of L'Engle at the 1984 Regina Medal presentation.]

After reading [Madeleine L'Engle's] books, one comes to feel a real kinship with this author, as if you'd known her long and well. With this feeling in mind, I'd like to sum up my thoughts in this way: As the words pour forth from pen to page / And we are caught up in your truth-telling / We learn of life. / We watch the struggle between good and evil / that is us. / And even though the dark forces surround us / all and all-ways, / You show us that there is love / And that too is real / And with that we can win.

Thank you Madeleine L'Engle for sharing your gifts with us, of all ages, in the celebration of life.

Kathleen M. Suchy, in an introduction to "Regina Medal Recipient—Madeleine L'Engle," in Catholic Library World, *Vol. 56, No. 1, July-August, 1984, p. 28.*

GARY D. SCHMIDT

One of the mainstays of children's literature over the past century has been the appearance of a character or set of characters in several successive novels. Most of these characters are as constant and unchanging as an Egyptian pyramid. Among others, Hugh Lofting's Dr. Dolittle, P. T. Travers' Mary Poppins, Eleanor Estes' Moffats, and Astrid Lindgren's Pippi dance gleefully from book to book, adventure to adventure. But they dance to a tune that moves into only slight variations. There is little chance that Mary Poppins or Pippi or Dr. Dolittle will be anything other than what they have been from the very first novel. And perhaps the reader would be chagrined if they did change. (p. 34)

But in the last thirty years or so, a quite different sort of series has emerged, a type practiced most skillfully by Madeleine L'Engle and Susan Cooper. In this type of sequence, narrative elements, theme, and character are all sustained and integrated, so that each book builds on the plot, experience, and meaning of the ones before. But—and this is a crucial matter—the novels build upon each other in a way that allows each novel of the sequence to stand independently, with its own meaning and its own artistic wholeness. This type of series is not, then, a traditional trilogy like that of Tolkien, where the conclusions of the first two novels leave so many things open that they might not properly be called conclusions. Instead, in what might be termed the integrated series, each book stands as a single complete and whole movement. But, as Susan Cooper notes, taken together these books form a symphony which contains its own unity and its own meaning because it is so much larger than any of its parts.

Of character, setting, and theme, the characters are most important in establishing the integration. The plots swirl around them, and they react and grow through the experience of the novel. The adventures of each novel are separate from the adventures of the preceding novels, yet the growth the characters have achieved and the new awareness they have gained from those past adventures determines their reactions to the present ones, and thus significantly affects later plots. There is consequently a long term development. Characters might

change in individual novels, but it is the cumulative change achieved by the end of the series that is most significant in terms of the meaning of the whole.

The structure of this kind of series generates an historical sense. By the end of the series, the author has developed several crucial moments in a character's growth. The reader, in effect, dips into moments of a character's life which the author has decided to flesh out. Long periods may pass between the action of these fleshing outs, periods when Meg and Charles Wallace grow and mature, when Taran does little but clean out the pig sty, when Will Stanton milks the cows rather than fights against the Dark. Whereas in a single novel gaps of any significant time are at best disconcerting, in an integrated series they are essential. Within these intervals the characters assimilate the meaning and experience of the previous novels.

The reader brings to each successive novel a knowledge of the character's past, and with that knowledge comes certain expectations. Characters must act consistently, and if they do not, there must be an apparent cause. Characters must act in light of what has happened in previous novels. And characters must act out of the context of what they have learned in the past. The very structure of the integrated series forces these criteria upon the plot of each novel.

The final effect of all this is that the reader, at the conclusion of a series, can step back and view the thing with an historical eye. Characters develop and grow and learn and change in stages, and all this is chronicled in each novel. But at the end, when the last page of the last novel is turned, the reader sees not just change in the confines of a single novel, but also change that has preceded over what might be called the lifetime of a character.

One result of this technique is the simultaneous establishment of familiarity and distance; the latter produces the greater sense of reality. The reader encounters the characters at moments far removed from each other, and consequently can see change and development more clearly and more truly than in other forms of sequences. (pp. 35-7)

Madeleine L'Engle's Time Trilogy is perhaps the best example of such a sequence. The first two novels, *A Wrinkle in Time* and *A Wind in the Door,* are divided by a full year, so that by the second novel Meg has, just by growing older, resolved some of her difficulties in self-acceptance that she had experienced in the first novel. At the same time the prodigious Charles Wallace, by moving into the first grade, has begun to learn the necessity of adapting. Between the second and the third novels nine years pass, so that in *A Swiftly Tilting Planet* Meg is married and pregnant and Charles Wallace has made it into adolescence with astonishing intuitive powers. The changes in their perceptions are in accord with their chronological growth, but their natures remain consistent with what we have previously seen, and their psychic powers and familial relationships are solidly based on what has gone before. In addition, their perceptions of goodness and mercy, and their understandings of the relationship between time and space, are all rooted in the adventures of the first two novels.

The integrated series gives the reader a significant entry into the worlds of the characters; by the time we reach the final novel of a series, we have a sense of the history of the characters. The author can manipulate this sense, so that as characters recall events in their past, we move back into time with them to something that both reader and character recall. So in L'Engle's *A Swiftly Tilting Planet,* Meg, sitting alone in her old brass bed because her husband is in London delivering a paper, hears Charles Wallace coming up the stairs for a conference:

> They had all got in the habit of automatically skipping the seventh step, which not only creaked when stepped on, but often made a sound like a shot. She and Charles Wallace had learned to put one foot on the extreme left of the step so that it let out only a long, slow sigh; when either one of them did this, it was a signal for a conference.
>
> She listened to his progress across the attic, heard the rocking of the old wooden horse as he gave it his usual affectionate slap on the rump, followed by the whing of a dart going into the corkboard: all the little signals they had built up over the years.
>
> He pushed through the long strands of patterned rice which curtained the doorway, stood at the foot of the bed, and rested his chin on the high brass rail of the footboard. He looked at her without smiling, then climbed over the footboard as he used to do when he was a little boy, and sat cross-legged on the foot of the bed. . . .

These are, of course, characters who are at least ten years older than when we first encounter them, and here L'Engle brings us back into their memories. The reader remembers with Meg what Charles Wallace was like, and we recognize with her how different he is now. The conversation of a high school freshman and a four year old brother merges with that of a married woman and her teenage brother, and fictional characters and real readers are both able to interpret the changes that the merger makes clear.

A similar case occurs during the first crucial ordeal of *A Wind in the Door*. Meg, faced with the trial of choosing the correct Mr. Jenkins from out of a possible three, is counselled by her companion cherubim to recall the time when she was most herself. The time that comes to her mind is one out of *A Wrinkle in Time* when she first met Calvin O'Keefe, who will become her husband between the second and third novels. Our memory moves back with hers, linking the two novels, yet also establishing the separate nature of this new adventure.

In L'Engle's novels, the reader is able to watch a developing history in the lives of the secondary characters as well. In *A Wrinkle in Time*, Mrs. Murry spends most of her time in a milk room converted into a laboratory. Here she stews dinner over a bunsen burner and conducts experiments, the nature of which are never revealed. In *A Wind in the Door* we find that the experiments involve the isolation of the oxygen-producing bodies of mitochondria. By the time of *A Swiftly Tilting Planet* she has not only isolated those bodies, but has won the Nobel Prize for her work. L'Engle is never one for half-hearted measures.

This process distances us from the previous novels by emphasizing the chronological leaps that occur between each one, thus endowing characters and events with greater historical reality and depth than they might otherwise have had. Such distancing between novels carries with it added chances of authorial manipulation. Readers of any sequence will come to the next book with certain expectations about the characters. . . . The chronological distance established in an integrated

sequence, however, gives greater freedom to the author to manipulate characters, as well as the reader's responses to them. Characters can develop in ways that are completely unexpected, though still consistent.

Recognition of this distancing and plot development as a consistent element of the series might provide at least a partial answer to the criticism of *A Wrinkle in Time* as a single novel. "The conceptual elements of this extraordinary novel," Justin Wintle writes, "are diffuse and never completely synthesized." John Townsend complains that her novels are "often complicated beyond endurance" [see excerpt in *CLR*, Vol. 1]. Marcus Crouch called it "an experiment, an uneasy blending of physics and metaphysics" which "proved almost too explosive to be controlled" and "failed to achieve total communication" [see excerpt in *CLR*, Vol. 2].

It is dangerous to assess the merits of a single book by comparing it to those which come after, but in the case of a sequence it seems necessary. The supposedly "uneasy blending of physics and metaphysics" in the first novel is lucidly explored and developed in the later novels. *A Wind in the Door* concentrates on the metaphysical side of events in the first book; the power and nature of love, examined in the first novel, are explained through the concept of naming. The third novel blends in the physics; the plot is based on Einstein's theories of space and time, as Charles Wallace moves back in time, though not space, to find a might-have-been to offset a coming catastrophe. Here the practice of kything—a form of telepathy first introduced in *A Wrinkle in Time*—is developed to a fine art. Taken as a whole, the sequence shows a stunning blend of physics and metaphysics. L'Engle's own response to such criticisms is that any story, if it is a good one, will be read; the success of the story is its own answer to criticism. (pp. 37-40)

> *Gary D. Schmidt, "See How They Grow: Character Development in Children's Series Books," in* Children's literature in education, *Vol. 18, No. 1 (Spring), 1987, pp. 34-44.*

A WRINKLE IN TIME (1962)

AUTHOR'S COMMENTARY

[The following excerpt is taken from L'Engle's Newbery Award acceptance speech.]

I believe that everyone of us here tonight has as clear and vital a vocation as anyone in a religious order. We have the vocation of keeping alive [Newbery Award founder Frederick G.] Melcher's excitement in leading young people into an expanding imagination. Because of the very nature of the world as it is today our children receive in school a heavy load of scientific and analytic subjects, so it is in their reading for fun, for pleasure, that they must be guided into creativity. There are forces working in the world as never before in the history of mankind for standardization, for the regimentation of us all, or what I like to call making muffins of us, muffins all like every other muffin in the muffin tin. This is the limited universe, the dying, dissipating universe, that we can help our children avoid by providing them with "explosive material capable of stirring up fresh life endlessly" [in the words of Bertha Mahony Miller].

So how do we do it? We can't just sit down at our typewriters and turn out explosive material. I took a course in college on Chaucer, one of the most explosive, imaginative, and far-reaching in influence of all writers. And I'll never forget going to the final exam and being asked why Chaucer used certain verbal devices, certain adjectives, why he had certain characters behave in certain ways. And I wrote in a white heat of fury, "I don't think Chaucer had any idea why he did any of these things. That isn't the way people write."

I believe this as strongly now as I did then. Most of what is best in writing isn't done deliberately.

Do I mean, then, that an author should sit around like a phony Zen Buddhist in his pad, drinking endless cups of espresso coffee and waiting for inspiration to descend upon him? That isn't the way the writer works, either. I heard a famous author say once that the hardest part of writing a book was making yourself sit down at the typewriter. I know what he meant. Unless a writer works constantly to improve and refine the tools of his trade, they will be useless instruments if and when the moment of inspiration, of revelation, does come. This is the moment when a writer is spoken through, the moment that a writer must accept with gratitude and humility, and then attempt, as best he can, to communicate to others.

A writer of fantasy, fairy tale, or myth must inevitably discover that he is not writing out of his own knowledge or experience, but out of something both deeper and wider. I think that fantasy must possess the author and simply use him. I know that this is true of *A Wrinkle in Time*. I can't possibly tell you how I came to write it. It was simply a book I had to write. I had no choice. And it was only *after* it was written that I realized what some of it meant.

Very few children have any problem with the world of the imagination; it's their own world, the world of their daily life, and it's our loss that so many of us grow out of it. Probably this group here tonight is the least grown-out-of-it group that could be gathered together in one place, simply by the nature of our work. We, too, can understand how Alice could walk through the mirror into the country on the other side; how often have our children almost done this themselves? And we all understand princesses, of course. Haven't we all been badly bruised by peas? And what about the princess who spat forth toads and snakes whenever she opened her mouth to speak, and the other whose lips issued forth pieces of pure gold? We all have had days when everything we've said has seemed to turn to toads. The days of gold, alas, don't come nearly as often.

What a child doesn't realize until he is grown is that in responding to fantasy, fairy tale, and myth he is responding to what Erich Fromm calls the one universal language, the one and only language in the world that cuts across all barriers of time, place, race, and culture. Many Newbery books are from this realm, beginning with Dr. Dolittle; books on Hindu myth, Chinese folklore, the life of Buddha, tales of American Indians, books that lead our children beyond all boundaries and into the one language of all mankind.

In the beginning God created the heaven and the earth. . . . The extraordinary, the marvelous thing about Genesis is not how unscientific it is, but how amazingly accurate it is. How could the ancient Israelites have known the exact order of an evolution that wasn't to be formulated for thousands of years? Here is a truth that cuts across barriers of time and space.

But almost all of the best children's books do this, not only an *Alice in Wonderland*, a *Wind in the Willows*, a *Princess and the Goblin*. Even the most straightforward tales say far more than they seem to mean on the surface. *Little Women,*

The Secret Garden, Huckleberry Finn—how much more there is in them than we realize at a first reading. They partake of the universal language, and this is why we turn to them again and again when we are children, and still again when we have grown up.

Up on the summit of Mohawk Mountain in northwest Connecticut is a large flat rock that holds the heat of the sun long after the last of the late sunset has left the sky. We take our picnics up there and then lie on the rock and watch the stars, one pulsing slowly into the deepening blue, and then another and another and another, until the sky is full of them.

A book, too, can be a star, "explosive material, capable of stirring up fresh life endlessly," a living fire to lighten the darkness, leading out into the expanding universe. (pp. 120-23)

> Madeleine L'Engle, "Newbery Award Acceptance: The Expanding Universe", in Newbery and Caldecott Medal Books: 1956-1965, *edited by Lee Kingman, The Horn Book, Incorporated, 1965, pp. 119-23.*

I have often wished it were not necessary to review a book immediately upon publication. Children's reactions and acceptances are always important and there should be time to be aware of them. The critic's own perspective on a book is often clearer months after it is read. I felt that way about . . . *A Wrinkle in Time*. I reviewed it favorably upon publication. Months later the books's extraordinary power began to show itself in the way incidents kept coming to mind, in the hold it had taken on my imagination.

I cannot forget the personalities of the children: precocious little Charles Wallace; Meg, whose faults alone—anger, impatience, stubbornness—could save her; the three strange beings who emerge at times as eccentric but very kind old ladies. The children reach a lost planet where they believe their father is imprisoned. I keep remembering the conversation with the man in the CENTRAL Central Intelligence Building who ran the number one spelling machine on the second-grade level; and the tense scene when Meg tried to break the rhythm of the dread thing that she felt absorbing her by reciting the Declaration of Independence, the periodic table of elements, and square roots; and the children's despair at their discovery that the earth was shadowed by the Powers of Darkness, followed by their growing courage as they began to recall the names of the earth's fighters against darkness. (p. 25)

Miss L'Engle has referred to her book as a parable; but it is first of all an exciting adventure story, with something important added—the overtones that will make it worth reading many times and will give new meanings with each new reading.

Here is a book which the analytical reviewer might characterize in this way:

> A mingling of realism and science fantasy which incorporates the concepts of time travel, extrasensory perception, and inhabited planets in outer space. Excellent writing style, involved plot. Vocabulary and literary references too difficult for the average fairy-tale audience.

An imaginative analyst might compare the three spirits with the witches of Macbeth, point out analogies to modern life, and cite the value (or confusion to the unread child) of the literary quotations. Both reviewers would be doing what C. S. Lewis calls judging "the instrument by anything rather than its power to do the work it was made for," criticizing "the lens after looking *at* it instead of *through* it."

We are so busy doing things with the work that we give it too little chance to work on us. Thus increasingly we meet only ourselves.

Here certainly is a book which should not be used but should be received, full of words which are "exquisitely detailed compulsions on a mind willing and able to be so compelled." Here is a book requiring an approach which allows margin for surprise. (pp. 26-7)

> *Ruth Hill Viguers, "Margin for Surprise: Reflections on the Pursuit of Excellence in Books for Children," in her* Margin for Surprise: About Books, Children, and Librarians, *Little, Brown and Company, 1964, pp. 3-34.*

A most popular and original book is *A Wrinkle in Time.* The book sparkles with the author's vitality and imagination and proceeds at a fast pace with recognizable character types. Her contributions are ingenious but not deep. The climactic scene in which Meg stands crying before Charles Wallace bothers me for two reasons. First of all, I find it hard to understand why she could not have done this before; secondly, if Mrs. Whatsit could tesser her and Charles Wallace away from IT, why couldn't she have been with them before and saved them from their father's inept tessering? Here, it seems to me, the ground rules of the plot have been violated. In the previous visit to IT, the children had to go alone; now Mrs. Whatsit is there to tesser them off. This may seem minor, but it is of a piece with the main criticism I have to make of this book; there is a facility about it, a slickness in characterization and dialogue which makes me feel that I have been dealt with less than directly. There is no question but that the book is good entertainment and that the writer carries the story along with a great deal of verve; there is some question about the depth of its quality. (p. 159)

> *Carolyn Horovitz, "Only the Best," in* Newbery and Caldecott Medal Books: 1956-65, *edited by Lee Kingman, The Horn Book, Incorporated, 1965, pp. 153-62.*

A Wrinkle in Time is a splendid fantasy; . . . it seldom violates reality. The Murry family relationships, Calvin's relationship to his parents, and Meg's relation to school authorities and the community, as well as the character portraits, are probable and realistic. Envy of the Murrys, gossip about the supposedly runaway father-husband, malice, selfishness, and even Charles Wallace's arrogance, are unflinchingly presented. Tesseracting, a seemingly instantaneous movement in time and/or place, is given a metamorphic fifth-dimension explanation. The witches who were formerly stars dying in the struggle against the evil shadow fight a symbolic battle steeped in classical and Gospel-of-John traditions, a battle that is psychically realistic even though symbolic. One can even relate Mrs. Whatsit's, Mrs. Who's, and Mrs. Which's actions to current theories of black holes in space and neutron stars; even the life style on Camazotz has an affinity to entropy. The only weakness in the novel is the confrontation with the It-brain by Mr. Murry and the children; the shift from the symbolic to the actual confrontation is a dramatic collapse of an antagonist from the infinite to the finite much like the cannon battle in *Paradise Lost.* (pp. 295-96)

> *Craig Wallace Barrow, in a review of "A Wrinkle in Time", in* Children's Literature: Annual of the Modern Language Association Seminar on Chil-

> dren's Literature and The Children's Literature Association, *Vol. 5, 1976, pp. 295-96.*

In literature involving any kind of a journey, whether psychological or literal, there are two major structural patterns. The first is a linear journey, in which the hero travels from Point A to Point B. Point B is generally more desirable than Point A, and the narrative explains why and shows how the hero reaches the desired location. Generally these are stories of wish fulfillment or actual achievement. . . .

More prevalent in children's fantasy, however, is the second structural pattern, the circular journey. The destination here is the same as the departure point. In these stories, the hero escapes from the normal world as defined by home and society, into a fantasy world where he undergoes experiences that ultimately allow him to return to the normal world a more self-confident, knowledgeable, and adjusted individual. (p. 25)

A variant of the circular pattern is one in which a child who is dissatisfied with his life moves into a new world, where, although apparently escaping reality, he is forced to confront his own problems and solve them, thus making possible his healthy return to his own world. Three particularly interesting examples shall be considered here: Virginia Hamilton's *Zeely,* in which a young girl daydreams because her life seems dull; Mordecai Richler's *Jacob Two-Two Meets the Hooded Fang* which examines the actual dream of a little boy who feels inadequate because he is the youngest of five children; and Madeleine L'Engle's *A Wrinkle in Time* which traces the interstellar journeys of a teenager who feels out of place both in her family and at school. In each, the escape to the different world is instrumental in helping the central character function more happily when he or she returns to everyday life. (pp. 25-6)

Like [Hamilton's] Elizabeth and [Richler's] Jacob, Meg Murry, heroine of *A Wrinkle in Time,* is dissatisfied with her life. And like them, she is transformed by an experience in another world. But there are considerable differences between this and the other books. Meg's dissatisfactions have a wider range, and the world she is transported to is objectively real. Still, *A Wrinkle in Time* contains the common theme which binds all these works together: in the strange and different world she visits, she must confront the very elements which had caused her dissatisfaction in her normal life.

Meg's sense of difference and unhappiness goes deeper than that of the other protagonists, and the circumstances of her life are more bizarre. She has a genius five-year-old brother named Charles Wallace who poses as a moron to the outside world, and two disgustingly average and efficient eleven-year-old brothers. Although she is very bright, she does poorly in school and gets into fights both with her teachers and with other children. Because she wears glasses and braces and has unmanageable hair, she feels hopelessly drab next to her beautiful, scientist mother. And worst of all, her father, a famous scientist at work on a government project, has suddenly disappeared.

The first stage of Meg's development begins as she goes to meet Mrs. Whatsit, Mrs. Which, and Mrs. Who, three extraterrestrial beings who have come to help the Murrys find their father. The three benevolent witches, whose names suggest their ability to make Meg ask basic questions about herself, take her, along with her brother Charles Wallace and her friend Calvin to a distant part of the galaxy.

They travel by a process known as tessering, and their first stop is the planet Uriel. The planet takes its name from the Archangel who was sent by God to answer the questions of Esdras and who was called by Milton "the sharpest sighted spirit of all in Heaven." Here the children see the evil black cloud enveloping the planet Camazotz and learn that their father is fighting this cloud. They receive this vision while riding Belleraphon-like on the back of Mrs. Whatsit, now transformed into a winged centaur. Like the boy hero from Greek mythology, Meg will be sent alone to combat the evil chimera which threatens to devour her little brother. At this point, Meg is not ready for her great task; she is alternately filled with fear, impatience, loneliness, and confusion.

On their visit to the second planet, the children meet a seer who presents them with further visions and informs Meg that she has an heroic mission. Shown a vision of the Earth, she sees that the dark cloud has attempted for centuries to envelop it and is told that great fighters from Christ to Einstein have held it at bay. She is told that she is to become one of these fighters. However, another vision reveals that heroism may require great sacrifice. She learns that Mrs. Whatsit, who had once been a beautiful star, has given up her light and star life to defeat the threatening darkness.

At this point, a small but significant change occurs within Meg. She has been impatient to find her father, feeling that he will solve all these difficulties, and in the meantime she had been relying on Calvin for support. But when she is presented with a vision of Calvin's unhappy home life, she reaches out to protect him:

> Now, instead of reaching out to Calvin for safety, Meg took his hand in hers, not saying anything in words, but trying to tell him by the pressure of her fingers what she felt. If anyone had told her only the day before that she, Meg, the snaggle-toothed, the myopic, the clumsy, would be taking a boy's hand to offer him comfort and strength, particularly a popular and important boy like Calvin, the idea would have been beyond her comprehension. But now it seemed as natural to want to help and protect Calvin as it did Charles Wallace.

The three children are now prepared for their trip to the dark planet, Camazotz, named appropriately after a malignant Mexican diety. The diety is worshipped as a vampire, a death-bat, a preying creature of darkness. The danger that awaits them becomes apparent as they tesser to the planet. . . . On the planet, Mrs. Whatsit explains to the children that they are to be alone and that they must face their challenges without help. However, Meg learns that the qualities of character which had often made her unhappy at home will be valuable here. Earlier Mrs. Whatsit had told her: "We can't take any credit for our talents. It's how we use them that counts". . . . Meg must be who she is, even if it makes her different, and she must make her uniqueness a positive asset.

When they first arrive on Camazotz, Meg is surprised to discover that the planet looks like earth. As is typical of science fiction, the new world satirizes the problems of her own, and, in the tradition of *1984*, offers a nightmare vision of the future. The residential areas resemble the little boxes of the 1960's folk song and the inhabitants uniformly perform uniform tasks. Deviant—we would say variant—behavior is swiftly corrected through painful reconditioning. In the city, the people mind-lessly attend to their duties, uncomplainingly submitting to red tape. They are controlled by the impersonal bureaucracy housed in the CENTRAL Central Intelligence Building and ultimately by IT, an oversized disembodied brain. . . . On Camazotz, all individual will is crushed. Clearly it is a magnified and distorted version of the conventional world of school and town from which Meg had felt separated back on Earth. In this light, Meg recognizes the value of her individuality. Conformity is revealed as dangerous, and her own angry response to it, which had gotten her into trouble at home, is now appropriate. When even Charles Wallace succumbs to the power of IT, Meg explains to him that conformity and equality are not the same. What is celebrated as equality on Camazotz is really the surrendering of one's will.

As the children are led off to see their father, Meg asserts her new sense of independence by not holding Calvin's hand. However, she still believes that when they reach her father, he will assume control. . . . But she is quickly disappointed to learn that her father can't rescue Charles Wallace "[He] had been found but he had not made everything all right. Instead, everything was worse than ever, and her adored father was bearded and thin and white and not omnipotent at all". . . .

It is appropriate that the title of the next chapter should be "Absolute Zero." Meg now lies on a third planet Ixchel, in a semi-coma, filled with bitterness, anger, and impatience toward her father, who, she feels, has failed her. It is both appropriate and ironic that the planet should be named Ixchel, after the Mayan Goddess of the Rainbow, the symbol of fecundity, patron of the art of medicine, and wife of Izanna, the Light God. For it is here that one of the planet's creatures cures Meg physically and mentally. But the planet is without visible light, a fact which puzzles Meg until she is told that the inhabitants are guided by the inner light of love, that they "look not at the things which are seen, but at the things which are unseen". . . . Meg also must look inward, must exorcise her faults and discover the love she possesses in her soul.

Her impatience is becoming dangerous because it puts her "as much in the power of the Black Thing as Charles Wallace". . . . With the aid of Aunt Beast, her Ixchelian nurse, she must "be as an infant again" . . . , and give up her anger. Only then can she rescue her brother. When she is ready to accept the challenge, she tells her father:

> I wanted you to do it all for me. I wanted everything to be all easy and simple. . . . So I tried to pretend that it was all your fault . . . because I was scared, and I didn't want to do anything for myself. . . .

Now she must go alone, without Mrs. Which to hold her hand, but with three gifts: Mrs. Whatsit's love, Mrs. Who's words about God's faith in the courage of the apparently weak of the world, and Mrs. Which's mysterious promise that Meg will find an inner strength that IT does not possess. What she has that IT does not is the ability to love. And with this recognition, she is able to complete her mission. At the end of the novel, reunited with her family, she has become stronger and more accepting of herself.

We have examined only three works which make use of the circular pattern to present the growth of their central characters. (pp. 34-8)

The important aspect of each of these stories is that the central character does return from his or her fantasy world, does complete the circular journey. For each there comes a crucial point when the character, in the midst of the fantasy world, must face the reality of his inner situation. Not to do so would be to become entrapped forever, never to return to the world from which he or she departed. . . . Meg in reaching ''absolute zero'' on the planet Ixchel [faces] just such crucial moments and [emerges] victorious. (pp. 38-9).

Jon C. Stott, ''Midsummer Night's Dreams: Fantasy and Self-Realization in Children's Fiction,'' in The Lion and the Unicorn, *Vol. 1, No. 2, Fall, 1977, pp. 25-39.*

[*A Wrinkle in Time* is a] watershed novel in children's science fiction of the 1960s. . . . L'Engle does not take an antiscience stand in this book—the parents of the children protagonists are renowned scientists—but when Meg, Charles Wallace, and Calvin confront the evil power threatening the universe, they learn that science is not enough; they discover that only science plus love can overcome the enemy. . . .

L'Engle introduced a metaphysical aspect to the genre. As in C. S. Lewis' science fiction, there is a religious aura which surrounds and infuses her work. The element of science which places her work in the realm of science fiction rather than mystical fantasy is sometimes overshadowed by this spiritual aspect. Still, her work paved the way for other authors' philosophically-oriented science fiction for children, and her character Meg opened the door for many more female protagonists in recent science fiction. The philosophical and feminist aspects of L'Engle's novel were innovations whose time had come. (p. 27)

Janice Antczak, ''The Growth and Development of a Genre,'' in her Science Fiction: The Mythos of a New Romance, *Neal-Schuman Publishers, Inc., 1985, pp. 15-37.*

[The] best stories written for children differ in degree, and not in kind, from the best stories written for adults. While children's literature may allow certain concessions to the nature of its intended audience, the critic may fairly expect that literature to heed Hamlet's advice to the players, and to show that the purpose of playing, even in literature written for children, ''both at the first and now, was and is to hold as 'twere the mirror up to Nature' ''. We may not always like what art's mirror shows us about human nature . . . , but its determination to reflect the complexity of the human psyche accurately is one criterion by which literature of all kinds—even, and perhaps especially, children's literature—is to be judged. Certainly it is one criterion by which Madeleine L'Engle's ambitious novel, *A Wrinkle in Time* . . . may usefully be judged, and its quality accurately assessed, for a child's encounter with and response to evil is central to this novel.

Certainly the zeal with which *A Wrinkle in Time* tackles ethical (and thus inevitably, psychological) issues distinguishes it from many other works of fantasy and science fiction written for children; and its moral earnestness has done much to secure its favorable reception by critics and the book-buying public. (pp. 123-24)

Because of its complexity of plot, character, and theme, *A Wrinkle in Time* merits the attention it has received. Meg's quest is perfectly suited to her character, and the novel artfully uses the traditional journey-to-the-Otherworld of fantasy to enrich its equally-traditional motif of the child's quest for the lost parent, a fruitful theme in children's literature since Te-

lemachus' search for his lost father at the opening of *The Odyssey*. *A Wrinkle in Time* is, in short, a remarkably ambitious novel, a novel which attempts to achieve at least three things, and which, in the opinion of many of its readers, achieves them very well.

First of all, it is a novel about self-discovery, a novel about an alienated teen-ager who finds within herself the resources to overcome that alienation. Those familiar with the contemporary adolescent novel will recognize this, or some trivial variation thereon, as the creaking mainstay of that genre. Suffice it to say that *A Wrinkle in Time* is superior to most of its plethora of imitators in its handling of this subject.

Second, the novel is a story of time travel and of journeys to other worlds; the flexibility of space and time provide circumstances in which Meg's growth can be accentuated and clearly understood; character and situation are mutually illuminating.

Finally, the novel attempts an anatomy of evil; in rescuing her father and Charles Wallace, Meg faces an evil power which not only threatens her personally, but is also presented as a power cosmic in its ambitions and operations. . . . It is in the matter of the presentation of evil that *A Wrinkle in Time* shows its greatest ambition—and its greatest weakness. In this, for all its virtues, it amply demonstrates the wisdom of another student of human misery, Lao-Tse, who once observed that ''It is difficult to use the Master Carpenter's tools without cutting one's fingers.''

In its treatment of Meg's alienation, and of the fantastic quest which enables her to resolve it, the novel is both artful and effective. The prime symptom of Meg's alienation is her strong sense ''of Meg Murry doing everything wrong,'' of herself as ''a monster'' because she is not like everyone else, and because she fails to fit in at school (which is also ''all wrong'' and where the principal helpfully describes her as ''the most belligerent, uncooperative child in school''). Meg's is the common confusion of adolescence, and her endemic sense of being ''an oddball,'' someone lost in time and space, is of course exacerbated by the unexplained absence of her father. Like most protagonists of quest-romance, Meg sets out in search of something external to herself; she does not suspect that she is simultaneously seeking her own identity. At first she believes what all children have a right to believe: that finding Daddy will solve all her problems. . . . Her father is, of course, only a man—and a man whose strength has been sapped by his long resistance to IT. . . . After their escape, when her father proves unable to return to Camazotz to rescue Charles Wallace, Meg's ''disappointment in her father's human fallibility rose like gorge in her throat.'' The failure of Meg's father to conform to her assumptions is one of the more astute snares lying in her path; the inhabitants of Camazotz are more pathetic than terrifying, and IT, for all its wiles, is obviously evil. Far more insidious is Meg's expectation of what her father should be and do; his failure to meet these expectations is crucial to her growth.

She is able to grow because her experience on Camazotz has taught her much about the evils of conformity, and her friendship with the three Mrs. W's . . . has helped her accept personal responsibility for her actions. To claim responsibility for one's actions is also, of course, to claim responsibility for one's self. In accepting herself as she is with all the irreducible difference this implies, Meg enables herself to accept her father. . . . Reconciled with her father, strengthened by her acceptance of herself as she is and of others as they are, Meg is able to resist IT and rescue her brother—for her love for Charles Wallace is now stronger than her fear of the individuality and uncertainty from which IT promises such certain deliverance. In this way, *A Wrinkle in Time* conforms to one of the most venerable formulae of fantasy: a journey to an Otherworld, an Otherworld where the quest in which the protagonist engages changes him or her irrevocably.... That *A Wrinkle in Time* handles the traditional elements of quest-romance so fruitfully, and with such an astute and sensitive grasp of the psychology of adolescence is one of the great sources of its success.

Now, given the novel's psychological insight, and given the fact that Meg Murry's confrontation with the evil power of IT is the climax for which the entire novel has prepared her, the sympathetic reader may be reluctant to see or concerned that there are also real problems with the anatomy of evil in *A Wrinkle in Time*. Such reluctance may well originate in the reader's hearty approbation of the novel's moral. After all, who among us really prefers not to believe that love is stronger than fear, or that love, not coercion, is the best foundation for social harmony? And yet it is precisely the enthusiasm of the moralist which can here betray the critic into what we might call the Horatian, or, more accurately, the Augustinian, fallacy. (Horace argued that poetry seeks both to instruct and to delight; between the fifteenth and the nineteenth centuries, most literature written for children assumed that useful instruction is much more important than gratuitous pleasure, and that, therefore, the lesson which literature has to teach is much more important than the fiction which is the vehicle of that teaching. This characteristic bias with which the name of Horace was associated actually reflects the influence of the Church Fathers, and of Augustine in particular: "it is a mark of good and distinguished minds," says Augustine, "to love the truth within words and not the words themselves." Letter is to meaning, runs his oft-quoted remark, as husk is to kernel.) The point at issue is not whether or not didacticism (in the broad sense) is a legitimate function of children's literature; after all, if we did not expect to gain something from our reading, few of us would bother with books at all. The point is that our fondness for the lesson conveyed in a work of literature, should not preempt our critical investigation of the fiction by which that lesson is conveyed. *A Wrinkle in Time* argues, most agreeably, that love is stronger than fear or coercion—but the novel's analysis of the evil over which love triumphs is far less agreeable than the novel's impeccable moral.

There are a number of reasons why this is so. Some readers may argue that the novel's treatment of evil is undermined by its overt Christian elements. Meg's father reminds her that "We were sent here for something. And we know that all things work together for good to them that love God, to them who are the called according to his purpose"—as if Meg were some sort of intergalactic missionary. Aunt Beast echoes this view when she tells Meg that "we are the called according to His purpose, and whom He calls, them He also justifies." Meg herself "must be as an infant again" before she can return to Camazotz to confront IT. And Charles Wallace's description of the three Mrs. W's as "Guardian angels ... Messengers. Messengers of God" likewise grates—because there is no necessity in the fiction for such an overt identification. The problem here is not with the Christian elements as such.... The problem is that these elements skew and direct our preception of evil, and that they are gratuitous to the novel throughout which they are so liberally sprinkled. Perhaps L'Engle could have paid more attention to the Narnia chronicles, where Lewis' fiction, though intimately conscious of Christian doctrine, never depends on that doctrine for justification. (pp. 124-27)

Other readers may object to *A Wrinkle in Time* on political as well as literary grounds. It is gratifying—but not necessarily accurate—to identify one's own party with those justified by the Lord and called according to His purpose. A similar facility with labels undermines the novel's depiction of evil on Camazotz. In its necessary attempt to give evil a local habitation and a name, *A Wrinkle in Time* too glibly suggests certain similarities between the cosmic struggle against evil and the Cold War of the early sixties. Ruled by a disembodied brain (a brain incapable of love—and itself a servant of the Black Thing), terrified inhabitants regimented into a ruthless and unswerving conformity (IT even insists that all children play the same way at the same time), Camazotz is not so much a planet as a bogeyman—an early sixties American image of life in a Communist state. The possibility of a totalitarianism of the Lord's Chosen, i.e., a totalitarianism of the American right, never casts so much as the flicker of a shadow across the serene pages of *A Wrinkle in Time*. (In 1962 we were always the ones in the white hats.) The novel makes it altogether too easy to identify the cosmic struggle of good against evil as the struggle of American libertarianism against Russian tyranny. Camazotz is "a planet which has given in"; its inhabitants are "all perfectly channeled" and "aberrations" are forbidden upon pain of death; even all the dwellings are identical. Meg's moral choice is perfectly clear, as clear as that facing the heroine of any fairy tale, and one may argue, as Bettelheim does, that here too "the basic decision, on which all later personality development will build, is facilitated by the polarizations of the fairy tale." ... But in fairy tales like those collected by the Brothers Grimm, evil merely exists, it is never explained. Though they depict many evil characters, the Hausmarchen never hang political labels on those characters. By contrast, in its readiness to identify cosmic evil with political opposition, and to suggest that evil is localized in readily identifiable groups or nations, *A Wrinkle in Time* sometimes comes deplorably close to an attitude parodied by the young Bob Dylan (a parody written in the same year in which *A Wrinkle in Time* appeared):

> A Russian has three and a half red eyes
> five flamin antennas
> drags a beet-colored ball and chain
> An wants to slip germs
> into my coke machine

Such moral polarization is altogether too facile, nor is it redeemed by such touches as having the children thwart IT by reciting, *inter alia,* the Gettysburg Address and the beginning of the Declaration of Independence. The novel pays insufficient heed to the fact that certain kingdoms are not of this world, and tends to confuse the spiritual and the political arenas.

So one may justly criticize the novel on literary and political grounds; we may applaud the presence of Christian elements in the novel, while wishing they had formed a substantial part of the feast, instead of being tossed about as a sort of garnish; and we can likewise wish that Camazotz were not quite so obviously a signatory to the Warsaw Pact. What is far more difficult to accept, particularly in a novel which is all about a quest for identity, the search for self, is the novel's psychology, and particularly its treatment of evil.

Some aspects of the novel's treatment of evil are of course, not problematical at all. When Meg first sees the Black Thing, she sees it as a shadow in the reaches of space, "a shadow that was so terrible that she knew that there had never been before or ever would be again, anything that would chill her, with a fear that was beyond shuddering, beyond anything crying or screaming, beyond the possibility of comfort." This description is altogether unexceptionable (if one makes allowances for a certain Gothic lushness); so is that of the avid shadow which surrounds earth (though one could perhaps have done without Mrs. Which's gratuitous observation that "Itt iss Eevill. Itt iss the Ppowers of Ddarkness"). This treatment of evil is too trite to be sinister (Come to that, it verges on the unintentionally hilarious; is it possible to read Mrs. Which's remark aloud without bursting into laughter?) But there are certain aspects of the treatment of evil in *A Wrinkle in Time* which are not so easy to accept, or to laugh away.

Many of the novel's real problems with the psychology of evil are illuminated by the author's decision to present IT as "A disembodied brain. . . ". There are certain obvious difficulties with the choice of a brain—even a disembodied brain—as a symbol of evil. The book as a whole refuses to address the dichotomy of head and heart, nor does it exhibit any consistent suspicion of the intellect. (Both Meg's parents are scientists.) The symbolism is also dubious because the brain has many tasks in addition to that of regulating the functioning of the body and the behavior of the body's cells. (Nor, in the microcosm, is such regulation necessarily sinister. Cancer cells are indeed diverse from those of their host, but they are not necessarily harbingers of freedom and virtue on that account.) For these reasons, the use of a brain as a symbol of evil is more puzzling than helpful.

But what is far more puzzling—and disturbing—still is that, despite its use of a brain as a figure for evil, *A Wrinkle in Time* insists on seeing evil as something external to the human psyche. (Hawthorne might well have used the same symbol; he would never have made the same mistake.) Meg always speaks of Charles Wallace as having been "taken" by IT: "'That isn't Charles! Charles is gone'" and "Charles Wallace was gone that . . . little boy in his place was only a copy of Charles Wallace, only a doll." When Charles argues in support of IT, Meg tells her father "that isn't Charles . . . Charles isn't like that. IT has him." Despite the occasional hint that evil may be internal as well as external, prompting from within as well as attacking from without (as when we are told of Meg that "disappointment was as dark and corrosive in her as the Black Thing"), the novel as a whole insists on depicting evil as foreign to human nature. . . . In fact, the novel goes to considerable pains to deny evil a home—as opposed to an outpost—anywhere in the human psyche, and this is why Meg finds IT "far more nauseating than anything she had ever imagined with her conscious mind, or that had ever tormented her in her most terrible nightmares." This is also why evil is always shown as something which assails both planets and individuals from without, as when Meg faces it and "the red miasma began to creep before her eyes again, and she was afraid that she was going to lose consciousness, and if she did that she would be completely in the power of IT."

One is prepared to concede a certain subjective validity to this characterization of evil. Evil often appears external to the conscious self, the ego. And there are also theological reasons for this characterization, for man was not originally created evil. . . . But, as C. G. Jung and others have noted "the ego knows only its own contents, not the unconscious and its contents." . . . And what meets the requirements of the theologican will not always satisfy those of the psychologist—particularly in a book which is all about the quest for identity. Fighting an external force, no matter how powerful the opponent or how painful the experience, is significantly different from confronting an

evil power which originates in oneself. (The difference is, in its way, at least as significant as the difference between the Neo-Platonic belief in creation by emanation and the orthodox Judeo-Christian belief in a creation *ex nihilo*.) The Black Thing can use Charles Wallace, just as it can use the pathetic inhabitants of Camazotz—but it always remains an invader, foreign to human nature. This is an exceedingly charming and comfortable view of evil, albeit one which perhaps takes too little cognizance of our condition as fallen creatures, and it has everything necessary to recommend it to our time—except plausibility. Jung observes that "we are always, thanks to our human nature, potential criminals. . . . None of us stands outside humanity's black collective shadow." Whether the crime lies many generations back or happens today, it remains the symptom of a disposition that is always and everywhere present—and one would therefore do well to possess some "imagination in evil," for only the fool can permanently neglect the conditions of his own nature.

We may not altogether agree with Jung's statement that "evil, as experience shows, lies in man," but this is a view which demands serious consideration unless, as he goes on to say, "in accordance with the Christian view one is willing to postulate a metaphysical principle of evil". . . . *A Wrinkle in Time* is clearly prepared to postulate such a principle, and this is the most telling weakness in its "imagination in evil." Meg's encounter with evil is central to the novel, and her struggle with it a fundamental condition of her growth, but that evil is always presented as foreign to her nature and that of her brother. This makes problems with the plot's resolution. Meg retrieves Charles from IT by loving him, but it is easy to love a brother possessed by an evil spirit—Meg and her creator both wisely recognize that "she was not strong enough to love IT"—and so her struggle with evil is limited because she does not struggle with someone who has chosen evil. Perhaps this is only to say that the novel confuses the ego with the total psyche—but such a confusion is especially pernicious in a novel which is all about a teen-ager's quest for identity. "Playing with space and time is a dangerous game," as Meg's father admits, but telling our children lies about the psyche is a pastime far more dangerous yet. It is not the business of literature to condone such lies.

And so, for all its strengths, *A Wrinkle in Time* shrinks from holding the mirror up to human nature; it shirks the task of providing the looking-glass we seek so fearfully, and so tenaciously. For despite our fears, we must see before we can understand, and we cannot hope to deal with evil until we come to terms with its presence within ourselves. Since it strenuously denies that presence, *A Wrinkle in Time* also denies us that hope; denying us a full 'imagination in evil,' it also denies us literature's power to lead us to the painful consciousness of our own full humanity, the true and piercing awareness of all we are and of all we might become.

Finally, however, the moral confusions of *A Wrinkle in Time* are a great part of what is fascinating about it. The novel is a touchstone even though it finally does fail, for the sources of its failure reveal much about children's literature and its relationship to the moral education of children. (pp. 127-31)

William Blackburn, "Madeleine L'Engle's 'A Wrinkle in Time': Seeking the Original Face," in Touchstones: Reflections on the Best in Children's Literature, Vol. 1, *edited by Perry Nodelman, Children's Literature Association, 1985, pp. 123-31.*

A WIND IN THE DOOR (1973)

Adult admirers of Miss L'Engle will appreciate this, her most virtuoso performance in fantasy to date, but I have a lingering doubt if any but the more virtuoso young readers will be able to escape a good deal of bewilderment. The plot is enormously exciting, though I have the same kind of reservations about the solution as some reviewers had about that in Alan Garner's *The Owl Service*. The book will not be for every child; a good many will find it puzzling, but for the discerning readers who are able to appreciate the symbolism it will make a lasting impression. (pp. 247-48)

> *Robert Bell, in a review of "A Wind in the Door," in* The School Librarian, *Vol. 23, No. 3, September, 1975, pp. 247-48.*

[*A Wind in the Door*] attempts to get to the spiritual by way of fantasy/science fiction. But [Madeleine L'Engle] also takes other routes as well: namely both the "dragon" road and that familiar street that runs through the unnoticed gap in the everyday and into the beyond. The result is that, in terms of wonder, we get nowhere. Mrs. L'Engle really can't make up her mind whether she wants the reader to be involved in the realistic dimension of her story (which is rendered with superfluous and unselective detail) or to be caught up in the discovery of the "other" in our lives. The idea for this story is a promising one: the discovery (by the children) of the presence, in the strange illness of one little boy, of a whole universe of struggle between good and evil, order and chaos, integration and disintegration. This is the same territory C. S. Lewis worked, both in the chronicles of Narnia and in the Perelandra series for adults. The difference is that genuine wonder is never present in *A Wind in the Door*. The problem appears to be one of writing, primarily. For not only is there a confusion of routes (lack of commitment?) but also the spiritual (galactic) dimension, once moved into, is simply too confusingly vague and obscure to win acceptance. In addition, the treatment of the realistic point of departure is too charmingly eccentric, even, finally, clichéd—that is, cliché ideas of charmingly eccentric people. Moreover, *A Wind in the Door* shares what appears to be the burden of all fantasy/science fiction: only the idea really interests the writer. (p. 174)

> *Wayne Dodd, "Mapping Numinous Ground," in* Children's Literature: Annual of the Modern Language Association Seminar on Children's Literature and The Children's Literature Association, *Vol. 4, 1975, pp. 173-75.*

'A novel is never anything but a philosophy expressed in images,' wrote Albert Camus. To this one might add that more is carried in an author's image than he intends or realizes. Fiction communicates covert as well as overt messages, unconscious as well as conscious attitudes about the world, society, man, God and morality. Images may contradict intent.

Children's literature is more than ordinarily vulnerable to such a split, and in contemporary children's fiction it may be seen particularly, I believe, in the extent to which pessimism and negativism are expressed, whether consciously or unconsciously. In a number of recent books written for children, beneath the affirmative philosophy which traditionally has been regarded as an appropriate convention in children's books, there runs an undercurrent of pessimism. . . . (p. 96)

Strangest and most paradoxical of all [the books considered, which also include Russell Hoban's *The Mouse and His Child*,

Chester Aaron's *An American Ghost*, and Eleanor Cameron's *The Court of the Stone Children*] is the pessimism emanating from Madeleine L'Engle's *Wind in the Door*. L'Engle evidently wrote with the intention of affirming life and the possibility of good; it is the thesis and theme of her story. But in its working out, I think, the thesis fails to carry conviction. In the end, the author's deeply felt dismay over the direction of contemporary American society seems stronger than her theoretical optimism about the conquest of evil and good.

Wind in the Door is a fantasy adventure involving the Murry family, particularly Meg and Charles Wallace, who were also the chief characters in *Wrinkle in Time*. Like *Wrinkle, Wind* moves from the real to the fantasy world and back again. The story begins in an atmosphere of tension and trouble. Charles Wallace, the extraordinarily intelligent six-year-old, is in school and in difficulties. He is set upon nearly every day by other boys, often older and bigger, who beat him up because he is different—too bright, beyond their understanding. He is also, his scientist mother discovers, ill with mitochondritis, a potentially fatal illness which ultimately provides the climactic struggle between life-affirming and life-denying forces.

The opening chapters of *Wind* are full of unhappy comment about the quality of contemporary life. Charles Wallace's troubles are only part of a more general state of things: 'Suddenly the whole world was unsafe and uncertain. Even their safe little village was revealing itself to be unpredictable and irrational and precarious.' Vandalism, lawlessness and violence come up again and again, both in Meg's thoughts and in her parents' conversation. 'Unreason has crept up on us so insidiously,' Mrs Murry says, and speaks despairingly of 'a world . . . so blunted by dishonor and violence that people casually take it for granted.'

The dichotomy is always clear. Good is intelligence, education, reason, order. Evil is 'war and hate and chaos'—but especially chaos. Mindlessness, represented by the vandalism, Calvin's family, the school children who cannot tolerate difference in other children, the teacher who has 'the mind of a grasshopper', is the enemy.

Yet the solutions, when they come, are neither reasoned nor rational. The story spins away from the actual world, with all its ugly, stubborn problems, into fantasy too fantastic by far to have any usable connection with reality. Confrontations with evil take place in outer space and within Charles Wallace's corpuscles. Charles Wallace is no longer a little boy with a specific problem at school, but a symbol for a society ill with irrational evil; his illness is a contest between life and nothingness, love and anti-love, as is, presumably, the sickness in the world.

The climax of the struggle soars into a kind of mystical exaltation. Whether Charles Wallace is to live or die depends upon whether the farandolae within his mitochondria, within his body cells, will consent to 'deepen', as they are meant to do. Meg and Calvin and Mr Jenkins, principal of Charles Wallace's school, are all there in the last chapters, inside Charles Wallace's cells, trying to persuade the farandolae to reject the blandishments of the forces of evil and 'deepen'. Everything is personified, and the outcome depends upon the assertion of love over the evil of nihilism. Of course, the love is sufficient here, as it was in *Wrinkle*, and all is well with Charles Wallace at the end.

My point is not whether *Wind* is a good book (I think it has a number of weaknesses), but whether, having brought into focus real problems of violence and irrationality and the decay of orderly social living, L'Engle's fantasy answers seem satisfying or applicable, or even as vivid as the problems she raises. The answer is quite clearly no.

L'Engle's metaphor fails to bridge the distance between the real and the symbolic experience. The gulf between the apprehension the author feels about the realities of the contemporary world and the affirmation she offers in the fantasy portion of the tale is too great; the reader cannot carry the lessons of fantasy to the problems of the reality. Nothing is transferable, nothing usable. The solution to the generic problem of evil is at one too simplistic—as it also was in *Wrinkle* (it is the same answer)—and too remote from the forms of evil touched on in the realistic portions of the book.

Moreover, the book does not accept its own premises. To irrational evil L'Engle has opposed a good quite as irrational, and has at the same time wrenched the discussion so far away from the terms of the real world that the answers she provides stay within the realm of fantasy, while the problems remain just as firmly part of the real world. The mystical triumph that takes place within Charles Wallace's mitochondria translates only into the lame advice that he must 'adjust' to his difficulties at school. There is really no answer here for Charles Wallace, as there is no answer for the rest of us confronted with a world in which unreason rules. The ultimate effect, it seems to me, is not hopeful, but despairing. (pp. 100-02)

> *Anne S. MacLeod, "Undercurrents: Pessimism in Contemporary Children's Fiction," in* Children's literature in education, *Vol. 21, (Summer), 1976, pp. 96-102.*

DRAGONS IN THE WATERS   (1976)

The O'Keefe family from *Arm of the Starfish* . . . are on hand to join Simon Bolivar Renier and his spooky Cousin Phair on a freighter voyage from Savannah to Venezuela which looks at the outset a bit like L'Engle's version of *Ship of Fools*. The O'Keefe kids haven't outgrown their arrogance—Poly is given to bragging about her family's doctorates real and potential, and excuses Simon's eavesdropping because this is the end of the century when "Things are falling apart. The center doesn't hold." But there's little time for metaphysical wrangles as we are introduced to the Orion's passengers and crew, while Simon survives several attempts on his life and Cousin Phair is murdered. We also learn that Simon's illustrious ancestor is viewed as a messiah and/or traitor (the contradiction is never really smoothed out) by the Quiztano Indians, an idyllically primitive Venezuelan tribe with unusual healing powers. In the rush of new developments . . . , one can be immune to the lure of the Quiztanos or even unimpressed by the murder mystery's solution and still be well entertained. Of all L'Engle's novels, we find this the most satisfying, perhaps because it doesn't demand to be taken with such deadly seriousness. Deduct ten points at the beginning for self-importance and enjoy the rest for a lark. (pp. 470-71)

> *A review of "Dragons in the Waters," in* Kirkus Reviews, *Vol. XLIV, No. 8, April 15, 1976, pp. 470-71.*

L'Engle writes a taut, intricately layered novel, charged with suspenseful twists and faceted into a thoughtful yet climactic conclusion. As in her other books, the power of love and cohesive force of caring are underlying themes, and the per-

ceptively drawn characters . . . are realistic in their conception, credible in their actions, and extremely human.

> *Barbara Elleman, in a review of "Dragons in the Waters," in* The Booklist, *Vol. 72, No. 17, May 1, 1976, p. 1266.*

Madeleine L'Engle's prose has a quality of elegance which charms both young and old alike. . . .

The author has taken many elements to produce a somewhat intricate plot. First and foremost, we have mystery on several levels. Who is Forsyth Phair? Why was he murdered? Who stole the portrait? Then there is an element of the occult, with Charles's dreams supplying some of the necessary clues. Anthropology, in an elementary way, is important too as we learn something of the Quiztano Indians. All in all, the result is a fairly complicated plot which is a bit baffling at times.

One of the merits of this junior novel is that, without being didactic, the author manages to present some high-level values of life which cannot help but impress the discerning reader.

> *Emily Weir, in a review of "Dragons in the Waters," in* Best Sellers, *Vol. 36, No. 5, August, 1976, p. 151.*

L'Engle blends a murder with contemporary politics and a mystical blend of past and present to create an adventure with overtones of a Gothic mystery. The three teen protagonists move throughout the many-layered novel in a rational manner. L'Engle manages to create logical reasons for the protagonists to be able to be the source of so much technical knowledge. Obviously well-researched for information on Venezuela, oil refining, and science, the book supplies a wealth of technical and historical information.

Simon, the hero, goes through a maturing process that is believable even in its mystical aspects. The story is essentially one of light and love which triumphs in the end. The complexity of the plot requires a mature reader who can keep track of several threads. Suspense is excellent and the resolution is plausible.

> *Leona Blum in a review of "Dragons in the Waters," in* The ALAN Review, *Vol. 10, No. 2, Winter, 1983, p. 25.*

The plot is complex and will demand an attentive reader. The ideas of healing, mystical experiences, and love will also demand a reader willing to reflect on the basic mysteries of life. Those who already love L'Engle's work will recognize in this book many of her themes, and it is perhaps a good introduction for those who are unfamiliar with her other work because of the exciting action and suspense. (p. 11)

> *A review of "Dragons in the Waters," in* Kliatt Young Adult Paperback Book Guide, *Vol. XVII, No. 1, January, 1983, pp. 10-11.*

A SWIFTLY TILTING PLANET   (1978)

The cast from the Newbery-award novel, *A Wrinkle in Time* and *A Wind in the Door* returns with the Murry children now grown. They join their parents, Nobel-Prize winners, at Thanksgiving dinner, interrupted by a phone call. The President of the United States calls with news of imminent nuclear war. Shivery and elegant twists of plot ensue as Meg and Charles Wallace employ time travel, telepathy, a Welsh rune and other means to prevent annihilation of the universe by a mad dictator. L'Engle's gifts are at their most impressive here. Her ability to draw attention to familiar details of settings and characters is such that she slips searingly abstract scientific and moral principles into the reader's consciousness, smoothly but surely.

A review of "A Swiftly Tilting Planet," in Publishers Weekly, *Vol. 214, No. 1, July 3, 1978, p. 65.*

[The idea] is for Charles to influence a Might-Have-Been which determines whether Branzillo is descended from the good or the bad line, and thus (?!) whether he will or will not start a nuclear war—a shaky if not asinine premise on which to build an earth-tilting adventure. The Madoc-Maddok-Maddox-Mad Dog family saga grows in interest as Charles gradually figures out all the connections, but—though his mission succeeds somewhere in the 19th century—we never see him as anything but a passive, if uniquely present, onlooker. Meg's role is even more passive and less engaging, as she alternates between wringing her hands in the family kitchen and stroking a strange dog on her attic bed while fretfully following Charles Wallace's adventures in her "kything" mind.

A review of "A Swiftly Tilting Planet," in Kirkus Reviews, *Vol. XLVI, No. 14, July 15, 1978, p. 754.*

This continuation of the Murry/O'Keefe cycle . . . proves that not only is success hard to improve upon, it's difficult to maintain. College-age Meg has married Calvin and is very pregnant, leaving the 15-year-old Charles Wallace to bear the brunt of their running battle with the forces of darkness and disharmony. Would you believe that a mad South American dictator, who just happens to be Calvin's distant cousin, is threatening the world with atomic obliteration in retaliation for the ecological/economic crimes of the developed countries? And that Charles Wallace defuses him by going back in time (with the help of a friendly time-and-space-hopping Unicorn) and altering his ancestry? A lot of readers may not either; most who are old enough to follow the complicated plot will be too old to be sufficiently credulous. Very little here is either exciting or fresh, and much seems carelessly done, e.g., the author has the Spanish still in control of Argentina just before the Civil War, when in reality they were gone by 1820. Though the Murrys are still their same loveable selves and engaged in the same noble struggle to save us all from disaster, this is not enough to compensate for the book's short-comings; fans of the first two books would be well advised to pass this by and switch to a more successfully culminated good versus evil series such as Susan Cooper's quintology. . . .

Chuck Schacht, in a review of "A Swiftly Tilting Planet," in School Library Journal, *Vol. 25, No. 1, September, 1978, p. 160.*

The author picks up themes from earlier books—time as a relative phenomenon, the interdependency of people and events, the importance of the individual—and presents them in an unusual framework. She considers the possibility of one person's altering the course of history by traveling back in time and entering the consciousness of other individuals: "What happens in one time can make a difference in what happens in another time, far more than we realize. . . . Nothing, no one, is too small to matter.". . . On one level the book takes place in the course of an evening; on another it spans centuries. Unfortunately, the different episodes are not well integrated, and the author's tendency to philosophize interrupts the smooth flow of the narrative. Characterization, though, is carefully

handled, and if the book is flawed on a structural level, it is impeccable on an emotional one. (pp. 525-26)

Karen M. Klockner, in a review of "A Swiftly Tilting Planet," in The Horn Book Magazine, *Vol. LV, No. 5, October, 1978, pp. 525-26.*

All modern fantasy has to relate its own private world to that of the existence we are familiar with. . . .

C. S. Lewis, in his Ransom trilogy, tried to bridge across the real and fantasy worlds, and mediate between them. L'Engle has followed Lewis's lead. That is a tricky business and may, unless done with great skill, cause a wrenching of the reader's mind as he leaps from one context to the other. Ideally, the two must be made to merge. In the case of a threatened nuclear war, which is something we have all thought about in starkly real terms, the leap must be aided with skillfully placed stepping stones.

Perhaps a reader who was familiar with the two previous Murry fantasies could make the leap successfully. One wonders, though, if the two worlds of the realistically horrifying and the bizarre context in which the problem is solved really merge for the new reader. While Charles Wallace's struggle is a severe one, and is dexterously handled, and while it involves all the lessons of loyalty, strength of character, and endurance that make modern fantasy such a vital literature, one may question its applicability to the saving of us all.

And yet it has its resemblance to the toils of [J. R. R. Tolkien's] faithful hobbit, Frodo, too insignificant to be noticed, yet holding, in the struggle between his character and the ring, the balance of power in the conflict between good and evil, finally turning the victory to the side of good.

If one can accept the difficult mixture of worlds L'Engle offers, her story is full of the charm and verve one has come to expect from her tales of the Murrys. The mature reader may question whether logic is so useless in solving problems, in fact is such a fault. But Obi-Wan Kenobi would not.

Ultimately, one accepts the story below the metaphorical level on which its action works, valuing the triumph of human freedom over domination; the strength of loyalty, good will, and love; the healing power of forgiveness; the uses of joy; and the recognition of the aid mankind has in his struggles to survive and improve.

A Swiftly Tilting Planet surely will be widely enjoyed. But its highly involved structure may mean that it will be one of those juvenile books read and admired by adults more than by the young.

Paul O. Williams, "L'Engle Travels through Time," in The Christian Science Monitor, *October 23, 1978, p. B8.*

Madeleine L'Engle's dynamic, imaginative fantasy coheres into a complex pattern of adventure and exploration, science and fiction, morality and myth. The time shifts are adroitly engineered and connexions are fused in a variety of ways—family ties, Welsh legends, a community in Patagonia, linguistic manipulation, a nineteenth century novel. Charles Wallace never loses touch with his contemporary world, as he and his sister, Meg, are capable of "kything", a facility which allows communication through thought and feeling.

Madeleine L'Engle's first book about Charles Wallace and his family, *A Wrinkle in Time,* won the Newbery Medal. *A Swiftly Tilting Planet* is in the award-winning class, too. (p. 126)

G. Bott, in a review of ''A Swiftly Tilting Planet,'' in The Junior Bookshelf, *Vol. 45, No. 3, June, 1981, pp. 125-26.*

LADDER OF ANGELS: SCENES FROM THE BIBLE   (1979)

Children aged eight through 14 from 26 countries participated in an art competition entitled ''Children of the World Illustrate the Old Testament,'' held in Jerusalem to mark the International Year of the Child. L'Engle, after traveling to the Middle East to view the paintings, briefly but inspirationally retells 65 Old Testament stories to accompany the full-color, imaginative pictures. The stories, which include Jacob's ladder, the tower of Babel, Noah and the flood, David and Goliath, and many lesser-known tales, will be most appreciated if shared with an adult who will discuss and interpret the selections. The author's intent in these one-page retellings is clearly not to give a message but to suggest and question as well as uplift her readers.

Barbara Elleman, in a review of ''Ladder of Angels: Scenes from the Bible,'' in Booklist, *Vol. 76, No. 9, January 1, 1980, p. 668.*

The venerable author of the children's classic *A Wrinkle in Time* [has written] a series of meditations in prose and poetry.... [This is a] captivating small book.... The interpretation, as expected, is very traditional and very literal. It is definitely Eve's fault; the Lord is elderly and bearded; a good wife is fruitful as the vine. L'Engle's text is steeped in the deceptive simplicity of deep faith.

GraceAnne A. DeCandido, in a review of ''Ladder of Angels: Scenes from the Bible Illustrated by Children of the World,'' in Library Journal, *Vol. 105, No. 1, January 1, 1980, p. 110*

Madeleine L'Engle's readers will not be surprised to find her illustrated account of the Old Testament, *Ladder of Angels,* the most directly and unequivocally religious [of the books reviewed, which also include Sue Ellen Bridgers's *All Together Now,* Joan W. Blos's *A Gathering of Days,* Boris Zhitkhov's *How I Hunted the Little Fellows,* and Ouida Sebestyen's *Words by Heart*]. What seems a bit new is the deftness and clarity with which she sets forth religious neo-orthodoxy within the bounds of the book's two defining elements: the Old Testament and children's art. She draws on both familiar and obscure scriptures to establish a clear theology of God's awfulness and man's fragility. From the beginning she exemplifies what she must see as modern man's greatest sin, Satan's timeless temptation: ''You shall be as God.'' The hubris of man is dramatized in her account of the ''clever but not wise'' erectors of the tower of Babel. She makes it clear that Noah, the intemperate imbiber, could only fashion his wonderful ark because of his obedience to God.

Beyond these famous passages L'Engle selects stories full of mystery and miracle, the very elements which Thomas Jefferson struck from his Bible and which are a scandal to the reasonable, modern mind: Moses' shining veil which radiates God's presence; Jacob's wrestle with the visitant angel at the foot of the ladder; Elijah's fiery ascent in the chariot; Gideon's visit from the Angel of the Lord; and Daniel's deliverance from the lion's den. She directly affirms the fact that ''angels are wholly

real as we'' and constantly proclaims a ''glory that is on the other side of daily life.''

Thus, the Old Testament is not translated into an easy humanism; justice and goodness are not given the same prominence as are God's grandeur and man's finitude. Though the passages are not without warnings against polluting God's world and affirmations of love's inextricable connectedness with life, the dramatization of Abraham's preparation to sacrifice his son Isaac confirms, as it did earlier for Kierkegaard, L'Engle's allegiance to the religious world-view rather than to the humanist one. (pp. 170-71)

Joseph O. Milner, ''The Emergence of Awe in Recent Children's Literature,'' in Children's Literature: Annual of the Modern Language Association Division on Children's Literature and The Children's Literature Association, *Vol. 10, 1982, pp. 169-77.*

A RING OF ENDLESS LIGHT   (1980)

Vicky Austin, 15, and her family have come to Seven Bay Island to be with their dying grandfather in his final months. It proves to be a difficult summer because Vicky faces not only her much-loved grandfather's ever-increasing deterioration but also the drowning of Commander Rodney, a good family friend who died saving a reckless suicide-bent teenager (and Vicky's sometime date); the death of a baby dolphin at the nearby Marine Biology Station; a near fatal accident of a scientist friend; and the death in her arms of a young epileptic child. Tempering these tragedies is the unfolding of Vicky as a person and her newfound relationships with three boys: Zack, who is seemingly repentant after his rescue; Leo Rodney, who wants comfort following his father's death; and especially Adam, with whom she feels a strong affinity while working on his dolphin project. Unexpectedly, Vicky also discovers that she can communicate telepathically with these dolphins; and it is her rapport with them—along with Adam's understanding—that eventually supports her when her despair over death nearly becomes too much. L'Engle writes eloquently about death and life with provocative passages that linger in the thoughts of the perceptive. In terms of action, the plot line is thin but not overly coincidental; though the characters' negative qualities are sometimes forced, their emotional reactions are true, and the story generally portrays people one would like to know. Inclusion of the dolphins brings a new dimension to the author's work, adding wildlife to her circle of concerns. (pp. 1366-67)

Barbara Elleman, in a review of ''A Ring of Endless Light,'' in Booklist, *Vol. 76, No. 18, May 15, 1980, pp. 1366-67.*

With customary grace and firm control of an intricate plot, L'Engle has created another irresistible novel about familiar characters, the Austin family.... [The] descriptions of the playful, intelligent and sensitive [dolphins] alone comprise a tale no one will forget. When a final and devastating blow from fate unhinges Vicky's mind, it is the dolphins who restore her to herself in a scene of incredible intensity.

A review of ''A Ring of Endless Light,'' in Publishers Weekly, *Vol. 217, No. 24, June 20, 1980, p. 87.*

The heroine of this first-person narrative is a fledgling poet who, during a summer, confronts both life's multiple-choices and the more demanding questions of death. The ''choice'' is among three young men: a gorgeous/sexy/rich/thrilling one, a plain/awkward/poor/dull one—and the winner, who falls predictably between these extremes. Vicky first sees Adam at the funeral of a family friend, and during the novel she must deal with her feelings about this death while she and her family also await the imminent demise of their grandfather. He, a former missionary-minister, and indeed the whole family (father, a brilliant but unambitious doctor, a gourmet-cooking, caring and understanding mother, sensitive small brother, et al.) are attractive if unreal characters. They meet the challenge of loss in an idealized but admirable way, calling on abundant reserves of faith and philosophy. There are no fewer than six deaths (as well as a dolphin's), two near misses, and several references to mass tragedies. Every single character is linked to the recent death of a loved one. . . . However worthy— and fashionable—the theme, it's overdone here. The first half is nevertheless interesting and readable, but the last half is strained when we are asked to believe that Vicky actually communicates—intuitively, immediately, unfailingly—with several dolphins who respond to her thought-commands. Most improbably this is placed in the context of a serious project at a marine biology research station. Fantasy and philosophy are L'Engle's forte, but they are not smoothly integrated in this novel.

> *Patricia Dooley, in a review of "A Ring of Endless Light," in* School Library Journal, *Vol. 27, No. 1, September, 1980, p. 73.*

As her confidant, Vicky's grandfather offers advice that combines mild, inoffensive piety and common-sense reflection. Here, Miss L'Engle displays her ability to invest her work with "messages," yet at the same time avoid a didactic tone. Occasionally, in his profound admonitions, the grandfather takes on larger-than-life dimensions that stretch the limits of credibility, and at times the Austins seem a little too good to be true. There's a predicablity about Miss L'Engle's characters that precludes real emotional intensity, but this small peculiarity is compensated for by the story's strength. . . .

[Despite] the story's concern with mortality, this is not a depressing book. Along with Vicky's work with dolphins, the Austins' solicitude for a family of swallows nested precariously over their door becomes a small demonstration of the pervading theme: a concern with preserving and serving life while at the same time accepting death as its inevitable companion. This may not be a particularly original notion, but it is handled with an originality of expression that lends substance to a nicely crafted story.

> *Marilyn Kaye, in a review of "A Ring of Endless Light," in* The New York Times Book Review, *January 11, 1981, p. 29.*

As the other stories about the Austins do, this one shows a spectrum of pleasing family relationships. Vicky is shown interacting with her parents and grandfather, as well as with John, sensitive seven-year-old Rob, and her bright and beautiful thirteen-year-old sister, Suzy, who wants to be a doctor like their father. Mrs. Austin does not work outside her home. Her primary interest is maintaining a happy home for her family, but her special talent is bringing words and music to life: in the evenings she reads aloud from Shakespeare and she sings to the family accompanying herself on a guitar. The values of the family are not materialistic. Spending time together in conversation is important to them. Family love and understanding sustain them in difficult times.

The author is adept at weaving into the story both philosophical and scientific ideas. The title comes from Henry Vaughan, a seventeenth-century English poet and divine admired by Grandfather who quotes him: "I saw eternity the other night/ Like a great ring of pure and endless light." Grandfather observes that "we're out of touch with death." Because he believes that to accept death as a friend is to affirm wholeness and life, he speaks of it to his family and his words bring them comfort. Although the dolphin theme appears incredible, we may be sure it is based on scientific data. While providing many interesting episodes, Vicky's relationship with the three young men seems devised. The emphasis on death may seem depressing to some, yet the author's intention obviously is to stress the beauty and naturalness of death, and not its pain. (pp. 224-25)

> *Marilyn Leathers Solt, "The Newbery Medal and Honor Books, 1922-1981: 'A Ring of Endless Light'," in* Newbery and Caldecott Medal and Honor Books: An Annotated Bibliography *by Linda Kauffman Peterson and Marilyn Leathers Solt, G. K. Hall & Co., 1982, pp. 224-25.*

This fourth book about the Austin family is a dramatic, involved, at times subtle philosophical novel that will appeal to mature readers. Vicky undergoes a massive emotional shock brought on by the death and pain all around her and by her own maturation struggles. She is helped to recover by the support of her family and friends, her grandfather's intelligence and sensitivity, the consolations of poetry and philosophy, and her love for Adam and the dolphins. This last angle, Vicky's communication with the dolphins, lends the book an almost fantasy-like quality that never detracts from the story's realism and believability. A rich brew, the book should reward readers with ample material for thought and discussion.

> *Sharon Spredemann Dreyer, "Annotations: 'A Ring of Endless Light'," in her* The Bookfinder, When Kids Need Books: Annotations of Books Published 1979 through 1982, *American Guidance Service, 1985, p. 206.*

THE ANTI-MUFFINS (1980)

L'Engle adds to the story of the Austin family . . . with Vicky's account of how she, her brother, and their friends accepted the orphaned Maggy, who lives with the Austins, into their anti-muffin group. Muffins are conformists, and the whole story— although it's told with L'Engle's usual grace—has the air of being a vehicle for the message of being oneself and accepting others for what they are. (pp. 154-55)

> *Zena Sutherland, in a review of "The Anti-Muffins," in* Bulletin of the Center for Children's Books, *Vol. 34, No. 8, April, 1981, pp. 154-55.*

Although the book is part of the United Church's series on The Education of the Public and the Public School, the story's theme is the importance of nonconformity rather than the value of education. . . . The characters' religious beliefs are important to them, and sometimes their conversations sound preachy but, in general, the book avoids moralizing. However, this story does not have the depth of L'Engle's full-length novels.

> *Kathy Piehl, in a review of "The Anti-Muffins," in* School Library Journal, *Vol. 28, No. 1, September, 1981, p. 110.*

A HOUSE LIKE A LOTUS (1984)

AUTHOR'S COMMENTARY

[The following excerpt is taken from L'Engle's Regina Medal acceptance speech.]

Last winter, spring, and summer, I spent writing two full 350 pages of a book about Vicky Austin. It wasn't until I had finished the complete second draft that I realized that the book was not meant to be about Vicky Austin at all, but about Polyhymnia O'Keefe, who first came to me in *The Arm of The Starfish*, and who loved Joshua deeply. She appears again in *Dragons in The Waters*. Changing the protagonist of a book is no mere matter of changing names. Poly and Vicky are very different people, with different families, growing up in different geographical parts of the world. But Poly has the intellectual sophistication and the total social naivete that was needed for what this book wanted to say. The theme of *A House Like a Lotus,* in three rather pompous words, is idolatry, disaster, and redemption. It will be out next autumn. It has now gone through five complete revisions, and many scenes have been written and rewritten more times than I can count.

So the honor I am receiving today is an affirmation that it is right to listen to the book, to go where it takes me, even if it is in directions I never expected to go. It is also a warning that I must not compromise, be cheap, capitulate to subtle pressures, and I am grateful for that warning. (p. 31)

> *Madeleine L'Engle, "Acceptance Speech: Regina Medal Recipient," in* Catholic Library World, *Vol. 56, No. 1, July-August, 1984, pp. 29-31.*

An intricate, ultimately overdrawn story about sixteen-year-old Polly O'Keefe and her coming of age. Geographically, Polly moves from her home on Benne Seed Island (off South Carolina) to Athens and Cyprus but what L'Engle really tracks is Polly's emotional course. L'Engle begins in Athens and, through present narrative and frequent recall, contrasts Polly's three days escorted by Zachary Gray to her previous eight months as the protegee of Maximiliana Horne, a wealthy neighbor who dazzled the teenager with art and champagne, philosophical conversations and timely encouragements. What the reader senses for a while—a betrayal back at Benne Seed—is disclosed by the time Polly reaches Cyprus. Max, who first concealed a fatal illness, loses control one night (bourbon for the pain) and reaches out to Polly for more than friendship. Recoiling, Polly runs to friend Renny, who first comforts and then seduces her. She has two more approaches from men before reaching a new equilibrium. L'Engle is such a practiced storyteller that although Max herself and the evolving relationship seem unoriginal, the actual telling is suspenseful. And she makes Zachary different enough from the others in Polly's life to make the Athens episode credible. But although the final revelations, made while Polly works at a conference in Cyprus, are fitting, the conference experience itself unbalances the book. Jammed with a complete set of new characters, customs, and themes, it makes the book too rich—like having three desserts after a roast beef dinner. L'Engle attempts a lot here and accomplishes much of it, but readers may well jump ship before Polly heads for home.

> *A review of "A House like a Lotus," in* Kirkus Reviews, *Juvenile Issue, Vol. LII, Nos. 18-21, November 1, 1984, p. J-105.*

In a sequel to *The Arm of the Starfish* and *Dragons in the Waters,* Polly . . . is the narrator, and her story is told partly in interpolated flashback sequences. The technique is not confusing, but it does grow a bit tedious as the explanation for what was clearly a traumatic event emerges very, very slowly. However, L'Engle writes effectively enough to compensate for this, and Polly's story at both levels is colorful: her present is a trip to Athens and Cyprus, where she makes an amazing variety of friends, gains an admirer, nearly drowns, and periodically voices the author's ideas on ethical or theistic issues; her past has the double crises of having an older woman, a beloved friend who is a lesbian, make advances while drunk and—while still in shock—losing her virginity. These are handled in dignified fashion; characters are vivid and well-differentiated; it's only the pace that's weakened by the structure.

> *Zena Sutherland, in a review of "A House like a Lotus," in* Bulletin of the Center for Children's Books, *Vol. 38, No. 4, December, 1984, p. 70.*

The attempted seduction is frenzied but oblique, and it may pass over some readers' heads. In fact, Polly's recollections are so obsessive, yet vague, that most readers won't understand the fuss. Polly is intelligent in the extreme, wise beyond her years, and she knew that Max was a lesbian with an alcohol problem dying of a rare disease. Her fear and fury seem disproportionate. However, characterization of both Max and Polly is superbly delineated, showing the very human complications of love and friendship. Conversation here takes a sometimes oppressively philosophical bent, but it is still a pleasure to read a leisurely, often powerful, novel for teens about people who think.

> *Roger D. Sutton, in a review of "A House like a Lotus," in* School Library Journal, *Vol. 31, No. 4, December, 1984, p. 91.*

L'Engle's novel is about the complexities of individual beings and of interpersonal relationships; it is about compassion and about loving people for what they are. A mere plot outline cannot do justice to the compelling story. . . . L'Engle's settings are an almost visually integral part of the story, her characterizations have a distinct vitality, and readers will come away with a feeling for what is good about humanity. An eminently caring book by an obviously caring writer.

> *Sally Estes, in a review of "A House like a Lotus," in* Booklist, *Vol. 81, No. 7, December 1, 1984, p. 518.*

Although the flashbacks are gracefully accomplished, the premonition of Max's eventual action comes well before the description of the actual event. Other flaws mar the book: The characters do not just talk; they tend to deliver lofty speeches; and Polly is almost too good to be true. Although the story has absorbing moments, it is hard to identify with Polly's exotic situations and to take her problems too seriously. (p. 59)

> *Ethel R. Twichell, in a review of "A House like a Lotus," in* The Horn Book Magazine, *Vol. LXI, No. 1, January-February, 1985, pp. 58-9.*

While this is a well written novel dealing with the sensitive issue of various kinds and levels of relationships, this reviewer was somewhat disappointed in L'Engle's newest work. Polly's character seems stiff and untouchable. The use of flashbacks can be an effective way to unravel and tell a story, but in this novel, the technique serves to distance the reader from Polly. As a result, the reader does not have an opportunity to truly feel and understand her confusion about Max's behavior. Indeed, only the discerning reader will interpret Max's actions as a pass for Polly and not just the stumbling ravings of a very ill and very drunk woman. As well, the presence of Zachary Gray (from **Moon by Night** and **Ring of Endless Light)** seems unnecessary. Why does aimless, undirected Zack pop from one series to another; is it one way to make this novel seem more realistic, or was his familiar personality needed for plot development? Despite these flaws, the story is not affected and will be welcome fare for the L'Engle fan. (p. 50)

> *Nancy E. Black, in a review of "A House like a Lotus," in* Voice of Youth Advocates, *Vol. 8, No. 1, April, 1985, pp. 49-50.*

MANY WATERS (1986)

Whisked through time after fooling around with their father's computer, the teenage Murry twins, Sandy and Dennys, find themselves stranded in a desert, their bodies ill-equipped to handle the merciless sun, their minds in shock at what has occurred. Rescued by a diminutive man who introduces himself as Japheth, the boys gradually begin to realize that they've time-tripped to a preflood Earth; their hosts are none other than the biblical Noah and his family; and they're all caught up in a struggle of good versus evil from which the ark may be the only escape. Biblical personalities, creatures of legend and imagination, and snippets of prehistory and science coalesce into a tantalizing backdrop for L'Engle's allegorical drama. But as committed as L'Engle obviously is to both her story and her message, the plot gains momentum only toward its close, and characters float in and out so rapidly it's easy to lose track of who's who. Nevertheless, this new episode in the adventures of the unique Murry family . . . is sure to be welcomed by L'Engle's many devoted fans. (pp. 1633-34)

> *Stephanie Zvirin, in a review of "Many Waters," in* Booklist, *Vol. 82, No. 22, August, 1986, pp. 1633-34.*

With a firm grounding in *Genesis,* this is the kind of intricate tale with complex characters and relationships that L'Engle's readers have come to expect. Her ancient world of desert and oasis are stark in their simplicity, yet the evils precipitating the Flood mirror today's. Old customs are flouted; even Noah has quarreled with his father, and young women are wedding nephilim, biblical "giants in the earth," drawn here as fallen angels who change from man to beast at will. . . .

Noah was before Babel; L'Engle's universal "Old Language" is spare, direct, without colloquialisms. Her reiterated descriptions—baboons clapping at dawn, the brilliance of the singing stars—lend a mythic timelessness to the setting. A carefully wrought fable, entwining disparate elements from unicorns to particle physics, this will be enjoyed for its suspense and humor as well as its other levels of meaning.

> *A review of "Many Waters," in* Kirkus Reviews, *Vol. LIV, No. 17, September 1, 1986, p. 1374.*

Like some of its predecessors, this is a mixture of inventive but heavily embroidered plot, strong characters and dialogue, competent writing style, and a mystical element that fails to fuse with the fantasy and thereby weakens the book. . . . Will [the twins] survive? How will they survive and return to their own time? How will the girl they both have come to love, Yalith, forbidden by the Lord to board the ark, be saved? In the end, there is a bit of contrivance, with the seraphim lending a helping hand.

> *Zena Sutherland, in a review of "Many Waters," in* Bulletin of the Center for Children's Books, *Vol. 40, No. 3, November, 1986, p. 54.*

[In] characteristic style, **Many Waters** tells the story of the way in which Sandy and Dennys resist kidnapping, attempted seduction and other nephil-inspired assaults, while helping to reconcile Noah with his dying father and persuading the seraphim to rescue Yalith from the impending Flood. Anyone disposed to carp by pointing out that Yalith, Sandy and Dennys are not recorded in the biblical history of Noah's Ark should be totally disarmed by Miss L'Engle's solution: before the rains come, Yalith is translated to heaven, like her great-great-grandfather Enoch who "walked with God and was not," and the twins are transported back to their parents' present-day laboratory on the backs of two time-traveling unicorns.

Analogies between the Flood and the possibility of nuclear destruction are suggested from time to time, but no didactic conclusion is forced out of them. A description of the bloody birth of a nephil-human baby won't comfort any young female reader prone to nightmares about difficult childbirth. But Miss L'Engle is above all a skillful storyteller, and every admirer of *A Wrinkle in Time* will have fun with **Many Waters**.

> *Susan Cooper, in a review of "Many Waters," in* The New York Times Book Review, *November 30, 1986, p. 40.*

Many Waters is rich with fascinating mythological characters such as the angelic, healing seraphim and the more threatening nephilim both of whom frequently change their earthly forms. . . . This novel does not have the richness of events with which L'Engle developed the age-old struggle between good and evil in *A Wrinkle in Time* and *A Swiftly Tilting Planet.* Still the possibility of modern humanity affecting the course of Biblical events is a novel and potentially controversial idea which will hold the interest of younger teens who have loved earlier L'Engle books.

> *Evie Wilson, in a review of "Many Waters," in* Voice of Youth Advocates, *Vol. 9, No. 5, December, 1986, p. 238.*

As usual, Madeleine L'Engle explores questions of faith, good and evil, the nature of reality, the power of love. She praises love in its "pure" sense but is chiefly concerned in this book with sexual love, from the innocent stirrings of youth to the destructive lust encouraged by the nephilim. Bare breasts, childbirth, interracial (human-nephil) marriage, and attempted seduction are presented graphically, though with propriety. This theme and others make **Many Waters** an eminently discussable book, thought-provoking and absorbing; but too many serious issues are raised and they are largely unrelieved by action or humor. Here there is no Mrs. Whatsit, no Progi-noskes, no urgent, world-saving activities as in the previous ''Time'' books, nothing comparable to balance the many messages and morals conveyed, some rather pointedly—for example, a comparison of the Flood to nuclear holocaust.

Even so, Madeleine L'Engle has given us a tale which firmly holds our attention from a whirlwind (if somewhat contrived) beginning to a reasoned, eucatastrophic conclusion. ***Many Waters*** adds much of interest to the mythology already established in the ''Time'' saga, though like its predecessors in the series it may be read with profit on its own. (p. 44)

Wayne G. Hammond, ''In L'Engle Waters,'' in
Mythlore, *Vol. 13, No. 3, Spring, 1987, pp. 43-4.*

Thomas Locker

1937-

American author/illustrator and illustrator of picture books.

With only three picture books to his credit, Locker is considered an illustrator of genius whose works bring a rare artistic quality to children's literature. Within the framework of remembered childhood experience, his simple, gentle stories address such themes as the companionship of children and their adult relatives, the joy in receiving an animal's trust, the passage of the seasons, and the impact of weather. Locker enhances his texts with panoramic landscapes and seascapes that reflect the terrain of the eastern United States; each of his alkyd and oil paintings emphasizes the beauty of nature and excludes the signs of modern society. Often compared to painters from nineteenth-century European Romanticism and the Hudson River School, Locker meshes the traditional with the contemporary by creating idealized versions of realistic outdoor scenes through sophisticated techniques. His richly textured illustrations are characterized by their expansive sense of space, lifelike detail, and illuminating use of light and shadow. A professional painter who has exhibited nationally and internationally, Locker achieved immediate recognition with *Where the River Begins* **(1984), which focuses on the quest of two young boys and their grandfather to find the source of the river that flows by their country home. In** *The Mare on the Hill* **(1985), the boys patiently gain the confidence of a skittish horse throughout a year depicted by colorful seasons. Locker has also published** *Sailing with the Wind* **(1986), in which a girl at the edge of adolescence and her beloved uncle take an exciting boat trip to the ocean. In addition to the works for which he created both text and pictures, Locker contributed the illustrations to** *The Ugly Duckling* **(1986), an adaptation of Hans Christian Andersen's tale by Marianna Mayer, and** *The Boy Who Held Back the Sea* **(1987), a Dutch tale retold by Lenny Hort.**

Locker's books are noted for successfully projecting enthusiasm for the country, for sustaining the interest of young children, and for involving their readers emotionally. Due to the sophistication of his pictures, some observers question the suitability of the books for children; reviewers are also divided in their appraisal of the texts, which are praised for their precision and thoughtfulness or categorized as bland background. However, critics applaud nearly every aspect of Locker's illustrations—especially his accuracy in reflecting the beauty and drama of nature, the excellence of his designs, his technical expertise, and his sure attention to detail—while acclaiming his picture books for providing readers of all ages with stunning visual experiences.

GENERAL COMMENTARY

LEIGH DEAN

Besides painting exquisite Constable-esque country scenes, Mr. Locker carefully chooses a particular rhythm of Nature to illustrate the passage of time and to provide his palette with the full spectrum of color, light and shadow. What makes his books so spectacularly successful is the harmonious marriage of tex-

tual theme and Nature's theme. . . . Three books, three distinct masterpieces, that's enough to convince me of Thomas Locker's genius.

Leigh Dean, in a review of "Sailing with the Wind," in Children's Book Review Service, *Vol. 15, No. 1, September, 1986, p. 7.*

WHERE THE RIVER BEGINS (1984)

Imagine a thread of a story running through a series of finely-brushed, majestic landscape paintings like those of the Hudson River School. "Once there were two boys named Josh and Aaron who lived with their family in a big yellow house. Nearby was a river. . . . Where, they wondered, did the river begin." Their grandfather agrees to take them on a camping trip to find out. The rest of the text then mostly tells, flatly, what the paintings show much better—unless one has an aversion to an Old Master painting showing two boys skipping over a river on rocks or setting up a campsite. But when the figures need only be specks in the landscape—crossing a drowned field or moving up a dirt lane, under stormy or clearing or twilit skies—then there's something of the experience that many of us have wished for as children, of actually living inside a picture. The boys and their grandfather do find the pond where the river begins, a satisfying quest in itself. But the only real drama is that of entering into this particular 19th-century romantic imagining.

A review of *"Where the River Begins,"* in Kirkus Reviews, *Juvenile Issue, Vol. LII, Nos. 10-17, September 1, 1984, p. J-63.*

Here is a truly beautiful book. The author and illustrator, Thomas Locker, is a painter in the traditional, academic mode. . . . The tale chiefly sustains a panoramic series of landscapes, done in a style reminiscent of the Hudson River School. The narrative itself is simple; the boys and their grandfather encounter very little adversity along the way. A certain tension is supplied by the grandfather's advanced age, which makes it difficult at times for him to keep up with his young charges, and the old man is given the last frame (as it were) of the pictorial narrative, back home again, watching by himself the sunset over the place where the river enters the sea, dual and conventional images of mortality that may or may not be comprehended by the intended audience.

Mr. Locker dedicates this book to his teacher, Joshua C. Taylor, the author of *America in Art* and a pioneering scholar in placing American painting in its cultural context. But perhaps as much of an influence on this book is more recent art criticism by Barbara Novak and others, with its emphasis on the Transcendental implication of the "luminist" tradition in 19th-century American art. Mr. Locker's use of light in his landscapes is clearly dependent not only on his models, like Thomas Cole, but on contemporary scholarship as well. His story, in which youth and age are contrasted, the boys associated with the source of the river, the grandfather with its final union with the ocean, may also owe something to Cole's "Voyage of Life" series.

All this is incidental to children, who will delight in the detailed accuracy of the pictures and will be able to participate vicariously in the two days' journey to the pond "where the river begins." What child growing up in the country has not followed a brook to its source? One does not need a Nile to be an explorer. Thoreau showed us that, and this book is very much in the Thoreauvian vein.

Many illustrators of modern children's literature take their cues from modern abstraction; still others continue to harken back to the pseudomedievalism of Randolph Caldecott. But Mr. Locker looks to the great American tradition of people in the landscape, a territory empty of modern features. There are no highways, no railroad tracks, not even a single telephone pole, and no jet planes or contrails punctuate the sky. The boys and their grandfather inhabit a distinctly anachronistic landscape. No power lines lead into the family home; no air conditioners protrude from the windows. The house has no garage, nor is an automobile or even a bicycle visible. The grandfather and his charges go by foot all the way—no recreational vehicles tear up the turf along the route. They sleep in a tent and cook over an open fire. Except for their clothes, particularly the jogging shoes worn by the youngest, these boys seem to have escaped into the dream world of Rip Van Winkle.

None of this detracts from—and, indeed, it adds to the beauty of—Mr. Locker's book. But it also helps define the nature of his experiment, for surely such it is, a kind of time travel that thrusts us backward. Sophisticated in technique, it is primitivistic in spirit. *The River* should appeal greatly to those of his (adult) readers who regard 19th-century American painting as the grandest natural resource we have, being a kind of portable window into a landscape long since disappeared, an infinite wilderness preserve.

John Seelye, *"Time Travel by Water,"* in The New York Times Book Review, *November 11, 1984, p. 49.*

Both of these elegant productions [*Where the River Begins* and *The Rose in My Garden,* written by Arnold Lobel and illustrated by Anita Lobel] are, I suspect, children's books for adults. This does not mean that they are beyond the reach of all children, but each depends for its effects on a degree of sophistication in the reader. (pp. 247-48)

Thomas Locker makes his debut with a set of superb landscapes, beautifully executed if rather static and lacking in drama. The accompanying text, which describes a rather uneventful camping trip to find the source of the river, is adequate but unexciting. Mr. Locker's pictures belong to the nineteenth-century tradition of American painting. No one would deny their great beauty, but do they really belong to book-art? With the figures blocked out they would look at least equally well hanging on a wall. (p. 248)

M. Crouch, in a review of *"Where the River Begins,"* in The Junior Bookshelf, *Vol. 48, No. 6, December, 1984, pp. 247-48.*

Spectacular paintings reminiscent of nineteenth-century landscape art are a unique and riveting anchor for this simple story. . . . Scenic expanses of eastern woodland hills and valleys glow with an inner light that invites the viewer to step into their beckoning vistas. Whether sunny, dusky, dark, or stormy, the pictures project a quiet drama that almost makes the story an afterthought. It isn't though; with the pictures as a backdrop, the events that occur as the trio traverses the back country prove interesting enough to keep listeners attentive to the end. A beautiful book with refined design, this will attract adults as well as children.

Denise M. Wilms, in a review of *"Where the River Begins,"* in Booklist, *Vol. 81, No. 8, December 15, 1984, p. 591.*

This is a picture book which does not readily fit into a familiar category. It is not clear which age group will enjoy it either, because young children will surely find the illustrations too adult in treatment, very different from the garish action pictures they are used to. Older children may appreciate the skill of the painter, but at the same time will find the text undemanding. Perhaps this is a case of an author falling between two stools. An adult reader could even believe that the artist had the landscapes to hand and added a bit of text and some figures in order to make a book for children. It does not quite come off in spite of the fact that the idea of tracing a mighty river back to its source is always fascinating. Probably adults will enjoy the artist's journey because of the realistic style of the traditionally American paintings. (pp. 220-21)

G. B. Harrison, in a review of *"Where the River Begins,"* in The School Librarian, *Vol. 33, No. 3, September, 1985, pp. 220-21.*

THE MARE ON THE HILL (1985)

The story [in *Where the River Begins*] was a simple one, told in a straightforward, unelaborate fashion, but one that would strike a chord for any reader, child or adult, who ever tossed

From Where the River Begins, *written and illustrated by Thomas Locker. Dial Books, 1984. Copyright © 1984 by Thomas Locker. All rights reserved. Reprinted by permission of the publisher, E. P. Dutton, Inc.*

a leaf in a gutter and then waited for it to come out the other end of a drainpipe. It conveyed, wonderfully, the suspense a person can feel at the bend of a river (or the turn of a page), waiting to see what's on the other side.

The pictures were oil paintings rather than illustrations—deep, richly textured landscapes that might almost have emerged from the Hudson River School. The book established Mr. Locker nearly instantly as an important figure in the world of children's books. His new book, ***The Mare on the Hill,*** is also a beauty. We are back at the same big yellow house where Grandpa and the two boys live, at the edge of the same wide river, next to the same steep cliff. But this time, instead of journeying, we stay close to home.

The story is about a white mare—mistreated by her original owner—whom Grandpa brings home one day as a mate for the family's stallion. The boys plead with Grandpa to let her run free in the pasture. He warns them they will never catch her, but consents. And then we watch as, for the next year, the boys and their horse slowly—very slowly—establish bonds of affection and trust.

Again, it is the paintings that linger in the mind. The scene elements remain constant: barn, house, pasture, gate. Sometimes the turn of a page reveals a nearly identical view to one

preceding it: all that changes is the season, the sky and the light. We see the trees redden and lose their leaves, watch the pasture become buried in snow and then witness its greening in the spring. Gradually, too, we watch the cautious mare move down the hill, closer to the house, until at last she enters the yard and eats a carrot from the hand of one of the boys. In late spring, at the book's close, she gives birth to a foal (that looks—the observant child may say—just like its father).

There is always a danger in picture books whose characters and settings remain this constant that a kind of claustrophobia will set in. Here, the illustrations reinforce and expand one another. The repetition—the way one comes to know even a particular group of trees, a particular bend in the river—provides a rare solidity and feeling of place. Looking at a painting of the barn, one knows what is behind it, where the stone wall is, where the house and silo stand. A child who had studied this book—and was then somehow transported to the spot Mr. Locker evokes in it—would know her way around.

If a weakness exists, it is probably Mr. Locker's portrayal of figures; they never possess the same lifelike quality as his landscapes. The three characters in this story (tiny figures set into the grand sweep of the fields and hillside) are virtually interchangeable, except that their heights differ. One can imagine they were painted in last.

That is a small quarrel though. *The Mare on the Hill* is a luminous, beautiful book (unusually well produced, incidentally, with resolution so fine that individual brushstrokes remain discernible). Mr. Locker's themes—of the changing seasons, the slow passing of time and the gradual development of trust between the boys and the horse—speak to many children. Realistic as the landscapes are, the book has elements of near-fantasy as well. The woods manage to be dark and wild but free of underbrush, the driveway is uncluttered by bicycles or a car, the skyline unbroken by power lines. Grandpa is gray without looking old. The horse simply appears one day. And the children run and play, with no limits but the horizon.

> *Joyce Maynard, in a review of "The Mare on the Hill," in* The New York Times Book Review, *October 27, 1985, p. 36.*

"By Constable out of Stubbs" might be the pedigree of the splendid oil paintings that face each page of text in this book. Traditional English bloodlines are suggested by Locker's handling of skies and horses, but the Connecticut landscape celebrated here is native, and lovingly observed through the changes of season and mutations of light. . . . There are no other buildings in the wide land, no power lines or vehicles in sight; except for some details of clothing, we might be at any point in the past 200 years. . . . As with *Where the River Begins* . . . , Locker allows his audience to contemplate anew—or for the first time—the traditional beauties of landscape.

> *Patricia Dooley, in a review of "The Mare on the Hill," in* School Library Journal, *Vol. 32, No. 3, November, 1985, p. 74.*

Locker, a painter whose works are gallery exhibits and prized by collectors, presents a beautiful successor to his acclaimed first book, *Where the River Begins.* Here he tells a solid story, in a minimum of well-chosen words, about young brothers and the wild mare they ache to befriend. . . . When they find the mare and her foal in their barn . . . , it is a glorious moment. Each event is printed on the reader's mind by Locker's ineffable paintings of the matchless terrain of the Hudson River Valley. The artist's rich colors emphasize changes wrought by the four seasons in the country, largely undisturbed by "progress," where people live in harmony with nature.

> *A review of "The Mare on the Hill," in* Publishers Weekly, *Vol. 228, No. 25, December 20, 1985, p. 66.*

Magnificent, archetypal illustrations glow from the pages of Thomas Locker's *The Mare on the Hill.* . . . Rarely has an illustrator reflected the changes of day and season with such accuracy. Chad [a primary student] says, "I know I have been to these places, but I don't know when."

> *Sam Leaton Sebesta and others, in a review of "The Mare on the Hill," in* The Reading Teacher, *Vol. 39, No. 9, May, 1986, p. 947.*

A farm nestled at the bottom of a cliff by the sea is the magnificent setting for this simple story. . . . The illustrations, as they were in Locker's *Where the River Begins* . . . , are museum-quality easel art reminiscent of the nineteenth century landscapes of Constable and Turner. Through detail, color, and light, Locker is able to convey seasonal weather changes that are truly awe-inspiring. He has also succeeded in this book to involve the reader emotionally in both his story and his pictures. This is difficult to achieve with art of this quality and style.

We often do feel somewhat emotionally removed from the paintings we see hanging on museum walls. An interesting activity for older children might be to visit a museum or look at a series of art prints to determine just how the artist was able to get that emotion across to his or her audience. The students could prepare for this by studying *The Mare on the Hill* and other books by a wide variety of illustrators, especially Donald Carrick, Trina Hyman, or Ann Grifalconi. A discussion about whether or not text helps convey emotion could be a part of this exploration.

> *Melissa Cain, in a review of "The Mare on the Hill," in* The Advocates' Newsletter, *February, 1987, p. 2.*

SAILING WITH THE WIND (1986)

Like Locker's *Where the River Begins* and *The Mare on the Hill,* a series of lovely oil landscapes in the spirit of the Hudson River School, masquerading as a picture book.

Elizabeth welcomes Uncle Jack, who arrives in a sailboat and arranges to take her down the river to the ocean, a trip they make the next day between sunrise and sunset; a few days later, restless, he says goodbye, promising to come back in a couple of years for another adventure. Although the waves loom at sea and there's a storm on the return trip, the pedestrian text completely fails to convey weather's drama (remember the excitement of the storm in McCloskey's *Time of Wonder?*); there are no other events of note. But what matter? The serene progression of earth, tree, and sky, from moonlit mist on the river to lowering clouds on a choppy sea, from sun shimmering through mid-morning pines to sun setting in crimson glory reflected in dappled water, conveys the drama of a beautiful setting, albeit conventionally idyllic.

Locker's high level of technical proficiency, excellence of design and careful detail are rare in books for children: a rewarding visual experience. (pp. 1119-20)

> *A review of "Sailing with the Wind," in* Kirkus Reviews, *Vol. LIV, No. 14, July 15, 1986, pp. 1119-20.*

[This] book is Locker's most visually stunning to date. The spare story . . . is illuminated by the clarity of Locker's narrative oil paintings. With wonderous accuracy, each one expresses a specific time and place, and more importantly, mood in nature. Of all the paintings, though, it is the episode with the coming of the storm, and then the nearness of the rocks, that will grip readers with its frightening reality. Locker has created an enduring work of art.

> *A review of "Sailing with the Wind," in* Publishers Weekly, *Vol. 230, No. 4, July 25, 1986, p. 182.*

Like Locker's first book, *Where the River Begins,* this is a childhood journey remembered. . . . The text mentions enough detail to evoke a sense of a highlight adventure, a special day that begins at 5:30 a.m. in an other-worldly mist. The paintings, a gallery of river scenes and seascapes, set a monumental tone to the episode. Each scene is arrestingly rich with dramatic colors in sky and deep shadings in foliage. Although the characters often appear posed in closeup composition, the overall vision is of an America the Beautiful, with sweeping natural panoramas untouched by factory or highway. That perspective at once moves and stills a viewer of any age.

From The Mare on the Hill, *written and illustrated by Thomas Locker. Dial Books, 1985. Copyright ©* *1985 by Thomas Locker. All rights reserved. Reprinted by permission of the publisher, E. P. Dutton,* *Inc.*

Betsy Hearne, in a review of "Sailing with the Wind," *in* Bulletin of the Center for Children's Books, *Vol.* *40, No. 1, September, 1986, p. 13.*

Locker's striking, luminous landscape paintings are again the stunning backdrop for what is perhaps his strongest story. . . . The river and ocean settings are the true focus of the paintings. The intensely colored scenes are sweeping, dominated by shifting skies, the movement of the water, and a strong sense of space. There is also surprising intimacy suggested by the still, controlled grace of the pictures. Handsome.

Denise M. Wilms, in a review of "Sailing with the *Wind," in* Booklist, *Vol. 83, No. 1, September 1,* *1986, p. 64.*

In the pencil-acrylic-watercolor world of children's books, Thomas Locker's Old-Masterly oil paintings cannot help but make an effect. His landscapes evoke such a rich tradition, and are composed of such idealized clouds, trees, and water, that objections may seem not only carping but a positive affront to High Art. His latest book again offers visual pleasures on a level not often reached in children's book illustration: that said, nevertheless it raises problems. Despite the river journey (entirely through an unpopulated and unpolluted wilderness—

a fantasy voyage) there is a certain monotony to the barely-differentiated settings, inadequately relieved by a sailboat as undetailed as a toy. No dramatically-lit horses, seasonal changes, or even remarkable features of landscape provide interest. The text asserts that this is an adventure, but the relentlessly poetic American pastoral unfolding in the pictures contradicts that claim. The second problem lies with the story. Its symbolic subtext is hardly ambiguous. Elizabeth's bachelor Uncle Jack carries the banner of Romance, and sails his pre-adolescent niece down the river to the ocean she's never seen. Before they're overtaken by a frightening storm they return: "My uncle was a fine sailor. Now I felt safe again." This initial venture onto the waters of adulthood, à deux with a strong and attractive, but "safe" and "understanding" man, with just enough danger to thrill, and a climactic baptism in a drenching rain, ends with the line, "I knew my parents were waiting for me and the day was just beginning." One must suppose that this book's ideal audience is the pre-pubescent girl, but will she look at a picture book? And if this book does find its readers, those readers will not find in it what they may need most: a hint that sailing *against* the wind might be what life is all about.

Patricia Dooley, in a review of "Sailing with the *Wind," in* School Library Journal, *Vol. 33, No. 2,* *October, 1986, p. 178.*

David (Alexander) Macaulay

1946-

English author/illustrator and illustrator of picture books.

Internationally acclaimed for creating striking, monochromatic informational books which characteristically demonstrate the step-by-step construction of monumental imaginary buildings, Macaulay is noted for making complex architectural and engineering procedures both intriguing and comprehensible. By using fictional storylines and characters to outline the development of such diverse structures as an ancient pyramid, a thirteenth-century cathedral, a Roman city, and the underground of a modern metropolis, he enlivens well-researched facts with humor, drama, and social commentary while portraying the political and economic climate of each period with authority. Macaulay initially intended his works to stimulate the curiosity of his audience about how things operate while celebrating the craftsmanship of an earlier age. Since *Castle* (1977), which tells of the erection and ironic destruction of an edifice designed for war, his books have become increasingly pessimistic, displaying evidence that human vanity, economic pressure, greed, and violence have fractured the unifying social and religious visions of the past. Macaulay utilizes a variety of styles in his later works, ranging from *Motel of the Mysteries* (1979), a comical parody directed at archaeologists, to *Baaa* (1985), a controversial fable on the fate of mankind. An architect and art teacher who resides in the United States but retains his British citizenship, Macaulay characteristically illustrates his books with precise pen-and-ink drawings featuring close-ups, cut-away sections, and panoramic double-page spreads. His pictures also reflect Macaulay's use of perspective to intensify size and space. Popular with both children and adults, several of Macaulay's works have been used in college classrooms, and *Underground* (1976) is considered a standard reference source by many architectural firms.

Critics admire Macaulay for his originality, wit, and technical virtuosity as well as for the beauty and exactness of his well-integrated, historically accurate drawings and texts. Before the publication of *Baaa*, reviewers pointed out only minor deficiencies in Macaulay's works, such as his rudimentary human figures and occasionally obtrusive comic details; in contrast, several observers strongly object to the nihilistic view he expresses in *Baaa*, an attitude they consider inappropriate for children. However, most comentators agree that Macaulay has made a distinctive contribution to children's literature by providing informative, entertaining, and thought-provoking books on buildings and the societies they illuminate.

Macaulay has won numerous American and European awards. Two of his works were designated Caldecott Honor Books, *Cathedral* in 1974 and *Castle* in 1978. *Cathedral* also received the Deutscher Jugendliteraturpreis and the Silver Slate Pencil Award in 1975. *Pyramid* was both a *Boston Globe-Horn Book Honor Book* and a *Christopher Award* winner in 1976. The American Institute of Architects presented Macaulay with their medal in 1977 for his contribution as "an outstanding illustrator and recorder of architectural accomplishment." He was nominated for the Hans Christian Andersen Illustrator Medal in 1984.

(See also *CLR*, Vol. 3; *Something about the Author*, Vols. 27, 46; *Contemporary Authors New Revision Series*, Vol. 5; *Contemporary Authors*, Vols. 53-56; and *Dictionary of Literary Biography*, Vol. 61: *American Writers for Children since 1960: Poets, Illustrators, and Nonfiction Writers.*)

GENERAL COMMENTARY

VALERIE ALDERSON

It is difficult to believe that David Macaulay's *Cathedral . . .* was his first book, for it conveys all the professionalism and authority of an established writer. Indeed, the unsuspecting reader might be forgiven for thinking the author-illustrator to be an established scholar who has turned to children's books to satisfy a need to find a wider audience for his enthusiasms.

In fact, *Cathedral* was written because its author wanted to become an illustrator and could not find a suitable text. That the book was an immediate success seems to have come as a complete surprise to its author and publisher although not to its readers.

David Macaulay is the first to deny any pretensions to being a writer, but he certainly has a gift for putting across the complexities of construction engineering which should be the

162

envy of most of our writers of children's non-fiction. No doubt his training as an architect has contributed much, giving him a thorough understanding of the principles behind the work he describes, but, in addition, he exploits his gifts as an illustrator to underline and expand his text.

It is in his stark, black and white illustrations that his books' great strength lies. Mr Macaulay is much pre-occupied with the use of perspective to give impressions of size and space and in *Cathedral* he demonstrates this par excellence.

Superficially, many of his drawings may seem strangely contorted, the lines twisted out of their conventional angles, but as one looks closer, one discovers the uncanny heights and depths of his buildings. The great west front of his cathedral leans up and back as though one were indeed standing in the precinct before it; or one can look dizzily down into the nave from the partially completed vaulting, teetering on a beam turned suddenly narrow by fear, reaching out for the comfort of chair or table to restore one to solid ground.

Despite three more books and another on the way, *Cathedral* is still David Macaulay's favourite, the one he feels comes closest to putting over his ideas.

In both *City . . .* and *Pyramid . . .*, he has tried to repeat the pattern begun in *Cathedral. Pyramid* comes closest, for again it relates the undertaking of a massive building project, with the minimum of mechanical equipment, depending primarily on unlimited manpower and a great deal of ingenuity. It is fascinating, for example, to discover at least one theory of how the Egyptians built without those essential aids of modern building, scaffolding and cranes.

City is somewhat different, for here the emphasis falls much more on the people who inhabit the buildings. Mr Macaulay has taken for his theme a hypothetical Roman city designed for a maximum of 50,000 inhabitants. He has followed through its building, from the construction of the outer walls, the aqueducts, cisterns and sewers, to the final completion of the buildings 125 years later when the population has reached its projected maximum.

In this book, the strength lies not only in his drawings of buildings, but in the way the author has brought the inhabitants to life. For most children, a Roman city is no more than so much rubble, but Mr Macaulay has taken the stones and rebuilt them into shops, tenements, houses, public baths, and filled them with the everyday bustle of a living town.

Suddenly, a Roman apartment begins to look very like its sparsely furnished modern counterpart; the eating places and their customers are not so very different from a modern snack bar.

One of David Macaulay's motives in his writing (and speaking) is the desire to make people, and especially children, look at the buildings around them; to activate in his audience a curiosity about how things are made and how they function. This finds specific expression in his book *Underground. . . .*

Here he has taken a new line, for he describes the book as a kind of guide to what happens *beneath* a modern city: the sewers, electric cables, water mains, subways and so on which are an unseen but essential part of that city's existence. Perhaps here there is more of the teacher coming out, for he admits to a sincere love of teaching, though as a two-way process rather than as instructor pontificating to unquestioning students.

And after *Underground* what? At present David Macaulay is working on *Castle* another "construction" story. He has done the reading, looked at examples and it now remains only for him to design the finished book, write the text and complete the illustrations. After that, he is adamant that there will be no more in that genre. . . . So while one regrets the endless possibilities that will not be taken up, it is good that David Macaulay knows enough to stop before he gets stale.

He has been working on a project for turning *Cathedral* and *City* into animated films, but is presently deadlocked over the use of colour which he considers unnecessary. . . .

Maybe a suitable text will come along, for he still protests he is not really a writer.

But it will have to be the right text, for he has decided views on the function of illustration. He does not subscribe to the popular opinion that all children's books should have pictures "to make them attractive". His view is that illustration should have a distinct function as an essential part of the book and that if the text can stand by itself, then it should do so. . . . Whatever Mr Macaulay does, however, one thing is certain: he is going to take time to sort out his ideas and let no one hustle him into a hastily conceived and ill-considered project.

Valerie Alderson, "A Sense of Size and Space," in The Times Educational Supplement, *No. 3197, September 10, 1976, p. 41.*

PAUL GOLDBERGER

When David Macaulay set out in 1973 to explain Gothic architecture, he contrived the story of an imaginary town in 13th-century France, a composite of many real towns, that took it upon itself to erect a cathedral. The cathedral was to be the biggest and the best in all of France, and the townspeople went methodically about their task for 86 years until it was finished.

Their story was told in *Cathedral,* Mr. Macaulay's first book and the model for four that have followed: *City, Pyramid, Underground* and the most recent, *Castle.* Each of the books has the author's splendid black-and-white line drawings, exquisitely intricate, precise communicators of information; each book tells an imaginary story much like the one in *Cathedral.*

In *Castle,* Macaulay traces the building of a 13th-century English castle in Wales. It is an ordered story told in an ordered style, with remarkable clarity: "Rounded towers were located along both walls, making it possible for soldiers to observe the entire perimeter of the structure," Macaulay writes, giving us in a single phrase not only a clear physical image but a concise understanding of how a certain architectural form we associate with castles actually evolved.

That is Macaulay's strength as a writer—he explains the making of a cathedral or a castle in terms of process, not merely product, and he defines process as broadly as possible. For example: In *Castle* we are told the story of England's conquest of Wales as well as the story of the making of a building; for indeed, the process of building the castle was as much part of a military scheme as it was an architectural one. And we are made to feel not only the life of the castle's residents, but also the life of the entire town that arose to service the castle and of the soldiers who attacked and defended it.

Macaulay sees the world with a writer's grace, but with an engineer's clarity. His drawings have been justly praised since his first book, and the set he has prepared for *Castle* is no letdown. His style as an artist has elegance and, on occasion,

From Cathedral: The Story of Its Construction, *written and illustrated by David Macaulay. Houghton Mifflin Company, 1973. Copyright © 1973 by David Macaulay. All rights reserved. Reprinted by permission of Houghton Mifflin Company.*

wit, although his talents were actually at their very best in *Cathedral* and in the unusual and impressive *Underground.*

The only problem with Macaulay's writings is that they are almost too methodical. There is a sense in all of these books of a neat, ordered world, of systems that, given enough calm and thoughtful attention, will reveal themselves clearly. Of course, it doesn't always happen that way in the physical environment; much of the design of things as great as cathedrals and as mundane as subway lines is by happenstance, and does not always fit into the orderly process he assigns to it. His book *City,* for example, which is a chronicle of a Roman settlement, tells of a place of civilized order, where chariots move only at specified hours and buildings respect what we would call zoning laws. In *Cathedral,* the design of the Gothic edifice is set at the start of work and not varied at all during construction.

But still, what a splendid teaching tool Mr. Macaulay's calm vision is! *Underground* could serve as an engineering primer, so clear and relaxed is its discussion of such usually deadening subjects as building foundations and sewage lines. *Cathedral* has not been surpassed as an introduction to the brilliance of Gothic architecture and the process of is creation. *Castle* has a topic that is slightly less easy to rhapsodize about—no Welsh castle is Chartres or the Pyramid of Cheops—but Mr. Macaulay does it honor nonetheless. The new book is a fine addition to what has become, in just four years, a set of standard works.

Paul Goldberger, "How to Build a Castle," in The New York Times Book Review, *November 13, 1977, p. 38.*

DORIS GRUMBACH

I have an apostolic purpose in this early fall column. I want to convert as many persons as possible to six books written and illustrated by David Macaulay. . . . The first five were clearly intended for intelligent children and adolescents: *Castle . . .* , *Cathedral . . .* , *City . . .* , *Pyramid . . .* , and *Underground. . . .* The last, *Great Moments in Architecture . . .* , is a wildly irreverent volume that makes fun with pictures of every kind of architectural subject. It is for an adult audience, though I can imagine a very informed child laughing at some of the drawings.

The five children's books are large—9½ inches by 11 inches. Each is a graphic, thorough exploration of the construction, and the workings, of its subject. *Underground* is the only book with a modern subject. . . .

My favorites are the ones with historic subjects. . . .

Macaulay's best achievements are his two medieval volumes, *Cathedral . . .* and *Castle. . . .*

[In *Cathedral* there] is one magnificent view from the beams and rafters of the unfinished roof, looking down from a great height to the nave. . . .

[In *Castle*], Macaulay's learning informs his imagination. We are provided with the best possible stance from which to watch the castle, its outer curtain, the moat, rooms, towers, and the outside huts go up. . . . Wonderful story, brilliant drawings.

I have left out *Pyramid,* an equally interesting book whose nature and contents you can gather from the others I have described. Lucky the child who learns about the past from David Macaulay's illuminating books. And, come to think of it, happy the adult who never quite understood how those stones were placed to make a pyramid, or what goes on under his feet on a city street, and now does. Me, for instance.

Doris Grumbach, "Well-Built Books," in Saturday Review, *Vol. 5, No. 24, September 16, 1978, p. 49.*

JOYCE A. THOMAS

Acknowledged as classic children's non-fiction, *Cathedral, Castle, City* and *Underground* exemplify some of the best in non-fiction illustration. . . . Although depicting imaginary structures and locales, Macaulay is always accurate, solidly rooting the imagined in historical reality. His detailed, black and white line drawings are placed directly alongside their appropriate text, with diagrams and labels completing the wealth of pictorial and textual information presented. Macaulay's illustrations are often impressive in themselves, always provide an accurate complement to his text, and extend his words in a way that allows the reader-viewer to live the building of that castle or that cathedral. Instead of passively witnessing, one imaginatively participates. Much of the drawings' lively quality derives from an effective use of size and scale: one literally sees each structure evolve and grow like any organism, while also observing the human creators who, in time, become dwarfed by their own child.

Detailed diagrams, perspectives ranging from the close-up to the aerial shot, small pictures, full-page and two-page spreads—all combine to yield a graphically comprehensive, always lively montage. The architectural subject is rendered in architectural drawings and diagrams which convey the spatial and structural perspectives of the architect as well as the stages of a structure's evolution: from idea to drawn plan, from boulder to laid stone, from inhabited building to empty ruin. Macaulay could have used photographs or turned to splashy colored images which might appear to suit the historical and romantic grandeur of the castle and cathedral, but none of these would have given that architectural activity he sought; none would have reactivated these structures of the past.

Joyce A. Thomas, in a review of "Cathedral," "Castle," "City," and "Underground," in Children's Literature Association Quarterly, *Vol. 6, No. 4, Winter, 1981-82, p. 27.*

RICHARD AMMON

Behind an unassuming, genuine friendliness is an articulate, well versed young artist who is acclaimed for his books on the construction of architectural structures.... "Although I'm grateful to children for my popularity, I do not necessarily create books just for them," Macaulay said. "Rather, I try to write and illustrate books for everyone to enjoy."

Indeed, Macaulay has brought a fresh, creative approach to the seemingly dull subject of construction. In *Cathedral, Pyramid,* and *Castle,* he has depicted the step-by-step process of constructing these great edifices. In each book, large pen-and-

From Cathedral: The Story of Its Construction, *written and illustrated by David Macaulay. Houghton Mifflin Company, 1973. Copyright © 1973 by David Macaulay. All rights reserved. Reprinted by permission of Houghton Mifflin Company.*

ink drawings invite the reader to pore over the rich details. From the authentic, easy-to-follow texts, one gains a sense of the tremendous achievement of the people who built these architectural monuments without modern technology or equipment. (p. 374)

After graduating from the Rhode Island School of Design in architecture, Macaulay taught one year of junior high school art. A year later, while working as a designer, he knew he wanted to create something with his name on it—namely a book. So he began submitting manuscripts to publishers in Boston. In one proposal, he had drawn a picture of some people standing in front of a cathedral. Although the editor didn't especially care for the story, he did like the picture of the cathedral. Soon David was off to Amiens, France to study and to make sketches of a real cathedral for his first book, *Cathedral.*

He wrote and illustrated his third book, *Pyramid,* because he wanted to go to Egypt. "Cairo is so mysterious," he said, "that I'm sure you could disappear into the night and no one would ever know. But I was able to climb to the top of the great Pyramid, something you're not legally permitted to do anymore."

As a child, Macaulay didn't play much with his sister or brother who is seven years younger. "I believe that playing alone helped to develop my imagination. In fact, to this day it is the dreaming of the ideas that is the most fun."

A Mickey Mouse telephone sits near one of the large drafting tables where David does much of his work. There he will often sit for hours doodling, thinking, and scribbling. But from these scratches will come a book. In his sketch books—large bound volumes—there are series of drawings that become more and more refined, reflecting the evolution of his stories.

Although developing his ideas is enjoyable for Macaulay, writing is laborious. To the reader the words seem to flow smoothly, belying what David readily admits is the most difficult aspect of making books. "I write and rewrite and revise and write some more until I'm satisfied," he said.

But the drawing of each line of detail is the most tedious part of composing a book.... [He] listens to music while carefully drawing each strand of hair, each brick, and each stone.

The development of Macaulay's artistry may be shown by a comparison of the shading techniques in *Cathedral* and in *Unbuilding.* For example, on page 50 of *Cathedral,* the textures are uniform, whereas on page 7 of *Unbuilding,* he produced the effect of sunlight filtering onto the city street. (p. 376)

Although most of his books are based upon facts, readers may have noticed certain subtle features. For example, *Underground* is a subterranean journey under the foundations of skyscrapers and through the utilities and subways buried beneath city streets. But in a picture of an excavation there is a hand and a skeleton protruding.... On other pages there are an elephant's feet ... and an alligator in the sewer....

In *Unbuilding* an Arab sheik buys the Empire State Building and has it dismantled for shipment to the Middle East—a startling but not too far-fetched idea. Young readers are most amused by the hand of a gorilla, presumably that of King Kong ..., extending onto the picture.

But it is in *Motel of the Mysteries* that Macaulay unleashed his humor and imagination. In this parody of the opening of King Tutankhamen's tomb, Howard Carson discovers the burial chamber (a locked motel room) of the ancient civilization Usa.

After cataloging every item, from the Great Altar (the television) to the Sacred Urn (the toilet), this hard-working archaeologist was not too busy to entertain his helpers by standing in front of a spotlight and making hand shadow images of a rabbit on the door of the tomb. (p. 377)

David rejects the notion that, because of his background in architecture, he was destined to write and illustrate books of this genre. Instead, he claims that his life has unfolded haphazardly and that he has no idea what he might be doing ten years from now. He ought to know, however, that there are a great many children, librarians, teachers, parents, and some architects who hope he continues writing and illustrating. (p. 378)

Richard Ammon, "Profile: David Macaulay," in
Language Arts, *Vol. 59, No. 4, April, 1982, pp.
374-78.*

MARY FURNESS

A rare combination of education and pleasure is to be found in David Macaulay's books. Each of them recounts the story of a construction, be it castle, city, pyramid or cathedral, from beginning to end, and each is illustrated by beautiful and clear black-and-white line drawings which make the most complicated building process comparatively easy to understand. The pictures are informative and at the same time full of charm and character; we are shown an imaginary Master Engineer in charge of building the thirteenth-century castle, and his dog, as well as the tools that were needed to build it. Each book has a glossary of technical terms.

The author takes in precise dimensions of parts of buildings and details such as, for example, the location and number of lavatories, as well as the wider social context. He explains how it came about that a castle, cathedral or city was built, what it was built for, where the money and materials came from and who were the different craftsmen involved. A blacksmith, for example, was always of primary importance in order to repair and replace tools as they wore out. . . .

The castle [in *Castle*] is besieged by Welsh soldiers using large timber catapults, battering rams, siege towers, and sappers try to dig tunnels to undermine the foundations. All these are shown in action so that it is possible to see exactly how they work. . . .

[In *Cathedral,* there] are vertigo-inducing drawings of men suspended on platforms high above the ground as they build the vaults or the steeple.

The account of the building of a Roman city, in *City,* is even more complex. . . .

Pyramid continues the excellent work. The only slightly odd one out in the series is *Underground,* an account of the workings and construction of everything that goes on underground—foundations of buildings, sewers, drains, gas and telephone cables, etc. The subject does not naturally appeal to the imagination as much as the others, nor is it conducive to such beautiful drawings especially as, in order to make them clearer, it has been found necessary to use a colour—a rather unattractive mustard yellow. But David Macaulay does much to lighten the rather technical bias of the drawings by inserting charming and irrelevant dogs all over the place. These are books which will be found equally fascinating by the technically-minded child and the adult alike.

Mary Furness, "The Art of Building," in The Times
Literary Supplement, *No. 4138, July 23, 1982, p.
797.*

JON STOTT

While it is generally recognized that many biographies and histories written for children contain the beliefs both of their authors and of the times in which they are written, it is not often noted that this is also true of other types of juvenile nonfiction. Each of the six architectural books written between 1973 and 1980 by English-American author-illustrator David Macaulay is a detailed and accurate description of the planning and consideration of a specific type of building or city in a particular setting. But taken individually and as a group, these books also present Macaulay's own interpretation of the nature and value of the interrelationship between the various constructions and the socio-cultural beliefs of their builders. While the author expresses in each of these books his admiration for the architectural and mechanical processes involved, he is critical of the human vanity and the economic pressures which often influence the builders. Macaulay salutes the unity of purpose which led to the creation of the pyramids, cathedrals, and Roman cities, and he disapproves of the destructive forces which led to the building of an early Renaissance castle and to the demolition of a modern skyscraper. In a sense, his books are nostalgic, although factually accurate, looks-back to earlier ways of life, and an implicit criticism of many of the attitudes of the modern world.

In *Cathedral . . . , City . . . ,* and *Pyramid . . . ,* Macaulay outlines the planning and construction of works in the High Middle

Ages, Augustan Rome, and Ancient Egypt respectively. Each of the constructions he describes, the Gothic cathedral at Chutreaux, the Po Valley city of Verbonia, and the pyramid of a twenty-fifth century B.C. pharaoh, are imaginary. As the prefaces note, however, the description of the building of each is based on known architectural and engineering practices.

What first strikes one on reading these three books is Macaulay's admiration for the careful planning and craftsmanship that went into the building of the cathedral, city, and pyramid. Most of the pages depict, in words and pictures, the development of plans, gathering of materials, and stage-by-stage construction. In all cases, hundreds of workers, performing countless different tasks, labor toward a preconceived goal, the completion of a clearly envisioned structure. In the case of the pyramid and cathedral, work is carried on under the direction of a master builder; for the Roman city, there is a master plan. There appears to be no wasted effort; even quarried blocks are numbered so that they may be fitted easily into the grand design. Pride in craftsmanship is evident. In painting an intricate maze on the roof of the cathedral vault, workers "were eager for the web to appear perfect even if no one could see the lines from the ground." When one considers the vastness of the structures, the length of time necessary to complete them, the limited scope of each worker's task, and the lack of motorized equipment, one can understand more fully Macaulay's admiration.

More evident on later readings of the books is Macaulay's interest in the motivating forces behind the construction. The author is well aware that the vanity of human wishes is an important factor. The cathedral of Chutreaux was conceived because, with other towns building similar structures, the villagers "did not wish to be outdone, on earth or especially in heaven," and so decided to build "the longest, widest, and most beautiful cathedral in all of France." Numerius Septimus donated money for a temple and a new market in the Roman town of Verbonia; then "so that everyone would know of his generosity, he commissioned a marble statue of himself holding a bust of Ceres." In deference to an eminent predecessor who had a magnificent pyramid, the pharaoh decrees that his own shall be ten feet lower, but makes sure that it is built on a site twenty feet higher.

While human vanity does influence the creation of these buildings and cities, it is not so important as are spiritual or cultural concerns. About the builders of the cathedral, Macaulay notes, "their singlemindedness, their spirit, and their incredible courage are typical of the people of twelfth-, thirteenth-, and fourteenth-century Europe, whose magnificent dreams still stand today." Similarly, "the pyramids continue to serve as a tribute to those who so skillfully organized the efforts of thousands of people in an attempt to deny the finality of death and the limitations of time by leaving behind something that would last forever." Although less permanent than these two buildings, and built for secular reasons, Roman cities like Verbonia were also created with a unity of purpose: "no matter what brought about their creation, they were designed to serve the needs of all the people who lived in them."

Through the details that he includes in both illustrations and text, Macaulay implicitly emphasizes the fact that although the huge buildings dominate the landscape, particularly in *Pyramid* and *Cathedral,* they are a part of the daily and seasonal rhythms of the life around them. Each book contains a series of panoramic double-spreads depicting the site and the building in various stages of construction. These illustrations suggest that the building or city is a part of the landscape, almost growing naturally from it, and indicate the time that passes while construction proceeds. Winter and the flooding of the Nile influence the erection of the cathedral and the pyramid respectively. Daily activities continue: children swim, birds raise their young, unbeknownst to each other a cat and mouse sleep in close proximity. Death takes its toll: master builders grow old and die, workers are killed in construction accidents.

One illustration that epitomizes the sense of unified purpose found in *Cathedral, Pyramid,* and *City* is found early in *Cathedral.* It illustrates the discussion of the early planning stages. Sitting on an ecclesiastical throne, a bishop offers a sign of benediction. In a semi-circle below him, the six dour-faced clergymen who comprise the chapter clasp bags and a chest of money. In front of them stands the master builder, smiling and holding a pair of dividers. Unnoticed to one side, a mouse scampers by. With the exception of the mouse, the figures in the picture are balanced. Spiritual power, money, and technical ability were all needed for building the cathedral. At the same time, the little mouse, unnoticed by the eight people, symbolizes the ordinary life which continues.

Underground . . . , Castle . . . , and *Unbuilding . . .* are markedly different in theme and tone from the three earlier books. While each follows a similar format to the earlier volumes—discussion of planning, materials, and implements, and stage-by-stage construction—none contains the only slightly qualified admiration found in the earlier books. As in the first three books, Macaulay notices that vanity and economics play important roles, but he does not notice the type of cultural or religious purpose that he had discovered before.

Written two years after *City, Underground* is almost the direct opposite of the earlier work. Whereas Verbonia is an example of careful, farsighted planning, and of the concept that a city should be designed to meet the needs of all its people, the modern metropolis is a disorganized, although relatively efficient hodge-podge. The earlier books had begun by asserting that, while the specific buildings were fictional, the processes were accurate. In *Underground,* the process itself is fictional: "although the information is accurate, the step-by-step way in which it is presented is somewhat idealistic. In most cities, especially those that have grown gradually over many years, the various functions are all happening at the same time and often in the same place."

Macaulay refers to "these amazing and often indispensable systems [which] work so well." But, in spite of his professed admiration for the utility of what he describes, he suggests, through many of his visual details, a certain uneasiness with modern subterranean architecture. In two illustrations there are billboards with ironically significant implications. On the title page, one states "This End Up," and another, "Things are Looking Down." Perhaps the first suggests that the modern world has lost a sense of direction and must be given one; the second, in addition to drawing attention to the focus of the following pages, may indicate the author's lack of optimism for the future: symbolically, things may not be looking up. Later, a peeling and faded billboard proclaims: "A Masterpiece: New Book by David Macaulay: Pyramid." While this may merely be a joke about an earlier work by the author (a not uncommon joke in picture books), it may also suggest that in the modern, cluttered metropolis, the architectural wonders of the old world are as easily ignored as an outdated sign.

Other visual details underscore the implicit ironies of *Underground.* Three workmen, one of whom leans on a shovel, look at an excavation, oblivious to a half-exposed skull; nearby a scowling dog eyes a fire hydrant which he cannot reach. The immediate problems of the underground network are more important than the just uncovered past. A catch basin contains modern artifacts: a broken whiskey bottle and beer cans. A double-spread cross-section drawing reveals an alligator slinking along a sewer pipe toward two unsuspecting rats, one reclining Stuart-Little-like with his legs crossed. As reviewers have noticed, this picture is humorous; but it also emphasizes unnaturalness. Alligators should be in jungle rivers, not urban pipes. Throughout the book, natural vegetation is noticeably absent, with the exception of scraggly potted trees.

On a first reading, *Castle* might appear to be a reversion to the style and themes of Macaulay's earlier works. As before, he describes the many years involved in planning and constructing, by manual labor, a major building. He even appears to begin the book with a note of praise similar to that found in *Cathedral* or *Pyramid:* ''this combination of castle and town in a military program displays both superior strategical skill and the farsightedness required for truly successful conquest.'' But, a careful reexamination, particularly of the pictures, suggests that this opening statement is ironic. Whereas the title pages in the earlier books had shown the sites before construction began and the final double-spread, the completed buildings, *Castle* marks a departure. The title page is similar, showing the sea-girt peninsula. The final page, however, is a nighttime view in which the moon shines down on the castle, now in ruins, two centuries after construction. The accompanying text states: ''by that time master James's mighty castle stood partially roofless and completely neglected except as a quarry for new buildings, and his once impressive town wall was now more of a nuisance to the town fathers than a necessity.''

What most differentiates the building of the castle from that of the cathedral or the pyramid is the motive underlying the construction. It is created neither as a monument to human vanity nor as an expression of religious beliefs. It is one of many bastions designed to subjugate the Welsh in the fifteenth century. But, in that respect it was unsuccessful; indeed, the Welsh nearly managed to overrun it. In the end, they are not subdued and are invited to become part of the new town. Interestingly, eight of the book's last twelve pages deal with the Welsh attack. Whereas *Pyramid* and *Cathedral* closed with a celebration of the completion of building, *Castle* ends with an account of the beginnings of destruction. Thus the opening remarks about ''the superior strategical skill and the farsightedness'' turn out to be ironic.

Interstingly, *Castle* bears the dedication ''to the past—farewell.'' It is as if Macaulay found in the fifteenth century the end of the types of ideals that had led to the creation of the other works he had so admired. Not surprisingly, then, his most recent work, *Unbuilding,* outlines destruction rather than construction, and is dedicated ''to those of us who don't always appreciate things until they are gone.'' Set in the future, 1989, it recounts the hypothetical demolition of an actual building, New York City's Empire State Building. Built in less than two years, it was ''forced to grow upward because of both the high cost of land and the desire to build as much rentable floor space as possible on it.'' Now, less than sixty years later, it is torn down so that the facing and other identifiable parts may be shipped to the near East by Prince Ali Smith, head of GRIP, Greater Riyadh Institute of Petroleum. He will use the salvaged parts in building a new headquarters for his oil business.

From Underground, *written and illustrated by David Macaulay. Houghton Mifflin Company, 1976. Copyright © 1976 by David Macaulay. All rights reserved. Reprinted by permission of Houghton Mifflin Company.*

As in the earlier works, Macaulay describes the step-by-step process, but there is no master builder, only the demolition firm of Krunchit and Sons. The plan is announced, appropriately, on April Fools' Day, and the project begun on September 5, the day after Labor Day. In the illustrations, one notes large numbers of men watching one or two others working, perhaps an implicit comment on modern labor. It is certainly a contrast to the almost total activity pictured on the pages of the earlier volumes. As well, one notices the lack of natural growth. Unlike the earlier buildings, which seemed to grow out of, and so to be a part of, the topography, the Empire State Building is completely surrounded by other skyscrapers. In one drawing, two men work dismantling girders, oblivious to a hairy, giant hand in one corner. The reference to King Kong is more than a visual joke. It is an implicit comment on the modern world's failure to recognize the legends associated with its architectural monuments.

Although the book ends with a May Day dedication of Empire State Park, built on the site of the historic building, and with the return of a tiny amount of green space into the concrete jungle, the dominant tone is satiric and critical. The motivation for both the building and dismantling have been almost totally economic. No unifying social or religious vision exists in the modern megapolis. For Krunchit and Sons, this is just another job. In fact, in the conclusion it is even reported that the company has presented Prince Ali Smith with another estimate, this one for dismantling the Chrysler Building.

The point of view that emerges from the six books is, in many ways, pastoral. While Macaulay admires the skilled planning and craftsmanship involved in all the processes, and while he recognizes that human vanity and economics have been important factors influencing building in each of the eras, his greatest admiration is for works of the pre-Renaissance period. The pyramid and the cathedral, and to a lesser extent, the Roman city: all grew naturally, products of both their time and place. They reflected the unified spiritual and cultural beliefs of the people involved in their creation. But the castle, built as an implement of war, is a destructive force; the modern city is a hodge-podge of underground service systems; and the Empire State Building was created to make money and torn down at the whim of a wealthy foreigner. These are not creations of societies possessing unified beliefs.

Like other ironic pastoralists, Macaulay first explores a simpler, more unified, more natural world, and then realizes that he must turn his back on it. This he does in **Castle,** as the above noted dedication indicates. He must face the reality of the modern world, specifically the motivating forces behind modern architecture. This modern world turns out to be one with no permanent, unifying values. Even such recent masterpieces as the Empire State Building have "life expectancies" of less than sixty years. At the conclusion of **Unbuilding,** spectators crowd the tiny Empire State Park, enjoying the green space and looking at the mast, the only remaining part of the famous landmark; the ship carrying parts of the building to the Near East has sunk in mid Atlantic; the rubble has been used as landfill in New Jersey. The spectators are oblivious to the fact that Prince Ali Smith is already considering dismantling another landmark. The implicit message of the final pages of this most recent Macaulay book is basically pessimistic; and, seen within the framework of the series, it reinforces the irony which is a major aspect of much pastoral literature. (pp. 15-17)

> *Jon Stott, "Architectural Structures and Social Values in the Nonfiction of David Macaulay," in* Children's Literature Association Quarterly, *Vol. 8, No. 1, Spring, 1983, pp. 15-17.*

JENNIFER WILSON

The text of both [*Cathedral* and *City*] is nicely peopled with the names of master masons and water engineers to make the stories convincing. But it is the pictures that are distinctive. The artist's black and white drawings display a craftsmanship equal to that which he is depicting. They give magnificent impressions of the scale of both enterprises and highlight the detail that may be missed in the finished edifice. In an age when vague impressions sometimes pass for information, such a detailed study, so beautifully presented, is a landmark among books that help us understand the past.

> *Jennifer Wilson, in a review of "Cathedral" and "City," in* The Signal Review of Children's Books, *1, 1983, p. 67.*

ALAN C. PURVES AND DIANNE L. MONSON

When visual appeal and writing style combine for an exceptionally good treatment of content, there is potential for a satisfying transaction between reader and book if the reader is interested and willing to be a part of the experience that the author/illustrator has set forth. So it is that adults as well as children find themselves engrossed in the lives of people living centuries ago when they study the architectural wonders described in books such as David Macaulay's **Pyramid, Castle,** and **Cathedral.**

Macaulay's work is especially sophisticated in this regard. His background in architecture makes him eminently well qualified for his writing. His knowledge of the field is evident in the way he treats the material, organizing it spatially, in the artistic sense, and also sequentially according to the processes involved in construction, whether it is of a pyramid, a Roman city, a cathedral, or a castle. Again, there is a hint of narrative. Beyond that, however, Macaulay gives us so much information about the *people* living at the time that we are compelled to wonder about them—to want to know how they lived and how they might have been like as well as different from us. We build a more elaborate story than he gives us. The experience is very similar to a reader's involvement with a work of fiction. Its success rests on the author's willingness and ability to research not only the bare facts but also the important social and cultural aspects of life.

Pyramid is one of David Macaulay's efforts to depict an existence far removed from ours in time. The presentation is primarily the revelation of an architectural wonder. Even so, there are meticulously detailed illustrations showing small but carefully planted plots of ground, homes in oases, boats bearing great stones from the quarries, numerous platoons of men carrying stones to the upper levels of the pyramids, and men dressed in animal skins as well as in white loincloths. All of these details add to our information about the times of the pharaohs and they also engage our curiosity about the lives of the vast community of people they governed. In that way, the information of the nonfiction combines with aspects of human existence which are the stuff of fiction. (p. 61)

> *Alan C. Purves and Dianne L. Monson, "Reading Prose: From Fact to Fantasy," in their* Experiencing Children's Literature, *Scott, Foresman and Company, 1984, pp. 57-87.*

ZENA SUTHERLAND AND MAY HILL ARBUTHNOT

David Macaulay has made a distinctive contribution to children's literature. His first book, **Cathedral: The Story of Its Construction** . . . was a Caldecott Honor Book and the winner of the Deutscher Jugendbuchpreis for the best nonfiction picture book of 1975, when it was published in the German edition. A student of architecture, Macaulay has, in this and in **City: A Story of Roman Planning and Construction** . . . and in **Pyramid** . . . , related significant architectural advances to the cultures from which they came. His humor is most evident in the bland spoof **Motel of the Mysteries** . . . , a book that will appeal primarily to older readers, as will **BAAA** . . . , a satire on society that is anything but bland. In **Unbuilding** . . . he shows the structure of the Empire State Building by dismantling it. His meticulously detailed drawings show, step by step, the construction procedures for the edifices. Whether the scene is a sweeping panorama of a city, a cutaway drawing that shows the architectural plan, or a small picture of one facet of ornamentation, the illustrations are impressive for the masterful handling of perspective and the consistency with which the artist combines informative drawing with visual beauty. (p. 158)

David Macaulay's books on architectural landmarks of the past . . . have been for many years, and are likely to be for many more, some of the best of their type. . . . (p. 485)

> *Zena Sutherland and May Hill Arbuthnot, "Artists and Children's Books: David Macaulay," and "Informational Books: Evaluating Informational Books," in their* Children and Books, *seventh edition, Scott, Foresman and Company, 1986, pp. 158, 484-87.*

CASTLE (1977)

Critics aren't likely to say, "He's done it again," but that Macaulay has surpassed all four of his brilliant books beginning with *Cathedral*. His clean text details each step in the creation of a 13th century castle and town, and the reasons for them. As in earlier works, people and places are fictional, but the information is authentic. In 1283, King Edward I of England appoints Kevin le Strange Lord of Aberwyvern in Wales. He is to build a castle and a settlement as a bulwark against rebellious Welsh forces. In 1288, the structure is complete and ready to ward off the army of attacking Prince Daffyd as well as to instruct entranced readers of all ages on the castle's defense mechanisms. The grand building is so beautiful and so real in the artist's awesome drawings that we regret seeing it deserted, in ruins on the last page, 200 years later. A prize for adults as well as children.

A review of "Castle," in Publishers Weekly, *Vol. 212, No. 1, July 4, 1977, p. 77.*

The enormous and complex task of constructing a castle in the Middle Ages has been clarified and reduced to understandable proportions by the artistic skill and thorough research of the author. . . . The illustrations—showing everything from arrow loops and siege engines to sanitary facilities—are superb, although one or two of the cutaway views are difficult to visualize. The book makes it clear that the fairy-tale vision of a completed castle masks a massive and well-engineered war machine.

Ann A. Flowers, in a review of "Castle," in The Horn Book Magazine, *Vol. LIII, No. 5, October, 1977, p. 544.*

There are any number of children's books which attempt to explain aspects of the world's workings, from the steam turbine to the electoral college. Few, however, can match the eloquence and calm confidence of David Macaulay's text and illustrations. And none is quite so successful at bringing the past to life, with the homely intricacies of its everyday tools and materials. . . .

With *Castle,* Macaulay returns to the Middle Ages to reconstruct not only how a Welsh castle and its adjacent town were built, but also the social and military factors that dictated their every detail. . . .

Macaulay's ability to convey architectural data through drawings at once exquisitely detailed and lucidly simple is outstanding, but his book's greatest virtue is the way text and pictures complement each other. It is as though he set out to restore the original meaning to the medieval term "illumination."

Castle is consequently a demanding book; there is no talking down or spoon-feeding. If a youngster can't figure out "cistern" from the text and drawings, then he had better get him to a dictionary.

The human figures are sometimes rudimentary, which is perhaps why Macaulay chooses to make his banquet scene so murky. On the other hand, such candlelit affairs were probably

From Castle, *written and illustrated by David Macaulay. Houghton Mifflin Company, 1977. Copyright © 1977 by David Macaulay. All rights reserved. Reprinted by permission of Houghton Mifflin Company.*

pretty murky in real life, and if the later "bokes of courtesie" are any indication, it's just as well not to see all those noble guests buttering their bread with their thumbs and trying to remember whether it's more polite to spit across or beside the table.

Anyway, Macaulay more than compensates for any deficiencies by the magnificence of his architectural renderings and by the whimsical humor with which he approaches people.

Macaulay covers every aspect of the castle and town from the selection of the site to the castle's eventual decay, including the machines and strategies of besiegers and the countermeasures of the castle's defenders. We also learn how a town draftsman displayed his wares, how the castle sink was supplied with running water, even how the castle's latrines or *garderobes*—in which Macaulay places a suitably glum churl with hose down-gyved, while a goat peers nervously over the cross-sectioned battlement—were built out from the wall, a practice which not only posed sanitary problems but exposed the defenders' ends to rough-hewing from below. . . .

There is a sense of wonder in David Macaulay's work. It is fresh and genuine, because Macaulay knows his subject, knows it well, loves it, and has something interesting to say about it. *Castle*'s only real liability is that parents are likely to find Macaulay's treatment so engrossingly thorough and cogent that many copies pried from dimpled hands for a casual perusal are going to wind up on the grown-ups' bookshelves for good.

> *Russell M. Griffin, "Within the Moat," in* Book World—The Washington Post, *November 13, 1977, p. E2.*

The drawings are just right: clear, unfussy, and a pleasure to look at. For younger pupils the language may not be too easy but I would hope that the combination of diagrams, pictures and commentary would make the growth of Aberwyfern Castle a good standby for project work, and for reading with first- and second-year pupils in secondary schools. The realities of castles (dungeons as well as garderobes) are acknowledged as well as the romantic appeal. There is a good glossary at the end. A good book for historians and anyone interested in the history of architecture. (pp. 176, 179)

> *Charles Hannam, in a review of "Castle," in* The School Librarian, *Vol. 26, No. 2, June, 1978, pp. 176, 179.*

Macaulay—need it be said?—combines a rare historical imagination, a keen eye, a gift for topographical and structural delineation, and a deep sense of the human condition. Watching his Welsh castle take shape, element by element, one enters into the lives of workers, farmers, townsfolk. The cutaway view is as characteristic of Macaulay, in one or another form, as the aerial panorama, in a variety of perspectives. . . . Yet mechanical drawing is no more to be found than a careless line. Timbered roof, thatched roof, and shingled roof each has its character, as each human figure, however minute, has a characterizing gesture, a characteristic stance. From raw beginnings to spectral end, virtuosity, sensitivity, and vision coalesce. (p. 291)

> *Barbara Bader, "The Caldecott Spectrum," in* Newbery and Caldecott Medal Books: 1976-1985, *edited by Lee Kingman, The Horn Book, Incorporated, 1986, pp. 279-314.*

MOTEL OF THE MYSTERIES (1979)

Popular crazes inevitably engender lampoons, takeoffs and pastiches. Tolkien and *Star Wars* have bred innumerable imitations—some reverent, some quite the reverse—so it is not surprising that even so sedate and scholarly a phenomenon as the Tutankhamen exhibit should inspire tributes of the purportedly humorous variety. Fortunately for the reading public one of the humorists moved to make his contribution is David Macaulay. My sole complaint about this witty and engaging book is its title, which telegraphs the punch line a little too soon.

The fun begins with Macaulay's brief but devastating description of the cataclysm which, overnight, buried the flourishing North American civilization of the 20th century. Two thousand years later tourists view the crumbling remains of the ancients with awe; but not until a gentleman named Howard Carson inadvertently tumbles into the buried shaft of a mysterious underground structure does the world of 4022 A.D. comprehend the true magnificence of the long-dead culture.

Carson immediately identifies the structure as a tomb (what else could it be?), and describes in painstaking detail the religious functions of the cult objects (what else could they be?) so miraculously preserved behind the sealed door. Macaulay's drawings make it clear that Carson must be descended from an ancestor of a similar name; the family resemblance is unmistakable.

Most of the humor can be easily appreciated by anyone at all familiar with the Tutankhamen discovery. There are a few "in" jokes, which may elude the casual reader, such as the sketch of Carson's assistant, Harriet Burton, decked out in the fabulous "jewelry" found in "Tomb 26." By a (no doubt) strange coincidence, this portrait bears a striking resemblance to that of another lady of archaeological leanings wearing the treasure discovered by her husband way back in the 19th century.

In fairness to the reader and the author I will not describe Harriet's "jewelry," or the other exquisite errors perpetuated by Carson, the brilliant amateur (more amateur, alas, than brilliant). But I can't resist one quote, which proves that Macaulay's satire is impartially aimed at archaeological weirdos as well as the archaeological establishment:

> the entire continent was covered by a complex network of gray and black stripes. . . . Because the various patterns can only be fully appreciated from the air, the German scholar Heinrich Von Hooligan believes the stripes were planned either as landing strips for extraterrestrial craft or as coded messages from the inhabitants of the continent to their many powerful gods.

Macaulay's superb drawings, familiar to readers of his serious books on architecture, add to the fun. There is joy on every page, but perhaps the most delectable section of the book is the one entitled "Souvenirs and Quality Reproductions," with its full page illustrations of the expensive adaptations of the items found in the tomb—bookends, tote bags and the like. Only someone like me, who has compulsively collected innumerable impractical imitations of Tutankhamens's tomb equipment, can fully appreciate the charm of this concept.

Successful humor is its own excuse for being. Indeed, it may be more important in the general scheme of things than such solemn matters as higher mathematics, General Motors or even archaeology. In this sense Macaulay's book is a triumph. It serves another function—as does all satire—in deflating pomposity and reminding us of our human susceptibility to error. Kathleen Kenyon, the excavator of Jericho and Jerusalem, once wryly remarked that archaeologists tend to label any artifact of unknown function as a ''cult object.'' **Motel of the Mysteries** illustrates this specific criticism so neatly that one is inclined to suspect that Macaulay shares Kenyon's opinion. I hope he sells a million copies. (pp. 9, 14)

> *Barbara Mertz, in a review of ''Motel of the Mysteries,'' in* Book World—The Washington Post, *October 7, 1979, pp. 9, 14.*

David Macaulay has a huge following among children, their parents and grandparents, and every other lover of the history of architecture, civilization and archeology. He is a superb draftsman and an imaginative writer and illustrator. (p. 15)

His new book is a marvel of imagination and a comfortable satire. . . . The motel room and bath behind the door is the [archeologist's] find, with its treasures of sacred collar (toilet seat), the ceremonial burial hat (shower cap), sacred pendant (bathtub stopper), the highly complex percussion instrument (telephone), and much more. The joke is a bit drawn-out, perhaps, but it is all good fun and, as always with Mr. Macaulay's books, wonderfully illustrated.

Best of all is the name of the buried motel of the mysteries: Toot'n'C'mon. My 8-year-old grandson found that hilarious. (pp. 15-16)

> *Doris Grumbach, in a review of ''Motel of the Mysteries,'' in* The New York Times Book Review, *December 9, 1979, pp. 15-16.*

In a clever and diverting spoof, Macaulay pokes fun at some of the aspects of our society, at archeologists, and at sensational journalese. His drawings are as meticulously detailed, as deftly executed, and as handsomely composed as in all of his earlier books, but more expressive of Macaulay's pointed wit and sense of humor. . . . The repeated allusions to Carter and his discovery of Tut's tomb may escape some readers, but there's enough sophisticated but obvious humor to entertain them anyway, and it's all given high polish by the serious and reverent tone of the writing. (pp. 99-100)

> *Zena Sutherland, in a review of ''Motel of the Mysteries,'' in* Bulletin of the Center for Children's Books, *Vol. 33, No. 5, January, 1980, pp. 99-100.*

UNBUILDING (1980)

David Macaulay's splendidly drawn, well-researched and written books about cathedrals, castles, pyramids and cities have been among the major phenomena of recent children's literature. Satisfying the questioner in us who by the age of 7 wonders about process and structure—how things work—they have found an international audience among both child and adult readers. In our curiosity about such matters we apparently remain children for life. Macaulay himself, undaunted in his fascination with monuments, has in his latest book, **Unbuilding,** also extended his range as a storyteller, changing forever, by this rare implausible triumph of fact over fiction and fiction over fact, our view of a landmark known from childhood by nearly everyone, the Empire State Building.

An eccentric, petro-rich Arab prince, in Macaulay's telling, has bought the Empire State Building in order to dismantle it and re-erect it in the Arabian Desert. American protests have proved fainthearted and shortlived; as a goodwill gesture (that New Yorkers gratefully accept!) the determined prince has also promised to pull down the World Trade Center some day. . . .

As Macaulay chronicles the complex ''unbuilding'' of the venerable New York tower, detailing as he goes its structural plan and something of its history, he publishes perhaps his finest series of visually expansive, black-and-white perspective drawings, incisive renderings of the skyscraper and its celebrated ''views.''

Olympic shifts of vantage point from one drawing to the next convince one immediately not only of the Empire State Building's commanding physical scale but of the brazen theatricality, the imaginative dimension, that is the very essence of its legend. Macaulay's tale of the famed tower's demise seems a strangely truthful homage, a mischievous wink at a distinguished (and a bit shopworn) symbol of protean change. **Unbuilding** is also of course a luscious spoof on changing world fortunes and a manic rehearsal of the universal urge to demolish one's favorite toy.

> *Leonard S. Marcus, ''Down with the Empire State Building,'' in* Book World—The Washington Post, *November 9, 1980, p. 12.*

[**Unbuilding**] is not a work of nonfiction but a work of fantasy, and not the story of the making of a skyscraper but the story of the un-making of a very particular one, the Empire State Building. . . .

It is a wonderful idea, firmly in the tradition of works of children's literature that are, at bottom, satires for adults. Mr. Macaulay's wit is quite biting—he tells of protests by historic preservationists over the Empire State Building's impending demolition, after which,

> On the brink of defeat, one desperate but clever preservationist suggested that the twin towers of the World Trade Center be offered instead— both for the price of the Empire State. In declining the offer Ali suggested that he would be willing to consider pulling them down as a goodwill gesture. With this final show of generosity, all remaining resistance crumbled.

Whether children who have not grown up in alert Manhattan households will pick up all of the subtleties of this is hard to know, but the joy of it for adults is clear. The exquisite drawing style that marked Mr. Macaulay's earlier works on architecture remains as whimsical as ever—this time, for example, there are skyline views of Manhattan containing a bizarre building with a pedimented top, a play on the A.T.&T. Building now under construction. All in all, **Unbuilding** is a splendid way to mark the fact that the Empire State Building will be a half-century old next year. (p. 54)

> *Paul Goldberger, ''From the Ground Up,'' in* The New York Times Book Review, *November 9, 1980, pp. 54, 67-8.*

In a mood of speculative spoofing and by blending factual information with wry, satiric humor, the author-artist describes the dismantling of the Empire State Building. . . . The ingenious plot enables Macaulay to make fine architectural drawings which describe in detail the construction of the building

From Unbuilding, *written and illustrated by David Macaulay. Houghton Mifflin Company, 1980. Copyright © 1980 by David Macaulay. All rights reserved. Reprinted by permission of Houghton Mifflin Company.*

by means of diagrams, cutaways, and double-page spreads. Drawn from unusual angles and consistently extending to the very limits of the pages, the pictures emphasize the structure's height and beautiful details. Verbal and visual jokes reinforce the satiric points of the story. . . . [The] book is humorous but cautionary, drawing attention to a handsome building while it still stands—perhaps the best method of preservation. Glossary.

> *Christine McDonnell, in a review of "Unbuilding,"*
> *in* The Horn Book Magazine, *Vol. LVI, No. 6, December, 1980, p. 655.*

David Macaulay can always be relied upon to produce an unusual and stimulating book and this is no exception. . . . [***Unbuilding***] makes fascinating reading, greatly aided by Macaulay's marvellously detailed drawings. It is an unusual book, detailed, highly imaginative, impressively illustrated and it is a mine of information for skilled and less technically minded readers alike. This must surely be one of the most original 'picture' books to be published for a long time and it definitely whets the appetite for more such imaginative productions from this talented author and illustrator.

> *Margaret Walker, in a review of "Unbuilding," in*
> Book Window, *Vol. 8, No. 3, Summer, 1981, p. 27.*

MILL (1983)

The New England cotton mills of the last century, mostly abandoned in the rush to new technologies, will never really be gone as long as David Macaulay's *Mill* has readers. His imaginary mills in an imaginary town in Rhode Island, and the generations of people who built and ran them, come to life in the mind and refuse to leave long after one has put his historical re-creation down. He reveals in detail the secrets of this man-made world but leaves one with the sense that it is part of nature, and just as surprising.

The first wooden mill of this book is begun in 1810 by a group of enterprising businessmen. One designs the mill, another its machinery; a third surveys land for the site. As workers cut a channel parallel to the river to divert a stream to turn the mill's great wheel, others build the structure to hold the machinery that is being made out of iron and wood on the site. When the mill begins to operate, we see how the raw cotton is prepared for the machines that card it, draw it into long strong fibers and finally twist and spin it into thread for sale to cloth weavers.

Twenty years later the owners decide to weave their own cloth and build a large stone mill across the river from the wooden one, with the newest spinning machinery and weaving looms. In another 20 years that mill is expanded and a water turbine is built to run its machinery. A generation later another company builds a vast mill run by a steam engine that drives acres of looms on many floors.

From Mill, *written and illustrated by David Macaulay. Houghton Mifflin Company, 1983. Copyright ©*
1983 by David Macaulay. All rights reserved. Reprinted by permission of Houghton Mifflin Company.

In his narrative, and in the superb drawings for which he has long been celebrated, Mr. Macaulay creates not only mills, but also a town and a society. Groups of immigrant workers succeed one another; company and private housing, churches and schools go up; railroads are built and decay; there are accidents in the mill, disputes over pay, new labor laws. The diaries and letters of mill owners and members of their families tell us of the passing generations and the changes in work, society and the nation. Mr. Macaulay does not make life always pleasant or work always equitable or decent: Children work; women are always subordinates; the early mills use cotton supplied from slave plantations. But the great milling machines he creates are wonderful giants that, because we have seen them made by men's hands, are companionable.

How well the machines will be understood by young readers it is hard to say. An older generation that grew up dismantling clocks for fun (the kind with gears, not just quartz crystals) or played with erector sets and watched their fathers working on simple old cars might understand Mr. Macaulay's mill machinery more easily than today's youngsters who have a quicker grasp of high technology than of simple mechanics. Mr. Macaulay is a superb storyteller and his drawings are vivid, but his readers will be on less familiar ground here than in any of his other books. *Mill* is not a book to be read when the television set is turned on in the background.

But for those of any age who make the effort, the reward is great. Mr. Macaulay is no simple romantic. The world he creates is real and rough, but its people are ingenious and purposeful and their machines just a bit enchanted. When at the end the last mill in the imagined village has been closed and turned into a condominium, there is a sense of loss—and of fulfillment.

> *D. J. R. Bruckner, in a review of "Mill," in* The New York Times Book Review, *September 25, 1983, p. 29.*

Macaulay's winning streak continues with this account of the development of four fictional 19th-Century Rhode Island cotton mills. . . . Well-written and readable, with clear technical explanations, the text traces the families of the characters involved with the mills throughout the century. . . . Illustrations are up to Macaulay's usual high level. Narrower in focus than Weitzman's *Windmills, Bridges, and Old Machines . . .* , but more detailed in its coverage of its topic, *Mill*, even without the intrinsic popular appeal of pyramids and cathedrals, is an attractive, attention-riveting effort.

> *Jeffrey A. French, in a review of "Mill," in* School Library Journal, *Vol. 30, No. 2, October, 1983, p. 160.*

[In *Mill*], admirers of *Cathedral* and *Pyramid . . .* will again find the same attention to architectural detail and the problems of construction. Unlike the other two books the new one includes a story line of sorts in the form of quotations from imaginary diaries and letters of those who either built or worked at the mills. This device lends insight into the vicissitudes of supply and demand in the mills' long history but may divert attention from the main focus, which is the construction of both the buildings and the machinery.... If the human figures appear rather wooden, the black-and-white drawings are, as always, wonderfully clear and compelling and offer a fine variety of cross sections, elevations, and diagrams of tools and machinery. The text is considerably longer than the ones in the author's previous books, but the handsome pictures alone could hold the reader's attention to the final pages.

> *Ethel R. Twichell, in a review of "Mill," in* The Horn Book Magazine, *Vol. LIX, No. 6, December, 1983, p. 726.*

This new book is as thorough and as brilliant in concept as David Macaulay's exploration of the building of castle and cathedral and other great projects. I must confess that I found it considerably less absorbing than its forerunners. Perhaps because the scale of operations is smaller,... the detail is correspondingly greater. Unlike cathedrals and castles the construction of these mills has been fully documented, and Mr. Macaulay faithfully passes all the facts on to us. Fine if you want to build a replica, or a working model; exhausting if you have only a layman's interest in industrial architecture and history. But for modern technological youth the book may well have an absorbing interest, as it demonstrates the ingenuity and resource of these millwrights of New England. The author's drawings are as beautiful as they are exact.

> *M. Crouch, in a review of "Mill," in* The Junior Bookshelf, *Vol. 48, No. 4, August, 1984, p. 177.*

BAAA (1985)

AUTHOR'S COMMENTARY

I'd been thinking of doing a series of drawings of famous places like St. Mark's Square in Venice, the Champs Élysée, places of that sort, places that you never see without people, where people have become part of the image.... I was going to do drawings that showed these places absolutely empty. So you would look at the picture and say, "Something is wrong." Where this idea came from I'm not entirely certain—a little bit of gloom and doom from news here and there. Maybe it's a personal response to the neutron bomb; I don't know.

And then I was in Washington, D.C. for a meeting. I was in the hotel at 3:15 in the morning when somebody kicked the door in down the hall because he'd been locked out. Tremendous ruckus. I woke up and couldn't get back to sleep. So I was lying there and started to think about these drawings again and thought, "Supposing animals wandered into these spaces that I've just made deserted in the drawings." Then I started to think about a flock of sheep wandering into St. Mark's. So I got up and grabbed the little telephone pad and pencil and... started scribbling down these ideas. Monday morning I went back to Providence (Rhode Island), sat down at the typewriter and by Thursday I had a draft of this story about sheep coming into an abandoned town and taking over. (p. 37)

> *Larry McCarthy, "Bright Lights—Big Season: David Macaulay," in* Saturday Review, *Vol. 11, No. 5, September-October, 1985, pp. 36-7.*

From Baaa, *written and illustrated by David Macaulay. Houghton Mifflin Company, 1985. Copyright © 1985 by David Macaulay. All rights reserved. Reprinted by permission of Houghton Mifflin Company.*

This is a fantasy in the Jean Merrill tradition, simple and sunny on the surface, refreshingly tart and sophisticated below, and liable—despite the simplicity of the writing style—to provoke some intricate ideas. In a world bereft of human beings, some sheep stray into houses and forage for food. Accidentally, they begin to acquire a language (from a VCR and television). They wear clothes, they travel, they pursue careers and move from simple division of labor to all complexities and problems of a technological civilization with a large population and a small food supply. Then numbers dwindle, and the sheep suffer the fate of the people who preceded them. In the end, a fish approaches the silent and empty land, and the reader may wonder if it's all going to happen again, the greed, the shortages, the corruption in high places. This is clever satire; what makes it comic are Macaulay's imaginative details in the black and white illustrations and in the text. Examples: when they first begin learning words from the VCR, the sheep are reciting "Play... it—Sam... a kiss... is just..." and later, when the pressure of life has brought crime and despair, the author says, "As more and more goods went to fewer and fewer sheep, the number of unhappy sheep grew." What the picture shows is an analyst with his patients reclining in a triple-tiered bunk bed. Pithy, hilarious, clever.

> *A review of "Baaa," in* Bulletin of the Center for Children's Books, *Vol. 39, No. 1, September, 1985, p. 13.*

If readers are anticipating the outright chuckles and sly, wry wit of Macaulay's **Motel of the Mysteries...**, **Baaa** is likely to be a surprise. Though it is funny at times, it is ultimately a somber portrait of modern materialism that pictures contemporary society as morally derelict and self-destructive. The story is simple and direct.... Macaulay uses black-and-white sketches and brief text to tell his tale. While he incorporates both visual and verbal humor, his book is more political statement than parody and his creation-myth-gone-askew ending is final proof of the holocaust he sees in the future. Filled with devices and allusions that beg for discussion, this should be provocative material out of as well as in the classroom.

Stephanie Zvirin, in a review of "Baaa," in Booklist, *Vol. 82, No. 1, September 1, 1985, p. 53.*

David Macaulay moves out of the past (**Castle, Cathedral, Pyramid**) and into the future—but not that of the fanciful **Motel of the Mysteries**. This time Macaulay tells a grimmer tale, a variant on Thurber's *The Last Flower,* Orwell's *Animal Farm* and Clifford Simak's *City.* Mankind has destroyed itself, and only sheep survive....

This is clearly a book with a message—don't repeat the mistakes about food, population and government that the sheep make—but Macaulay's didacticism has a whimsical rather than preacherly character. The drawings are super: for all their mighty achievements the sheep always look like really dumb animals, perpetually startled by the world about them, mildly ridiculous in their human clothing. Macaulay's captions possess a deadpan rightness: on one page he shows a tapestry of numbers—a huge graph—proving that the starving animals have enough to eat. The sheep leaders on a balustrade repeat, a la Newspeak or *Newsweek,* that "Everything is just fine" and "See the chart." The crowd below holds placards. But there is, of course, not enough: The hungry sheep look up and are not fed.

This is an odd album, one that will appeal to thoughtful children even as it worries their parents. I liked the book, especially for its fatalistic character—Macaulay offers the sheep no hope of altering their destiny—but prospective buyers would do well to read it before automatically buying it.

Michael Dirda, in a review of "Baaa," in Book World—The Washington Post, *September 8, 1985, p. 9.*

[**Baaa**] is being marketed for children as well as adults. It is difficult to understand why. True, the picture-book format seems visually suited to the young reader. True, the black-and-white illustrations are indeed funny—at least they start out funny—and the scenes of sheep dressed up in high heels and trench coats, riding a tricycle and watching old Bogart movies are amusing kid stuff. But not for long. Soon the funny pictures are succeeded by those of have-nots and criminals; of broken bodies, savaged cities, abandoned homes; and of a bloodied balcony where, it is chillingly suggested, sheep leaders have come to a very unpleasant end.

As do all the sheep in this cautionary tale that cautions ... what?

That the human race is composed of consumers and killers? That human beings, and any creatures adopting human characteristics, are doomed? That given a choice, you should better remain a grazing sheep in a meadow, a fish in the sea? That if you are reading this book it is already too late to choose—and too late to save yourself? What is the reader supposed to do with this news?

Adults may wrestle with it, may come up with some hey-wait-a-minute arguments about the nature of man, may challenge the book's sentimentality about the lower forms of animal life (we all know what the big fish do to the little fish), may appreciate the black humor while firmly rejecting the thesis, may even agree with Mr. Macaulay's desolate view which has evolved since his popular earlier books, **Cathedral, Castle,** even the futurist **Motel of the Mysteries.** Young readers, on the other hand, are more likely just to be frightened and depressed by a book that says there is no humanity in the human race and absolutely no hope for its future.

I am certainly not suggesting that books for children should exclude life's tougher realities. Those tough realities dwell in every child's home. But perhaps a crucial distinction between writing for children and for adults is the duty to instruct our children in hope. Because David Macaulay's **Baaa** withholds all hope, I would not choose to buy it for children I love.

Judith Viorst, in a review of "Baaa," in The New York Times Book Review, *December 1, 1985, p. 38.*

Patricia (Pritzkau) MacLachlan

1938-

American author of fiction and picture books.

MacLachlan is recognized as the creator of warm, unconventional family stories for both primary and middle grade readers which highlight intergenerational relationships while expressing her optimism and belief in the preciousness of life. Noted for her wisdom, quiet humor, and disciplined yet lyrical prose, she tells simple, sensitive tales about unusual, personable characters whom she portrays with conviction and charm. A former teacher and social worker, MacLachlan began her writing career with picture books such as *The Sick Day* (1979), which describes how daughter Emily's aches and pains are nursed by her father, and *Through Grandpa's Eyes* (1980), which depicts how small John learns to see the world through his blind grandfather's fingers. *Mama One, Mama Two* (1982) is regarded as one of the most successful examples of presenting foster parenting and mental illness to primary readers; MacLachlan establishes an intimate bond between Katherine and her charge, Maudie, and provides frank but hopeful references to Maudie's absent, unstable mother. MacLachlan's books for middle graders frequently deal with children learning both about themselves and how to care for others. Her best-known book, *Sarah, Plain and Tall* (1985), is told from the viewpoint of the prairie children who yearn for their father's mail-order wife from Maine to stay as a permanent member of the family. Prompted by a vignette that appeared in *Arthur, for the Very First Time* (1980), MacLachlan's first novel for the middle age group, *Sarah* is based on the author's family history and reveals her interest in the links between the past and the present. In addition to her realistic accounts of everyday problems and resolutions, MacLachlan has written a fairy tale about a frog prince and a whimsical collection of short stories about a wizard, his apprentice, and a talking horse.

Critics generally praise MacLachlan for her lifelike, endearing protagonists, natural tenderness, droll wit, and fluid language, which they find conducive to oral reading. Although a few reviewers point out that the pace of some of her works is slow and the plots occasionally predictable, most agree that MacLachlan's skillful craftsmanship, subtle nondidactic style, and emphasis on nurturing familial relationships combine to make books that comfort, satisfy, and entertain young readers.

MacLachlan has received several awards for her books. In 1984, *Unclaimed Treasures* was designated a *Boston Globe-Horn Book* Honor Book. *Sarah, Plain and Tall* won the Newbery Medal and the Scott O'Dell Historical Fiction Award in 1986.

(See also *Something about the Author*, Vol. 42 and *Contemporary Authors*, Vol. 118.)

AUTHOR'S COMMENTARY

[The following excerpt is from an interview by Ann Courtney in the "Profile" section of Language Arts *magazine.]*

Profile: What originally took you into writing children's books?

Courtesy of Dick Carnes

Ms. MacLachlan: First, let me say that as a child I made a conscious decision not to be a writer because I thought writers had all the answers. My teachers did not encourage writing like teachers do today. Teachers are often cast in the role as critic, sometimes without regard to the person behind the writing, and sometimes children do not want to risk revealing themselves and I did not. I think I always wanted to write all my life, but was afraid to do so because I think it is personal, risky, and a rather fearful experience.

I think my parents had a lot to do with it. When I was young, I read everything. My father and mother invited me into books and we discussed the characters and acted them out. So in a way books and characters in particular became very real. I also had a wonderful fantasy life. I invented brothers and sisters, kings and queens.

As I grew older and my children grew older, I thought I was doing all the things I ought to be doing. I went back to school and started taking graduate courses and studying cello. One day when I was talking to my cello instructor, she asked whether I was enjoying this and I said not really. One of us said, "You only grow old and die, so why don't you do what you want to do best." I decided right then that I wanted to write children's books. I continued reading some wonderful books and I thought, "This is marvelous and this is what I want to do."

Also, this area is full of writers and when you get to know them I think it becomes a more accessible thing for you to do. I think if writers had come into the classroom, as I often do, when I was a child, it would have seemed like something I could do also. I didn't start writing until my children were in school. I said to my husband once, my one regret was that I wasn't writing all these years. My writing career began when I was thirty-five years old.

Profile: Do you remember any books or writers which particularly influenced you when you were a child?

Ms. MacLachlan: All books and all writers influenced me. Not until I was older and in my thirties and beginning to think about writing did I find writers that really had in a way shaped my taste. I love Natalie Babbitt, William Steig, and an English writer, Jane Gardam. In fact, when I'm having a hard time writing, I get these books out and I read them. I can always tell when I'm about to start writing. I go through cycles in reading. When I'm beginning to want to write something, I start reading what I think of as good literature. I read things with wonderful language. The rest of the time I read everything.

Profile: Are there any adult writers that have influenced your writing?

Ms. MacLachlan: I love William Blake and Rumer Godden. I'm reading E. B. White's essays and they make me breathless sometimes because they say something and I have to go write it down right away and keep it and save it and think about it. So it's not so much that an entire book may have impact, but certain ways of saying things do.

Profile: How do your books begin? Where do you get your ideas?

Ms. MacLachlan: I always begin with a character. I write a chapter about the character and what he or she is doing, thinking, but I don't know what the story is about yet. I can't sit down with a full view of how a book is going to unfold and what is going to happen in the end. In a sense, I think I'm a participant that way. I go through every chapter with the character and participate, which is often tiring. Actually, the new book I'm writing is giving me a great deal of trouble because I consciously thought about writing about my family. I did it consciously which is a bad thing for me to do. One child in a school I was visiting said to me, "You take the facts and then you reach, don't you?" I think that's what I try to do.

Profile: You say you begin with the characters. How long is it before you know what's going to happen in the middle of a story and how it's going to end?

Ms. MacLachlan: It's hard to pinpoint a time, but usually by the fourth or fifth chapter I begin to see what's happening. For me the plot comes out of the characters. So the better I get to know my characters the more the plot unfolds naturally. I like the word "organic" because I think it is an organic quality; one chapter leading to the next chapter leading to events leading to thoughts, all unfolding on a page.

Profile: Do you usually do some type of research before you begin writing?

Ms. MacLachlan: I read good books when I'm ready to write and I listen to good music. Then all of a sudden I wake up in the morning one day and I go to the typewriter and I'm ready to write. I don't think I do any formal research. Life is my research, I suppose.

Profile: Do you have a specific writing space that you write in?

Ms. MacLachlan: No, I can pretty much write anywhere. I can write very well when everyone is bumping around the house talking or asking me questions because it just seems like a normal kind of thing. I have to have a window somehow and a typewriter.

Profile: How long does it take you to write a children's book?

Ms. MacLachlan: I think it takes often about six months if I'm going well and doing well on a book. But there are times when I get in the middle of a book and I have trouble and put it aside and do other things. I read it all out loud so that I can hear how the words come to the ear.

Profile: Your books are generally optimistic. Is this self-censorship?

Ms. MacLachlan: I have to think about that a little. I remember getting offended when I read a review of one of my books that said they're gentle and not much is happening. A friend of mine said maybe that's so, but the characters are always on the edge of something bad happening. I think that's the way life is. I think life is a mixture of humor and sadness and poignancy and grief, all these things mixed in together. I think that books in a sense maybe don't change lives, but they have a great impact on children's lives. There's a good deal in this world that is not happy and yet there are moments here or there that I try to illuminate, the kind of thoughtful, pensive moments. We spend a lot of time inside our heads. I don't know if it's censorship or not but it's just a reflection of how I think and I must be optimistic.

Profile: Are any of your books autobiographical?

Ms. MacLachlan: Most are to some degree. Cassie in **Cassie Binegar** is. For instance, when I was a child, I spent a lot of time in hidden places observing and listening to conversations that I thought seemed very important—I was a listener. Cassie, of course, sits under this huge and ugly tablecloth listening to the conversations and watching feet. After my mother read the manuscript, she brought the tablecloth out and there it was and I hadn't realized that that was certainly me as Cassie underneath the table listening to things. Also Willa in **Unclaimed Treasures.**

Profile: Are your books intended as a way through the barriers between children and their parents?

Ms. MacLachlan: I never thought of that. I don't think they're intended that way. I think they're rather common, everyday kinds of things that most children go through in one way or another. It's really funny when you say "intended" because I don't intend to do anything but tell a story and tell it to myself as well as to someone who will read it.

Profile: Which of your books did you most enjoy writing?

Ms. MacLachlan: Well, I really enjoyed writing **The Sick Day.** It just worked beautifully and was about my husband and my child. But I think I probably most liked writing **Arthur, For the Very First Time** and **Unclaimed Treasures.** At the time **Arthur** was an intensely personal thing. I knew I was writing about a lot of me, a lot of my family, a lot of what I was thinking about at that time. Secondly, it was the first time I'd written in the novel form. Previously I had written picture books and they are so tight. A novel allowed me a little more space. **Unclaimed Treasures** is really a love story, a romance. I always wanted to write about falling in love.

Profile: Rewriting—how difficult is it for you?

Ms. MacLachlan: It is difficult, very difficult at times, and then sometimes illuminating. I guess the hardest part is that it is not spontaneous. That's why I love the initial writing because it's all so spontaneous. What I try for is to get it as well written as I can the first time so that I don't have to do a lot of rewriting.

Profile: How do you see the major themes in your books developing?

Ms. MacLachlan: I can only see them developing as I look back on them. I cannot see them as I'm writing them. I notice space is something I'm concerned with a lot of the time. Arthur is looking for his space; Cassie is looking for hers; Willa and Nicholas are certainly looking for theirs. I hope that as adults we still think about and reevaluate where we fit into life. That's why I think that children's books are concerned with the same themes as adult books are. I do notice that the themes are loyalty, honesty, families, and relationships and this wonderful personal issue of tidiness vs neatness. I think the theme throughout all my books is how is the world really? What I think I try to do in my books, if I try to do anything consciously, is to not overwrite. I would rather unravel a story and have the character say it rather than I the author having to tell it. I would rather show it instead of tell it.

Profile: What's coming out now?

Ms. MacLachlan: I have a new book *Sarah, Plain and Tall* just out which is the story of a mail-order bride who comes from the coast of Maine inland to the prairies to be a mother and a wife. It is told in the voice of the children waiting for her to come. It comes out of my family past and through *Arthur, For the Very First Time.* Now I'm in the middle of a novel geared to the same middle age group as *Arthur, For the Very First Time, Cassie Binegar,* and *Unclaimed Treasures.* It's the story of a little girl whose mother is a writer for children and her father is a psychologist. The little girl feels that she is not getting the proper attention, the same attention as her mother's readers, so she writes to her mother under another name.

Profile: It's really evident that you enjoy what you are doing. Do you have any words of wisdom to offer aspiring writers?

Ms. MacLachlan: I would certainly say only write books for children if you really love children's books and want to do it. Writing for children is special because I think children read with a great true belief in what they're reading. The other thing is to read. One must understand the far reaches of children's books because they're really about many of the same subjects as adults are concerned with. Don't be condescending. I hate the didacticism that sometimes comes through in children's books. I would read and read and read. There is no better model than a good book. (pp. 783-87)

Patricia MacLachlan and Ann Courtney in a conversation, in Language Arts, *Vol. 62, No. 7, November, 1985, pp. 783-87.*

GENERAL COMMENTARY

ETHEL L. HEINS

With her wonderfully eccentric characters, her preoccupation with intergenerational affinities, and her calm, lucid prose, the author reached a high point in the artlessly crafted *Unclaimed Treasures.* . . . Now [in *Sarah, Plain and Tall*] she tells a much more simple, but no less subtle, story of a motherless pioneer family living on the great prairie. . . . Some writers might have been tempted to flesh out the story into a full-length novel, but the brief, well-rounded tale has its own satisfying completeness. (pp. 557-58)

Ethel L. Heins, in a review of "Sarah, Plain and Tall," in The Horn Book Magazine, *Vol. LXI, No. 5, September-October, 1985, pp. 557-58.*

EDEN ROSS LIPSON

[The 66th John Newbery Medal was] presented to Patricia MacLachlan for *Sarah, Plain and Tall.* The 58-page book, accessible to early readers, perfect for reading aloud, poignant and affecting even to jaded teen-agers and weary adults, is, as a New York Times reviewer said last year, "the simplest of love stories expressed in the simplest of prose" [see excerpt dated May 19, 1985 for *Sarah, Plain and Tall*]. . . .

In addition to the Newbery, *Sarah, Plain and Tall* won the third Scott O'Dell Award for Historical Fiction. . . . At the presentation ceremony. . . , Mr. O'Dell noted that when Willa Cather began a new book, she tried to strike a "mental tuning fork." He said that Mrs. MacLachlan had also done this, beginning with the ringing, lingering double L of the last word of the title. Short as the book is, Mr. O'Dell said, it so caught him that he "turned to the back to see if she was going to stay.". . .

[Mrs. MacLachlan's] first book, *The Sick Day,* was published in 1979 and is out of print. She writes slowly, "sitting in my window overlooking the field." Her books "do not have slam-bang plots," but she is getting tired of hearing that they are "gentle," although the word is apt.

She writes "as a participant, to see what will happen." An only child herself, she said, "looking back I see that I write books about brothers and sisters, about what makes up a family, what works and what is nurturing." For *Mama One, Mama Two,* a picture book about a foster mother, she thought her interest in the theme came from her experience in the social work field and as a teacher of young children. But an observant child told her recently that the story was another way of thinking about Sarah, who becomes a foster mother. *Seven Kisses in a Row,* written for her daughter Emily, is about what happens when Emma and Zachary's parents go off to a professional meeting and leave Aunt Evelyn and Uncle Elliot, who are expecting a baby, to mind the children and learn the rules of family life. *Arthur, for the Very First Time* is about a tense 10-year-old boy, whose mother is pregnant, spending the summer with eccentric relatives in the country. It contains the Sarah story as a short vignette. . . .

The connections between past and present interest her deeply. Each spring she teaches a popular introductory course on children's literature at Smith College for the local five-college consortium. In addition to the substantial reading list and one critical paper, she requires that her students begin ("they couldn't possibly finish") a picture book, a fable and a piece of historical fiction that establishes character, time and place. She reads those assignments and takes "the 11 o'clock phone calls."

She also goes into many classrooms, mostly in Massachusetts, and works with children, which "takes much more energy than anything. . . . If an author had come to my classroom I might have written earlier. I did a class the other day where they were doing rewrites. They were doing work at 10 or 11 I had to learn at 35. I love to talk to children about making mistakes. It's important that I tell them about how I don't get it right the first time. We live in such a perfectionist society and they see so many finished products and polished performances.''

While Mrs. MacLachlan would like to write for teen-agers, she is drawn repeatedly to the special demands of writing for younger children:''I have to write what I can write, and writing the text of a picture book is like walking a tightrope, if you ramble off. . . . As my friend Julius Lester says, a picture book is the essence of an experience.''

> *Eden Ross Lipson, ''A Children's Author Joins the Immortals,'' in* The New York Times Book Review, *June 29, 1986, p. 31.*

THE SICK DAY (1979)

''I have a stomach ache in my head.'' Emily's opening words could be any child's cute saying, but even at that level MacLachlan overdoes it by following up with ''. . . and a headache in my throat.'' What's more, Emily's speech from then on is a cloying cascade of cute sayings: ''My toe . . . hurts on and off. The ons are long''; ''My stomach feels bad. I think I have to swallow up''; ''Do you think I'm going to die, float up to heaven, and fly around with fedders all over me?'' Emily's father is foolishly indulgent toward her icky talk and sickbed demands; so far, the result of his upbringing is a child who sleeps with money under her pillow because ''it makes me dream about fur coats and plastic jewelry.''. . . Emily is a child only a doting parent could love.

> *A review of ''The Sick Day,'' in* Kirkus Reviews, *Vol. XLVII, No. 9, May 1, 1979, p. 514.*

The story sounds like an eavesdropped scene, with dialogue and action set down straight from a real and very familiar situation. . . . [This is a] slice-of-life picture book, which may prove to be an especially diverting read-aloud for sick preschoolers.

> *Betsy Hearne, in a review of ''The Sick Day,'' in* Booklist, *Vol. 75, No. 18, May 15, 1979, p. 1441.*

[This is a] read-aloud story told with a polished ease that belies the fact that this is MacLachlan's first book for children. The dialogue between father and daughter as one, then the other, is ill, has a natural spontaneity, and the same quality carries over into exposition. . . . Just try to read this one aloud without a grin of recognition. (pp. 11-12)

> *Zena Sutherland, in a review of ''The Sick Day,'' in* Bulletin of the Center for Children's Books, *Vol. 33, No. 1, September, 1979, pp. 11-12.*

Emily complains of a stomachache in her head and a headache in her throat. Her gentle, all-wise father has the right medicine, which includes fixing Emily's hair into 3 ponytails (making her look like a fountain) and putting a plastic giraffe in her otherwise plain broth. These are nice touches, but the book is overplayed with cute child-sayings. There is no tension, no plot building, and the climax—Dad gets sick and Emily nurses him—is weak. [William Pène du] Bois' full-color palette infuses warmth and humor into this overblown story and makes the medicine a lot easier to swallow.

> *Anne McKeithen-Boes, in a review of ''The Sick Day,'' in* School Library Journal, *Vol. 26, No. 1, September, 1979, p. 116.*

THROUGH GRANDPA'S EYES (1980)

The high quality of this book deserves a long, close look. There are too few children's books that explore feelings, values, and sensitivities. ''Grandpa is blind. He has his own way of seeing.'' Grandpa *feels* the sun by its warmth. He *hears* his grandson come to his bedroom. He *smells* eggs frying. He urges his grandson John to close his eyes to share the same experiences. . . . The book makes you want to slow the pace of life to appreciate the beauties we so often take for granted. It needs to be a part of every child's experience. Children and grown-ups, too, should read it for its sensitivity to people's interrelationships and other, sometimes forgotten, values: life is precious, nature is interdependent. It should be on every child's bookshelf to be reread many times.

> *Ruth W. Bauer, in a review of ''Through Grandpa's Eyes,'' in* Children's Book Review Service, *Vol. 8, No. 9, April, 1980, p. 84.*

How a little boy, whose grandfather is blind, learns in the course of a day to see ''through Grandpa's eyes'': an idea with possibilities that are only partially realized here. Problem number one is that the idea is thrust upon us rather than allowed to grow out of the story (to an early question, Grandpa replies, ''Close your eyes, John, and look through my eyes''). Other problems are a meandering text that sometimes uses language more for sound than for meaning (''his eyes are sharp blue though they are not sharp seeing''); rarefied examples of the capacities of the blind (Grandma sculpts Grandpa's head—and he pronounces it a good likeness; he and the little-boy narrator play the cello together, and he is the more adept player); and a tenuousness overall that . . . virtually labels the situation ''special handling.'' Now and again, however, we see—more interestingly and impressively—just how Grandpa copes: his breakfast is arranged on the plate like a clock (''Two eggs at nine o'clock and toast at two o'clock''); he pours his own tea ''by putting his finger just inside the rim of the cup to tell him when it is full.'' And in an occasional exchange between grandfather and grandson the author does achieve the tenderness she's aiming for. A more down-to-earth treatment, however, would have accomplished more.

> *A review of ''Through Grandpa's Eyes,'' in* Kirkus Reviews, *Vol. XLVIII, No. 12, June 15, 1980, p. 777.*

The text is slow-paced and gentle but deliberate in its introduction of information. The message is clear: Grandpa is bright, active, and independent. Told in the first person by John, the narration is so evenly paced and controlled that it is not convincingly childlike. It succeeds, however, in conveying the loving, close bond between John and his grandfather and depicts an elderly couple sharing an active, happy life. Although the message is clear, the book is not a didactic lesson but rather a sensory exploration of the world of a blind person.

> *Christine McDonnell, in a review of ''Through Grandpa's Eyes,'' in* The Horn Book Magazine, *Vol. LVI, No. 4, August, 1980, p. 398.*

This little story is an attempt, largely successful, to demonstrate the fact that when sight is gone, our other four senses—plus memory—can still inform us handsomely about our environment. And in the process, it has something nicely positive to say about a child's relationship with his grandparents. . . .

Though the tone of this story is gentle and warm, it also has well-measured moments of humor, and is never sentimental. The child narrator accepts his grandfather's blindness matter-of-factly because Grandpa accepts it that way, and the relationship between the two is natural and satisfying. . . .

Because of its subject, this story may find only a limited audience, but it should by no means be considered useful only for the handicapped or their families. It has a lot of good things to say about our physical surroundings and how we perceive them, things that would be interesting to any young reader who has ever worn a blindfold or lain awake in the dark.

> *Natalie Babbitt, in a review of "Through Grandpa's Eyes," in* The New York Times Book Review, *Vol. LXXXV, No. 39, September 28, 1980, p. 36.*

ARTHUR, FOR THE VERY FIRST TIME   (1980)

Arthur is ten. A quiet, literal child, he is unhappy because his parents squabble; he is unhappy because he has guessed his mother is pregnant; he is not totally enthralled at being taken to stay with Great-Aunt Elda and Great-Uncle Wrisby for the summer. He meets a lively girl his own age, Moira, who calls him "Mouse" rather than Arthur, and advises him to think less and do more; it is because Arthur changes and makes his mark that Moira, at the end of the story, calls him Arthur for the very first time. By then Arthur has learned a great deal about himself, has learned to care more for other people, and has gained self-confidence. Other people he cares about (Moira, her grandfather, his aunt and uncle, some animals) are well worth loving; MacLachlan has created a wonderfully original and lovable group of people. The story has a deep tenderness, a gentle humor, and a beautifully honed writing style. (pp. 15-16)

> *Zena Sutherland, in a review of "Arthur, for the Very First Time," in* Bulletin of the Center for Children's Books, *Vol. 34, No. 1, September, 1980, pp. 15-16.*

Good-hearted good humor relieves this from the mawkishness of therapeutic novels about kids with problems who invariably get transformed. . . . The colorfulness of the characters is unrelenting; each is more exaggeratedly unique and zany than the other. But the intensity of their collective impact does make Arthur's reprogramming plausible—and fun.

> *Marilyn R. Singer, in a review of "Arthur, for the Very First Time," in* School Library Journal, *Vol. 27, No. 2, October, 1980, p. 149.*

Fine characterization, an intriguing mix of people and problems, and the author's remarkable knack for leaving between the lines things best unsaid are some of the strengths of the novel. . . . Meaningful writing that's entertaining as well—a rare combination of qualities that often contradict each other. (pp. 328-29)

> *Judith Goldberger, in a review of "Arthur, for the Very First Time," in* Booklist, *Vol. 77, No. 4, October 15, 1980, pp. 328-29.*

An often humorous recounting of ten-year-old Arthur's activities and introspections during a summer spent with a great-uncle and a great-aunt. . . . An observant child, Arthur jots down in his notebook vivid descriptions and conversations which interest him. He could look at the pig Bernadette for whom he was building a pen and consider her to be, even with her wet

snout and bristly ears, *"almost pleasant."* The story may seem inconsequential, but the central interest is an engaging, very real child.

> *Virginia Haviland, in a review of "Arthur, for the Very First Time," in* The Horn Book Magazine, *Vol. LVII, No. 1, February, 1981, p. 51.*

MOON, STARS, FROGS, AND FRIENDS   (1980)

A rather silly frog story with a different twist, but frog stories are always popular with children and this one will have frequent check-outs. Randall is a lonely frog who finally finds a frog friend, Rupert, who is a prince turned frog by Witch Esme. Esme really didn't intend to turn her friend Rupert into a frog, she just used the wrong spell. The princess whom Esme finds to kiss Rupert turns into a lovely green frog after the kiss. Still, everything works out as Rupert and Esme marry and have fourteen daughters, while Randall and the princess marry and have 441 children. . . . [Tomie de Paola's] colorful, humorous illustrations dominate the book.

> *Margaret M. Nichols, in a review of "Moon, Stars, Frogs, and Friends," in* Children's Book Review Service, *Vol. 9, No. 2, October, 1980, p. 15.*

It's all silly but it's fun, and the ending is a nice variation of the usual princess-frog-prince story. One quibble—Witch Esme is described as "foxy-looking," which is a bit of slang already showing its age, and the preschoolers who will be the book's primary audience aren't going to understand it anyway.

> *Elaine Fort Weischedel, in a review of "Moon, Stars, Frogs, and Friends," in* School Library Journal, *Vol. 27, No. 7, March, 1981, p. 134.*

MAMA ONE, MAMA TWO   (1982)

Softly-crayoned pastel pictures, simply and tenderly composed [by Ruth Lercher Bornstein] and nicely fitting the mood of the story, show the love that is the mortar of the text. In the quiet night dialogue between Katherine and small Maudie, as together they feed and comfort the baby, Maudie's story emerges. Her mother, increasingly disturbed, had needed to go away for therapy, and Maudie was taken to a second (foster) mother, Mama Two. The author does a good job, within the story, of having a social worker explain to a child, in very simple terms, why her mother has become unstable and what will happen. The tone is candid, the approach positive. It is not until the end of the story that the reader knows that the loving, gentle Katherine is Mama Two; the book ends with her telling Maudie, who has asked, "When is spring?" that "Whenever Mama One comes home will be spring." There have been other books in which foster parents were sympathetically portrayed; this is the nicest yet for the primary grades reader. (pp. 153-54)

> *Zena Sutherland, in a review of "Mama One, Mama Two," in* Bulletin of the Center for Children's Books, *Vol. 35, No. 8, April, 1982, pp. 153-54.*

[Katherine and Maudie] discuss Maudie's feelings and her hopes for her mother's quick recovery. This articulation of her fears calms the troubled child. Although a model for expressing painful emotions is presented, the tone is so mild and serene that the seriousness of the problem is much too understated. Both text and illustrations have a pastoral quality that seems incompatible with the traumatic kinds of events that are the subject of the book.

> *Karen Harris, in a review of "Mama One, Mama Two," in* School Library Journal, *Vol. 28, No. 8, April, 1982, p. 59.*

This is a tender, loving story of a young child in the care of a foster mother. The warmth and caring that "Mama Two" communicates defines a singular relationship, which the reader experiences through the story. A real winner.

> *Beverly Woods, in a review of "Mama One, Mama Two," in* Children's Book Review Service, *Vol. 10, No. 10, May, 1982, p. 94.*

TOMORROW'S WIZARD (1982)

Warm humor and a gift for language plus an eye for improbable characters ("... a whiny, complaining woman named Mona who was as homely as a mushroom gone by") are the hallmarks of this delightful storybook about a wizard, his apprentice, and their talking horse. The wizard is able to make wishes come true, and each wish is a new and highly entertaining story. This reads as well aloud as silently. A real charmer.

> *Jane Yolen, in a review of "Tomorrow's Wizard," in* Children's Book Review Service, *Vol. 10, No. 9, April, 1982, p. 85.*

This collection of six warm, humorous and gentle vignettes follows the adventures of three colorful characters: Tomorrow's Wizard, his young apprentice Murdoch and a philosophical horse saved from an ill-tempered owner. The Wizard and Murdoch are charged with fulfilling the most important wishes and curses uttered by the humans who inhabit the nearby villages of this unnamed land. Watched over by the High Wizard, the three companions go about making surprising matches between very different individuals and solving a variety of problems in a way that reveals much about the human heart and the meaning of true happiness and contentment. The style is warm and comforting without becoming syrupy and burdensome. While there is much to challenge young readers' imagination and understanding, the message at the heart of these stories is sometimes handed over a bit too easily. But this is a trifle compared to the overall effect. The bittersweet ending is to be appreciated because it is based on human longing and experience.... A winner.... (pp. 72-3)

> *Jerry Spiegler, in a review of "Tomorrow's Wizard," in* School Library Journal, *Vol. 28, No. 8, April, 1982, pp. 72-3.*

Wizards, as we all know, perch in clouds, rattle their wands, and shower the earth with promises. What we don't know—but what Patricia MacLachlan tells us in her most magical of books—is that wizards are often cranky, prone to indecision, and blighted with incompetent assistants....

Tomorrow's Wizard is a quietly stunning book, filled with poetry and parables. Kathy Jacobi's illustrations perfectly complement Patricia MacLachlan's lyrical storytelling. A book that should stand permanently on every child's shelf.

> *Alexandra Johnson, "Meet a Cranky Wizard," in* The Christian Science Monitor, *May 14, 1982, p. B9.*

Somewhat reminiscent in its drollness of Natalie Babbitt's *The Devil's Storybook* ..., the book is notable for its elliptical style, which fosters a feeling of wonder, and its warm, affectionate view of life.

> *Ann A. Flowers, in a review of "Tomorrow's Wizard," in* The Horn Book Magazine, *Vol. LVIII, No. 3, June, 1982, p. 290.*

CASSIE BINEGAR (1982)

Cassie—whose family is loving, boisterous and original—longs to have a family like her friend, Margaret Mary. MM's parents are coldly unimaginative bores, but Cassie finds them "serene." Meanwhile, proper MM basks in the warmth of Cassie's casual but big-hearted clan. The problem is that Cass is changing—aware for the first time of other people, and feeling the natural "anguish" of growing up. She hides in her secret places: observing, listening and judging her loved ones, often unfairly. She despises change and, when her grandmother comes for the summer, Cass is shocked that "Gran" has aged. But Gran's still the blunt and sharply empathic woman Cass remembers, and readers discover that the old and the young have much to give each other. The only conflict is Cassie's war with herself, and this is taken in stride by her understanding family. By the end of the story, Cass is "learning how to look through other people's eyeglasses"—as Gran has advised—and beginning to understand how they feel about things. The characters in this sensitive story are pleasant and kindly, and most of them are philosophical. MacLachlan flattens her lyric style with occasional clichés, but her writing is luminous and readable, and romantic 10- and 12-year-old girls will love it all.

> *Wendy Dellett, in a review of "Cassie Binegar," in* School Library Journal, *Vol. 29, No. 1, September, 1982, p. 124.*

Since nothing rings of the American here-and-now, one's first thought is that this is some Highland fastness, some redoubt of eccentricity, poetry, and romance. But though Margaret Mary is said to come from England, the Binegars are truly of no time and place—and that's both an attraction and a weakness.... Every motif has its opposite number—for a story about waywardness and flux, this is highly patterned—and almost every moment is a rapt one. But introspective girls will readily put themselves in Cassie's place.

> *A review of "Cassie Binegar," in* Kirkus Reviews, *Vol. L, No. 17, September 1, 1982, p. 998.*

It is not the plot (there really isn't one) that makes this so readable and distinctive a novel, but the flow of the writing, the easy mingling of exposition and dialogue, the polished merging of colorful characters and shifting relationships, and Cassie's continuing and believable growth in understanding herself and others.... Still waters run deep and clear here.

> *Zena Sutherland, in a review of "Cassie Binegar," in* Bulletin of the Center for Children's Books, *Vol. 36, No. 4, December, 1982, p. 73.*

Cassie Binegar worried for fear she could never find a place of her own in her disorganized, loving family. Her father and brothers were fishermen, and the family had recently moved to the seashore to manage a colony of summer cottages. There they were joined by Uncle Hat, who spoke in rhyme; the divorced Cousin Coralinda, who wore too many feathers; her daughter, Baby Binnie, who spoke only gibberish except when it suited her; and Jason, an aspiring writer. . . . The final chapter is a splendid account of Coralinda's wedding to Jason—an unconventional, delightful wedding. The writing style is elegant and evocative, and the symbolic use of an ever-changing kaleidoscope does justice to the theme of growth and acceptance. (pp. 45-6)

> *Ann A. Flowers, in a review of ''Cassie Binegar,''* in The Horn Book Magazine, *Vol. LIX, No. 1, February, 1983, pp. 45-6.*

SEVEN KISSES IN A ROW   (1983)

With her parents off at an ''eyeball doctors''' convention, Emma is left with an aunt and uncle who know nothing about giving seven wake-up kisses in a row, not to mention sectioned grapefruit for breakfast. As this book gently reminds readers, adults don't have exclusive rights to eccentric, stubborn habits. Change also comes hard for children, who quickly become accustomed to familiar routines.

That's exactly 7-year-old Emma's problem. Her amusing rituals frequently clash with Aunt Evelyn and Uncle Elliot's rules. And they ''came with lots of rules.'' But with the help of her empathetic brother, Zach, Emma begins to see the merit of ''different strokes for different folks.''

By the book's end, Elliot and Evelyn, who are expectant parents, have received Emma's crash (and nonsexist) course in how to be a good father and mother as well as a top-notch uncle and aunt. In return Emma learns the value of flexibility.

Some might consider this book too idyllic—there is never any screaming, hitting or serious throwing of tantrums. Instead its relaxed pacing and reassuring tone are accentuated by [Maria Pia Marrella's] warm, folksy pen-and-ink illustrations—a refreshing change from the tendency to overplay blood, guts and fear in books for younger children. Flashes of humor thrown in at odd moments—before running away from home, Emma signs her note ''fondest regards to the family''—lightly move the action along to a comfortable close for everyone, including the reader.

> *E. A. Hass, in a review of ''Seven Kisses in a Row,''* in The New York Times Book Review, *March 20, 1983, p. 31.*

This warm story of family ties emphasizes accepting others as they are. The plot develops slowly, but moves at a relaxed pace. The characters are interesting, but not fully developed. MacLachlan creates a laidback mood that is humorous and pleasing to read, although the slow pace may discourage some readers.

> *Lizz Timmons, in a review of ''Seven Kisses in a Row,''* in School Library Journal, *Vol. 29, No. 8, April, 1983, p. 115.*

Emma's character is right on target, and the text is simply written—just right for unseasoned readers looking for something to tackle independently. The warmth is beguiling. (p. 1278)

> *Denise M. Wilms, in a review of ''Seven Kisses in a Row,''* in Booklist, *Vol. 79, No. 19, June 1, 1983, pp. 1277-78.*

UNCLAIMED TREASURES   (1984)

Willa, almost twelve, is an imaginative and sensitive girl who yearns to be interesting, to do something extraordinary. She thinks she's in love with the man next door, an artist for whom she poses while his wife is away; when she finally sees that the model in the white dress has his wife's face, Willa leaves a note that brings the estranged pair together. That's one of the ways Willa learns about love, in a tender and subtle book that has strong characters, a flowing style, and a perceptive depiction of familial problems and loyalties. (pp. 151-52)

> *Zena Sutherland, in a review of ''Unclaimed Treasures,''* in Bulletin of the Center for Children's Books, *Vol. 37, No. 8, April, 1984, pp. 151-52.*

MacLachlan has crafted an extraordinary story from ordinary daily events and filled it with unique neighborhood characters including Old Pepper, ancient and wrinkled; Horace's maiden aunts, the Unclaimed Treasures; and Matthew, Horace's tall and solemn father. MacLachlan's penetration into the dreams of youth merges with her keen sense of humor and fluid writing style to give a new perspective on chicken pot pie, Czerny exercises and practicing on the bedpost for that first kiss. Romantic young girls will quickly claim this treasure.

> *Cynthia K. Leibold, in a review of ''Unclaimed Treasures,''* in School Library Journal, *Vol. 30, No. 8, April, 1984, p. 116.*

This is romance and moonshine: layer upon layer, meaning interknit with meaning—totally unreal, and hugely seductive. . . . That it all does hold together, at least for the duration, is a testament to MacLachlan's structural finesse and heady atmospherics.

> *A review of ''Unclaimed Treasures,''* in Kirkus Reviews, *Juvenile Issue, Vol. LII, Nos. 6-9, May 1, 1984, p. J-40.*

Things both ordinary and extraordinary happen to Willa the summer she is twelve, and MacLachlan tells about them in a retrospective story deepened with evocative writing. . . . [The] incidents, which unfold introspectively—and somewhat slowly—from Willa's point of view, are set in the aura of a soft summer night and will be savored by young readers looking for a romantic, tender tale, sensitively told.

> *Barbara Elleman, in a review of ''Unclaimed Treasures,''* in Booklist, *Vol. 80, No. 21, July, 1984, p. 1550.*

Fragments of two stories contrapuntally enrich the sprightly main story. . . . An array of delightfully eccentric characters and comic scenes—akin to those of Ellen Raskin—add to the story, which exudes spontaneity yet rests on fine craftsmanship.

> *Nancy C. Hammond, in a review of ''Unclaimed Treasures,''* in The Horn Book Magazine, *Vol. LX, No. 4, August, 1984, p. 467.*

SARAH, PLAIN AND TALL (1985)

AUTHOR'S COMMENTARY

[*The following excerpt is taken from MacLachlan's Newbery Award acceptance speech of June 29, 1986.*]

I would like to tell you about the roots of [*Sarah, Plain and Tall*], in the process of which you will probably know more about me than you care to know.

When I learned that I had won the Newbery, it was after lunch with friends, not my best time of day, even though my fortune cookie was the only one with a prophetic message. It said: "Your talents will soon be recognized." Honest it did. I will carry it with me always so that when I am in the middle of a book or a speech, where I am always convinced that I am tedious or dull or self-conscious, I will remember that once upon a time I was talented.

My best time of day as a writer . . . is between five-thirty and eight in the morning, when I make what at the time seem to me to be the most startling observations. The observations, mind you, that later as I write them become as common as the odd glass of water, the coffee dregs, the garbage of the day—those things, surprise or no surprise, that are what life and literature are made up of. The sunrise and I are close friends; we are well connected. Good word, *connection*, for if I feel connected to the sunrise, I am even more connected to childhood. Once when I was young, I had a dream that the sun did not rise because I had overslept. Ah, the wonderful self-centeredness that is allowed, that is *necessary* in childhood, suspicious in adulthood. Dare I admit that I have had the same dream as an adult? You bet I do. My daughter gave me permission when she exclaimed one day, "When are we grown up anyway?" When, indeed. E. L. Konigsburg, writing in *Celebrating Children's Books* . . . , confesses to the same thing after describing a trip to New York after winning the Newbery: "But because I retain this ability to see myself as the center of the universe, I can write for children. And because the adult part of me can see how absolutely ridiculous I am when I am doing it, my writings are readable." I wonder if there really is that adult part of me, for every morning as the sun comes up I crash downstairs, first one up, to clamp myself against the kitchen sink and watch the sun come up over the hills. It does not seem ridiculous. It is serious business. (pp. 408-09)

Sarah, Plain and Tall grew out of . . . what my mother used to call the heroics of a common life. When Julius Lester praises children's literature as the "literature that gives full attention to the ordinary," he echoes my parents' belief that it is the daily grace and dignity with which we survive that children most need and wish to know about in books. My parents believed in the truths of literature, and it was my mother who urged me to "read a book and find out who you are," for there are those of us who read or write to slip happily into the characters of those we'd like to be. It is, I believe, our way of getting to know the good and bad of us, rehearsing to be more humane, "revising our lives in our books," as John Gardner wrote, "so that we won't have to make the same mistakes again." My father and I played out daily scenes in the cloaks of characters, engaging in extended plots that we changed as we wished. More rehearsal. It was a safe way to bump up against life, and exciting because my father always invited questions and disagreement. Our plots could make you cry, and I don't mean tears of joy. His enthusiasm—coupled with my mother's incredible tolerance for the eccentricities and subtleties of people, particularly children—meant that I could risk being a rascal. And I was, like the horse Jack in *Sarah,*

Plain and Tall. It is the essence of my parents' acceptance reflected in the character of Anna and Caleb's father when he complains that Jack was feisty in town. "'Rascal,' murmured Papa, smiling, because no matter what Jack did Papa loved him."

My mother told me early on about the real Sarah, who came from the coast of Maine to the prairie to become a wife and mother to a close family member. My mother remembered her fondly. "Is that real?" demanded a school child. "Just what are the facts?" This is the question most asked by children, I suppose because part of childhood is concerned with sorting out the facts from the fiction, both truths of life. (pp. 410-11)

[I] am still trying to sort out facts for myself, though with little luck. "I've noticed," said a friend recently, "that you don't pay much attention to facts. They are not," she added, "of great importance to you." I confess to this. Facts are like an oil painting which begins with a figure and soon succumbs to layers of paint so that the original is lost underneath. Facts are, for me, close to what the writer Harriet Doerr describes as memories in *Stones for Ibarra* . . . , when she writes that "memories are like corks left out of bottles. They swell. They no longer fit." I will believe anything, fact or fiction, if it's written or told well, as Jane Yolen will tell you. She called me once to read a passage she was writing about a dragon giving birth, laying its eggs in the sand. "Tell me if this works for you," she said. After she read I was incredulous. "I didn't know dragons laid eggs," I said. "I thought they had live young." There was silence. "Patty," she said, "dragons are imaginary." Oh. "It works," I muttered.

So the fact of Sarah was there for years, though the book began, as books often do, when the past stepped on the heels of the present; or backward, when something *now* tapped something *then*. Two of my children began to prepare to leave home for college, first one, then the other. But before they left, my parents took us on a trip west to the prairie, where they and I had been born. It was a gift for all of us, for the children to see a land they had never seen, to know family they had never met, to stand on the vast North Dakota farm where my father had been born in a sod house and, as Anna observes, "the prairie reached out and touched the places where the sky came down." Maya Angelou said recently that when Thomas Wolfe said you can't go home again, he was right. But he was also wrong, for you can't really ever leave either. It was a startling connection from the past to open the door of the granary, the only building still standing, and find a gopher filling his cheeks with grain.

But mostly it was an important and poignant connection for my mother who was, because of Alzheimer's disease, beginning to lose her memory. How splendid if memories swell like corks out of a bottle! How cruel when they diminish and disappear. First there is no more present. Then there is no past. At last there are no more words. "Words, words, words," complained a frustrated young writer in a letter to me. "Is that all writers have?" Yes and no. Sarah speaks for me and my mother, for whom there are few words left, when she writes in the book: "My brother William is a fisherman, and he tells me that when he is in the middle of a fogbound sea the water is a color for which there is no name." This is my favorite sentence in the book, and I know why. It makes an attempt to say what I have always thought and only been able to say in Sarah's voice: that words are limiting, an odd thing for a writer to say. There is an entire world, complex and layered and full, behind each word or between words, that is often present but not spoken. And it is often what is left unsaid that shapes and empowers a moment, an experience, a book. Or a life. Actors know this. Musicians know it, too.

When I began *Sarah,* I wished for several things and was granted something unexpected. Most of all I wished to write my mother's story with spaces, like the prairie, with silences that could say what words could not. I began the story as a picture book, and it is clear to me that I wanted to wrap the land and the people as tightly as I could and hand this small piece of my mother's past to her in a package as perfect as Anna's sea stone, as Sarah's sea. But books, like children, grow and change, borrowing bits and pieces of the lives of others to help make them who and what they are. And in the end we are all there, my mother, my father, my husband, my children, and me. We gave my mother better than a piece of her past. We gave her the same that Anna and Caleb and Sarah and Jacob received—a family. (pp. 411-12)

> *Patricia MacLachlan, "Newbery Medal Accep-tance," in* The Horn Book Magazine, *Vol. LXII, No. 4, July-August, 1986, pp. 407-13.*

Anna, the narrator, has been running the family's modest prai-rie home since her mother died giving birth to Caleb; both of them are excited when their father says he has been corre-sponding with a woman in Maine who may become his bride. Sarah, who writes of herself as "plain and tall," comes west for a month's trial and the two children try in every way to make her love them as they instantly love her. So this is a love story, but a most unusual one, and it is told with distinction, in a style that is imbued with lyricism although it is simple prose. The structure is spare and strong, the characters firmly established.

> *Zena Sutherland, in a review of "Sarah, Plain and Tall," in* Bulletin of the Center for Children's Books, *Vol. 38, No. 9, May, 1985, p. 171.*

A book that is filled with wisdom, gentle humor and the prac-tical concerns necessary for a satisfying life. Terse writing and poetic rhythm flow to create a tender story about the fragile beginnings of a family relationship on its way to perma-nence. . . . The characters emerge through dialogue, Sarah's letters and the family's responses to her. Through a simple sentence or phrase, aspects of each character's personality—strength, stubbornness, a sense of humor—are brought to light. Refreshingly, this novel portrays children as receptive to the love, nurturing and attention that a step-parent can offer—and the willingness to return the affection. Throughout the story, MacLachlan weaves in the colors of the prairie as the seasons pass. Readers will hold their breaths with Anna and Caleb, wondering if indeed Sarah will stay, and breathe a sigh of relief when she does. A short but moving book that is anything but plain—for those who prefer quality to quantity. (pp. 92-3)

> *Trev Jones, in a review of "Sarah, Plain and Tall," in* School Library Journal, *Vol. 31, No. 9, May, 1985, pp. 92-3.*

A near-perfect miniature novel that fulfills the ideal of different levels of meaning for children and adults. . . . The simplicity of plot, style, and characterization is deceptive. Sarah proves not only plain and tall, but also kind and good, coming like water to three people thirsty for someone caring. . . . The dia-

logue is natural, varied but always vivid, ranging from scenes of soft singing to a romp in the cow pond to a raging storm. When Sarah comes back from town, a trip that the children fear signals her permanent departure, the reader is as deeply moved to happiness as the family itself. . . . Poignant but never sentimental, this is a worthy successor to Wilder's Little House books and a prime choice for reading aloud. (pp. 1254, 1256)

> *Betsy Hearne, in a review of "Sarah, Plain and Tall," in* Booklist, *Vol. 81, No. 17, May 1, 1985, pp. 1254, 1256.*

This is an exquisite, sometimes painfully touching little tale. . . .

It is the simplest of love stories expressed in the simplest of prose. Embedded in these unadorned declarative sentences about ordinary people, actions, animals, facts, objects and colors are evocations of the deepest feelings of loss and fear, love and hope.

The characters have no vocabulary or taste for elaborate dis-cussions. Like them, the book has a magical kind of tact. The author never disfigures what is implicit by spelling it out. . . .

This gentle book cannot fail to touch readers.

> *Martha Saxton, in a review of "Sarah, Plain and Tall," in* The New York Times Book Review, *May 19, 1985, p. 20.*

Subject and style combine to give this brief book a strong emotional impact. It is a story of longings fulfilled, of a family being made instead of broken. Anna is cast as the narrator, but the use of first person does not make the language ordinary, as is often the case with first-person accounts. Anna's telling is almost musical in its rhythm, and while the words are simple they are artfully arranged. This would be a natural choice for reading aloud so that children can savor the sound of the language.

> *Janet Hickman, in a review of "Sarah, Plain and Tall," in* Language Arts, *Vol. 62, No. 8, December, 1985, p. 883.*

A month's trial can apply to many situations but few will seem as strange to modern readers than the month in which Caleb and Anna get to know the wife Papa had advertised for in the newspapers after several years of managing with the limited support of housekeepers. Sarah Wheaton from Maine showed a marked individuality in her reply to the advertisement—'I am strong and I work hard and I am willing to travel. But I am not mild mannered'—and the point of identification she offered when the trial period was agreed ('I will come by train. I will wear a yellow bonnet. I am plain and tall') is seen at once to be as veracious as everything she says. Her character fairly bursts out of the pages.

Prairie customs of a century ago may differ from ours but people don't change so much, nor does the problem faced by the writer who is trying to convey a delicate web of relation-ships within the limits of a junior story, and in this case a very short one. It has become a convention that a child or children shall stand in the centre of a narrative as touchstones for sub-ordinate characters. Not so in *Sarah, Plain and Tall.* There is no artificial centre but the pattern of four people approaching one another in goodwill and with a good deal of care. . . . Time is measured, in this infinitely selective, delicately allusive tale, by the almost imperceptible changes and adjustments in the four people whose feelings are measured with the same quiet, sober accuracy. . . . The end is as piercingly simple and as satisfying as the rest of this finely wrought tale. Not a word is wasted, not a nuance missed in the quiet tenor of a narrative which creates, seemingly without any effort, the family's world of sky and prairies and Sarah's remembered world of sea and sand, the day to day work and weather of a family community and the vulnerable tender affections with which this family achieves an enormous, important change in its constitution. This small masterpiece should prove to young readers once and for all the power and scope which words well managed have to follow the intricate tracks of human relationships.

> *Margery Fisher, in a review of "Sarah, Plain and Tall," in* Growing Point, *Vol. 25, No. 6, March, 1987, p. 4750.*

Eve Merriam

1916-

American poet; author of picture books, fiction, and nonfiction; and reteller.

One of America's most popular contemporary poets for children, Merriam is noted for her versatility, freshness, wit, nonsexist attitude, and concern with social issues. A prolific author for over twenty-five years, she has written numerous collections of verse as well as biographies, picture books including an alphabet book and a counting book, nonfiction about nature, original fantasies, a lexicon of imaginary terms, and a pithy adaptation of a folktale. She is best known for her poetry, which ranges from playful verbal nonsense and melodic lyrics rich with imagery to satirical verse on such topics as television addiction, computerization, urban renewal, and war. Like David McCord, to whom she has been compared, Merriam excels in creating verse that is both instructive and entertaining. Continually experimenting with the sounds, shapes, and meanings of words, Merriam expresses herself through a variety of subjects and moods, utilizing forms ranging from free verse and structured stanzas to concrete poetry; her poems are often noted for their appeal both on a page and when read aloud. Her collections, such as the well-known trilogy *There Is No Rhyme for Silver* (1962), *It Doesn't Always Have to Rhyme* (1964), and *Catch a Little Rhyme* (1966), demonstrate Merriam's freedom from the restrictions of traditional rhyming meters and illustrate her skillful use of inner rhyme, alliteration, assonance, onomatopoeia, and rhythm. Merriam invites children of all ages to delight in poetry through the inventive wordplay, multisensory appeal, amusing observations of everyday experiences, and strong, contagious beats with which she invests her verses. Characteristically unconventional as a biographer, Merriam's cast of American heroes and heroines includes the first female physician Elizabeth Blackwell, New York mayor Fiorello La Guardia, black abolitionist Frederick Douglass, and Jewish poet Emma Lazarus.

Critics generally applaud Merriam's craftsmanship, the currentness of her language and themes, and her lively, approachable style. They also praise her success in bringing her audience to poetry by turning the genre into an enjoyable game, her understanding and depiction of the child's viewpoint, and her ability to keep her social criticism sharp but light. Although some reviewers express disappointment with the occasionally uneven quality of her works, most agree that Merriam's infectious playfulness, challenging social commentary, and evocative verses, whether rhymed or unrhymed, have inspired children to appreciate poetry as both readers and writers.

Merriam received the National Council of Teachers of English Award for excellence in poetry for children in 1981 for her body of work.

(See also *Something about the Author,* Vols. 3, 40; *Contemporary Authors,* Vols. 5-8, rev. ed.; and *Dictionary of Literary Biography,* Vol. 61: *American Writers for Children since 1960: Poets, Illustrators, and Nonfiction Writers.*)

AUTHOR'S COMMENTARY

[The following excerpt is from an interview by Glenna Sloan.]

Eve Merriam derives satisfaction from all aspects of her writing career, but nothing is more important to her than bringing children and poetry together. Not only does she write poetry for children, when possible, she also goes into schools like an evangelist, to spread the good news that reading and writing poetry is fun. "I try to transmit to children and their teachers something of my lust for the language of poetry."

For Eve Merriam, poetry read aloud has always elicited a physical response. "I find it difficult to sit still when I hear poetry or read it out loud. I feel a tingling all over, particularly in the tips of my fingers and in my toes, and it just seems to go right from my mouth all the way through my body. It's like a shot of adrenalin or oxygen when I hear rhymes and word play."

It is this kind of response to poetry that Eve Merriam wants to help children to experience for themselves. She goes on: "I try to give young people a sense of the sport and playfulness of language, because I think it's like a game. There's a physical element in reading poetry aloud; it's like jumping rope or throwing a ball."

Poetry and children form a natural partnership, Eve Merriam insists. Poetry's musical effects of rhyme, rhythm, and alliteration, extensions of children's own speech, naturally appeal to them. Children, like poets, are intrigued by the wonderful things that words can do: how their sounds mimic what is being described, how puns are possible, how language can be made, in Eve Merriam's words, to "natter, patter, chatter, and prate."

If children turn away from poetry, Eve Merriam thinks that the adults in their lives, particularly their teachers, are probably responsible. From her acquaintance with textbooks and her experience in holding workshops for teachers, Ms. Merriam concludes that many teachers take a wrong approach to poetry. For some reason, perhaps because they were themselves poorly taught, too many teachers seem intimidated by poetry.

According to Ms. Merriam, their intimidation causes teachers to intellectualize poetic experience. They ask their pupils for analyses of poems; they feel a need to force the ferreting out of Great Thoughts and Noble Notions, even though a poem may contain none. They ask dreary factual questions. More often than not, teachers in Eve Merriam's experience take the whole business of poetry far too seriously, making the study of it heavy and sanctimonious when it can be light and delightful.

What is her advice to teachers? "Start light. Give children the whole spectrum. Low taste can only be raised by experiencing poetry of all literary levels. Just relax. There are only two rules for poetry: A poem must be read aloud once for the sense or nonsense; then it must be read aloud again for the music. Read, enjoy, then talk about the poem. Do away with questions. Examine the poem instead, reading and re-reading bits of it in turn, picking out words that start the same or sound alike."

She continues: "Take, for instance, my poem, '**Lullaby:**'

    Sh   sh   what do you wish
    sh   sh   the windows are shuttered
    sh   sh   a magical fish
    swims out from the window and down to the river

    lap   lap   the waters are lapping
    sh   sh   the shore slips away
    glide   glide   glide with the current
    sh   sh   the shadows are deeper

    sleep   sleep   tomorrow is sure

For children to count how many times the sound *sh* is in the poem, they will have to hear the poem read aloud. Just looking at the printed page doesn't give you the sound *sh* found in the word *sure*. Nor is the *sh* always at the beginning of a word; you can hear it in *wish* and *fish, if* you read the poem *out loud.*"

Out Loud is not only the title of a book of poems by Eve Merriam, it is also her teaching philosophy in two words. She maintains that no one learns to love poetry without hearing it read out loud. Teachers must force themselves to read aloud and not be deterred by their mistakes. All the better if they flounder and flub, says Ms. Merriam. "Begin over again when that happens. Repetition can only help comprehension and it lets the music of the language sink in. If we can get teachers to read poetry, lots of it, out loud to children, we'll develop a generation of poetry readers; we may even have some poetry writers, but the main thing, we'll have language appreciators."

To share with teachers and children the joys of expression through poetry, Eve Merriam includes in her collections of poetry for children what she calls "open-ended poems," blue-

prints for children to use in writing their own poetry. Here is one example:

"A Rhyme Is a Jump Rope"

A rhyme is a jump rope—
Let's begin.
Take a turn and
Jump right in.

What can we do with a rhyme for *today?*

Perhaps we'll go sailing in the *bay.*
We could feel the silver dots of *spray.*
We might watch the white gulls fly *away.*

In Turkey a king is known as a *bey.*
In Paris there's a street called Rue de la *Paix.*
Olé in Spanish means the same as *hooray.*

How long do you think this rhyme will *stay?*
Until the sky turns dark and *gray?*
(If you were a horse you could answer *neigh* . . .)

                                                    (pp. 959-61)

Eve Merriam sees three main strains throughout her poetry and other writing. The first is her delight in word play, in the ridiculous side of language, its oddities and eccentricities. She loves "kidding around with language," doing slapstick nonsense, making puns and working out word puzzles. . . .

Eve Merriam considers its social aspect to be the second important strain in all her work. She reports being astonished when an anthologist once told her that she was the only poet who wrote poetry for children on social issues. While she agrees that these issues may be overdone in literature to the point of propaganda, she believes that the pain of war, pollution, the evils of technology without humanity, sexism, racism, and the like are matters that touch the lives of children and concern them. (p. 961)

The third strain evident throughout her work is, in her own words, "an affirmation of the joy of being alive." She speaks of the sensuality of her feelings for trees, for the ocean, for the natural world in general. Poems like **"Vacation"** in *It Doesn't Always Have to Rhyme,* with its appeal to all of the senses and its runaway rhythm do reflect Eve Merriam's joy in living fully, in exploring experience with all the senses. The images, lovingly detailed, of **"Simile: Willow and Ginkgo"** in the same collection, are those created by a poet who knows the trees she describes both by sight and by heart.

Asked what early influences are reflected in her work, Eve Merriam spoke first of being read aloud to when she was a child. The sonorous cadences of the Psalms in the Bible had a strong appeal for her. "The Psalms echo in my work, sometimes directly. For one of my city poems, I borrowed form and language from a psalm: 'Thou shalt not be afraid of the terror by night, the fear by day.'"

Eve Merriam grew up in the Philadelphia suburb of Germantown. . . . She found the cultural life there to be rich and varied. Eve was a regular at Friday afternoon children's concerts and at try-out performances of shows bound for New York. Those who enjoy the polysyllabic playfulness of the rhymes in Gilbert and Sullivan operas will hear their echoes in Ms. Merriam's poetry. As a child, she attended many D'Oyly Carte productions of Gilbert and Sullivan works.

Hearing the language of master playwright George Bernard Shaw was a part of her early experience. Eve Merriam's brother-in-law, who loved the theater, took her often to Rose Valley to Jasper Deeter's Hedgerow Theater where Shaw's plays were performed. Eve read with delight Tom Daley's humorous column in the Philadelphia *Bulletin*. Her eyes sparkle as she recalls how much she and her brother enjoyed the funny parodies of Mother Goose rhymes by Guy Wetmore Carryl and his brother Charles. "Obviously those parodies had something to do with my writing *Inner City Mother Goose*" [an adult work]!

In Helen Heffer's (1980) study of her work [*A Checklist of Works By and About Eve Merriam* (unpublished master's thesis, University of Maryland)], Eve Merriam comments about the writers who influenced her most, Gerard Manley Hopkins, W. H. Auden and Jacques Prévert:

> With Hopkins, there is a certain tremendous density of language, of passion, which is so compressed. I think it's the principal reason I'm a poet. . . . It's only half a joke, one definition I give of poetry: It's like condensed orange juice; add the three cans of water and you get prose. Hopkins is so dense and so packed. I get bored or impatient using descriptions or articles and he rarely will say "the," "an" or whatever. The words are just there in tremendous clusters.
>
> Auden was my god as an undergraduate. . . . The things Auden said, like that great sonnet, "The Unknown Citizen." "Was he free? Was he happy? The question is absurd: Had anything been wrong, we would certainly have heard." Tremendous irony. And I think that with Auden there is a cleverness in some of his work where he has taken song forms and adapted them. He did "Refugee Blues" and that kind of thing. So he would often deal with deep material in what would seem on the surface a fairly light way. . . . There is a line of his that I can never forget every day of my life and I can't even remember what poem it's in. But he talks about himself as "a fathom of earth alive in air." And it just seemed such a wonderful image to me. . . .

(pp. 961-63)

Eve Merriam admires in Prévert and Auden their social awareness of the world and their urban sensibility, themes that recur in her own work. Of Prévert she adds:

> Prévert was very interested in songwriting as well as poems. He's very playful; there are lots of puns in his work. And at the same time he has tremendous empathy for the condition of women. And he loves writing for children, too. So I think there was almost a calling out to a sort of soul mate, not that I put myself in that category, I'm much lesser, but that sort of personality. . . .

Eve Merriam's two sons, Guy and Dee Michel, taught her first-hand about children's natural love of the oddities and delights of language. In her interview with Helen Heffer, Ms. Merriam tells how her young sons inspired her first poetry for children:

> I just started with the playful aspect of enjoying the sounds of language. I began to find with my own children that children don't know the

meanings of words, but things are automatically punful. Guy, when he was very young, had been taught to wave bye-bye. My husband and I were talking and somebody used the word "bicycle." Guy heard "bi" and he started to wave bye-bye. . . . The two of them, Guy and Dee, thought the word *encyclopedia* was hysterically funny, and I realized that it was because they could accent the "pe" and that was a naughty thing to do. . . . That's the aspect that I would *love* people of all ages to continue to have with language—that's what attracted me to rhyming and playing around with it: that's the enjoyment of the verbal felicity of language. . . .

Today Eve Merriam is proud of her two sons and her influence on *them*. "It delights me that we are a family of word lovers," she says. Guy, an illustrator, illustrated *The Birthday Cow*, a book of her poems, and did the dust jacket for another, *Rainbow Writing*. He also collaborated with his mother to produce, for Pied Piper Productions, a filmstrip and cassette about her poetry. Dee, Eve Merriam's younger son, is a student of linguistics. "And we are all terrible punsters," Eve admits with obvious delight.

Asked for her advice to aspiring poets of all ages, Eve Merriam said this: "Read a lot. Sit down with anthologies and decide what pleases you. Copy out your favorites in your own handwriting. Buy a notebook and jot down images and descriptions. Be specific; use all the senses. Use your whole body as you write. It might even help sometimes to stand up and move with your words. Don't be afraid of copying a form or a convention, especially in the beginning. And, to give yourself scope and flexibility, remember: It doesn't *always* have to rhyme." (p. 963)

> *Glenna Sloan, "Profile: Eve Merriam," in* Language Arts, *Vol. 58, No. 8, November-December, 1981, pp. 957-64.*

GENERAL COMMENTARY

MAY HILL ARBUTHNOT and ZENA SUTHERLAND

Eve Merriam's verse is varied in form, inventive, and often humorous. It usually speaks directly to the child's experience and is especially appealing to the reader who enjoys word-play. Her essay on **"Writing a Poem,"** in *Finding a Poem*, describes the poet's search for the exact word or phrase to express and illuminate her meaning. Both this essay and the chapter entitled "'I,' Says the Poem" in Nancy Larrick's *Somebody Turned on a Tap in These Kids* are good reading for anyone working with children.

Some notion of the range of Eve Merriam's poetry can be seen in two contrasting poems:

"Landscape"

What will you find at the edge of the world?
A footprint,
a feather,
desert sand swirled?
A tree of ice,
a rain of stars,
or a junkyard of cars?

What will there be at the rim of the world?
A mollusc,
a mammal,
a new creature's birth?
Eternal sunrise,
immortal sleep,
or cars piled up in a rusty heap?

"Ping-Pong"

Chitchat
wigwag
rickrack
zigzag

knickknack
gewgaw
riffraff
seesaw

crisscross
flip-flop
ding-dong
tiptop

singsong
mishmash
King Kong
　　　bong.

"Landscape" has the provocative imagery and the concern with today's problems that are typical of Eve Merriam's poetry and are qualities that she encourages in the writing of her students. . . .

"Ping-Pong" is a good example of the way she uses words for aural effect; bouncy and rhythmic, the poem evokes the patterned clicking of the game's sound. In *There Is No Rhyme for Silver, It Doesn't Always Have to Rhyme,* and *Catch a Little Rhyme,* Merriam—like David McCord—uses poems to illustrate such terms as cliché, homonym, limerick, onomatopoeia, simile, and metaphor.

> *May Hill Arbuthnot and Zena Sutherland, "Poets and Children's Poetry: Eve Merriam," in their* Children and Books, *fourth edition, Scott, Foresman and Company, 1972, p. 377*

CHARLOTTE S. HUCK

Eve Merriam has written a trilogy of books for children about the nature of poetry, including *There Is No Rhyme for Silver, It Doesn't Always Have to Rhyme,* and *Catch a Little Rhyme.* Her poetry has a lilt and bounce that will capture the most disinterested child's attention, beginning with **"How to Eat a Poem."** Such poems as **"Metaphor," "Cliché," "Simile,"** and **"Onomatopoeia"** are excellent for the language class. The poems in *Catch a Little Rhyme* are for children in the primary grades. City boys and girls who are accustomed to slum clearance will appreciate **"Bam Bam Bam."** They will also enjoy the ironic twist to **"The Stray Cat."** Humor is found in **"Teevee,"** and **"Alligator on the Escalator."** In her books *Finding a Poem* and *Out Loud* Merriam continues her interest in playing with language, and at the same time shows her increasing interest in social and political satire. Thus, **"The Wholly Family"** is really a wholly plastic family, while **"Basic for Irresponsibility"** suggests that everything can be blamed on **"It."** Some of the poetry in this book is concrete; while other poems, such as **"A Charm for Our Time,"** are chants of newly created words and products such as "freeze-dry, high-fi." *Independent*

Voices includes seven long poems on persons whom Merriam admires: Benjamin Franklin, Elizabeth Blackwell, Frederic Douglass, Henry Thoreau, Lucretia Mott, Ida B. Wells, and Fiorello La Guardia. Merriam has also written *I Am a Man: An Ode to Martin Luther King, Jr.,* which appears in a picture-book format. Her political satire, written primarily for adults, has received much acclaim. These books include *The Inner City Mother Goose* and *The Nixon Poems.* Obviously, Eve Merriam writes on many subjects and for all ages. (p. 353)

> *Charlotte S. Huck, "Poetry: Selecting Poetry for Children," in her* Children's Literature in the Elementary School, *third edition, Holt, Rinehart and Winston, 1976, pp. 324-53.*

REBECCA LUKENS

To paint without a palette,
To dance without music

The three senses implied in these lines—and more—are teased in the poetry of Eve Merriam. The poems even taste good. In **"How to Eat a Poem,"** she gives permission to be voracious, to gobble each last nibble of sound. **"Inside a Poem"** encourages us to "hear with / our / heels," to inhale, to "swerve in a curve," and to feel with our eyes "what they never touched before." Reading Merriam through, end to end, awakens all our senses to sharpness, but touches our intellects, too. The unexpected juxtapositions, the keen contrasts, the onomatopoeic series, even the clichés freshened to surprise—all are parts of Merriam's own pleasure, and now of ours.

Taking the everyday not for granted but for novelty, Merriam alerts us to a **"Thumbprint,"** "My signature, / thumbing the pages of my time. / My universe key," and thus shows that each person is startlingly singular. Or take socks. In **"The Hole Story"** we find we needn't worry about mending that hole. No need to say, "'Oh, darn,' / For I'm spinning you a yarn." The hole's at the top. Merriam's words play with us, surprising us with double meanings—three in two short lines.

Further delight in words shows in her contrasts. **"Argument"** is a series of one term oppositions like a confrontation between two obstinate speakers shouting "Over. / Under. / Cloudless. / Thunder" and concluding "By way . . .? / MY WAY!" Even clichés are fresh as the visual poem **"Euphemistic"** forms a page pattern including every known phrase for what has happened to great-great-great-great Uncle Clyde, then ends abruptly with the single line *"died."*

Merriam loves the sensory opposition, the surprising synergy of image and metaphor. Her series of sensory appeals in **"What Makes a Poem?"** is filled with surprises as she speaks of the "secrets of rain," and opposes "the touch of grass / Or an icy glass," the "shout of noon" and "the silent moon." In **"A Matter of Taste"** she asks, "What does your tongue like the most?" Contrast sharpens our tastebuds to appreciate anew chewy meat and crunchy toast, "soft marshmallow or a hard lime drop," "hot pancakes or a sherbet freeze."

In addition to this sharply honed sensory awareness, a continuous sense of play spurs us to savor words and explore new meanings. Merriam does not stop with words we know; she creates more. In **"Mean Song,"** which rings of "Jabberwocky," she builds a series of mean wishes, begins with short sounds (snickles and podes, / Ribble and grodes"), crescendoes to "A nox in the groot, / A root in the stoot," and reduces us to shudders with the threat of "one flack snack in the bave." In **"One, Two, Three—Gough!"** her rhymes are proof of the irrationality of English; rhyming dough/sough, through/blough. With equal wit she introduces us to the absurd bird called "Gazinta"; "Two gazinta four two times. . . ."

Merriam is highly skilled in use of sound. Her onomatopoeia in describing a rusty spigot in **"Onomatopoeia"** for example, the internal rhyme in **"What in the World,"** and her frequent yet not cloying assonance and consonance make her poems exactly the stuff for reading aloud. We hear the spondees and sprung rhythm. But the *look* of the poem matters too. *Out Loud,* for example, seems inadequately titled; out loud is not enough, not nearly. Without the book before us, we miss the engaging visual form of short lines and long, broken words and portmanteaus.

The conclusion to draw from a close look at Merriam's poetry remains delight—delight in its freshness and its deceptive spontaneity worked with high craftsmanship. Merriam's own definitions of poetry describe what she creates: acute sensory awareness and the joy of words and wit.

> *Rebecca Lukens, "Eve Merriam," in* Children's Literature Association Quarterly, *Vol. 5, No. 4, Winter, 1981, p. 45.*

SHEILA A. EGOFF

[In *Finding a Poem*], Eve Merriam's dexterous handling of blank verse, free verse, and verbal nonsense is allied with social satire and a fierce political conscience. Contemporary sociological issues are the subject of ironic, angry, sometimes didactic or simply nonmusical flat verse, as expressed in these lines from **"The Wholly Family"**:

> Baby's got a plastic bottle,
> plastic pacifier to chew;
> plastic pillows on the sofa,
> plastic curtains frame the view;
> plastic curlers do up Mama,
> Mama's hairdo plastic, too. . . .
>
> > Praise of plastic thus we sing,
> > plastic over everything
> > keeps us cool and safe and dry:
> > it may not pain us much to die.
>
> (p. 228)

Recognizing that children are not bound rigidly to neat, regular meter and rhyme, [May Swenson, David McCord, Eve Merriam, and Robert Froman] have shared with them delight in the playful visual, aural, and intellectual concepts of shaped verse, concrete poetry, found poetry, and a host of collage and typographical verse forms. . . . Eve Merriam also challenges readers to involve themselves in the fun, accentuating the playful communion between poet and reader. In *Finding a Poem* . . . , she imaginatively explains language terminology, poetic devices, syntax, and grammar, as found in her poem, **"Markings: The Semicolon"**:

> Diver on the board
> lunges toward the edge;
> hedges;
> takes a deep breath;
> hesitates;
> plunges.

She similarly manipulates poetic forms so that they describe themselves, illustrating their structure within the context of the poem itself. Her emphasis on snappy, linguistic wit and clever

wordplay is evident in such collections as *It Doesn't Always Have to Rhyme.* . . . (pp. 235-36)

> *Sheila A. Egoff, "Poetry," in her* Thursday's Child: Trends and Patterns in Contemporary Children's Literature, *American Library Association, 1981, pp. 221-46.*

NANCY LARRICK

When children of [the late sixties and early seventies] were asked why they preferred one poem over another, the usual answer was "I like this one because it's real. The other one is too sweet." I came to believe that "too sweet" is the most damning judgment today's child can make about a poem.

Eve Merriam is never too sweet. Indeed she takes a strong and often minority stand on such issues as pollution, phony advertising, television addiction, and the threat of war. But like Tom Leher, she uses a light satire that is amusing while being sharply critical. (p. 598)

> *Nancy Larrick, "From Tennyson to Silverstein: Poetry for Children, 1910-1985," in* Language Arts, *Vol. 63, No. 6, October, 1986, pp. 594-600.*

THE REAL BOOK ABOUT FRANKLIN D. ROOSEVELT   (1952)

A readable summing up of a great career, though at times one feels the anecdotal handling of the family circle and friends is somewhat bland for so vigorous a subject. Thanks to the accessibility of material since his death, Roosevelt's story is already part of history, and this author had available more than did Rita Kleeman for her *Young Franklin Roosevelt* . . . and Alden Hatch for his *Franklin Roosevelt.* . . . She has used it competently, though her book is less distinguished writing than either of these mentioned. His personal as well as his public life is given full attention. His tremendous vitality, versatility and courage are evident from his youthful exploits, triumphs and hobbies, through his school years at Groton and Harvard, his first ventures into public life as a State Senator, successive steps to the Presidency, his part in national and global policies, his last years.

> *A review of "The Real Book about Franklin D. Roosevelt," in* Virginia Kirkus' Bookshop Service, *Vol. 19, No. 24, December 15, 1951, p. 705.*

THE REAL BOOK ABOUT AMAZING BIRDS   (1955)

Astounding information about the hornbill, the ostrich, the hummingbird, the umbrella bird and other such feathered oddities, dots the pages of a book that is also a good general introduction to ornithological study. Although the author states at the outset that her choice of examples will be in the realm of the more unusual birds, the themes of her chapters are generally informative. The origin of birds from reptiles, feather structure, beaks, nests, birds that dance and skip, migration, non-flying birds—these are the subjects that orient and entertain and that have a good chance of making bird watchers out of even the most apathetic, as they begin to realize that even the general run of bird is amazing too.

> *A review of "The Real Book about Amazing Birds," in* Virginia Kirkus' Service, *Vol. XXIII, No. 13, July 1, 1955, p. 427.*

What child is not full of questions about [animals]? *The Real Book of Amazing Birds* . . . is full of answers. Here authentic nature lore is presented in ways that stress the curious and unusual. The child learns of birds that cooperate, of birds in many lands that build amazing nests, birds that "play hide-and-seek," and other characteristics to intrigue the child. Particularly good is the chapter on "dancers, skippers, and strutters," which describes some of the interesting courtship ritual.

> *Millicent Taylor, "Making the Acquaintance of Some Very Unusual Creatures," in* The Christian Science Monitor, *November 10, 1955, p. 3B.*

Eve Merriam rouses interest by introducing us to examples of the curious, the ornate and the exotic. There are, for instance, the Australian bower bird . . . ; the sociable African weaver-bird; and the game little American roadrunner. . . . These and many other birds are sorted into chapters bearing such provocative headings as **"Beaks and Freaks," "Birds that Hunt"** and **"Dancers, Skippers and Strutters."** Her final chapter on the mystery of migration is excellent.

> *Robert K. Plumb, "From Dinohyus to Jaguar," in* The New York Times Book Review, *Part II, November 13, 1955, p. 34.*

In the same fine literary style which characterizes her writing for children. . . . Species included are not all dealt with in equal detail, the index is incomplete and the illustrations [by Paul Wenck] do not always appear opposite text. Otherwise, this might have been as useful for reference as it is absorbing reading. Humor makes it ideal for reading aloud in groups.

> *A review of "The Real Book about Amazing Birds," in* Bulletin of the Children's Book Center, *Vol. X, No. 5, January, 1957, p. 69.*

THE VOICE OF LIBERTY: THE STORY OF EMMA LAZARUS (1959)

The story of a woman with a great heart, this volume constitutes a fictionalized biography of the Jewish patriot whose lines are immortalized on the base of the Statue of Liberty. A brilliant poet and prose writer, Emma Lazarus championed the cause of the Jewish refugees from Russian persecution and fought an intellectual and active battle against the forces of anti-Semitism in this country. . . . The author paints her subject in a moving, clear and dramatic way, that should prove interesting and inspiring to her young readers.

> *A review of "Voice of Liberty: The Story of Emma Lazarus," in* Virginia Kirkus' Service, *Vol. XXVII, No. 2, January 15, 1959, p. 48.*

[Emma Lazarus] is vividly portrayed. Her spirit, sensitivity, and facile mind are captured in this brief biography. A good picture of the period is given through a view of her acquaintances among literary figures and philanthropists. This account, fuller than others for children, is one of the best in the "Covenant" series.

> *Julia J. Brody, in a review of "The Voice of Liberty: The Story of Emma Lazarus," in* Junior Libraries, *Vol. 5, No. 7, March, 1959, p. 146.*

Although exceedingly adulatory, the portrayal of [Emma Lazarus's] life in a wealthy, well-established Jewish family, her career as a writer, her growing consciousness of her Jewish heritage, and her crusade to help Jewish refugees in America and to further Jewish nationalism is nonetheless inspiring.

> *A review of "The Voice of Liberty: The Story of Emma Lazarus," in* The Booklist and Subscription Books Bulletin, *Vol. 55, No. 15, April 1, 1959, p. 426.*

A GAGGLE OF GEESE (1960)

Among word-collectors some of the most prized items are those nouns describing an assemblage or "company" of beasts and birds. The collection, comparison and usage of such archaic, fanciful terms as a skulk of foxes or a gam of whales has generally been an adult diversion but now the poet, Eve Merriam, and illustrator Paul Galdone have provided a picture-book introduction to the subject. Granted that 5-year-olds and possibly even 8-year-olds may not fully recognize the appropriateness of "a shrewdness of apes," "a murmuration of starlings," or even "a murder of crows," but they will, I think, get a lot of fun out of the sound and rhythm of the phrases and from Paul Galdone's amusing pictures. A child needs little encouragement to play with words and who, in this game, doesn't like to run a bit before settling down to a walk?

> *Ellen Lewis Buell, "Company Words," in* The New York Times Book Review, *August 7, 1960, p. 26.*

Here is a picture book for the age that is just outgrowing Mother Goose, offering new and curious words. A poet, Eve Merriam suitably enough, has . . . collected and commented in verse on nearly forty names used to indicate a group of one kind of animal. . . . Some of the names are odd, some quaint and all are singularly appropriate, especially the *murder* of crows, an *exaltation* of larks and, most familiar of all, a *pride* of lions. Stimulating and fun.

> *Margaret Sherwood Libby, in a review of "A Gaggle of Geese," in* Lively Arts and Book Review, *March 5, 1961, p. 35.*

Play with the group names of animals, birds, and fish, and full-page illustrations in two colors . . . make a picture book that should be fun for the child who enjoys words and for the adult who wishes to stimulate interest in words. I couldn't help wishing that the emphasis had been more on the text than on the pictures, with many others of these fascinating words included, for children beyond the picture-book age are the ones who will take the greatest pleasure in discovering "a lepe of leopards," "a kindle of kittens," "a labor of moles," "a husk of jackrabbits," and the rest.

> *Ruth Hill Viguers, in a review of "A Gaggle of Geese," in* The Horn Book Magazine, *Vol. XXXVII, No. 2, April, 1961, p. 154.*

MOMMIES AT WORK (1961)

Beginning with how mommies work in the home to keep baby happy and comfortable, this goes on to portray the many different outside roles many different mommies fill in the wide world away from home. There are mommies who are teachers, dancers, office workers, doctors, cashiers, etc., etc., but each one comes home at the end of the day to fill that one role young listeners know best. An excellent original conception, designed to provide understanding of career mothers for their very young offspring. . . .

A review of "Mommies at Work," in Virginia Kirkus'
Service, *Vol. 29, No. 16, August 15, 1961, p. 727.*

The text is slight: mommies kiss you, tie laces, wash dishes,
etc.; mommies do all kinds of work, with many examples of
the kinds of work mommies do; and mommies love best of all
to be coming home to you. The reassurance of that affection
gives the book some value, but the listing of activities at home
and varieties of jobs is not liable to interest a small child whose
interest is probably only in his own mother's job.

*Zena Sutherland, in a review of "Mommies at Work,"
in* Bulletin of the Center for Children's Books, *Vol.
XV, No. 2, October, 1961, p. 31.*

THERE IS NO RHYME FOR SILVER   (1962)

The acid test for poetry designed for small listeners is how
quickly it lends itself to rereading and memorizing. This collection of small poems affords many examples that children
will claim as their own. They will love the use of words, made-
up as well as real, appealing in form and sound, varied in
rhythmic use. They will find quick recognition in concepts and
images and associations:—city and country, travel and stay-
at-home, fun and games and imaginative flights, laughter—all
this and more.

A review of "There Is No Rhyme for Silver," in
Virginia Kirkus' Service, *Vol. 30, No. 13, July 1,
1962, p. 555.*

Because poetry is so personal, there are poems here for everyone, though no reader will be happy with them all. **"To Meet
Mr. Lincoln"** is a welcome addition to the holiday material;
"Associations" is clever and childlike; **"Exploring"** is a miniature history lesson, painlessly given. The best of this collection will last a long time and will appear in future anthologies.

*Dorothy M. Broderick, in a review of "There Is No
Rhyme for Silver," in* School Library Journal, *an
appendix to* Library Journal, *Vol. 9, No. 1, September, 1962, p. 124.*

There are many truly poetic elements in this first collection of
Eve Merriam's light verse for children, a delight in melody,
in the sound effects of certain words (**"A Yell for Yellow"**)
and in word pictures. All the poems express the child's point-
of-view, but they are not childish and we think those that suit
the sound to the sense will be great favorites for learning by
heart (**"Toaster Time"** and **"The Motor Boat Song"**). Our
favorites are the splendid nonsense bits called **"A Mean Song"**
wishing you "snickles and podes, ribbles and grodes" and
telling you to "keep out of sight for fear that I might glom
you a gravely snave," or give you "one flack on the bave",
and the **"Sappy Heasons"** (all spoonerisms). . . . Crazy, but
enjoyably so.

*Margaret Sherwood Libby, in a review of, "There
Is No Rhyme for Silver," in* Books, *November 11,
1962, p. 2.*

The child's viewpoint is often tellingly reflected in these poems;
nonsense ideas are pushed to their extravagant limits, and a
few serious notes are struck in just the right way at appropriate
times. An ocelot fond of cranberry sauce and a moose devoted
to automatic car brakes enliven the proceedings, but there is
still room for shrewd reflection on the greatness of Washington,
the pathos of Lincoln.

*William Turner Levy, "Voices That Know How to
Say It in Verse," in* The New York Times Book
Review, *Part II, November 11, 1962, p. 61.*

A light and pleasant collection of poems, suitable also for
reading aloud to younger children. Only a few of the selections
are serious, most of them being humorous or whimsical; many
of the selections simply play with words in a fashion children
enjoy. Some few of the poems seem slight. . . . The humor is
at an appropriate level, the writing—although it is not uniformly good—is competent and occasionally fresh and imaginative, and the collection has variety of form, subject, and
mood. Some of the poems are based on a subject or a concept
that seems rather sophisticated or mature for the level of the
reader.

*Zena Sutherland, in a review of "There Is No Rhyme
for Silver," in* Bulletin of the Center for Children's
Books, *Vol. XVI, No. 4, December, 1962, p. 63.*

IT DOESN'T ALWAYS HAVE TO RHYME   (1964)

It doesn't have to rhyme, but it frequently does, in this volume
of gay verse for children small and not so small. Rhyming or
not, it romps along like uninhibited brook water, inviting a
child to adventure. It does not hesitate to take him a little out
of his reading depth, and so he has the joy of learning to swim.
Although it is mostly for fun, the book offers several pieces
that assume the stature of serious and lovely poetry.

*Silence Buck Bellows, in a review of "It Doesn't
Always Have to Rhyme," in* The Christian Science
Monitor, *May 7, 1964, p. 6B.*

Fresh, rippling poems about the very fun of poetry and its
infinite possibilities. Both individual children and teachers with
classes should gather new insight into the delights offered by
play with words. Beginning with **"Inside a Poem"** ("It doesn't
always have to rhyme, / but there's the repeat of a beat, somewhere / an inner chime that makes you want to / tap your feet
or swerve in a curve . . ."), the poet includes jolly sequences
of homonyms and homographs and her ideas about metaphor,
simile, cliché, limerick, and onomatopoeia. Of wide interest.

*Virginia Haviland, in a review of "It Doesn't Always
Have to Rhyme," in* The Horn Book Magazine, *Vol.
XL, No. 3, June, 1964, p. 299.*

Like a genie summoning numberless treasures, Eve Merriam
takes everyday occurrences and transforms them into unexpected discoveries of delight. Even puns are spirited by her
magic touch into refreshing humor, making children want to
read them out loud so grown-ups can share the laughter. Much
of the enjoyment comes from the ease with which she twists
and turns the illogical into a logic of its own. Yet, for all the
poems' crisp originality, each is rooted in common sense. One
presents us with a formula for telling the difference between
stalactites and stalagmites. One gives a lovely answer to a
reader searching for identity, while another presents an indef-
inite, temporary solution to the same problem. There is also
practical advice on **"How to Eat a Poem,"** and suggestions
for avoiding clichés like "warm as toast." Miss Merriam's
last poem tells us that no poem is complete without a reader.
Hers deserve a great many.

*Gloria Vanderbilt, in a review of "It Doesn't Always
Have to Rhyme," in* The New York Times Book
Review, *August 16, 1964, p. 18.*

This unusual volume is not so much a classical collection of poems as an unrestrained and effervescent compendium of word games in poetic format. In **"One, Two, Three—Gough,"** the variant pronunciations of the vowel/consonant cluster "ough" are wittily explored.

> To make some bread you must have dough,
> Isn't that sough?

"Why I Did Not Reign" is concerned with violations of the orthographic rule requiring "I before E, except after C." **"Be My Non-Valentine"** proposes thirty-seven derogatory, obscure adjectives as being properly descriptive of the character addressed in the poem. **"Mr. Zoo"** arrays a series of depictions of human behavior in terms derived from animal sources.

The predominant concern, however, is with the way the sounds of words suggest meaning and evoke response. Alliteration, figurative language, onomatopoeia, echoic phrases, and subtle variations among synonymous words are the primary devices exploited by Merriam. Of particular interest in this regard is **"A Spell of Weather,"** which, when read out loud, is so carefully structured that it forces a change in speaking tempo and stress as different climatic conditions are described. The images in the collection are sometimes startling, the vocabulary is impressive, and the puns a delight—when they work. (pp. 194-95)

Although the literal meaning of these poems will be readily accessible to most youngsters, this collection has specific validity for high-ability readers. A lighthearted, amusing, and occasionally wry volume, *It Doesn't Always Have to Rhyme* demonstrates remarkable sensitivity to the playful possibilities inherent in language. (p. 195)

> *Barbara H. Baskin and Karen H. Harris, "A Selected Guide to Intellectually Demanding Books: 'It Doesn't Always Have to Rhyme',"* in their Books for the Gifted Child, R. R. Bowker Company, 1980, pp. 194-95.

WHAT CAN YOU DO WITH A POCKET? (1964)

An oversize picture book, the text of which makes quite elaborate suggestions for imaginative play, each suggestion based on an object often found in pockets. Example: "If you have a BUTTON in your pocket / you can balance / it on your nose / and be a seal / at the / CIRCUS. Sit up, seal, and flap your flippers!" . . . The book has some humor, and it does suggest independent imaginative play, but this kind of play comes without suggestion to an imaginative child; to a stolid and unimaginative child, the book may have little effect as a stimulus.

> *Zena Sutherland, in a review of "What Can You Do with a Pocket?"* in Bulletin of the Center for Children's Books, Vol. XVIII, No. 3, November, 1964, p. 40.

SMALL FRY (1965)

The lean pickings of both text and [Garry MacKenzie's] illustrations are a check to the instant appeal of baby animals and their identifying terms. Pictures of the young ones of quite a number of familiar and popular species are accompanied with the specific word for the type of baby. The names are tied together with some irrelevant and pretty meaningless verses, which occasionally chirrup off into italicized lines for the adults

reading this aloud to gag over: "Hoo, little owlet, hooeee. / Who, me? / Yes, you, little owlet, youee."

> *A review of "Small Fry,"* in Virginia Kirkus' Service, Vol. XXXIII, No. 5, March 1, 1965, p. 232.

The delightful pictures in this bright little book for 5-8's appealingly illustrate some odd tidbits of information. Adults may know what type of small fry is called a joey, a farrow, a blinker or tinker, an eyas or poult. They may even know what a squearer is, or a squealer, or a squeaker. They may also know everything called a cub or an infant. In which case this book should be bought only for the education of children.

> *Guernsey Le Pelley, in a review of "Small Fry,"* in The Christian Science Monitor, May 6, 1965, p. 2B.

The apparent objective of this colorful yet over-embellished little book appears to be the presentation of pictures and the appropriate names assigned to the offspring of various birds and mammals. . . . Nonsense verses in italics occasionally follow the name designations: e.g., following "frog and tadpole," one reads "Kerplunk and kerplunklet. Greensplash and dunkit." For whom or for what purpose is this rubbish intended?

> *A review of "Small Fry,"* in Science Books: A Quarterly Review, Vol. 1, No. 3, December, 1965, p. 158.

CATCH A LITTLE RHYME (1966)

According to the publisher's afterword, this book, ". . . completes a trilogy of poetry books for children that really begins with this book. For here she has poems that will appeal to the primary child. . . ." The two previous books were the excellent *There Is No Rhyme For Silver* and *It Doesn't Always Have to Rhyme*. . . . Miss Merriam's approach is consistently fresh and she is no slave to either meter or rhyme in these short poems. She has a special flair for the humor small children enjoy—a parrot making a riot screaming "QUIET!"; what the animals in the zoo think of the people who come to stare; and plays on simple words. Most of them transcend the level of nonsense to present an idea, a new way of looking at or listening to things.

> *A review of "Catch a Little Rhyme,"* in Virginia Kirkus' Service, Vol. XXXIV, No. 2, January 15, 1966, p. 54.

Sprightly verse written for younger children than those poems in the poet's two previously published volumes of excellent children's poetry: *There Is No Rhyme for Silver* and *It Doesn't Always Have to Rhyme*. Varied verse forms, interesting rhythms, arresting images, clever employment of the inherent musical quality of words, and subjects of childish concern distinguish these poems. (p. 225)

> *Elva Harmon, in a review of "Catch a Little Rhyme,"* in School Library Journal, an appendix to Library Journal, Vol. 12, No. 7, March, 1966, pp. 225-26.

This one shares the delights of words, and the fresh views they disclose of familiar things. *Catch a Little Rhyme* completes a trilogy of poetry books which Eve Merriam has written for children; this is the one to begin with. All three beg to be read out loud; this one shouts to be shared.

> *A review of "Catch a Little Rhyme,"* in Publishers Weekly, Vol. 189, No. 14, April 4, 1966, p. 62.

Eve Merriam's poems remind me of a kitten playing with a thimble on a wooden floor—and that means no disrespect. She writes about a place, Schenectady, and plays with the word, enjoying the metallic clink with uninhibited delight: "I'll take any trek to Schenectady, / Even wash my neck for Schenectady, / So expect me next at Schenectady." As poet-kitten she sits on the fence watching the city's "great demolition show," describing it with pop action words: "Crash goes a chimney, / Pow goes a hall, / Zowie goes a doorway, / Zam goes a wall." She stretches in front of the window on a rainy day to notice the "Spack a spack speck / Freckling the windowpane." The kitten has claws, too; she can give a gentle raking, as she does in the poem **"Teevee,"** about what TV has done in the house of Mr. and Mrs. Spouse. Mostly, though, in these 27 poems, she is gracefully, amusingly at play. And with a kitten's proclivity to furl in a ball after a vigorous romp, she purrs: "Close your eyes and within the stillness / You will hear the silent tune / Of the spinning of the planets / And the circling round of the moon."

> *George A. Woods, in a review of "Catch a Little Rhyme," in* The New York Times Book Review, *April 10, 1966, p. 20.*

ANDY ALL YEAR ROUND: A PICTURE BOOK OF FOUR SEASONS AND FIVE SENSES (1967)

This picture book attempts a lyrical instruction in appreciating the changing seasons through the full use of the five senses. In summer Andy plays at the beach: "LOOK at the sand, all tawny-colored like a lion." Readers are encouraged to feel, taste, listen to and smell the sand as Andy performs these actions. Similar activities are presented with autumn leaves, winter snow, and spring grass.... Eve Merriam's onomatopoeic text is at times too difficult for new readers. Read aloud the book makes an adequate though obvious and pretentious introduction to the concepts of changing seasons and the five senses.

> *Joan Sragow, in a review of "Andy All Year Round," in* School Library Journal, *an appendix to* Library Journal, *Vol. 14, No. 3, November, 1967, p. 61.*

Aimed at sharpening sensuous awareness of the natural world, this book encourages readers to experience with young Andy each season through all of their senses.... Meant to be shared by an adult, the book makes the child aware of his sense impressions, stimulating in him a desire to develop them further. For the adult the book evokes memories of his own early childhood.

> *Marion Marx, in a review of "Andy All Year Round: A Picture Book for Four Seasons and Five Senses," in* The Horn Book Magazine, *Vol. XLIII, No. 6, December, 1967, p. 743.*

EPAMINONDAS (1968)

A new version of an old storytelling favorite.... "Careful how you step on those pies!" his mother said, and Epaminondas, "good and careful," went out on the porch where the pies were cooling and stepped precisely in the middle of each one. The story ends with a kiss rather than a spank, an expression of Mama's acceptance of the fact that Epaminondas will not change, and of her love. The retelling has an engaging

quality of simplicity and a bland humor; some storytellers may prefer their accustomed versions, some may prefer this.

> *Zena Sutherland, in a review of "Epaminondas," in* Bulletin of the Center for Children's Books, *Vol. 21, No. 11, July-August, 1968, p. 178.*

Collins used to publish *Epaminondas* in a version by Constance Egan: pocket-size, cheap, and showing Epaminondas himself, not unnaturally, as coal black. Now, the same publisher gives us Epaminondas retold by Eve Merriam, larger, dearer, and ... white—at least, a sort of sandy beige. "Eve Merriam gives Epaminondas a universal quality with which every young reader can identify...." In the tale chosen here the gormless boy gets hopelessly confused.... It seems a pity we may no longer laugh at little black boys, but good stories have a way of seeping through....

> *"... And Page to Screen," in* The Times Literary Supplement, *No. 3051, April 3, 1969, p. 358.*

[*Epaminondas* will] ring a bell. Eve Merriam economically retells Sara Cone Bryant's story of the boy who does obey his mother's instructions about how to bring home presents from his grandmother's house but is always one out of step.... Trina Schart Hyman draws the little boy a trifle cutely ... but the volume has coherence. (p. 703)

> *John Fuller, "Beginners," in* New Statesman, *Vol. 77, No. 1992, May 16, 1969, pp. 702-03.*

INDEPENDENT VOICES (1968)

It Doesn't Always Have to Rhyme but these panegyrics also lack grace, strength and restraint. Seven notable Americans, chosen "because they seemed to be not heroic," are subjected individually to fawning and gimmick-y eulogies. Ben Franklin picks up that loaf of bread in Philadelphia and does enough "for twenty men! / ... Became a city planner, / and Postmaster Gen." Elizabeth Blackwell lives through three pages of medical school rejections, several stanzas of Victorian scorn from the ladies of Geneva until "The perfect happy ending / came to pass: / Elizabeth graduated ... / ... at the head of her class." Also Frederick Douglass, Thoreau, Lucretia Mott, Ida B. Wells (Barnett), La Guardia. There are some better passages (La Guardia's New York where "Garbage trucks bang. / Honk squawk squawk beep beep skureech / YIKES HEY Whynchamove outathe way?") but each of the portraits is bloated and seven at a blow is too much.

> *A review of "Independent Voices," in* Kirkus Service, *Vol. 36, No. 19, October 1, 1968, p. 1170.*

Rosemary and Stephen Vincent Benét turned many American historical characters into people with their *Book of Americans*.... Eve Merriam is Pygmalion to American historical characters who appealed to her especially for "their gumption—not hesitating to look and act like a fool—and the pinch of mischief along with the high purpose in each of their personalities." Her verses about these cantankerous figures will take them out of the history books and into the hearts of all young people who are, or yearn to be, "drop-outs from Graceful Social Behavior Under Any and All Circumstances."

> *A review of "Independent Voices," in* Publishers Weekly, *Vol. 194, No. 17, October 21, 1968, p. 51.*

A collection of seven profiles in verse of Americans who to Eve Merriam exemplify characteristics that most of us would agree are attractive: to her they are heroic, but more than that, approachable, lovable, and "along with the high purpose and morality in each of their personalities," mischievous. Unfortunately, they fail to come through this way.

Ben Franklin . . . appears to be meanly frugal, grimly inventive, and deadly dull. He is also said to be "bowering," which if it signifies anything to anyone signifies nothing to me. Elizabeth Blackwell has a ramrod will and a nice middle-class virtue. . . . Frederick Douglass is dedicated to the right things— labor, education, equal rights for Negroes and for women— and has a fancy funeral. Transcendentalism I grant to be a complex idea, but there's old Henry Thoreau basking rustically for small apparent reason. Finally, Fiorello H. La Guardia, "At his fullgrown height, five feet two / (Napoleon, move over, company for you.)"

Pictorially [illustrations are by Arvis Stewart] as well as textually little humanity let alone humor animates this group. The sis-boom-bah seems mechanically injected, and the mini-biographies, neither history nor poetry, are classic simplified American success stories out of the movies of the thirties and forties. Many words seem wrong and the rhythms strained, except for a few bouncing passages, where the material reads comfortably (either silently, or as Miss Merriam prefers, aloud.) These are notably those setting Thoreau in his country context and La Guardia in his city context. All in all, Miss Merriam writes out of a mix that is at once stiff, sweet and oh so good for you. Jell-o.

> *Nora L. Magid, in a review of "Independent Voices,"* in The New York Times Book Review, *March 2, 1969, p. 32.*

Naturally lively and provocative, the subjects were chosen not for any grand heroism but for their high purposes, energy, zest, and daring. The author intends group presentation with choral counterpoint and individual speakers. The verse, both rhymed and unrhymed, varies in poetic quality and emotional impact; but much of it reads aloud extremely well. (p. 182)

> *Ethel L. Heins, in a review of "Independent Voices,"* in The Horn Book Magazine, *Vol. XLV, No. 2, April, 1969, pp. 182-83.*

FINDING A POEM   (1970)

You will find, in this collection of Eve Merriam's poems, a feast as varied as must be the facets of Miss Merriam's mind. There are poems of despair, cries of a poet, "in a plastic age of time for everything and time for nothing, of masses of people and lonely individuals, of new discovery and numbing sameness." There are poems as bright as quicksilver that in a few words reveal a mood of awe, of surprise, of wonder. And there is a record, noted down step by step, word by word, of how she created a poem, that is as fascinating to follow as the birth of a baby.

> *A review of "Finding a Poem," in* Publishers Weekly, *Vol. 198, No. 7, August 17, 1970, p. 50.*

A collection of 39 excellent poems, most of which protest the artificiality and computerization of contemporary life. Included also are some which glory in the flexibility of language and draw striking work portraits of such diverse things as spaghetti and semicolons. The book ends with a candid, step-by-step

account of the writing of one poem, an essay that should be of great help to young readers inspired by the freshness and deceptive simplicity of the author's work to try their own hand at poetry.

> *Margaret A. Dorsey, in a review of "Finding a Poem,"* in School Library Journal, *an appendix to* Library Journal, *Vol. 17, No. 1, September 15, 1970, p. 119.*

An irresistible collection of poems that satirize our empty, "plastic" society, the verses reflect some of the slick sheen of contemporary life and should have "instant" appeal for those seeking instant satisfactions as well as an enduring attraction for thoughtful young people and the young-in-heart. . . . The poet is playing games with her readers—writing hilarious poems that contain sobering communication; inventing word games which show how the poet juggles and juxtaposes words to extract more-than-dictionary meaning from her phrases. . . . A bonus is an extraordinary essay on **"Writing a Poem,"** in which the author details each thought, association, image, and idea that contributed to the development or "finding" of the poem **"Landscape."**

> *Diane Farrell, in a review of "Finding a Poem," in* The Horn Book Magazine, *Vol. XLVI, No. 5, October, 1970, p. 486.*

Word plays and weirdos and modern discomforts: these are recurring themes in *Finding a Poem*. Miss Merriam throws a quizzical light on the everyday: a transistor is umbilical, a bargain sale ritualistic, spaghetti **"A Round"** without end. A modern angel is rebuffed . . . , and the neuter computer is deplored along with plastics, billboards, and other targets of recent protest. Some poems attempt more genial subjects: e.g., **"Calendar"** (oneday . . . moonday .. whensday") or the breezy, sneezy **"Llude Sig Kachoo"** ("Wed flowers bloob / with sweet perfube / . . . the cobbod code / its gerbs / doth brig"). Not all are equally engaging; some begin with strength then settle into lazy detail.

The last 12 pages record the construction of the poem **"Landscape"**. . . . An openhanded exercise, it reveals the vagaries— and limitations—of poetic choice.

It's a modest collection of uneven quality and only occasional insight.

> *Nancy Klein, in a review of "Finding a Poem," in* The New York Times Book Review, *October 25, 1970, p. 38.*

Two characteristics dominate *Finding a Poem:* language playfulness—for which this author is justifiably well known—and sardonic, wry commentaries on contemporary topics. The latter are expressed in such poems as **"The Wholly Family,"** **"Umbilical,"** and **"Alarm Clock,"** in which humanity's need for the latitude to pursue individual, unfettered, and natural interests conflicts with the demands of a highly structured, technologically obsessed, and plasticized world. People caught in various traps—sometimes of their own devising, but more commonly as a spinoff from the rat race they were scarcely aware they had entered—is a recurring theme in this collection.

Merriam uses punctuation marks as a stimulus for some poetic musings, taking off from either the meaning or function of these mundane, omnipresent, but virtually unremarked little writing props. Some minor poems are devoted to responses to the sounds of words, as in **"Ping-Pong,"** which consists exclusively of two-syllable words with identical consonants and varying vowels, as in "chitchat / wigwag / rickrack," and so on. (p. 193)

Although the verses in this slim volume give insight into particular aspects of poetry that have utility in developing sensitivity to language and particularly to tone, it is the last section that is of special interest. Here the poet has shared with the reader the eleven separate revisions of a single poem, explaining the alternatives she considered, their virtues and faults, and why each was accepted or rejected, until the end product was finally massaged and coaxed into shape. In doing so, she has provided an unusual opportunity for a backstage look at this genre. (p. 194)

> *Barbara H. Baskin and Karen H. Harris, "A Selected Guide to Intellectually Demanding Books: 'Finding a Poem',"* in their *Books for the Gifted Child, R. R. Bowker Company, 1980, pp. 193-94.*

I AM A MAN: ODE TO MARTIN LUTHER KING, JR. (1971)

If response to the man alive was universal, response to his death is personal. And this is personal: muted charcoal sketches [by Suzanne Verrier] and mood-conscious couplets—a picture-book eulogy/elegy. The lines, suggestive variously of image and event, here and there fleetingly touch, elsewhere border on the mawkish, elsewhere on cliche . . . and the rhyme is anyhow too circumscribing when it's forced. Self-readers can *Meet Martin Luther King, Jr.* in James T. de Kay's meaningfully rounded, simple profile . . . , where he's a person first and only then a symbol. Older children who know him will bridle at both the format and the merchandised sentiment, however appreciative, however soberly purveyed.

> *A review of "I Am a Man: Ode to Martin Luther King, Jr.,"* in Kirkus Reviews, Vol. 39, No. 5, March 1, 1971, p. 240.

An idealistic summary in verse of the life and philosophy of the famous black leader. . . . This mood book adds no informative material but would be fine for browsing; for reading aloud if one can avoid the sing-song rhythm the form employs (e.g., "'Fight to be equal, fight to be free, / but only fight non-violently.'"); and for additional reading on King and the non-violent movement.

> *Margaret Riddell, in a review of "I Am a Man: Ode to Martin Luther King, Jr.,"* in School Library Journal, *an appendix to* Library Journal, Vol. 17, No. 9, May, 1971, p. 68.

Eve Merriam's distinctive poem, dedicated to the memory of Dr. Martin Luther King, Jr. . . . , is a loving tribute that can be enjoyed by children and adults everywhere. For younger readers especially, more basic information from another source needs to be provided as Miss Merriam only fleetingly refers to events and personalities.

> *A review of "I Am a Man: Ode to Martin Luther King, Jr.,"* in Publishers Weekly, Vol. 199, No. 19, May 10, 1971, p. 43.

PROJECT 1-2-3 (1971)

A housing project that is "as big as a town" is the focal point of this imaginative counting book. Many clever, unobtrusive applications of the numbers, from 1 to 10, are neatly incorporated into the text which, along with the pictures [by Harriet

Sherman], concisely and accurately portrays the physical organization and life style in a typical urban housing project. "There are 3 playgrounds with 3 jungle gyms . . . 4 groundsmen dig 4 holes to plant 4 bushes in the spring . . ." etc. Among the maintenance needs: "Replace 7 glasspanes," "7 stuffed toilets," "check 7 incinerator hoppers," etc. . . . All in all, this book is a welcome and overdue departure from the traditional, ubiquitous animal counting books.

> *Melinda Schroeder, in a review of "Project 1-2-3,"* in School Library Journal, *an appendix to* Library Journal, Vol. 18, No. 3, November, 1971, p. 108.

This colorful, imaginative romp through a big-city housing project, a numerical counting book—is given a fresh, lively treatment. . . . An ideal book for city children to gain a wider insight into their world; but there is no reason why suburban children should miss out on all the fun—there's enough here for everyone.

> *A review of "Project 1-2-3,"* in Publishers Weekly, Vol. 200, No. 20, November 15, 1971, p. 71.

A book that introduces numbers one to ten is set in a large urban housing project, its dual purpose being that of describing the setting as well as being a counting book. Since not all of the pages have to do with numbers, and since some of the illustrations are not really clear . . . , this is not wholly successful as a counting book. As an introduction to a mammoth interracial housing project, the book is more effective.

> *Zena Sutherland, in a review of "Project 1-2-3,"* in Bulletin of the Center for Children's Books, Vol. 25, No. 4, December, 1971, p. 62.

While not entirely successful as a counting book for young children unable to read, the picture book . . . gives a fascinating first view of a huge big-city housing complex—its physical appearance, maintenance, conveniences, and tenants. For some children, an introduction to a different way of living; for others, a game of recognition.

> *Aileen Howard, in a review of "Project 1-2-3,"* in The Booklist, Vol. 68, No. 10, January 15, 1972, p. 434.

BAM! ZAM! BOOM! A BUILDING BOOK (1972)

Miss Merriam, an accomplished poet in her own right, has apparently brainwashed herself into thinking like a kid in this one, if thinking like a kid is defined as being addicted to violent demolition and comic-strip onomatopoeia. There's this condemned brownstone, see—let me shed a tear for it and a more gracious past, since Miss Merriam doesn't—and the author can't wait to tear into it with the wrecking ball of doggerel:

> Crack goes the wall
> as it starts to crumble
>   Slam
>   bam
>   zoom DOOM!
> Fall, wall . . .
>   Zonk!
>   Smash!

The elegance of the verse is nicely matched by the perfectly hideous layout [by William Lightfoot]. . . .

L. E. Sissman, "Poems Good and Otherwise," in
The New York Times Book Review, *June 25, 1972,*
p. 8.

Fast-moving verse emphasizes the sounds and action of construction; the illustrations give a knot-hole view of demolition
and high-rising. Social conscience might wonder if displaced
tenants get the new building, but that is not to deny the appeal
this has for children who enjoy looking and listening as building
goes on.

Lois Belfield Watt, in a review of "Bam! Zam! Boom!
A Building Book," in Childhood Education, *Vol. 49,*
No. 3, (December, 1972), p. 149.

BOYS AND GIRLS, GIRLS AND BOYS   (1972)

Marvin & Marcia, Annie & Andy and Lee B. & Lee G. demonstrate that anything boys can do girls can do as well, and
vice versa—a lesson which effectively counters the stereotyped
sex roles of [Robert] Kraus' by now notorious *I'm Glad I'm*
a Boy, I'm Glad I'm a Girl. The pairs play together with dolls
and tools and catcher's mitts; they take music lessons . . . ; they
help both their mothers and fathers interchangeably; and they
dream together of becoming ballet dancers and lion tamers,
forest rangers, lighthouse keepers and letter carriers. To make
up for the absence of a plot, [illustrator] Harriet Sherman animates the children's fantasies aggressively. . . . The message
is certainly well taken, and if the mix and match kids aren't
individualized enough to encourage close acquaintance, their
zappy appearance and playful improvisation makes them worth
at least one good look.

A review of "Boys & Girls, Girls & Boys," in Kirkus
Reviews, *Vol. XL, No. 23, December 1, 1972, p.*
1351.

This book energetically tries to stamp out separate roles for
males and females and show that boys and girls are really alike.
Since the pairs of children are integrated (whites, blacks and
an Oriental), the message is extended to cover equality of races
as well as sexes. The theme is an admirable one, but the heavy-
handed execution is not much fun. . . . A concept book rather
than a story, by the middle, the cataloging of activities and
ambitions shared by boys and girls gets tiresome. The first 13
pages about Marvin and Marcia are the best because text and
pictures are well coordinated, and the idea has novelty. The
same kind and amount of material follow about two more
couples, but it is crammed into six pages each, which slows
down the book's pace and makes the layouts look cluttered.
For the fourth boy-girl team the pages open up again, but it's
not enough to perk up the tedium. All in all, while this book
is certainly better than *I'm Glad I'm a Boy, I'm Glad I'm a*
Girl [illustrated by Whitney] Darrow . . . , children would prefer doing the activities mentioned here more than reading about
them.

Marilyn R. Singer, in a review of "Boys & Girls,
Girls & Boys," in School Library Journal, *an ap-*
pendix to Library Journal, *Vol. 19, No. 6, February,*
1973, p. 62.

The book presents a refreshing alternative to the traditional
male-female sex roles described in children's literature. These
girls and boys share career dreams, activities, games, likes and
dislikes. The book is flawed by a weak story line and an obvious
self-conscious feminism. Despite these, the book is highly rec-

ommended because of the general lack of such treatment in
this field.

A review of "Boys & Girls, Girls & Boys," in Children's Book Review Service, *Vol. 1, No. 7, March,*
1973, p. 40.

OUT LOUD   (1973)

For anyone who still hopes to be surprised by this once Younger
Yale Poet, *Out Loud* is another disappointment. The rhymes,
never as innovative as [Harriet] Sherman's zappy non-linear
design makes them look, include a smattering of Merriam's
typical socio-political noncommentary . . . but the emphasis
here is on repetitive sounds and word play. With none of (say)
Swenson's verbal clicks and collisions the effect is usually
monotonous (as in . . . **"Leak"** which ends "all things may
stop / but not the drip drop / of the drip drip drip drip in the
sink. / Drip drip drip / d / r / i / p *drip*") and sometimes just
silly—as in **"The Stuck Horn"** which relies for effect on long
strings of O's and ends

> somebody please
> dooooooooooooooo
> something soooooooooooooooooooooooon.

Like stop the leak?

A review of "Out Loud," in Kirkus Reviews, *Vol.*
XLI, No. 8, April 15, 1973, p. 460.

The pictures are ingeniously designed as integral parts of each
of Miss Merriam's modern and provocative lyrics. Here is
admirable experimentation from a poet and an artist who are
obviously in love with words and images. **"Evergreen"** is
written so that the lines form the shape of hemlocks and other
winter beauties and the artist encloses the poem in the outline
of an evergreen with the title forming the trunk. The other
poems are similarly evocative of shapes as well as emotions.

A review of "Out Loud," in Publishers Weekly, *Vol.*
203, No. 26, June 25, 1973, p. 74.

I found the poems very difficult to read. The designs were
unusual and the titles were often written in such a way that I
was unable to read them. If you were to try to read these poems
"Out Loud" to children I'm afraid you would get tongue-tied
and disgusted before you had read very many. I do not think
children would have the patience to read them themselves.

Judy N. Staley, in a review of "Out Loud," in Children's Book Review Service, *Vol. 1, No. 12, August,*
1973, p. 79.

Most of the 41 poems in this collection rely heavily on onomatopoeia. . . . These efforts at sound effects are interspersed
with more effective traditional compositions, . . . all reminiscent of Merriam's delightful *Catch a Little Rhyme*. . . . Unfortunately, here the poetry must be sorted out from the noise,
and the flights of imagination from mere word play. Further-
more, young children will need explanations of "idiosyncratic," "deciduous," "metaphor," and other adult words.

Daisy Kouzel, in a review of "Out Loud," in School
Library Journal, *an appendix to* Library Journal, *Vol.*
20, No. 1, September, 1973, p. 60.

If a young reader were to get nothing else from Eve Merriam's
poetry, it would be worth reading and rereading for the way

in which words are relished; her writing sparkles with freshets and cascades of words used for meaning or just for the pleasure of their sound. In this new collection there is more, however: bright imagery, fresh ideas, humor, and—while there is some lyricism—a stress on here and now.

> *Zena Sutherland, in a review of "Out Loud," in*
> Bulletin of the Center for Children's Books, *Vol. 27,
> No. 2, October, 1973, p. 32.*

RAINBOW WRITING (1976)

In verses of a page or less, or not more than two, the poet comments epigrammatically on a variety of subjects, ranging from **"Pigeons"** and **"Ice-Creepers"** to **"Advice from a Visiting Poet"** and **"I'm Sorry Says the Machine."** The lines vary in length, long and short verses are frequently juxtaposed, and rhyming as well as other forms of repetition is occasional. Precise and provocative, the images often indulge in word play, such as "marinating toadstools in the mushroom sauce"; "*Belt* / class-conscious neutralist / dividing line between / upper and lower"; or "the iron gates on Dimondstein's drugstore / folding up like his wheelchair." A keen but joyful book, in which the poet seizes what casually comes into her perspective and finds right and telling words to snare her observations. (pp. 635-36)

> *Paul Heins, in a review of "Rainbow Writing," in*
> The Horn Book Magazine, *Vol. LII, No. 6, December, 1976, pp. 635-36.*

In her latest poetry collection Merriam once again demonstrates her ability to capture vivid images and moods with an economy of words. She views the world in fresh, invigorating terms—e.g., a cat is a "self-made rug / a furry hug / welcome mat"; love is "a single drop of wine / in a crystal goblet."—and she is careful not to allow her clever word plays (reminiscent of e.e. cummings) to overwhelm the content. Containing both simple and complex poems, this collection offers something for everyone and can be used successfully in poetry workshops.

> *Connie Serina, in a review of "Rainbow Writing," in* School Library Journal, *Vol. 23, No. 6, February, 1977, p. 73.*

As she often does, Merriam includes some poems that play with words, like **"Ego-Tripping,"** or **"By the Shores of Pago-Pago,"** which use repeat-syllables like pawpaw, dodo, froufrou, and names like Mimi and Bebe. But most of the selections in this new collection are lyric, some direct and some convoluted, or they are tart comments on aspects of our society like **"Prodigal Returns,"** in which the friendly, heterogeneous old neighborhood has given way to the "plastic banners of McDonald's."

> *Zena Sutherland, in a review of "Rainbow Writing," in* Bulletin of the Center for Children's Books, *Vol. 30, No. 7, March, 1977, p. 110.*

Reflective poems for the older reader capture elusive moments in a vast array of experiences. Forty poems in the modern vein, by a well-known poet, comprise unusual imagery and a nonconformist view of life. Merriam has the poet's eye and ear, spiced by a wry sense of humor and wonder. Unusual are her **"Counting-out Rhyme,"** using names of apples; her teams in **"Twogether";** her **"Notions,"** with its "*Buttons* / unable to bear a single life / must always make a match"; and the solution to her **"Whodunnit."** Explore and share her small moments.

> *Ruth M. Stein, in a review of "Rainbow Writing," in* Language Arts, *Vol. 54, No. 3, March, 1977, p. 329.*

It is worrisome that Eve Merriam, usually a good prose writer, can get by with writing and publishing a book of poetry so sloppy in craftsmanship. There are places were line breaks seem arbitrary and punctuation and capitalization are random throw-around affairs. There are also internal errors such as faulty imagery, dangling symbolism and confusion of unity within lines and within poems. How is one supposed to take the lines: "Ling Chee's laundry tickets drift in the gutter / moaning with stomach cancer?"

Technical errors aside, there are major flaws in the conception and content of the work. Certainly one of these is the writer's assumption that if you use enough unusual words and use them often enough and cleverly enough then you're sure to turn out a poem. This leads at times to senseless, silly poems. At other times it is the direct cause of imperfect diction that leaves even the serious poems lacking in depth and meaning.

Miss Merriam has a fine ear for words that are pleasing in themselves, and she has a vivacious way of looking at life. This could serve children well if she would only pay closer attention to her craft.

> *Ardis Kimzey, in a review of "Rainbow Writing," in* The New York Times Book Review, *March 13, 1977, p. 16.*

AB TO ZOGG: A LEXICON FOR SCIENCE-FICTION AND FANTASY READERS (1977)

In the form of a small glossary of imaginary terms—mostly nouns—complete with a punning etymology for each . . . , this is a less clever spoof of sci fi and fantasy staples than private, arcane whimsy for an undetermined audience. There is amusing word play in some of the definitions ("Mog. . . . A magic potion, compounded of cinnamoon and nightmeg.") and in the names themselves, as befits a poet of Merriam's renown. . . . But the puns and definitions are too often belaboredly un-funny, arch and adult in nature, and generally call for more familiarity with elements parodied than children are apt to have.

> *Ruth M. McConnell, in a review of "Ab to Zogg: A Lexicon for Science-Fiction and Fantasy Readers," in* School Library Journal, *Vol. 24, No. 2, October, 1977, p. 126.*

Seldom has the realm of science fiction provided for its devotees such witty diversion as this lexicon of science fiction and fantasy. All the words are original (to say the least), with the pronunciation, derivation, and definition given for each. Many of the creatures presented . . . have appearances that defy description. Though brief, this little gem will surely be popular and much quoted by YAs. We recommend especially the words *Jyk, Lillizizz,* and *XIVLCMXXXVILXVM!*

> *Evie Wilson and Michael McCue, in a review of "Ab to Zogg," in* Wilson Library Bulletin, *Vol. 52, No. 2, October, 1977, p. 177.*

With spoofy entries such as Eldron tablets ("the pre-Hammurabi Code of Ethics . . . adhered to by all citizens, citizanissaries, and citizorians . . ."), hoberry (". . . blooms on holidays and private happiness days"), and Ogrimony (guess), Merriam proves herself capable of spinning fantasy fabrications with the genre's dippiest. She also takes off on foolish derivations, as in Cheen (from the Cappek *ch*, complaint or crying out, therefore alive + the suffix *een*, corruption of *ayn*, i.e., own or one) and at least once breaks from satire to be just plain funny: "XIVLCMXXXVILXVM—Reincarnated Roman gladiator whose quarked tunic conceals deadly microwaves and whose name none dare pronounce aloud!" But Merriam will lose most young readers with WY ("the metamorphic river that winds from Synechdoche to Simile as it leads on and on past the reverberating caves into the analagous springs of Aska") and the cry of Wishtawee! ("... in daemonic dialect can be roughly translated as agitato, pronto, tempus fugit, vite alors"). And that leaves you wondering who might be entertained. A full-blown parody incorporating such terms could be tedious; Merriam spares us that but, at a scant 43 illustrated pages, this is flimsy whimsy indeed—more suited to the *New York Times Magazine* "Endpapers" where it first appeared—and too clever by a demixtrk.

> *A review of "Ab to Zogg: A Lexicon for Science Fiction and Fantasy Readers," in* Kirkus Reviews, *Vol. XLV, No. 22, November 15, 1977, p. 1209.*

For a real example of how to waste your money, ... take a look at—but DON'T BUY—*AB to Zogg*.... They call this thing "a Lexicon for Science-Fiction and Fantasy Readers." And it's full ... of such enthralling entries as Hershebehemoth and Ritipox and Wockups, with the *ke-you-test* definitions relating to absolutely nothing having anything to do with science fiction or fantasy.

Apparently Merriam thinks that fantasy and science fiction are made up of nothing but gobbledygook terms without any referents. The blurb says she has captured some of "the most elusive whimsy of science fiction and fantasy"—but there's no evidence internally that she has ever seen a book of science fiction.

It's enough to turn any child who gets it off fantasy or science fiction forever. Isn't there a law about misrepresentation in advertising? If not, this should cause one to be passed—and enforced, in this instance.

Carry a woops bag with you when you go to look at it.

> *Lester del Rey, in a review of "Ab to Zogg," in* Analog Science Fiction/Science Fact, *Vol. XCVII, No. 12, December, 1977, p. 170.*

Ab to Zogg is a glossary of nonexistent but likely-sounding science fiction terms. A traditional dictionary format is used, including didactic pronunciation guides, etymological explanations of derivations, variant forms of words, and, of course, definitions. The defined words look like conventional dictionary entries. The definitions appear at first glance to provide legitimate, if obscure, explanations. Caveat emptor! This seemingly scholarly effort is in reality a collection of outrageous puns, plays on words, literary and historical parodies, and obscure, obtuse, and unlikely allusions. Subsequent readings will uncover new word games in some passages originally read too quickly. (p. 192)

Ab to Zogg is a highly cerebral game in which geographic, mathematical, scientific, mythic, literary, linguistic, and historical sources are tapped. Self-contradictory expressions such as *singularly plural* proliferate. The book demands not only close concentration and a willingness to engage in tomfoolery, but also prodigious feats of memory and association. Missed allusions are more enticing than frustrating, and the under-

standing that finally dawns after multiple attempts to discern just what game is being played, if any, with a particular entry is marvelously satisfying. *Ab to Zogg* is intended only for an extraordinarily bright child who is singularly knowledgeable and well read. (p. 193)

> *Barbara H. Baskin and Karen H. Harris, "A Selected Guide to Intellectually Demanding Books: 'Ab to Zogg: A Lexicon for Science-Fiction and Fantasy Readers',*" in their *Books for the Gifted Child, R. R. Bowker Company, 1980, pp. 192-93.*

UNHURRY HARRY (1978)

Everyone tries to hurry Harry but for whom is the book intended, the harriers, or the Harrys? Often predictable in its jibes at parents and teachers who rush through life, the book reaches its literary highpoint with a bedtime story that is read too fast: "ONCE UPON TIME KING HAD THREE HORSES GALLOP FLEW BEAUTIFUL PRINCESS...." But ... the device is too condensed and cerebral for the very young children likely to hear this story.

> *Joan W. Blos, in a review of "Unhurry Harry," in* School Library Journal, *Vol. 25, No. 2, October, 1978, p. 137.*

The story is nicely told if at times seeming forced in situation; for example, the class starts with reading, but the reading period is over by the time Harry has inspected the covers of his reader. Not much strength in plot, but a palatable expansion of a situation. (p. 48)

> *Zena Sutherland, in a review of "Unhurry Harry," in* Bulletin of the Center for Children's Books, *Vol. 32, No. 3, November, 1978, pp. 47-8.*

A unique read-aloud book for the child in every classroom whose daydreams get in the way of everyday living. It may be comforting for this youngster, often the despair of teachers and parents, to realize that he is not alone in his leisurely world. The book offers no resolution, just acceptance.... A charming story for the "Harry" in all of us.

> *Beverly Woods, in a review of "Unhurry Harry," in* Children's Book Review Service, *Vol. 7, No. 3, November, 1978, p. 22.*

Any story with a title like Tag-along Tommy or Absent-Minded Annie has almost got to be one-dimensional, and it's no surprise that this is all about how Harry ... dawdles through the day's routine.... Merriam's examples, of course, have lots of recognition value, and a bit more color than most such: at lunch, Harry presses on his sandwich to smooth the lumpy filling and "jelly and peanut butter began to ooze over the edge. Volcano erupting. Watch out everybody!" She also gives a nice rendition of Harry's father rushing through a bedtime story ..., and she knows better than to impose some artificial resolution.

> *A review of "Unhurry Harry," in* Kirkus Reviews, *Vol. XLVI, No. 21, November 1, 1978, p. 1186.*

GOOD NIGHT TO ANNIE (1980)

An alphabet book with a sleepytime theme. Although the text is minimal (one sentence per letter of the alphabet), the book is not a basic one; it is rather sophisticated, presenting lyrical ideas and concepts, with quaint turns of phrase and made-up words. The illustrations [by John Wallner] are soft and gentle, in keeping with the hushed tone of the book. An added bonus: the alphabet is shown throughout in both capital and small letters. Despite an occasional insipid sentence ("Grass is silently growing"), the book is very appealing and offers an added dimension for the young imagination.

> *Maureen O'Connor, in a review of "Good Night to Annie," in* Children's Book Review Service, *Vol. 8, No. 10, May, 1980, p. 93.*

This bedtime alphabet book will ease children into a marvelous slumber. If they're lucky, their dreams will be . . . as peaceful as Merriam's understated text presenting alligators dozing in warm mud, nightingales nodding in their nests, and waves washing over the shore.

> *Gemma DeVinney, in a review of "Good Night to Annie," in* School Library Journal, *Vol. 26, No. 9, May, 1980, p. 61.*

A bedtime ABC featuring a moppet in a polka-dot mobcap and assorted entities—Alligators, Cats, Inchworms, Jets—doing their nighttime thing. Now and again one finds a pleasant word-and-picture configuration ("Elephants are curling in with their dark trunks"; "Penguins are folding in their flippers"); often, though, the imagery is strained beyond the natural order of things. . . . A very few felicities, then, along with many fey imaginings. . . .

> *A review of "Good Night to Annie," in* Kirkus Reviews, *Vol. XLVIII, No. 9, May 1, 1980, p. 578.*

A WORD OR TWO WITH YOU: NEW RHYMES FOR YOUNG READERS (1981)

Merriam doesn't even seem to be trying very hard in this latest collection of 17 unexciting small rhymes. The longest promises also to be the most ambitious, but instead of responding with thought or wit to the title question, **"What Is a Rhyme?,"** it settles mostly for mindless doggerel ("You can rhyme with two / out of the zoo: / a hare and a bear, / a cow and a sow, / a moose and a goose, / a cat and a rat / and how about a wombat?")—and never takes up the challenge of the most interesting lines, "What else can you do with a rhyme? / You can take a rhyme and shake it / and wake it up. . . ." Elsewhere we have lesser lessons on **"Portmanteaux"** and **"Fiddle-Faddle"** ("Said the razor, 'Be keen,' / 'String along,' said the bean . . ."), both of which do too little with what might have been bright ideas. And the faint echoes of Merriam's old satire are just that—with the added offense of throwing "cotton flannel" into a TV-commercial collage as a repeated rhyme for "switch the channel." Weak.

> *A review of "A Word or Two with You," in* Kirkus Reviews, *Vol. XLIX, No. 21, November 1, 1981, p. 1348.*

Some of the contents [of *A Word or Two with You*] deal with everyday concerns—**"Tube Time,"** for instance, with its sprightly take-off on TV commercials that leave a child sated—while others deal with things as bizarre as **"The Dreadful Drawkcab,"** a monster. As ever, Eve Merriam has a sharp ear for verbal music (a supermarket sells "shreddable edible paper towels"); in fact, her work will be useful in acquainting young readers with rhyme. She even defines this basic ingredient of traditional poetry for us: "A rhyme is a chime / that rings in time." Try reading the whole book aloud. (p. 60)

> *X. J. Kennedy, "A Rhyme Is a Chime," in* The New York Times Book Review, *November 15, 1981, pp. 51, 60.*

A brief collection of light verse catches the quick beat of modern living with titles like **"Tube Time,"** **"Supermarket, Supermarket,"** and **"Frying Pan in the Moving Van."** Varying the pace are a few lyrical pieces—**"Secret Talk"** is a gentle description of friendship—but most are simply amusing and accessible to children, with some energetic word combinations and chanting rhythms.

> *A review of "A Word or Two with You: New Rhymes for Young Readers," in* Booklist, *Vol. 78, No. 7, December 1, 1981, p. 500.*

Too thin to be a "best buy," this collection is a modest salmagundi of poetical forms and devices by a poet who makes the difficult look easy. Merriam's touch remains authoritative, whether in the display of intricate patterns or in her trust that a neat compound sentence can be whittled to earn its way as a poem. Nothing, Merriam asserts by her choice of subjects, need be beyond a poet's attention. As frequently in her work, there are poems about poetry, demonstrating the craft even as Merriam mouths, chews, masticates, gulps, or nibbles words. She abides by what Auden said was the poet's disposition: to "have fun hanging around words." She ever remains graceful, skilled, unstuffy. And by her own seeming unself-consciousness in the presence of poetry, by her demonstration of the manner in which poetry may attend mundane reality, she can encourage children to attend as well.

> *Peter Neumeyer, in a review of "A Word or Two with You: New Rhymes for Young Readers," in* School Library Journal, *Vol. 28, No. 5, January, 1982, p. 68.*

Despite her playful proclamation in an earlier volume, *It Doesn't Always Have to Rhyme* . . ., the poet usually finds that it does; rhyme, rhythm, and wordplay characterize her verses, which often instruct as well as entertain. . . . Unevenness haunts both the poems and the volume. With only seventeen poems—compared with the several dozen typical of her other collections—weak ones are glaring. Yet who can keep muscles motionless while chanting the sprightly **"Supermarket, Supermarket"** jump-rope rhyme with its "Vegetable soapflakes, / filtertip milk, / frozen chicken wings ready to fly, / shreddable edible paper towels, / banana detergent, / deodorant pie."? (pp. 176-77)

> *Nancy C. Hammond, in a review of "A Word or Two with You: New Rhymes for Young Readers," in* The Horn Book Magazine, *Vol. LVIII, No. 2, April, 1982, pp. 176-77.*

IF ONLY I COULD TELL YOU: POEMS FOR YOUNG LOVERS AND DREAMERS (1983)

Merriam's latest collection of poetry for adolescents is a disappointment. Several of the poems entice with the quality of language and emotion one expects from Merriam, notably **"Expression,"** a poem about crushes and **"Like Bookends,"** about families. Unfortunately most of the poems are simplistic, often trite in their expression of feeling. Peck's *Pictures That Storm Inside My Head* . . . and Dunning's anthologies offer poems of more depth for adolescents interested in poetry about feelings. . . . This collection . . . seems designed for the same mass appeal as the teen romance series.

Barbara Chatton, in a review of "If Only I Could Tell You: Poems for Young Lovers and Dreamers," in School Library Journal, *Vol. 30, No. 6, February, 1984, p. 82.*

In a collection of short, tender poems, Merriam captures the delight and wonder of young love, the feeling that the love is unique, the absorption in self and the loved one, the desolation when separation comes. The poetry is deceptively simple, controlled in style and deep in its empathy and insight. A few of the selections are on other themes, other kinds of love, but most have to do with the aching romantic love of adolescence.

Zena Sutherland, in a review of "If Only I Could Tell You," in Bulletin of the Center for Children's Books, *Vol. 37, No. 7, March, 1984, p. 131.*

For the starry-eyed young romantic who adores Rod McKuen's verse, some 50 rapturous short and short-short love poems. . . . [Montages by Donna Diamond] help carry out the dreamy mood and enhance the Hallmark card-type format. Hokey and inconsequential but sure to be dog-eared.

A review of "If Only I Could Tell You: Poems for Young Lovers and Dreamers," in Booklist, *Vol. 80, No. 14, March 15, 1984, p. 1036.*

The jacket notes say this book "grew out of Ms. Merriam's readings . . . where she was frequently asked by young people to write a book of love poems especially for them." I assume that's what the poet tried to do with *If Only I Could Tell You.* And that, I fear, is why this book is disappointing. Merriam has written down to adolescents. She has given them lifeless, colorless poems that are little more exciting than greeting card verse. (p. 47)

This collection, from a poet who has written some interesting poems, perpetuates the myth that young adults should not be given high quality poetry because they will not be able to handle it. I say, "Nonsense!" I say the same thing to this book. (p. 48)

Paul B. Janeczko, in a review of "If Only I Could Tell You," in Voice of Youth Advocates, *Vol. 7, No. 1, April, 1984, pp. 47-8.*

BLACKBERRY INK: POEMS (1985)

Suggested by topics familiar to small children, the pithy verses lift off with a paean to berry-picking: "Look at my mouth, / It's huckleberry purple. / Look at my tongue, / It's blackberry ink." Dizzy Bella is one of the types kids will love to laugh at, seeing her striding through a storm with a new umbrella she won't use. . . . A pizza with everything, a hole in a pocket, a cat's tongue, a night light, snow and lots of other things are transformed into rollicking amusements by the poet and [Hans Wilhelm, the illustrator]. (pp. 117-18)

A review of "Blackberry Ink," in Publishers Weekly, *Vol. 227, No. 20, May 17, 1985, pp. 117-18.*

Most of the selections are light in concept, lilting, agreeably silly; although few have the depth or nuance of which Merriam has shown herself capable in the past, all of the poems have a yeasty quality and good form.

Zena Sutherland, in a review of "Blackberry Ink," in Bulletin of the Center for Children's Books, *Vol. 38, No. 10, June, 1985, p. 191.*

An agreeable collection of 23 light poems for reading aloud, this has the look and appeal of a picture book. . . . Merriam is playing with words here, bouncing rhythms and juggling rhymes. There's the feel of an insouciant child on a very familiar playground, and indeed some of the poems bounce along like jumprope rhymes. While not as technically proficient as the verse, the watercolor illustrations are a good match in humor, verve, and innocent enjoyment. . . . Merriam is a poet sure of her craft and capable of committing nonsense with style.

Carolyn Phelan, in a review of "Blackberry Ink: Poems," in Booklist, *Vol. 81, No. 21, July, 1985, p. 1558.*

These 24 simple poems touch everyday objects and occurrences—elusive butterflies, seasonal happenings, favorite foods, bedtime routine, animal antics and more. They overflow with descriptive rhythms and rhymes both pure and nonsensical. . . . Merriam's poems are great fun to read. They may even make children want to grab a pen (and some blackberry ink?) and write a few of their own! Sure to tickle small funny-bones everywhere and to provide many moments of pleasure.

Susan Scheps, in a review of "Blackberry Ink," in School Library Journal, *Vol. 32, No. 1, September, 1985, p. 122.*

THE CHRISTMAS BOX (1985)

Obviously, all the members of a very large family believe in Santa Claus, since the adults are just as surprised and disappointed as the children when they come downstairs on Christmas morning to find only one box under the tree. That's the part of the story that even small listeners may find hard to believe; the fact that the box is magic in its capacity, providing one substantial present (a flute, a fishing rod, a hammock, a kite) for each member of the family is standard fantasy. Amusing, but it's an extension of a one-gag situation.

A review of "The Christmas Box," in Bulletin of the Center for Children's Books, *Vol. 39, No. 2, October, 1985, p. 33.*

Never before has the awakening scene on Christmas morning been described so well as in Merriam's sparkling book. Seemingly simple actions ("Mother left the bed unmade and didn't even brush her hair. Father left the top off the toothpaste tube") will tickle children as they recall their own harried Christmas mornings. . . . [Illustrator David] Small uses this somewhat curious story to portray the family excitement on Christmas morn in a hilarious fashion. . . . Together, Merriam and Small have created a special scene of family solidarity and fun that is especially appropriate for Christmas. (pp. 190-91)

A review of "The Christmas Box," in School Library Journal, *Vol. 32, No. 2, October, 1985, pp. 190-91.*

Eve Merriam's *The Christmas Box* . . . is so unobtrusively inventive that it may have been overlooked at a time of year-end budget skimping. In descriptive passages, as well as drawings, there are some fresh images.

David Small has preserved the whimsical, warm quality of Merriam's text and, like her story, has made the drawings exude practicality and no-nonsense simplicity.

Donnarae MacCann and Olga Richard, in a review of "The Christmas Box," in Wilson Library Bulletin, *Vol. 60, No. 9, May, 1986, p. 46.*

THE BIRTHDAY DOOR   (1986)

A small girl deciphers a series of rhymed clues leading to her birthday gift of a dollhouse and a cake already lit with candles. . . .

Helen follows simple clues (''Find the door that hides a light, / where it's cold all day and night.''—refrigerator) from door to door, ten in all from birdhouse to attic.

All rather tame, then, and a disappointment from poet Merriam, who has often shown that she can write livelier verse than this. Beginning readers might enjoy answering the easy riddles.

> *A review of "The Birthday Door," in* Kirkus Reviews, *Vol. LIV, No. 12, June 15, 1986, p. 932.*

Few children can resist fantasizing about their birthdays and birthday surprises, and, although the text is somewhat unimaginative, Merriam's book will hold appeal for young audiences as they follow Helen and her cat Clio from clue to clue on the morning of her birthday. . . . Both illustrations and text have a touch of nostalgia and an old-fashioned charm. Nevertheless, some children may wonder about the ''clunk thunk'' of the garage door or the ''chig choog whoosh'' of the dishwasher. In any case, the rhythm and rhyme of the clues will delight listeners and pique their imaginations, and trying to unravel the clues should keep readers engaged until the last page.

> *Janice L. Amicone, in a review of "The Birthday Door," in* School Library Journal, *Vol. 33, No. 3, November, 1986, p. 80.*

FRESH PAINT: NEW POEMS   (1986)

Forty-five new poems, colorful, humorous, thoughtful, and bursting with energy—poems on colors, nature, nonsense, and love. . . .

It is hard to choose a favorite. Among the color poems, **"Strike Me Pink,"** where ''Rose became madder'' and then reels off a catalog of reds, is a wonderful word play. **"Sunset,"** ''Yellow and pink as a peach left to ripen on a tree,'' explores color and texture in a softer mood. **"A New Pencil"** tells a story within a story, pulling together images of the simple act of sharpening a pencil and an immigrant grandmother's view of the world, past and future.

Not all the poems work; **"Quest"** is a didactic complaint about pollution, awkwardly phrased; **"Excursion,"** a nonsense dialogue between a bear and a flea, is more interesting for its play with the sounds of words than humorous; but at their best, these poems are very good indeed. A collection to savor.

> *A review of "Fresh Paint: New Poems," in* Kirkus Reviews, *Vol. LIV, No. 14, July 15, 1986, p. 1126.*

Ms. Merriam exhibits her talent for inventive expression and appealing imagery in this collection. . . . Short, pithy observations on nature and human activities, they range from comments on new shoes, a new suit, and fresh paint to problem-solving and composing haiku. The appeal to the senses is short and memorable and the sound patterns arresting. Although the set on the whole seems slighter than Merriam's early collections, the poems are nevertheless very good. They should be read aloud for maximum appreciation.

> *Alethea K. Helbig, in a review of "Fresh Paint: New Poems," in* Children's Book Review Service, *Vol. 15, No. 1, September, 1986, p. 10.*

Some of the best writing Merriam has done surfaces in these 45 poems, which achieve a light, effortless tone with echoes of meaning. The title poem, **"Fresh Paint,"** sets the pace with fresh images of color blended into an invitation: ''. . . and look / how the word *don't* is painted out / so the sign reads / touch.'' **"A New Pencil"** subtly sketches the portrait of an immigrant grandmother; **"Flying for the First Time"** catches the thrill of an airplane ride with a comparison to swimming in the sea. Some of these—**"New Love," "Skip Rope Rhyme for Our Time"** (about junk mail), and **"Artichoke"**—reach toward an older awareness than the audience implied by the format. . . . On the whole, however, the language is simple and ideas lyrical.

> *Betsy Hearne, in a review of "Fresh Paint," in* Bulletin of the Center for Children's Books, *Vol. 40, No. 2, October, 1986, p. 32.*

A singularly apt title reinforces what quickly becomes apparent in a collection of crisply written poems; they are as bright and welcome as the season's first strawberries. Like that early fruit, they are often a bit tart, have an individual texture, and awaken old memories and new ideas. Nostalgic or vivid, thoughtful or downright funny, each is an entirely satisfying unit; yet the collection, like a large, noisy, and affectionate family, would be diminished by the removal of even one. Some are merely simple listings, but the musings in **"Questions for an Angel"**— ''Do you take it off when you go to sleep? / Do they fold back so you can put on a jacket? / Do you have memories?''—are also provocative. Others, such as **"Mushroom,"** develop an image through skillful appeal to all the senses: ''Squat / it will never rule the world from on high / soft as eyelashes / soft / without even the memory of bones / its stem so gray it turns to silver / and smells more like the earth / than the earth itself.'' The variety of rhyming patterns, the freshness of vision, and the deceptive ease with which image and idea are summoned up contribute a liveliness, sophistication, and vitality often missing in poetry for the young.

> *Ethel R. Twichell, in a review of "Fresh Paint: New Poems," in* The Horn Book Magazine, *Vol. LXII, No. 6, November-December, 1986, p. 753.*

[Merriam's] eloquent message to children is that poetry is to be touched and tasted. She delights in the sounds of language, savoring a rich variety of rhymes and rhythms from the lovely litany of **"Giving Thanks Giving Thanks"** to the gentle haiku of **"Frame for a Picture."** Some of the poems provide delicate extended imagery, while others move wildly from one image to another. . . . As always, Merriam's great gift to children is in providing poems that make them think and wonder and laugh about the world as they read or listen.

> *Barbara Chatton, in a review of "Fresh Paint," in* School Library Journal, *Vol. 33, No. 4, December, 1986, p. 106.*

A SKY FULL OF POEMS   (1986)

What to do with precocious young students who have devoured every Shel Silverstein poetry book and are getting older and more competent at handling the mechanics of creating poetry themselves? Try *A Sky Full of Poems* by Eve Merriam, guaranteed to provide long hours of relief for teachers and enjoyment for their students.

A Sky Full of Poems is divided into five sections. There is "Poet's Play," a selection of 18 poems that basically fool around with our language, ruminating on the oddities of a 29-letter word, the "i before e" rule, and the reasons for the varying rhymes for "through," "bough," and "enough." There is a section called "Poet's Tools," which contains poems on punctuation, clichés, and onomatopoeia. "Poet's Talk" consists of more challenging poems that illustrate the topics of poetry, the themes it can touch and enlarge. "Poet's People" is much the same, a parade of personalities for students to enjoy, emulate, or write about. The last section, "A Sky Full of Poems," combines all the elements of the previous sections and ends the book with a flourish of sheer creativity, poems both playful and philosophical, all sufficient for motivation and/or lessons in writing. Merriam even includes a prose piece on the making of one of her poems to give students an insight into the process behind the final product.

This wonderful collection . . . is destined to bring pleasure to readers of all ages in classrooms across the country.

> *John T. Hodgen, in a review of "A Sky Full of Poems,"*
> *in* Kliatt Young Adult Paperback Book Guide, *Vol.*
> *XX, No. 6, September, 1986, p. 34.*

(Alice) Patricia (Furlonger) Wrightson

1921-

Australian author of fiction and editor.

Wrightson is perhaps the most respected Australian author currently writing for children. Combining realistic characters and locales with native folklore and legends, she produces fiction which interweaves past and present to explore the child's significance in the universe. Her books challenge older elementary and young adult readers to examine such meaningful topics as the ownership and preservation of land and alternative ways of defining reality. Wrightson's most unique contribution is her advancement of Australian fantasy through the creation of a body of aboriginal folk literature which deals with ancient nature spirits, such as those of water, rock, and tree. Considered her most significant achievement, the *Book of Wirrun* trilogy—*The Ice Is Coming* (1977), *The Dark Bright Water* (1979), and *Behind the Wind* (1981; U.S. edition as *Journey behind the Wind*)—is a well-received example of Wrightson's accomplishment; it revolves around the aborigine Wirrun, who represents the people, land, and peaceful spirits as they battle to vanquish malicious spirits causing havoc with nature. Notable among Wrightson's other books are *Down to Earth* (1965), which spotlights a young Martian and remains her sole venture into science fiction; *'I Own the Racecourse!'* (1968; U.S. edition as *A Racecourse for Andy*), a work of realistic fiction which centers on an illusion harbored by a retarded boy; *The Nargun and the Stars* (1973), which features a powerful rock spirit who rebels against the desecration of his land by humans; and *A Little Fear* (1983), which depicts the struggles of an elderly, independent woman to keep her land from an age-old gnome. Wrightson's most recent work, *Night Outside* (1985), uses a realistic framework to introduce fantastical night people who help two children search for their missing bird.

Reviewers consistently praise Wrightson for the originality and depth of her subject matter. While some critics find that *Night Outside* lacks cohesiveness, they admire the strong plots, perceptive characterizations, descriptive settings, and lyrical prose which generally distinguish her works. Wrightson is regarded not only as an important regional author but as a stimulating international writer whose portrayals of Australian folklore hold universal appeal.

In 1978, *The Ice Is Coming* was placed on the International Board on Books for Young People (IBBY) Honor List. In 1982, *Behind the Wind* was highly commended by the Australian Children's Book of the Year committee. In 1984, *A Little Fear* won the Australian Children's Book of the Year Award and the *Boston Globe-Horn Book* Award. In the same year, Wrightson was nominated for the Hans Christian Andersen Medal, an award she won in 1986. Wrightson was also chosen as the 1985 May Hill Arbuthnot Honor Lecturer.

(See also *CLR*, Vol. 4; *Something about the Author Autobiography Series*, Vol. 4; *Something about the Author*, Vol. 8; *Contemporary Authors New Revision Series*, Vols. 3, 19; and *Contemporary Authors*, Vols. 45-48.)

Courtesy of Patricia Wrightson

AUTHOR'S COMMENTARY

[The following excerpt is from a speech given by Wrightson on April 16, 1985 as presenter of the 1985 May Hill Arbuthnot Honor Lecture.]

On that exciting day when I was invited to deliver the May Hill Arbuthnot Honor Lecture, I at once went into a state of panic. That was quite usual, only perhaps more justified than usual. The organizers were kind enough to send me copies of previous papers in the series: it didn't help. They were all by notable people, qualified people, whose long experience was built on a sound base of study; people who knew what they did and why they did it.

I'm not one of those. I'm not really sure what I do or why I do it. So you must accept that I can speak only from my experience, and that what is true for me may not be true for anyone else, and even that I may be discovering it as I go along.

I probably would have been better for a college course in writing—but, true to my empiricism and my native obstinacy, I don't really believe that writing *can* be taught. I know it is taught, commonly in your country [the United States] and increasingly in mine; I've even been called on now and then to teach it. Yet I can't be convinced that it can or should be taught. . . .

Is there a right way to tell a story? Surely there is: a different one for every writer. And just as surely, this is what gives life and strength to literature. The same stories are told and retold and told again, and still they're fresh and different and alive: as alive and different and fresh as their authors, who are as different, fresh and alive as other people. Every writer has to discover the inner vision, as well as the techniques, that are secretly and only his. You find them by needing them: when you're wholly engrossed in a story, urgently trying to grasp and shape and convey it. Writing teaches writing. (p. 284)

But probably I'm being unfair to the college course and they don't really aim to teach the skill of achieving publication. That would be more valid, for publication matters acutely, and writers may need to learn it since it's a separate skill. In fact, at the deep-down level at which I find myself thinking, publication has nothing at all to do with writing.

Editors and royalties and up-front payments; reviews and critical studies and literary values; libraries and audiovisual and reluctant readers; all of these are important, matter acutely, and yet are quite irrelevant. They're the complex superstructure that we've built around the skills of writing. Writers may need to work within this superstructure, but I don't believe they work for it.

Let the superstructure collapse, and writers will go on writing. Allow them a personal happy-ending of fame and fortune, and they'll thank you warmly and go on writing. Assure them of immortality, promise them that their names are now preserved for all time, and they'll thank you warmly and go on writing. As they learn from story, so they're slaves to story. Practical purposes can be achieved, but the old, simple-minded motive can never be satisfied: the motive of story itself.

Even today, in spite of the complex structure of which this meeting is a part, I don't believe many stories are written for reputation or royalties, for reviews or posterity, or even for children. They're written for a stranger, for Someone Out There: that rare, unknown precious soul who will respond. Given one warm and seeing response from somewhere in the world, a writer standing in the dole queue will glow with success. Publication may serve its hundred useful purposes for society; to the writer it's the way to reach the stranger.

But even when you've reached them, responsive strangers are often shy. They don't often write to give you their response; and there's no longer a circle of faces round the fire, faces rapt or restless, to let you see the power of the story. As for letters, people write to ask for information and advice; children spurred on by teachers write to ask questions and display your reply; but only a handful write to say, "I loved it. I felt . . . I thought . . .". And that, I promise you, is the real reason why reviewers were invented. They may serve a dozen useful purposes for society; to the writer they are faces round the fire.

We have grown accustomed, you see, to thinking in terms of books and literature; and so we sometimes get the emphasis wrong. Books are simply a packaging of story. Literature exists on the authority of story and not the other way around. You don't need to examine a story to see whether it measures up to literature—though you may need to examine literature to see whether it measures up to story—for every story exists in its own right. If you don't like it, better read something else; this story wasn't written for you but for some other stranger.

Story is something much larger, more fundamental, more invincible, than books or literature.

It may be solemn or poetic or the purest fun, but it's always something more. It's a system of thought for exploring life in terms of circumstances and people; a system that proposes by example, and defines and illuminates by demonstration. But its particular skill, as well as its particular power, lies in its directness of communication: it's a system of thinking directly into someone else's mind. It conveys not an argument drawn from experience but the experience itself, illuminated; it is a direct extension of my life and thought and experience to you and yours to me. Story is communication so finely tuned that it sounds like silence.

Because it thinks always about life and people in a framework of circumstance, its conclusions are not mathematically final, to be ruled off neatly like a sum. They always lead on: back into life, on into fresh thought and new conclusions. So story moves on with life itself, and the same story may be relevant in new ways at new times; a tale that explored the concept of the sun as a burning chariot travelling over the sky may be relevant in the age of radio-telescopes for its illumination of fear or vanity, and of man's own questioning habits of thought.

Story explores the intangible as science can't do, defining through experience what can't be defined in words. It explores the unknown, speculating in human terms. It extends not only mind to mind but mind itself, teaching it the freedom to explore and the power to see what isn't there; and this is a power that can't be taught by visual means. If we build around it a complexity that, for any reason, fences any child off from story, we do well to worry: we have cut that child off from the thinking, the defining, the shared experience, of its kind. Story is a mark of Man.

So now, perhaps, if you wanted to know what it is that writers do I might answer, in my wrong-headed way, that they drop stones into pools: finding a visionary stone, handling and weighing it; dropping it into a pool of another mind; watching for the ripples to spread, and perhaps for the stirred water to give something back. And if you asked why they do it I might answer that everyone shares in story, but writers happen, some of the time, to be on the transmitting rather than the receiving end. They are just a few accidental words of the book itself in all its forms: painted in caves, impressed into clay, penned on papyrus, spoken by firelight, or fingered into a word-processor.

The novel is a modern invention—if you ignore, for instance, the *budaram:* long traditional tales with songs interspersed, that were continued over several nights in the camps of some of the Australian Aborigines. They were not ritual stories. They were told and sung for entertainment and for literature; just as my father would read us, say, *David Copperfield* night after night before bed. The *budaram* were still being told and sung within recent memory, yet they could be twice as old as a papyrus scroll.

There are even older Australian stories still alive. Some of them tell of the time when our deserts were lush and green, some of extinct giant animals whose bones have indeed been found among bones of the people. The current estimate is that the Aborigines have occupied Australia for something like forty-thousand years: almost halfway back to Neanderthal Man. This is no reliable dating of the stories, of course, but we don't need that to establish the age of story. For Neanderthal Man himself, one-hundred-thousand years ago, buried his dead with ceremony, and it is not humanly possible to believe that he did it in silence. He must have conveyed, at least to each generation, the story of why, and in what manner. Story begins when man begins, and flows forward with him out of the ages.

We haven't long been aware of this river of continuity: of life and experience flowing down to us out of the whole country of mankind. Until lately we thought of continuity in terms of Greece and Rome. Only since the Brothers Grimm and folklore, since the finding and decoding of Ancient Egypt and Sumeria, have we had a longer view. Now we know that if you could look back all that long, dark way through the ages, right back to the painted caves, the whole way would be lined with human figures slumped in thought and struggling to convey: fingering and weighing their visionary stones, judging how to drop or slip them into the pools of other minds, wondering if the minds would stir and the ripples spread.

I'm certainly no student, either of folklore or of archaeology. I've read only a little, for my own purposes, and I read always like a writer: in terms of life, circumstance and humanity. And what this reading has given me is, more than anything else, a warm sense of familiarity, of recognition, of experience passed on from Man to men. A sense of mankind seen whole. (pp. 285-87)

For here is the record revealed, and the differences are swallowed up in the sameness. Here are school exercises, careful sentences impressed in clay, painted on shards, and pencilled along pale-blue lines in an exercise-book. Here is a code of law set down four thousand years ago and old even then; we never saw it till lately, but its ripples have spread forward into our own laws. Here is a nation's heroicised view of itself, a successful man's self-satisfaction, a love-song, a law-suit, a traveller's tale, a list of taxes; all ancient, long-forgotten, and relevant and modern. And here is story exploring life, the known and unknown and the intangible: proposing and testing and defining by the same system; conveying with the same power directly into other minds, reaching conclusions that lead back into life and on into new thought. Dropping stones into pools.

And the ripples reached us even when we didn't see them. You and I as persons may often be in doubt or disagree; we may hotly debate terms, or means, or applications. As a kind we are not in doubt; we know our values and purposes. We have shared in the experience of mankind.

"No man is an island; pride is arid; personal power is a dangerous evil." Modern maxims proved by recent history, themes for a hundred modern novels—but they reached us long ago in the ripples of old stories. Unspoken, they came to us in tales of great hunters rescued by tiny beasts, of proud princesses and swineherds, of the dangerous evil of witches. "Simple goodwill is worth more than a devious mind"; a hundred triumphant simpletons have shown it. "The greatest beauty is kindness"; dozens of cruel stepmothers, though they worked through magic, have proved the point in terms of life and humanity. These are our foundation-values, often rethought, retested, reexplored, but never questioned. We don't question them because we have not merely learnt them; we have directly shared the experience of them in story.

These were the stories of simple people, whose journeys were short and made on foot over muddy forest tracks; for whom a neighborhood was a world, and even natural science was generally magic. Life for us, materially, could hardly be more different; yet what comes through is sameness, a brotherhood

in life. Those early people thought by our system and passed it on to us. They had no glimpse of our century's massive knowledge, but their questioning thought began it. Their storytelling broke the ground for science, as well as for literature.

It's no wonder that so many of their stories are of the kind we know as fantasy. They had a huge unknown to explore, and fantasy best explores the unknown. They had to define the intangible without the aid of a jargon, and fantasy substitutes symbols for jargon; it's the algebra of literature. The stories that reached us have lasted because they were memorable, and fantasy, dealing in the extraordinary, is most memorable. A simple verbal form, when it deals with emotions, should step easily into poetry, and fantasy steps easily into poetry. It's not remarkable that, of the folktales we know, so many should be fantasy. What does seem remarkable is that we of today should be divided, some of us uncertain, in our approach to fantasy.

This oldest and freest kind of thinking—which abandons restrictive detail in favour of essentials, or which in its search for a wider view demands the freedom to fly—is an inheritance as old as story itself. Neanderthal Man, explaining the rituals of death, must have done so through fantasy. We should be perfectly at home with it, should know with the experience of millennia what it is doing and how. Yet somewhere, somehow, understanding has broken down.

When you mention fantasy to any large group, there's often an uneasy shuffling. Half of the company, or rather less, sits forward with a happy smile; the rest sit back looking baffled. What has happened? (pp. 287-88)

To me this is saddening. To like or dislike so ancient a system of thought is one thing; to be baffled by it is another. But one can't help noticing that, to many keen readers, fantasy is a doubtful sort of lightweight nonsense fit only for tinies. They would like to reject it outright, but this is a problem because every now and then someone produces another fantasy that can't be rejected or labelled as lightweight nonsense. And so, with puzzled resignation, they can only regret that some substantial authors should over-indulge their imagination in this way, or perhaps retreat from reality.

This is a lack of comprehension, for substantial authors don't generally aim to produce either fantasy or realism; they aim to produce a story, exploring a certain concept. They will produce it in whatever form the story seems to demand. They will go on using fantasy because story, that powerful system of thought, will go on demanding it. Luckily.

Even the makers of visual story, on stage or film, can't resist fantasy. This is less fortunate; for fantasy, which most extends the power and freedom of the mind, most often also *depends* on that power and freedom. Even the sort of trick photography that merely shrinks or enlarges characters can't do it with the rightness and realness of a mental picture; and puppets or animations can be quite destructive. Fantasy is a natural region only of the mind. Yet one can't blame any maker of story for extending creativity into fantasy. One can only ask what has happened at the receiving end.

Perhaps the attempts to make fantasy visual must share in the blame. And perhaps that stern old nineteenth-century materialism has confused us all, writers and readers too. For one has to admit that there has been some basis for an uneasy approach to fantasy, and some writers have seemed as uncertain as some readers. A lot has been written that is truly lightweight and nonsensical; fantasy has sometimes been truly a self-indulgence.

Surely anyone with experience as a children's editor must know how often children are an excuse for the sort of whimsical non-story that I used to call "personal daydream," inflicted on this captive audience in the name of fantasy. But fantasy is story; it shares the object of story. It may be solemn or poetic or the purest fun, but it is always concerned with life. It may speak in symbols, or abandon the restrictions of life, but it should always explore and illuminate life.

In my childhood, when fantasy was suspect but-of-course-there-was-Lewis-Carroll, confused writers used to avoid the problem of unreality by writing stories that ended, "and then she woke up. It was only a dream." I remember how letdown I used to feel, having the rug pulled out from under me like that. But *Alice in Wonderland* is not a fantasy; it's the very successful, lifelike story of a dream. In fantasy the dream is always real.

I don't know which came first, the hen or the egg—whether pesudo-fantasy, from writers without purpose, caused the dichotomy among readers, or whether a helplessly uncritical approach by readers encouraged the pseudo-fantasy; but I should think it very likely, by now, that each of these factors works on and helps to perpetuate the other. Librarians will know, as I do not, who first uttered the famous apology that one still hears quoted: "Fantasy begins by asking you to suspend disbelief." No greater disservice could have been done to fantasy than to offer for it this apology and excuse. A thousand maiden ladies, on first-name terms with raindrops and roses, must have rubbed their hands and reached for their pens.

Fantasy is story, no story has any business to begin by asking you weakly to suspend disbelief. It is the business of story to require and work for your belief. It may be more difficult in fantasy, but that is the writer's affair; no one is forcing him to try. If he invites you to go flying with him, the very least he can do is to build a strong pair of wings. The freedom of fantasy is not license: if it abandons the laws and logic of reality, it must provide other laws and logic to govern itself. It may invent circumstances to suit its purpose, but the purpose must be story's obligation to explore life and humanity. It has great strengths: the power of the extraordinary, the broad definition of symbol, the evocative voice of poetry; having them, it mustn't also ask for your weak and complaisant credulity. If fantasy is not strong, it is nothing.

If you begin, as a special concession to fantasy, by abandoning disbelief, you begin by abandoning your critical judgement on all these functions. You wouldn't dream of approaching a real-life story in such a way. So it's hardly a wonder if the approach to fantasy is often uncertain, if writers as well as readers lose their conviction and purpose.

It would be a strange defeat for our knowledgeable age: the loss of a mental skill that was used confidently by men and women wearing string or skins or homespun. People who stood on the verge of a world seen but not yet known used it to explore their visions of the stars and the wind. Having no safeguards against material want, yet they had room in their thinking to explore intangibles: the fear and fascination of the sea, the silent mystery of snow, the terrible stroke of lightning, the menace of the dark, the lurking unknown of the forest. They explored emotion: fear and jealousy, loss and endurance, loneliness and companionship. And their thinking is still relevant, still human and moving.

There's the Australian story of Balyet, the lovely young girl who faded into an echo: not for love, as the Greek Echo did

but few living people have done, but for loneliness, frustration, and despair as many people have done.

And how can you read without compassion those universal tales of the vanishing fairy-wife?—beautiful, tender, romantic—and vanishing, because the human husband could not fulfil her terms. It's a theme that will be relevant as long as men and women fall in love with their dreams and ache to find reality only human; the theme of a million stories and poems to come. And none of them will handle it with a deeper or more poetic insight than the tales of the fairy-wife who is always lost.

The pervasive theme of man-into-beast, as we know it best, has been taken over by the nursery; frog princes, cat princesses, caged-bird heroines, Beauty and the Beast, have all their happy endings. But I have met the theme in a folklore that never reached the nursery, and I can't believe in the happy ending. The theme is too painful; for me it threw a whole book into shadow. Nor could I feel it as some old nightmare, irrelevant to life. In those days too there must have been deforming accidents and diseases, insanity with flashes of insight, a moment's breaking of tabu. Men could suddenly become beasts then as now, when they may wake from a blind red mist, or a drink too many, to find themselves monsters; when a trained, athletic body can become in one moment a quadriplegic hulk.

And we whose vision is so much broader, who have turned magic into mathematics and walked on the magic moon—we who have advanced so far that some of us have lost touch with fantasy—do we use it only from habit and tradition, or by caprice? Not always, at any rate. There's the Earthsea trilogy, exploring the darkness of self: in what different form could that have been better done?

There's science fiction, pouring out under the pressure of demand: you'd almost think that we too, like the people from the age of folklore, stood on the verge of a world seen but not yet known. There was the sweeping success of The Lord of the Rings: it almost seems as if we too had felt a darkness of Mordor. Supermen, bionic men, Dr Who: you could almost believe that we too needed heroes.

The Borrowers, Mistress Masham's Repose, The Lost Forum, The Mouse and His Child: you'd almost think that we, in our turn, explored the conditions of being very small in a world of superpowers. Talking animals still, and in spite of wiser counsels: you might think we suspected that man's dominion ought to be more brotherly.

No, I don't think we're in danger of losing fantasy; not as long as we go on needing it. In fact, I might suggest to a superpower or two that whenever they notice a regrettable upsurge of fantasy they should take heed: the people are exploring values and imponderables. They're trying on new visions, debating questions, working it out in algebra.

And to those who believe that reality is solidest and soundest I might say, in my Australian way, fair enough; but how do you decide, in this century, what is real and what is fantasy? Since Einstein has shown that truth is what you see from a certain point of view, since physics has proved by its own laws that it can't exist, since it's now all right to wear a copper band for rheumatism and almost all right to spank your child if he's naughty, since the planet Venus is an intruder into our universe, since as many minor mysteries as ever remain unexplained, who will have the temerity to say, "This is real," without adding cautiously, "as far as we know?" In the 1940s we plumbed the horrors of fantasy and they were real. Is there no room in reality for wonder too?

There's a new story hovering at the edge of my mind—or it may be a story, that will have to be proved. I would have been working at it, weighing and handling the stone, if I hadn't been trying to work out what writers do and why. But if this wild idea does prove to be a story, it will be a fantasy in which two children wander for a long time in my country and discover magical things. They'll find a mountain being burnt away underneath by fire; a sleeping pool whose waters rise and fall as it breathes; a beach where they can gather gems instead of shells; a lake that vanishes and is restored; another whose waters wander round its bed, now here, now there. They will meet, in darkness, their ancient ancestor made of opal; camp by a salt-water river where, at evening, fresh water rises through the rocks for thirsty travellers; tumble through a swamp into mysterious gardens deep under crystal water. The story will be fantasy, yet all these magical things will in fact be real; places and things that do exist, or did until lately. So perhaps it's only because I'm Australian that I think there should be room in reality for wonder.

For fantasy is only a way of looking at things: looking at them with wonder. And surely wonder is a real and hopeful experience. We who share in story the visions and values, the humour and sadness, the poetry and the whole homely business of living, surely we would choose to share wonder too. (pp. 289-92)

Patricia Wrightson, "Stones into Pools," in Top of the News, *Vol. 41, No. 3, Spring, 1985, pp. 283-92.*

GENERAL COMMENTARY

DONALD A. YOUNG

At first glance, Patricia Wrightson's award-winning novel *The Crooked Snake* appears to belong to the story category so cleverly exploited by Enid Blyton. Six children form a secret society for holiday fun. They undertake a sensible project of recording the local district and its industries which brings them up against the somewhat coyly described Dangerous Persons. These D.P.s are older children violating the local reserves and doing things which ought not to be done in areas designated by the Department of Conservation as sanctuaries or flora reserves. The children outwit the D.P.s and in the tradition of such stories are rewarded by grown-ups who have remained discreetly out of the story until then.

We must remember that *The Crooked Snake* appeared in 1955: that it is set in N.S.W. [New South Wales]: that the plot is neatly contrived: that the conservationist theme is strong and the setting described skilfully. There is plenty of action and both the staff work and the working out of the final confrontation are well handled, hinting at powers which will find their full fruition some twenty years later. All these qualities were no doubt much in the minds of those who selected *The Crooked Snake* to win the Children's Book Council of New South Wales Award for the best Australian Children's Book of the Year. The author was off to a good start.

In *The Bunyip Hole* which appeared two years later in 1957 we find the same formula at work. The rival gangs of children range in conflict over the North Coast Country just south of the Queensland border. The cave which gives the title to the book plays an important part in the workings of the plot. The Bunyip itself lives in the imagination of the children and is

perhaps Patricia Wrightson's first attempt to make use of the spirit world of the aborigine which came to dominate her later writings. Here she is at pains to provide normal explanations for abnormal manifestations. She is not yet free to accord a reality to the mysterious paranormal powers which are the heritage of the vast continent where she lives and writes.

A more determined attempt to make use of indigenous material came with *The Rocks of Honey*. The school is still the meeting place of the white and abo children but in the middle of the schoolboy fun, there are serious farming and practical lessons. Patricia Wrightson devotes a whole chapter to the legend of Warrimai and his stone axe. Inadvertently he breaks a taboo which turns the axe into an instrument of evil. The evil can be neutralised by hiding the axe in the Rocks of Honey. The style of writing of this chapter is in marked contrast to the able but somewhat stilted account of the day to day activities. The seriousness and the sacredness of the folkmemory she re-tells gives an intensity and power to this new voice. Such a difference makes for an uneven story which young readers might find difficult to grasp after enjoying her two previous adventure stories. The practical world of the small bush school does not align itself happily with the spirit world of the abos. The axe is found but a series of inexplicable accidents convince the children that it is best returned to the neutralising safety of the Rocks of Honey. The children settle down to their lessons and their catapults, and the magic seeps away.

In *The Feather Star* she abandons both the child gang warfare and mythology in favour of the more delicate sensitivities of adolescent girlhood. There is an avid demand for stories in which 14-16 year old girls can find self-identification and discover the mysteries of womanhood and gain some understanding of a relationship with those outside the family circle. Written in 1962 the book does not give the brash revelations of Judy Blume or Paul Zindel. It is true that 15-year-old Lindy is confused and bemused by Bill and Ian, local boys who are introduced by Felice to make up a holiday foursome. They argue, fish, explore caves and discuss their future. The girls talk clothes and the boys tease them clumsily because they are girls. There are some moments of strange tenderness as Linda shares Bill's poetic interest and in the delicate beauty of the feather star as it swims in the darkened cave, they discover a common awareness of things that are good. In contrast the Bible-quoting alcoholic Abel rants and roars at them and reminds them of the misery and bitterness that awaits all those who turn their backs upon life, beauty and friendship.

The slow tempo, more thoughtful theme and perhaps the older reader, allow for a more developed descriptive style. (pp. 235-36)

The setting is still the coastal district of New South Wales and its flora and fauna help to create the atmosphere and surroundings to enhance an account of adolescent yearnings for all that is best in the world. Adults are suitably supportive in the background. It is an optimistic view quite free from the cynicism which some writers think essential to depictions of adolescence. There were no sequels to *The Feather Star*.

Patricia Wrightson next tried her hand at Sci-Fi. Woolloomooloo is visited by beings from another planet. To the ordinary observer these strange beings are so cleverly camouflaged as normal Woolloomooloo inhabitants as to be quite indistinguishable from them—except, of course, to the perceptive George, David and Cathy who meet the strange boy who lives by himself in an empty house. It turns out that Martin the Martian, as he is nicknamed, is not the only visitor of this kind. So when his unusual habits of bouncing, glowing and living on dog biscuits bring him into conflict with the law, help is at hand. Grown-ups refuse to believe Martin's story in the classical tradition of rejecting those who are outside the range of normal experience. In the country of the blind the one-eyed man is not king but an odd freak who is best normalised. Martin and his colleagues meet the space-ship sent to collect them and another adventure is over. In theme and style *Down to Earth* is a richer book than the first two adventure stories. The new dimension is handled well and the topographical detail together with the lively dialogue and good characterisation all work together to make the story a success. The author is fully at home with the supernatural either in the form of Sci-Fi or mythology. It was the latter to which she returned in 1972 with *An Older Kind of Magic.* In between came *I Own the Racecourse,* the Runner-up for the Children's Book of the Year Award in Australia and nominated for the 1970 Hans Christian Andersen Award Honours List. . . . In Andy, the twelve-year-old E.S.N. [Educationally Subnormal] boy who goes to a Special school, she has created a memorable character. His simplicity shields him from the consequences of his actions. It is a story of fantasy but the fantasy is in Andy's mind and the picture of the world as he sees it is unshakeable. His two friends know that reality will break through eventually and the reader shares their sighs of relief as the dilemma is resolved.

Andy and his friends have a game they play in which they 'own' and sell real estate. When an old tramp offers the Racecourse to Andy for three dollars it is a bargain his simple mind cannot refuse. What starts out as a joke amongst the racecourse staff of treating Andy as 'the owner' spreads dangerously until the Committee have to act. They buy back the course from Andy for ten dollars. The story is told very much through the thoughts of Andy. It says something about the quality of life which is positive and heartwarming. We rejoice when the meek inherit the earth. *I Own the Racecourse* proved that Patricia Wrightson could do without the gimmicks of science-fiction and the deus ex machina of folk-lore. She can create characters in sufficient depth to hold our interest. The emphasis is on people and their relationships rather than the mechanics of a plot. This book looks back to *The Feather Star* and forward to *The Ice is Coming.*

An increasing interest in the beliefs and traditions of the original inhabitants of the Australian Continent turned Particia Wrightson's thoughts away from Western mythology as a source for the elements of magic and fantasy she needed for her stories. She could do without elves, fairies, giants and dragons when the strange denizens of the outback were tumbling in and out of the rocks and caverns which surrounded her and began to form the furniture of her mind. She chose the Botanical Gardens of a 20th century city as the venue of *An Older Kind of Magic.* The remaining area free from the layer of man-made rock— that concrete layer that is the mark of man's subjugation of the earth—becomes the scene of the battle between the ecologists and the interests of commerce and industry. Against the forces of exploitation led by Sir Mortimer Wyvern is arrayed a lively group of children with such allies as the small hairy Net-Net, the Nyols and Pot-Koorok who lives in a pond. It is the small, stone-grey and shadowy Nyols who come out of the crevices in the rocks to kidnap Sir Mortimer, tease him unmercifully and then abandon him to his fate. Turned to stone he becomes just one of the statues in the Botanical Gardens he sought to turn into a car-park. Despite the somewhat extravagant plot the style is lyrical and poetic.

Wrightson, age four, seated between her sisters. Courtesy of Patricia Wrightson.

> Through dark lanes below, Selina's cat went silently. A thousand years of cat history prickled in its fur. Old mysteries tingled in its whiskers, a witch's spell twitched at its tail: and it padded into the street to sit under the bearded man's window.
>
> Farther off, in an underground tunnel where no trains ran, little brown shadows crept out of the land.

Such is a typical chapter ending which sets up a delicate frisson down the backbone of the sensitive reader and impels a quick turn of the page to read on.

The balance which she did not quite achieve with *The Rocks of Honey* is certainly found in her next book. In 1973 she turned once more to the folk memory of the abos and wrote convincingly of the Nargun, a monster of rock which moves painfully across the country at night and rests by day indistinguishable from the other rocks amongst which it moves. Sometimes it kills for food and sometimes through a sudden crushing rage. The havoc it causes is countered by young Simon but much happens before the Nargun is trapped once more within the mountain. Simon is helped by Potkoorok, the Turongs and the Nyols. So masterly is the writing that a total suspension of disbelief is attained. The brilliant descriptions, the heightened sensitivity of the characters and the magical prose all work together with great success. *The Nargun and the Stars* looks back to her earlier works and forward to the trilogy which has the aboriginal boy Wirrun as a central character and a rich tapestry of myth and legend as a background. The schoolroom is finally abandoned and the main roles are no longer allotted to the children of the white settlers now somewhat insignificantly referred to as the Happy People.

Wirrun is the archetypal Boy-Saviour rather than a child and his companions and helpers are the host of beings with which the aboriginal imagination has peopled the harsh land. The schoolboy fun gives way to the seriousness of the Quest and the school playground becomes an arena for the titanic struggle between the forces of good and evil.

Like Hercules, Wirrun has tasks to perform to save his people. He is sent for and he goes reluctantly to do what a Hero must do no matter what the cost. In *The Ice is Coming,* it is the Ninya who are the enemy bringing about startling climatic changes which are even noted in the newspapers of the Happy People. Ice appears where it has not been seen before and the prospect of the land becoming an icy waste unites all the spirits of the Dreamtime in a fierce battle against the green-eyed Ninya whose blood is white and whose beards shed needles of ice as they sing and howl for their freedom to emerge from their deep fastness and to range over the surface of the land once more smothered in glacial ice.

Wirrun's second task, to tame the unruly water-spirits whose wild behaviour is turning water-holes dry and making the barren desert flower, is featured in *The Dark Bright Water.* The third and final volume [*Behind the Wind*] brings Wirrun face to face with the greatest enemy of all, Death itself. He rides the winds with his companion, the water-spirit Yunggamurra in search of Wulgaru. The fight to the death against Death is as dramatic as any combat in the chronicles of Western mythology.

To make the folk memories of a culture alien to European thought so convincingly acceptable is a tribute to the literary skill of the author. That she should arrive at such a successful treatment of such a theme by way of stories written for children is in itself intriguing. Tracing the growth of her interest in the land of Australia and the legends of its indigenous people from its small beginnings in *The Crooked Snake* to the full-blown development in her last three books makes a fascinating study in itself. There were some false starts and excursions into different genres but always the mythology which demanded to be taken seriously persisted and the craftsmanship evidenced in *The Nargun and the Stars* led triumphantly to the Wirrun trilogy.

It will be interesting to see if her work is instrumental in clarifying the quest for identity that is always the preoccupation of a population whose roots are elsewhere than in the country in which they live. (pp. 236-37, 240-41)

> *Donald A. Young, "Patricia Wrightson, O.B.E.,"*
> *in* The Junior Bookshelf, *Vol. 45, No. 6, December,*
> *1981, pp. 235-37, 240-41.*

AUDREY LASKI

[*The Book of Wirrun* is] the most distinguished . . . , indeed the most outstanding of this whole batch [of books being reviewed]. *The Book of Wirrun* is a three-part epic (*The Ice is Coming, The Dark Bright Water, Behind the Wind* . . .), which draws on the myths and folktales of the Aboriginals to produce

a fantasy of great freshness and distinction. . . . [This] is fantasy on a grand scale, resonant in the imagination.

> *Audrey Laski, in a review of "The Book of Wirrun,"*
> *in* The Times Educational Supplement, *No. 3521,*
> *December 23, 1983, p. 23.*

JOHN ROWE TOWNSEND

[Patricia Wrightson's] work does not fit into any neat descriptive pigeonhole, for she has regarded each of her books as an individual challenge and has never used anything resembling a formula. *The Rocks of Honey* . . . is in the main a realistic story; yet one of its chief points is that 'reality' is not enough; that there is more to life than common sense can take account of. . . . [*Down to Earth*] could be labelled as fantasy or science fiction, but more than anything it is about contemporary life in Sydney: how it might appear to, and might be affected by, a visitor from another world.

'I Own the Racecourse!' (. . . American title *A Racecourse for Andy*) is Mrs Wrightson's best book so far. . . . [The] author ends it perfectly. The final twist to the story-line is unexpected but not arbitrary; it is the one way out of Andy's delusion that will solve everybody's problems and not do Andy any harm. The vivid life of the city (above all, the racecourse in action), the relationships of the boys, and Andy's simplicity—a perilous quality, this, to portray in print—are handled with a skill and insight that make this one of the outstanding children's books of its decade. (pp. 285-86)

> *John Rowe Townsend, "Realism, Wider-Range," in*
> *his* Written for Children: An Outline of English-Language Children's Literature, *second revised edition,*
> *J. B. Lippincott, 1983, pp. 283-90.*

ETHEL HEINS

Patricia Wrightson, for me Australia's foremost contemporary writer for young people, has never created a book that is not exciting in its freshness and originality. Perhaps one of the reasons is the fact that she grew up in a remote area and received part of her education through the state correspondence school— but only part of it. For she says she was also educated by her father in "literature, philosophy, and wonder"—quite a legacy for a future novelist, and especially a children's novelist.

Patricia Wrightson lays claim to two major preoccupations: the richness of fantasy as a means of exploring ideas and the use of Aboriginal folk-spirits to enrich her writing. About fantasy, she is absolutely definite: "Not the escape from life that some people see as fantasy, nor the symbolism that is some fantasy, but that strangeness and fullness of life that spills out of the bucket of reality—the human experience of fantasy." As for the other preoccupation, she remarked that her kind of fantasy "needs to be rooted in the profound and primitive experience of folklore, and I had to discover . . . the folklore. When it was found, and found so rich and strong, the folklore made demands in its own right." Thus, for herself she rejects the traditional stuff of European folk material in favor of legendary Australian Aboriginal spirits inhabiting water, forest, and rock. "Many of them are beliefs still living," she has said. "And I claim a writer's leave to employ them in my own stories in my own way."

In an article that appeared in the December 1980 *Horn Book* [see Author's Commentary in *CLR*, Vol. 4], Patricia Wrightson wrote: "Folklore is no amusing invention but the record of a long struggle with the strangeness of life, and a new strangeness calls up a new speculation. And I think this authenticity, this lived and remembered experience, explains the lasting power of folklore. It is why fantasy, the exploring-outward-and-beyond branch of literature, clings like mistletoe to the root and branch of folklore.''

Just as her extraordinary novel *A Racecourse for Andy* . . . might have seemed important to some readers only because it centers on a handicapped boy, so her latest book, *A Little Fear,* might conceivably cause rejoicing. ''Aha, at last we have geriatrics for children; a good strong book about the elderly.'' But Patricia Wrightson elegantly transcends both issues and fashions. In the book a tough-minded, canny old woman—Mrs. Tucker—seethes with impatience at being cooped up in a clean, bright, sterile, insufferably dull home for elder citizens, so she plans and executes a brilliant escape. Unbeknown to her family, she has inherited an isolated cottage in the country, and she contrives a journey to the remote, steamy place, alive with clouds of insects, bandicoots, and cunning swamp-rats. But, unseen by the old woman, an eternal, ancient gnome watches her activities, furiously, resentfully—a small powerful spirit that has lived there ''while the forests grew and fell and the men came and went.'' And thus a battle is joined: Two fiercely independent creatures engage in a desperate struggle to possess the place, until Mrs. Tucker, battered but unvanquished, finally arrives at a courageous and perfectly logical decision. With its almost tangible sense of place, its sensitive, trenchant character portrayals, its sly humor and rich, graphic prose, *A Little Fear* emerged the winner of the Boston Globe-Horn Book Award for fiction. (pp. 38-9)

> Ethel Heins, in an introduction to ''The Fellowship of Man and Beast,'' by Patricia Wrightson, in The Horn Book Magazine, *Vol. LXI, No. 1, January-February, 1985, pp. 38-9.*

BOOKBIRD

Mrs. Wrightson's talent as a writer has shown remarkable progression both in style of writing and in her range of subject matter. Whilst certain themes endure—for example the nature of reality and what constitutes ownership (especially of the land)—her subject matter ranges from simple adventure, through the process of growing up and discovering one's identity (black or white), to the process of dealing with mental handicap (*I Own the Racecourse*).

She has written science-fiction, realistic stories and fantasy. By giving literary form to Australian Aboriginal mythological spirits, notably in the trilogy *The Ice Is Coming, The Dark Bright Water* and *Behind the Wind,* and in her evocation of the Australian landscape Mrs. Wrightson has made a unique statement which is undeniably Australian but which is international and universal in the deepest sense.

> ''1986 Hans Christian Andersen Medalists,'' in Bookbird, *No. 2, June 15, 1986, p. 4.*

MAURICE SAXBY

Patricia Wrightson's books reveal a sure and firm growth in the writer both as a thinker and as a craftsman. Her art is a steadily developing one. Whilst certain underlying themes remain constant, and whilst her writing always bears the stamp of her personality—her style—she is not narrow in her range of subjects. Rather she extends these outwards, book by book. Her underlying theme is that of the relationship of people (children and adults) with their environment, and of people with people. This theme is given individual expression in each of her books and in that expression the author is able to explore related themes and further facets of human experience. But because of the underlying theme and the strength of expression, Patricia Wrightson's work, as a body of writing, has unity, harmony and cohesion. In all it adds up to a radiant sharing of her own wise perceptions of life with her readers.

Mrs. Wrightson's books span the period during which Australian books for children came to maturity. Indeed they did much to bring that maturity into being. She is the most acclaimed children's writer in her country and she has an international reputation and following.

Her first book, *The Crooked Snake* . . . , helped establish what is now recognised as the 'modern' Australian novel for children. Real life children discover adventure as they interact with their environment.

In 1974 Patricia Wrightson again won the Australian Children's Book of the Year with *The Nargun and the Stars.* . . . This book ushered in the 'contemporary' phase of Australian children's literature; marked by realism carried beyond the knowable, the touchable, the explainable—through fantasy. A fantasy which draws on ancient Aboriginal non-sacred mythology for its images and symbols. The land and its early inhabitants has now become a profound force: a force which had gradually been asserting itself in Patricia Wrightson's earlier books (the patient, knowing land of *The Rocks of Honey* . . .); and which was to become fully manifest in the Book of Wirrun Trilogy—[*The Ice Is Coming, The Dark Bright Water, Behind the Wind*]. . . . Here the land itself, which in *The Rocks* is felt as ''a deep pulse like a heartbeat'' by the Aboriginal boy, Barney, becomes the life-force motivating both mankind and the spirit world. (pp. 5-6)

[*A Little Fear*] has proved to be enormously popular with children and adults in Australia and overseas. It represents a world trend in writing for children; a realistic story with an underlying thread of fantasy. The social realism is that of a remarkably doughty old lady who refuses to give up her independence and become institutionalised; the fantasy is in the form of an ancient imp, an Aboriginal land spirit—the Njimbin—who is not much more than a shadow but who (as is the way of the spirits of any 'place' the world over) resists Mrs. Tucker's intrusion. The fact that there are no children as such in the book has not detracted from its popularity and only proves that children are able and willing to enter into a fictional relationship with the elderly and to understand their problems.

Between *The Crooked Snake* and *A Little Fear* have been some twelve books, which have been part of the development of children's literature in Australia and have won acclaim and awards at home and overseas. (p. 6)

The Nargun and the Stars and *I Own the Racecourse* . . . have been filmed and televised. *I Own the Racecourse,* which is a sympathetic and moving story of a handicapped boy, has been called ''one of the outstanding English language books of its decade: a triumph in the mode of contemporary realism.''

Mrs. Wrightson's books have now been translated into nine languages; and she is represented in libraries around the world. (p. 7)

> Maurice Saxby, ''The Art of Patricia Wrightson,'' in Bookbird, *No. 2, June 15, 1986, pp. 4-7.*

SUSAN COOPER

[*In the following excerpt, Cooper, author of the acclaimed* The Dark Is Rising *quintet, praises* The Nargun and the Stars. *For a further discussion of* The Nargun and the Stars, *see the title entry in* CLR, *Vol. 4.*]

Once in a great while a story will hit you so hard that you never forget the first hearing of it. When I was a child, that lovely shock came from a magical BBC radio adaptation of John Masefield's *The Box of Delights . . .* , when I was an undergraduate, from a book called *The Fellowship of the Ring . . .* , written most astonishingly by the jovial chap who taught us Anglo-Saxon Literature. Out of all the years since, only two other books have instantly sandbagged me in quite the same way: Alan Garner's *The Owl Service . . .* and Patricia Wrightson's *The Nargun and the Stars. . . .*

Now that Patricia Wrightson has deservedly won the Hans Christian Andersen Medal, perhaps our label-besotted society will take a second look at her books. For twelve years I've shared the bafflement of her publisher . . . over the low American sales not only of *The Nargun and the Stars* but of the haunting trio of fantasies that followed it: *The Ice Is Coming, The Dark Bright Water,* and *Journey Behind the Wind. . . .* (p. 572)

The Nargun and the Stars is a wonderful book, with a hypnotic sense of place. Patricia Wrightson is deeply Australian, and she makes her fantasies out of the relationships and conflicts between ordinary, everyday human beings and the folk-spirits of the first Australians, the Aborigines—"not the ritual figures of the creative myths but the gnomes and heroes and monsters of Australia." The real and the magical are interwoven, in the powerful landscape of that astonishing continent; these are fantasies not of good and evil but of unjudging, unjudged creatures who are, above all, *old*.

Simon Brent's parents die. He is sent to live with two distant aging cousins, Charlie and Edie Waters, on their five-thousand-acre sheep run, Wongadilla. He's too shy and gruff to call them Charlie and Edie, yet. They're patient and gentle, and they let him learn the place for himself: the lonely house among the hills and ridges, the green swamp below, and the high dark gully above. Ancient creatures live in those hills: the mischievous Potkoorok in the swamp, the ethereal Turongs rustling in the trees. They show themselves to Simon, and he nurses his private, amazing discovery of them—only to find, quite soon, that Edie and Charlie have shared the secret since they, too, were young. Charlie smiles at him. "'*You're* all right, then. That's about what Edie and I always reckoned.'"

But something else also shows itself to Simon: the Nargun, a powerful, dreadful rock that is more than a rock, which has been sleeping in the wild places of Australia since time began and is now, very gradually, on the move. It has reached Wongadilla, and in its slow mind are the ancient longings and formless rage that can drive it, sometimes, to kill. Simon narrowly escapes it, and a sheep lies dead instead. Since the Nargun cannot be destroyed, the story of the book is the story of how—by the ingenuity of the old creatures, and the wit and courage of a man, a woman, and a boy—it is driven away.

The satisfying turns of that story, which I don't propose to reveal, are clear and simple but at the same time full of the kind of unconscious metaphor that marks all true fantasy writing. The roaring yellow bulldozer which erupts into Wongadilla, shattering its silence and stripping its trees, becomes also in a most unpredictable manner the means by which the land and its people are saved from the Nargun. Yet one is left with a lingering resentment of the world of bulldozers, and an irrational sympathy for the timeless Nargun, which Simon shares.

"That granite face turned to the sky seemed to bear all age, all emptiness, all evil and good; without hope or despair; with rocklike patience. [Simon] was shaken by a sudden storm of pity and fear."

Patricia Wrightson makes her world startlingly vivid. When Simon first comes to Wongadilla, we feel his uneasiness as the car's engine stops and he is enveloped in the huge silence of the land, "waiting, coiled like a spring between earth and sky." The bleat of a sheep, the laugh of a kookaburra, the scratching crash of possums jumping on the roof—they all make the reader jump as nervously as Simon jumps. And an unexpected image can make a sentence glow, as when one is suddenly inside Simon's surprised head, with "questions and alarms rolling about in his mind like marbles," or listening on a windy day to sounds which "were blown away and came sweeping back like sheets on a clothesline."

Above all, Patricia Wrightson is a marvellous storyteller. The most remarkable quality of this remarkable book is its wire-tight suspense; the Nargun is so ancient and immutable a monster, how can its implacable advance ever be checked? Listen to this, as Simon and Charlie are driven home by darkness, having tried once more and failed:

> It had grown so dark that the stars hung close and brilliant. They fumbled through the gate to the back door, and Charlie pulled it open on yellow light, warmth, and Edie's face turned to them from the stove. Simon had one foot in the door when the night reached out and held them frozen. Sudden and savage came the Nargun's cry, bellowing down from the mountain, full of all time and the darkness behind the stars. It held them at the door while it rang between mountains and died away. Charlie pushed Simon inside and shut the door.
>
> "*We made it angry,*" whispered Simon.

That's the kind of passage that makes for immensely satisfying reading aloud. "Don't stop *there!*" the children cry, in an anguish of suspense. It ranks with another section in which Charlie and Edie, after the first encounter with the Nargun, sit up all night, watchful, listening. "Peering through dark windows into darkness, they saw nothing. Only once, strained wires creaked when something heavy leaned against the gate." Perhaps the reading aloud should not be done at night.

But under whatever circumstances, this book should be read. It is fantasy of a very uncommon kind: accessible yet profound, immensely readable yet graced with the rhythms and images of poetry in its distinguished prose. It's the kind of story which children seize upon when young and never, thereafter, let go. (pp. 572-74)

Susan Cooper, "A Second Look: 'The Nargun and the Stars'," in The Horn Book Magazine, *Vol. LXII, No. 5, September-October, 1986, pp. 572-74.*

ZENA SUTHERLAND AND MAY HILL ARBUTHNOT

Patricia Wrightson has been a channel through which children of her own and other countries have learned the beauty and dignity of the legendary creatures of Aborigine mythology. In *An Older Kind of Magic . . .* the theme is conservation, as some of the little people use their magic to foil a plan to destroy the botanical garden where they play. Here, and in *The Nargun and the Stars,* the lives of human children and of ancient spirits are credibly intermeshed in a story that is structured with craft and affection for the mighty and mysterious spirits of an ancient world. . . .

Unlike *Down to Earth* . . . , a humorous story of a visitor from Mars, [*The Ice Is Coming* and *The Dark Bright Water*] are serious in tone, cadenced and stately in style, yet filled with suspense and action.

> *Zena Sutherland and May Hill Arbuthnot, "Modern Fantasy: Patricia Wrightson," in their* Children and Books, *seventh edition, Scott, Foresman and Company, 1986, p. 232.*

A LITTLE FEAR (1983)

AUTHOR'S COMMENTARY

[*The following acceptance speech for the 1984* Boston Globe-Horn Book *Award was written by Wrightson and delivered for her on October 1, 1984.*]

To describe what I felt about the news of this award, I have to fall back on the word *delight*. There are other words—*pride, pleasure, glow, excitement,* and so on; but for me *delight* has a special quality of warm astonishment as well as pleasure and all the rest. And it has been warm, astonishing, delightful to find *A Little Fear* so well and widely received.

It seemed such a small and personal story. I have always responded to places. Finding myself living in an isolated fisherman's cottage on the edge of a broad, shallow water, it was inevitable that sooner or later I would need to reproduce that place. But I didn't expect that many readers would want to share it.

I remember, when the idea was working, talking about it to Joan Phipson by telephone. We were both trying to describe new ideas and having the usual trouble.

"I want," I said, "a story that's crawling alive with insects."

"Oh," said Joan as warmly as possible. "That—should be—different."

It was also, of course, inaccurate. I didn't really want insects for their own sake; what I wanted was something more like life at the smaller end of the scale. That's the kind of life I live with now. It replaces crowded streets and city traffic.

But living with it is not coldly observing it. That's a matter for animal behaviorists and books on natural history, of which I have and constantly use my share. Living with it is being one thread in the fabric and knowing it; being aware of a crowd of other lives driving in different directions yet interlocking; knowing that your land belongs also to a complex population who find you a threat, a resource, or wholly negligible; knowing that your walls and gutters belong also to rats and ants and frogs. And you can't live with it without interpreting it.

The cold observer insulates himself against any such thing— as, of course, he must—to produce cold and objective facts. He deliberately closes the door to any sense of sharing, thinks in terms of organisms, and regards anthropomorphism as a dangerous sin. Fair enough (as we say in Australia), but I didn't realize, until I came across a few dire warnings about *A Little Fear,* that there are still some teachers or librarians or critics who take the same position. If this prickly attitude does still exist, even in corners, it seems worth an argument.

"Stories about talking animals are bad." But folklore is full of them; recent literature warm and alive with them. To lose them we must support the loss not only of Puss-in-Boots, the Three Bears, Brer Rabbit and Brer Fox, an assortment of frog princes, Faralda's horse, and those Australian dogs whose speech, if overheard, will turn you into stone, but also of *Alice in Wonderland, The Wind in the Willows, The Jungle Book, Charlotte's Web* . . . , *The Story of Babar* . . . , *Watership Down* . . . , and so on. It seems a poor bargain to exchange all that for *Tarka the Otter* . . . , *A Ring of Bright Water* . . . , *King Solomon's Ring,* and a few more, splendid though they are. It also seems a deliberate rejection of fellowship between man and beast.

On the evidence of literature, this fellowship, this sense of sharing, is a very old and general experience of mankind. "Stories about talking animals are bad" simply means "bad stories about bad talking animals are bad." There are enough of those, heaven knows—as there are about fairies, ghosts, love, machines, families, school, history. We needn't support any of them.

It's true, I'm afraid, that interpretation does humanize. But interpretation in nonhuman terms is meaningless to us, and we can't help being human. We can only try to rise above it. In what nonhuman terms can we brood over the other life around us: the relationship between the farmer and the farmed; the estrangement between caterpillar and butterfly; a hen's emotional instability; a dog's sense of humor fighting with its sense of dignity; the mischievous teasing of one animal by another? These don't cease to be facts simply because they are not cold. I can't note or explore them except in human terms, and I live with them.

You have to plan for a story in order to get it going, but it helps to know that once it is going it will do what it likes with your plan. So *A Little Fear* refused children and required a bony and intrepid old lady instead. I knew it would cause qualms, but as a matter of fact I think the story was right. I have seen older children become, suddenly, understanding of old people: a sudden illumination quite different from the response of the very young. I think it's a stage in maturing, and it ought to be allowed to happen. Certainly Mrs. Tucker—old, defeated, but indomitable—seems to have touched a wide concern. So perhaps I was wrong about the story. Obstinate and willful to the end, perhaps it succeeded in spite of me. This may have been the right moment for humanized animals and indomitable old ladies, and I thank you on their behalf. (pp. 39-41)

> *Patricia Wrightson, "The Fellowship of Man and Beast," in* The Horn Book Magazine, *Vol. LXI, No. 1, January-February, 1985, pp. 39-41.*

Patricia Wrightson has a peculiar ability in evoking an uncanny and menacing atmosphere, as evidenced in this story of an old woman living with her dog in a derelict cottage. She incurs the anger of one of the elemental spirits of the land, the Njimbin, who lives in an old shed in the garden. The Njimbin has learnt the ways of men over the centuries and cunningly makes use of them for its own ends. The old woman and her dog are an intrusion which must be driven away.

The ways in which the Njimbin tries to rid himself of the unwelcome visitor are malicious and frightening. The old woman is subjected to an invasion of frogs, then of ants, then rats and, worst of all, swarms of midges, 'a great dark mass that cuts off the northern stars', and invades every crevice and the air

Wrightson, with her children Peter and Jenny: "the new writer and the children she began writing for." Courtesy of Patricia Wrightson.

itself so that the old woman nearly dies. The cottage is swarming with unseen life and the old woman must admit defeat, but, indomitable still, she plans 'to go out with a bang', although she cannot fight the spirit of the land itself.

A chilling story, suggesting to a horrified imagination, what could happen if that 'unseen life' of insects and animals were to be free to invade our homes.

> *E. Colwell, in a review of "A Little Fear," in* The Junior Bookshelf, *Vol. 47, No. 5, October, 1983, p. 215.*

[Wrightson] has grown so comfortable with her Australian spirit-presences that she's domesticated them; the Njimbin, or gnome, . . . could almost be one of those mischief-makers, protecting his territory, common to Scottish and Irish lore. The crucial difference, which queers this almost-childless book for child-readers (in particular), is that the Njimbin turns into a mere instrument—for getting Mrs. Tucker from regimented Sunset House to a little-house-of-her-own in town, now with her foolish, lovable dog Hector *and* near her worried family. But because "she hated to go meekly back to town and leave the land's old thing victorious in her fowlhouse," she gets the building ready for a conflagration. Thus, she acknowledges

she couldn't beat the Njimbin. . . . She knows, after young Ivan has fired his gun, that it would be open warfare with the Njimbin. But, in conceding defeat (and selling the rural property to purchase her house-in-town), she can't bear to leave the Njimbin, it seems, in even temporary possession. Since the story is involving only to the extent that the Njimbin and Mrs. Tucker are evenly matched (and tacit counterparts), the ending falsifies what has gone before. A good deal of Wrightson's typically fine descriptive detail (the behavior of rattled hens, the sound of a strong rower, the whirl of a column of midges) is expended on a rigged situation.

> *A review of "A Little Fear," in* Kirkus Reviews, *Juvenile Issue, Vol. LI, No. 21, November 1, 1983, p. J-210.*

Just when you decide there are no new stories to be told, something utterly new comes along to refresh your viewpoint. Old Mrs. Tucker is angry at having to live in Sunset House—and what a name that is for a home for the elderly! The reader of *A Little Fear* is at once on her side. . . .

The outcome [of this book] is neat and appropriate, and Mrs. Tucker, losing the battle, finds a way to win the war.

I did not find the storyline of *A Little Fear* particularly scary—much as I dislike insects—mostly because the Njimbin was hard to believe in. So for me the title of the book is exactly descriptive. But because of the fine writing, Mrs. Tucker, her dog Hector, all the creatures of nature, even the landscape and the cottage, are brightly drawn in fascinating detail. Hector is resting outside the cottage when "an ant, laboriously toiling through the grass, mounted the tower of his nose. He snorted and shook it off." The frogs croak with "leather throats pumping." And a line of ants are "endlessly moving like people on an escalator."

I think it would not much matter what Patricia Wrightson wrote about; her work is special for the quality of the writing alone.

> *Natalie Babbitt, "Danger, Defiance and Survival," in* The New York Times Book Review, *November 13, 1983, p. 41.*

[*A Little Fear*] is an excellent performance. It might very well become a minor classic. . . .

[Mrs. Tucker] is a memorable and realistic heroine caught in a fantastic struggle to maintain her personal dignity and her homestead. The characterizations and the plot are equally admirable. And the ending, although triumphant, is unexpected. *A Little Fear* is a superb children's tale with special meaning. Highly recommended.

> *Kenneth McNamee, in a review of "A Little Fear," in* Best Sellers, *Vol. 43, No. 9, December, 1983, p. 351.*

There are some terrifying moments as the mighty forces of the land are turned against [Mrs Tucker] through the medium of insignificant creatures. . . .

Patricia Wrightson is a fine storyteller who writes with clarity and economy. Mrs Tucker is an unusual and memorable creation. The details of the Australian scene are skilfully handled and the nerve endings twitch at the evocation of the old magic. (p. 362)

> *Peter Kennerley, in a review of "A Little Fear," in* The School Librarian, *Vol. 31, No. 4, December, 1983, pp. 361-62.*

Set in an Australian marsh area, the pervading mood is one of respect for nature and for the mysteries of those who trace their roots to the ways of the old land. Within this context the author dramatically portrays the two struggling forces: the Njimbin with his rats, Hairy Man, and hoardes of mites and Mrs. Tucker with her dog Hector, the young neighbor boy Ivan, and her can of insect spray.

Patricia Wrightson evolves a remarkable depth of character in her depiction of Mrs. Tucker. The reader realizes, for perhaps the first time, the full implication of being old: its frustrations and hopelessness. However, there is also the sense of independence and determination to struggle for self-reliance. (p. 297)

> *Ronald A. Jobe, in a review of "A Little Fear," in* Language Arts, *Vol. 61, No. 3, March, 1984, pp. 296-97.*

NIGHT OUTSIDE (1985)

The distinguished Australian author of *A Little Fear, The Ice Is Coming* and other electrifying novels presents a haunting and spirit-elevating story arising out of an inauspicious beginning. Dad's temper explodes in the evening when he's been sick with the flu and Mum's late getting home. Grabbing the budgerigar William, Dad tosses it out the window. Anne and her small brother James run out into the dark streets to rescue their dear pet. Large, white letters spelling "ETERNITY" on the sidewalks seem to guide the search and lead the children to ask help from a bag lady and her friend, a junk collector. They take Anne and James to a shop/dwelling to meet the owner, Mrs. Haitch, and Cyril, a mysterious man. Cyril is the writer of "eternity," and his theory on the concept is intriguing. The strange story peaks with Anne and James embraced by Dad who has come after them, just as Mrs. Haitch had predicted. Wrightson builds her lyrical evocation of night and its people on reassuring facts about human nature. Sure, gremlins can occasionally push the most loving parents into choleric displays. But the love remains constant when the fireworks fizzle.

> *A review of "Night Outside," in* Publishers Weekly, *Vol. 228, No. 9, August 30, 1985, p. 423.*

From a major Australian writer, a book first published in 1979 [as a school supplement] is, unlike most of the Wrightson fantasy titles published in the United States, a realistic story. It is also less cohesive, weak in structure although not in writing style. . . . Too diffuse for its length, this might have been a taut short story.

> *A review of "Night Outside," in* Bulletin of the Center for Children's Books, *Vol. 39, No. 2, October, 1985, p. 40.*

Unlike Wrightson's previous fantasies (for somewhat older readers), this is almost an anti-fantasy, as Anne discovers the trees behind shadows, flashlighted trash cans, the humanity within her "strange spirits of the night": "Don't you go turning us all into fairies, love, or monsters, either . . . *We're all old losers, making do.*" The novel occasionally veers off into the obscure, particularly when discussing Eternity, and the narrative, like the children, wanders uncertainly before reaching a comforting end. But the language and characters . . . are evocative of this "special, different, once-only night."

> *Roger D. Sutton, in a review of "Night Outside," in* School Library Journal, *Vol. 32, No. 4, December, 1985, p. 96.*

Sometimes the mundane can be transformed into the magical without the intervention of extraordinary or otherworldly powers. It is this kind of enchantment which permeates Patricia Wrightson's novella, set in a working-class neighborhood of what is undoubtedly an Australian city. The action begins realistically enough with a family quarrel, precipitated by cramped living quarters, fatigue, illness, and financial worries. . . . Mood rather than plot is the dominant element in the story. Descriptions, although evocative, are almost like stage directions, an impression reinforced by the emphasis on dialogue and Anne's unspoken reflections. For the right reader, the book is a haunting and provocative experience, for it has the wistful charm so often associated with the plays of James Barrie. And because of its short chapters, style, and imagery, it also works as a read-aloud for a small group. (pp. 64-5)

> *Mary M. Burns, in a review of "Night Outside," in* The Horn Book Magazine, *Vol. LXII, No. 1, January-February, 1986, pp. 64-5.*

APPENDIX

The following is a listing of all sources used in Volume 14 of *Children's Literature Review*. Included in this list are all copyright and reprint rights and acknowledgments for those essays for which permission was obtained. Every effort has been made to trace copyright, but if omissions have been made, please let us know.

THE EXCERPTS IN CLR, VOLUME 14, WERE REPRINTED FROM THE FOLLOWING PERIODICALS:

The Academy, n.s. v. XIV, November 16, 1878.

The Advocates' Newsletter, February, 1987. Reprinted by permission of the publisher.

The ALAN Review, v. 10, Winter, 1983. Reprinted by permission of the publisher.

American Artist, v. 42, November, 1978. Copyright © 1978 by Billboard Publications, Inc. Reprinted by permission of the publisher.

Analog Science Fiction/Science Fact, v. XCVII, December, 1977. Copyright © 1977 by the Condé Nast Publications, Inc. Reprinted by permission of the author.

The Art Journal, 1881.

The Artful Reporter, June, 1985. Reprinted by permission of the publisher.

Best Sellers, v. 36, August, 1976; v. 41, January, 1982; v. 43, December, 1983. Copyright © 1976, 1982, 1983 Helen Dwight Reid Educational Foundation. All reprinted by permission of the publisher.

Black Enterprise, v. 12, December, 1981. Copyright December, 1981, The Earl G. Graves Publishing Co., Inc., 130 Fifth Avenue, New York, NY 10011. All rights reserved. Reprinted by permission of the publisher.

Book Week—The Sunday Herald Tribune, October 31, 1965. © 1965, *The Washington Post.* Reprinted by permission of the publisher.

Book Window, v. 8, Summer, 1981 for a review of ''Unbuilding'' by Margaret Walker. © 1981 S.C.B.A. and contributors. Reprinted by permission of the publisher.

Book World—The Washington Post, November 11, 1973. Copyright © 1973 The Washington Post Company. Reprinted by permission of the publisher./ November 13, 1977; October 7, 1979; November 9, 1980; May 10, 1981; November 7, 1982; September 8, 1985. © 1977, 1979, 1980, 1981, 1982, 1985, *The Washington Post.* All reprinted by permission of the publisher.

Bookbird, n. 1 & 2, March 15 & June 15, 1982; n. 2, June 15, 1984; n. 4, December 15, 1984; n. 2, June 15, 1986; n. 3 & 4, September 15 & October 15, 1986. All reprinted by permission of the publisher.

The Classical Journal, v. XXXII, December, 1936.

Fantasy Review, v. 7, May, 1984 for "Brilliant Invention, or Endless Tedium?" by Brian Stableford; v. 8, April, 1985 for "Semi-Allegory Delights in Spite of Flaws" by E. F. Bleiler. Copyright © 1984, 1985 by the respective authors. Both reprinted by permission of the respective authors.

The Five Owls, v. 1, May-June, 1987. Copyright © 1987 by The Five Owls, Inc. Both reprinted by permission of the publisher.

The Gentleman's Magazine, v. CCXLVI, January-June, 1880.

Growing Point, v. 14, July, 1975; v. 17, July, 1978; v. 21, January, 1983; v. 22, January, 1984; v. 24, May, 1985; v. 25, March, 1987. All reprinted by permission of the publisher.

The Horn Book Magazine v. XXV, September-October, 1949 for "Distinction in Picture Books" by Marcia Brown; v. LXI, January-February, 1985 for "The Fellowship of Man and Beast" by Patricia Wrightson; v. LXII, July-August, 1986 for "Newbery Medal Acceptance" by Patricia MacLachlan. Copyright, 1949, 1985, 1986, by the respective authors. All reprinted by permission of the respective authors./ v. LXI, January-February, 1985 for "Turning History Inside Out" by Jean Fritz. Copyright © 1985 by the author. Reprinted by permission of Gina Maccoby Literary Agency./ v. XXII, March-April, 1946; v. XXXIV, June, 1958; v. XXXV, April, 1959; v. XXXVII, April, 1961; v. XL, June, 1964; v. XL, August, 1964; v. XLIII, October, 1967; v. XLIII, December, 1967; v. XLV, April, 1969; v. XLVI, October, 1970; v. LII, June, 1976; v. LII, October, 1976; v. LII, December, 1976; v. LIII, October, 1977; v. LV, October, 1978; v. LV, October, 1979; v. LVI, June, 1980; v. LVI, August, 1980; v. LVI, December, 1980; v. LVII, February, 1981; v. LVII, June, 1981; v. LVIII, April, 1982; v. LVIII, June, 1982; v. LVIII, August, 1982; v. LVIII, December, 1982; v. LIX, February, 1983; v. LIX, April, 1983; v. LIX, October, 1983; v. LIX, December, 1983; v. LX, August, 1984; v. LXI, January-February, 1985; v. LXI, September-October, 1985; v. LXII, January-February, 1986; v. LXII, July-August, 1986; v. LXII, September-October, 1986; v. LXII, November-December, 1986; v. LXIII, July-August, 1987. Copyright, 1946, 1958, 1959, 1961, 1964, 1967, 1969, 1970, 1976, 1977, 1978, 1979, 1980, 1981, 1982, 1983, 1984, 1985, 1986, 1987, by The Horn Book, Inc., Boston. All rights reserved. All reprinted by permission of the publisher.

Instructor, v. 94, August, 1984 for "Is That a Fact, Jean Fritz?" by Verna Bargsley, Nita Beckman, Joan Dilger, Irene Pedersen and others. Copyright © 1984 by The Instructor Publications, Inc. Reprinted by permission of the respective authors.

Interracial Books for Children, v. 15, 1984. Reprinted by permission of the Council on Interracial Books for Children, 1841 Broadway, New York, NY 10023.

Interracial Books for Children Bulletin, v. 12, 1981. Reprinted by permission of the Council on Interracial Books for Children, 1841 Broadway, New York, NY 10023.

The Journal of Negro Education, v. XLIII, Summer, 1974. Copyright © Howard University 1974. Reprinted by permission of the publisher.

The Junior Bookshelf, v. 10, March, 1946./ v. 39, June, 1975; v. 41, October, 1977; v. 42, June, 1978; v. 43, April, 1979; v. 45, April, 1981; v. 45, June, 1981; v. 45, December, 1981; v. 46, February, 1982; v. 46, October, 1982; v. 47, October, 1983; v. 48, August, 1984; v. 48, October, 1984; v. 48, December, 1984; v. 49, June, 1985; v. 49, August, 1985; v. 50, June, 1986. All reprinted by permission of the publisher.

Junior Libraries, v. 5, October, 1958./ v. 5, March, 1959. Copyright © 1959. Reprinted from *Junior Libraries*, published by R. R. Bowker Co./ A Xerox Corporation, by permission.

Kirkus Reviews, v. XXXIX, March 1, 1971; v. XL, December 1, 1972; v. XLI, April 15, 1973; v. XLIII, December 1, 1975; v. XLIV, April 15, 1976; v. XLIV, June 1, 1976; v. XLIV, December 1, 1976; v. XLV, May 1, 1977; v. XLV, August 15, 1977; v. XLV, November 15, 1977; v. XLVI, April 1, 1978; v. LXVI, July 15, 1978; v. XLVI, November 1, 1978; v. XLVII, February 15, 1979; v. XLVII, May 1, 1979; v. XLVII, July 1, 1979; v. XLVIII, February 15, 1980; v. XLVIII, March 15, 1980; v. XLVIII, May 1, 1980; v. XLVIII, June 15, 1980; v. XLIX, January 15, 1981; v. XLIX, March 1, 1981; v. XLIX, November 1, 1981; v. L, September 1, 1982; v. LIV, March 1, 1986; v. LIV, June 15, 1986; v. LIV, July 15, 1986; v. LIV, September 1, 1986; v. LV, April 15, 1987. Copyright © 1971, 1972, 1973, 1975, 1976, 1977, 1978, 1979, 1980, 1981, 1982, 1986, 1987 The Kirkus Service, Inc. All rights reserved. All reprinted by permission of the publisher.

Kirkus Reviews, Juvenile Issue, v. LI, November 1, 1983; v. LII, May 1, 1984; v. LII, September 1, 1984; v. LII, November 1, 1984; v. LIII, March 1, 1985. Copyright © 1983, 1984, 1985 The Kirkus Service, Inc. All rights reserved. All reprinted by permission of the publisher.

Kirkus Service, v. 36, October 1, 1968. Copyright © 1968 The Kirkus Service, Inc. Reprinted by permission of the publisher.

THE EXCERPTS IN CLR, VOLUME 14, WERE REPRINTED FROM THE FOLLOWING BOOKS:

Alderson, Brian. From *Sing a Song for Sixpence: The English Picture-Book Tradition and Randolph Caldecott*. Cambridge University Press, 1986. © Cambridge University Press and the British Library Board, 1986. Reprinted with permission of the publisher.

Anno, Mitsumasa. From a postscript to *The Unique World of Mitsumasa Anno: Selected Works (1968-1977)*. Edited and translated by Samuel Crowell Morse. Philomel Books, 1980. Copyright © 1980 by Philomel Books. All rights reserved. Reprinted by permission of The Putnam Publishing Group.

Antczak, Janice. From *Science Fiction: The Mythos of a New Romance*. Neal-Schuman, 1985. Copyright © 1985 by Neal-Schuman Publishers, Inc. All rights reserved. Reprinted by permission of the publisher.

Arbuthnot, May Hill. From *Children and Books*. Third edition. Scott, Foresman and Company, 1964. Copyright © 1964 by Scott, Foresman and Company. All rights reserved. Reprinted by permission of the publisher.

Arbuthnot, May Hill and Zena Sutherland. From *Children and Books*. Fourth edition. Scott, Foresman, 1972. Copyright © 1972, 1964, 1957, 1947 by Scott, Foresman and Company. All rights reserved. Reprinted by permission of the publisher.

Bader, Barbara. From ''The Caldecott Spectrum,'' in *Newbery and Caldecott Medal Books: 1976-1985*. Edited by Lee Kingman. Horn Book, 1986. Copyright © 1986 by The Horn Book, Inc. All rights reserved. Reprinted by permission of the publisher.

Baskin, Barbara H. and Karen H. Harris. From *Books for the Gifted Child*. Bowker, 1980. Copyright © 1980 by Reed Publishing, USA, Division of Reed Holdings, Inc. All rights reserved. Reprinted with permission of the publisher.

Billington, Elizabeth T. From *The Randolph Caldecott Treasury*. Edited by Elizabeth T. Billington. Frederick Warne, 1978. Copyright © 1978 Elizabeth T. Billington. All rights reserved. Reprinted by permission of Viking Penguin Inc.

Blackburn, Henry. From *Randolph Caldecott: A Personal Memoir of His Early Art Career*. Sampson Low & Co., 1886.

Blackburn, William. From ''Madeleine L'Engle's 'A Wrinkle in Time': Seeking the Original Face,'' in *Touchstones: Reflections on the Best in Children's Literature, Vol. 1*. Edited by Perry Nodelman. Children's Literature Association, 1985. © 1985 ChLA Publishers. Reprinted by permission of the publisher.

Blount, Margaret. From *Animal Land: The Creatures of Children's Fiction*. William Morrow & Company, Inc., 1975. Copyright © 1974 by Margaret Ingle-Finch. Reprinted by permission of the author.

Caldecott, Randolph. From *Yours Pictorially: Illustrated Letters of Randolph Caldecott*. Edited by Michael Hutchins. Warne, 1976. © Frederick Warne & Co. Ltd., 1976.

Chesterton, G. K. From an introduction to *Aesop's Fables*. Translated by V. S. Vernon Jones. Doubleday Page & Co., 1912.

Childress, Alice. From ''A Candle in a Gale Wind,'' in *Black Women Writers (1950-1980): A Critical Evaluation*. Edited by Mari Evans. Anchor Books, 1984. Copyright © 1984 by Mari Evans. All rights reserved. Reprinted by permission of Doubleday, a division of Bantam, Doubleday, Dell Publishing Group, Inc.

Childress, Alice. From ''The People behind the Books: 'A Hero Ain't Nothin' but a Sandwich','' in *Literature for Today's Young Adults*. By Kenneth L. Donelson and Alleen Pace Nilsen. Scott, Foresman, 1980. Copyright © 1980 Scott, Foresman and Company. Reprinted by permission of Flora Roberts, Inc.

Crane, Walter. From *An Artist's Reminiscences*. Methuen & Co., 1907.

Cullinan, Bernice E., with Mary K. Karrer and Arlene M. Pillar. From *Literature and the Child*. Harcourt Brace Jovanovich, 1981. Copyright © 1981 by Harcourt Brace Jovanovich, Inc. Reprinted by permission of the publisher.

Darton, F. J. Harvey. From *Children's Books in England: Five Centuries of Social Life*. Third Edition. Cambridge University Press, 1982. Copyright © 1958, 1982, Cambridge University Press. Reprinted with permission of the publisher.

Davis, Mary Gould. From *Randolph Caldecott, 1846-1886: An Appreciation*. J. B. Lippincott Company, 1946. Copyright, 1946, renewed 1974, by Mary Gould Davis. Reprinted by permission of Harper & Row, Publishers, Inc.

Dixon, Bob. From *Catching Them Young 2: Political Ideas in Children's Fiction*. Pluto Press, 1977. Copyright © Pluto Press 1977. Reprinted by permission of the publisher, 11-21 Northbown Street, London N1 9BN, England.

Downs, Robert B. From *Famous Books: Ancient and Medieval*. Barnes & Noble, 1964. © copyright, 1964 by Barnes & Noble, Inc. All rights reserved. Reprinted by permission of the publisher.

Dreyer, Sharon Spredemann. From *The Bookfinder, When Kids Need Books: Annotations of Books Published 1979 through 1982*. American Guidance Service, 1985. © 1985 American Guidance Service, Inc. All rights reserved. Reprinted by permission of the publisher.

Eaton, Anne. From "Widening Horizons, 1840-1890: Illustrators Who Were More Than Illustrators," in *A Critical History of Children's Literature*. By Cornelia Meigs and others, edited by Cornelia Meigs. Macmillan, 1953. Copyright, 1953, by Macmillan Publishing Company. Renewed 1981 by Charles H. Eaton. All rights reserved. Reprinted with permission of Macmillan Publishing Company.

Eaton, Anne Thaxter. From *Reading with Children*. The Viking Press, 1940. Copyright 1940 by Anne Thaxter Eaton. Renewed © 1967 by Anne Thaxter Eaton. Reprinted by permission of Viking Penguin Inc.

Egoff, Sheila A. From *Thursday's Child: Trends and Patterns in Contemporary Children's Literature*. American Library Association, 1981. Copyright © 1981 by the American Library Association. All rights reserved. Reprinted by permission of the publisher.

Evans, Edmund. From *The Reminiscences of Edmund Evans*. Edited by Ruari McLean. Oxford at the Clarendon Press, 1967. © Oxford University Press 1967. Reprinted by permission of Oxford University Press.

Ewing, Juliana Horatia. From letters in *Yours Pictorially: Illustrated Letters of Randolph Caldecott*. Edited by Michael Hutchins. Frederick Warne, 1976. © Frederick Warne & Co. Ltd., 1976.

Ewing, Mrs. From a letter in *Mrs. Gatty and Mrs. Ewing*. By Christabel Maxwell. Constable Publishers, 1949.

Fadiman, Clifton. From an afterword to *The Fables of Aesop*. Edited by Joseph Jacobs. Macmillan, 1964. Afterword copyright © Macmillan Publishing Company, 1964. All rights reserved. Reprinted with permission of Macmillan Publishing Company.

Fritz, Jean. From *Homesick: My Own Story*. G. P. Putnam's Sons, 1982. Text and photographs copyright © 1982 by Jean Fritz. All rights reserved. Reprinted by permission of the Putnam Publishing Group.

Gardner, Martin. From a foreword to *The Unique World of Mitsumasa Anno: Selected Works (1968-1977)*. Edited and translated by Samuel Crowell Morse. Philomel Books, 1980. Copyright © 1980 by Philomel Books. All rights reserved. Reprinted by permission of The Putnam Publishing Group.

Gillespie, John T. From *More Juniorplots: A Guide for Teachers and Librarians*. Bowker, 1977. Copyright © 1977 by John Gillespie. All rights reserved. Reprinted by permission of R. R. Bowker Company, Division of Reed Publishing, USA.

Gillespie, Margaret C. From *History and Trends*. Brown, 1970. Copyright © 1970 by Wm. C. Brown Company Publishers. Reprinted by permission of the author.

Goldsmith, Oliver. From "Life of Aesop," in *Bewick's Select Fables of Aesop*. By Aesop. T. Saint, 1784.

Greenaway, Kate. From a letter in *Kate Greenaway*. By M. H. Spielmann and G. S. Layard. G. P. Putnam's Sons, 1905.

Hardie, Martin. From *English Coloured Books*. Methuen and Company, 1906.

Hearn, Michael Patrick. From an introduction to *The Caldecott Aesop*. By Alfred Caldecott. Doubleday & Company, Inc., 1978. Introduction copyright © 1978 by Michael Patrick Hearn. All rights reserved. Reprinted by permission of Doubleday, a division of Bantam, Doubleday, Dell Publishing Group, Inc.

Hill, Elbert R. From "A Hero for the Movies," in *Children's Novels and the Movies*. Edited by Douglas Street. Ungar, 1983. Copyright © 1983 by The Ungar Publishing Company. Reprinted by permission of the publisher.

Hogarth, Grace Allen. From "Biographies of Illustrators Active 1967-1976: Mitsumasa Anno," in *Illustrators of Children's Books: 1967-1976*. Lee Kingman, Grace Allen Hogarth, Harriet Quimby, eds. Horn Book, 1978. Copyright © 1978 by The Horn Book, Inc. All rights reserved. Reprinted by permission of the publisher.

Horovitz, Carolyn. From "Only the Best," in *Newbery and Caldecott Medal Books: 1956-1965*. Edited by Lee Kingman. Horn Book, 1965. Copyright © 1965 by The Horn Book, Inc. All rights reserved. Reprinted by permission of the publisher.

Huck, Charlotte S. and Doris Young Kuhn. From *Children's Literature in the Elementary School*. Second edition. Holt, Rinehart and Winston, 1968. Copyright © 1961, 1968 by Holt, Rinehart and Winston, Inc. All rights reserved. Reprinted by permission of Holt, Rinehart and Winston, Inc.

Huck, Charlotte S. From *Children's Literature in the Elementary School*. Third edition. Holt, Rinehart and Winston, 1976. Copyright © 1961, 1968 by Holt, Rinehart and Winston, Inc. Copyright © 1976 by Charlotte S. Huck. All rights reserved. Reprinted by permission of Holt, Rinehart and Winston, Inc.

Hürlimann, Bettina. From *Three Centuries of Children's Books in Europe*. Edited and translated by Brian W. Alderson. Oxford University Press, London, 1967. © Oxford University Press 1967. Reprinted by permission of the publisher.

Hutchins, Michael. From *Yours Pictorially: Illustrated Letters of Randolph Caldecott*. Edited by Michael Hutchins. Frederick Warne, 1976. © Frederick Warne & Co. Ltd., 1976.

Jacobs, Joseph. From a preface and "A Short History of the Aesopic Fable," in *The Fables of Aesop*. Edited by Joseph Jacobs. N.p., 1894.

Lang, Andrew. From *The Fables of Aesop: History of the Aesopic Fable, Vol. I*. Edited by Joseph Jacobs. David Nutt, 1889.

L'Engle, Madeleine. From "Newbery Award Acceptance: The Expanding Universe," in *Newbery and Caldecott Medal Books: 1956-1965*. Edited by Lee Kingman. Horn Book, 1965. Copyright © 1965 by The Horn Book, Inc. All rights reserved. Reprinted by permission of the publisher.

L'Engle, Madeleine. From "Through the Eyes of an Author: The Search for Truth," in *Through the Eyes of a Child: An Introduction to Children's Literature*. By Donna E. Norton. Second edition. Merrill, 1987. Copyright © 1987, 1983, by Merrill Publishing Company. Reprinted by permission of Madeleine L'Engle.

Locke, John. From *Some Thoughts Concerning Education*. A. and J. Churchill, 1693.

Locker-Lampson, Frederick. From an extract in *Randolph Caldecott: A Personal Memoir of His Early Art Career*. By Henry Blackburn. Sampson Low & Co., 1886.

Meigs, Cornelia. From "The Multiplying Leaves: The Printed Word—Caxton, Aesop, Malory," in *A Critical History of Children's Literature*. By Cornelia Meigs and others, edited by Cornelia Meigs. Revised edition. Macmillan, 1969. Copyright 1953, 1969 by Macmillan Publishing Company. All rights reserved. Reprinted with permission of Macmillan Publishing Company.

Moss, Elaine. From *Picture Books for Young People 9-13*. The Thimble Press, 1981. Copyright © 1981 Elaine Moss. Reprinted by permission of the publisher.

Muir, Percy. From *Victorian Illustrated Books*. B. T. Batsford Ltd., London, 1971. © Percy Muir 1971. Reprinted by permission of the publisher.

Nesbitt, Elizabeth. From "A Rightful Heritage, 1890-1920: The March of Picture Books," in *A Critical History of Children's Literature*. By Cornelia Meigs and others, edited by Cornelia Meigs. Macmillan, 1953. Copyright, 1953, by Macmillan Publishing Company. Renewed 1981 by Charles H. Eaton. All rights reserved. Reprinted with permission of Macmillan Publishing Company.

Nilsen, Alleen Pace and Kenneth L. Donelson. From *Literature for Today's Young Adults*. Second edition. Scott, Foresman, 1985. Copyright © 1985, 1980 Scott, Foresman and Company. All rights reserved. Reprinted by permission of the publisher.

Norton, Donna E. From *Through the Eyes of a Child: An Introduction to Children's Literature*. Second edition. Merrill, 1987. Copyright © 1987, 1983, by Merrill Publishing Company, Columbus, OH. All rights reserved. Reprinted by permission of the publisher.

Overton, Jacqueline. From "'Tuppence Colored': Walter Crane, Randolph Caldecott and Kate Greenaway," in *Contemporary Illustrators of Children's Books*. Edited by Bertha E. Mahony and Elinor Whitney. The Bookshop for Boys and Girls, 1930.

Parker, Willis L. From an introduction to *The Fables of Aesop*. Edited by Willis L. Parker. Illustrated Editions Company, 1931. Copyright, 1931, by Illustrated Editions Co., Inc. Reprinted by permission of the publisher.

Pennell, Joseph. From *Pen Drawing and Pen Draughtsmen: Their Work and Their Methods*. The Macmillan Company, 1920. Copyright, 1920, by Macmillan Publishing Company. Renewed 1948 by the Literary Estate of Joseph Pennell. All rights reserved. Reprinted with permission of Macmillan Publishing Company.

Potter, Beatrix. From *Beatrix Potter's Americans: Selected Letters*. Edited by Jane Crowell Morse. Horn Book, 1982. Copyright © 1982 by The Horn Book, Inc. All rights reserved. Reprinted by permission of the publisher.

Purves, Alan C. and Dianne L. Monson. From *Experiencing Children's Literature*. Scott, Foresman, 1984. Copyright © 1984 Scott, Foresman and Company. All rights reserved. Reprinted by permission of the publisher.

Reeves, James. From an introduction to *Fables from Aesop*. Adapted by James Reeves. Henry Z. Walck, Inc., 1962. Copyright © 1961 by James Reeves and Blackie & Sons Ltd. All rights reserved. Reprinted by permission of Random House, Inc.

Richardson, Samuel. From a preface and ''The Life of Aesop,'' in *Aesop's Fables*. Edited by Samuel Richardson. J. F. and C. Rivington, 1740.

Sebesta, Sam Leaton and William J. Iverson. From *Literature for Thursday's Child*. Science Research Associates, 1975. © 1975, Science Research Associates, Inc. All rights reserved. Reprinted by permission of the authors.

Sendak, Maurice. From ''Randolph Caldecott: An Appreciation,'' in *The Randolph Caldecott Treasury*. Edited by Elizabeth T. Billington. Frederick Warne, 1978. Appreciation copyright © 1978 Maurice Sendak. All rights reserved. Reprinted by permission of Viking Penguin Inc.

Seta, Teiji and Momoko Ishii. From ''Where the Old Meets the New: The Japanese Picture Book,'' in *Illustrators of Children's Books: 1967-1976*. Lee Kingman, Grace Allen Hogarth, Harriet Quimby, eds. Horn Book, 1978. Copyright © 1978 by The Horn Book, Inc. All rights reserved. Reprinted by permission of the publisher.

Smith, Irene. From *A History of the Newbery and Caldecott Medals*. The Viking Press, 1957. Copyright © 1957, renewed 1985, by Irene Smith. Reprinted by permission of Viking Penguin Inc.

Smith, Lillian H. From *The Unreluctant Years: A Critical Approach to Children's Literature*. American Library Association, 1953. Copyright 1953, renewed 1981, by the American Library Association. All rights reserved. Reprinted by permission of the publisher.

Solt, Marilyn Leathers. From ''The Newbery Medal and Honor Books, 1922-1981: 'A Ring of Endless Light','' in *Newbery and Caldecott Medal and Honor Books: An Annotated Bibliography*. By Linda Kauffman Peterson and Marilyn Leathers Solt. G. K. Hall & Co., 1982. Copyright © 1982 by Marilyn Solt and Linda Peterson. Reprinted by permission of Marilyn Leathers Solt.

Stott, Jon C. From *Children's Literature from A to Z: A Guide for Parents and Teachers*. McGraw-Hill Book Company, 1984. Copyright © 1984 by McGraw-Hill, Inc. All rights reserved. Reproduced with permission.

Sutherland, Zena and May Hill Arbuthnot. From *Children and Books*. Seventh edition. Scott, Foresman, 1986. Copyright © 1986, 1981, 1977, 1972, 1964, 1957, 1947 Scott, Foresman and Company. All rights reserved. Reprinted by permission of the publisher.

Thwaite, Mary F. From *From Primer to Pleasure in Reading*. Revised edition. The Horn Book, Inc., 1972. Copyright © 1963 by Mary F. Thwaite. All rights reserved. Reprinted by permission of the publisher.

Townsend, John Rowe. From *A Sense of Story: Essays on Contemporary Writers for Children*. J. B. Lippincott Company, 1971. Copyright © 1971 by John Rowe Townsend. All rights reserved. Reprinted by permission of Harper & Row, Publishers, Inc.

Townsend, John Rowe. From *Written for Children: An Outline of English-Language Children's Literature*. Revised edition. Kestrel Books, 1974, J. B. Lippincott, 1975. Copyright © 1965, 1974 by John Rowe Townsend. All rights reserved. Reprinted by permission of Harper & Row, Publishers, Inc. In Canada by Penguin Books, Ltd.

Townsend, John Rowe. From *Written for Children: An Outline of English-Language Children's Literature*. Second revised edition. J. B. Lippincott, 1983, Penguin Books, 1983. Copyright © 1965, 1974, 1983 by John Rowe Townsend. All rights reserved. Reprinted by permission of Harper & Row, Publishers, Inc. In Canada by Penguin Books Ltd.

Van Doren, Mark. From ''Aesop and Jean De La Fontaine: Fables,'' in *The New Invitation to Learning*. Edited by Mark Van Doren. Random House, 1942. Copyright, 1942, by the Columbia Broadcasting System, Inc. Renewed 1970 by Mark Van Doren. Reprinted by permission of the Literary Estate of Mark Van Doren.

Viguers, Ruth Hill. From "Golden Years and Time of Tumult, 1920-1967: Worlds without Boundaries and Experiences to Share," in *A Critical History of Children's Literature*. By Cornelia Meigs and others, edited by Cornelia Meigs. Revised edition. Macmillan, 1969. Copyright 1953, 1969 by Macmillan Publishing Company. All rights reserved. Reprinted with permission of Macmillan Publishing Company.

Viguers, Ruth Hill. From *Margin for Surprise: About Books, Children, and Librarians*. Little, Brown, 1964. Copyright © 1964 by Ruth Hill Viguers. All rights reserved. Reprinted by permission of Little, Brown and Company.

Yutang, Lin, Jacques Barzun, and Mark Van Doren. From ''Aesop and Jean De La Fontaine: Fables,'' in *The New Invitation to Learning*. Edited by Mark Van Doren. Random House, 1942. Copyright, 1942, by the Columbia Broadcasting System, Inc. Renewed 1970 by Mark Van Doren. Reprinted by permission of the Literary Estate of Mark Van Doren.

CUMULATIVE INDEX TO AUTHORS

This index lists all author entries in *Children's Literature Review* and includes cross-references to them in other Gale sources. References in the index are identified as follows:

AITN: *Authors in the News*, Volumes 1-2
CA: *Contemporary Authors* (original series), Volumes 1-120
CANR: *Contemporary Authors New Revision Series*, Volumes 1-20
CAP: *Contemporary Authors Permanent Series*, Volumes 1-2
CA-R: *Contemporary Authors* (revised editions), Volumes 1-44
CLC: *Contemporary Literary Criticism*, Volumes 1-45
CLR: *Children's Literature Review*, Volumes 1-14
DLB: *Dictionary of Literary Biography*, Volumes 1-61
DLB-DS: *Dictionary of Literary Biography Documentary Series*, Volumes 1-4
DLB-Y: *Dictionary of Literary Biography Yearbook*, Volumes 1980-1986
NCLC: *Nineteenth-Century Literature Criticism*, Volumes 1-16
SAAS: *Something about the Author Autobiography Series*, Volume 1-4
SATA: *Something about the Author*, Volumes 1-49
TCLC: *Twentieth-Century Literary Criticism*, Volumes 1-23
YABC: *Yesterday's Authors of Books for Children*, Volumes 1-2

Author Index

Author Index

CUMULATIVE INDEX TO NATIONALITIES

AMERICAN

Adkins, Jan 7
Adoff, Arnold 7
Alcott, Louisa May 1
Alexander, Lloyd 1, 5
Aliki 9
Anglund, Joan Walsh 1
Armstrong, William H. 1
Aruego, Jose 5
Asimov, Isaac 12
Aylesworth, Thomas G. 6
Babbitt, Natalie 2
Bacon, Martha 3
Bang, Molly 8
Baylor, Byrd 3
Bemelmans, Ludwig 6
Benary-Isbert, Margot 12
Bendick, Jeanne 5
Bethancourt, T. Ernesto 3
Blume, Judy 2
Bond, Nancy 11
Bontemps, Arna 6
Bova, Ben 3
Branley, Franklyn M. 13
Brown, Marcia 12
Brown, Margaret Wise 10
Burton, Virginia Lee 11
Byars, Betsy 1
Cameron, Eleanor 1
Carle, Eric 10
Charlip, Remy 8
Childress, Alice 14
Cleary, Beverly 2, 8
Cleaver, Bill 6
Cleaver, Vera 6
Clifton, Lucille 5
Coatsworth, Elizabeth 2
Cobb, Vicki 2
Cohen, Daniel 3

Cole, Joanna 5
Collier, James Lincoln 3
Conford, Ellen 10
Corbett, Scott 1
Cormier, Robert 12
Crews, Donald 7
de Angeli, Marguerite 1
DeJong, Meindert 1
de Paola, Tomie 4
Donovan, John 3
du Bois, William Pène 1
Emberley, Barbara 5
Emberley, Ed 5
Engdahl, Sylvia Louise 2
Enright, Elizabeth 4
Estes, Eleanor 2
Feelings, Muriel L. 5
Feelings, Tom 5
Fitzgerald, John D. 1
Fitzhugh, Louise 1
Fleischman, Sid 1
Foster, Genevieve 7
Fox, Paula 1
Fritz, Jean 2, 14
Gág, Wanda 4
Geisel, Theodor Seuss 1
George, Jean Craighead 1
Gibbons, Gail 8
Giovanni, Nikki 6
Glubok, Shirley 1
Goffstein, M. B. 3
Graham, Lorenz B. 10
Greene, Bette 2
Greenfield, Eloise 4
Guy, Rosa 13
Hamilton, Virginia 1, 11
Haskins, James 3
Henry, Marguerite 4
Hentoff, Nat 1

Hinton, S. E. 3
Hoban, Russell 3
Hoban, Tana 13
Hogrogian, Nonny 2
Howe, James 9
Hunt, Irene 1
Hunter, Kristin 3
Isadora, Rachel 7
Jarrell, Randall 6
Jonas, Ann 12
Jordan, June 10
Keats, Ezra Jack 1
Kellogg, Steven 6
Klein, Norma 2
Konigsburg, E. L. 1
Kotzwinkle, William 6
Krementz, Jill 5
Kuskin, Karla 4
Langstaff, John 3
Lasky, Kathryn 11
Lawson, Robert 2
Le Guin, Ursula K. 3
L'Engle, Madeleine 1, 14
LeShan, Eda J. 6
Lester, Julius 2
Lionni, Leo 7
Livingston, Myra Cohn 7
Lobel, Arnold 5
Locker, Thomas 14
Lowry, Lois 6
MacLachlan, Patricia 14
Manley, Seon 3
Mathis, Sharon Bell 3
Mayer, Mercer 11
McCloskey, Robert 7
McClung, Robert M. 11
McCord, David 9
McDermott, Gerald 9
McHargue, Georgess 2

McKinley, Robin 10
Meltzer, Milton 13
Merriam, Eve 14
Monjo, F. N. 2
Mukerji, Dhan Gopal 10
Myers, Walter Dean 4
Ness, Evaline 6
O'Brien, Robert C. 2
O'Dell, Scott 1
Oneal, Zibby 13
Paterson, Katherine 7
Peet, Bill 12
Petry, Ann 12
Pfeffer, Susan Beth 11
Pinkwater, D. Manus 4
Prelutsky, Jack 13
Pringle, Laurence 4
Provensen, Alice 11
Provensen, Martin 11
Raskin, Ellen 1, 12
Rau, Margaret 8
Rey, H. A. 5
Rey, Margret 5
Rockwell, Thomas 6
Sachs, Marilyn 2
Scarry, Richard 3
Schwartz, Alvin 3
Selden, George 8
Selsam, Millicent E. 1
Sendak, Maurice 1
Seredy, Kate 10
Seuss, Dr. 9
Showers, Paul 6
Shulevitz, Uri 5
Silverstein, Shel 5
Simon, Seymour 9
Singer, Isaac Bashevis 1
Slote, Alfred 4
Smucker, Barbara 10

235

CUMULATIVE INDEX TO TITLES

Title Index

Title Index

Title Index

Title Index

Title Index